CENSUS OF INDIA 1931

Census of India 1871-1951, 9 Sets In 384 Bindings (9788121258876) Rs. 700000

Census of India 1931, 28 Vols. In 52 Bindings (9788121271233) Rs. 102000

1. India - Report (9788121276153) Rs. 2820 (Vol. I, Pt. 1)
2. India - Imperial Tables (9788121276139) Rs. 3210 (Vol. I, Pt. 2)
3. India - Ethnographical and Administration Report (9788121276115) Rs. 2900 (Vol. I, Pt. 3 & 5)
4. The Andaman And Nicobar Islands - Report, Tables (9788121276078) Rs. 720 (Vol. II, Pt. 1, Pt. 2)
5. Assam - Report (9788121276054) Rs. 1340 (Vol. III, Pt. 1)
6. Assam - Tables and Administrative Report (9788121276030) Rs. 1830 (Vol. III, Pt. 2 & 3)
7. Baluchistan - Report, Imeprial and Provincial Tables and Administrative Report (9788121276016) Rs. 2320 (Vol. IV, Pt. 1 & 2 & 3)
8. Bengal & Sikkim - Report (9788121275972) Rs. 2860 (Vol. V, Pt. 1)
9. Bengal & Sikkim - Tables (9788121275958) Rs. 1660 (Vol. V, Pt. 2)
10. Calcutta (9788121275910) Rs. 960 (Vol. VI, Pt. 1 & 2)
11. Bengal, Sikkim And Calcutta - Administrative Report (9788121275934) Rs. 580 (Vol. V & VI, Pt. 3)
12. Bihar And Orissa - Report (9788121275897) Rs. 1780 (Vol. VII, Pt. 1)
13. Bihar And Orissa - Tables and Administrative Report (9788121275873) Rs. 1190 (Vol. VII, Pt. 2 & 3)
14. Bombay Presidency - General Report (9788121275835) Rs. 3620 (Vol. VIII, Pt. 1)
15. Bombay - Statistical tables (9788121275811) Rs. 3060 (Vol. VIII, Pt. 2)
16. Bombay Presidency Aden - report and tables and Administrative report (9788121275798) Rs. 520 (Vol. VIII, Pt. 3 & 4)
17. Cities of the Bombay Presidency Report & Statistical tables (9788121275750) Rs. 2020 (Vol. IX, Pt. 1 & 2)
18. The Western India States Agency, In Two Parts - The Report & The Statistical Tables (9788121275736) Rs. 2560 (Vol. X, Pt. 1 & 2)
19. Burma - Report (9788121275712) Rs. 1860 (Vol. XI, Pt. 1)
20. Burma - Tables and Administrative Report (9788121275699) Rs. 1690 (Vol. XI, Pt. 2 & 3)
21. Central Provinces & Berar - Report (9788121275651) Rs. 2340 (Vol. XII, Pt. 1)
22. Central Provinces & Berar - Tables and Administrative Report (9788121275637) Rs. 3120 (Vol. XII, Pt. 2 & 3)
23. Coorg - Report And Tables and Madras - Report (9788121275613) Rs. 2680 (Vol. XIV, Pt. 1)
24. Madras - Imperial And Provincial Tables and The Administration Report (9788121275576) Rs. 1950 (Vol. XIV, Pt. 2 & 4)
25. North - West Frontier Province - Report & Tables (9788121275538) Rs. 2300 (Vol. XV, Pt. 1 & 2)
26. Delhi - Report & Tables (9788121275514) Rs. 1180 (Vol. XVI, Pt. 1 & 2)
27. Punjab - Report (9788121275491) Rs. 2070 (Vol. XVII, Pt. 1)
28. Punjab - Tables (9788121275477) Rs. 1690 (Vol. XVII, Pt. 2)
29. United Provinces of Agra And Oudh - Report (9788121275453) Rs. 3380 (Vol. XVIII, Pt. 1)
30. United Provinces of Agra And Oudh - Imperial And Provincial Tables and Administrative (9788121275439) Rs. 3600 (Vol. XVIII, Pt. 2 & 3)
31. Baroda - Report (9788121275415) Rs. 2800 (Vol. XIX, Pt. 1)
32. Baroda - Tables (9788121275392) Rs. 730 (Vol. XIX, Pt. 2)
33. Baroda - Administrative (9788121275378) Rs. 780 (Vol. XIX, Pt. 3)
34. Central India Agency - Report (9788121275354) Rs. 1690 (Vol. XX, Pt. 1)
35. Central India Agency - Tables and Administrative Volume (9788121275330) Rs. 2260 (Vol. XX, Pt. 2 & 3)
36. Cochin - Report & Tables (9788121275293) Rs. 2460 (Vol. XXI, Pt. 1 & 2 - A & B.)
37. Gwalior - Report (9788121275279) Rs. 1470 (Vol. XXII, Pt. 1)
38. Gwalior - Tables (9788121275255) Rs. 980 (Vol. XXII, Pt. 2)
39. H. E. H. The Nizam's Dominions (Hyderabad State) - Report (9788121275231) Rs. 1540 (Vol. XXIII, Pt. 1)
40. H. E. H. The Nizam's Dominions (Hyderabad State) - Tables (9788121275217) Rs. 1510 (Vol. XXIII, Pt. 2)
41. Jammu & Kashmir State - Report (9788121275194) Rs. 2060 (Vol. XXIV, Pt. 1)
42. Jammu & Kashmir State - Imperial & State Tables (9788121275170) Rs. 1940 (Vol. XXIV, Pt. 2 & 3)
43. Mysore - Report (9788121275156) Rs. 1950 (Vol. XXV, Pt. 1)
44. Mysore - Tables (9788121275132) Rs. 1380 (Vol. XXV, Pt. 2)
45. Ajmer-Merwara - Report And Tables (9788121275118) Rs. 780 (Vol. XXVI)
46. Rajputana Agency And Ajmer-Merwara - Report and Tables and Administrative (9788121275095) Rs. 2380 (Vol. XXVII, Pt. 1 & 2)
47. Travancore - Report (9788121276092) Rs. 2960 (Vol. XXVIII, Pt. 1)
48. Travancore - Tables & Administrative (9788121275996) Rs. 1360 (Vol. XXVIII, Pt. 2 & 4)
49. Jaipur State- Report (9788121275859) Rs. 1280 (Pt. 1)
50. Jaipur State- Tables (9788121275774) Rs. 2030 (Pt. 2)
51. Mayurbhanj state- Report (9788121275675) Rs. 3180 (Pt. 1)
52. Mayurbhanj state- Tables (9788121275552) Rs. 3070 (Pt. 2)

Owing to the antiquity and rarity of this book, certain pages are regrettably absent, and readability is compromised due to the blurring of the original text. If you possess any insights regarding the availability of these missing sections, kindly inform us. Your assistance is crucial in ensuring the completion of this significant work for the benefit of future generations.

CENSUS OF INDIA, 1931

BOOK - 40: VOLUME - XXIII

H. E. H. THE NIZAM'S DOMINIONS

(HYDERABAD STATE)

PART II - TABLES

GULAM AHMED KHAN

GYAN

Published by

Gyan Publishing House
5, Ansari Road
Daryaganj, New Delhi-110002
Phone: 011-47034999, 9811692060
E-mail: books@gyanbooks.com

Distribution Network
gyanbooks.com
India, USA, Canada, UK, Australia

ISBN: 978-81-212-7123-3 (Set) 28 Vols. In 52 Bindings

ISBN: 978-81-212-7521-7 (PB) Vol. XXIII, Pt. II

First Published, 1933

2nd Impression 2024

Printed at: Gyan Press, Delhi.

CENSUS OF INDIA 1931

Census of India, 1931

VOLUME XXIII

H.E.H. the Nizam's Dominions

(HYDERABAD STATE)

PART II.—TABLES

BY

GULAM AHMED KHAN

Census Commissioner

1933

PRINTED BY THE SUPERINTENDENT, GOVERNMENT CENTRAL PRESS

HYDERABAD-DECCAN.

Price B.G. Rs. 6 or O.S. Rs. 7.

FOREWORD

1. All the Imperial tables contained in this volume are in accord with the prescribed form and cover the whole population of 14,436,148 persons enumerated in the Dominions of His Exalted Highness the Nizam on the night of 26th of February, 1931. There was no non-synchronous area this time and, therefore, there is no estimated population of any tract included in the above figure.

2. In all tables, in which statistics are given by districts, the Dominions have been divided into two natural divisions, Marathwara and Telangana. Districts being the unit of administration, subahs have been left out of consideration. Telangana includes the city of Hyderabad, which embraces the metropolis, the British Administered Areas and the British cantonments of Secunderabad and Bolarum. Aurangabad (cantonment included), Gulbarga, and Warangal towns have been treated as cities. The last is comprised of Fort Warangal, Matwada, Hanamkonda, and Urus Karimabad and the figures of the previous censuses have been grouped together to admit of comparison.

3. The samastan of Amarchinta has this time been assigned its proper place, in Mahbubnagar district. For the purpose of comparison, therefore, its population figures at the preceding censuses have been deducted from the Raichur district total and added to that of Mahbubnagar.

4. In the age tables the individual ages have been reckoned from the nearest births and not from the number of completed years as in 1921.

5. For the first time separate figures for Urdu literates have been shown along with English figures in the Imperial table.

6. Imperial table XX is an additional feature presenting in a nutshell the area, population, density and religions of each district. The table of literate unemployed was not compiled as the schedules returned were too inadequate and entries too unreliable to be of any use.

7. Among the State tables, an innovation has been made in II by showing literacy by religions and English literacy by taluks. The other useful additions are III in three parts regarding Infirmities, IV on cottage industries and V population of wards of the Hyderabad city.

GULAM AHMED KHAN,
Census Commissioner.
1931.

HYDERABAD, DECCAN,
31*st March*, 1933.
27*th Urdibehisht*, 1342 *F.*

TABLE OF CONTENTS

Imperial Tables

State Tables

Table I.

AREA, HOUSES AND POPULATION

THIS table shows for each district the area, the number of towns and inhabited villages, the number of occupied houses and the total urban and rural population—males and females.

2. During the decade (1921-1931) there was no other jurisdictional change in the districts save that of Amarchinta Samasthan which was transferred from Raichur to Mahbubnagar district in 1334 F. Also, the Samasthan of Gopalpet has been included in Nagarkarnul Taluk, within whose jurisdiction the villages of the Samasthan lie.

3. Figures for the four divisions (subhas) have been deleted on this occasion as they do not serve any ethnological or statistical purpose.

4. The difference between the areas here shown and those in the corresponding table of 1921 is due to changes referred to in para. 2 *supra*.

5. The Cantonment of Secunderabad including Bolarum and the Residency Bazaars have been, as heretofore, treated as part of the City of Hyderabad; and the Cantonment of Aurangabad, as part of the Aurangabad City. Details of the area and population of these places, which are administered areas, are shown below :—

Locality	Area in Sq. miles	Occupied Houses	Population		
			Persons	Males	Females
1. Residency Bazaar ..	0·576	4,524	14,472	8,116	6,356
2. Secunderabad including Bolarum Cantonment ..	19·0	31,057	120,801	64,738	56,063
Military	..	5,700	13,708	9,798	3,910
Civil	19·0	25,357	107,093	54,940	52,153
3. Aurangabad Cantonment ..	3·53	1,455	7,582	4,490	3,092

6. The areas of Residency Bazaars and Secunderabad Cantonment have been slightly increased, due to more accurate information.

7. The main statistics for taluks will be found in State Tables I and II at the end of this Volume.

TABLE I.

Area, Houses and Population.

DISTRICT	Area in square miles	Towns	Villages	OCCUPIED HOUSES			POPULATION								
							Persons			Males			Females		
				Total	In towns	In villages	Total	Urban	Rural	Total	Urban	Rural	Total	Urban	Rural
1	2	3	4	5	6	7	8	9	10	11	12	13	14	15	16
HYDERABAD STATE.	82,698	133	21,697	3,312,222	395,482	2,916,740	14,436,148	1,616,981	12,819,167	7,370,010	836,874	6,533,136	7,066,138	780,107	6,286,031
1. Hyderabad City	53	1	..	116,807	116,807	..	466,894	466,894	..	247,623	247,623	..	219,271	219,271	..
2. Atraf-i-Balda	2,651	2	982	128,871	2,348	126,523	499,661	11,838	487,823	253,975	5,935	248,040	245,686	5,903	239,783
3. Warangal	7,944	7	1,443	232,340	22,134	210,206	1,117,693	117,579	1,000,114	575,819	62,482	513,337	541,874	55,097	486,777
4. Karimnagar	5,722	11	1,217	264,619	17,890	246,729	1,241,405	82,818	1,158,587	634,416	41,883	592,533	606,989	40,935	566,054
5. Adilabad	7,294	9	2,068	157,438	8,987	148,451	762,030	48,084	713,946	389,754	24,272	365,482	372,276	23,812	348,464
6. Medak	3,198	8	938	168,531	12,492	156,039	738,665	51,783	686,882	373,475	25,818	347,657	365,190	25,965	339,225
7. Nizamabad	3,265	10	857	159,296	24,176	135,120	623,225	64,599	558,626	313,556	32,448	281,108	309,669	32,151	277,518
8. Mahbubnagar	5,326	3	1,373	225,039	7,893	217,146	971,616	32,401	939,215	494,061	16,347	477,714	477,555	16,054	461,501
9. Nalgonda	6,049	3	1,286	237,793	6,423	231,370	1,133,409	25,702	1,107,707	580,897	12,925	567,972	552,512	12,777	539,735
10. Aurangabad	6,212	5	1,953	225,371	27,529	197,842	944,793	79,918	864,875	480,498	41,652	438,846	464,295	38,266	426,029
11. Bir	4,132	8	1,039	154,792	12,332	142,460	633,690	57,751	575,939	325,396	29,583	295,813	308,294	28,168	280,126
12. Nander	3,771	8	1,394	190,366	21,716	168,650	722,081	69,863	652,218	367,170	35,684	331,486	354,911	34,179	320,732
13. Parbhani	5,125	12	1,566	186,341	24,756	161,585	853,760	98,312	755,448	434,777	51,006	383,771	418,983	47,306	371,677
14. Gulbarga	6,975	12	1,698	298,571	30,711	267,860	1,225,008	145,773	1,079,235	621,687	74,387	547,300	603,321	71,386	531,935
15. Osmanabad	3,526	7	813	156,623	15,460	141,163	691,068	74,211	616,857	357,489	38,879	318,610	333,579	35,332	298,247
16. Raichur	6,630	16	1,748	202,860	27,390	175,470	937,535	117,935	819,600	473,161	59,237	413,924	464,374	58,698	405,676
17. Bidar	4,825	11	1,422	206,564	16,438	190,126	873,615	71,520	802,095	446,256	36,713	409,543	427,359	34,807	392,552

Table II.

VARIATION IN POPULATION SINCE 1881

This table compares the population as now obtained with the figures of the last five decades. Changes due to inter-district transfers during the decade 1921-1931 have been taken into account and figures adjusted accordingly.

(2) During the ten years, there was no other inter-district change save that of the transfer of Samasthan of Amarchinta from Raichur to Mahbubnagar district.

TABLE II.

Variation in Population during last fifty years.

DISTRICT	PERSONS						VARIATION (+) Increase (—) Decrease					Net variation in period 1881 to 1931
	1931	1921	1911	1901	1891	1881	1921 to 1931	1911 to 1921	1901 to 1911	1891 to 1901	1881 to 1891	
1	2	3	4	5	6	7	8	9	10	11	12	13
HYDERABAD STATE ..	14,436,148	12,471,770	13,374,676	11,141,142	11,537,040	9,845,594	+1,964,378	— 902,906	+2,233,534	— 395,898	+1,691,446	+4,590,554
1. Hyderabad City	*466,894*	*404,187*	*501,646*	*463,173*	*428,731*	*379,643*	+ 62,707	— 97,459	+ 38,473	+ 34,442	+ 49,088	+ 87,251
2. Atraf-i-Balda	*499,661*	*497,498*	*537,025*	*445,551*	*424,348*	*387,835*	+ 2,163	— 39,527	+ 91,474	+ 21,208	+ 36,513	+ 111,826
3. Warangal	*1,117,693*	*925,041*	*905,522*	*716,261*	*640,358*	*506,653*	+ 192,652	+ 19,519	+ 189,261	+ 75,903	+ 133,705	+ 611,040
4. Karimnagar	*1,241,405*	*1,095,444*	*1,129,198*	*833,293*	*870,567*	*743,479*	+ 145,961	— 33,754	+ 295,905	— 37,274	+ 127,088	+ 497,926
5. Adilabad	*762,030*	*655,536*	*620,426*	*484,281*	*449,875*	*406,904*	+ 106,494	+ 35,110	+ 136,145	+ 34,406	+ 42,971	+ 355,126
6. Medak	*738,665*	*642,796*	*682,030*	*527,105*	*530,032*	*464,049*	+ 95,869	— 39,234	+ 154,925	— 2,927	+ 65,983	+ 274,616
7. Nizamabad	*623,225*	*499,765*	*565,890*	*495,804*	*499,619*	*449,434*	+ 123,460	— 66,125	+ 70,086	— 3,815	+ 50,185	+ 173,791
8. Mahbubnagar	*971,616*	*792,632*	*792,777*	*648,343*	*621,780*	*513,530*	+ 178,984	— 145	+ 144,434	+ 26,563	+ 108,250	+ 458,086
9. Nalgonda	*1,133,409*	*948,301*	*1,035,770*	*862,900*	*769,202*	*608,635*	+ 185,108	— 87,469	+ 172,870	+ 93,698	+ 160,567	+ 524,774
10. Aurangabad	*944,793*	*714,008*	*869,787*	*725,556*	*833,699*	*733,813*	+ 230,785	— 155,779	+ 144,231	— 108,143	+ 99,886	+ 210,980
11. Bir	*633,690*	*467,616*	*622,531*	*492,258*	*642,722*	*558,745*	+ 166,074	— 154,915	+ 130,273	— 150,464	+ 83,977	+ 74,945
12. Nander	*722,081*	*671,019*	*698,411*	*575,132*	*698,894*	*690,698*	+ 51,062	— 27,392	+ 123,279	— 123,762	+ 8,205	+ 31,392
13. Parbhani	*853,760*	*765,787*	*779,379*	*646,800*	*805,145*	*685,617*	+ 87,973	— 13,592	+ 132,579	— 158,345	+ 119,528	+ 168,143
14. Gulbarga	*1,225,008*	*1,095,753*	*1,190,327*	*1,086,918*	*975,209*	*781,175*	+ 129,255	— 94,574	+ 103,409	+ 111,709	+ 194,034	+ 443,833
15. Osmanabad	*691,068*	*615,216*	*641,005*	*534,765*	*648,172*	*542,541*	+ 75,852	— 25,789	+ 106,240	— 113,407	+ 105,631	+ 148,527
16. Raichur	*937,535*	*880,420*	*953,324*	*888,286*	*852,494*	*652,040*	+ 57,115	— 72,904	+ 65,038	+ 35,792	+ 200,454	+ 285,495
17. Bidar	*873,615*	*800,751*	*849,628*	*714,716*	*846,193*	*740,812*	+ 72,864	— 48,877	+ 134,912	— 131,477	+ 105,381	+ 132,803

2

TABLE II.

Variation in Population during last fifty years.

DISTRICT	Males						Females					
	1931	1921	1911	1901	1891	1881	1931	1921	1911	1901	1891	1881
1	14	15	16	17	18	19	20	21	22	23	24	25
HYDERABAD STATE ..	7,370,010	6,345,071	6,797,118	5,673,629	5,873,129	5,002,137	7,066,138	6,126,699	6,577,558	5,467,513	5,663,911	4,843,457
1. Hyderabad City	247,623	208,705	258,998	240,036	223,495	194,220	219,271	195,392	242,648	223,187	205,236	185,423
2. Atraf-i-Balda	258,975	252,202	273,834	226,737	216,192	196,606	245,086	245,296	263,191	218,814	208,156	191,229
3. Warangal	575,819	475,785	467,496	374,575	380,744	259,435	541,874	449,256	438,026	341,086	309,614	247,218
4. Karimnagar	634,416	562,241	585,029	434,775	448,005	378,335	606,989	533,203	544,160	398,318	422,472	365,144
5. Adilabad	380,734	336,024	314,428	243,525	225,610	203,734	372,276	319,512	305,998	210,736	224,265	203,170
6. Medak	373,475	325,698	345,706	270,382	260,485	234,381	365,190	317,098	336,324	256,723	260,547	229,068
7. Nizamabad	313,536	248,016	282,505	250,005	251,580	226,410	309,669	251,749	283,385	245,799	248,030	223,024
8. Mahbubnagar	494,061	400,857	402,380	327,664	314,423	258,122	477,555	391,775	390,238	320,679	307,857	255,408
9. Nalgonda	580,897	485,273	532,740	457,839	393,029	308,679	552,512	463,028	503,030	405,061	376,173	299,956
10. Aurangabad	480,498	358,629	437,495	363,191	423,414	374,784	464,295	355,379	432,292	362,365	410,285	359,029
11. Bir	325,396	238,492	314,738	248,151	328,530	286,170	308,294	220,124	307,793	244,107	314,192	272,575
12. Nander	367,170	338,178	349,619	286,666	352,951	350,310	354,011	332,841	348,792	288,466	345,943	340,379
13. Parbhani	434,777	387,123	391,088	324,044	410,538	351,824	418,983	378,664	388,201	322,756	394,607	333,793
14. Gulbarga	621,687	555,105	602,385	530,482	404,582	394,689	603,321	540,648	587,942	586,486	480,627	386,486
15. Osmanabad	357,489	319,517	327,535	270,833	331,216	277,850	333,579	295,699	313,470	263,932	316,956	264,691
16. Raichur	473,161	446,168	481,861	445,880	430,645	329,600	464,874	434,252	471,463	442,397	421,849	322,440
17. Bidar	440,256	406,968	429,122	358,885	428,600	376,988	427,350	393,783	420,506	355,831	417,593	363,824

Table III.

TOWNS AND VILLAGES CLASSIFIED BY POPULATION

Note.—The following statement explains the variation in the number of towns and villages in the State :—

CITIES.

Number shown in 1921	1
Number shown in 1931	4

The towns of Aurangabad (including cantonment), Gulbarga and Warangal have now been treated as cities owing to their special characteristics—historical, educational and civic—which have been greatly developed since the last decade.

The City of Warangal has been formed by the amalgamation of four former towns, viz ; Fort Warangal, Mathwada, Hanamkonda and Urs-Karimabad, which no longer find a place separately as independent units.

The town of Muhammadnagar (Fort Golconda)—a civil area lying close to and being interwoven with the metropolis—has been abandoned as a separate town and included in the City of Hyderabad.

TOWNS.

Number shown in 1921	88
Deduct:—	
(*a*) Towns which have been amalgamated into a city	4
(*b*) Towns which have been treated as cities in 1931	3
Add :—	
Villages which have become towns in 1931 ..	48
Number shown in 1931	129

VILLAGES.

Number shown in 1921	21,223
Deduct :—	
Villages treated as towns in 1931 ..	48
Add :—	
As a result of accurate enumeration ..	522
Number shown in 1931	21,697

N.B.—Figures for cantonments have been shown in Tables IV and V.

TABLE III.

Towns and villages classified by Population.

DISTRICT	Total number of inhabited Villages and Towns	Population	Under 500		500-1,000		1,000-2,000		2,000-5,000		5,000-10,000		10,000-20,000		20,000-50,000		50,000-100,000		100,000 and over		Encampment, Boat, and Railway Population.
			Number	Population	Number	Population	Number	Population	Number	Population	Number	Population	Number	Population	Number	Population	Number	Population	Number	Population	
1	2	3	4	5	6	7	8	9	10	11	12	13	14	15	16	17	18	19	20	21	22
STATE.	21,830	14,436,148	12,601	2,851,391	5,439	3,819,128	2,808	3,843,747	884	2,440,955	64	422,849	26	343,042	6	186,023	1	62,119	1	466,894	..
1. Hyderabad City ..	1	*466,894*	..	..	..	..	..	..	..	..	..	..	..	..	..	..	..	..	1	466,894	..
2. Atraf-i-Balda ..	934	*499,661*	587	112,956	200	135,065	113	156,503	32	82,399	2	11,838	..	..	..	..	..	..	..	..	..
3. Warangal ..	1,450	*1,117,693*	742	114,810	332	248,478	280	397,284	89	244,542	4	22,586	2	32,874	..	..	1	62,119	..	..	..
4. Karimnagar ..	1,228	*1,241,405*	394	93,993	342	254,862	353	483,399	129	328,674	8	38,692	2	24,785	..	..	..	..	..	..	..
5. Adilabad ..	2,077	*762,030*	1,393	260,588	316	218,219	138	187,875	27	66,916	2	15,847	1	12,585	..	..	..	..	..	..	..
6. Medak ..	946	*738,665*	416	122,186	313	221,473	164	218,141	48	186,102	3	18,347	2	22,416	..	..	..	..	..	..	..
7. Nizamabad ..	867	*623,225*	462	103,179	204	147,936	132	204,687	45	125,529	3	23,085	1	18,809	..	..	..	..	..	..	..
8. Mahbubnagar ..	1,376	*971,616*	696	137,627	385	271,447	228	318,368	69	191,773	1	5,076	2	27,325	..	..	..	..	..	..	..
9. Nalgonda ..	1,239	*1,133,409*	435	108,460	399	294,536	300	430,103	102	274,608	2	14,843	1	10,859	..	..	..	..	..	..	..
10. Aurangabad ..	1,958	*944,793*	1,364	308,555	426	288,838	130	168,079	33	99,408	3	20,640	..	..	2	59,278	..	..	..	..	..
11. Bir ..	1,047	*633,690*	629	168,987	298	208,867	82	112,583	31	88,746	5	28,743	2	25,814	..	..	..	..	..	..	..
12. Nander ..	1,402	*722,081*	945	223,245	330	229,559	91	122,011	30	85,557	5	34,717	..	..	1	26,992	..	..	..	..	..
13. Parbhani ..	1,578	*853,760*	1,044	261,152	384	262,863	108	146,106	32	94,600	6	37,680	4	51,359	..	..	..	..	..	..	..
14. Gulbarga ..	1,710	*1,225,008*	950	242,144	449	303,888	220	307,050	80	230,800	5	34,231	5	65,812	1	41,083	..	..	..	..	..
15. Osmanabad ..	820	*691,068*	344	114,248	276	194,363	152	193,629	42	118,973	4	27,829	1	11,266	1	30,760	..	..	..	..	..
16. Raichur ..	1,764	*937,535*	1,186	250,783	381	261,687	134	178,066	54	159,628	7	46,479	1	12,982	1	27,910	..	..	..	..	..
17. Bidar ..	1,433	*873,615*	814	208,478	404	281,152	168	217,913	41	112,700	4	27,216	2	26,156	..	..	..	..	..	..	..

Table IV.

TOWNS CLASSIFIED BY POPULATION WITH VARIATION SINCE 1881

At the present time, three former towns, viz., Aurangabad, Gulbarga and Warangal, having grown into importance, are classed as cities.

2. The new City of Warangal now comprises four former towns—Matwada, Hanamkonda, Urs-Karimabad and Warangal Fort, and these as well as the civil town of Muhammadnagar (Fort Golconda), which has been absorbed in the city of Hyderabad, do no longer come under the category of independent towns and the population of these towns for previous Census is included in the totals of the year concerned.

3. Forty-eight new towns (marked with an asterisk) are included in the Table and figures for these towns for previous years are given in brackets as far as possible from the Village Lists and these are omitted from the total urban population as they were rural units then.

4. Figures for the Cantonment within the Aurangabad City for previous years are given only as much as available, and no previous Census figures for the Cantonments within the City of Hyderabad are available, as this is the first time that figures for Cantonments are exhibited separately from towns.

5. Hyderabad City and Aurangabad City include the Cantonments. The Units composing them are detailed below :—

Unit	Persons	Males	Females
1. Hyderabad City			
(a) Hyderabad Municipality ..	306,646	160,889	145,757
(b) H.E.H. the Nizam's Cantonments	24,975	13,880	11,095
(c) Residency Bazaars ..	14,472	8,116	6,356
(d) Secunderabad including Trimulgherry and Bolarum ..	120,801	64,738	56,063
1. (Civil)	107,093	54,940	52,153
2. (Military)	13,708	9,798	3,910
Total ..	466,894	247,623	219,271
2. Aurangabad City	29,288	15,132	14,156
Do Cantonment ..	7,582	4,490	3,092
Total ..	36,870	19,622	17,248

TABLE IV.

TOWNS CLASSIFIED BY POPULATION WITH VARIATION SINCE 1881.

TABLE

Towns classified by Population

Town	District	Description of Town (Municipality, suburbs, Cantonment, &c.)	POPULATION 1931	1921	1911	1901	1891	1881
1	2	3	4	5	6	7	8	9
Total ..	..	..	1,616,981	1,187,297	1,295,305	1,126,948	1,074,899	884,567
1. Hyderabad City ..	..	M. & C.	*466,894*	404,187	500,623	448,466	415,039	367,417
Do *Cantonment* ..	..	..	*38,683*	..	..	..	..	..
2. Warangal City† ..	Warangal ..	M.	*62,119*	5,422	5,542	4,741	3,433	..
3. Gulbarga City† ..	Gulbarga ..	do ..	*41,083*	35,820	32,437	29,228	28,200	22,834
4. Aurangabad City† ..	Aurangabad ..	M. & C. ..	*36,870*	36,876	34,902	36,837	33,887	30,219
Do *Cantonment* ..	..	..	*7,582*	*8,336*	*11,953*	..	..	..
5. Latur ..	Osmanabad	M. ..	*30,760*	16,233	7,574	10,479	9,063	8,648
6. Raichur ..	Raichur ..	do ..	*27,910*	26,374	25,034	22,165	23,174	15,887
7. Nander	Nander ..	do ..	*26,992*	21,470	17,625	14,184	13,105	14,091
8. Jalna	Aurangabad ..	do ..	*22,408*	16,912	18,993	20,270	19,128	16,199
9. Yellandlapad ..	Warangal ..	do ..	*19,872*	22,938	15,914	12,877	..	..
10. Yadgir . ..	Gulbarga ..	do ..	*19,380*	11,092	10,945	9,865	..	..
11. Nizamabad ..	Nizamabad ..	do ..	*18,809*	15,672	17,353	12,871	11,482	10,264
12. Parbhani ..	Parbhani ..	do ..	*16,830*	14,755	9,081	9,958	10,102	7,996
13. Bidar	Bidar ..	do ..	*15,198*	12,434	12,684	11,367	11,815	9,730
14. Bir	Bir	do ..	*14,840*	13,547	16,010	17,671	18,994	17,898
15. Narayanpet ..	Mahbubnagar ..	do ..	*14,025*	12,944	12,449	12,011	11,888	11,290
16. Jagtial ..	Karimnagar ..	do ..	*13,882*	9,682	11,688	11,181	9,538	7,302
17. Mahbubnagar ..	Mahbubnagar ..	do ..	*13,300*	9,991	8,651	7,605	6,222	4,680
18. Khammam ..	Warangal ..	do ..	*13,002*	11,532	9,117	8,713	9,062	..
19. Gadwal . ..	Raichur ..	S. ..	*12,982*	10,104	12,082	10,195	14,672	12,207
20. Aland	Gulbarga ..	P. ..	*12,924*	11,431	12,051	10,130	9,588	6,201
21. Shorapur ..	Do ..	M. ..	*12,673*	12,748	8,048	8,271	9,754	9,900
22. Hingoli	Parbhani ..	do ..	*12,667*	10,298	17,507	17,256	11,966	14,804
23. Nirmal ..	Adilabad ..	do ..	*12,585*	9,457	9,588	7,751	10,932	10,577
24. Osmanabad ..	Osmanabad ..	do ..	*11,266*	9,056	10,221	10,607	10,511	8,801
25. Sid lipet ..	Medak ..	do ..	*11,260*	8,044	9,583	8,302	7,671	7,002
26. Basmath ..	Parbhani ..	do ..	*11,207*	10,137	10,599	8,445	11,361	11,022
27. Medak ..	Medak ..	do	*11,156*	10,432	9,125	8,511	7,556	7,026
28. Mominabad ..	Bir ..	do ..	*10,974*	9,280	11,073	12,628	13,923	12,052
29. Ekeli (Zahirabad) ..	Bidar ..	P. ..	*10,958*	4,875	5,889	4,920	5,138	..
30. Karimnagar ..	Karimnagar ..	M. ..	*10,903*	9,399	8,847	5,752	6,848	5,486
31. Bhongir ..	Nalgonda ..	do ..	*10,859*	5,845	7,842	5,806	4,938	..
32. Manwath ..	Parbhani ..	do ..	*10,655*	9,091	11,002	7,395	10,912	8,767
33. Kosgi	Gulbarga ..	J. ..	*10,494*	7,203	9,683	8,228	8,418	7,946
34. Kalyani ..	Do ..	do ..	*10,341*	9,187	11,077	11,191	13,026	11,092
35. Kopbal	Raichur ..	do ..	*9,979*	9,187	7,558	8,903	6,991	5,088
36. Nalgonda ..	Nalgonda ..	M. ..	*9,711*	7,814	7,582	5,889	5,900	5,283
37. Peddapalli ..	Karimnagar ..	J. ..	*8,945*	5,340	7,260	2,783	5,995	..
38. Shahabad ..	Gulbarga ..	P. ..	*8,896*	6,895	5,607	5,105	3,452	..
39. Achampet* ..	Nizamabad ..	..	*8,761*	(444)	..	..	..	..
40. Thair	Osmanabad ..	..	*8,541*	8,691	7,948	7,827	8,015	3,984
41. Bhainsa ..	Nander ..	..	*8,525*	8,311	8,444	7,126	7,688	6,701
42. Tandur	Gulbarga ..	J. ..	*8,462*	7,430	6,504	5,930	4,278	..
43. Udgir	Bidar ..	M. ..	*8,308*	7,178	7,213	5,984	6,722	7,141
44. Adilabad ..	Adilabad ..	do ..	*8,096*	7,271	7,560	6,303	6,084	5,522
45. Sadaseopet ..	Medak ..	do ..	*8,071*	7,146	8,625	6,672	7,350	8,775
46. Sailu	Parbhani ..	..	*7,967*	5,525	4,819	..	..	..
47. Qadirabad ..	Aurangabad ..	M. ..	*7,909*	8,978	10,270	11,159	11,402	9,876
48. Parli	Bir ..	..	*7,759*	8,474	7,478	7,289	7,659	7,090
49. Chinnur ..	Adilabad ..	..	*7,751*	5,705	6,989	6,501	5,719	5,721
50. Vemalwada ..	Karimnagar ..	J.	*7,645*	5,986	8,075	5,372	6,511	6,007
51. Manthani ..	Do ..	..	*7,560*	6,731	7,759	6,680	6,046	5,794
52. Chitgopa ..	Bidar ..	P. ..	*7,447*	3,640	4,427	..	..	..
53. Armur	Nizamabad ..	M. ..	*7,279*	7,121	7,530	9,031	7,015	5,530
54. Bodhan . ..	Do ..	do ..	*7,045*	4,188	6,996	6,438	5,841	5,898
55. Koratla . ..	Karimnagar ..	..	*6,996*	6,004	6,068	5,524	5,892	5,522
56. Moram ..	Osmanabad ..	..	*6,879*	6,098	6,150	5,692	5,874	4,079
57. Kondalwadi ..	Nander ..	P. ..	*6,840*	7,178	7,018	6,557	5,986	7,570
58. Gangawati ..	Raichur ..	M. ..	*6,722*	6,027	6,663	6,245	6,188	..
59. Mukher ..	Nander ..	..	*6,614*	5,072	6,584	6,148	6,019	5,795
60. Deglur	Do ..	M. ..	*6,553*	7,695	7,800	6,917	6,578	6,808
61. Homnabad ..	Atraf-i-Balda ..	..	*6,550*	5,182	6,798	7,136	7,736	7,199
62. Manvi	Raichur ..	M. ..	*6,500*	6,250	6,679	6,253	5,669	..
63. Gangakher ..	Parbhani ..	J. ..	*6,446*	5,437	5,997	5,007	6,653	5,517
64. Vaijapur ..	Aurangabad ..	M. ..	*6,437*	5,756	5,406	5,451	5,411	5,300
65. Deodrug ..	Raichur ..	do	*6,412*	6,652	6,837	6,778	7,213	4,587
66. Owsa	Osmanabad ..	..	*6,352*	5,754	5,446	6,026	6,091	5,640
67. Paithan ..	Aurangabad ..	M. ..	*6,294*	5,330	6,989	8,638	8,788	10,874
68. Huzurabad* ..	Karimnagar ..	do ..	*6,251*	(4,534)	..	..	..	..
69. Kodangal ..	Gulbarga ..	do ..	*6,228*	5,812	6,062	5,099	5,296	..
70. Hasanparti* ..	Warangal ..	..	*6,198*	(4,780)	..	..	..	..
71. Mudhol ..	Nander ..	M. ..	*6,185*	5,451	6,876	6,040	6,024	6,177
72. Purna* . ..	Parbhani ..	.. ..	*6,082*	(4,648)	..	..	..	..
73. Partur* . ..	Do ..	J. ..	*6,075*	(4,570)	..	..	..	..
74. Tuljapur ..	Osmanabad ..	M. ..	*6,057*	5,921	5,451	6,612	6,862	5,988
75. Rajuli*	Raichur ..	S. ..	*5,980*	(5,238)	..	..	..	..
76. Bhalki	Bidar ..	P. ..	*5,912*	4,081	6,268	5,788	5,383	5,168
77. Jintur*	Parbhani ..	M. ..	*5,825*	(4,832)	..	..	..	..
78. Mahbubabad* ..	Warangal ..	do ..	*5,824*	(3,499)	..	..	..	..
79. Sirsilla* . ..	Karimnagar ..	do ..	*5,752*	(4,360)	..	..	..	..
80. Sindhnur ..	Raichur ..	do ..	*5,553*	4,648	5,578	5,242	4,768	..

† Newly created cities (Warangal is formed by merging of Warangal, Hanamkonda, Warangal Fort and Urs-Karimabad) Golconda (Civil Station) is included in the Hyderabad City. *New towns.

IV.

for the last fifty years.

TABLE IV.

TOWNS CLASSIFIED BY POPULATION WITH VARIATION SINCE 1881.

VARIATION (+) INCREASE (—) DECREASE					Variation in period 1881 to 1931 Increase (+) Decrease (—)	MALES			FEMALES		
1921 to 1931	1911 to 1921	1901 to 1911	1891 to 1901	1881 to 1891		1931	1921	1911	1931	1921	1911
10	11	12	13	14	15	16	17	18	19	20	21
+ 429,684	— 108,008	+ 168,357	+ 52,049	+ 190,332	+ 732,414	836,874	607,395	660,940	780,107	579,902	634,365
+ 62,707	— 96,486	+ 52,157	+ 38,427	+ 47,622	+ 99,477	247,623	208,795	258,454	219,271	195,392	242,169
..	..	..	..	..	..	23,678	..	..	15,005	..	..
+ 56,697	— 120	+ 801	+ 1,308	..	..	33,326	2,781	2,754	28,793	2,691	2,788
+ 5,263	+ 3,388	+ 8,209	+ 1,028	+ 5,366	+ 18,249	21,567	18,720	16,849	19,516	17,100	15,588
— 6	+ 1,974	— 1,935	+ 2,950	+ 3,668	+ 6,651	19,622	19,237	17,902	17,248	17,639	16,910
— 754	— 3,617	..	..	..	..	4,490	4,708	6,699	3,092	3,628	5,254
+ 14,527	+ 8,659	— 2,905	+ 1,416	+ 415	+ 22,112	16,609	8,767	3,843	14,151	7,466	3,731
+ 1,536	+ 1,340	+ 2,869	— 1,009	+ 7,787	+ 12,323	14,026	13,323	12,681	13,884	13,051	12,358
+ 5,522	+ 3,845	+ 3,441	+ 1,079	— 986	+ 12,901	14,332	11,435	9,281	12,660	10,035	8,344
+ 5,496	— 2,081	— 1,277	+ 1,142	+ 2,929	+ 6,209	11,764	8,660	9,711	10,644	8,252	9,282
— 3,066	+ 7,024	+ 3,537	..	..	..	11,077	13,465	9,891	8,795	9,473	6,023
+ 7,388	+ 1,047	+ 1,580	..	..	..	9,520	5,761	5,241	9,860	6,231	5,704
+ 3,137	— 1,681	+ 4,482	+ 1,389	+ 1,218	+ 8,545	9,550	8,864	9,135	9,259	6,808	8,218
+ 2,075	+ 5,674	— 877	— 144	+ 2,106	+ 8,834	9,035	7,839	4,817	7,795	6,916	4,264
+ 2,764	— 250	+ 1,317	+ 52	+ 1,585	+ 5,468	7,767	6,267	6,316	7,431	6,167	6,368
+ 1,293	— 2,463	— 1,661	— 1,323	+ 1,596	— 2,558	7,577	6,814	8,074	7,263	6,733	7,936
+ 1,081	+ 495	+ 438	+ 123	+ 598	+ 2,735	6,959	6,498	6,206	7,066	6,446	6,248
+ 4,200	— 2,006	+ 507	+ 1,643	+ 2,236	+ 6,580	7,071	4,880	6,032	6,811	4,802	5,656
+ 3,809	+ 1,840	+ 1,046	+ 1,383	+ 1,542	+ 8,620	6,820	5,156	4,470	6,480	4,835	4,181
+ 1,470	+ 2,415	+ 401	— 849	..	..	6,448	5,748	4,539	6,554	5,784	4,578
+ 2,878	— 1,978	+ 1,887	— 4,477	+ 2,465	+ 775	6,538	4,962	5,965	6,444	5,142	6,117
+ 1,493	— 620	+ 1,921	+ 392	+ 3,337	+ 6,723	6,643	5,792	6,158	6,281	5,639	5,893
— 75	+ 4,705	— 228	— 1,488	— 146	+ 2,773	6,239	6,177	3,899	6,434	6,571	4,144
+ 2,374	— 7,214	+ 251	+ 5,200	— 2,838	— 2,137	6,588	5,376	9,199	6,079	4,917	8,308
+ 3,128	— 131	+ 1,837	— 3,181	+ 855	+ 2,008	6,064	4,518	4,580	6,521	4,939	5,008
+ 2,210	— 1,165	— 386	+ 96	+ 1,710	+ 2,465	5,878	4,678	5,235	5,388	4,378	4,966
+ 3,216	— 1,539	+ 1,281	+ 631	+ 669	+ 4,258	5,582	3,976	4,964	5,678	4,068	4,619
+ 1,070	— 462	+ 2,154	— 2,916	+ 339	+ 185	5,660	5,075	5,336	5,547	5,062	5,263
+ 724	+ 1,307	+ 614	+ 955	+ 530	+ 4,130	5,543	5,187	4,880	5,613	5,245	4,743
+ 1,694	— 1,793	— 1,555	— 1,295	+ 1,871	— 1,078	5,611	4,630	5,581	5,363	4,650	5,492
+ 6,083	— 1,014	+ 969	— 213	..	..	5,670	2,460	2,914	5,288	2,415	2,975
+ 1,501	+ 1,052	+ 2,595	— 596	+ 912	+ 5,467	5,580	4,756	4,393	5,323	4,648	3,954
+ 5,014	— 1,497	+ 1,536	+ 868	..	..	5,411	3,052	3,816	5,448	2,793	3,326
+ 1,564	— 1,911	+ 3,607	— 3,517	+ 2,145	+ 1,888	5,476	4,652	5,740	5,179	4,439	5,262
+ 3,291	— 2,480	+ 1,455	— 190	+ 472	+ 2,548	5,237	3,572	4,850	5,257	3,631	4,883
+ 1,154	— 1,890	— 114	— 1,835	+ 1,934	— 751	5,212	4,585	5,458	5,129	4,602	5,619
+ 792	+ 1,629	— 1,345	+ 1,912	+ 1,908	+ 4,896	5,157	4,661	3,916	4,822	4,526	3,642
+ 1,897	+ 282	+ 1,643	— 17	+ 623	+ 4,428	4,927	3,794	3,736	4,784	4,020	3,796
+ 3,605	— 1,920	+ 4,477	— 3,212	..	..	4,600	2,620	3,745	4,345	2,720	3,515
+ 2,001	+ 1,288	+ 502	+ 1,653	..	..	4,581	3,570	2,886	4,315	3,325	2,721
+ 8,317	..	..	..	..	..	4,682	(206)	..	4,079	(238)	..
— 150	+ 743	+ 621	— 688	+ 4,031	+ 4,557	4,320	4,397	3,991	4,221	4,294	3,957
+ 214	— 133	+ 1,318	— 562	+ 987	+ 1,824	4,267	4,206	4,108	4,258	4,105	4,341
+ 1,026	+ 932	+ 574	+ 1,632	..	..	4,265	3,872	3,344	4,197	3,564	3,160
+ 1,130	— 35	+ 1,229	— 738	— 419	+ 1,167	4,306	3,763	3,619	4,002	3,415	3,594
+ 825	— 289	+ 1,257	+ 219	+ 562	+ 2,574	4,097	3,525	3,689	3,999	3,746	3,871
+ 925	— 1,479	+ 1,953	— 678	— 1,425	— 704	4,106	3,563	4,415	3,965	3,583	4,210
+ 2,442	+ 706	..	..	..	..	4,222	2,899	2,463	3,745	2,626	2,356
— 1,064	— 1,297	— 889	— 243	+ 1,526	— 1,967	3,943	4,280	5,180	3,966	4,693	5,090
— 715	+ 996	+ 189	— 370	+ 569	+ 669	3,937	4,301	3,888	3,822	4,173	3,640
+ 2,046	— 1,284	+ 428	+ 842	— 2	+ 2,030	3,887	2,849	3,435	3,864	2,856	3,554
+ 1,659	— 2,089	+ 2,703	— 1,139	+ 414	+ 1,548	3,757	3,027	4,060	3,888	2,959	4,015
+ 820	— 1,028	+ 1,070	+ 634	+ 232	+ 1,766	3,791	3,476	3,814	3,769	3,255	3,945
+ 3,807	— 787	..	..	..	..	3,688	1,824	2,184	3,759	1,816	2,243
+ 158	— 409	— 1,501	+ 2,016	+ 1,485	+ 1,749	3,582	3,843	3,028	3,697	3,778	3,902
+ 2,857	— 2,808	+ 558	+ 597	— 57	+ 1,147	3,510	2,049	3,335	3,535	2,139	3,661
+ 992	— 64	+ 544	— 368	+ 370	+ 1,474	3,479	3,042	3,010	3,517	2,962	3,058
+ 781	— 52	+ 458	— 182	+ 1,795	+ 2,800	3,555	3,104	3,126	3,324	2,994	3,024
— 833	+ 155	+ 461	+ 621	— 1,634	— 730	3,356	3,284	3,408	3,484	3,889	3,615
+ 693	— 636	+ 418	+ 107	..	..	3,356	2,970	3,238	3,366	3,057	3,425
+ 1,342	— 1,512	+ 436	+ 120	+ 224	+ 819	3,391	2,503	3,308	3,223	2,569	3,276
— 1,142	— 105	+ 883	+ 339	— 230	— 255	3,310	3,729	3,772	3,243	3,966	4,028
+ 1,418	— 1,666	— 338	— 600	+ 537	— 649	3,230	2,568	3,322	3,320	2,564	3,476
+ 250	— 429	+ 426	+ 584	..	..	3,250	3,098	3,359	3,250	3,152	3,320
+ 1,009	— 560	+ 990	— 1,646	+ 1,136	+ 929	3,206	2,682	2,878	3,240	2,755	3,119
+ 681	+ 350	— 45	+ 40	+ 111	+ 1,137	3,225	2,889	2,719	3,212	2,917	2,687
— 240	— 185	+ 64	— 440	+ 2,626	+ 1,825	3,107	3,219	3,334	3,305	3,433	3,503
+ 598	+ 808	— 580	— 65	+ 451	+ 712	3,186	2,886	2,716	3,166	2,868	2,730
+ 964	— 1,659	— 1,649	— 150	— 2,086	— 4,580	3,098	2,541	3,376	3,196	2,789	3,613
+ 1,717	..	..	..	..	..	3,317	(2,828)	..	2,934	(2,206)	..
+ 416	— 250	+ 963	— 197	..	..	3,129	2,917	3,010	3,099	2,895	3,052
+ 1,418	..	..	..	..	..	3,199	(2,360)	..	2,999	(2,420)	..
+ 734	— 1,425	+ 886	— 584	+ 447	+ 8	2,997	2,558	3,811	3,188	2,808	3,565
+ 1,434	..	..	..	..	..	3,225	(2,257)	..	2,857	(2,391)	..
+ 1,505	..	..	..	..	..	3,232	(2,248)	..	2,843	(2,327)	..
+ 136	+ 470	— 1,161	— 250	+ 924	+ 119	3,110	3,028	2,766	2,947	2,893	2,685
+ 742	..	..	..	..	..	3,107	(2,656)	..	2,873	(2,582)	..
+ 1,831	— 2,187	+ 480	+ 405	+ 220	+ 749	3,025	2,044	3,158	2,887	2,087	3,110
+ 993	..	..	..	..	..	2,936	(2,422)	..	2,889	(2,410)	..
+ 2,325	..	..	..	..	..	3,044	(1,791)	..	2,780	(1,708)	..
+ 1,392	..	..	..	..	..	2,944	(2,256)	..	2,808	(2,104)	..
+ 910	— 935	+ 336	+ 479	..	..	2,731	2,256	2,733	2,822	2,387	2,845

TABLE IV.

TOWNS CLASSIFIED BY POPULATION WITH VARIATION SINCE 1881.

TABLE

Towns classified by Population

Town	District	Description of Town (Municipality, suburbs, Cantonment, &c.)	POPULATION 1931	1921	1911	1901	1891	1881
1	2	3	4	5	6	7	8	9
81. Kohir ..	.. Bidar ..	..	5,549	5,932	6,486	6,379	6,557	7,027
82. Dharmapuri*	.. Karimnagar ..	J. ..	5,537	(5,082)	..	..	..	..
83. Chitapur	.. Gulbarga ..	P. ..	5,365	5,879	9,335	8,150	8,818	..
84. Dacha* .	.. Raichur ..	S. ..	5,333	(4,165)	..	..	..	..
85. Paloncha*	.. Warangal ..	do ..	5,330	(4,082)	..	..	..	..
86. Fatehabad*	.. Bhir ..	..	5,304	(4,081)	..	..	..	..
87. Qila Shahpur*	.. Atraf-i-balda ..	..	5,288	(3,962)	..	..	..	..
88. Kalamnuri*	.. Parbhani ..	M. .	5,285	(4,419)	..	..	..	..
89. Seram* ..	.. Gulbarga ..	do ..	5,280	(7,666)	..	..	..	..
90. Manjlegaon	.. Bir ..	..	5,260	4,668	5,640	5,698	5,556	..
91. Mandarpalli*	.. Warangal ..	..	5.234	(4,492)	..	..	..	..
92. Sangareddipet	.. Medak ..	M. ..	5,227	4,588	5,947	4,809	4,993	..
93. Georai* .	.. Bir ..	do	5,218	(3,440)	..	..	..	..
94. Paignon*	.. Bir ..	..	5,202	(4,011)	..	..	..	..
95. Chirial Jangoan *	.. Nalgonda ..	M.	5,132	(3,822)	..	..	..	..
96. Wanparthi	.. Mahbubnagar ..	S. ..	5,076	4,586	4,429	..	..	..
97. Jogipet ..	.. Medak ..	..	5,049	5,462	3,046	..	..	..
98. Gambiraopet*	.. Karimnagar ..	..	5,006	(4,453)	..	..	..	..
99. Mudgal ..	.. Raichur ..	..	4,955	4,507	6,947	7,729	6,641	5,064
100. Pathri .	.. Parbhani ..	..	4,904	5,548	7,095	5,828	6,726	6,572
101. Balkonda*	.. Nizamabad ..	J. ..	4,814	(3,701)	..	..	..	..
102. Gurmatkal*	.. Gulbarga ..	..	4,647	(2,937)	..	..	..	..
103. Alampur*	.. Raichur ..	M. ..	4,646	(4,466)	..	..	..	..
104. Kadoli*	.. Do ..	..	4,634	(2,846)	..	..	..	..
105. Ibrahimpatan*	.. Medak ..	..	4,610	(4,989)	..	..	..	..
106. Rajeswari*	.. Bidar ..	P.	4,585	(4,516)	..	..	..	..
107. Kushtagi*	.. Raichur ..	M. ..	4,460	(4,016)	..	..	..	..
108. Banswada*	.. Nizamabad ..	..	4,454	(3,840)	..	..	..	..
109. Qandahar*	.. Nander ..	M. ..	4,452	(4,029)	..	..	..	..
110. Sonepet	.. Parbhani ..	J. ..	4,369	5,406	5,551	5,759	8,090	6,407
111. Wasi ..	.. Osmanabad ..	..	4,356	4,167	4,927	..	..	..
112. Manakundur*	.. Karimnagar ..	..	4,341	(4,302)	..	..	..	..
113. Hamsagar*	.. Raichur ..	..	4,339	(3,552)	..	..	..	..
114. Nilanga*	.. Bidar ..	M. ..	4,139	(3,780)	..	..	..	..
115. Deoni	.. Do ..	J. ..	3,951	3,729	3,545	..	..	..
116. Sirpur*	.. Adilabad ..	M. ..	3,877	(2,959)	..	..	..	..
117. Jalhally*	.. Raichur ..	..	3,871	(4,204)	..	..	..	..
118. Yellareddipet	.. Nizamabad ..	M. ..	3,839	2,841	3,247	..	..	..
119. Tekmal*	.. Medak	..	3,800	(3,329)	..	..	..	..
120. Kotgir .	.. Nizamabad ..	P. ..	3,749	3,706	4,200	..	..	..
121. Madnur*	.. Nander ..	J. ..	3,702	(1,905)	..	..	..	..
122. Kodaikal	.. Raichur ..	..	3,659	3,223	3,829	..	..	..
123. Boath*	.. Adilabad ..	M. ..	3,351	(3,067)	..	..	..	..
124. Ahmadpur*	.. Bidar ..	..	3,274	(4,088)	..	..	..	..
125. Kinwat*	.. Adilabad ..	M. ..	3,257	(2,970)	..	..	..	..
126. Kaij* ..	.. Bir ..	..	3,194	(2,122)	..	..	..	..
127. Lakshattipet*	.. Adilabad ..	M. ..	3,124	(1,839)	..	..	..	..
128. Asifabad*	.. do ..	do ..	3,075	(2,590)	..	..	..	..
129. Rodrur*	.. Nizamabad ..	..	3,060	(2,940)	..	..	..	..
130. Rajura*	.. Adilabad ..	M. ..	2,968	(2,685)	..	..	..	..
131. Bhimgal*	.. Nizamabad ..	..	2,789	(2,597)	..	..	..	..
132. Audol*	.. Medak ..	M. ..	2,610	(2,471)	..	..	..	..
133. Janwada*	.. Bidar ..	..	2,199	(2,326)	..	..	..	..

IV.

for the last fifty years.

TABLE IV.

TOWNS CLASSIFED BY POPULATION WITH VARIATION SINCE 1881.

VARIATION + INCREASE — DECREASE					Variation in period 1881 to 1931 Increase + Decrease —	MALES			FEMALES		
1921 to 1931	1911 to 1921	1901 to 1911	1891 to 1901	1881 to 1891		1931	1921	1911	1931	1921	1911
10	11	12	13	14	15	16	17	18	19	20	21
— 383	— 554	+ 107	— 178	— 470	— 1,478	*2,805*	2,939	3,154	*2,744*	2,993	3,332
+ 455	..	..	..	..	..	*2,751*	(2,488)	..	*2,786*	(2,594)	..
— 14	— 3,976	+ 1,205	— 668	..	..	*2,963*	2,669	4,676	*2,402*	2,710	4,679
+ 1,168	..	..	..	..	..	*2,771*	(2,215)	..	*2,562*	(1,950)	..
+ 1,248	..	..	..	..	..	*2,686*	(2,028)	..	*2,644*	(2,034)	..
+ 1,223	..	..	..	..	..	*2,780*	(2,055)	..	*2,524*	(2,026)	..
+ 1,826	..	..	..	..	..	*2,705*	(2,031)	..	*2,583*	(1,931)	..
+ 866	..	..	..	..	..	*2,620*	(2,167)	..	*2,665*	(2,252)	..
— 2,386	..	..	..	..	..	*2,721*	(3,856)	..	*2,559*	(3,810)	..
+ 592	— 972	— 58	+ 142	..	..	*2,747*	2,459	2,905	*2,513*	2,209	2,785
+ 742	..	..	..	..	..	*2,702*	(2,263)	..	*2,532*	(2,229)	..
+ 639	— 1,359	+ 1,138	— 184	..	..	*2,650*	2,286	3,006	*2,577*	2,302	2,941
+ 1,778	..	..	..	..	..	*2,607*	(1,778)	..	*2,611*	(1,662)	..
+ 1,191	..	..	..	..	..	*2,660*	(2,068)	..	*2,542*	(1,943)	..
+ 1,810	..	..	..	..	..	*2,587*	(1,904)	..	*2,545*	(1,918)	..
+ 490	+ 157	..	..	..	..	*2,568*	2,230	2,137	*2,508*	2,336	2,292
— 418	+ 416	..	..	..	..	*2,530*	2,756	2,423	*2,519*	2,706	2,623
+ 553	..	..	..	..	..	*2,466*	(2,173)	..	*2,540*	(2,280)	..
+ 448	— 2,440	— 782	+ 1,088	+ 1,577	— 109	*2,403*	2,242	3,455	*2,552*	2,265	3,492
— 644	— 1,547	+ 1,267	— 898	+ 154	— 1,668	*2,638*	2,822	3,501	*2,266*	2,726	3,594
+ 1,113	..	..	..	..	..	*2,288*	(1,675)	..	*2,526*	(2,026)	..
+ 1,710	..	..	..	..	..	*2,310*	(1,479)	..	*2,337*	(1,458)	..
+ 180	..	..	..	..	..	*2,338*	(2,212)	..	*2,308*	(2,254)	..
+ 1788	..	..	..	..	..	*2,277*	(1,506)	..	*2,357*	(1,340)	..
— 379	..	..	..	..	..	*2,324*	(2,486)	..	*2,286*	(2,503)	..
+ 69	..	..	..	..	..	*2,288*	(2,348)	..	*2,297*	(2,168)	..
+ 441	..	..	..	..	..	*2,287*	(2,072)	..	*2,173*	(1,944)	..
+ 614	..	..	..	..	..	*2,211*	(1,884)	..	*2,243*	(1,936)	..
+ 428	..	..	..	..	..	*2,226*	(1,938)	..	*2,226*	(2,001)	..
— 1,037	— 145	— 208	— 2,331	+ 1,683	— 2,038	*2,168*	2,624	2,689	*2,201*	2,782	2,862
+ 189	— 760	..	..	..	..	*2,221*	2,159	2,554	*2,135*	2,008	2,873
+ 89	..	..	..	..	..	*2,127*	(2,069)	..	*2,214*	(2,233)	..
+ 787	..	..	..	..	..	*2,197*	(1,821)	..	*2,142*	(1,731)	..
+ 359	..	..	..	..	..	*2,165*	(1,926)	..	*1,974*	(1,854)	..
+ 222	+ 184	..	..	..	..	*2,131*	1,936	1,776	*1,820*	1,793	1,769
+ 918	..	..	..	..	..	*1,969*	(1,466)	..	*1,908*	(1,493)	..
— 333	..	..	..	..	..	*1,817*	(2,015)	..	*2,054*	(2,189)	..
+ 1,498	— 906	..	..	..	..	*1,895*	1,136	1,617	*1,944*	1,205	1,630
+ 471	..	..	..	..	..	*1,845*	(1,647)	..	*1,955*	(1,682)	..
+ 43	— 494	..	..	..	..	*1,853*	1,816	2,018	*1,896*	1,890	2,182
+ 1,797	..	..	..	..	..	*1,805*	(905)	..	*1,897*	(1,000)	..
+ 436	— 606	..	..	..	..	*1,875*	1,636	1,873	*1,784*	1,587	1,956
+ 284	..	..	..	..	..	*1,710*	(1,644)	..	*1,641*	(1,423)	..
— 814	..	..	..	..	..	*1,758*	(2,080)	..	*1,516*	(2,008)	..
+ 287	..	..	..	..	..	*1,722*	(1,586)	..	*1,535*	(1,384)	..
+ 1,072	..	..	..	..	..	*1,664*	(1,106)	..	*1,530*	(1,016)	..
+ 1,285	..	..	..	..	..	*1,669*	(915)	..	*1,455*	(924)	..
+ 485	..	..	..	..	..	*1,633*	(1,343)	..	*1,442*	(1,247)	..
+ 120	..	..	..	..	..	*1,521*	(1,845)	..	*1,539*	(1,595)	..
+ 283	..	..	..	..	..	*1,521*	(1,410)	..	*1,447*	(1,275)	..
+ 192	..	..	..	..	..	*1,356*	(1,185)	..	*1,433*	(1,412)	..
+ 139	..	..	..	..	..	*1,238*	(1,182)	..	*1,372*	(1,339)	..
— 127	..	..	..	..	..	*1,110*	(1,160)	..	*1,089*	(1,166)	..

N.B.—M.—Municipality. C.—Cantonment. P.—Paigah. ⁖.—Samasthan. J.—Jagir.

Hyderabad Census, 1931

Table V.

TOWNS ARRANGED TERRITORIALLY WITH POPULATION BY RELIGION

TABLE V.

Towns arranged Territorially with Population by Religion.

DISTRICTS	TOWN, MUNICIPALITY SUBURBS, CANTONMENTS, ETC.	POPULATION			HINDU														
					Brahmanic Hindu			Adi-Hindu			Arya			Brahmo			Total		
		Persons	Males	Females	Persons	Males	Females	Persons	Males	Females	Persons	Males	Females	Persons	Males	Females	Persons	Males	Females
1	2	3	4	5	6	7	8	9	10	11	12	13	14	15	16	17	18	19	20
All Towns ..	.. ..	**1,616,981**	**836,874**	**780,107**	**841,600**	**433,585**	**408,015**	**206,201**	**104,612**	**101,589**	**1,019**	**496**	**523**	**81**	**46**	**35**	**1,048,901**	**538,739**	**510,162**
Hyderabad City.	Hyderabad City (M & C)	**466,894**	**247,623**	**219,271**	**172,279**	**90,790**	**81,489**	**79,839**	**41,120**	**38,719**	**382**	**196**	**186**	**77**	**44**	**33**	**252,577**	**132,150**	**120,427**
	Municipality ..	*428,211*	223,945	204,266	*163,602*	85,428	78,179	*75,769*	38,890	36,879	*329*	166	163	*77*	44	33	*239,777*	124,528	115,254
	Cantonment ..	*38,683*	23,678	15,005	*8,677*	5,367	3,310	*4,070*	2,230	1,840	*53*	30	23	..	..	..	*12,800*	7,627	5,173
Atraf-i-Balda ..		**11,838**	**5,935**	**5,903**	**6,740**	**3,377**	**3,363**	**1,770**	**875**	**895**	..	..	..	..	..	..	**8,510**	**4,252**	**4,258**
	Homnabad ..	*6,550*	3,230	3,320	*3,219*	1,572	1,647	*616*	292	324	..	..	..	..	..	..	*3,835*	1,864	1,971
	Khilashahpur ..	*5,288*	2,705	2,583	*3,521*	1,805	1,716	*1,154*	583	571	..	..	..	..	..	..	*4,675*	2,388	2,287
Warangal ..		**117,579**	**62,482**	**55,097**	**65,306**	**34,825**	**30,481**	**22,019**	**11,427**	**10,592**	**83**	**40**	**43**	..	..	..	**87,408**	**46,292**	**41,116**
	Warangal City (M) ..	*62,119*	33,826	28,798	*35,199*	18,926	16,273	*11,336*	5,812	5,524	..	..	..	..	..	..	*46,535*	24,738	21,797
	Yellandlapad (M) ..	*19,872*	11,077	8,795	*10,166*	5,792	4,374	*5,806*	3,103	2,703	..	..	..	..	..	..	*15,972*	8,895	7,077
	Khammam (M) ..	*13,002*	6,448	6,554	*7,794*	3,819	3,975	*1,692*	863	829	*83*	40	43	..	..	..	*9,569*	4,722	4,847
	Hasanparthi ..	*6,198*	3,199	2,999	*4,364*	2,264	2,100	*1,104*	578	526	..	..	..	..	..	..	*5,468*	2,842	2,626
	Mahbubabad (M) ..	*5,824*	3,044	2,780	*4,221*	2,165	2,056	*546*	285	261	..	..	..	..	..	..	*4,767*	2,450	2,317
	Paloncha (S) ..	*5,330*	2,686	2,644	*1,307*	695	612	*670*	337	333	..	..	..	..	..	..	*1,977*	1,032	945
	Mandarpalli ..	*5,234*	2,702	2,532	*2,255*	1,164	1,091	*865*	449	416	..	..	..	..	..	..	*3,120*	1,613	1,507
Karimnagar ..	..	**82,818**	**41,883**	**40,935**	**56,802**	**28,579**	**28,223**	**10,182**	**5,135**	**5,047**	**111**	**48**	**63**	..	..	..	**67,095**	**33,762**	**33,333**
	Jagtial (M) ..	*13,882*	7,071	6,811	*9,804*	4,995	4,809	*1,431*	742	689	*9*	6	3	..	..	..	*11,244*	5,743	5,501
	Karimnagar (M) ..	*10,903*	5,580	5,323	*5,550*	2,869	2,681	*1,398*	684	714	*102*	42	60	..	..	..	*7,050*	3,595	3,455
	Manthani ..	*7,560*	3,791	3,769	*6,711*	3,323	3,388	*331*	171	160	..	..	..	..	..	..	*7,042*	3,494	3,548
	Koratla ..	*6,996*	3,479	3,517	*4,939*	2,490	2,449	*745*	369	376	..	..	..	..	..	..	*5,684*	2,859	2,825
	Huzurabad (M) ..	*6,251*	3,317	2,934	*4,697*	2,457	2,240	*836*	439	397	..	..	..	..	..	..	*5,533*	2,896	2,637
	Vemalwada (J) ..	*7,645*	3,757	3,888	*6,257*	3,028	3,229	*597*	298	299	..	..	..	..	..	..	*6,854*	3,326	3,528
	Peddapalli (J) ..	*8,945*	4,600	4,345	*5,940*	3,018	2,922	*955*	496	459	..	..	..	..	..	..	*6,895*	3,514	3,381
	Sirsilla (M) ..	*5,752*	2,944	2,808	*3,997*	2,047	1,950	*1,192*	596	596	..	..	..	..	..	..	*5,189*	2,643	2,546
	Dharmapuri (J) ..	*5,537*	2,751	2,786	*4,520*	2,231	2,289	*748*	379	369	..	..	..	..	..	..	*5,268*	2,610	2,658
	Gambhiraopet ..	*5,006*	2,466	2,540	*1,710*	820	890	*1,420*	699	721	..	..	..	..	..	..	*3,130*	1,519	1,611
	Manakundur ..	*4,341*	2,127	2,214	*2,677*	1,301	1,376	*529*	262	267	..	..	..	..	..	..	*3,206*	1,563	1,643

TABLE V.
TOWNS ARRANGED TERRITORIALLY WITH POPULATION BY RELIGION.

TABLE V.

Towns arranged Territorially with Population by Religion.

DISTRICTS	TOWN, MUNICIPALITY, SUBURBS, CANTONMENTS, ETC.	JAIN			SIKH			MUSLIM			CHRISTIAN			ZOROASTRIAN			BUDDHIST			JEW			TRIBAL		
		Persons	Males	Females	Persons	Males	Females	Persons	Males	Females	Persons	Males	Females	Persons	Males	Females	Persons	Males	Females	Persons	Males	Females	Persons	Males	Females
1	2	21	22	23	24	25	26	27	28	29	30	31	32	33	34	35	36	37	38	39	40	41	42	43	44
All Towns ..	.. ..	6,141	3,263	2,878	3,441	2,226	1,215	514,281	269,005	245,276	26,261	14,407	11,854	1,520	793	727	38	20	18	27	11	16	16,371	8,410	7,961
Hyderabad City	Hyderabad City (M & C)	312	194	118	1,002	690	312	192,343	103,095	89,248	16,123	9,217	6,906	1,092	548	544	38	20	18	27	11	16	3,380	1,698	1,682
	Municipality ..	*312*	194	118	*796*	516	280	*171,594*	91,052	80,542	*11,291*	5,435	5,836	*1,092*	548	544	*38*	20	18	*27*	11	16	*3,284*	1,646	1,638
	Cantonment ..	..	..	..	*206*	174	32	*20,749*	12,043	8,706	*4,832*	3,782	1,050	..	..	..	..	..	..	..	..	..	*96*	52	44
Atraf-i-Balda..		24	9	15	..	..	..	2,841	1,427	1,414	11	3	8	..	..	..	..	..	..	..	..	..	452	244	208
	Homnabad (M) ..	*24*	9	15	..	..	..	*2,680*	1,354	1,326	*11*	3	8	..	..	..	..	..	..	..	..	..	..	..	..
	Khilashahpur ..	..	..	..	..	..	..	*161*	73	88	..	..	..	..	..	..	..	..	..	..	..	..	*452*	244	208
Warangal ..		..	..	..	132	86	46	22,303	12,178	10,125	1,815	903	912	40	30	10	..	..	..	..	..	..	5,881	2,993	2,888
	Warangal City (M) ..	..	..	..	*114*	72	42	*14,460*	8,003	6,457	*748*	357	391	*7*	7	..	..	..	..	..	..	..	*255*	149	106
	Yellandlapad (M) ..	..	..	..	*10*	6	4	*2,905*	1,619	1,286	*757*	401	356	*24*	16	8	..	..	..	..	..	..	*204*	140	64
	Khammam (M) ..	..	..	..	..	..	..	*3,153*	1,004	1,549	*167*	71	96	*9*	7	2	..	..	..	..	..	..	104	44	60
	Hasanparti ..	..	..	..	..	..	..	606	293	313	98	49	49	..	..	..	..	..	..	..	..	..	26	15	11
	Mahbubabad (M) ..	..	..	..	*2*	2	..	*1,041*	584	457	*6*	2	4	..	..	..	..	..	..	..	..	..	*8*	6	2
	Paloncha (S) ..	..	..	..	6	6	..	133	73	60	*39*	23	16	..	..	..	..	..	..	..	..	..	*3,175*	1,552	1,623
	Mandarpalli ..	..	..	..	..	..	..	5	2	3	..	..	..	..	..	..	..	..	..	..	..	..	*2,109*	1,087	1,022
Karimnagar ..	..	19	2	17	25	16	9	14,677	7,615	7,062	936	457	479	4	2	2	..	..	..	..	..	..	62	29	33
	Jagtial (M) ..	..	..	..	..	..	..	*2,398*	1,211	1,187	*240*	117	123	..	..	..	..	..	..	..	..	..	..	..	..
	Karimnagar (M) ..	..	..	..	*16*	9	7	*3,485*	1,814	1,671	*351*	161	190	*1*	1	..	..	..	..	..	..	..	..	..	..
	Manthani ..	..	..	..	..	..	..	*518*	297	221	..	..	..	..	..	..	..	..	..	..	..	..	..	..	..
	Koratla ..	..	..	..	..	..	..	*1,312*	620	692	..	..	..	..	..	..	..	..	..	..	..	..	..	..	..
	Huzurabad (M) ..	*15*	..	15	..	..	..	*530*	330	200	*162*	86	76	*3*	1	2	..	..	..	..	..	..	..	..	..
	Vemalwada (J) ..	..	..	..	*6*	4	2	*744*	408	336	..	..	..	..	..	..	..	..	..	..	..	..	*8*	4	4
	Peddapalli (J) ..	*4*	2	2	*3*	3	..	*1,847*	982	865	*183*	93	90	..	..	..	..	..	..	..	..	..	*41*	19	22
	Sirsilla (M) ..	..	..	..	..	..	..	*563*	301	262	..	..	..	..	..	..	..	..	..	..	..	..	*13*	6	7
	Dharmapuri (J) ..	..	..	..	..	..	..	*269*	141	128	..	..	..	..	..	..	..	..	..	..	..	..	..	..	..
	Gambhiraopet ..	..	..	..	..	..	..	*1,876*	947	929	..	..	..	..	..	..	..	..	..	..	..	..	..	..	..
	Manakundur ..	..	..	..	..	..	..	*1,135*	564	571	..	..	..	..	..	..	..	..	..	..	..	..	..	..	..

TABLE V.

Towns arranged Territorially with Population by Religion.

DISTRICTS	TOWN, MUNICIPALITY, SUBURBS, CANTONMENTS, ETC.	POPULATION			HINDU														
					Brahmanic Hindu			Adi-Hindu			Arya			Brahmo			Total		
		Persons	Males	Females	Persons	Males	Females	Persons	Males	Females	Persons	Males	Females	Persons	Males	Females	Persons	Males	Females
1	2	3	4	5	6	7	8	9	10	11	12	13	14	15	16	17	18	19	20
Adilabad ..	..	**48,084**	**24,272**	**23,812**	**32,074**	**15,936**	**16,138**	**4,027**	**2,067**	**1,960**	..	..	..	..	..	..	**36,101**	**18,003**	**18,098**
	Nirmal (M) ..	12,585	6,064	6,521	8,201	3,933	4,268	1,103	505	598	..	..	..	..	..	..	9,304	4,438	4,866
	Adilabad (M) ..	8,096	4,097	3,999	4,864	2,406	2,458	622	368	254	..	..	..	..	..	..	5,486	2,774	2,712
	Chinnur ..	7,751	3,887	3,864	6,155	3,073	3,082	328	174	154	..	..	..	..	..	..	6,483	3,247	3,236
	Asifabad (M) ..	3,075	1,633	1,442	1,999	990	1,009	83	44	39	..	..	..	..	..	..	2,082	1,034	1,048
	Rajura (M) ..	2,968	1,521	1,447	1,992	1,004	988	316	159	157	..	..	..	..	..	..	2,308	1,163	1,145
	Lakshatipet (M) ..	3,124	1,669	1,455	1,995	1,072	923	330	170	160	..	..	..	..	..	..	2,325	1,242	1,083
	Sirpur (M) ..	3,877	1,969	1,908	2,278	1,138	1,140	610	331	279	..	..	..	..	..	..	2,888	1,469	1,419
	Boath (M) ..	3,351	1,710	1,641	2,469	1,212	1,257	172	88	84	..	..	..	..	..	..	2,641	1,300	1,341
	Kinwat (M) ..	3,257	1,722	1,535	2,121	1,108	1,013	463	228	235	..	..	..	..	..	..	2,584	1,336	1,248
Medak ..	..	**51,783**	**25,818**	**25,965**	**33,723**	**16,707**	**17,016**	**4,872**	**2,442**	**2,430**	..	..	..	..	..	.	**38,595**	**19,149**	**19,446**
	Medak (M) ..	11,156	5,543	5,613	5,686	2,812	2,874	1,478	746	732	..	..	..	..	..	.	7,164	3,558	3,606
	Siddipet (M) ..	11,260	5,582	5,678	9,222	4,595	4,627	..	..	..	..	..	..	..	..	..	9,222	4,595	4,627
	Sadaseopet (M) ..	8,071	4,106	3,965	5,782	2,927	2,855	349	169	180	..	..	..	..	..	..	6,131	3,096	3,035
	Jogipet (M) ..	5,049	2,530	2,519	4,009	1,980	2,029	248	126	122	..	..	..	..	..	..	4,257	2,106	2,151
	Sangareddipet (M) ..	5,227	2,650	2,577	2,396	1,129	1,267	601	291	310	..	..	..	..	..	..	2,997	1,420	1,577
	Andol (M) ..	2,610	1,238	1,372	1,431	687	744	459	214	245	..	..	..	..	..	..	1,890	901	989
	Tekmal ..	3,800	1,845	1,955	2,321	1,150	1,171	531	269	262	..	..	..	..	..	..	2,852	1,419	1,433
	Ibrahimpatan ..	4,610	2,324	2,286	2,876	1,427	1,449	1,206	627	579	..	..	..	..	..	..	4,082	2,054	2,028
Nizamabad ..	..	**64,599**	**32,448**	**32,151**	**41,749**	**20,728**	**21,021**	**7,691**	**3,723**	**3,968**	..	..	..	..	..	..	**49,440**	**24,451**	**24,989**
	Nizamabad ..	18,809	9,550	9,259	11,375	5,797	5,578	2,093	1,003	1,090	..	..	..	..	..	..	13,468	6,800	6,668
	Armur (M) ..	7,279	3,582	3,697	5,557	2,706	2,851	487	241	246	..	..	..	..	..	..	6,044	2,947	3,097
	Bodhan (M) ..	7,045	3,510	3,535	4,253	2,125	2,128	930	465	465	..	..	..	..	..	..	5,183	2,590	2,593
	Kotgir (P) ..	3,749	1,853	1,896	2,041	1,026	1,015	533	259	274	..	..	..	..	..	..	2,574	1,285	1,289
	Achampet ..	8,761	4,682	4,079	6,095	3,161	2,934	995	522	473	..	..	..	..	..	..	7,090	3,683	3,407
	Yellareddipet (M) ..	3,839	1,895	1,944	2,230	1,111	1,119	629	293	336	..	..	..	..	..	..	2,859	1,404	1,455
	Banswada ..	4,454	2,211	2,243	2,885	1,432	1,453	803	379	424	..	..	..	..	..	..	3,688	1,811	1,877
	Rodrur ..	3,060	1,521	1,539	2,241	1,115	1,126	324	143	181	..	..	..	..	..	..	2,565	1,258	1,307
	Bimgal ..	2,789	1,356	1,433	2,023	992	1,031	377	191	186	..	..	..	..	..	..	2,400	1,183	1,217
	Balkonda (J) ..	4,814	2,288	2,526	3,049	1,263	1,786	520	227	293	..	..	..	..	..	..	3,569	1,490	2,079

4

TABLE V.

Towns arranged Territorially with Population by Religion.

DISTRICTS	TOWN, MUNICIPALITY, SUBURBS CANTONMENTS ETC.	JAIN			SIKH			MUSLIM			CHRISTIAN			ZOROASTRIAN			BUDDHIST			JEW			TRIBAL		
		Persons	Males	Females	Persons	Males	Females	Persons	Males	Females	Persons	Males	Females	Persons	Males	Females	Persons	Males	Females	Persons	Males	Females	Persons	Males	Females
1	2	21	22	23	24	25	26	27	28	29	30	31	32	33	34	35	36	37	38	39	40	41	42	43	44
Adilabad ..	..	23	12	11	7	1	6	10,918	5,724	5,194	250	130	120	24	14	10	..	..	..	..	..	..	761	388	373
	Nirmal (M) ..	3	2	1	4	..	4	3,175	1,570	1,605	12	6	6	8	4	4	..	..	..	..	..	..	79	44	35
	Adilabad (M) ..	..	..	..	..	..	..	2,578	1,310	1,268	..	..	..	..	..	..	..	..	..	..	..	..	32	13	19
	Chinnur ..	..	..	..	..	..	..	1,173	594	579	5	2	3	..	..	..	..	..	..	..	..	..	90	44	46
	Asifabad (M) ..	6	4	2	..	..	..	968	587	381	..	..	..	9	3	6	..	..	..	..	..	..	10	5	5
	Rajura (M) ..	8	4	4	..	..	..	539	294	245	..	..	..	7	7	..	..	..	..	..	..	..	106	53	53
	Lakshatipet (M) ..	..	..	..	..	..	..	587	318	269	212	109	103	..	..	..	..	..	..	..	..	..	..	..	..
	Sirpur (M) ..	6	2	4	..	..	..	914	464	450	..	..	..	..	..	..	..	..	..	..	..	..	69	34	35
	Boath (M) ..	..	..	..	3	1	2	405	254	151	21	13	8	..	..	..	..	..	..	..	..	..	281	142	139
	Kinwat (M) ..	..	..	..	..	..	..	579	333	246	..	..	..	..	..	..	..	..	..	..	..	..	94	53	41
Medak ..		91	59	32	12	5	7	11,854	5,939	5,915	1,231	666	565	..	..	..	..	..	..	..	..	..	..	..	..
	Medak (M) ..	10	4	6	4	2	2	2,918	1,402	1,516	1,060	577	483	..	..	..	..	..	..	..	..	..	..	..	..
	Siddipet (M) ..	..	..	..	..	..	..	2,038	987	1,051	..	..	..	..	..	..	..	..	..	..	..	..	..	..	..
	Sadaseopet (M) ..	47	30	17	1	1	..	1,789	924	865	103	55	48	..	..	..	..	..	..	..	..	..	..	..	..
	Jogipet (M) ..	21	13	8	..	..	..	771	411	360	..	..	..	..	..	..	..	..	..	..	..	..	..	..	..
	Sangareddipet (M) ..	13	12	1	7	2	5	2,210	1,216	994	..	..	..	..	..	..	..	..	..	..	..	..	..	..	..
	Andol (M) ..	..	..	..	..	..	..	720	337	383	..	..	..	..	..	..	..	..	..	..	..	..	..	..	..
	Teknal (M) ..	..	..	..	..	..	..	948	426	522	..	..	..	..	..	..	..	..	..	..	..	..	..	..	..
	Ibrahimpatan (M) ..	..	..	..	..	..	..	460	236	224	68	34	34	..	..	..	..	..	..	..	..	..	..	..	..
Nizamabad ..	..	306	168	138	175	92	83	13,699	7,212	6,487	262	134	128	23	12	11	..	..	..	..	..	..	694	379	315
	Nizamabad ..	17	12	5	79	40	39	5,046	2,605	2,441	181	84	97	3	2	1	..	..	..	..	..	..	15	7	8
	Armur (M) ..	..	..	..	..	..	..	1,072	556	516	26	17	9	6	2	4	..	..	..	..	..	..	131	60	71
	Bodhan (M) ..	..	..	..	..	..	..	1,837	899	938	..	..	..	..	..	..	..	..	..	..	..	..	25	21	4
	Kotgir (P) ..	..	..	..	..	..	..	1,171	566	605	..	..	..	4	2	2	..	..	..	..	..	..	..	..	..
	Achampet ..	289	156	133	95	51	44	873	557	316	1	1	..	1	..	1	..	..	..	..	..	..	412	234	178
	Yellareddipet (M) ..	..	..	..	1	1	..	883	439	444	54	32	22	6	3	3	..	..	..	..	..	..	36	16	20
	Banswada ..	..	..	..	..	..	..	763	397	366	..	..	..	3	3	..	..	..	..	..	..	..	..	..	..
	Rodrur ..	..	..	..	..	..	..	435	234	201	..	..	..	..	..	..	..	..	..	..	..	..	60	29	31
	Bimgal ..	..	..	..	..	..	..	374	161	213	..	..	..	..	..	..	..	..	..	..	..	..	15	12	3
	Balkonda (J) ..	..	..	..	..	..	..	1,245	798	447	..	..	..	..	..	..	..	..	..	..	..	..	..	..	..

TABLE V.

Towns arranged Territorially with Population by Religion.

DISTRICTS	TOWN, MUNICIPALITY, SUBURBS, CANTONMENTS, ETC.	POPULATION			HINDU														
					Brahmanic Hindu			Adi-Hindu			Arya			Brahmo			Total		
		Persons	Males	Females	Persons	Males	Females	Persons	Males	Females	Persons	Males	Females	Persons	Males	Females	Persons	Males	Females
1	2	3	4	5	6	7	8	9	10	11	12	13	14	15	16	17	18	19	20
Mahbubnagar..	..	32,401	16,347	16,054	22,389	11,137	11,252	2,454	1,298	1,156	21	11	10	..	..	..	24,864	12,446	12,418
	Narayanpet (M) ..	14,025	6,959	7,066	9,005	4,419	4,586	541	276	265	..	..	..	..	..	..	9,546	4,695	4,851
	Mahbubnagar (M) ..	13,300	6,820	6,480	10,092	5,100	4,992	1,330	711	619	..	..	..	..	..	..	11,422	5,811	5,611
	Wanparthi (S) ..	5,076	2,568	2,508	3,292	1,618	1,674	583	311	272	21	11	10	..	..	..	3,896	1,940	1,956
Nalgonda ..	..	25,702	12,925	12,777	13,871	6,942	6,929	3,863	1,944	1,919	..	..	..	..	..	..	17,734	8,886	8,848
	Nalgonda (M) ..	9,711	4,927	4,784	3,929	2,010	1,919	1,320	652	668	..	..	..	..	..	..	5,249	2,662	2,587
	Bhongir (M) ..	10,859	5,411	5,448	7,028	3,464	3,564	1,237	634	603	..	..	..	..	..	..	8,265	4,098	4,167
	Chiriala (Jangaon) (M).	5,132	2,587	2,545	2,914	1,468	1,446	1,306	658	648	..	..	..	..	..	..	4,220	2,126	2,094
Aurangabad ..	..	79,918	41,652	38,266	39,707	20,588	19,119	6,452	3,122	3,330	145	60	85	2	1	1	46,306	23,771	22,535
	Aurangabad City (M&C)	36,870	19,622	17,248	15,520	8,372	7,148	3,212	1,494	1,718	145	60	85	2	1	1	18,879	9,927	8,952
	Aurangabad (M) ..	29,288	15,132	14,156	12,511	6,510	6,001	2,335	1,085	1,250	125	59	66	2	1	1	14,973	7,655	7,318
	Aurangabad (C) ..	7,582	4,490	3,092	3,009	1,862	1,147	877	409	468	20	1	10	..	..	..	3,906	2,272	1,634
	Jalna (M) ..	22,408	11,764	10,644	12,030	6,289	5,741	1,701	858	843	..	..	..	..	..	..	13,731	7,147	6,584
	Qadirabad (M) ..	7,909	3,943	3,966	4,354	2,102	2,252	658	338	320	..	..	..	..	..	..	5,012	2,440	2,572
	Vaijapur (M) ..	6,437	3,225	3,212	3,863	1,917	1,946	561	276	285	..	..	..	..	..	..	4,424	2,193	2,231
	Paithan (M) ..	6,294	3,098	3,196	3,940	1,908	2,032	320	156	164	..	..	..	..	..	..	4,260	2,064	2,196
Bir ..	..	57,751	29,583	28,168	36,500	18,778	17,722	4,599	2,270	2,329	199	98	101	..	..	..	41,298	21,146	20,152
	Bir (M)	14,840	7,577	7,263	8,641	4,407	4,234	553	278	275	3	3	..	..	..	..	9,197	4,688	4,509
	Mominabad (M) ..	10,974	5,611	5,363	7,444	3,820	3,624	687	330	357	..	..	..	..	..	..	8,131	4,150	3,981
	Manjlegaon (M) ..	5,260	2,747	2,513	3,371	1,782	1,589	387	184	203	3	1	2	..	..	..	3,761	1,967	1,794
	Georai (M) ..	5,218	2,607	2,611	3,574	1,779	1,795	434	201	233	..	..	..	..	..	..	4,008	1,980	2,028
	Parli (J)	7,759	3,937	3,822	5,253	2,676	2,577	576	277	299	..	..	..	..	..	..	5,829	2,953	2,876
	Kaij ..	3,194	1,664	1,530	1,639	862	777	469	240	220	..	..	..	..	..	..	2,108	1,111	997
	Fatehabad ..	5,304	2,780	2,524	2,914	1,542	1,372	567	293	274	193	94	99	..	..	..	3,674	1,929	1,745
	Paigaon (J) ..	5,202	2,660	2,542	3,664	1,910	1,754	926	458	468	..	..	..	..	..	..	4,590	2,368	2,222

TABLE V.

Towns arranged Territorially with Population by Religion.

DISTRICTS	TOWN, MUNICIPALITY, SUBURBS, CANTONMENTS, ETC.	Jain			Sikh			Muslim			Christian			Zoroastrian			Buddhist			Jew			Tribal		
		Persons	Males	Females	Persons	Males	Females	Persons	Males	Females	Persons	Males	Females	Persons	Males	Females	Persons	Males	Females	Persons	Males	Females	Persons	Males	Females
1	2	21	22	23	24	25	26	27	28	29	30	31	32	33	34	35	36	37	38	39	40	41	42	43	44
Mahbubnagar..	..	1	1	..	17	8	9	6,483	3,303	3,180	215	110	105	1	1	..	..	..	..	..	..	..	820	478	342
	Narayanpet (M) ..	*1*	1	..	*3*	1	2	*4,472*	2200	2,212	*1*	1	..	*1*	1	..	..	..	..	..	..	..	*1*	..	1
	Mahbubnagar (M) ..	..	..	..	*8*	5	3	*971*	483	488	*87*	46	41	..	..	..	..	..	..	..	..	..	*812*	475	337
	Wanparthi (S) ..	..	..	..	*6*	2	4	*1,040*	560	480	*127*	63	64	..	..	..	..	..	..	..	..	..	*7*	3	4
Nalgonda ..	..	6	2	4	87	47	40	7,556	3,814	3,742	273	142	131	2	1	1	..	..	..	..	..	..	44	33	11
	Nalgonda (M) ..	..	..	..	*74*	40	34	*4,111*	2,070	2,041	*254*	132	122	..	..	..	..	..	..	..	..	..	*23*	23	..
	Bhongir (M) ..	6	2	4	*13*	7	6	*2,554*	1,293	1,261	*19*	10	9	*2*	1	1	..	..	..	..	..	..	*21*	10	11
	Chiriala (Jangoan) (M) .	..	..	..	..	..	..	*891*	451	440	..	..	..	..	..	..	..	..	..	..	..	..	..	..	..
Aurangabad ..	..	908	509	399	385	302	83	29,775	15,757	14,018	1,647	876	771	207	105	102	..	..	..	..	..	..	690	332	358
	Aurangabad City (M&C)	*361*	215	146	*374*	296	78	*16,104*	8,567	7,537	*788*	440	348	*197*	101	96	..	..	..	..	..	..	*167*	76	91
	Aurangabad (M) ..	*328*	196	132	*157*	87	70	*13,492*	7,023	6,469	*12*	7	5	*159*	88	71	..	..	..	..	..	..	*167*	76	91
	Aurangabad (C) ..	*33*	19	14	*217*	209	8	*.612*	1,544	1,068	*776*	433	343	*38*	*13*	*25*	..	..	..	..	..	..	..	..	..
	Jalna (M) ..	*378*	204	174	*8*	4	4	*7,447*	3,992	3,455	*655*	330	325	*10*	4	6	..	..	..	..	..	..	*179*	83	96
	Qadirabad (M) ..	*62*	33	29	..	..	..	*2,602*	1,349	1,253	*81*	41	40	..	..	..	..	..	..	..	..	..	*152*	80	72
	Vaijapur ..	*87*	50	37	*3*	2	1	*1,644*	837	807	*114*	60	54	..	..	..	..	..	..	..	..	..	*165*	83	82
	Paithan (M) ..	*20*	7	13	..	..	..	*1,978*	1,012	966	*9*	5	4	..	..	..	..	..	..	..	..	..	*27*	10	17
Bir ..	..	710	354	356	13	7	6	15,118	7,756	7,362	12	6	6	3	3	..	..	..	..	..	..	..	597	311	286
	Bir (M)	*319*	159	160	*9*	4	5	*5,183*	2,655	2,328	*2*	2	..	*2*	2	..	..	..	..	..	..	..	*128*	67	61
	Mominabad (M) ..	*180*	87	93	..	..	..	*2,653*	1,370	1,283	*10*	4	6	..	..	..	..	..	..	..	..	..	..	..	..
	Manjlegaon (M) ..	6	4	2	*4*	3	1	*1,408*	727	681	..	..	..	*1*	1	..	..	..	..	..	..	..	*80*	45	35
	Georai (M) ..	*62*	31	31	..	..	..	*1,138*	591	547	..	..	..	..	..	..	..	..	..	..	..	..	*10*	5	5
	Parli	*49*	23	26	..	..	..	*1,881*	961	920	..	..	..	..	..	..	..	..	..	..	..	..	..	..	..
	Kaij ..	*53*	24	29	..	..	..	*1,033*	529	504	..	..	..	..	..	..	..	..	..	..	..	..	..	..	..
	Fatehabad ..	*17*	12	5	..	..	..	*1,261*	659	602	..	..	..	..	..	..	..	..	..	..	..	..	*352*	180	172
	Paigaon(J) ..	*24*	14	10	..	..	..	*561*	264	297	..	..	..	..	..	..	..	..	..	..	..	..	*27*	14	13

TABLE V.

Towns arranged Territorially with Population by Religion.

DISTRICTS	TOWN, MUNICIPALITY, SUBURBS, CANTONMENTS, ETC.	POPULATION			HINDU																
					Brahmanic Hindu			Adi-Hindu			Arya			Brahmo			Total		
		Persons	Males	Females	Persons	Males	Females	Persons	Males	Females	Persons	Males	Females	Persons	Males	Females	Persons	Males	Females
1	2	3	4	5	6	7	8	9	10	11	12	13	14	15	16	17	18	19	20
Nander ..	..	69,863	35,684	34,179	38,545	19,695	18,850	8,885	4,487	4,398	5	5	..	..	..	..	47,435	24,187	23,248
	Nander (M) ..	*26,992*	14,332	12,660	*13,343*	7,065	6,278	*3,656*	1,930	1,726	..	..	..	..	..	..	*16,999*	8,995	8,004
	Bhainsa ..	*8,525*	4,267	4,258	*4,044*	2,047	1,997	*979*	477	502	5	5	..	..	..	..	*5,028*	2,529	2,499
	Deglur (M) ..	*6,553*	3,310	3,243	*4,079*	2,066	2,013	*1,613*	820	793	..	..	..	..	..	..	*5,692*	2,886	2,806
	Kondalwadi (P) ..	*6,840*	3,356	3,484	*4,991*	2,418	2,573	*495*	260	235	..	..	..	..	..	..	*5,486*	2,678	2,808
	Mudhol (M) ..	*6,185*	2,997	3,188	*3,180*	1,586	1,594	*548*	240	308	..	..	..	..	..	..	*3,728*	1,826	1,902
	Mukher ..	*6,614*	3,391	3,223	*4,393*	2,258	2,135	*573*	274	299	..	..	..	..	..	..	*4,966*	2,532	2,434
	Madnur ..	*3,702*	1,805	1,897	*2,735*	1,336	1,399	*427*	196	231	..	..	..	..	..	..	*3,162*	1,532	1,630
	Qandahar (M) ..	*4,452*	2,226	2,226	*1,780*	919	861	*594*	290	304	..	..	..	..	..	..	*2,374*	1,209	1,165
Parbhani ..		98,312	51,006	47,306	57,462	30,205	27,257	7,330	3,580	3,750	..	..	..	..	..	..	64,792	33,785	31,007
	Parbhani (M)	*16,830*	9,035	7,795	*8,566*	4,650	3,916	*1,002*	492	510	..	..		..	..	..	*9,568*	5,142	4,426
	Hingoli (M)	*12,667*	6,588	6,079	*7,069*	3,770	3,299	*1,420*	665	755	..	..		..	..	..	*8,489*	4,435	4,054
	Basmath (M)	*11,207*	5,660	5,547	*7,014*	3,572	3,442	*275*	130	145	..	..	..	..	..	..	*7,289*	3,702	3,587
	Manwath (M)	*10,655*	5,476	5,179	*8,514*	4.375	4,139	..	..	..	..	..	..	..	..	..	*8,514*	4,375	4,139
	Pathri	*4,904*	2,638	2,266	*2,129*	1,268	861	..	..	..	..	..	..	..	..	..	*2,129*	1,268	861
	Sailu ..	*7,967*	4,222	3,745	*5,336*	2,868	2,468	*911*	419	492	..	..	..	..	..	..	*6,247*	3,287	2,960
	Gangakhed (J) ..	*6,446*	3,206	3,240	*4,130*	2,067	2,063	*626*	315	311	..	..	..	..	..	..	*4,756*	2,382	2,374
	Partur (J) ..	*6,075*	3,232	2,843	*3,581*	1,933	1,648	*690*	358	332	..	..		..	..	..	*4,271*	2,291	1,980
	Jintur (M) ..	*5,825*	2,936	2,889	*2,599*	1,294	1,305	*403*	191	212	..	..		..	..	..	*3,002*	1,485	1,517
	Purna ..	*6,082*	3,225	2,857	*3,360*	1,761	1,599	*1,142*	598	544	..	..	..	..	..	..	*4,502*	2,359	2,143
	Kalamnuri (M) ..	*5,285*	2,620	2,665	*2,198*	1,113	1,085	*566*	280	286	..	..	..	..	..	..	*2,764*	1,393	1,371
	Sonepet (J) ..	*4,369*	2,168	2,201	*2,966*	1,534	1,432	*295*	132	163	..	..	..	..	..	..	*3,261*	1,666	1,595
Gulbarga ..	..	145,773	74,387	71,386	71,455	36,823	34,632	14,635	7,409	7,226	..	..	..	..	..	..	86,090	44,232	41,858
	Gulbarga City (M) ..	*41,083*	21,567	19,516	*17,509*	9,465	8,044	*3,428*	1,715	1,713	..	..	..	..	..	..	*20,937*	11,180	9,757
	Shorapur (M) ..	*12,673*	6,239	6,434	*7,519*	3,663	3,856	*346*	193	153	..	..		..	..	..	*7,865*	3,856	4,009
	Yadgir(M) ..	*19,380*	9,520	9,860	*7,790*	3,892	3,898	*3,261*	1,690	1,571	..	..		..	..	..	*11,051*	5,582	5,469
	Kalyani (J) ..	*10,341*	5,212	5,129	*3,853*	1,951	1,902	*674*	325	349	..	..	..	..	..	..	*4,527*	2,276	2,251
	Aland (P) ..	*12,924*	6,643	6,281	*5,150*	2,672	2,478	*506*	246	260	..	..	..	..	..	..	*5,656*	2,918	2,738
	Tandur (J) ..	*8,462*	4,265	4,197	*5,178*	2,592	2,586	*1,882*	990	892	..	..	..	..	..	..	*7,060*	3,582	3,478
	Kosgi (J) ..	*10,494*	5,237	5,257	*7,427*	3,680	3,747	*1,467*	740	727	..	..	..	..	..	..	*8,894*	4,420	4,474
	Shahabad (P) ..	*8,896*	4,581	4,315	*4,672*	2,467	2,205	*1,337*	646	691	..	..	..	..	..	..	*6,009*	3,113	2,896
	Kodangal (M) ..	*6,228*	3,129	3,099	*3,820*	1,932	1,888	*685*	334	351	..	..	..	..	..	..	*4,505*	2,266	2,239
	Chitapur (J) ..	*5,365*	2,963	2,402	*3,047*	1,745	1,302	*347*	185	162	..	..	..	..	..	..	*3,394*	1,930	1,464
	Gurmatkal ..	*4,647*	2,310	2,337	*2,643*	1,315	1,328	*233*	109	124	..	..	..	..	..	..	*2,876*	1,424	1,452
	Seram (M) ..	*5,280*	2,721	2,559	*2,847*	1,449	1,398	*469*	236	233	..	..	..	..	..	..	*3,316*	1,685	1,631

TABLE V.

Towns arranged Territorially with Population by Religion.

DISTRICTS	TOWN, MUNICIPALITY, SUBURBS, CANTON MENTS, ETC.	Jain			Sikh			Muslim			Christian			Zoroastrian			Buddhist			Jew			Tribal		
		Persons	Males	Females	Persons	Males	Females	Persons	Males	Females	Persons	Males	Females	Persons	Males	Females	Persons	Males	Females	Persons	Males	Females	Persons	Males	Females
1	2	21	22	23	24	25	26	27	28	29	30	31	32	33	34	35	36	37	38	39	40	41	42	43	44
Nander ..	..	227	105	122	1,148	642	506	20,611	10,543	10,068	210	117	93	10	3	7	..	..	..	..	..	..	222	87	135
	Nander (M) ..	110	52	58	1,104	615	489	8,540	4,546	3,994	194	108	86	3	1	2	..	..	..	..	..	..	42	15	27
	Bhainsa ..	3	1	2	..	..	..	3,482	1,733	1,749	5	2	3	7	2	5	..	..	..	..	..	..	..	..	..
	Deglur (M) ..	4	2	2	20	11	9	735	379	356	11	7	4	..	..	..	..	..	..	..	..	..	91	25	66
	Kondalwadi (P) ..	..	..	..	..	..	..	1,354	678	676	..	..	..	..	..	..	..	..	..	..	..	..	..	..	..
	Mudhol ..	..	..	..	..	..	..	2,457	1,171	1,286	..	..	..	..	..	..	..	..	..	..	..	..	..	..	..
	Mukher ..	52	26	26	..	..	..	1,507	786	721	..	..	..	..	..	..	..	..	..	..	..	..	89	47	42
	Madnur ..	..	..	..	14	9	5	526	264	262	..	..	..	..	..	..	..	..	..	..	..	..	..	..	..
	Qandahar (M) ..	58	24	34	10	7	3	2,010	986	1,024	..	..	..	..	..	..	..	..	..	..	..	..	..	..	..
Parbhani ..	..	1,317	679	638	49	27	22	31,574	16,215	15,359	370	192	178	72	44	28	..	..	..	..	..	..	138	64	74
	Parbhani (M) ..	119	65	54	7	4	3	7,095	3,798	3,297	21	13	8	20	13	7	..	..	..	..	..	..	..	..	..
	Hingoli (M) ..	227	116	111	9	8	1	3,888	2,007	1,881	43	17	26	11	5	6	..	..	..	..	..	..	..	..	..
	Basmath (M) ..	65	35	30	4	3	1	3,816	1,906	1,910	..	..	..	..	..	..	..	..	..	..	..	..	33	14	19
	Manwath (M) ..	296	153	143	..	..	..	1,838	945	893	..	..	..	..	..	..	..	..	..	..	..	..	7	3	4
	Pathri (M) ..	11	6	5	..	..	..	2,763	1,363	1,400	1	1	..	..	..	..	..	..	..	..	..	..	..	..	..
	Sailu (M) ..	85	49	36	6	3	3	1,597	865	732	3	2	1	9	6	3	..	..	..	..	..	..	20	10	10
	Gangakhed (J) ..	72	27	45	3	1	2	1,615	796	819	..	..	..	..	..	..	..	..	..	..	..	..	..	..	..
	Partur (J) ..	17	12	5	..	..	..	1,715	892	823	2	1	1	6	6	..	..	..	..	..	..	..	64	30	34
	Jintur (M) ..	66	33	33	..	..	..	2,757	1,418	1,339	..	..	..	..	..	..	..	..	..	..	..	..	..	..	..
	Purna ..	63	38	25	7	3	4	1,179	653	526	293	158	140	24	12	12	..	..	..	..	..	..	14	7	7
	Kalamnuri (M) ..	226	110	116	..	..	..	2,292	1,114	1,178	3	3	..	..	..	..	..	..	..	..	..	..	..	..	..
	Sonepet (J) ..	70	35	35	13	5	8	1,019	458	561	4	2	2	2	2	..	..	..	..	..	..	..	..	..	..
Gulbarga ..	..	850	452	398	117	68	49	56,741	28,628	28,113	959	471	488	35	23	12	..	..	..	..	..	..	981	513	468
	Gulbarga City (M) ..	181	88	93	4	4	..	19,792	10,228	9,564	145	50	95	16	9	7	..	..	..	..	..	..	8	8	..
	Shorapur (M) ..	63	39	24	..	..	..	4,743	2,343	2,400	..	..	..	2	1	1	..	..	..	..	..	..	..	..	..
	Yadgir (M) ..	52	28	24	8	8	..	8,155	3,844	4,311	34	20	14	..	..	..	..	..	..	..	..	..	80	38	42
	Kalyani (J) ..	18	9	9	..	..	..	5,787	2,920	2,867	5	3	2	4	4	..	..	..	..	..	..	..	..	..	..
	Aland (P) ..	514	273	241	..	..	..	6,754	3,452	3,302	..	..	..	..	..	..	..	..	..	..	..	..	..	..	..
	Tandur (J) ..	..	..	..	..	..	..	565	258	307	269	133	136	..	..	..	..	..	..	..	..	..	568	292	276
	Kosgi (J) ..	..	..	..	..	..	..	1,589	811	778	11	6	5	..	..	..	..	..	..	..	..	..	..	..	..
	Shahabad (P) ..	8	5	3	2	2	..	2,802	1,417	1,385	63	36	27	12	8	4	..	..	..	..	..	..	..	..	..
	Kodangal (M) ..	..	..	..	..	..	..	1,454	715	739	254	135	119	1	1	..	..	..	..	..	..	..	14	12	2
	Chitapur (J) ..	..	..	..	..	..	..	1,782	935	847	4	3	1	..	..	..	..	..	..	..	..	..	185	95	90
	Gurmatkal ..	..	..	..	102	53	49	1,496	749	747	173	84	89	..	..	..	..	..	..	..	..	..	..	..	..
	Seram (M) ..	14	10	4	1	1	..	1,822	956	866	1	1	..	..	..	..	..	..	..	..	..	..	126	68	58

TABLE V.

Towns arranged Territorially with Population by Religion.

DISTRICTS	TOWN, MUNICIPALITY, SUBURBS, CANTONMENTS, ETC.	POPULATION			HINDU														
					Brahmanic Hindu			Adi-Hindu			Arya			Brahmo			Total		
		Persons	Males	Females	Persons	Males	Females	Persons	Males	Females	Persons	Males	Females	Persons	Males	Females	Persons	Males	Females
1	2	3	4	5	6	7	8	9	10	11	12	13	14	15	16	17	18	19	20
Osmanabad ..	..	74,211	38,879	35,332	44,073	23,408	20,665	10,127	5,205	4,922	..	..	..	..	..	..	54,200	28,613	25,587
	Latur ..	30,760	16,609	14,151	17,372	9,662	7,710	3,848	1,972	1,876	..		..	..	..	..	21,220	11,634	9,580
	Osmanabad (M) ..	11,266	5,878	5,388	5,973	3,175	2,798	1,460	740	720	..	..	..	..	..	..	7,433	3,915	3,518
	Thair ..	8,541	4,320	4,221	6,594	3,340	3,254	1,085	554	531	..		..	..	..	..	7,679	3,894	3,785
	Moram ..	6,879	3,555	3,324	3,971	2,052	1,919	1,100	567	533	..	..	..	..	..	..	5,071	2,619	2,452
	Tuljapur ..	6,057	3,110	2,947	4,562	2,345	2,217	700	362	338	..	..	..	..	..	..	5,262	2,707	2,555
	Ousa	6,352	3,186	3,166	2,990	1,523	1,467	728	365	363	..	..	..	..	..	..	3,718	1,888	1,830
	Wasi	4,356	2,221	2,135	2,611	1,311	1,300	1,206	645	561	..	..	..	..	..	..	3,817	1,956	1,861
Raichur ..	..	117,935	59,237	58,698	74,285	37,277	37,008	11,035	5,228	5,807	4	3	1	..	..	..	85,324	42,508	42,816
	Gadwal (S) ..	12,982	6,538	6,444	9,000	4,503	4,497	882	457	425	..	..	..	..	..	..	9,882	4,960	4,922
	Kopbal (J) ..	9,979	5,157	4,822	5,728	2,978	2,750	438	210	228	..	..	..	..	..	..	6,166	3,188	2,978
	Deodrug (M) ..	6,412	3,107	3,305	3,928	1,897	2,031	445	206	239	..	..	..	..	..	..	4,373	2,103	2,270
	Manvi (M) ..	6,500	3,250	3,250	4,020	2,019	2,001	446	201	245	..	..	..	..	..	..	4,466	2,220	2,246
	Gangawati (M) ..	6,722	3,356	3,366	3,748	1,853	1,895	702	334	368	..	..	..	..	..	..	4,450	2,187	2,263
	Raichur (M) ..	27,910	14,026	13,884	16,500	8,251	8,249	3,845	1,772	2,073	..	..	..	..	..	..	20,345	10,023	10,322
	Sindhnur (M) ..	5,553	2,731	2,822	3,264	1,613	1,651	224	81	143	..	..	..	..	..	..	3,488	1,694	1,794
	Mudgal ..	4,955	2,403	2,552	2,547	1,276	1,271	299	140	159	..	..	..	..	..	..	2,846	1,416	1,430
	Kodaikal ..	3,659	1,875	1,784	2,240	1,150	1,090	288	120	168	4	3	1	..	..	..	2,532	1,273	1,259
	Jalhally ..	3,871	1,817	2,054	3,041	1,426	1,615	330	150	180	..	..	..	..	..	..	3,371	1,576	1,795
	Kadoli ..	4,634	2,277	2,357	2,877	1,406	1,471	378	177	201	..	..	..	..	..	..	3,255	1,583	1,672
	Kushtagi (M) ..	4,460	2,287	2,173	3,304	1,686	1,618	294	135	159	..	..	..	..	..	..	3,598	1,821	1,777
	Hamsagar ..	4,339	2,197	2,142	3,351	1,698	1,653	266	135	131	..	..	..	..	..	..	3,617	1,833	1,784
	Alampur (M) ..	4,646	2,338	2,308	2,195	1,094	1,101	666	324	342	..	..	..	..	..	..	2,861	1,418	1,443
	Dacha (S) ..	5,333	2,771	2,562	3,854	1,995	1,859	823	428	395	..	..	..	..	..	..	4,677	2,423	2,254
	Rajoli (S) ..	5,980	3,107	2,873	4,688	2,432	2,256	709	358	351	..	..	..	..	..	..	5,397	2,790	2,607
Bidar ..	..	71,520	36,713	34,807	34,640	17,790	16,850	6,421	3,280	3,141	69	35	34	2	1	1	41,132	21,106	20,026
	Bidar (M) ..	15,198	7,767	7,431	5,273	2,733	2,540	931	485	446	27	17	10	..	..	..	6,231	3,285	2,996
	Udgir (M) ..	8,308	4,306	4,002	4,080	2,110	1,970	928	478	450	39	16	23	2	1	1	5,049	2,605	2,444
	Kohir ..	5,549	2,805	2,744	1,650	818	832	304	160	144	..	..	..	..	..	..	1,954	978	976
	Ekeli (P) ..	10,958	5,670	5,288	4,719	2,416	2,303	1,157	591	566	..	..	..	..	..	..	5,876	3,007	2,869
	Bhalki (P) ..	5,912	3,025	2,887	3,955	2,054	1,901	584	285	299	..	..	..	..	..	..	4,539	2,339	2,200
	Deoni (J) ..	3,951	2,131	1,820	2,378	1,260	1,118	443	239	204	..	..	..	..	..	..	2,821	1,499	1,322
	Chitgopa (P) ..	7,447	3,688	3,759	3,974	1,959	2,015	509	254	255	..	..	..	..	..	..	4,483	2,213	2,270
	Ahmadpur (M) ..	3,274	1,758	1,516	2,259	1,200	1,059	236	140	96	..	..	..	..	..	..	2,495	1,340	1,155
	Janwada ..	2,199	1,110	1,089	1,413	703	710	177	90	87	..	..	..	..	..	..	1,590	793	797
	Nilanga (M) ..	4,139	2,165	1,974	2,220	1,162	1,058	473	236	237	..	..	..	..	..	..	2,693	1,398	1,295
	Rajeshwar (P) ..	4,585	2,288	2,297	2,719	1,375	1,344	679	322	357	3	2	1	..	..	..	3,401	1,699	1,702

TABLE V.

Towns arranged Territorially with Population by Religion.

DISTRICTS	TOWN, MUNICIPALITY, SUBURBS, CANTONMENTS, ETC.	JAIN			SIKH			MUSLIM			CHRISTIAN			ZOROASTRIAN			BUDDHIST			JEW			TRIBAL		
		Persons	Males	Females	Persons	Males	Females	Persons	Males	Females	Persons	Males	Females	Persons	Males	Females	Persons	Males	Females	Persons	Males	Females	Persons	Males	Females
1	2	21	22	23	24	25	26	27	28	29	30	31	32	33	34	35	36	37	38	39	40	41	42	43	44
Osmanabad ..		888	467	421	30	29	1	18,926	9,666	9,260	26	20	6	3	3	..	..	..	..	..	..	..	138	81	57
	Latur (M) ..	474	267	207	26	26	..	8,993	4,649	4,344	..	..	..	2	2	..	..	..	..	..	..	..	45	31	14
	Osmanabad (M) ..	279	132	147	3	2	1	3,529	1,813	1,716	21	15	6	1	1	..	..	..	..	..	..	..	..	..	..
	Thair ..	9	4	5	..	..	..	853	422	431	..	..	..	..	..	..	..	..	..	..	..	..	..	..	..
	Moram ..	65	32	33	..	..	..	1,650	854	796	..	..	..	..	..	..	..	..	..	..	..	..	93	50	43
	Tuljapur (M) ..	57	28	29	1	1	..	732	369	363	5	5	..	..	..	..	..	..	..	..	..	..	..	..	..
	Ousa	4	4	..	..	..	..	2,630	1,294	1,336	..	..	..	..	..	..	..	..	..	..	..	..	..	..	..
	Wasi	..	..	..	..	..	..	539	265	274	..	..	..	..	..	..	..	..	..	..	..	..	..	..	..
Raichur ..	..	304	173	131	236	204	32	30,490	15,533	14,957	666	342	324	3	3	..	..	..	..	..	..	..	912	474	438
	Gadwal (S) ..	..	..	..	24	10	14	2,829	1,442	1,387	139	72	67	2	2	..	..	..	..	..	..	..	106	52	54
	Kopbal (J) ..	114	59	55	..	..	..	3,628	1,873	1,755	9	5	4	..	..	..	..	..	..	..	..	..	62	32	30
	Deodrug (M) ..	..	..	..	..	..	..	1,843	904	939	3	1	2	1	1	..	..	..	..	..	..	..	192	98	94
	Manvi (M) ..	..	..	..	..	..	..	2,001	1,011	990	7	4	3	..	..	..	..	..	..	..	..	..	26	15	11
	Gangawati (M) ..	2	2	..	..	..	..	2,236	1,148	1,088	..	..	..	..	..	..	..	..	..	..	..	..	34	19	15
	Raichur (M) ..	61	35	26	212	194	18	6,856	3,565	3,291	130	61	69	..	..	..	..	..	..	..	..	..	306	148	158
	Sindhnur (M) ..	101	63	38	..	..	..	1,964	974	990	..	..	..	..	..	..	..	..	..	..	..	..	..	..	..
	Mudgal ..	11	5	6	..	..	..	2,062	963	1,099	..	..	..	..	..	..	..	..	..	..	..	..	36	19	17
	Kodaikal ..	..	..	..	..	..	..	1,068	566	502	5	5	..	..	..	..	..	..	..	..	..	..	54	31	23
	Jalhally ..	..	..	..	..	..	..	482	231	251	..	..	..	..	..	..	..	..	..	..	..	..	18	10	8
	Koadoli ..	..	..	..	..	..	..	1,012	504	508	367	190	177	..	..	..	..	..	..	..	..	..	..	..	..
	Kushtagi (M) ..	15	9	6	..	..	..	845	455	390	..	..	..	..	..	..	..	..	..	..	..	..	2	2	..
	Hamsagar ..	..	..	..	..	..	..	702	353	349	..	..	..	..	..	..	..	..	..	..	..	..	20	11	9
	Alampur (M) ..	..	..	..	..	..	..	1,779	916	863	6	4	2	..	..	..	..	..	..	..	..	..	..	..	..
	Dacha (S) ..	..	..	..	..	..	..	620	323	297	..	..	..	..	..	..	..	..	..	..	..	..	36	25	11
	Rajoli (S) ..	..	..	..	..	..	..	563	305	258	..	..	..	..	..	..	..	..	..	..	..	..	20	12	8
Bidar ..	..	155	77	78	6	2	4	28,372	14,600	13,772	1,255	621	634	1	1	..	..	..	..	..	..	..	599	306	293
	Bidar (M) ..	27	15	12	5	2	3	8,400	4,241	4,159	456	230	226	1	1	..	..	..	..	..	..	..	78	43	35
	Udgir (M) ..	88	42	46	1	..	1	3,095	1,613	1,482	6	4	2	..	..	..	..	..	..	..	..	..	69	42	27
	Kohir ..	..	..	..	..	..	..	3,071	1,573	1,498	490	240	250	..	..	..	..	..	..	..	..	..	34	14	20
	Ekeli (P) ..	..	..	..	..	..	..	4,765	2,508	2,257	303	147	156	..	..	..	..	..	..	..	..	..	14	8	6
	Bhalki (P) ..	11	6	5	..	..	..	1,362	680	682	..	..	..	..	..	..	..	..	..	..	..	..	..	..	..
	Deoni (J) ..	1	..	1	..	..	..	1,097	614	483	..	..	..	..	..	..	..	..	..	..	..	..	32	18	14
	Chitgopa (P) ..	..	..	..	..	..	..	2,894	1,449	1,445	..	..	..	..	..	..	..	..	..	..	..	..	70	26	44
	Ahmadpur (M) ..	27	13	14	..	..	..	454	252	202	..	..	..	..	..	..	..	..	..	..	..	..	298	153	145
	Janwada ..	..	..	..	..	..	..	609	317	292	..	..	..	..	..	..	..	..	..	..	..	..	..	..	..
	Nilanga (M) ..	1	1	..	..	..	..	1,441	764	677	..	..	..	..	..	..	..	..	..	..	..	..	4	2	2
	Rajeshwar (P) ..	..	..	..	..	..	..	1,184	589	595	..	..	..	..	..	..	..	..	..	..	..	..	..	..	..

Table VI.

BIRTHPLACE

This table deals with the statistics of birthplace for the State. It is divided into eight parts according to the following scheme of classification :—

PART	BIRTHPLACE.
A.—Born in India.—	(I) Born within the State.
	(II) Born in provinces and States beyond the State.
B.—Born in other Asiatic countries.	
C.—Born in Europe.	
D.—Born in Africa.	
E.—Born in America.	
F.—Born in Australasia.	
G.—Born at Sea.	
H.—Birthplace unspecified or not returned.	

N.B.—G. and H. are new.

2. On the present occasion details of birthplaces beyond India are not exhaustive. They have been recorded for certain important countries only within and without British Dominions.

3. Out of 14,436,148 persons (7,370,010 males and 7,066,138 females) enumerated in the Hyderabad State, 14,431,167 persons (7,366,000 males and 7,065,167 females) were born in India with a population of 14,188,358 persons (7,203,129 males and 6,985,224 females) returning their birthplace within the State itself.

4. In the Capital of the State, Hyderabad City, the foreign population predominates, it being as much as 2,375 out of a total foreign population of 2,665 for the whole State.

TABLE VI.

Birthplace.

S. No.	District, State, Province, or Country where born	Population of the State: Persons	Population of the State: Males	Population of the State: Females	Hyderabad City: Persons	Hyderabad City: Males	Hyderabad City: Females	Atraf-i-Balda: Persons	Atraf-i-Balda: Males	Atraf-i-Balda: Females	Warangal: Persons	Warangal: Males	Warangal: Females	Karimnagar: Persons	Karimnagar: Males	Karimnagar: Females	Adilabad: Persons	Adilabad: Males	Adilabad: Females
	1	2	3	4	5	6	7	8	9	10	11	12	13	14	15	16	17	18	19
	TOTAL POPULATION ..	14,436,148	7,370,010	7,066,138	466,894	247,623	219,271	499,661	253,975	245,686	1,117,693	575,819	541,874	1,241,405	634,416	606,989	762,030	389,754	372,276
	A. BORN IN INDIA ..	14,431,167	7,366,000	7,065,167	463,580	244,759	218,821	499,647	253,965	245,682	1,117,653	575,796	541,857	1,241,369	634,396	606,973	762,012	389,736	372,276
	(i) Born within the State..	14,188,353	7,203,129	6,985,224	408,636	209,706	198,930	496,634	252,317	244,317	1,088,177	552,098	536,079	1,239,928	633,544	606,384	703,886	342,918	360,968
1	Hyderabad City	*373,249*	191,265	181,984	*325,163*	164,453	160,710	*13,540*	8,063	5,477	*4,481*	2,031	2,450	*1,129*	657	472	*2,653*	1,234	1,419
2	Atraf-i-Balda	*464,282*	238,669	225,613	*15,794*	8,246	7,548	*426,278*	221,529	204,749	*635*	270	365	*764*	188	576	*878*	362	516
3	Warangal	*1,069,360*	543,271	526,089	*7,256*	5,215	2,041	*1,464*	610	854	*1,045,717*	530,671	515,046	*2,170*	967	1,203	*2,885*	1,473	1,412
4	Karimnagar	*1,292,515*	659,477	633,038	*5,750*	3,784	1,966	*1,510*	570	940	*19,572*	10,877	8,695	*1,227,313*	627,492	599,821	*21,808*	9,573	12,235
5	Adilabad	*657,184*	320,507	336,677	*1,438*	649	789	*906*	441	465	*673*	396	277	*713*	401	312	*649,403*	316,768	332,685
6	Medak	*755,488*	382,511	372,977	*16,074*	6,247	9,827	*13,616*	6,866	6,750	*799*	310	489	*2,667*	954	1,713	*2,126*	1,298	828
7	Nizamabad	*634,205*	318,780	315,425	*5,186*	2,858	2,328	*1,470*	684	786	*530*	318	212	*1,543*	664	879	*7,189*	3,555	3,634
8	Mahbubnagar	*990,793*	500,557	490,236	*6,228*	3,650	2,578	*7,567*	2,169	5,398	*224*	108	116	*192*	123	69	*932*	479	453
9	Nalgonda	*1,165,428*	590,733	574,695	*7,260*	4,242	3,018	*17,274*	5,148	12,126	*14,767*	6,681	8,086	*1,436*	1,016	420	*1,915*	999	916
10	Aurangabad	*938,758*	479,066	459,692	*4,247*	2,272	1,975	*535*	358	177	*114*	75	39	*1,364*	707	657	*1,115*	642	473
11	Bir	*647,342*	330,190	317,152	*1,037*	544	493	*14*	14	..	*11*	6	5	*102*	101	1	*1,854*	1,145	709
12	Nander	*707,442*	359,611	347,831	*1,797*	999	798	*1,829*	986	843	*98*	69	29	*161*	108	53	*4,794*	2,186	2,608
13	Parbhani	*821,778*	418,257	403,521	*940*	518	422	*417*	86	331	*21*	12	9	*54*	41	13	*1,978*	804	1,174
14	Gulbarga	*1,212,711*	611,765	600,946	*3,971*	2,368	1,603	*5,314*	2,328	2,986	*195*	90	105	*85*	64	21	*1,378*	763	615
15	Osmanabad	*680,590*	353,771	326,819	*554*	335	219	*231*	101	130	*8*	8	..	*28*	24	4	*1,192*	720	472
16	Raichur	*909,739*	462,696	447,043	*1,979*	1,201	778	*571*	335	236	*144*	47	97	*35*	16	19	*117*	84	33
17	Bidar	*867,489*	442,003	425,486	*3,962*	2,125	1,837	*4,098*	2,029	2,069	*188*	129	59	*172*	21	151	*1,669*	833	836
	(ii) Born in Provinces and States beyond the State.	242,814	162,871	79,943	54,944	35,053	19,891	3,013	1,648	1,365	29,476	23,698	5,778	1,441	852	589	58,126	46,818	11,308
	(a) Provinces adjacent to the State.	214,975	145,884	69,091	37,894	24,450	13,444	2,839	1,536	1,303	28,929	23,438	5,491	1,141	686	455	57,068	46,231	10,837
18	Bombay	*67,734*	36,637	31,097	*12,170*	6,063	6,107	*816*	510	306	*191*	98	93	*92*	60	32	*1,829*	1,181	648
19	Central Provinces and Berar ..	*14,289*	6,702	7,587	*3,032*	1,155	1,877	*67*	18	49	*563*	427	136	*128*	112	16	*2,827*	1,770	1,057
20	Madras	*132,952*	102,545	30,407	*22,692*	17,232	5,460	*1,956*	1,008	948	*28,175*	22,913	5,262	*921*	514	407	*52,412*	43,230	9,182

TABLE VI.

Birthplace.

S. No.	District, State, Province, or Country where born	Population of the State			Districts where enumerated														
					Hyderabad City			Atraf-i-Balda			Warangal			Karimnagar			Adilabad		
		Persons	Males	Females	Persons	Males	Females	Persons	Males	Females	Persons	Males	Females	Persons	Males	Females	Persons	Males	Females
	1	2	3	4	5	6	7	8	9	10	11	12	13	14	15	16	17	18	19
	(b) Other Provinces in India.	14,148	8,745	5,403	10,644	6,672	3,972	112	87	25	223	112	111	120	87	33	247	111	136
21	Ajmer-Merwara	1,525	602	928	600	211	389	3	3	..	..	..	..	10	8	2	110	25	85
22	Assam	5	2	3	5	2	3	..	..	..	..	..	..	..	..	..	..	..	..
23	Andamans	..	..	..	..	..	..	..	..	..	..	..	..	..	..	..	..	..	..
24	Baluchistan (British administered area)	21	17	4	5	5	..	4	4	..	1	1	..	4	1	3	1	1	..
25	Bengal	313	167	146	220	100	120	1	1	..	5	3	2	3	3	..	2	2	..
26	Bihar and Orissa	564	354	210	264	225	39	..	..	..	..	..	..	..	..	..	52	41	11
27	Burma	105	36	69	92	25	67	1	..	1	2	2	..	..	..	..	..	..	..
28	Coorg	6	3	3	6	3	3	..	..	..	..	..	..	..	..	..	..	..	..
29	Delhi	949	641	308	463	298	165	1	..	1	5	4	1	14	9	5	1	1	..
30	North West Frontier Provinces (British Administered) ..	184	145	39	112	97	15	..	..	..	1	1	..	..	..	..	1	..	1
31	Punjab	3,190	2,220	970	2,882	2,210	672	46	35	11	55	40	15	20	8	12	64	29	35
32	United Provinces of Agra and Oudh	7,286	4,558	2,728	5,995	3,496	2,499	56	44	12	154	61	93	69	58	11	16	12	4
	(c) States and Agencies. ..	12,509	7,646	4,863	6,269	3,844	2,425	62	25	37	319	143	176	105	44	61	209	122	87
33	Baroda	37	26	11	22	16	6	..	..	..	..	..	..	..	..	..	..	..	..
34	Bombay States	324	192	132	148	59	89	..	..	..	..	..	..	..	..	..	6	4	2
35	Central India Agency ..	558	293	265	56	31	25	1	..	1	26	5	21	17	1	16	2	2	..
36	Cochin	31	22	9	25	18	7	..	..	..	3	2	1	..	..	..	..	..	..
37	Gwalior	717	528	189	342	292	50	..	..	..	17	13	4	..	..	..	88	59	29
38	Jammu and Kashmir ..	42	26	16	35	21	14	..	..	..	..	..	..	..	..	..	..	..	..
*39	Madras States	2	..	2	..	..	..	..	..	..	..	..	..	..	..	..	..	..	..
40	Mysore	2,869	1,728	1,141	1,779	1,125	654	17	5	12	50	28	22	9	5	4	21	19	2
41	Punjab States	541	422	119	493	386	107	..	..	..	..	..	..	..	..	..	..	..	..
42	Rajputana Agency ..	6,608	4,040	2,568	2,669	1,576	1,093	44	20	24	215	90	125	79	38	41	92	38	54
43	Travancore	28	16	12	18	8	10	..	..	..	6	5	1	..	..	..	..	..	..
44	United Provinces States ..	752	353	399	682	312	370	..	..	..	2	..	2	..	..	..	..	..	..
	(d) French and Portuguese Settlements	157	98	59	137	87	50	..	..	..	5	5	..	..	..	..	2	..	2
45	French and Portuguese Settlements	157	98	59	137	87	50	..	..	..	5	5	..	..	..	..	2	..	2
	(e) India, Unspecified ..	1,025	498	527	..	..	..	..	..	..	..	..	..	75	35	40	600	354	246
46	India, Unspecified ..	1,025	498	527	..	..	..	..	..	..	..	..	..	75	35	40	600	354	246

* Excluding Travancore and Cochin States.

TABLE VI.

Birthplace.

S. No.	District, State, Province, or Country where born	Population of the State: Persons	Population of the State: Males	Population of the State: Females	Hyderabad: Persons	Hyderabad: Males	Hyderabad: Females	Atraf-i-Balda: Persons	Atraf-i-Balda: Males	Atraf-i-Balda: Females	Warangal: Persons	Warangal: Males	Warangal: Females	Karimnagar: Persons	Karimnagar: Males	Karimnagar: Females	Adilabad: Persons	Adilabad: Males	Adilabad: Females
	1	2	3	4	5	6	7	8	9	10	11	12	13	14	15	16	17	18	19
	B. BORN IN OTHER ASIATIC COUNTRIES	2,258	1,659	599	881	765	116	11	10	1	25	18	7	20	13	7	18	18	..
	(i) Within British Dominions	15	14	1	10	9	1	..	..	..	..	..	..	1	1	..	..	..	..
47	Ceylon	11	10	1	6	5	1	..	..	..	..	..	..	1	1	..	..	..	..
48	Strait Settlements and Malaya.	2	2	..	2	2	..	..	..	..	..	..	..	..	..	..	..	..	..
49	Elsewhere	2	2	..	2	2	..	..	..	..	..	..	..	..	..	..	..	..	..
	(ii) Outside British Dominions	2,235	1,637	598	871	756	115	11	10	1	25	18	7	19	12	7	18	18	..
50	Afghanistan	181	154	27	117	94	23	5	5	..	12	11	1	..	..	..	9	9	..
51	China	13	5	8	6	5	1	..	..	..	..	..	..	7	..	7	..	..	..
52	Nepal	14	8	6	8	5	3	..	..	..	..	..	..	..	..	..	..	..	..
53	Elsewhere	2,027	1,470	557	740	652	88	6	5	1	13	7	6	12	12	..	9	9	..
	(iii) Asia, Unspecified ..	8	8	..	..	..	..	..	..	..	..	..	..	..	..	..	..	..	..
54	Asia, Unspecified ..	8	8	..	..	..	..	..	..	..	..	..	..	..	..	..	..	..	..
	C. BORN IN EUROPE ..	2,548	2,234	314	2,270	1,990	280	2	..	2	14	5	9	16	7	9	..	..	..
	(i) Great Britain and Ireland. ..	2,086	1,942	144	1,885	1,773	112	2	..	2	13	4	9	14	5	9	..	..	..
55	Great Britain and Ireland ..	2,086	1,942	144	1,885	1,773	112	2	..	2	13	4	9	14	5	9	..	..	..
	(ii) British possessions in Europe. ..	2	2	..	2	2	..	..	..	..	..	..	..	..	..	..	..	..	..
56	British possessions in Europe .	2	2	..	2	2	..	..	..	..	..	..	..	..	..	..	..	..	..
	(iii) Continental Europe ..	237	131	106	220	115	105	..	..	..	1	1	..	..	..	..	..	..	..
57	Continental Europe ..	237	131	106	220	115	105	..	..	..	1	1	..	..	..	..	..	..	..
	(iv) Europe, Unspecified ..	223	159	64	163	100	63	..	..	..	..	..	..	2	2	..	..	..	..
58	Europe, Unspecified ..	223	159	64	163	100	63	..	..	..	..	..	..	2	2	..	..	..	..

TABLE VI.

Birthplace.

S. No.	District, State, Province, or Country where born.	POPULATION OF THE STATE			DISTRICTS WHERE ENUMERATED: HYDERABAD CITY			ATRAF-I-BALDA			WARANGAL			KARIMNAGAR			ADILABAD		
		Persons	Males	Females	Persons	Males	Females	Persons	Males	Females	Persons	Males	Females	Persons	Males	Females	Persons	Males	Females
	1	2	3	4	5	6	7	8	9	10	11	12	13	14	15	16	17	18	19
	D. BORN IN AFRICA.	4	3	1	4	3	1	..	..	..	..	..	..	..	..	..	..	..	..
	(i) Within British Dominions	4	3	1	4	3	1	..	..	..	..	..	..	..	..	..	..	..	..
59	Kenya (British East Africa) ..	4	3	1	4	3	1	..	..	..	..	..	..	..	..	..	..	..	..
	E. BORN IN AMERICA.	92	70	22	80	62	18	1	..	1	1	..	1	..	..	..	..	..	..
	(i) Within British Dominions.	22	19	3	19	16	3	..	..	..	..	..	..	..	..	..	..	..	..
60	Canada	22	19	3	19	16	3	..	..	..	..	..	..	..	..	..	..	..	..
	(ii) Outside British Dominions. ..	46	30	16	37	25	12	1	..	1	1	..	1	..	..	..	..	..	..
61	United States	46	30	16	37	25	12		..	1	1	..	1	..	..	..	..	..	..
	(iii) America, (Unspecified)	24	21	3	24	21	3	..	..	..	..	..	..	..	..	..	..	..	..
62	America, Unspecified ..	24	21	3	24	21	3	..	..	..	..	..	..	..	..	..	..	..	..
	F. BORN IN AUSTRALASIA	21	12	9	21	12	9	..	..	..	..	..	..	..	..	..	..	..	..
	(i) Within British Dominions.	21	12	9	21	12	9	..	..	..	..	..	..	..	..	..	..	..	..
63	Australia	17	12	5	17	12	5	..	..	..	..	..	..	..	..	..	..	..	..
64	New Zealand	4	..	4	4	..	4	..	..	..	..	..	..	..	..	..	..	..	..
	G. BORN AT SEA. ..	..	..	..	..	..	..	..	..	..	..	..	..	..	..	..	..	..	..
65	Born at sea	..	..	..	..	..	..	..	..	..	..	..	..	..	..	..	..	..	..
	H. BIRTHPLACE UNSPECIFIED OR NOT RETURNED. ..	58	32	26	58	32	26	..	..	..	..	..	..	..	..	..	..	..	..
66	Birthplace unspecified or not returned	58	32	26	58	32	26	..	..	..	..	..	..	..	..	..	..	..	..

TABLE VI.

Birthplace.

S. No.	District, State, Province or Country where born	DISTRICTS WHERE ENUMERATED																	
		Medak			Nizamabad			Mahbubnagar			Nalgonda			Aurangabad			Bir		
		Persons	Males	Females	Persons	Males	Females	Persons	Males	Females	Persons	Males	Females	Persons	Males	Females	Persons	Males	Females
		20	21	22	23	24	25	26	27	28	29	30	31	32	33	34	35	36	37
	TOTAL POPULATION ..	738,665	373,475	365,190	623,225	313,556	309,669	971,616	494,061	477,555	1,133,409	580,897	552,512	944,793	480,498	464,295	633,690	325,396	308,294
	A. BORN IN INDIA	738,640	373,459	365,181	623,157	313,516	309,641	971,578	494,031	477,547	1,133,383	580,879	552,504	944,514	480,232	464,282	633,647	325,361	308,286
	(i) Born within the State ..	736,110	372,036	364,074	621,079	312,211	308,868	969,028	492,408	476,620	1,122,833	572,441	550,392	929,197	473,376	455,821	625,845	320,464	305,381
1	Hyderabad City	*3,298*	1,799	1,409	*2,118*	1,259	859	*991*	515	476	*2,376*	1,544	832	*1,929*	922	1,007	*526*	323	203
2	Atraf-i-Balda	*11,593*	4,659	6,934	*348*	246	102	*2,675*	793	1,882	*2,600*	1,256	1,344	*153*	62	91	*103*	59	44
3	Warangal	*497*	251	246	*836*	428	408	*1,558*	845	1,213	*3,470*	1,465	2,005	*61*	14	47	*39*	8	31
4	Karimnagar	*4,397*	1,508	2,889	*7,150*	3,070	4,080	*574*	230	344	*690*	377	313	*45*	20	25	*47*	41	6
5	Adilabad	*85*	57	28	*500*	292	208	*42*	27	15	*213*	32	181	*264*	75	189	*114*	9	105
6	Medak	*702,033*	357,852	344,181	*4,257*	2,102	2,155	*5,293*	2,790	2,503	*3,142*	1,251	1,891	*390*	327	63	*31*	16	15
7	Nizamabad	*2,846*	967	1,879	*602,010*	302,571	299,439	*335*	280	55	*240*	177	63	*1,440*	790	650	*96*	74	22
8	Mahbubnagar	*1,860*	924	936	*272*	192	80	*942,023*	480,492	461,531	*1,061*	618	443	*408*	173	235	*10*	9	1
9	Nalgonda	*5,524*	2,494	3,030	*522*	269	253	*5,278*	2,159	3,119	*1,108,597*	565,519	543,078	*77*	63	14	*16*	9	7
10	Aurangabad	*245*	81	164	*222*	103	119	*39*	30	9	*113*	89	24	*911,810*	465,056	446,754	*2,368*	1,078	1,290
11	Bir	*117*	8	9	*114*	90	24	*30*	14	16	*9*	..	9	*5,102*	2,143	2,959	*611,874*	313,145	298,729
12	Nander	*441*	123	318	*1,332*	689	643	*118*	24	94	*46*	24	22	*2,079*	1,258	821	*617*	470	147
13	Parbhani	*106*	24	82	*122*	93	29	*75*	38	37	*4*	2	2	*3,536*	1,292	2,244	*2,880*	1,539	1,341
14	Gulbarga	*555*	264	291	*256*	199	57	*7,326*	3,740	3,586	*69*	46	23	*588*	306	282	*273*	116	157
15	Osmanabad	*265*	50	215	*68*	34	34	*26*	8	18	*13*	3	10	*429*	278	151	*4,192*	2,458	1,734
16	Raichur	*388*	159	229	*154*	85	69	*2,287*	873	1,414	*29*	11	18	*506*	355	151	*88*	43	45
17	Bidar	*1,960*	816	1,144	*798*	489	309	*358*	50	308	*161*	27	134	*380*	242	138	*2,571*	1,067	1,504
	(ii) Born in Provinces and States beyond the State	2,530	1,423	1,107	2,078	1,305	773	2,550	1,623	927	10,550	8,438	2,112	15,317	6,856	8,461	7,802	4,897	2,905
	(a) Provinces adjacent to the State ..	1,964	1,135	829	1,544	1,031	513	2,375	1,525	850	10,405	8,333	2,072	12,735	5,314	7, 421	6,950	4,240	2,710
18	Bombay	*261*	134	127	*282*	215	67	*106*	48	58	*29*	21	8	*9,148*	3,978	5,170	*6,828*	4,173	2,655
19	Central Provinces and Berar ..	*119*	46	73	*49*	39	10	*10*	5	5	*12*	12	..	*3,126*	1,038	2,088	*112*	60	52
20	Madras	*1,584*	955	629	*1,213*	777	436	*2,259*	1,472	787	*10,364*	8,300	2,064	*461*	298	163	*10*	7	3

TABLE VI.

Birthplace.

S. No.	District, State, Province or Country where born	DISTRICTS WHERE ENUMERATED																	
		MEDAK			NIZAMABAD			MAHBUBNAGAR			NALGONDA			AURANGABAD			BIR		
		Persons	Males	Females	Persons	Males	Females	Persons	Males	Females	Persons	Males	Females	Persons	Males	Females	Persons	Males	Females
	1	20	21	22	23	24	25	26	27	28	29	30	31	32	33	34	35	36	37
	(b) Other Provinces in India ..	295	138	157	106	51	55	41	23	18	64	49	15	851	510	341	178	108	70
21	Ajmer-Merwar	112	45	67	41	10	31	2	..	2	4	4	..	162	39	123	..	..	..
22	Assam	..	..	..	..	..	..	..	..	..	..	..	..	..	..	..	..	..	..
23	Andamans	..	..	..	..	..	..	..	..	..	..	..	..	..	..	..	..	..	..
24	Baluchistan (British Administered area)..	..	..	..	..	..	..	..	..	..	..	..	..	..	..	..	1	1	..
25	Bengal	10	6	4	5	5	..	..	..	..	..	..	..	26	14	12	2	..	2
26	Bihar and Orissa	22	6	16	..	..	..	11	5	6	1	1	..	149	49	100	61	26	35
27	Burma	..	..	..	..	..	..	..	..	..	..	..	..	2	2	..	1	1	..
28	Coorg	..	..	..	..	..	..	..	..	..	..	..	..	..	..	..	..	..	..
29	Delhi	20	1	19	3	3	..	5	2	3	..	..	..	327	265	62	11	5	6
30	North West Frontier Provinces ..	..	..	..	1	1	..	..	..	..	..	..	..	4	4	..	31	26	5
31	Punjab	39	22	17	6	4	2	12	10	2	22	21	1	96	89	7	45	28	17
32	United Provinces of Agra and Oudh ..	92	58	34	50	28	22	11	6	5	37	23	14	85	48	37	26	21	5
	(c) States and Agencies	236	145	91	371	183	188	64	40	24	81	56	25	1,672	1,013	659	674	549	125
33	Baroda	..	..	..	..	..	..	..	..	..	1	1	..	4	4	..	1	1	..
34	Bombay States	..	..	..	..	..	..	..	..	..	17	16	1	51	35	16	..	..	..
35	Central India Agency	21	20	1	6	1	5	..	..	..	15	10	5	35	7	28	173	173	..
36	Cochin	..	..	..	..	..	..	..	..	..	..	..	..	3	2	1	..	..	..
37	Gwalior	..	..	..	..	..	..	..	..	..	2	1	1	262	160	102	4	1	3
38	Jammu and Kashmir	..	..	..	..	..	..	..	..	..	..	..	..	..	..	..	2	..	2
*39	Madras States	..	..	..	..	..	..	..	..	..	..	..	..	..	..	..	..	..	..
40	Mysore	118	76	42	32	21	11	32	16	16	19	12	7	207	98	109	..	..	..
41	Punjab States	..	..	..	..	..	..	..	..	..	..	..	..	48	36	12	..	..	..
42	Rajputana Agency	94	47	47	293	141	152	32	24	8	27	16	11	1,052	666	386	494	374	120
43	Travancore	3	2	1	..	..	..	..	..	..	..	..	..	..	..	..	..	..	..
44	United Provinces States	..	..	..	40	20	20	..	..	..	..	..	..	10	5	5	..	..	..
	(d) French and Portuguese Settlements	..	..	..	..	..	..	..	..	..	..	..	..	..	..	..	..	..	..
45	French, and Portuguese Settlements ..	..	..	..	..	..	..	..	..	..	..	..	..	..	..	..	..	..	..
	(e) India, Unspecified	35	5	30	57	40	17	70	35	35	..	..	..	59	19	40	..	..	..
46	India, Unspecified	35	5	30	57	40	17	70	35	35	..	..	..	59	19	40	..	..	..

*Excluding Travancore and Cochin states

TABLE VI.

Birthplace.

S. No.	District, State, Province or Country where born.	DISTRICTS WHERE ENUMERATED																	
		MEDAK			NIZAMABAD			MAHBUBNAGAR			NALGONDA			AURANGABAD			BIR		
		Persons	Males	Females	Persons	Males	Females	Persons	Males	Females	Persons	Males	Females	Persons	Males	Females	Persons	Males	Females
	1	20	21	22	23	24	25	26	27	28	29	30	31	32	33	34	35	36	37
	B. BORN IN OTHER COUNTRIES. ..	16	12	4	65	37	28	36	29	7	11	6	5	68	60	8	42	34	8
	(i) Within British Dominions ..	..	..	..	1	1	..	..	..	..	..	..	..	3	3	..	..	..	..
47	Ceylon	..	..	..	*1*	1	..	..	..	..	..	..	..	3	3	..	..	..	..
48	Strait Settlements and Malaya ..	..	..	..	..	..	..	..	..	..	..	..	..	..	..	..	..	..	..
49	Elsewhere	..	..	..	..	..	..	..	..	..	..	..	..	..	..	..	..	..	..
	(ii) Outside British Dominions ..	16	12	4	64	36	28	28	21	7	11	6	5	65	57	8	42	34	8
50	Afghanistan	..	..	..	..	..	..	*1*	1	..	..	..	..	*8*	8	..	..	..	..
51	China	..	..	..	..	..	..	..	..	..	..	..	..	..	..	..	..	..	..
52	Nepal	..	..	..	..	..	..	..	..	..	..	..	..	*1*	1	..	*1*	..	1
53	Elsewhere	*16*	12	4	*64*	36	28	*27*	20	7	*11*	6	5	*56*	48	8	*41*	34	7
	(iii) Asia, Unspecified	..	..	..	..	..	..	8	8	..	..	..	..	..	..	..	..	..	..
54	Asia, Unspecified	..	..	..	..	..	..	*8*	8	..	..	..	..	..	..	..	..	..	..
	C. BORN IN EUROPE. ..	7	4	3	3	3	..	2	1	1	14	11	3	204	199	5	1	1	..
	(i) Great Britian and Ireland ..	7	4	3	3	3	..	..	..	..	13	11	2	133	128	5	1	1	..
55	Great Britain and Ireland ..	*7*	4	3	*3*	3	..	..	..	..	*13*	11	2	*133*	128	5	*1*	1	..
	(ii) British possessions in Europe ..	..	..	..	..	..	..	..	..	..	..	..	..	..	..	..	..	..	..
56	British possessions in Europe ..	..	..	..	..	..	..	..	..	..	..	..	..	..	..	..	..	..	..
	(iii) Continental Europe	..	..	..	..	..	..	..	..	..	1	..	1	15	15	..	..	..	..
57	Continental Europe	..	..	..	..	..	..	..	..	..	*1*	..	1	15	15	..	..	..	..
	(iv) Europe, Unspecified ..	..	..	..	..	..	..	2	1	1	..	..	..	56	56	..	..	..	..
58	Europe, Unspecified	..	..	..	..	..	..	2	1	1	..	..	..	*56*	56	..	..	..	..

TABLE VI.

Birthplace.

S. No.	District, State, Province or Country where born.	DISTRICT WHERE ENUMERATED																	
		MEDAK			NIZAMABAD			MAHBUBNAGAR			NALGONDA			AURANGABAD			BIR		
		Persons	Males	Females	Persons	Males	Females	Persons	Males	Females	Persons	Males	Females	Persons	Males	Females	Persons	Males	Females
	1	20	21	22	23	24	25	26	27	28	29	30	31	32	33	34	35	36	37
	D. BORN IN AFRICA. ..	..	..	..	..	..	..	..	..	..	..	..	..	..	..	..	..	..	..
	(i) Within British Dominions ..	..	..	..	..	..	..	..	..	..	..	..	..	..	..	..	..	..	..
59	Kenya (British East Africa) ..	..	..	..	..	..	..	..	..	..	..	..	..	..	..	..	..	..	..
	E. BORN IN AMERICA. ..	2	..	2	..	..	..	..	..	..	1	1	..	7	7	..	..	..	..
	(i) Within British Dominions. ..	..	..	..	..	..	..	..	..	..	..	..	..	3	3	..	..	..	..
60	Canada	..	..	..	..	..	..	..	..	..	..	..	..	3	3	..	..	..	..
	(ii) Outside British Dominions. ..	2	..	2	..	..	..	..	..	..	1	1	..	4	4	..	..	..	..
61	United States	2	..	2	..	..	..	..	..	..	1	1	..	4	4	..	..	..	..
62	America, Unspecified	..	..	..	..	..	..	..	..	..	..	..	..	..	..	..	..	..	..
	F. BORN IN AUSTRALASIA.	..	..	..	..	..	..	..	..	..	..	..	..	..	..	..	..	..	..
	(i) Within British Dominions.	..	..	..	..	..	..	..	..	..	..	..	..	..	..	..	..	..	..
63	Australia	..	..	..	..	..	..	..	..	..	..	..	..	..	..	..	..	..	..
64	New Zealand	..	..	..	..	..	..	..	..	..	..	..	..	..	..	..	..	..	..
	G. BORN AT SEA.	..	..	..	..	..	..	..	..	..	..	..	..	..	..	..	..	..	..
65	Born at Sea	..	..	..	..	..	..	..	..	..	..	..	..	..	..	..	..	..	..
	H. BIRTH PLACE UNSPECIFIED OR NOT RETURNED. ..	..	..	..	..	..	..	..	..	..	..	..	..	..	..	..	..	..	..
66	Birthplace Unspecified or not returned ..	..	..	..	..	..	..	..	..	..	..	..	..	..	..	..	..	..	..

TABLE VI.

Birthplace.

S. No.	District, State, Province or Country where born	DISTRICTS WHERE ENUMERATED																	
		NANDER			PARBHANI			GULBARGA			OSMANABAD			RAICHUR			BIDAR		
		Persons	Males	Females	Persons	Males	Females	Persons	Males	Females	Persons	Males	Females	Persons	Males	Females	Persons	Males	Females
	1	38	39	40	41	42	43	44	45	46	47	48	49	50	51	52	53	54	55
	TOTAL POPULATION ..	722,081	367,170	354,911	853,760	434,777	418,983	1,225,008	621,687	603,321	691,068	357,489	333,579	937,535	473,161	464,374	873,615	446,256	427,359
	A. BORN IN INDIA	722,014	367,103	354,911	852,825	434,248	418,577	1,224,984	621,667	603,317	691,040	357,461	333,579	937,511	473,137	464,374	873,613	446,254	427,359
	(i) Born within the State ..	716,121	363,284	352,837	846,241	430,617	415,624	1,216,888	617,870	599,018	678,452	351,954	326,498	917,203	460,515	456,688	872,095	445,370	426,725
1	Hyderabad City	2,046	1,195	851	2,899	1,717	1,182	6,658	3,519	3,139	1,008	356	652	1,003	845	158	1,431	833	598
2	Atraf-i-Balda	442	156	286	188	103	85	972	393	579	252	118	134	40	3	37	567	226	341
3	Warangal	661	453	208	641	164	477	959	482	477	51	22	29	94	64	30	1,001	639	362
4	Karimnagar	1,828	1,214	614	798	314	484	193	117	76	8	1	7	20	15	5	812	274	538
5	Adilabad	1,339	665	674	181	118	63	214	95	119	102	19	83	20	5	15	977	458	519
6	Medak	1,303	866	437	509	195	314	870	473	397	272	102	170	144	70	74	1,962	792	1,170
7	Nizamabad	7,418	4,317	3,101	1,210	421	789	819	463	356	259	84	175	246	240	6	1,368	817	1,051
8	Mahbubnagar	592	160	432	297	290	7	8,798	5,383	3,415	35	9	26	19,389	5,365	14,024	905	413	492
9	Nalgonda	583	490	93	176	91	85	811	497	314	21	8	13	29	6	23	1,142	1,042	100
10	Aurangabad	1,737	742	995	10,199	4,860	5,339	1,371	1,057	314	1,324	703	621	39	32	7	1,916	1,181	735
11	Bir	4,607	2,215	2,392	14,847	6,580	8,267	262	152	110	5,251	2,514	2,737	95	55	40	2,116	1,464	652
12	Nander	680,787	345,833	334,954	8,649	4,250	4,399	556	338	218	1,564	600	964	83	57	26	2,491	1,597	894
13	Parbhani	8,638	2,955	5,683	800,182	409,294	390,888	525	136	389	694	262	432	2	2	..	1,604	1,159	445
14	Gulbarga	1,018	442	576	2,026	355	1,671	1,179,724	595,818	583,906	3,457	1,750	1,707	1,839	591	1,248	4,637	2,525	2,112
15	Osmanabad	497	271	226	712	356	356	2,037	1,466	571	659,502	343,422	316,080	57	34	23	10,779	4,203	6,576
16	Raichur	211	59	152	233	215	18	7,599	5,428	2,171	253	138	115	894,052	453,110	440,942	1,093	537	556
17	Bidar	2,414	1,251	1,163	2,494	1,294	1,200	4,520	2,053	2,467	4,399	1,846	2,553	51	21	30	837,294	427,710	409,584
	(ii) Born in Provinces and States beyond the State	5,893	3,819	2,074	6,584	3,631	2,953	8,096	3,797	4,299	12,588	5,507	7,081	20,308	12,622	7,686	1,518	884	634
	(a) Provinces adjacent to the State ..	4,791	3,020	1,771	6,105	3,371	2,734	7,213	3,260	3,953	12,207	5,291	6,916	19,711	12,321	7,390	1,104	702	402
18	Bombay	2,514	1,741	773	4,297	2,549	1,748	6,523	2,922	3,601	11,866	5,120	6,746	10,095	7,357	2,738	687	467	229
19	Central Provinces and Berar ..	1,866	909	957	1,709	782	927	61	35	26	274	140	134	23	10	13	311	144	167
20	Madras	411	370	41	99	40	59	629	303	326	67	31	36	9,593	4,954	4,639	106	91	15

TABLE VI.

Birthplace.

S. No.	District, State, Province or Country where born	DISTRICTS WHERE ENUMERATED																	
		NANDER			PARBHANI			GULBARGA			OSMANABAD			RAICHUR			BIDAR		
		Persons	Males	Females	Persons	Males	Females	Persons	Males	Females	Persons	Males	Females	Persons	Males	Females	Persons	Males	Females
		38	39	40	41	42	43	44	45	46	47	48	49	50	51	52	53	54	55
	(b) Other Provinces in India ..	296	208	88	419	232	187	331	210	121	27	12	15	30	24	6	164	111	53
21	Ajmer-Merwar	*99*	76	23	*223*	87	136	*127*	77	50	*8*	1	7	*2*	2	..	*22*	14	8
22	Assam	..	..	..	..	..	..	..	..	..	..	..	..	..	..	..	..	..	..
23	Andamans	..	..	..	..	..	..	..	..	..	..	..	..	..	..	..	..	..	..
24	Baluchistan (British Administered area)..	1	..	1	..	..	..	*1*	1	..	*1*	1	..	..	..	..	*2*	2	..
25	Bengal	..	..	..	*4*	2	2	*32*	28	4	*1*	1	..	*2*	2	..	..	..	..
26	Bihar and Orissa	..	..	..	..	..	..	*4*	1	3	..	..	..	..	..	..	..	..	..
27	Burma	..	..	..	*6*	5	1	..	..	..	..	..	..	*1*	1	..	..	..	..
28	Coorg	..	..	..	..	..	..	..	..	..	..	..	..	..	..	..	..	..	..
29	Delhi	..	..	..	*6*	5	1	*24*	21	3	*5*	5	..	*8*	6	2	*56*	16	40
30	North West Frontier Provinces ..	*28*	10	18	*4*	4	..	*2*	2	..	..	..	..	..	..	..	..	..	..
31	Punjab	*100*	79	21	*59*	42	17	*60*	50	10	*5*	4	1	*4*	3	1	*10*	10	..
32	United Provinces of Agra and Oudh ..	*68*	43	25	*117*	87	30	*81*	30	51	*7*	..	7	*13*	10	3	*74*	69	5
	(c) States and Agencies	744	591	153	59	28	31	549	326	223	349	199	150	563	277	286	183	61	122
33	Baroda	*1*	1	..	..	..	..	*2*	2	..	*4*	..	4	*2*	1	1	..	..	..
34	Bombay States	..	..	..	*6*	4	2	*2*	2	..	*91*	71	20	*3*	1	2	..	..	..
35	Central India Agency	*3*	3	..	*28*	13	15	*7*	6	1	*4*	2	2	*74*	16	58	*90*	3	87
36	Cochin	..	..	..	..	..	..	..	..	..	..	..	..	..	..	..	..	..	..
37	Gwalior	..	..	..	*2*	2	..	..	..	..	..	..	..	..	..	..	..	..	..
38	Jammu and Kashmir	*1*	1	..	*1*	1	..	*3*	3	..	..	..	..	..	..	..	..	..	..
*39	Madras States	..	..	..	*2*	..	2	..	..	..	..	..	..	..	..	..	..	..	..
40	Mysore	*21*	5	16	*20*	8	12	*76*	44	32	*20*	7	13	*428*	239	189	*20*	20	..
41	Punjab States	..	..	..	..	..	..	..	..	..	..	..	..	..	..	..	..	..	..
42	Rajputana Agency	*707*	570	137	..	..	..	*453*	263	190	*230*	119	111	*56*	20	36	*71*	38	33
43	Travancore	*1*	1	..	..	..	..	..	..	..	..	..	..	..	..	..	..	..	..
44	United Provinces States	10	10	..	..	..	..	6	6	..	..	..	..	..	..	..	*2*	..	2
	(d) French and Portuguese Settlements	..	..	..	1	..	1	3	1	2	5	5	..	4	..	4	..	..	..
45	French and Portuguese Settlements ..	..	..	..	*1*	..	1	*3*	1	2	*5*	5	..	*4*	..	4	..	..	..
	(e) India, Unspecified	62	..	62	..	..	..	..	..	..	..	..	..	..	..	..	67	10	57
46	India, Unspecified	*62*	..	62	..	..	..	..	..	..	..	..	..	..	..	..	*67*	10	57

* Excluding Travancore and Cochin States.

TABLE VI.

Birthplace.

S. No.	District, State, Province or Country, where born	DISTRICTS WHERE ENUMERATED																	
		Nander			Parbhani			Gulbarga			Osmanabad			Raichur			Bidar		
		Persons	Males	Females	Persons	Males	Females	Persons	Males	Females	Persons	Males	Females	Persons	Males	Females	Persons	Males	Females
	1	38	39	40	41	42	43	44	45	46	47	48	49	50	51	52	53	54	55
	B. BORN IN OTHER ASIATIC COUNTRIES. ..	67	67	..	935	529	406	19	17	2	28	28	..	14	14	..	2	2	..
	(i) Within British Dominions ..	..	..	..	..	..	..	..	..	..	..	..	..	..	..	..	..	..	..
47	Ceylon	..	..	..	..	..	..	..	..	..	..	..	..	..	..	..	..	..	..
48	Strait Settlements and Malaya ..	..	..	..	..	..	..	..	..	..	..	..	..	..	..	..	..	..	..
49	Elsewhere	..	..	..	..	..	..	..	..	..	..	..	..	..	..	..	..	..	..
	(ii) Outside British Dominions ..	67	67	..	935	529	406	19	17	2	28	28	..	14	14	..	2	2	..
50	Afghanistan	*1*	1	..	*12*	10	2	7	6	1	7	7	..	..	..	..	2	2	..
51	China	..	..	..	..	..	..	..	..	..	..	..	..	..	..	..	..	..	..
52	Nepal	*1*	1	..	*3*	1	2	..	..	..	..	..	..	..	..	..	..	..	..
53	Elsewhere	*65*	65	..	*920*	518	402	*12*	11	1	*21*	21	..	*14*	14	..	..	..	..
	(iii) Asia, Unspecified	..	..	..	..	..	..	..	..	..	..	..	..	..	..	..	..	..	..
54	Asia, Unspecified	..	..	..	..	..	..	..	..	..	..	..	..	..	..	..	..	..	..
	C. BORN IN EUROPE. ..	..	..	..	..	..	..	5	3	2	..	..	..	10	10	..	..	..	..
	(i) Great Britain and Ireland ..	..	..	..	..	..	..	5	3	2	..	..	..	10	10	..	..	..	..
55	Great Britain and Ireland ..	..	..	..	..	..	..	*5*	3	2	..	..	..	*10*	10	..	..	..	..
	(ii) British possessions in Europe ..	..	..	..	..	..	..	..	..	..	..	..	..	..	..	..	..	..	..
56	British possessions in Europe ..	..	..	..	..	..	..	..	..	..	..	..	..	..	..	..	..	..	..
	(iii) Continental Europe	..	..	..	..	..	..	..	..	..	..	..	..	..	..	..	..	..	..
57	Continental Europe	..	..	..	..	..	..	..	..	..	..	..	..	..	..	..	..	..	..
	(iv) Europe, Unspecified ..	..	..	..	..	..	..	..	..	..	..	..	..	..	..	..	..	..	..
58	Europe, Unspecified	..	..	..	..	..	..	..	..	..	..	..	..	..	..	..	..	..	..

TABLE VI.

Birthplace.

S. No.	District, State, Province or Country where born	DISTRICT WHERE ENUMERATED																	
		Nander			Parbhani			Gulbarga			Osmanabad			Raichur			Bidar		
		Persons	Males	Females	Persons	Males	Females	Persons	Males	Females	Persons	Males	Females	Persons	Males	Females	Persons	Males	Females
1	2	38	39	40	41	42	43	44	45	46	47	48	49	50	51	52	53	54	55
	D. BORN IN AFRICA. ..	..	..	..	..	..	..	..	..	..	..	..	..	..	..	..	..	..	..
	(i) Within British Dominions ..	..	..	..	..	..	..	..	..	..	..	..	..	..	..	..	..	..	..
59	Kenya (British East Africa) ..	..	..	..	..	..	..	..	..	..	..	..	..	..	..	..	..	..	..
	E. BORN IN AMERICA. ..	..	..	..	..	..	..	..	..	..	..	..	..	..	..	..	..	..	..
	(i) Within British Dominions. ..	..	..	..	..	..	..	..	..	..	..	..	..	..	..	..	..	..	..
60	Canada	..	..	..	..	..	..	..	..	..	..	..	..	..	..	..	..	..	..
	(ii) Outside British Dominions. ..	..	..	..	..	..	..	..	..	..	..	..	..	..	..	..	..	..	..
61	United States	..	..	..	..	..	..	..	..	..	..	..	..	..	..	..	..	..	..
	(iii) America, Unspecified ..	..	..	..	..	..	..	..	..	..	..	..	..	..	..	..	..	..	..
62	America, Unspecified	..	..	..	..	..	..	..	..	..	..	..	..	..	..	..	..	..	..
	F. BORN IN AUSTRALASIA.	..	..	..	..	..	..	..	..	..	..	..	..	..	..	..	..	..	..
	(i) Within British Dominions.	..	..	..	..	..	..	..	..	..	..	..	..	..	..	..	..	..	..
63	Australia	..	..	..	..	..	..	..	..	..	..	..	..	..	..	..	..	..	..
64	New Zealand	..	..	..	..	..	..	..	..	..	..	..	..	..	..	..	..	..	..
	G. BORN AT SEA.	..	..	..	..	..	..	..	..	..	..	..	..	..	..	..	..	..	..
65	Born at Sea	..	..	..	..	..	..	..	..	..	..	..	..	..	..	..	..	..	..
	H. BIRTHPLACE UNSPECIFIED OR NOT RETURNED. ..	..	..	..	..	..	..	..	..	..	..	..	..	..	..	..	..	..	..
66	Birthplace Unspecified or not returned ..	..	..	..	..	..	..	..	..	..	..	..	..	..	..	..	..	..	..

Table VII.

AGE, SEX AND CIVIL CONDITION

Note.—This table is divided into three parts and shows the distribution of the population by age, sex and civil condition. Part I shows the distribution for the State as a whole of the total population, male and female, by each religion; part II shows similar statistics of the total district population and for main religion only and part III gives similar information for the four cities.

2. The ages shown in this table are smoothed according to the method recommended by the Actuary to the Government of India,—the method being conversion of ternary and septenary groups into quinary groups. The individual ages recokoned in the present Census are from the *nearest* birthday and not (like 1921) from the number of completed years.

TABLE VII.

AGE, SEX & CIVIL CONDITION.

TABLE VII.—

Age, Sex and

RELIGION AND AGE	TOTAL POPULATION			UNMARRIED		
	Persons	Males	Females	Persons	Males	Females
1	2	3	4	5	6	7
All Religions	14,436,148	7,370,010	7,066,138	5,323,888	3,124,066	2,199,822
0–1	*437,224*	206,994	230,230	*429,824*	203,708	226,116
1–2	*488,250*	234,050	254,200	*476,652*	229,064	247,588
2–3	*490,396*	233,577	256,819	*472,354*	226,193	246,161
3–4	*475,857*	232,359	243,498	*439,706*	218,253	221,453
4–5	*536,492*	251,849	284,648	*459,780*	227,604	232,086
Total 0–5	2,428,219	1,158,829	1,269,390	2,278,316	1,104,912	1,173,404
5–10	*1,758,013*	914,853	843,160	*1,339,548*	784,278	555,270
10–15	*1,575,481*	827,213	748,268	*926,163*	616,285	309,878
15–20	*1,294,390*	638,789	655,601	*328,568*	273,315	55,253
20–25	*1,360,945*	673,215	687,730	*200,616*	168,628	31,988
25–30	*1,259,758*	635,407	624,351	*84,991*	65,374	19,617
30–35	*1,060,369*	553,799	506,570	*51,553*	36,700	14,853
35–40	*889,841*	474,600	415,241	*30,865*	19,744	11,121
40–45	*755,754*	406,456	349,298	*24,090*	15,401	8,689
45–50	*593,770*	324,795	268,975	*17,617*	11,329	6,288
50–55	*473,350*	256,884	216,466	*14,188*	9,751	4,437
55–60	*351,869*	185,613	166,256	*10,410*	7,338	3,072
60–65	*288,606*	147,839	140,767	*7,517*	4,920	2,597
65–70	*150,688*	76,921	73,767	*4,022*	2,565	1,457
70 and over	*195,095*	94,797	100,298	*5,424*	3,526	1,898
Hindu (Brahmanic)	9,699,615	4,948,408	4,751,207	3,439,233	2,039,805	1,399,428
0–1	*288,238*	135,820	152,418	*283,896*	134,070	149,826
1–2	*316,253*	151,236	165,017	*308,858*	147,815	161,043
2–3	*318,446*	150,945	167,501	*306,305*	146,012	160,293
3–4	*310,269*	149,024	161,245	*283,817*	139,039	144,778
4–5	*356,598*	160,845	195,753	*300,097*	144,495	155,602
Total 0–5	1,589,804	747,870	841,934	1,482,973	711,431	771,542
5–10	*1,170,888*	610,169	560,710	*862,021*	517,412	344,609
10–15	*1,064,485*	559,251	505,234	*591,586*	405,399	186,187
15–20	*872,670*	431,572	441,098	*205,047*	174,338	30,709
20–25	*917,159*	457,589	459,570	*127,436*	108,473	18,963
25–30	*849,468*	432,872	416,596	*55,568*	43,589	11,979
30–35	*717,859*	376,922	340,937	*35,142*	25, 835	9,307
35–40	*600,319*	321,146	279,173	*20,936*	13,690	7,246
40-45	*510,653*	273,939	236,714	*15,967*	10,336	5,631
45–50	*404,659*	219,420	185,239	*12,305*	8,050	4,255
50–55	*323,284*	173,844	149,440	*10,782*	7,799	2,983
55–60	*242,781*	126,719	116,062	*7,696*	5,575	2,121
60–65	*200,267*	102,801	97,466	*5,245*	3,658	1,587
65–70	*103,705*	52,578	51,127	*2,912*	1,911	1,001
70 and over	*131,614*	61,716	69,898	*3,617*	2,309	1,308
Adi Hindu	2,473,230	1,252,651	1,220,579	923,136	530,431	392,705
0–1	*80,159*	38,272	41,887	*78,347*	37,459	40,888
1–2	*93,995*	44,724	49,271	*91,557*	44,005	47,552
2–3	*92,460*	43,611	48,849	*89,224*	42,544	46,680
3–4	*88,153*	45,081	43,072	*82,920*	43,004	39,916
4–5	*95,147*	49,452	45,695	*82,943*	45,071	37,872
Total 0–5	449,914	221,140	228,774	424,991	212,083	212,908
5–10	*305,760*	157,591	148,169	*235,463*	135,984	99,520
10–15	*264,014*	137,882	126,132	*154,716*	103,415	51,301
15–20	*212,404*	101,139	111,265	*48,034*	39,327	8,707
20–25	*225,662*	107,938	117,724	*26,470*	20,550	5,920
25–30	*215,266*	104,593	110,673	*10,922*	6,668	4,250
30–35	*180,843*	91,436	89,407	*6,511*	3,528	2,983
35–40	*153,083*	80,437	72,646	*4,544*	2,364	2,180
40 45	*129,693*	69,807	59,886	*3,947*	2,260	1,687
45–50	*100,394*	54,757	45,637	*2,559*	1,427	1,132
50–55	*79,201*	43,620	35,581	*1,585*	794	791
55–60	*55,691*	30,175	25,516	*1,252*	759	493
60–65	*45,821*	23,179	22,642	*933*	517	416
65–70	*24,072*	12,419	11,653	*546*	347	199
70 and over	*31,412*	16,538	14,874	*663*	463	200

PART I.

Civil Condition.

TABLE VII.

AGE, SEX & CIVIL CONDITION.

RELIGION AND AGE	MARRIED			WIDOWED		
	Persons	Males	Females	Persons	Males	Females
1	8	9	10	11	12	13
All Religions	**7,641,784**	**3,878,362**	**3,763,422**	**1,470,476**	**367,582**	**1,102,894**
0–1	7,183	3,207	3,976	217	79	138
1–2	11,273	4,891	6,382	325	95	230
2–3	17,280	7,111	10,169	762	273	489
3–4	33,839	13,361	20,478	2,312	745	1,567
4–5	72,619	23,004	49,615	4,093	1,151	2,942
Total 0–5	**142,194**	**51,574**	**90,620**	**7,709**	**2,343**	**5,366**
5–10	403,381	126,537	276,844	15,084	4,038	11,046
10–15	627,649	205,207	422,442	21,669	5,721	15,948
15–20	928,427	355,928	572,499	37,395	9,546	27,849
20–25	1,102,905	489,033	613,872	57,424	15,554	41,870
25–30	1,083,669	548,201	535,468	91,098	21,832	69,266
30–35	899,474	491,849	407,625	109,342	25,250	84,092
35–40	705,699	420,299	285,400	153,277	34,557	118,720
40–45	567,774	353,829	213,945	163,890	37,226	126,664
45–50	397,221	270,308	126,913	178,932	43,158	135,774
50–55	296,605	206,644	89,961	162,557	40,489	122,068
55–60	187,456	138,432	49,024	154,003	39,843	114,160
60–65	144,579	107,791	36,788	136,510	35,128	101,382
65–70	70,913	52,043	18,870	75,753	22,313	53,440
70 and over	83,838	60,687	23,151	105,833	30,584	75,249
Hindu (Brahmanic)	**5,204,303**	**2,641,439**	**2,562,864**	**1,056,079**	**267,164**	**788,915**
0–1	4,207	1,707	2,500	135	43	92
1–2	7,202	3,376	3,826	193	45	148
2–3	11,612	4,753	6,859	529	180	349
3–4	24,527	9,374	15,153	1,925	611	1,314
4–5	53,432	15,451	37,981	3,069	899	2,170
Total 0–5	**100,980**	**34,661**	**66,319**	**5,851**	**1,778**	**4,073**
5–10	296,892	89,615	207,277	11,975	3,142	8,833
10–15	455,967	149,429	306,538	16,932	4,423	12,509
15–20	639,416	249,720	389,696	28,207	7,514	20,693
20–25	747,087	337,153	409,934	42,636	11,963	30,673
25–30	726,998	372,937	354,061	66,902	16,346	50,556
30–35	603,341	332,430	270,911	79,376	18,657	60,719
35–40	469,975	282,740	187,235	109,408	24,716	84,692
40–45	377,628	236,723	140,905	117,058	26,880	90,178
45–50	264,671	180,232	84,439	127,683	31,138	96,545
50–55	197,862	137,427	60,435	114,640	28,618	86,022
55–60	125,438	92,677	32,761	109,647	28,467	81,180
60–65	96,958	72,823	24,135	98,064	26,320	71,744
65–70	47,540	34,294	13,246	53,253	16,373	36,880
70 and over	53,550	38,578	14,972	74,447	20,829	53,618
Adi Hindu	**1,323,693**	**666,299**	**657,394**	**226,401**	**55,921**	**170,480**
0–1	1,777	800	977	35	13	22
1–2	2,390	717	1,673	48	2	46
2–3	3,143	1,051	2,092	93	16	77
3–4	5,030	2,020	3,010	203	57	146
4–5	11,588	4,246	7,342	616	135	481
Total 0–5	**23,928**	**8,834**	**15,094**	**995**	**223**	**772**
5–10	68,396	21,123	47,273	1,901	534	1,367
10–15	106,324	33,614	72,710	2,974	853	2,121
15–20	158,784	60,696	98,088	5,586	1,116	4,470
20–25	190,864	85,522	105,342	8,328	1,866	6,462
25–30	190,872	95,175	95,697	13,472	2,755	10,717
30–35	157,733	84,551	73,182	16,599	3,357	13,242
35–40	123,638	72,295	51,343	24,901	5,778	19,123
40–45	99,285	61,381	37,904	26,461	6,166	20,295
45–50	69,504	46,250	23,254	28,331	7,080	21,251
50–55	51,426	35,804	15,622	26,190	7,022	19,168
55–60	30,836	22,827	8,009	23,603	6,589	17,014
60–65	25,119	18,211	6,908	19,769	4,451	15,318
65–70	12,179	9,228	2,951	11,347	2,844	8,503
70 and over	14,805	10,788	4,017	15,944	5,287	10,657

TABLE VII—

Age, Sex and

TABLE VII.

AGE, SEX & CIVIL CONDITION.

RELIGION AND AGE	TOTAL POPULATION			UNMARRIED		
	Persons	Males	Females	Persons	Males	Females
1	2	3	4	5	6	7
Arya	3,700	1,896	1,804	1,520	924	596
0–1	178	92	86	176	90	86
1–2	133	58	75	130	58	72
2–3	143	67	76	135	62	73
3–4	115	59	56	106	53	53
4–5	122	69	53	108	62	46
Total 0–5	691	345	346	655	325	330
5–10	375	205	170	298	177	121
10–15	379	229	150	251	177	74
15–20	284	142	142	78	55	28
20–25	358	189	169	98	77	21
25–30	281	122	159	49	32	17
30–35	242	121	121	41	33	8
35–40	215	114	101	22	22	..
40–45	204	106	98	14	14	..
45–50	186	99	87	5	4	1
50–55	131	57	74	1	1	..
55–60	110	40	70	2	2	..
60–65	100	45	55	4	3	1
65–70	73	45	28	1	1	..
70 and over	71	37	34	1	1	..
Brahmo	182	98	84	43	20	23
0–1	2	1	1	2	1	1
1–2	4	3	1	4	3	1
2–3	5	2	3	5	2	3
3–4	2	1	1	2	1	1
4–5	2	1	1	1	..	1
Total 0–5	15	8	7	14	7	7
5–10	7	2	5	4	1	3
10–15	7	4	3	3	2	1
15–20	17	7	10	5	2	3
20–25	12	6	6	1	1	..
25–30	26	16	10	4	2	2
30–35	28	13	15	3	1	2
35–40	27	13	14	4	2	2
40–45	17	8	9	1	..	1
45–50	16	14	2	2	1	1
50–55	2	1	1	..	..	..
55–60	4	4	..	1	1	..
60–65	3	1	2	1	..	1
65–70	1	1	..	..	..	..
70 and over	..	..	..	..	..	..
Jain	21,543	11,456	10,087	7,631	4,539	3,092
0–1	677	323	354	658	311	347
1–2	624	315	309	601	299	302
2–3	648	329	319	597	303	294
3–4	613	309	304	521	269	252
4–5	745	366	379	576	282	294
Total 0–5	3,307	1,642	1,665	2,953	1,464	1,489
5–10	2,553	1,383	1,170	1,871	1,106	765
10–15	2,277	1,151	1,126	1,226	773	453
15–20	1,986	1,022	964	523	428	95
20–25	2,051	1,056	995	340	275	65
25–30	1,717	918	799	174	131	43
30–35	1,563	917	646	128	105	23
35–40	1,422	766	656	131	77	54
40–45	1,205	596	609	95	51	44
45–50	951	565	386	57	46	11
50–55	805	504	301	39	35	4
55–60	651	374	277	23	22	1
60–65	488	261	227	32	10	22
65–70	315	154	161	28	7	21
70 and over	252	147	105	11	9	2

PART I.

Civil Condition.

TABLE VII.

AGE, SEX & CIVIL CONDITION.

RELIGION AND AGE	MARRIED			WIDOWED		
	Persons	Males	Females	Persons	Males	Females
1	8	9	10	11	12	13
Arya	1,852	855	997	328	117	211
0-1	2	2	..	..	..	..
1-2	3	..	3	..	..	..
2-3	8	5	3	..	..	..
3-4	9	6	3	..	..	..
4-5	12	7	5	2	..	2
Total 0-5	34	20	14	2	..	2
5-10	75	28	47	2	..	2
10-15	123	48	75	5	4	1
15-20	197	83	114	9	4	5
20-25	247	109	138	13	3	10
25-30	202	79	123	30	11	19
30-35	185	87	98	16	1	15
35-40	169	82	87	24	10	14
40-45	159	81	78	31	11	20
45-50	150	85	65	31	10	21
50-55	89	42	47	41	14	27
55-60	75	30	45	33	8	25
60-65	66	31	35	30	11	19
65-70	44	29	15	28	15	13
70 and over	37	21	16	33	15	18
Brahmo	112	68	44	27	10	17
0-1	..	..	..	..	..	..
1-2	..	..	..	..	..	..
2-3	..	..	..	..	..	..
3-4	..	..	..	..	..	..
4-5	1	1	..	..	..	..
Total 0-5	1	1	..	..	..	..
5-10	3	1	2	..	..	..
10-15	4	2	2	..	..	..
15-20	10	4	6	2	1	1
20-25	8	4	4	3	1	2
25-30	17	12	5	5	2	3
30-35	15	7	8	10	5	5
35-40	19	11	8	4	..	4
40-45	13	7	6	3	1	2
45-50	14	13	1	..	..	..
50-55	2	1	1	..	..	..
55-60	3	3	..	..	..	..
60-65	2	1	1	..	..	..
65-70	1	1	..	..	..	..
70 and over	..	..	..	..	..	..
Jain	11,412	5,994	5,418	2,500	923	1,577
0-1	18	11	7	1	1	..
1-2	23	16	7	..	..	..
2-3	46	26	20	5	..	5
3-4	86	39	47	6	1	5
4-5	154	79	75	15	5	10
Total 0-5	327	171	156	27	7	20
5-10	664	270	394	18	7	11
10-15	1,007	365	642	44	13	31
15-20	1,399	572	827	64	22	42
20-25	1,586	731	855	125	50	75
25-30	1,382	741	641	161	46	115
30-35	1,247	752	495	188	60	128
35-40	1,072	611	461	219	78	141
40-45	868	466	402	242	79	163
45-50	598	400	198	296	119	177
50-55	473	341	132	293	128	165
55-60	333	241	92	295	111	184
60-65	233	169	64	223	82	141
65-70	124	81	43	163	66	97
70 and over	99	83	16	142	55	87

TABLE VII.

AGE, SEX & CIVIL CONDITION.

RELIGION AND AGE	TOTAL POPULATION			UNMARRIED		
	Persons	Males	Females	Persons	Males	Females
1	2	3	4	5	6	7
Sikh	5,178	3,064	2,114	1,990	1,254	736
0–1	*137*	71	66	*135*	71	64
1–2	*128*	65	63	*124*	63	61
2–3	*161*	83	78	*155*	81	74
3–4	*142*	78	64	*129*	68	61
4–5	*182*	95	87	*145*	82	63
Total 0–5	750	392	358	688	365	323
5–10	*502*	262	240	*396*	229	167
10–15	*506*	237	269	*323*	173	150
15–20	*512*	288	224	*192*	147	45
20–25	*587*	375	212	*159*	143	16
25–30	*463*	309	154	*65*	58	7
30–35	*369*	245	124	*41*	34	7
35–40	*322*	190	132	*31*	18	13
40–45	*315*	199	116	*28*	24	4
45–50	*220*	142	78	*23*	21	2
50–55	*179*	121	58	*13*	12	1
55–60	*154*	111	43	*13*	13	..
60–65	*110*	79	31	*8*	8	..
65–70	*78*	46	32	*5*	3	..
70 and over	*111*	68	43	*5*	4	1
Muslim	1,534,666	791,435	743,231	638,010	370,211	267,799
0–1	*45,459*	21,480	23,979	*44,618*	20,988	23,630
1–2	*50,171*	24,662	25,509	*49,102*	24,121	24,981
2–3	*50,129*	24,784	25,345	*48,397*	23,858	24,539
3–4	*48,351*	24,169	24,182	*45,674*	22,828	22,846
4–5	*54,888*	26,940	27,948	*49,830*	24,576	25,254
Total 0–5	248,998	122,035	126,963	237,621	116,371	121,250
5–10	*182,954*	95,048	87,906	*156,917*	83,629	73,288
10–15	*164,680*	86,439	78,241	*121,223*	71,590	49,633
15–20	*147,168*	75,384	71,784	*55,022*	43,803	11,219
20–25	*151,417*	74,626	76,791	*34,038*	29,447	4,591
25–30	*133,044*	66,238	66,806	*12,938*	10,874	2,064
30–35	*111,137*	58,837	52,300	*6,953*	5,262	1,691
35–40	*94,788*	50,292	44,496	*3,793*	2,782	1,011
40–45	*80,217*	43,190	37,027	*2,992*	2,130	862
45–50	*62,900*	35,737	27,163	*1,995*	1,398	597
50–55	*50,251*	27,953	22,298	*1,310*	856	454
55–60	*38,412*	20,593	17,819	*1,007*	671	336
60–65	*29,954*	15,059	14,895	979	565	414
65–70	*15,936*	8,281	7,655	*348*	195	153
70 and over	*22,810*	11,723	11,087	*874*	638	236
Christian	151,382	79,444	71,938	62,758	36,674	26,084
0–1	*4,290*	2,206	2,084	*4,253*	2,180	2,073
1–2	*4,986*	2,535	2,451	*4,940*	2,512	2,428
2–3	*5,096*	2,577	2,519	*5,021*	2,546	2,475
3–4	*4,837*	2,408	2,429	*4,676*	2,836	2,840
4–5	*5,642*	2,482	3,160	*5,206*	2,301	2,905
Total 0–5	24,851	12,208	12,643	24,796	11,875	12,221
5–10	*17,624*	9,805	8,819	*15,063*	8,450	6,613
10–15	*16,506*	9,187	7,319	*11,451*	7,391	4,050
15–20	*14,087*	7,376	6,711	*5,016*	3,785	1,231
20–25	*15,259*	8,073	7,186	*3,476*	2,758	718
25–30	*13,624*	7,228	6,396	*1,567*	1,254	313
30–35	*11,178*	5,774	5,404	*737*	489	248
35–40	*9,347*	4,810	4,537	*373*	192	181
40–45	*8,034*	4,364	3,670	*351*	176	175
45–50	*6,165*	3,346	2,819	*247*	109	138
50–55	*4,815*	2,536	2,279	*130*	69	61
55–60	*3,388*	1,802	1,586	*98*	60	38
60–65	*2,699*	1,460	1,239	*54*	28	26
65–70	*1,613*	820	793	*47*	17	30
70 and over	*2,192*	1,155	1,037	*52*	21	31
Zoroastrian	1,784	937	847	764	426	338
0–1	*35*	17	18	*35*	17	18
1–2	*40*	22	18	*40*	22	18
2–3	*43*	22	21	*42*	21	21
3–4	*37*	21	16	*33*	19	14
4–5	*49*	25	24	*45*	22	23
Total 0-5	204	107	97	195	101	94

PART I.

Civil Condition.

TABLE VII.

AGE, SEX & CIVIL CONDITION.

RELIGION AND AGE	MARRIED			WIDOWED		
	Persons	Males	Females	Persons	Males	Females
1	8	9	10	11	12	13
Sikh	**2,710**	**1,620**	**1,090**	**478**	**190**	**288**
0–1						
1–2	*2*	..	2	..	..	..
2–3	*3*	1	2	*1*	1	..
3–4	*6*	2	4	..	..	..
4–5	*12*	9	3	*1*	1	..
	32	11	21	*5*	2	3
Total 0–5	**55**	**23**	**32**	**7**	**4**	**3**
5–10	*99*	30	69	*7*	3	4
10–15	*173*	57	116	*10*	7	3
15–20	*305*	182	173	*15*	9	6
20–25	*409*	222	187	*19*	10	9
25–30	*364*	239	125	*34*	12	22
30–35	*292*	194	98	*36*	17	19
35–40	*238*	159	79	*53*	13	40
40–45	*238*	159	79	*49*	16	33
45–50	*156*	105	51	*41*	16	25
50–65	*120*	94	26	*46*	15	31
55–60	*96*	80	16	*45*	18	27
60–65	*68*	52	16	*34*	19	15
65–70	*38*	26	12	*35*	15	20
70 and over	*59*	48	11	47	16	31
Muslim	**758,433**	**390,149**	**368,284**	**138,223**	**31,075**	**107,148**
0–1	*806*	474	332	*35*	18	17
1–2	*1,022*	515	507	*47*	26	21
2–3	*1,640*	875	765	*92*	51	41
3–4	*2,538*	1,281	1,257	*139*	60	79
4–5	*4.767*	2,281	2,486	*291*	83	208
Total 0–5	**10,773**	**5,426**	**5,347**	**604**	**238**	**366**
5–10	*25,187*	11,175	14,012	*850*	244	606
10–15	*42,222*	14,564	27,658	*1,235*	285	950
15–20	*89,518*	30,973	58,545	*2,628*	608	2,020
20–25	*112,565*	44,063	68,502	*4,814*	1,116	3,698
2g–30	*112,131*	53,496	58,635	*7,975*	1,868	6,107
30–35	*94,089*	51,260	42,829	*10,095*	2,315	17,780
35–40	*76,790*	44,610	32,180	*14,205*	2,900	11,303
40–45	*62,090*	38,099	23,991	*15,135*	2,961	12,174
45–50	*44,062*	30,931	13,131	*16,843*	3,408	13,485
50–55	*32,972*	23,739	9,233	*15,969*	3,358	12,611
55–60	*22,159*	16,565	5,594	*15,246*	3,357	11,889
60–65	*15,311*	11,371	3,940	*13,664*	3,123	9,541
65–70	*7,590*	5,919	1,671	*7,998*	2,167	5,831
70 and over	*10,974*	7,958	3,016	*10,962*	3,127	7,835
Christian	**76,130**	**39,332**	**36,798**	**12,494**	**3,438**	**9,056**
0–1	*36*	25	11	*1*	1	..
1–2	*46*	23	23	..	..	..
2–3	*72*	29	43	*3*	2	1
3–4	*155*	69	86	*6*	3	3
4–5	*415*	176	239	*21*	5	16
Total 0–5	**724**	**322**	**402**	**31**	**11**	**20**
5–10	*2,492*	846	1,646	*69*	9	60
10–15	*4,943*	1,761	3,182	*112*	35	77
15–20	*8,855*	3,525	5,330	*216*	66	150
20–25	*11,431*	5,204	6,227	*352*	111	241
25–30	*11,367*	5,759	5,608	*690*	215	475
30–35	*9,564*	4,996	4,568	*877*	289	588
35–40	*7,664*	4,263	3,401	*1,310*	355	055
40–45	*6,276*	3,853	2,423	*1,407*	335	1,072
45–50	*4,323*	2,833	1,490	*1,595*	404	1,191
50–55	*3,214*	2,115	1,099	*1,471*	352	1,119
55–60	*1,994*	1,416	578	*1,296*	326	070
60–65	*1,489*	1,133	356	*1,156*	299	857
65–70	*842*	595	247	*724*	208	516
70 and over	*952*	711	241	*1,188*	423	765
Zoroastrian	**863**	**453**	**410**	**157**	**58**	**99**
0–1	..	..	..	..	..	..
1–2	..	..	..	..	..	..
2–3	*1*	1	..	..	..	..
3–4	*4*	2	2	..	..	..
4–5	*4*	3	1	..	..	..
Total 0–5	**9**	**6**	**3**	..	..	..

TABLE VII.
AGE, SEX & CIVIL CONDITION.

TABLE VII.—
Age, Sex and

RELIGION AND AGE	TOTAL POPULATION			UNMARRIED		
	Persons	Males	Females	Persons	Males	Females
1	2	3	4	5	6	7
Zoroastrian—(*contd.*)						
5–10	*120*	78	42	*106*	71	35
10–15	*154*	69	85	*129*	60	69
15–20	*158*	58	100	*101*	44	57
20–25	*161*	76	85	*88*	47	41
25–30	*141*	77	64	*48*	33	15
30–35	*144*	70	74	*26*	17	9
35–40	*139*	69	70	*24*	18	6
40–45	*130*	78	52	*20*	15	5
45–50	*133*	73	60	*11*	5	6
50–55	*108*	54	54	*6*	5	1
55–60	*59*	38	21	..	..	..
60–65	*58*	40	18	*4*	4	..
65–70	*33*	25	8	*5*	5	..
70 and over	*42*	25	17	*1*	1	..
Buddhist	**52**	**26**	**26**	**19**	**9**	**10**
0–1	..	..	..	..	..	..
1–2	*1*	..	1	*1*	..	1
2–3	*2*	1	1	*2*	1	1
3–4	*2*	1	1	*2*	1	1
4–5	*2*	2	..	*1*	1	..
Total 0–5	**7**	**4**	**3**	**6**	**3**	**3**
5–10	*2*	1	1	..	..	..
10–15	*5*	3	2	*2*	1	1
15–20	*6*	2	4	*1*	..	1
20–25	*10*	6	4	*3*	2	1
25–30	*7*	4	3	*4*	2	2
30–35	*2*	..	2	..	..	..
35–40	*3*	1	2	*1*	..	1
40–45	*4*	2	2	..	..	..
45–50	*1*	1	..	..	..	..
50–55	*5*	2	3	*2*	1	1
55–60	..	..	..	..	..	..
60–65	..	..	..	..	..	..
65–70	..	..	..	..	..	..
70 and over	..	..	..	..	..	..
Jew	**27**	**11**	**16**	**10**	**4**	**6**
0–1	..	..	..	..	..	..
1–2	..	..	..	..	..	..
2–3	..	..	..	..	..	..
3–4	*1*	..	1	*1*	..	1
4–5	*2*	1	1	*2*	1	1
Total 0–5	**3**	**1**	**2**	**3**	**1**	**2**
5–10	..	..	..	..	..	..
10–15	*3*	1	2	*1*	..	1
15–20	*3*	1	2	..	..	..
20–25	*3*	1	2	*2*	1	1
25–30	*2*	1	1	..	..	..
30–35	*9*	4	5	*4*	2	2
35–40	*2*	1	1	..	..	..
40–45	..	..	..	..	..	..
45–50	*1*	..	1	..	..	..
50–55	*1*	1	..	..	..	..
55–60	..	..	..	..	..	..
60–65	..	..	..	..	..	..
65–70	..	..	..	..	..	..
70 and over	..	..	..	..	..	..
Tribal	**544,789**	**280,584**	**264,205**	**248,774**	**139,769**	**109,005**
0–1	*18,049*	8,712	9,387	*17,704*	8,521	9,183
1–2	*21,915*	10,430	11,485	*21,295*	10,166	11,129
2–3	*23,263*	11,156	12,107	*22,471*	10,763	11,708
3–4	*23,335*	11,208	12,127	*21,825*	10,635	11,190
4–5	*23,113*	11,571	11,542	*20,826*	10,801	10,025
Total 0-5	**109,675**	**53,077**	**56,598**	**104,121**	**50,886**	**53,235**
5 –10	*77,228*	40,809	36,419	*67,409*	37,269	30,140
10–15	*62,465*	32,760	29,705	*45,252*	27,304	17,948
15–20	*45,095*	21,798	23,297	*14,549*	11,386	3,163
20–25	*48,266*	23,280	24,986	*8,505*	6,854	1,651
25–30	*45,719*	23,029	22,690	*3,652*	2,736	916
30–35	*36,995*	19,460	17,535	*1,967*	1,394	573
35–40	*30,174*	16,761	13,413	*10,06*	579	427
40–45	*25,282*	14,167	11,115	*675*	395	280
45–50	*18,144*	10,641	7,503	*413*	268	145
50–55	*14,568*	8,191	6,377	*320*	179	141
55–60	*10,619*	5,757	4,862	*318*	235	83
60–65	*9,106*	4,914	4,192	*257*	127	130
65–70	*4,862*	2,552	2,310	*130*	77	53
70 and over	*6,591*	3,388	3,203	*200*	80	120

PART I.

Civil Condition.

TABLE VII.

AGE, SEX & CIVIL CONDITION

RELIGION AND AGE	MARRIED			WIDOWED		
	Persons	Males	Females	Persons	Males	Females
1	8	9	10	11	12	13
Zoroastrian—(*contd.*)						
5–10	*14*	7	7	..	..	..
10–15	*24*	9	15	*1*	..	1
15–20	*56*	14	42	*1*	..	1
20–25	*68*	27	41	*5*	2	3
25–30	*86*	38	48	*7*	6	1
30–35	*113*	53	60	*5*	..	5
35–40	*105*	49	56	*10*	2	8
40–45	*100*	59	41	*10*	4	6
45–50	*99*	60	39	*23*	8	15
50–55	*79*	43	36	*23*	6	17
55–60	*41*	31	10	*18*	7	11
60–65	*31*	26	5	*23*	10	18
65–70	*15*	14	1	*13*	6	7
70 and over	*23*	17	6	*18*	7	11
Buddhist	30	17	13	3	..	3
0–1	..	..	..	..	..	..
1–2	..	..	..	..	..	..
2–3	..	..	..	..	..	..
3–4	..	..	..	..	..	..
4–5	*1*	1	..	..	..	..
Total 0–5	1	1	..	..	..	..
5–10	*2*	1	1	..	..	..
10–15	*3*	2	1	..	..	..
15–20	*5*	2	3	..	..	..
20–25	*7*	4	3	..	..	..
25–30	*3*	2	1	..	..	..
30–35	*2*	..	2	..	..	..
35–40	*2*	1	1	..	..	..
40–45	*2*	2	..	*2*	..	..
45–50	*1*	1	..	..	..	..
50–55	*2*	1	1	*1*	..	1
55–60	..	..	..	..	..	..
60–65	..	..	..	..	..	..
65–70	..	..	..	..	..	..
70 and over	..	..	..	..	..	..
Jew	15	6	9	2	1	1
0–1	..	..	..	..	..	..
1–2	..	..	..	..	..	..
2–3	..	..	..	..	..	..
3–4	..	..	..	..	..	..
4–5	..	..	..	..	..	..
Total 0–5	..	..	..	..	..	..
5–10	..	..	..	..	..	..
10–15	*2*	1	1	..	..	..
15–20	*3*	1	2	..	..	..
20–25	*1*	..	1	..	..	..
25–30	*2*	1	1	..	..	..
30–35	*5*	2	3	..	..	..
35–40	*2*	1	1	..	..	..
40–45	..	..	..	..	..	..
45–50	..	..	..	*1*	..	1
50–55	..	..	..	*1*	1	..
55–60	..	..	..	..	..	..
60–65	..	..	..	..	..	..
65–70	..	..	..	..	..	..
70 and over	..	..	..	..	..	..
Tribal	262,231	132,130	130,101	33,784	8,685	25,099
0–1	*335*	188	147	*10*	8	7
1–2	*584*	243	341	*36*	21	15
2–3	*752*	369	383	*40*	24	16
3–4	*1,478*	561	917	*32*	12	20
4–5	*2,213*	748	1,465	*74*	22	52
Total 0–5	5,362	2,109	3,253	192	82	110
5–10	*9,557*	3,441	6,116	*262*	99	163
10–15	*16,857*	5,355	11,502	*356*	101	255
15–20	*29,879*	10,206	19,673	*667*	206	461
20–25	*38,632*	15,994	22,638	*1,129*	432	697
25–30	*40,245*	19,722	20,523	*1,822*	571	1,251
30–35	*32,888*	17,517	15,371	*2,140*	540	1,591
35–40	*26,025*	15,477	10,548	*3,143*	705	2,438
40–45	*21,115*	12,999	8,116	*3,492*	773	2,719
45–50	*13,643*	9,398	4,245	*4,088*	975	3,113
50–55	*10,366*	7,037	3,829	*3,882*	975	2,907
55–60	*6,481*	4,562	1,919	*3,820*	960	2,860
60–65	*5,302*	3,974	1,328	*3,547*	813	2,734
65–70	*2,540*	1,856	684	*2,192*	619	1,573
70 and over	*3,339*	2,488	856	*3,052*	825	2,227

TABLE VII.

Age, Sex and Civil Condition Part II.—Districts.

District	Religion and Age	POPULATION			UNMARRIED			MARRIED			WIDOWED		
		Persons	Males	Females	Persons	Males	Females	Persons	Males	Females	Persons	Males	Females
1	2	3	4	5	6	7	8	9	10	11	12	13	14
Atraf-i-Balda ..	**All Religions**	499,661	253,975	245,686	198,212	119,097	79,115	246,108	123,332	122,776	55,341	11,546	43,795
	0—1	*16,433*	7,759	8,674	*16,272*	7,687	8,585	*148*	72	76	*13*	..	13
	1—5	*72,365*	35,697	36,668	*69,642*	34,716	34,926	*2,483*	936	1,547	*240*	45	195
	5—10	*62,029*	33,324	28,705	*51,524*	30,750	20,774	*10,074*	2,521	7,553	*431*	53	378
	10—15	*50,969*	27,819	23,150	*34,664*	23,716	10,948	*15,778*	4,023	11,755	*527*	80	447
	15—20	*37,764*	18,258	19,506	*12,176*	10,660	1,516	*24,485*	7,352	17,133	*1,103*	246	857
	20—30	*83,291*	38,033	45,258	*10,072*	8,831	1,241	*67,965*	28,130	39,835	*5,254*	1,072	4,182
	30—40	*69,649*	36,458	33,191	*2,161*	1,612	549	*58,153*	33,261	24,892	*9,335*	1,585	7,750
	40—50	*50,180*	26,892	23,288	*904*	608	296	*36,343*	23,920	12,423	*12,933*	2,364	10,569
	50—60	*31,115*	16,526	14,589	*494*	335	159	*18,587*	13,593	4,994	*12,034*	2,598	9,436
	60 and over	*25,866*	13,209	12,657	*303*	182	121	*12,092*	9,524	2,568	*13,471*	3,503	9,968
	Hindu (Brahmanic) ..	333,919	169,509	164,410	132,125	80,537	51,588	162,423	80,802	81,621	39,371	8,170	31,201
	0—1	*10,659*	5,071	5,588	*10,585*	5,009	5,576	*69*	62	7	*5*	..	5
	1—5	*47,535*	23,888	23,647	*45,790*	23,210	22,580	*1,624*	666	958	*121*	12	109
	5—10	*42,644*	23,125	19,519	*35,657*	21,405	14,252	*6,666*	1,678	4,988	*321*	42	279
	10—15	*34,734*	19,253	15 481	*23,742*	16,635	7,107	*10,595*	2,555	8,040	*397*	63	334
	15—20	*24,333*	12,208	12,125	*7,702*	7,032	670	*15,803*	4,983	10,820	*828*	193	635
	20—30	*53,857*	23,515	30,342	*6,318*	5,638	680	*43,674*	17,059	26,615	*3,865*	818	3,047
	30—40	*46,940*	24,148	22,792	*1,241*	880	361	*39,126*	22,157	16,969	*6,573*	1,111	5,462
	40—50	*34,463*	18,526	15,937	*583*	402	181	*24,647*	16,437	8,210	*9,233*	1,687	7,546
	50—60	*21,239*	11,118	10,121	*320*	217	103	*12,294*	9,006	3,288	*8,625*	1,895	6,730
	60 and over	*17,515*	8,657	8,858	*187*	109	78	*7,925*	6,199	1,726	*9,403*	2,349	7,054
	Adi Hindu	98,366	50,243	48,123	41,056	24,266	16,790	47,713	23,853	23,860	9,597	2,124	7,473
	0—1	*3,475*	1,687	1,788	*3,451*	1,680	1,771	*18*	7	11	*6*	..	6
	1—5	*15,913*	7,484	8,429	*15,412*	7,336	8,076	*444*	146	298	*57*	2	55
	5—10	*13,164*	6,886	6,278	*10,809*	6,467	4,342	*2,292*	411	1,881	*63*	8	55
	10—15	*10,158*	5,862	4,296	*6,990*	5,012	1,978	*3,093*	842	2,251	*75*	8	67
	15—20	*7,030*	3,220	3,810	*2,172*	2,016	156	*4,689*	1,174	3,515	*169*	30	139
	20—30	*15,858*	7,499	8,359	*1,547*	1,332	215	*13,437*	6,002	7,435	*874*	165	709
	30—40	*13,225*	7,241	5,984	*344*	218	126	*11,152*	6,720	4,432	*1,729*	303	1,426
	40—50	*8,958*	4,517	4,441	*172*	105	67	*6,568*	3,984	2,584	*2,218*	428	1,790
	50—60	*5,811*	3,213	2,598	*102*	69	33	*3,684*	2,682	1,002	*2,025*	462	1,563
	60 and over	*4,774*	2,634	2,140	*57*	31	26	*2,336*	1,885	451	*2,381*	718	1,663

TABLE VII.

Age, Sex and Civil Condition Part II.—Districts.

District	Religion and Age	POPULATION			UNMARRIED			MARRIED			WIDOWED		
		Persons	Males	Females	Persons	Males	Females	Persons	Males	Females	Persons	Males	Females
1	2	3	4	5	6	7	8	9	10	11	12	13	14
Atraf-i-Balda ..	Muslim	50,412	25,417	24,995	16,819	9,684	7,135	28,363	14,769	13,594	5,230	964	4,266
	0—1	*1,719*	740	973	*1,703*	743	960	*15*	3	12	*1*	..	1
	1—5	*5,814*	2,822	2,992	*5,571*	2,766	2,805	*224*	55	169	*19*	1	18
	5—10	*3,771*	2,021	1,750	*2,897*	1,720	1,177	*841*	299	542	*33*	2	31
	10—15	*3,960*	1,583	2,377	*2,408*	1,106	1,302	*1,512*	471	1,041	*40*	6	34
	15—20	*4,895*	2,087	2,808	*1,813*	1,194	619	*2,994*	876	2,118	*88*	17	71
	20—30	*11,139*	5,721	5,418	*1,710*	1,555	155	*8,996*	4,009	4,897	*433*	67	366
	30—40	*7,644*	4,061	3,583	*504*	457	47	*6,264*	3,474	2,790	*876*	130	746
	40—50	*5,386*	3,105	2,281	*122*	82	40	*4,023*	2,829	1,194	*1,241*	194	1,047
	50—60	*3,231*	1,740	1,491	*56*	38	18	*2,045*	1,519	526	*1,130*	183	947
	60 and over	*2,853*	1,531	1,322	*35*	23	12	*1,449*	1,144	305	*1,369*	364	1,005
	Christian	3,154	1,573	1,581	1,382	738	644	1,481	764	717	291	71	220
	0—1	*87*	39	48	*87*	39	48	..	..	..	..	..	..
	1—5	*490*	220	270	*478*	216	262	*9*	4	5	*3*	..	3
	5—10	*413*	203	210	*367*	188	179	*40*	15	25	*6*	..	6
	10—15	*377*	186	191	*262*	156	106	*110*	30	80	*5*	..	5
	15—20	*258*	109	149	*90*	68	22	*164*	39	125	*4*	2	2
	20—30	*444*	250	194	*59*	50	9	*367*	196	171	*18*	4	14
	30—40	*405*	218	187	*14*	9	5	*345*	196	149	*46*	13	33
	40—50	*357*	178	179	*11*	6	5	*277*	155	122	*69*	17	52
	50—60	*166*	84	82	*6*	2	4	*89*	61	28	*71*	21	50
	60 and over	*157*	86	71	*8*	4	4	*80*	68	12	*69*	14	55

TABLE VII.

Age, Sex and Civil Condition Part II.—Districts.

District	Religion and Age	POPULATION			UNMARRIED			MARRIED			WIDOWED		
		Persons	Males	Females	Persons	Males	Females	Persons	Males	Females	Persons	Males	Females
1	2	3	4	5	6	7	8	9	10	11	12	13	14
Warangal ..	All Religions	1,117,693	575,819	541,874	455,841	265,140	190,701	559,172	289,424	269,748	102,680	21,255	81,425
	0—1	31,874	15,626	16,248	31,825	15,599	16,226	47	27	20	2	..	2
	1—5	152,214	73,636	78,578	149,574	72,021	77,553	2,532	1,587	945	108	28	80
	5—10	142,556	72,643	69,913	123,518	68,158	55,360	18,529	4,413	14,116	509	72	437
	10—15	122,725	64,312	58,413	86,410	55,709	30,701	35,422	8,487	26,935	893	116	777
	15—20	100,558	50,512	50,046	32,102	26,650	5,448	66,002	23,469	42,538	2,454	384	2,070
	20—30	210,171	104,086	106,085	23,067	19,436	3,631	176,008	82,777	93,231	11,096	1,873	9,223
	30—40	148,213	80,299	67,914	4,822	3,948	874	125,399	73,157	52,242	17,992	3,194	14,798
	40—50	100,273	56,375	43,898	2,466	1,970	496	73,356	49,695	23,661	24,451	4,710	19,741
	50—60	57,884	31,977	25,907	1,268	1,028	240	34,529	25,914	8,615	22,087	5,035	17,052
	60 and over	51,225	26,353	24,872	789	612	177	27,348	19,898	7,450	23,088	5,843	17,245
	Hindu (Brahmanic) ..	705,102	362,125	342,977	272,420	158,972	113,448	361,091	189,374	171,717	71,591	13,779	57,812
	0—1	19,464	9,642	9,822	19,443	9,629	9,814	20	13	7	1	..	1
	1—5	90,209	43,189	47,020	88,470	42,078	46,397	1,671	1,102	569	68	14	54
	5—10	89,431	44,871	44,560	74,865	41,671	33,194	14,219	3,158	11,061	347	42	305
	10—15	77,303	40,654	36,649	51,319	34,263	17,056	25,345	6,322	19,023	639	69	570
	15—20	64,071	33,021	31,050	19,265	16,053	3,212	43,019	16,747	26,272	1,787	221	1,566
	20—30	132,997	67,034	65,963	14,209	11,533	2,676	110,857	54,410	56,447	7,931	1,091	6,840
	30—40	94,265	51,102	43,163	2,799	2,253	546	79,066	46,855	32,211	12,400	1,994	10,406
	40—50	64,676	35,355	29,321	1,157	876	281	46,721	31,423	15,298	16,798	3,056	13,742
	50—60	37,667	20,125	17,542	578	418	160	21,985	16,474	5,511	15,104	3,233	11,871
	60 and over	35,019	17,132	17,887	315	203	112	18,188	12,870	5,318	16,516	4,059	12,457
	Àdi Hindu	175,687	90,922	84,765	71,998	42,289	29,709	89,365	44,878	44,487	14,324	3,755	10,569
	0—1	5,404	2,570	2,834	5,393	2,568	2,825	10	2	8	1	..	1
	1—5	26,882	13,045	13,837	26,562	12,923	13,639	301	117	184	19	5	14
	5—10	21,114	10,906	10,208	18,543	10,354	8,189	2,470	543	1,927	101	9	92
	10—15	18,295	9,511	8,784	12,700	8,396	4,304	5,456	1,095	4,361	139	20	119
	15—20	15,272	7,364	7,908	4,224	3,838	386	10,692	3,424	7,268	356	102	254
	20—30	33,066	15,697	17,369	2,555	2,335	220	28,978	12,974	16,004	1,533	388	1,145
	30—40	23,770	12,940	10,830	731	666	65	20,265	11,606	8,659	2,774	668	2,106
	40—50	15,547	9,069	6,478	602	555	47	11,403	7,720	3,683	3,542	794	2,748
	50—60	8,853	5,367	3,486	439	412	27	5,291	4,012	1,279	3,123	943	2,180
	60 and over	7,484	4,453	3,031	249	242	7	4,499	3,885	1,114	2,736	826	1,910

TABLE VII.

Age, Sex and Civil Condition Part II.—Districts.

District	Religion and Age	POPULATION			UNMARRIED			MARRIED			WIDOWED		
		Persons	Males	Females	Persons	Males	Females	Persons	Males	Females	Persons	Males	Females
1	2	3	4	5	6	7	8	9	10	11	12	13	14
Warangal ..	Muslim	67,820	36,176	31,644	31,088	18,686	12,402	31,433	16,402	15,031	5,299	1,088	4,211
	0—1	*1,714*	831	883	*1,712*	830	882	*2*	1	1	..	..	..
	1—5	*8,767*	4,698	4,069	*8,541*	4,551	3,990	*220*	146	74	*6*	1	5
	5—10	*8,759*	4,616	4,143	*8,086*	4,349	3,737	*654*	261	393	*19*	6	13
	10—15	*8,248*	3,987	4,261	*6,474*	3,708	2,766	*1,743*	272	1,471	*31*	7	24
	15—20	*6,918*	3,161	3,757	*3,050*	2,319	731	*3,766*	826	2,940	*102*	16	86
	20—30	*12,376*	6,271	6,105	*2,104*	1,941	163	*9,714*	4,255	5,459	*558*	75	483
	30—40	*8,235*	4,597	3,638	*429*	372	57	*6,894*	4,093	2,801	*912*	132	780
	40—50	*6,057*	3,913	2,144	*401*	366	35	*4,350*	3,263	1,087	*1,306*	284	1,022
	50—60	*3,809*	2,365	1,444	*151*	130	21	*2,436*	1,933	503	*1,222*	302	920
	60 and over	*2,937*	1,737	1,200	*140*	120	20	*1,654*	1,352	302	*1,143*	265	878
	Christian	28,952	14,955	13,997	12,310	7,015	5,295	14,446	7,428	7,018	2,196	512	1,684
	0—1	*958*	487	471	*954*	483	471	*4*	4	..	..	..	..
	1—5	*4,134*	2,044	2,090	*4,076*	1,992	2,084	*54*	48	6	*4*	4	..
	5—10	*3,404*	1,729	1,675	*3,151*	1,615	1,536	*245*	113	132	*8*	1	7
	10—15	*2,992*	1,675	1,317	*2,388*	1,464	924	*595*	211	384	*9*	..	9
	15—20	*2,409*	1,266	1,143	*911*	777	134	*1,470*	486	984	*28*	3	25
	20—30	*5,726*	2,713	3,013	*610*	511	99	*4,917*	2,151	2,766	*199*	51	148
	30—40	*4,110*	2,180	1,930	*130*	102	28	*3,607*	1,998	1,609	*373*	80	293
	40—50	*2,595*	1,398	1,197	*40*	32	8	*1,965*	1,246	719	*590*	120	470
	50—60	*1,493*	861	632	*22*	19	3	*963*	729	234	*508*	113	395
	60 and over	*1,131*	602	529	*28*	20	8	*626*	442	184	*477*	140	337
	Tribal	139,499	71,305	68,194	67,748	38,003	29,745	62,532	31,187	31,345	9,219	2,115	7,104
	0—1	*4,316*	2,088	2,228	*4,305*	2,081	2,224	*11*	7	4	..	..	..
	1—5	*22,155*	10,627	11,528	*21,860*	10,450	11,410	*285*	174	111	*10*	3	7
	5—10	*19,782*	10,486	9,296	*18,811*	10,135	8,676	*937*	336	601	*34*	15	19
	10—15	*15,819*	8,446	7,373	*13,477*	7,845	5,632	*2,267*	581	1,686	*75*	20	55
	15—20	*11,824*	5,664	6,160	*4,620*	3,647	973	*7,024*	1,976	5,048	*180*	41	139
	20—30	*25,870*	12,298	13,572	*3,552*	3,084	468	*21,444*	8,946	12,498	*874*	268	606
	30—40	*17,739*	9,432	8,307	*725*	547	178	*15,488*	8,566	6,922	*1,526*	319	1,207
	40—50	*11,334*	6,605	4,729	*264*	139	125	*8,871*	6,011	2,860	*2,199*	455	1,744
	50—60	*6,032*	3,246	2,786	*77*	48	29	*3,840*	2,736	1,084	*2,115*	442	1,673
	60 and over	*4,628*	2,413	2,215	*57*	27	30	*2,365*	1,834	531	*2,206*	552	1,654

TABLE VII.

Age, Sex and Civil Condition Part II.—Districts.

District	Religion and Age	POPULATION			UNMARRIED			MARRIED			WIDOWED		
		Persons	Males	Females	Persons	Males	Females	Persons	Males	Females	Persons	Males	Females
1	2	3	4	5	6	7	8	9	10	11	12	13	14
Karimnagar ..	**All Religions**	1,241,405	634,416	606,989	450,583	275,857	174,726	667,414	333,473	333,941	123,408	25,086	98,322
	0—1	36,583	17,403	19,180	36,536	17,395	19,141	47	8	39	..	..	..
	1—5	187,028	82,605	104,423	181,615	80,907	100,708	5,235	1,677	3,558	178	21	157
	5—10	137,284	82,321	54,963	102,371	74,871	27,500	34,283	7,351	26,932	630	99	531
	10—15	138,056	74,026	64,030	79,020	58,903	20,117	57,356	14,893	42,463	1,680	230	1,450
	15—20	117,634	58,380	59,254	26,300	23,435	2,865	87,993	34,474	53,519	3,341	471	2,870
	20—30	228,288	113,097	115,191	18,192	16,430	1,762	198,504	94,881	103,623	11,592	1,786	9,806
	30—40	162,694	84,416	78,278	2,679	1,802	877	138,338	78,950	59,388	21,677	3,664	18,013
	40—50	115,788	61,414	54,374	1,705	994	711	83,812	54,525	29,287	30,271	5,895	24,376
	50—60	68,650	35,985	32,665	1,066	505	561	40,116	29,266	10,850	27,468	6,214	21,254
	60 and over	49,400	24,769	24,631	1,099	615	484	21,730	17,448	4,282	26,571	6,706	19,865
	Hindu (Brahmanic) ..	933,527	476,884	456,643	325,619	202,645	122,974	509,416	253,858	255,558	98,492	20,381	78,111
	0—1	26,822	13,033	13,789	26,778	13,025	13,753	44	8	36	..	..	..
	1—5	137,909	57,717	80,192	134,213	56,963	77,250	3,555	741	2,814	141	13	128
	5—10	97,927	61,637	36,290	69,468	55,900	13,568	27,919	5,643	22,276	540	94	446
	10—15	105,062	56,915	48,147	57,409	44,453	12,956	46,119	12,246	33,873	1,534	216	1,318
	15—20	89,703	44,584	45,119	18,635	16,687	1,948	68,139	27,500	40,639	2,929	397	2,532
	20—30	174,430	86,881	87,549	13,643	12,439	1.204	151,320	73,011	78,309	9,467	1,431	8,036
	30—40	122,978	63,824	59,154	2,088	1,395	693	103,743	59,435	44,308	17,147	2,994	14,153
	40—50	86,838	45,297	41,541	1,428	801	627	61,594	39,724	21,870	23,816	4,772	19,044
	50—60	52,997	27,642	25,355	922	410	512	30,425	22,192	8,233	21,650	5,040	16,610
	60 and over	38,861	19,354	19,507	1,035	572	463	16,558	13,358	3,200	21,268	5,424	15,844
	Adi Hindu	227,274	116,291	110,983	88,847	52,012	36,835	120,169	60,770	59,399	18,258	3,509	14,749
	0—1	7,293	3,104	4,189	7,290	3,104	4,186	3	..	3	..	..	..
	1—5	37,762	19,282	18,480	36,190	18,877	17,313	1,539	897	642	33	8	25
	5—10	29,052	15,457	13,595	23,520	13,919	9,601	5,461	1,335	3,926	71	3	68
	10—15	23,452	12,118	11,334	14,132	9,865	4,267	9,198	2,242	6,956	122	11	111
	15—20	20,431	10,022	10,409	4,715	4,286	429	15,412	5,680	9,732	304	56	248
	20—30	39,580	19,186	20,394	2,338	2,027	311	35,650	16,878	18,772	1,592	281	1,311
	30—40	29,237	15,069	14,168	309	199	110	25,573	14,390	11,183	3,355	480	2,875
	40—50	20,853	11,279	9,374	190	134	56	15,861	10,307	5,554	4,802	838	3,964
	50—60	11,321	6,050	5,271	113	70	43	6,965	5 075	1,890	4,243	905	3,338
	60 and over	8,293	4,724	3,569	50	31	19	4,507	3,766	741	3,736	927	2,809

TABLE VII.

Age, Sex and Civil Condition Part II.—Districts.

District	Religion and Age	POPULATION			UNMARRIED			MARRIED			WIDOWED		
		Persons	Males	Females	Persons	Males	Females	Persons	Males	Females	Persons	Males	Females
1	2	3	4	5	6	7	8	9	10	11	12	13	14
Karimnagar ..	Muslim ..	55,802	28,256	27,546	25,610	15,075	10,535	25,454	12,379	13,075	4,738	802	3,936
	0—1 ..	*1,775*	926	849	*1,775*	926	849	..	..	..	..	..	..
	1—5 ..	*7,708*	3,825	3,883	*7,646*	3,812	3,834	*59*	13	46	*3*	..	8
	5—10 ..	*7,276*	3,720	3,556	*6,746*	3,610	3,136	*513*	108	405	*17*	2	15
	10—15 ..	*6,571*	3,389	3,182	*5,383*	3,239	2,144	*1,171*	148	1,023	*17*	2	15
	15—20 ..	*5,018*	2,419	2,599	*2,110*	1,768	342	*2,825*	639	2,186	*83*	12	71
	20—30 ..	*9,877*	4,723	5,154	*1,695*	1,528	167	*7,777*	3,139	4,038	*405*	56	349
	30—40 ..	*7,171*	3,722	3,449	*161*	119	42	*6,182*	3,489	2,693	*828*	114	714
	40—50 ..	*4,978*	2,651	2,327	*64*	46	18	*3,764*	2,426	1,338	*1,150*	179	971
	50—60 ..	*3,081*	1,658	1,423	*21*	19	2	*1,965*	1,463	502	*1,095*	176	919
	60 and over ..	*2,347*	1,223	1,124	*9*	8	1	*1,198*	954	244	*1,140*	261	879
	Christian ..	13,622	7,188	6,434	5,140	3,057	2,083	7,352	3,899	3,453	1,130	232	898
	0—1 ..	*351*	198	153	*351*	198	153	..	..	..	..	..	..
	1—5 ..	*1,868*	908	960	*1,804*	885	919	*64*	23	41	..	..	..
	5—10 ..	*1,678*	887	791	*1,388*	835	553	*288*	52	236	*2*	..	2
	10—15 ..	*1,645*	907	738	*1,023*	704	319	*615*	202	413	*7*	1	6
	15—20 ..	*1,422*	763	659	*365*	296	69	*1,036*	463	573	*21*	4	17
	20—30 ..	*2,409*	1,264	1,145	*167*	123	44	*2,164*	1,130	1,034	*78*	11	67
	30—40 ..	*1,799*	954	845	*28*	10	18	*1,568*	896	672	*203*	48	155
	40—50 ..	*1,250*	673	577	*10*	4	6	*931*	614	317	*309*	55	254
	50—60 ..	*718*	370	348	*4*	2	2	*433*	314	119	*281*	54	227
	60 and over ..	*482*	264	218	..	..	..	*253*	205	48	*229*	59	170
	Tribal ..	10,394	5,384	5,010	5,060	2,873	2,187	4,597	2,358	2,239	737	153	584
	0—1 ..	*306*	122	184	*306*	122	184	..	..	..	..	..	..
	1—5 ..	*1,633*	797	836	*1,618*	797	821	*14*	..	14	*1*	..	1
	5—10 ..	*1,298*	582	716	*1,203*	570	633	*95*	12	83	..	..	..
	10—15 ..	*1,244*	646	598	*1,019*	601	418	*225*	45	180	..	..	..
	15—20 ..	*999*	563	436	*460*	384	76	*536*	178	358	*3*	1	2
	20—30 ..	*1,872*	987	885	*340*	304	36	*1,485*	676	809	*47*	7	40
	30—40 ..	*1,395*	776	619	*91*	78	13	*1,166*	670	496	*138*	28	110
	40—50 ..	*799*	474	325	*13*	9	4	*602*	416	186	*184*	49	135
	50—60 ..	*476*	246	230	*5*	4	1	*286*	205	81	*185*	37	148
	60 and over ..	*372*	191	181	*5*	4	1	*188*	156	32	*179*	31	148

TABLE VII.

Age, Sex and Civil Condition Part II.—Districts.

District	Religion and Age	POPULATION			UNMARRIED			MARRIED			WIDOWED		
		Persons	Males	Females	Persons	Males	Females	Persons	Males	Females	Persons	Males	Females
1	2	3	4	5	6	7	8	9	10	11	12	13	14
Adilabad ..	All Religions	762,030	389,754	372,276	284,409	161,772	122,637	411,284	211,532	199,752	66,337	16,450	49,887
	0—1	30,033	13,323	10	29,456	13,058	16,398	568	262	306	9	3	6
	1—5	111,721	55,113	56,608	102,722	51,668	51,054	8,309	3,165	5,144	690	280	410
	5—10	99,627	53,549	46,078	72,578	42,578	30,000	25,776	10,511	15,265	1,273	460	818
	10—15	83,810	44,943	38,867	43,822	28,496	15,326	38,644	16,031	22,613	1,344	416	928
	15—20	66,092	32,136	33,956	12,779	9,819	2,960	51,529	21,891	29,638	1,784	426	1,358
	20—30	138,822	70,112	68,710	11,802	8,747	3,055	119,938	59,438	60,500	7,082	1,927	5,155
	30—40	100,561	53,274	47,287	5,398	3,252	2,146	83,203	47,170	36,033	11,960	2,852	9,108
	40—50	65,940	35,430	30,510	3,080	2,149	931	47,380	29,647	17,733	15,480	3,634	11,846
	50—60	37,883	19,473	18,410	1,517	1,117	400	22,572	15,018	7,554	13,794	3,338	10,456
	60 and over	27,541	12,401	15,140	1,255	888	367	13,365	8,399	4,966	12,921	3,114	9,807
	Hindu (Brahmanic) ..	491,088	252,021	239,067	176,408	101,853	74,555	266,090	137,930	128,160	48,590	12,238	36,352
	0—1	19,817	8,495	11,322	19,523	8,420	11,103	290	72	218	4	3	1
	1—5	68,375	34,289	34,086	62,739	32,284	30,455	5,092	1,756	3,336	544	240	295
	5—10	63,081	34,742	28,339	43,932	26,901	17,031	18,092	7,435	10,657	1,057	406	651
	10—15	54,766	29,427	25,339	26,217	17,264	8,953	27,461	11,821	15,640	1,088	342	746
	15—20	43,567	21,075	22,492	7,927	5,890	2,037	34,294	14,876	19,418	1,346	309	1,037
	20—30	89,433	45,956	43,477	7,759	5,612	2,147	76,293	38,922	37,371	5,381	1,422	3,959
	30—40	65,107	34,403	30,704	4,221	2,485	1,736	52,131	29,786	22,345	8,755	2,132	6,623
	40—50	43,132	23,064	20,068	2,310	1,548	762	29,503	18,748	10,755	11,319	2,768	8,551
	50—60	25,075	12,568	12,507	1,021	785	236	14,247	9,370	4,877	9,807	2,413	7,394
	60 and over ..	18,735	8,002	10,733	759	664	95	8,687	5,144	3,543	9,289	2,194	7,095
	Adi Hindu	115,554	57,843	57,711	43,825	24,025	19,800	63,662	32,137	31,525	8,067	1,681	6,386
	0—1	4,512	2,103	2,409	4,468	2,084	2,384	39	19	20	5	..	5
	1—5	18,774	8,828	9,946	17,097	8,299	8,798	1,597	524	1,073	80	5	75
	5—10	15,097	8,029	7,068	11,613	6,627	4,986	3,388	1,390	1,998	96	12	84
	10—15	12,247	6,455	5,792	7,053	4,541	2,512	5,077	1,884	3,193	117	30	87
	15—20	9,825	4,865	4,960	1,689	1,347	342	7,934	3,466	4,468	202	52	150
	20—30	21,289	10,137	11,152	1,305	835	470	19,222	9,122	10,100	762	180	582
	30—40	15,021	7,684	7,337	297	164	133	13,163	7,247	5,916	1,561	273	1,288
	40—50	9,912	5,246	4,666	141	79	62	7,855	4,768	3,087	1,916	399	1,517
	50—60	5,438	2,840	2,598	100	37	63	3,558	2,428	1,130	1,780	375	1,405
	60 and over	3,439	1,656	1,783	62	12	50	1,829	1,289	540	1,548	355	1,193

TABLE VII.

Age, Sex and Civil Condition Part II.—Districts.

District	Religion and Age	POPULATION			UNMARRIED			MARRIED			WIDOWED		
		Persons	Males	Females	Persons	Males	Females	Persons	Males	Females	Persons	Males	Females
1	2	3	4	5	6	7	8	9	10	11	12	13	14
Adilabad ..	**Muslim** ..	**45,821**	**24,030**	**21,791**	**19,976**	**11,783**	**8,193**	**22,659**	**11,465**	**11,194**	**3,186**	**782**	**2,404**
	0—1 ..	*1,628*	823	805	*1,588*	787	801	*40*	36	4	..	..	..
	1—5 ..	*6,237*	3,073	3,164	*5,766*	2,788	2,978	*450*	281	169	*21*	4	17
	5—10 ..	*6,393*	2,931	3,462	*5,010*	2,473	2,537	*1,360*	455	905	*23*	3	20
	10—15 ..	*5,099*	2,787	2,312	*3,597*	2,190	1,407	*1,471*	590	881	*31*	7	24
	15—20 ..	*4,261*	2,243	2,018	*1,398*	1,207	191	*2,784*	1,016	1,708	*79*	20	59
	20—30 ..	*9,001*	4,716	4,285	*1,310*	1,166	144	*7,387*	3,480	3,907	*304*	70	234
	30—40 ..	*6,038*	3,376	2,662	*398*	338	60	*5,034*	2,871	2,163	*606*	167	439
	40—50 ..	*3,591*	2,012	1,579	*438*	418	20	*2,380*	1,445	935	*773*	149	624
	50—60 ..	*2,051*	1,148	903	*286*	248	38	*1,046*	730	316	*719*	170	549
	60 and over	*1,522*	921	601	*185*	168	17	*707*	561	146	*630*	192	438
	Christian ..	**4,244**	**2,092**	**2,152**	**1,516**	**856**	**660**	**2,379**	**1,167**	**1,212**	**349**	**69**	**280**
	0—1 ..	*173*	97	76	*173*	97	76	..	..	..	..	..	..
	1—5 ..	*707*	316	391	*694*	310	384	*12*	5	7	*1*	1	..
	5—10 ..	*439*	264	175	*341*	223	118	*96*	40	56	*2*	1	1
	10—15 ..	*382*	214	168	*205*	146	59	*174*	67	107	*3*	1	2
	15—20 ..	*348*	169	179	*54*	49	5	*284*	119	165	*10*	1	9
	20—30 ..	*802*	381	421	*40*	26	14	*718*	346	372	*44*	9	35
	30—40 ..	*605*	315	290	*5*	4	1	*516*	293	223	*84*	18	66
	40—50 ..	*439*	190	249	*1*	1	..	*340*	172	168	*98*	17	81
	50—60 ..	*253*	97	156	*2*	..	2	*184*	86	98	*67*	11	56
	60 and over	*96*	49	47	*1*	..	1	*55*	39	16	*40*	10	30
	Tribal ..	**104,807**	**53,513**	**51,294**	**42,456**	**23,130**	**19,326**	**56,247**	**28,716**	**27,531**	**6,104**	**1,667**	**4,437**
	0—1 ..	*3,877*	1,797	2,080	*3,679*	1,662	2,017	*198*	135	63	..	..	..
	1—5 ..	*17,552*	8,572	8,980	*16,364*	7,956	8,408	*1,144*	595	549	*44*	21	23
	5—10 ..	*14,562*	7,558	7,004	*11,639*	6,332	5,307	*2,829*	1,188	1,641	*94*	38	56
	10—15 ..	*11,259*	6,031	5,228	*6,721*	4,336	2,385	*4,434*	1,659	2,775	*104*	36	68
	15—20 ..	*8,048*	3,765	4,283	*1,696*	1,318	378	*6,205*	2,403	3,802	*147*	44	103
	20—30 ..	*18,201*	8,875	9,326	*1,363*	1,091	272	*16,251*	7,539	8,712	*587*	245	342
	30—40 ..	*13,712*	7,449	6,263	*453*	243	210	*12,310*	6,944	5,366	*949*	262	687
	40—50 ..	*8,821*	4,897	3,924	*185*	101	84	*7,271*	4,497	2,774	*1,365*	299	1,066
	50—60 ..	*5,046*	2,811	2,235	*108*	47	61	*3,526*	2,397	1,129	*1,412*	367	1,045
	60 and over	*3,729*	1,758	1,971	*248*	44	204	*2,079*	1,359	720	*1,402*	355	1,047

TABLE VII.

Age, Sex and Civil Condition Part II.—Districts.

District	Religion and Age	POPULATION			UNMARRIED			MARRIED			WIDOWED		
		Persons	Males	Females	Persons	Males	Females	Persons	Males	Females	Persons	Males	Females
1	2	3	4	5	6	7	8	9	10	11	12	13	14
Medak	**All Religions**	738,665	373,475	365,190	255,138	157,392	97,746	402,655	199,982	202,673	80,872	16,101	64,771
	0—1	*21,067*	10,003	10,164	*20,995*	10,878	10,117	*72*	25	47	..	..	..
	1—5	*107,696*	47,915	59,781	*94,977*	47,340	47,637	*12,551*	569	11,982	*168*	6	162
	5—10	*83,485*	41,369	42,116	*58,206*	37,783	20,423	*24,237*	3,550	20,687	*1,042*	36	1,006
	10—15	*76,726*	34,891	41,835	*39,907*	26,216	13,691	*35,008*	8,589	26,419	*1,811*	86	1,725
	15—20	*67,722*	31,380	36,342	*16,255*	14,131	2,124	*48,715*	17,045	31,670	*2,752*	204	2,548
	20—30	*136,497*	69,147	67,350	*15,914*	14,210	1,704	*112,445*	53,746	58,699	*8,138*	1,191	6,947
	30—40	*95,746*	54,263	41,483	*4,430*	3,557	873	*78,645*	48,426	30,219	12,671	2,280	10,391
	40—50	*69,682*	40,488	29,194	*2,350*	1,740	610	*49,139*	35,140	13,999	*18,193*	3,608	14,585
	50—60	*43,035*	24,013	19,022	*1,024*	734	290	*24,800*	19,444	5,356	*17,211*	3,885	13,376
	60 and over	*37,009*	19,106	17,903	*1,080*	808	277	*17,043*	13,448	3,595	*18,886*	4,855	14,031
	Hindu (Brahmanic) ..	508,690	256,911	251,779	168,160	105,405	62,755	282,134	139,852	142,282	58,396	11,654	46,742
	0—1	*14,502*	7,856	6,646	*14,464*	7,844	6,620	*38*	12	26	..	..	..
	1—5	*75,004*	32,431	42,573	*63,037*	32,034	31,003	*11,848*	393	11,455	*119*	4	115
	5—10	*62,183*	30,644	31,539	*41,606*	27,990	13,616	*19,691*	2,630	17,061	*886*	24	862
	10—15	*51,556*	21,864	29,692	*23,636*	15,278	8,358	*26,477*	6,518	19,950	*1,443*	68	1,375
	15—20	*46,089*	20,441	25,648	*9,299*	8,368	931	*34,479*	11,923	22,556	*2,311*	150	2,161
	20—30	*91,848*	47,531	44,317	*9,598*	8,810	788	*76,113*	37,838	38,275	*6,137*	883	5,254
	30—40	*64,485*	38,229	26,256	*3,239*	2,621	618	*52,380*	33,936	18,444	*8,866*	1,672	7,194
	40—50	*48,029*	28,515	19,514	*1,631*	1,204	427	*33,420*	24,727	8,693	*12,978*	2,584	10,394
	50—60	*29,537*	16,712	12,825	*814*	607	207	*16,693*	13,360	3,333	*12,030*	2,745	9,285
	60 and over	*25,457*	12,688	12,769	*836*	649	187	*10,995*	8,515	2,480	*13,626*	3,524	10,102
	Adi Hindu	133,599	67,943	65,656	47,270	27,848	19,422	73,530	37,281	36,249	12,799	2,814	9,985
	0—1	*4,242*	1,907	2,335	*4,222*	1,897	2,325	*20*	10	10	..	..	..
	1—5	*19,733*	9,707	10,026	*19,314*	9,567	9,747	*399*	138	261	*20*	2	18
	5—10	*13,010*	6,419	6,591	*9,215*	5,691	3,524	*3,715*	717	2,998	*80*	11	69
	10—15	*14,456*	7,065	7,391	*7,986*	5,588	2,398	*6,257*	1,463	4,794	*213*	14	199
	15—20	*12,312*	5,801	6,511	*2,711*	2,200	511	*9,342*	3,569	5,773	*259*	32	227
	20—30	*25,039*	12,107	12,932	*2,376*	1,811	565	*21,448*	10,121	11,327	*1,215*	175	1,040
	30—40	*18,087*	9,509	8,578	*640*	487	153	*15,264*	8,635	6,629	*2,183*	387	1,796
	40—50	*12,515*	7,181	5,334	*522*	415	107	*9,024*	6,081	2,943	*2,969*	685	2,284
	50—60	*7,425*	4,252	3,173	*119*	68	51	*4,490*	3,476	1,014	*2,816*	708	2,108
	60 and over	*6,780*	3,995	2,785	*165*	124	41	*3,571*	3,071	500	*3,044*	800	2,244

TABLE VII.

Age, Sex and Civil Condition Part II.—Districts.

District	Religion and Age	POPULATION			UNMARRIED			MARRIED			WIDOWED		
		Persons	Males	Females	Persons	Males	Females	Persons	Males	Females	Persons	Males	Females
1	2	3	4	5	6	7	8	9	10	11	12	13	14
Medak ..	**Muslim**	71,518	35,396	36,122	30,315	18,483	11,832	33,833	15,868	17,965	7,370	1,045	6,325
	0—1	*1,789*	868	921	*1,776*	865	911	*13*	3	10	..	..	..
	1—5	*10,046*	4,314	5,732	*9,787*	4,286	5,501	*237*	28	209	*22*	..	22
	5—10	*5,580*	2,819	2,761	*5,080*	2,697	2,383	*432*	121	311	*68*	1	67
	10—15	*7,962*	4,333	3,029	*6,392*	4,066	2,326	*1,427*	264	1,163	*143*	3	140
	15—20	*6,814*	3,693	3,121	*3,304*	2,883	421	*3,358*	797	2,561	*152*	13	139
	20—30	*15,197*	7,265	7,932	*3,319*	3,147	172	*11,245*	4,033	7,212	*633*	85	548
	30—40	*9,637*	4,694	4,943	*444*	387	57	*7,928*	4,173	3,755	*1,265*	134	1,131
	40—50	*6,579*	3,401	3,178	*115*	86	29	*4,743*	3,115	1,628	*1,721*	200	1,521
	50—60	*4,492*	2,239	2,253	*56*	41	15	*2,628*	1,952	676	*1,808*	246	1,562
	60 and over	*3,422*	1,770	1,652	*42*	25	17	*1,822*	1,382	440	*1,558*	363	1,195
	Christian	19,662	10,488	9,174	7,068	4,331	2,737	10,810	5,744	5,066	1,784	413	1,371
	0—1	*384*	191	193	*383*	191	192	*1*	..	1	..	..	..
	1—5	*2,109*	1,060	1,049	*2,060*	1,053	1,007	*48*	7	41	*1*	..	1
	5—10	*2,131*	1,177	954	*1,772*	1,106	666	*351*	71	280	*8*	..	8
	10—15	*2,214*	1,365	849	*1,431*	1,029	402	*775*	335	440	*8*	1	7
	15—20	*2,076*	1,218	858	*742*	550	192	*1,314*	666	648	*20*	2	18
	20—30	*3,585*	1,828	1,757	*488*	340	148	*3,001*	1,468	1,533	*96*	20	76
	30—40	*2,842*	1,462	1,380	*83*	44	39	*2,468*	1,353	1,115	*291*	65	226
	40—50	*2,037*	1,070	967	*58*	12	46	*1,548*	954	594	*431*	104	327
	50—60	*1,231*	612	619	*18*	3	15	*783*	508	275	*430*	101	329
	60 and over	*1,053*	505	548	*33*	3	30	*521*	382	139	*499*	120	379
	Tribal	4,570	2,396	2,174	2,100	1,200	900	2,031	1,045	986	439	151	288
	0—1	*147*	80	67	*147*	80	67	..	..	..	..	..	..
	1—5	*736*	374	362	*723*	374	349	*13*	..	13	..	..	..
	5—10	*550*	290	260	*505*	282	223	*45*	8	37	..	..	..
	10—15	*508*	259	249	*439*	251	188	*65*	8	57	*4*	..	4
	15—20	*359*	188	171	*167*	113	54	*183*	68	115	*9*	7	2
	20—30	*701*	353	348	*90*	78	12	*571*	257	314	*40*	18	22
	30—40	*604*	313	291	*14*	12	2	*530*	279	251	*60*	22	38
	40—50	*424*	251	173	*5*	4	1	*342*	216	126	*77*	31	46
	50—60	*287*	154	133	*6*	4	2	*169*	119	50	*112*	31	81
	60 and over	*254*	134	120	*4*	2	2	*113*	90	23	*137*	42	95

TABLE VII.

Age, Sex and Civil Condition Part II.—Districts.

District	Religion and Age	POPULATION			UNMARRIED			MARRIED			WIDOWED		
		Persons	Males	Females	Persons	Males	Females	Persons	Males	Females	Persons	Males	Females
1	2	3	4	5	6	7	8	9	10	11	12	13	14
Nizamabad ..	**All Religions**	623,225	313,556	309,669	202,434	119,566	82,868	351,114	177,637	173,477	69,677	16,353	53,324
	0—1	*18,697*	9,301	9,396	*17,922*	8,906	9,016	*774*	395	379	*1*	..	1
	1—5	*81,765*	40,235	41,530	*72,797*	37,399	35,398	*8,819*	2,818	6,001	*149*	18	131
	5—10	*73,247*	37,848	35,399	*48,236*	29,398	18,838	*24,525*	8,336	16,189	*486*	114	372
	10—15	*64,874*	33,100	31,774	*30,149*	21,370	8,779	*33,647*	11,493	22,154	*1,078*	237	841
	15—20	*56,236*	26,285	29,951	*10,711*	8,363	2,348	*43,722*	17,506	26,216	*1,803*	416	1,387
	20—30	*116,883*	58,392	58,491	*11,425*	7,888	3,537	*99,088*	49,024	50,064	*6,370*	1,480	4,890
	30—40	*85,154*	44,900	40,254	*5,154*	2,949	2,205	*68,096*	39,319	28,777	*11,904*	2,632	9,272
	40—50	*61,720*	32,122	29,598	*3,434*	1,859	1,575	*40,983*	26,117	14,866	*17,303*	4,146	13,157
	50—60	*36,316*	18,116	18,200	*1,516*	897	619	*19,415*	13,766	5,649	*15,385*	3,453	11,932
	60 and over	*28,333*	13,257	15,076	*1,090*	537	553	*12,045*	8,863	3,182	*15,198*	3,857	11,341
	Hindu (Brahmanic)	439,962	220,875	219,087	132,659	79,743	52,916	256,672	128,624	128,048	50,631	12,508	38,123
	0—1	*12,531*	5,986	6,545	*12,128*	5,592	6,536	*402*	394	8	*1*	..	1
	1—5	*54,814*	26,886	27,928	*49,699*	24,400	25,299	*4,995*	2,471	2,524	*120*	15	105
	5—10	*52,641*	26,908	25,733	*32,367*	19,818	12,549	*19,874*	6,990	12,884	*400*	100	300
	10—15	*46,801*	23,726	23,075	*19,028*	14,156	4,872	*26,895*	9,367	17,528	*878*	203	675
	15—20	*40,468*	19,064	21,404	*5,860*	5,135	725	*33 285*	13,584	19,701	*1,323*	345	978
	20—30	*83,662*	42,291	41,371	*6,205*	5,357	848	*72,882*	35,762	37,120	*4,575*	1,172	3,403
	30—40	*59,802*	31,688	28,114	*2,921*	2,389	532	*48,253*	27,241	21,012	*8,628*	2,058	6,570
	40—50	*43,918*	22,637	21,281	*2,465*	1,613	852	*28,751*	17,750	11,001	*12,702*	3,274	9,428
	50—60	*26,211*	12,829	13,382	*1,157*	814	343	*13,741*	9,453	4,288	*11,313*	2,562	8,751
	60 and over	*19,114*	8,860	10,254	*829*	469	360	*7,594*	5,612	1,982	*10,691*	2,779	7,912
	Adi-Hindu	103,061	51,751	51,310	38,212	21,290	16,922	54,123	28,223	25,900	10,726	2,238	8,488
	0—1	*3,424*	1,801	1,623	*3,052*	1,800	1,252	*372*	1	371	..	..	..
	1—5	*15,065*	7,018	8,047	*11,433*	6,762	4,671	*3,619*	253	3,366	*13*	3	10
	5—10	*11,614*	6,236	5,378	*8,185*	5,370	2,815	*3,379*	855	2,524	*50*	11	39
	10—15	*10,349*	5,351	4,998	*5,835*	3,991	1,844	*4,409*	1,336	3,073	*105*	24	81
	15—20	*9,372*	4,161	5,211	*3,081*	1,776	1,305	*6,003*	2,339	3,664	*288*	46	242
	20—30	*19,038*	9,273	9,765	*3,740*	1,291	2,449	*14,160*	7,788	6,372	*1,138*	194	944
	30—40	*14,164*	7,389	6,775	*1,730*	173	1,557	*10,530*	6,884	3,646	*1,904*	332	1,572
	40—50	*9,860*	5,365	4,495	*742*	76	666	*6,409*	4,756	1,653	*2,709*	533	2,176
	50—60	*5,667*	3,089	2,578	*271*	27	244	*3,117*	2,553	564	*2,279*	509	1,770
	60 and over	*4,508*	2,068	2,440	*143*	24	119	*2,125*	1,458	667	*2,240*	586	1,654

TABLE VII.

Age, Sex and Civil Condition Part II.—Districts.

District	Religion and Age	POPULATION			UNMARRIED			MARRIED			WIDOWED		
		Persons	Males	Females	Persons	Males	Females	Persons	Males	Females	Persons	Males	Females
1	2	3	4	5	6	7	8	9	10	11	12	13	14
Nizamabad ..	Muslim	48,769	24,761	24,008	19,682	11,565	8,117	23,680	12,281	11,399	5,407	915	4,492
	0—1	*1,848*	1,078	770	*1,848*	1,078	770	..	..	..	..	..	..
	1—5	*7,366*	4,065	3,301	*7,273*	4,013	3,260	*82*	52	30	*11*	..	11
	5—10	*5,398*	2,742	2,656	*4,783*	2,508	2,275	*597*	234	363	*18*	..	18
	10—15	*4,484*	2,310	2,174	*3,243*	1,925	1,318	*1,175*	380	795	*66*	5	61
	15—20	*3,889*	1,825	2,064	*1,086*	871	215	*2,661*	939	1,722	*142*	15	127
	20—30	*8,630*	4,132	4,498	*902*	763	139	*7,247*	3,298	3,949	*481*	71	410
	30—40	*6,796*	3,530	3,266	*333*	291	42	*5,494*	3,101	2,393	*969*	138	831
	40—50	*4,750*	2,330	2,420	*77*	54	23	*3,457*	2,091	1,366	*1,216*	185	1,031
	50—60	*2,543*	1,180	1,363	*53*	36	17	*1,363*	934	429	*1,127*	210	917
	60 and over	*3,065*	1,569	1,496	*84*	26	58	*1,604*	1,252	352	*1,377*	291	1,086
	Christian	13,856	7,128	6,728	4,056	2,408	1,648	8,334	4,349	3,985	1,466	371	1,095
	0—1	*376*	190	186	*376*	190	186	..	..	..	..	..	..
	1—5	*1,676*	836	840	*1,583*	810	773	*89*	26	63	*4*	..	4
	5—10	*1,416*	792	624	*966*	632	334	*440*	160	280	*10*	..	10
	10—15	*1,444*	735	709	*677*	467	210	*749*	264	485	*18*	4	14
	15—20	*1,080*	531	549	*170*	142	28	*888*	383	505	*22*	6	16
	20—30	*2,463*	1,298	1,165	*178*	125	53	*2,195*	1,147	1,048	*90*	26	64
	30—40	*2,113*	1,110	1,003	*54*	24	30	*1,833*	1,015	818	*226*	71	155
	40—50	*1,572*	829	743	*26*	11	15	*1,236*	741	495	*310*	77	233
	50—60	*945*	488	457	*11*	4	7	*603*	393	210	*331*	91	240
	60 and over	*771*	319	452	*15*	3	12	*301*	220	81	*455*	96	359
	Tribal	17,358	8,925	8,433	7,756	4,526	3,230	8,195	4,092	4,103	1,407	307	1,100
	0—1	*512*	244	268	*512*	244	268	..	..	..	..	..	..
	1—5	*2,815*	1,416	1,399	*2,781*	1,401	1,380	*33*	15	18	*1*	..	1
	5—10	*2,161*	1,163	998	*1,924*	1,065	859	*230*	96	134	*7*	2	5
	10—15	*1,776*	969	807	*1,357*	825	532	*409*	143	266	*10*	1	9
	15—20	*1,411*	695	716	*511*	437	74	*873*	254	619	*27*	4	23
	20—30	*3,044*	1,373	1,671	*391*	348	43	*2,568*	1,008	1,560	*85*	17	68
	30—40	*2,243*	1,163	1,080	*114*	71	43	*1,958*	1,059	899	*171*	33	138
	40—50	*1,592*	948	644	*123*	104	19	*1,118*	768	350	*351*	76	275
	50—60	*942*	525	417	*24*	16	8	*585*	428	157	*333*	81	252
	60 and over	*862*	429	433	*19*	15	4	*421*	321	100	*422*	98	329

TABLE VII.

Age, Sex and Civil Condition Part II.—Districts.

District	Religion and Age	POPULATION			UNMARRIED			MARRIED			WIDOWED		
		Persons	Males	Females	Persons	Males	Females	Persons	Males	Females	Persons	Males	Females
1	2	3	4	5	6	7	8	9	10	11	12	13	14
Mahbubnagar..	**All Religions**	971,616	494,061	477,555	377,641	222,603	155,038	488,143	246,916	241,227	105,832	24,542	81,290
	0—1	*26,463*	12,860	13,603	*26,402*	12,843	13,559	*43*	17	26	*18*	..	18
	1—5	*141,302*	68,881	72,421	*128,652*	64,579	64,073	*11,087*	4,226	6,861	*1,563*	76	1,487
	5—10	*119,405*	59,362	60,043	*94,447*	53,355	41,092	*22,811*	5,778	17,033	*2,147*	229	1,918
	10—15	*106,725*	54,454	52,271	*65,599*	43,139	22,460	*39,147*	10,989	28,158	*1,979*	326	1,653
	15—20	*89,684*	33,147	46,537	*24,904*	20,089	4,815	*61,667*	22,261	39,406	*3,113*	797	2,316
	20—30	*177,624*	89,811	87,813	*21,152*	17,541	3,611	*145,359*	69,304	76,055	*11,113*	2,966	8,147
	30—40	*126,577*	67,914	58,663	*6,597*	4,681	1,916	*102,037*	59,688	42,349	*17,943*	3,545	14,398
	40—50	*85,671*	46,630	39,041	*4,333*	2,759	1,574	*59,316*	39,492	19,824	*22,022*	4,379	17,643
	50—60	*53,097*	28,398	24,699	*3,675*	2,710	965	*28,127*	20,276	7,851	*21,295*	5,412	15,883
	60 and over	*45,068*	22,604	22,464	*1,880*	907	973	*18,549*	14,885	3,664	*24,639*	6,812	17,827
	Hindu (Brahmanic) ..	637,927	323,041	314,886	235,951	139,515	96,436	321,217	164,455	156,762	80,759	19,071	61,688
	0—1	*16,457*	8,055	8,402	*16,399*	8,041	8,358	*40*	14	26	*18*	..	18
	1—5	*91,045*	43,671	47,374	*79,212*	39,813	39,399	*10,324*	3,802	6,522	*1,509*	56	1,453
	5—10	*75,866*	36,382	39,484	*56,100*	31,476	24,624	*17,733*	4,700	13,033	*2,033*	206	1,827
	10—15	*68,617*	34,447	34,170	*38,956*	25,801	13,155	*27,915*	8,381	19,534	*1,746*	265	1,481
	15—20	*59,880*	28,913	30,967	*16,347*	12,768	3,579	*40,962*	15,459	25,503	*2,571*	686	1,885
	20—30	*119,150*	61,776	57,374	*15,449*	12,722	2,727	*94,992*	46,726	48,266	*8,709*	2,328	6,381
	30—40	*81,595*	43,377	38,218	*5,135*	3,654	1,481	*62,957*	37,029	25,928	*13,503*	2,694	10,809
	40—50	*57,382*	30,746	26,636	*3,495*	2,133	1,362	*37,422*	25,402	12,020	*16,465*	3,211	13,254
	50—60	*36,418*	19,811	16,607	*3,253*	2,397	856	*17,429*	13,211	4,218	*15,736*	4,203	11,533
	60 and over	*31,517*	15,863	15,654	*1,605*	710	895	*11,443*	9,731	1,712	*18,469*	5,422	13,047
	Adi Hindu	197,784	100,913	96,871	79,382	46,515	32,867	103,727	51,204	52,523	14,675	3,194	11,481
	0—1	*6,145*	2,902	3,243	*6,143*	2,900	3,243	*2*	2	..	..	..	..
	1—5	*29,677*	14,876	14,801	*29,382*	14,744	14,638	*245*	112	133	*50*	20	30
	5—10	*24,855*	12,783	12,072	*21,123*	12,162	8,961	*3,633*	599	3,034	*99*	22	77
	10—15	*22,122*	11,430	10,692	*14,425*	9,665	4,760	*7,504*	1,713	5,791	*193*	52	141
	15—20	*17,732*	8,390	9,342	*4,076*	3,634	442	*13,262*	4,672	8,590	*394*	84	310
	20—30	*35,768*	17,099	18,669	*2,683*	2,267	416	*31,526*	14,434	17,092	*1,559*	398	1,161
	30—40	*27,086*	14,440	12,646	*604*	388	216	*23,634*	13,511	10,123	*2,848*	541	2,307
	40—50	*17,270*	9,975	7,295	*532*	440	92	*13,481*	8,835	4,646	*3,257*	700	2,557
	50—60	*9,786*	5,328	4,458	*232*	171	61	*6,398*	4,459	1,939	*3,156*	698	2,458
	60 and over	*7,343*	3,690	3,653	*182*	144	38	*4,042*	2,867	1,175	*3,119*	679	2,440

TABLE VII.

Age, Sex and Civil Condition Part II.—Districts.

District	Religion and Age	POPULATION			UNMARRIED			MARRIED			WIDOWED		
		Persons	Males	Females	Persons	Males	Females	Persons	Males	Females	Persons	Males	Females
1	2	3	4	5	6	7	8	9	10	11	12	13	14
Mahbubnagar	Muslim	84,604	43,281	41,323	37,617	22,291	15,326	39,794	19,691	20,103	7,193	1,299	5,894
	0—1	*2,083*	1,058	1,025	*2,082*	1,057	1,025	*1*	1	..	..	..	..
	1—5	*11,260*	5,624	5,636	*11,158*	5,538	5,620	*102*	86	16	..	..	..
	5—10	*11,162*	5,974	5,188	*10,411*	5,722	4,689	*743*	251	492	*8*	1	7
	10—15	*10,097*	5,388	4,709	*7,918*	4,979	2,939	*2,156*	404	1,752	*23*	5	18
	15—20	*7,878*	3,767	4,111	*3,059*	2,566	493	*4,697*	1,177	3,520	*122*	24	98
	20—30	*14,511*	7,019	7,492	*2,192*	1,907	285	*11,731*	4,970	6,761	*588*	142	446
	30—40	*11,656*	6,792	4,864	*446*	326	120	*10,109*	6,254	3,855	*1,101*	212	889
	40—50	*7,254*	3,774	3,480	*212*	119	93	*5,431*	3,402	2,029	*1,611*	253	1,358
	50—60	*4,599*	1,958	2,641	*98*	63	35	*2,799*	1,621	1,178	*1,702*	274	1,428
	60 and over	*4,104*	1,927	2,177	*41*	14	27	*2,025*	1,525	500	*2,038*	388	1,650
	Christian	2,705	1,410	1,295	1,293	680	613	1,208	690	518	204	40	164
	0—1	*103*	57	46	*103*	57	46	..	..	..	..	..	..
	1—5	*420*	211	209	*407*	206	201	*13*	5	8	..	..	..
	5—10	*367*	190	177	*296*	166	130	*71*	24	47	..	..	..
	10—15	*308*	156	152	*204*	125	79	*104*	31	73		..	..
	15—20	*228*	113	115	*93*	62	31	*131*	51	80	*4*	..	4
	20—30	*485*	260	225	*108*	49	59	*362*	208	154	*15*	3	12
	30—40	*340*	192	148	*60*	11	49	*249*	177	72	*31*	4	27
	40—50	*195*	113	82	*16*	4	12	*136*	100	36	*43*	9	34
	50—60	*126*	68	58	*3*	..	3	*81*	60	21	*42*	8	34
	60 and over	*133*	50	83	*3*	..	3	*61*	34	27	*69*	16	53
	Tribal	47,881	25,049	22,832	23,133	13,444	9,689	21,842	10,710	11,132	2,906	895	2,011
	0—1	*1,644*	771	873	*1,644*	771	873	..	..	..	..	..	..
	1—5	*8,805*	4,446	4,359	*8,403*	4,230	4,173	*398*	216	182	*4*	..	4
	5—10	*7,077*	3,991	3,086	*6,457*	3,793	2,664	*613*	198	415	*7*	..	7
	10—15	*5,526*	3,007	2,519	*4,068*	2,549	1,519	*1,443*	456	987	*15*	2	13
	15—20	*3,912*	1,940	19,72	*1,308*	1,043	265	*2,584*	895	1,689	*20*	2	18
	20—30	*7,571*	3,595	3,976	*698*	583	115	*6,648*	2,920	3,728	*225*	92	133
	30—40	*5,798*	3,057	2,741	*346*	299	47	*5,011*	2,672	2,339	*441*	86	355
	40—50	*3,508*	1,985	1,523	*77*	62	15	*2,802*	1,726	1,076	*629*	197	432
	50—60	*2,129*	1,216	913	*87*	78	9	*1,396*	913	483	*646*	225	421
	60 and over	*1,911*	1,041	870	*45*	36	9	*947*	714	233	*919*	291	628

TABLE VII.

Age, Sex and Civil Condition Part II.—Districts.

District	Religion and Age	POPULATION			UNMARRIED			MARRIED			WIDOWED		
		Persons	Males	Females	Persons	Males	Females	Persons	Males	Females	Persons	Males	Females
1	2	3	4	5	6	7	8	9	10	11	12	13	14
Nalgonda ..	All Religions	1,133,409	580,897	552,512	455,748	274,799	180,949	576,842	288,587	288,255	100,819	17,511	83,308
	0—1	*35,418*	16,738	18,680	*35,385*	16,735	18,650	*33*	3	30	..	..	..
	1—5	*158,767*	78,237	80,530	*153,244*	77,274	75,970	*5,330*	947	4,383	*193*	16	177
	5—10	*147,732*	76,174	71,558	*123,003*	71,501	51,502	*24,105*	4,640	19,465	*624*	33	591
	10—15	*130,205*	70,399	59,806	*84,567*	58,721	25,846	*44,678*	11,614	33,064	*960*	64	896
	15—20	*104,454*	52,080	52,374	*29,593*	26,528	3,065	*72,740*	25,339	47,401	*2,121*	213	1,908
	20—30	*201,848*	98,595	103,253	*22,525*	19,712	2,813	*169,367*	77,461	91,906	*9,956*	1,422	8,534
	30—40	*146,629*	75,740	70,889	*3,712*	2,370	1,342	*124,464*	70,849	53,615	*18,453*	2,521	15,932
	40—50	*99,874*	55,600	44,274	*1,764*	997	767	*74,382*	50,673	23,709	*23,728*	3,930	19,798
	50—60	*61,750*	33,886	27,864	*983*	543	440	*39,147*	29,046	10,101	*21,620*	4,297	17,323
	60 and over	*46,732*	23,448	23,284	*972*	418	554	*22,596*	18,015	4,581	*23,164*	5,015	18,149
	Hindu (Brahmanic) ..	780,440	399,249	381,191	304,032	184,166	119,866	401,111	201,897	199,214	75,297	13,186	62,111
	0—1	*23,810*	11,196	12,614	*23,794*	11,193	12,601	*16*	3	13	..	..	..
	1—5	*106,598*	51,863	54,735	*102,156*	51,126	51,030	*4,288*	724	3,564	*154*	13	141
	5—10	*102,084*	52,200	49,884	*82,498*	48,525	33,973	*19,063*	3,649	15,414	*523*	26	497
	10—15	*90,497*	48,993	41,504	*56,010*	39,745	16,265	*33,766*	9,190	24,576	*721*	58	663
	15—20	*73,121*	36,453	36,668	*19,213*	17,339	1,874	*52,257*	18,954	33,303	*1,651*	160	1,491
	20—30	*138,764*	67,813	70,951	*14,904*	13,038	1,866	*116,095*	53,692	62,403	*7,765*	1,083	6,682
	30—40	*100,691*	52,361	48,330	*2,666*	1,794	872	*84,194*	48,622	35,572	*13,831*	1,945	11,886
	40—50	*68,097*	37,844	30,253	*1,305*	673	632	*49,261*	34,193	15,068	*17,531*	2,978	14,553
	50—60	*43,946*	24,197	19,749	*786*	425	361	*27,113*	20,549	6,564	*16,047*	3,223	12,824
	60 and over	*32,832*	16,329	16,503	*700*	308	392	*15,058*	12,321	2,737	*17,074*	3,700	13,374
	Adi Hindu	208,980	106,897	102,083	85,605	51,687	33,918	107,552	52,644	54,908	15,823	2,566	13,257
	0—1	*7,054*	3,151	3,903	*7,046*	3,151	3,895	*8*	..	8	..	..	..
	1—5	*31,015*	15,323	15,692	*30,424*	15,206	15,218	*561*	115	446	*30*	2	28
	5—10	*26,058*	13,607	12,451	*22,513*	13,069	9,444	*3,487*	535	2,952	*58*	3	55
	10—15	*23,010*	12,649	10,361	*15,499*	11,055	4,444	*7,319*	1,590	5,729	*192*	4	188
	15—20	*18,876*	9,390	9,486	*5,502*	5,176	326	*13,006*	4,186	8,820	*368*	28	340
	20—30	*37,774*	18,179	19,595	*3,875*	3,581	294	*32,365*	14,362	18,003	*1,534*	236	1,298
	30—40	*27,593*	13,847	13,746	*371*	240	131	*24,171*	13,264	10,907	*3,051*	343	2,708
	40—50	*20,006*	10,939	9,067	*181*	112	69	*15,778*	10,269	5,509	*4,047*	558	3,480
	50—60	*10,430*	5,800	4,630	*107*	55	52	*6,955*	5,106	1,849	*3,368*	639	2,729
	60 and over	*7,164*	4,012	3,152	*87*	42	45	*3,902*	3,217	685	*3,175*	753	2,422

E

TABLE VII.

Age, Sex and Civil Condition Part II.—Districts.

District	Religion and Age	POPULATION			UNMARRIED			MARRIED			WIDOWED		
		Persons	Males	Females	Persons	Males	Females	Persons	Males	Females	Persons	Males	Females
1	2	3	4	5	6	7	8	9	10	11	12	13	14
Nalgonda ..	**Muslim**	**62,233**	**31,842**	**30,391**	**27,075**	**16,327**	**10,748**	**29,706**	**14,615**	**15,091**	**5,452**	**900**	**4,552**
	0—1	*1,908*	1,005	903	*1,904*	1,005	899	*4*	..	4	..	..	..
	1—5	*8,247*	4,689	3,558	*8,139*	4,667	3,472	*104*	22	82	*4*	..	4
	5—10	*7,538*	4,074	3,464	*7,107*	3,967	3,140	*410*	107	303	*21*	..	21
	10—15	*6,435*	3,386	3,049	*5,277*	3,117	2,160	*1,129*	269	860	*29*	..	29
	15—20	*5,242*	2,737	2,505	*2,274*	1,912	362	*2,921*	819	2,102	*47*	6	41
	20—30	*11,156*	5,381	5,625	*1,690*	1,389	301	*9,117*	4,099	5,018	*349*	43	306
	30—40	*8,731*	4,044	4,687	*355*	101	254	*7,471*	3,834	3,637	*905*	109	796
	40—50	*5,686*	3,065	2,621	*165*	128	37	*4,347*	2,735	1,612	*1,174*	202	972
	50—60	*3,624*	1,864	1,760	*35*	20	15	*2,375*	1,620	755	*1,214*	224	990
	60 and over	*3,666*	1,447	2,219	*129*	21	108	*1,828*	1,110	718	*1,709*	316	1,393
	Christian	**23,689**	**12,324**	**11,365**	**10,314**	**6,027**	**4,287**	**11,837**	**6,017**	**5,820**	**1,538**	**280**	**1,258**
	0—1	*659*	346	313	*659*	346	313	..	..	..	..	..	..
	1—5	*3,309*	1,626	1,683	*3,265*	1,615	1,650	*43*	11	32	*1*	..	1
	5—10	*3,210*	1,708	1,502	*2,945*	1,644	1,301	*256*	64	192	*9*	..	9
	10—15	*2,740*	1,463	1,277	*2,084*	1,343	741	*646*	120	526	*10*	..	10
	15—20	*2,169*	1,045	1,124	*793*	627	166	*1,357*	416	941	*19*	2	17
	20—30	*4,250*	2,057	2,193	*463*	383	80	*3,670*	1,656	2,014	*117*	18	99
	30—40	*3,123*	1,711	1,412	*57*	31	26	*2,805*	1,632	1,173	*261*	48	213
	40—50	*2,095*	1,216	879	*35*	27	8	*1,684*	1,124	560	*376*	65	311
	50—60	*1,239*	656	583	*7*	6	1	*875*	585	290	*357*	65	292
	60 and over	*895*	496	399	*6*	5	1	*501*	409	92	*388*	82	306
	Tribal	**57,549**	**30,321**	**27,228**	**28,553**	**16,504**	**12,049**	**26,354**	**13,258**	**13,096**	**2,642**	**559**	**2,083**
	0—1	*1,956*	1,027	929	*1,951*	1,027	924	*5*	..	5	..	..	..
	1—5	*9,552*	4,713	4,839	*9,215*	4,637	4,578	*333*	75	258	*4*	1	3
	5—10	*8,799*	4,561	4,238	*7,905*	4,277	3,628	*881*	280	601	*13*	4	9
	10—15	*7,480*	3,887	3,593	*5,666*	3,447	2,219	*1,806*	438	1,368	*8*	2	6
	15—20	*5,011*	2,439	2,572	*1,800*	1,467	333	*3,175*	955	2,220	*36*	17	19
	20—30	*9,806*	4,968	4,838	*1,585*	1,317	268	*8,039*	3,610	4,429	*182*	41	141
	30—40	*6,400*	3,728	2,672	*261*	202	59	*5,747*	3,453	2,294	*392*	73	319
	40—50	*3,930*	2,504	1,426	*77*	56	21	*3,264*	2,326	938	*589*	122	467
	50—60	*2,470*	1,346	1,124	*45*	34	11	*1,805*	1,171	634	*620*	141	479
	60 and over	*2,145*	1,148	997	*48*	40	8	*1,299*	950	349	*798*	158	640

TABLE VII.

Age, Sex and Civil Condition Part II.—Districts.

District	Religion and Age	POPULATION			UNMARRIED			MARRIED			WIDOWED		
		Persons	Males	Females	Persons	Males	Females	Persons	Males	Females	Persons	Males	Females
1	2	3	4	5	6	7	8	9	10	11	12	13	14
Aurangabad ..	**All Religions**	944,793	480,498	464,295	335,575	194,579	140,996	531,071	266,654	264,417	78,147	19,265	58,882
	0—1	*28,555*	13,941	14,614	*27,813*	13,632	14,181	*713*	306	407	*29*	3	26
	1—5	*126,367*	64,182	62,185	*115,759*	59,052	56,707	*10,474*	5,081	5,393	*134*	49	85
	5—10	*120,491*	62,636	57,855	*88,021*	49,922	38,099	*31,911*	12,517	19,394	*559*	197	362
	10—15	*106,672*	54,727	51,945	*58,521*	37,127	21,394	*47,135*	17,302	29,833	*1,016*	298	718
	15—20	*87,004*	41,359	45,645	*18,697*	15,027	3,670	*66,556*	25,943	40,613	*1,751*	389	1,362
	20—30	*171,411*	85,906	85,505	*17,829*	13,965	3,864	*146,845*	70,129	76,716	*6,737*	1,812	4,925
	30—40	*127,118*	66,141	60,977	*4,542*	3,185	1,357	*108,674*	59,451	49,223	*13,902*	3,505	10,397
	40—50	*86,284*	45,686	40,598	*2,468*	1,445	1,023	*64,465*	39,478	24,987	*19,351*	4,763	14,588
	50—60	*52,714*	27,162	25,552	*955*	600	355	*33,827*	22,361	11,466	*17,932*	4,201	13,731
	60 and over	*38,177*	18,758	19,419	*970*	624	346	*20,471*	14,086	6,385	*16,736*	4,048	12,688
	Hindu (Brahmanic) ..	641,214	325,257	315,957	218,084	128,695	89,389	366,499	182,620	183,879	56,631	13,942	42,689
	0—1	*19,199*	9,420	9,779	*18,701*	9,193	9,508	*471*	225	246	*27*	2	25
	1—5	*83,903*	43,090	40,813	*76,860*	39,846	37,014	*6,956*	3,218	3,738	*87*	26	61
	5—10	*80,346*	41,519	38,827	*56,677*	32,800	23,877	*23,241*	8,570	14,671	*428*	149	279
	10—15	*71,054*	36,795	34,259	*37,353*	24,833	12,520	*32,878*	11,718	21,160	*823*	244	579
	15—20	*58,810*	27,681	31,129	*11,490*	9,538	1,952	*46,054*	17,843	28,211	*1,266*	300	966
	20—30	*118,152*	59,347	58,805	*11,474*	8,983	2,491	*101,614*	49,073	52,541	*5,064*	1,291	3,773
	30—40	*87,099*	44,706	42,393	*2,803*	1,800	1,003	*74,328*	40,583	33,745	*9,968*	2,323	7,645
	40—50	*60,234*	31,554	28,680	*1,575*	900	675	*44,476*	27,068	17,408	*14,183*	3,586	10,597
	50—60	*36,835*	18,510	18,325	*608*	378	230	*23,338*	15,075	8,263	*12,889*	3,057	9,832
	60 and over	*25,582*	12,635	12,947	*543*	424	119	*13,143*	9,247	3,896	*11,896*	2,964	8,932
	Adi Hindu	140,336	70,323	70,013	49,538	26,560	22,978	81,177	41,299	39,878	9,621	2,464	7,157
	0—1	*4,507*	2,205	2,302	*4,360*	2,172	2,188	*146*	32	114	*1*	1	..
	1—5	*20,120*	10,056	10,064	*18,625*	9,314	9,311	*1,472*	727	745	*23*	15	8
	5—10	*17,600*	8,768	8,832	*13,532*	7,246	6,286	*3,991*	1,492	2,499	*77*	30	47
	10—15	*15,906*	7,676	8,230	*8,359*	5,000	3,359	*7,450*	2,648	4,802	*97*	28	69
	15—20	*12,344*	5,511	6,833	*2,186*	1,464	722	*10,000*	4,007	5,993	*158*	40	118
	20—30	*24,218*	12,116	12,102	*1,524*	831	693	*21,944*	11,066	10,878	*750*	219	531
	30—40	*19,428*	10,186	9,242	*377*	237	140	*17,089*	9,347	7,742	*1,962*	602	1,360
	40—50	*12,995*	6,830	6,165	*334*	181	153	*10,167*	6,044	4,123	*2,494*	605	1,889
	50—60	*7,684*	4,102	3,582	*120*	45	75	*5,387*	3,526	1,861	*2,177*	531	1,646
	60 and over	*5,534*	2,873	2,661	*121*	70	51	*3,531*	2,410	1,121	*1,882*	393	1,489
	Muslim	124,441	65,065	59,376	52,487	30,642	21,845	62,642	32,216	30,426	9,312	2,207	7,105
	0—1	*3,602*	1,755	1,847	*3,540*	1,722	1,818	*61*	33	28	*1*	..	1
	1—5	*16,402*	8,431	7,971	*14,972*	7,586	7,386	*1,415*	842	573	*15*	3	12
	5—10	*17,219*	9,462	7,757	*13,688*	7,450	6,238	*3,497*	2,001	1,496	*34*	11	23
	10—15	*15,214*	7,845	7,369	*10,256*	5,636	4,620	*4,883*	2,191	2,692	*75*	18	57
	15—20	*12,225*	6,345	5,880	*4,122*	3,281	841	*7,827*	3,029	4,798	*276*	35	241
	20—30	*22,214*	10,897	11,317	*3,984*	3,467	517	*17,511*	7,182	10,329	*719*	248	471
	30—40	*15,612*	8,564	7,048	*1,127*	949	178	*12,924*	7,173	5,751	*1,561*	442	1,119
	40—50	*9,977*	5,670	4,307	*371*	292	79	*7,519*	4,929	2,590	*2,087*	449	1,638
	50—60	*6,352*	3,535	2,817	*187*	144	43	*3,957*	2,942	1,015	*2,208*	449	1,759
	60 and over	*5,624*	2,561	3,063	*240*	115	125	*3,048*	1,894	1,154	*2,336*	552	1,784

TABLE VII.

Age, Sex and Civil Condition Part II.—Districts.

District	Religion and Age	POPULATION			UNMARRIED			MARRIED			WIDOWED		
		Persons	Males	Females	Persons	Males	Females	Persons	Males	Females	Persons	Males	Females
1	2	3	4	5	6	7	8	9	10	11	12	13	14
Aurangabad ..	Christian	10,576	5,393	5,183	4,258	2,342	1,916	5,717	2,924	2,793	601	127	474
	0—1	290	146	144	278	138	140	12	8	4	..	..	..
	1—5	1,497	737	760	1,378	676	702	118	61	57	1	..	1
	5—10	1,499	757	742	1,209	643	566	288	114	174	2	..	2
	10—15	1,352	732	620	797	466	331	552	264	288	3	2	1
	15—20	1,017	564	453	255	208	47	753	352	401	9	4	5
	20—30	1,799	981	818	214	189	25	1,537	785	752	48	7	41
	30—40	1,503	690	813	15	10	5	1,352	627	725	136	53	83
	40—50	812	411	401	57	7	50	606	388	218	149	16	133
	50—60	467	228	239	54	4	50	281	200	81	132	24	108
	60 and over	340	147	193	1	1	..	218	125	93	121	21	100
	Jain	5,313	2,906	2,407	1,793	1,092	701	2,978	1,616	1,362	542	198	344
	0—1	153	75	78	149	72	77	4	3	1	..	..	..
	1—5	617	312	305	547	274	273	64	34	30	6	4	2
	5—10	574	322	252	422	257	165	145	61	84	7	4	3
	10—15	590	308	282	310	202	108	277	105	172	3	1	2
	15—20	503	250	253	91	80	11	397	164	233	15	6	9
	20—30	985	528	457	102	91	11	823	421	402	60	16	44
	30—40	790	516	274	65	55	10	651	434	217	74	27	47
	40—50	485	265	220	37	34	3	323	182	141	125	49	76
	50—60	339	214	125	20	19	1	183	129	54	136	66	70
	60 and over	277	116	161	50	8	42	111	83	28	116	25	91
	Tribal	22,137	11,066	11,071	9,178	5,103	4,075	11,594	5,678	5,916	1,365	285	1,080
	0—1	736	320	416	717	315	402	19	5	14	..	..	..
	1—5	3,192	1,487	1,705	2,748	1,288	1,460	442	198	244	2	1	1
	5—10	3,436	1,778	1,658	2,685	1,498	1,187	740	277	463	11	3	8
	10—15	2,786	1,341	1,445	1,694	972	722	1,078	364	714	14	5	9
	15—20	2,076	989	1,087	568	450	118	1,483	535	948	25	4	21
	20—30	3,924	1,959	1,965	536	400	136	3,300	1,534	1,766	88	25	63
	30—40	2,589	1,423	1,166	155	133	22	2,247	1,242	1,005	187	48	139
	40—50	1,636	892	744	44	31	13	1,294	810	484	298	51	247
	50—60	1,003	501	502	16	10	6	612	424	188	375	67	308
	60 and over	759	376	383	15	6	9	379	289	90	365	81	284

TABLE VII.

Age, Sex and Civil Condition Part II.—Districts.

District	Religion and Age	POPULATION			UNMARRIED			MARRIED			WIDOWED		
		Persons	Males	Females	Persons	Males	Females	Persons	Males	Females	Persons	Males	Females
1	2	3	4	5	6	7	8	9	10	11	12	13	14
Bir ..	All Religions	633,690	325,396	308,294	230,556	132,962	97,594	343,495	172,441	171,054	59,639	19,993	39,646
	0—1	19,016	8,728	10,298	18,600	8,637	9,963	408	82	326	8	4	4
	1—5	87,687	41,090	46,597	80,040	39,226	40,814	7,226	1,600	5,626	421	264	157
	5—10	72,752	38,584	34,168	54,890	33,508	21,382	17,257	4,770	12,487	605	306	299
	10—15	69,249	37,106	32,143	39,523	27,043	12,480	28,695	9,782	18,913	1,031	281	750
	15—20	55,340	26,342	28,998	13,845	10,152	3,693	39,830	15,742	24,088	1,665	448	1,217
	20—30	112,818	56,037	56,781	13,882	9,440	4,442	92,021	44,214	47,807	6.915	2,383	4,532
	30—40	88,834	46,245	42,589	6,183	3,439	2,744	71,279	39,029	32,250	11,372	3,777	7,595
	40—50	61,812	34,050	27,762	2,336	871	1,465	46,494	29,050	17,444	12,982	4,129	8,853
	50—60	38,885	22,541	16,344	891	410	481	25,307	17,984	7,323	12,687	4,147	8,540
	60 and over	27,297	14,678	12,619	366	236	130	14,978	10,188	4,790	11,953	4,254	7,699
	Hindu (Brahmanic) ..	473,445	243,844	229,601	168,782	97,650	71,132	258,198	129,434	128,764	46,465	16,760	29,705
	0—1	13,960	6,174	7,786	13,707	6,105	7,602	251	67	184	2	2	..
	1—5	63,382	29,215	34,167	57,062	27,706	29,356	6,003	1,252	4,751	317	257	60
	5—10	53,522	28,491	25,031	40,160	24,905	15,255	12,895	3,300	9,595	467	286	181
	10—15	50,548	26,711	23,837	28,140	19,218	8,922	21,544	7,238	14,306	864	255	609
	15—20	42,075	20,170	21,905	10,279	7,708	2,571	30,394	12,067	18,327	1,402	395	1,007
	20—30	86,521	43,323	43,198	11,250	7,630	3,620	69,548	33,592	35,956	5,723	2,101	3,622
	30—40	67,939	35,978	31,961	5,343	3,098	2,245	53,426	29,593	23,833	9,170	3,287	5,883
	40—50	46,775	26,196	20,579	1,833	742	1,091	34,905	21,999	12,906	10,037	3,455	6,582
	50—60	28,172	16,489	11,733	731	340	391	17,860	12,738	5,122	9,581	3,361	6,220
	60 and over	20,551	11,147	9,404	277	198	79	11,372	7,588	3,784	8,902	3,361	5,541
	Adi Hindu	95,051	47,701	47,350	34,594	19,388	15,206	53,126	26,704	26,422	7,331	1,609	5,722
	0—1	3,140	1,517	1,623	3,029	1,508	1,521	109	8	101	2	1	1
	1—5	14,507	7,230	7,277	13,766	7,106	6,660	727	122	605	14	2	12
	5—10	10,901	5,378	5,523	7,858	4,363	3,495	2,998	1,005	1,993	45	10	35
	10—15	11,632	6,470	5,162	6,719	4,699	2,020	4,850	1,755	3,095	63	16	47
	15—20	7,811	3,356	4,455	1,503	961	542	6,180	2,358	3,822	128	37	91
	20—30	15,470	7,038	8,432	1,008	558	450	13,900	6,328	7,572	562	152	410
	30—40	12,439	6,001	6,438	374	102	272	10,875	5,661	5,214	1,190	238	952
	40—50	8,881	4,737	4,144	216	53	163	6,904	4,389	2,515	1,761	295	1,466
	50—60	6,258	3,883	2,375	78	25	58	4,461	3,470	991	1,719	388	1,331
	60 and over	4,012	2,091	1,921	43	18	30	2,122	1,608	514	1,847	470	1,377

TABLE VII.

Age, Sex and Civil Condition Part II.—Districts.

District	Religion and Age	POPULATION			UNMARRIED			MARRIED			WIDOWED		
		Persons	Males	Females	Persons	Males	Females	Persons	Males	Females	Persons	Males	Females
1	2	3	4	5	6	7	8	9	10	11	12	13	14
Bir ..	**Muslim**	53,421	27,691	25,730	21,897	12,887	9,010	26,447	13,444	13,003	5,077	1,360	3,717
	0—1	*1,537*	824	713	*1,494*	818	676	*42*	5	37	*1*	1	..
	1—5	*7,752*	3,547	4,205	*7,346*	3,442	3,904	*333*	100	233	*73*	5	68
	5—10	*6,722*	3,706	3,016	*5,558*	3,346	2,212	*1,097*	352	745	*67*	8	59
	10—15	*5,803*	3,302	2,501	*3,816*	2,667	1,149	*1,901*	629	1,272	*86*	6	80
	15—20	*4,445*	2,340	2,105	*1,673*	1,242	431	*2,652*	1,085	1,567	*120*	13	107
	20—30	*9,011*	4,678	4,333	*1,356*	1,063	293	*7,079*	3,510	3,569	*576*	105	471
	30—40	*6,987*	3,612	3,375	*341*	206	135	*5,754*	3,195	2,559	*892*	211	681
	40—50	*5,090*	2,621	2,469	*215*	59	156	*3,822*	2,225	1,597	*1,053*	337	716
	50—60	*3,787*	1,829	1,958	*65*	32	33	*2,514*	1,475	1,039	*1,208*	322	886
	60 and over	*2,287*	1,232	1,055	*33*	12	21	*1,253*	868	385	*1,001*	352	649
	Jain	3,183	1,728	1,455	1,213	775	438	1,619	783	836	351	170	181
	0—1	*90*	54	36	*86*	53	33	*4*	1	3	..	..	..
	1—5	*319*	170	149	*280*	158	122	*35*	12	23	*4*	..	4
	5—10	*415*	265	150	*327*	247	80	*85*	17	68	*3*	1	2
	10—15	*283*	147	136	*168*	108	60	*110*	36	74	*5*	3	2
	15—20	*299*	183	116	*126*	105	21	*171*	77	94	*2*	1	1
	20—30	*495*	269	226	*86*	65	21	*381*	188	193	*28*	16	12
	30—40	*489*	212	277	*74*	21	53	*351*	161	190	*64*	30	34
	40—50	*403*	165	238	*58*	10	48	*286*	131	155	*59*	24	35
	50—60	*222*	170	52	*5*	5	..	*125*	113	12	*92*	52	40
	60 and over	*168*	93	75	*3*	3	..	*71*	47	24	*94*	43	51
	Tribal	8,280	4,273	4,007	3,975	2,204	1,771	3,907	1,979	1,928	398	90	308
	0—1	*283*	154	129	*279*	153	126	*1*	1	..	*3*	..	3
	1—5	*1,690*	910	780	*1,552*	796	756	*125*	114	11	*13*	..	13
	5—10	*1,148*	725	423	*961*	631	330	*174*	93	81	*13*	1	12
	10—15	*958*	463	495	*664*	340	324	*281*	122	159	*13*	1	12
	15—20	*682*	277	405	*257*	129	128	*412*	146	266	*13*	2	11
	20—30	*1,281*	704	577	*176*	118	58	*1,071*	577	494	*34*	9	25
	30—40	*937*	424	513	*50*	12	38	*834*	401	433	*53*	11	42
	40—50	*622*	305	317	*14*	7	7	*537*	281	256	*71*	17	54
	50—60	*419*	205	214	*12*	8	4	*323*	174	149	*84*	23	61
	60 and over	*260*	106	154	*10*	10	..	*149*	70	79	*101*	26	75

TABLE VII.

Age, Sex and Civil Condition Part II.—Districts.

District	Religion and Age	POPULATION			UNMARRIED			MARRIED			WIDOWED		
		Persons	Males	Female	Persons	Males	Females	Persons	Males	Females	Persons	Males	Females
1	2	3	4	5	6	7	8	9	10	11	12	13	14
Nander ..	**All Religions**	722,081	367,170	354,911	232,290	138,551	93,739	414,053	208,240	205,813	75,738	20,379	55,359
	0—1	*22,203*	11,479	10,724	*21,624*	11,068	10,556	*566*	405	161	*13*	6	7
	1—5	*92,814*	45,949	46,865	*85,651*	43,234	42,417	*6,685*	2,578	4,107	*478*	137	341
	5—10	*90,159*	47,756	42,403	*62,387*	37,520	24,867	*26,799*	9,864	16,935	*973*	372	601
	10—15	*77,995*	41,202	36,793	*37,220*	25,417	11,803	*39,510*	15,262	24,248	*1,265*	523	742
	15—20	*64,123*	31,652	32,471	*10,826*	9,331	1,495	*51,715*	21,627	30,088	*1,582*	694	888
	20—30	*130,983*	65,448	65,535	*8,644*	7,465	1,179	*115,796*	55,594	60,202	*6,543*	2,389	4,154
	30—40	*96,499*	48,050	48,449	*2,612*	1,998	614	*80,521*	42,484	38,087	*13,366*	3,568	9,798
	40—50	*74,277*	38,392	35,885	*1,566*	1,134	432	*54,049*	32,799	21,250	*18,662*	4,459	14,203
	50—60	*42,106*	22,174	19,932	*1,062*	842	220	*24,230*	17,255	6,975	*16,814*	4,077	12,737
	60 and over	*30,922*	15,068	15,854	*698*	542	156	*14,182*	10,372	3,810	*16,042*	4,154	11,888
	Hindu (Brahmanic) ..	479,445	244,003	235,442	144,364	87,400	56,964	280,325	141,355	138,970	54,756	15,248	39,508
	0—1	*14,255*	7,214	7,041	*14,016*	7,044	6,972	*233*	166	67	*6*	4	2
	1—5	*58,253*	29,492	28,761	*53,349*	27,646	25,703	*4,679*	1,783	2,896	*225*	63	162
	5—10	*58,477*	31,252	27,225	*38,891*	24,098	14,793	*18,925*	6,907	12,018	*661*	247	414
	10—15	*52,005*	27,334	24,671	*23,469*	16,256	7,213	*27,637*	10,718	16,919	*899*	360	539
	15—20	*42,167*	20,463	21,704	*6,076*	5,223	853	*34,946*	14,733	20,213	*1,145*	507	638
	20—30	*86,653*	43,204	43,449	*4,635*	4,004	631	*77,319*	37,427	39,892	*4,699*	1,773	2,926
	30—40	*66,461*	33,144	33,317	*1,606*	1,256	350	*55,169*	29,238	25,931	*9,686*	2,650	7,036
	40—50	*50,311*	25,915	24,396	*1,070*	855	215	*35,636*	21,608	14,028	*13,605*	3,452	10,153
	50—60	*29,466*	15,637	13,829	*823*	683	140	*16,421*	11,851	4,570	*12,222*	3,103	9,119
	60 and over	*21,397*	10,348	11,040	*429*	335	94	*9,360*	6,924	2,436	*11,608*	3,089	8,519
	Adi Hindu	141,820	71,492	70,328	46,495	27,449	19,046	83,141	40,929	42,212	12,184	3,114	9,070
	0—1	*5,015*	2,843	2,172	*4,741*	2,614	2,127	*270*	228	42	*4*	1	3
	1—5	*19,153*	9,431	9,722	*17,701*	8,914	8,787	*1,270*	469	801	*182*	48	134
	5—10	*18,359*	9,619	8,740	*12,599*	7,550	5,049	*5,552*	1,977	3,575	*208*	92	116
	10—15	*15,222*	7,800	7,422	*6,575*	4,418	2,157	*8,391*	3,255	5,136	*256*	127	129
	15—20	*12,742*	6,317	6,425	*1,789*	1,514	275	*10,719*	4,690	6,029	*234*	113	121
	20—30	*26,834*	13,371	13,463	*1,894*	1,642	252	*23,895*	11,339	12,556	*1,045*	390	655
	30—40	*17,778*	8,825	8,953	*565*	407	158	*15,019*	7,795	7,224	*2,194*	623	1,571
	40—50	*13,663*	6,549	7,114	*326*	162	164	*10,306*	5,757	4,549	*3,031*	630	2,401
	50—60	*7,572*	4,068	3,504	*116*	73	43	*4,887*	3,438	1,449	*2,569*	557	2,012
	60 and over	*5,482*	2,669	2,813	*189*	155	34	*2,832*	1,981	851	*2,461*	533	1,928
	Muslim	81,155	41,667	39,488	33,102	19,120	13,982	40,955	21,178	19,777	7,098	1,369	5,729
	0—1	*2,237*	1,098	1,139	*2,174*	1,087	1,087	*60*	10	50	*3*	1	2
	1—5	*12,096*	5,359	6,737	*11,453*	5,118	6,335	*596*	229	367	*47*	12	35
	5—10	*10,719*	5,546	5,173	*8,740*	4,723	4,017	*1,905*	811	1,094	*74*	12	62
	10—15	*8,658*	5,020	3,638	*5,850*	3,989	1,861	*2,726*	1,014	1,712	*82*	17	65
	15—20	*7,630*	4,142	3,488	*2,548*	2,272	276	*4,942*	1,842	3,100	*140*	28	112
	20—30	*14,220*	7,290	6,930	*1,749*	1,533	216	*11,823*	5,617	6,206	*648*	140	508
	30—40	*9,961*	4,878	5,083	*329*	244	85	*8,390*	4,421	3,969	*1,242*	213	1,029
	40—50	*8,677*	5,034	3,643	*113*	69	44	*6,885*	4,704	2,181	*1,679*	261	1,418
	50—60	*3,939*	1,855	2,084	*88*	55	33	*2,212*	1,504	708	*1,639*	296	1,343
	60 and over	*3,018*	1,445	1,573	*58*	30	28	*1,416*	1,026	390	*1,544*	389	1,155

TABLE VII.

Age, Sex and Civil Condition Part II.—Districts.

District	Religion and Age	POPULATION			UNMARRIED			MARRIED			WIDOWED		
		Persons	Males	Females	Persons	Males	Females	Persons	Males	Females	Persons	Males	Females
1	2	3	4	5	6	7	8	9	10	11	12	13	14
Nander ..	Jain	1,085	556	529	367	215	152	575	288	287	143	53	90
	0—1	*31*	16	15	*31*	16	15	..	..	..	..	..	..
	1—5	*150*	97	53	*121*	75	46	*28*	22	6	*1*	..	
	5—10	*138*	73	65	*98*	52	46	*40*	21	19	..	..	1
	10—15	*126*	60	66	*62*	34	28	*62*	24	38	*2*	2	..
	15—20	*104*	44	60	*25*	16	9	*76*	26	50	*3*	2	1
	20—30	*196*	94	102	*24*	16	8	*160*	71	89	*12*	7	5
	30—40	*131*	76	55	*6*	6	..	*103*	60	43	*22*	10	12
	40—50	*100*	53	47	..	..	..	*68*	41	27	*32*	12	20
	50—60	*66*	28	38	..	..	..	*31*	18	13	*35*	10	25
	60 and over	*43*	15	28	..	..	..	*7*	5	2	*36*	10	26
	Sikh	1,588	869	719	563	346	217	806	440	366	219	83	136
	0—1	*41*	14	27	*41*	14	27	..	..	..	..	..	..
	1—5	*181*	71	110	*160*	63	97	*16*	5	11	*5*	3	2
	5—10	*153*	76	77	*115*	63	52	*34*	11	23	*4*	2	2
	10—15	*141*	66	75	*81*	48	33	*51*	11	40	*9*	7	2
	15—20	*122*	63	59	*34*	30	4	*83*	30	53	*5*	3	2
	20—30	*249*	155	94	*43*	41	2	*184*	102	82	*22*	12	10
	30—40	*222*	124	98	*24*	24	..	*158*	93	65	*40*	7	33
	40—50	*214*	117	97	*26*	24	2	*146*	80	66	*42*	13	29
	50—60	*141*	99	42	*23*	23	..	*74*	61	13	*44*	15	29
	60 and over	*124*	84	40	*16*	16	..	*60*	47	13	*48*	21	27
	Tribal	16,369	8,231	8,138	7,151	3,871	3,280	7,930	3,868	4,062	1,288	492	796
	0—1	*603*	281	322	*600*	280	320	*3*	1	2	..	..	..
	1—5	*2,879*	1,449	1,430	*2,778*	1,374	1,404	*86*	64	22	*15*	11	4
	5—10	*2,243*	1,148	1,095	*1,886*	996	890	*333*	133	200	*24*	19	5
	10—15	*1,773*	883	890	*1,134*	642	492	*622*	231	391	*17*	10	7
	15—20	*1,289*	592	697	*341*	266	75	*896*	285	611	*52*	41	11
	20—30	*2,713*	1,262	1,451	*291*	223	68	*2,310*	973	1,337	*112*	66	46
	30—40	*1,863*	950	913	*74*	54	20	*1,614*	833	781	*175*	63	112
	40—50	*1,270*	706	564	*29*	22	7	*977*	595	382	*264*	89	175
	50—60	*900*	470	430	*12*	8	4	*590*	371	219	*298*	91	207
	60 and over	*836*	400	346	*6*	6	..	*499*	382	117	*331*	102	229

TABLE VII.

Age, Sex and Civil Condition Part II.—Districts.

District	Religion and Age	POPULATION			UNMARRIED			MARRIED			WIDOWED		
		Persons	Males	Females	Persons	Males	Females	Persons	Males	Females	Persons	Males	Females
1	2	3	4	5	7	7	8	9	10	11	12	13	14
Parbhani ..	**All Religions**	**853,760**	**434,777**	**418,983**	**285,850**	**162,724**	**123,126**	**483,401**	**248,136**	**235,265**	**84,509**	**23,917**	**60,592**
	0—1	*24,644*	11,769	12,875	*24,151*	11,532	12,619	*471*	231	240	*22*	6	16
	1—5	*122,567*	56,584	65,983	*110,075*	53,438	56,637	*12,004*	2,922	9,082	*488*	224	264
	5—10	*113,918*	58,473	55,445	*76,369*	45,428	30,946	*36,457*	12,636	23,821	*1,092*	414	678
	10—15	*100,765*	51,783	48,982	*47,875*	31,585	16,290	*51,408*	19,566	31,842	*1,482*	632	850
	15—20	*72,843*	35,609	37,234	*11,466*	9,326	2,140	*59,071*	25,128	33,943	*2,306*	1,155	1,151
	20—30	*145,635*	75,622	70,013	*9,027*	7,423	1,604	*127,562*	63,978	63,584	*9,046*	4,221	4,825
	30—40	*109,987*	57,069	52,918	*3,539*	1,937	1,602	*92,258*	51,500	40,758	*14,190*	3,632	10,558
	40—50	*78,860*	42,830	36,030	*1,684*	1,009	675	*58,020*	37,407	20,613	*19,156*	4,414	14,742
	50—60	*49,192*	26,907	22,285	*937*	538	399	*29,527*	21,775	7,752	*18,728*	4,594	14,134
	60 and over	*35,349*	18,,131	17,218	*727*	513	214	*16,623*	12,993	3,630	*17,999*	4,625	13,374
	Hindu (Brahmanic)	**589 ,258**	**301,611**	**287,647**	**190,410**	**111,102**	**79,308**	**335,419**	**171,407**	**164,012**	**63,429**	**19,102**	**44,327**
	0—1	*16,720*	7,920	8,800	*16,453*	7,793	8,660	*256*	127	129	*11*	..	11
	1—5	*79,552*	36,388	43,164	*71,673*	34,515	37,158	*7,659*	1,801	5,858	*220*	72	148
	5—10	*78,024*	40,380	37,644	*51,747*	31,737	20,010	*25,494*	8,354	17,140	*783*	289	494
	10—15	*71,193*	37,211	33,982	*32,691*	22,328	10,363	*37,467*	14,453	23,014	*1,035*	430	605
	15—20	*51,162*	25,069	26,093	*7,484*	6,384	1,100	*41,823*	17,683	24,140	*1,855*	1,002	853
	20—30	*101,754*	53,589	48,165	*5,894*	5,271	623	*88,771*	44,709	44,062	*7,089*	3,609	3,480
	30—40	*76,120*	39,757	36,363	*2,209*	1,429	780	*63,213*	35,417	27,796	*10,698*	2,911	7,787
	40—50	*54,985*	29,679	25,306	*1,036*	785	251	*39,580*	25,321	14,259	*14,369*	3,573	10,796
	50—60	*34,273*	18,583	15,690	*670*	431	239	*19,665*	14,597	5,068	*13,938*	3,555	10,383
	60 and over	*25,475*	13,035	12,440	*553*	429	124	*11,491*	8,945	2,546	*13,431*	3,661	9,770
	Adi Hindu	**153,030**	**76,344**	**76,686**	**50,560**	**27,480**	**23,080**	**90,389**	**46,409**	**43,980**	**12,081**	**2,455**	**9,626**
	0—1	*5,012*	2,444	2,568	*4,870*	2,381	2,489	*140*	63	77	*2*	..	2
	1—5	*24,293*	11,073	13,220	*21,740*	10,393	11,347	*2,478*	667	1,811	*75*	13	62
	5—10	*21,258*	11,195	10,063	*12,832*	7,534	5,298	*8,225*	3,593	4,632	*201*	68	133
	10—15	*18,173*	9,293	8,880	*7,684*	5,085	2,599	*10,189*	4,061	6,128	*300*	147	153
	15—20	*12,896*	6,447	6,449	*1,660*	1,148	512	*11,008*	5,218	5,790	*228*	81	147
	20—30	*24,786*	12,528	12,258	*911*	630	281	*22,813*	11,594	11,219	*1,062*	304	758
	30—40	*19,106*	9,297	9,809	*430*	132	298	*16,640*	8,802	7,838	*2,036*	363	1,673
	40—50	*13,740*	7,177	6,563	*282*	71	211	*10,589*	6,653	3,936	*2,869*	453	2,416
	50—60	*8,709*	4,585	4,124	*75*	47	28	*5,835*	4,018	1,817	*2,799*	520	2,279
	60 and over	*5,057*	2,305	2,752	*76*	59	17	*2,472*	1,740	732	*2,509*	506	2,003

TABLE VII.

Age, Sex and Civil Condition Part II.—Districts.

District	Religion and Age	POPULATION			UNMARRIED			MARRIED			WIDOWED		
		Persons	Males	Females	Persons	Males	Females	Persons	Males	Females	Persons	Males	Females
1	2	3	4	5	6	7	8	9	10	11	12	13	14
Parbhani ..	**Muslim**	88,425	45,332	43,093	34,995	18,978	16,017	45,835	24,403	21,432	7,595	1,951	5,644
	0—1	*2,205*	1,046	1,159	*2,126*	1,004	1,122	*70*	36	34	*9*	6	3
	1—5	*14,050*	7,312	6,738	*13,112*	6,780	6,332	*757*	399	358	*181*	133	48
	5—10	*10,970*	5,331	5,639	*9,113*	4,715	4,398	*1,766*	566	1,200	*91*	50	41
	10—15	*8,671*	4,074	4,597	*5,792*	3,156	2,636	*2,765*	878	1,887	*114*	40	74
	15—20	*7,087*	3,333	3,754	*1,900*	1,530	370	*5,009*	1,752	3,257	*178*	51	127
	20—30	*15,980*	7,930	8,050	*1,771*	1,284	487	*13,485*	6,398	7,087	*724*	248	476
	30—40	*12,212*	6,468	5,744	*678*	304	374	*10,319*	5,869	4,450	*1,215*	295	920
	40—50	*8,494*	4,936	3,558	*273*	131	142	*6,579*	4,483	2,096	*1,642*	322	1,320
	50—60	*5,142*	3,029	2,113	*151*	54	97	*3,301*	2,551	750	*1,690*	424	1,266
	60 and over	*3,614*	1,873	1,741	*79*	20	59	*1,784*	1,471	313	*1,751*	382	1,369
	Jain	3,685	1,924	1,761	1,242	717	525	2,067	1,077	990	376	130	246
	0—1	*133*	45	88	*130*	42	88	*3*	3	..	..	..	..
	1—5	*504*	245	259	*451*	220	231	*51*	25	26	*2*	..	2
	5—10	*482*	243	239	*326*	188	138	*153*	54	99	*3*	1	2
	10—15	*437*	222	215	*212*	153	59	*213*	68	145	*12*	1	11
	15—20	*372*	184	188	*56*	53	3	*303*	128	175	*13*	3	10
	20—30	*629*	328	301	*41*	38	3	*553*	283	270	*35*	7	28
	30—40	*436*	238	198	*15*	14	1	*363*	204	159	*58*	20	38
	40—50	*325*	200	125	*6*	6	..	*236*	162	74	*83*	32	51
	50—60	*240*	134	106	*2*	1	1	*133*	97	36	*105*	36	69
	60 and over	*127*	85	42	*3*	2	1	*59*	53	6	*65*	30	35
	Tribal	17,580	8,648	8,932	7,810	3,948	3,862	8,877	4,471	4,406	893	229	664
	0—1	*506*	276	230	*504*	274	230	*2*	2	..	..	..	..
	1—5	*3,884*	1,414	2,470	*2,833*	1 391	1,442	*1,043*	18	1,025	*8*	5	3
	5—10	*2,967*	1,218	1,749	*2,190*	1,168	1,022	*765*	45	720	*12*	5	7
	10—15	*2.066*	864	1,202	*1,345*	771	574	*703*	80	623	*18*	13	5
	15—20	*1,189*	515	674	*325*	188	137	*835*	311	524	*29*	16	13
	20—30	*2,131*	1,054	1,077	*319*	118	201	*1,692*	892	800	*120*	44	76
	30—40	*1,876*	1,192	684	*163*	20	143	*1,555*	1,139	416	*158*	33	125
	40—50	*1,161*	756	405	*78*	11	67	*918*	718	200	*165*	27	138
	50—60	*759*	545	214	*38*	4	34	*555*	489	66	*166*	52	114
	60 and over	*1,041*	814	227	*15*	3	12	*809*	777	32	*217*	34	183

TABLE VII.

Age, Sex and Civil Condition Part II.—Districts.

District	Religion and Age	POPULATION			UNMARRIED			MARRIED			WIDOWED		
		Persons	Males	Females	Persons	Males	Females	Persons	Males	Females	Persons	Males	Females
1	2	3	4	5	6	7	8	9	10	11	12	13	14
Gulbarga ..	All Religions	1,225,008	621,687	603,321	438,854	255,561	183,293	657,515	332,369	325,146	128,639	33,757	94,882
	0—1	32,923	15,376	17,547	31,650	14,598	17,052	1,214	732	482	59	46	13
	1—5	157,873	76,617	81,256	143,308	68,494	74,814	13,699	7,757	5,942	866	366	500
	5—10	146,342	74,670	71,672	112,388	61,296	51,092	32,955	13,002	19,953	999	372	627
	10—15	129,572	68,599	60,973	78,542	50,546	27,996	49,684	17,473	32,211	1,346	580	766
	15—20	104,008	51,550	52,458	26,847	22,787	4,060	74,809	27,950	46,859	2,352	813	1,539
	20—30	224,251	110,028	114,223	25,070	20,812	4,258	187,986	86,299	101,687	11,195	2,917	8,278
	30—40	175,144	92,425	82,719	8,770	6,711	2,059	143,255	80,272	62,983	23,119	5,442	17,677
	40—50	117,657	62,710	54,947	4,870	4,018	852	82,830	51,494	31,336	29,957	7,198	22,759
	50—60	76,409	39,077	37,332	4,847	4,208	639	42,767	27,445	15,322	28,795	7,424	21,371
	60 and over	60,829	30,635	30,194	2,562	2,091	471	28,316	19,945	8,371	29,951	8,599	21,352
	Hindu (Brahmanic) ..	785,929	398,524	387,405	266,412	156,347	110,065	429,533	217,282	212,251	89,984	24,895	65,089
	0—1	20,043	91,32	10,911	19,430	8,808	10,622	582	297	285	31	27	4
	1—5	93,752	44,750	49,002	84,985	39,599	45,386	8,086	4,815	3,271	681	336	345
	5—10	90,906	45,242	45,664	67,595	36,457	31,138	22,720	8,584	14,136	591	201	390
	10—15	82,999	43,648	39,351	48,760	31,918	16,842	33,374	11.377	21,997	865	353	512
	15—20	67,441	33,452	33,989	16,316	14,341	1,975	49,522	18,562	30,960	1,603	549	1,054
	20—30	143,517	71,003	72,514	15,286	13,069	2,217	120,444	55,815	64,629	7,787	2,119	5,668
	30—40	114,954	60,645	54,309	5,562	4,503	1,059	93,200	52,108	41,092	16,192	4,034	12,158
	40—50	77,860	41,535	36,325	3,038	2,639	399	53,849	33,524	20,325	20,973	5,372	15,601
	50—60	53,476	27,790	25,686	3,874	3.630	244	29,329	18,604	10,725	20,273	5,556	14,717
	60 and over	40,981	21,327	19,654	1,566	1,383	183	18,427	13,596	4,831	20,988	6,348	14,640
	Adi Hindu	194,810	98,250	96,560	70,621	41,045	29,576	106,008	53,141	52,867	18,181	4,064	14,117
	0—1	5,947	2,786	3,161	5,674	2,626	3,048	266	153	113	7	7	..
	1—5	29,189	14,743	14,446	26,077	13,223	12,854	3,023	1,505	1,518	89	15	74
	5—10	23,992	12,898	11,094	18,085	10,580	7,505	5,701	2,228	3,473	206	90	116
	10—15	19,989	10,833	9,156	11,308	7,634	3,674	8,402	3,054	5,348	279	145	134
	15—20	14,873	7,331	7,542	3,442	2,910	526	11,104	4,298	6,806	327	117	210
	20—30	35,364	16,880	18,484	3,247	2,434	813	30,514	14,040	16,474	1,603	406	1,197
	30—40	27,506	14,459	13,047	1,339	794	545	22,803	12,988	9,815	3,364	677	2,687
	40—50	18,905	9,957	8,948	867	577	290	13,583	8,473	5,110	4,455	907	3,548
	50—60	10,408	4,814	5,594	301	126	175	6,068	3,857	2,211	4,039	831	3,208
	60 and over	8,637	3,549	5,088	281	135	146	4,544	2,545	1,999	3,812	869	2,943
	Muslim	195,586	99,636	95,950	80,311	46,130	34,181	97,699	49,470	48,229	17,576	4,036	13,540
	0—1	5,517	2,759	2,758	5,190	2,519	2,671	308	230	78	19	10	9
	1—5	26,877	13,248	13,629	24,822	12,045	12,777	1,971	1,190	781	84	13	71
	5—10	24,630	12,819	11,811	20,879	10,948	9,931	3,569	1,797	1,772	182	74	108
	10—15	21,270	11,308	9,962	14,902	8,868	6,034	6,202	2,370	3,832	165	70	96
	15—20	17,729	8,740	8,989	5,940	4,643	1,297	11,425	3,966	7,459	364	131	233
	20—30	36,383	17,325	19,058	5,363	4,499	864	29,466	12,512	16,954	1,554	314	1,240
	30—40	26,705	14,285	12,420	1,384	1,153	231	22,212	12,511	9,701	3,109	621	2,488
	40—50	16,802	9,079	7,723	752	635	117	12,153	7,678	4,475	3,897	766	3,131
	50—60	10,253	5,230	5,023	426	289	137	5,981	4,060	1,921	3,846	881	2,965
	60 and over	9,420	4,843	4,577	653	531	122	4,412	3,156	1,256	4,355	1,156	3.199

TABLE VII.

Age, Sex and Civil Condition Part II.—Districts.

District	Religion and Age	POPULATION			UNMARRIED			MARRIED			WIDOWED		
		Persons	Males	Females	Persons	Males	Females	Persons	Males	Females	Persons	Males	Females
1	2	3	4	5	6	7	8	9	10	11	12	13	14
Gulbarga ..	Christian	5,645	2,861	2,784	2,203	1,226	977	2,998	1,560	1,438	444	75	369
	0—1	*166*	88	78	*152*	75	77	*13*	12	1	*1*	1	..
	1—5	*780*	397	383	*723*	369	354	*54*	28	26	*3*	..	3
	5—10	*662*	352	310	*556*	309	247	*99*	41	58	*7*	2	5
	10—15	*491*	194	297	*262*	119	143	*217*	70	147	*12*	5	7
	15—20	*515*	238	277	*106*	78	28	*400*	156	244	*9*	4	5
	20—30	*1,402*	844	558	*146*	96	50	*1,206*	733	473	*50*	15	35
	30—40	*745*	364	381	*102*	56	46	*576*	295	281	*67*	13	54
	40—50	*460*	203	257	*96*	80	16	*255*	110	145	*109*	13	96
	50—60	*251*	108	143	*50*	41	9	*101*	57	44	*100*	10	90
	60 and over	*173*	73	100	*10*	3	7	*77*	58	19	*86*	12	74
	Jain	1,948	1,013	935	781	441	340	937	500	437	230	72	158
	0—1	*60*	31	29	*55*	27	28	*4*	3	1	*1*	1	..
	1—5	*277*	152	125	*216*	109	107	*61*	43	18	..	..	..
	5—10	*251*	126	125	*199*	92	107	*52*	34	18	..	..	..
	10—15	*221*	103	118	*147*	72	75	*68*	28	40	*6*	3	3
	15—20	*148*	75	73	*52*	40	12	*89*	32	57	*7*	3	4
	20—30	*302*	156	146	*56*	47	9	*219*	100	119	*27*	9	18
	30—40	*282*	170	112	*40*	40	..	*206*	115	91	*36*	15	21
	40—50	*174*	90	84	*9*	8	1	*126*	72	54	*39*	10	29
	50—60	*120*	64	56	*5*	5	..	*66*	44	22	*49*	15	34
	60 and over	*113*	46	67	*2*	1	1	*46*	29	17	*65*	16	49
	Tribal	40,468	21,061	19,407	18,282	10,231	8,051	20,004	10,238	9,766	2,182	592	1,590
	0—1	*1,171*	571	600	*1,132*	536	596	*39*	35	4	..	..	..
	1—5	*6,904*	3,285	3,619	*6,418*	3,119	3,209	*478*	164	314	*8*	2	6
	5—10	*5,836*	3,203	2,633	*5,036*	2,890	2,146	*787*	308	479	*13*	5	8
	10—15	*4,540*	2,481	2,059	*3,129*	1,917	1,212	*1,393*	560	833	*18*	4	14
	15—20	*3,236*	1,693	1,543	*981*	766	215	*2,214*	919	1,295	*41*	8	33
	20—30	*7,133*	3,735	3,398	*941*	638	303	*6,026*	3,048	2,978	*166*	49	117
	30—40	*4,889*	2,461	2,428	*334*	158	176	*4,212*	2,225	1,987	*343*	78	265
	40—50	*3,389*	1,791	1,598	*85*	57	28	*2,832*	1,610	1,222	*472*	124	348
	50—60	*1,890*	1,038	852	*188*	115	73	*1,220*	815	405	*482*	128	354
	60 and over	*1,480*	783	697	*38*	35	3	*803*	554	249	*639*	194	445

TABLE VII.

Age, Sex and Civil Condition Part II.—Districts.

District	Religion and Age	POPULATION			UNMARRIED			MARRIED			WIDOWED		
		Persons	Males	Females	Persons	Males	Females	Persons	Males	Females	Persons	Males	Females
1	2	3	4	5	6	7	8	9	10	11	12	13	14
Osmanabad ..	All Religions	691,068	357,489	333,579	244,934	138,524	106,410	374,132	192,076	182,056	72,002	26,889	45,113
	0—1	*24,449*	12,199	12,250	*23,176*	11,922	11,254	*1,256*	270	986	*17*	7	10
	1—5	*94,661*	46,381	48,280	*84,775*	42,429	42,346	*9,444*	3,704	5,740	*442*	248	194
	5—10	*85,887*	43,378	42,509	*62,152*	34,460	27,692	*22,879*	8,517	14,362	*856*	401	455
	10—15	*77,831*	40,909	36,922	*43,047*	27,733	15,314	*33,570*	12,676	20,894	*1,214*	500	714
	15—20	*58,731*	29,458	29,273	*13,293*	10,742	2,551	*43,650*	17,955	25,695	*1,788*	761	1,027
	20—30	*118,651*	59,611	59,040	*10,735*	7,384	3,351	*99,929*	49,475	50,454	*7,987*	2,752	5,235
	30—40	*93,982*	49,487	44,495	*4,213*	2,066	2,147	*76,449*	42,863	33,586	*13,320*	4,558	8,762
	40—50	*63,590*	34,591	28,999	*1,995*	977	1,018	*45,539*	28,107	17,432	*16,056*	5,5 7	10,549
	50—60	*39,266*	22,425	16,841	*867*	414	453	*23,994*	16,694	7,300	*14,405*	5,317	9,088
	60 and over	*34,020*	19,050	14,970	*681*	397	284	*17,422*	11,815	5,607	*15,917*	6,838	9,079
	Hindu (Brahmanic) ..	464,455	241,373	223,082	159,857	90,984	68,873	251,218	129,809	121,409	53,380	20,580	32,800
	0—1	*15,847*	7,933	7,914	*14,792*	7,827	6,965	*1,047*	105	942	*8*	1	7
	1—5	*61,390*	30,370	31,020	*53,835*	27,330	26,505	*7,236*	2,830	4,406	*319*	210	109
	5—10	*57,038*	28,702	28,336	*40,072*	22,278	17,799	*16,347*	6,117	10,230	*619*	312	307
	10—15	*52,679*	27,803	24,876	*28,407*	18,495	9,912	*23,289*	8,884	14,405	*983*	424	559
	15—20	*40,066*	20,389	19,677	*9,247*	7,537	1,710	*29,402*	12,213	17,189	*1,417*	639	778
	20—30	*80,060*	40,436	39,624	*7,583*	4,987	2,596	*66,358*	33,237	33,121	*6,119*	2,212	3,907
	30—40	*63,875*	33,932	29,943	*3,301*	1,422	1,879	*50,747*	28,990	21,757	*9,827*	3,520	6,307
	40—50	*43,384*	23,596	19,788	*1,517*	603	914	*29,950*	18,735	11,215	*11,917*	4,258	7,659
	50—60	*26,912*	15,345	11,567	*689*	308	381	*15,666*	11,065	4,601	*10,557*	3,972	6,585
	60 and over	*23,204*	12,867	10,337	*414*	202	212	*11,176*	7,633	3,543	*11,614*	5,082	6,582
	Adi Hindu	131,904	66,921	64,983	46,989	26,135	20,854	74,389	37,257	37,132	10,526	3,529	6,997
	0—1	*4,852*	2,415	2,437	*4,680*	2,270	2,410	*168*	142	26	*4*	3	1
	1—5	*19,368*	9,069	10,299	*18,055*	8,617	9,438	*1,225*	417	808	*88*	35	53
	5—10	*16,892*	8,628	8,264	*12,577*	7,155	5,422	*4,141*	1,401	2,740	*174*	72	102
	10—15	*14,412*	7,602	6,810	*7,931*	5,284	2,647	*6,373*	2,280	4,093	*108*	38	70
	15—20	*10,516*	4,994	5,522	*1,767*	1,435	332	*8,567*	3,503	5,064	*182*	56	126
	20—30	*22,630*	0,912	11,718	*1,193*	861	332	*20,472*	9,797	10,675	*965*	254	711
	30—40	*17,669*	8,934	8,735	*357*	218	139	*15,405*	8,225	7,180	*1,907*	491	1,416
	40—50	*11,706*	6,287	5,419	*199*	142	57	*9,212*	5,451	3,761	*2,295*	694	1,601
	50—60	*7,318*	4,243	3,075	*79*	45	34	*4,972*	3,419	1,553	*2,267*	779	1,488
	60 and over	*6,541*	3,837	2,704	*151*	108	43	*3,854*	2,022	1,232	*2,536*	1,107	1,429

TABLE VII.

Age, Sex and Civil Condition Part II.—Districts.

District	Religion and Age	POPULATION			UNMARRIED			MARRIED			WIDOWED		
		Persons	Males	Females	Persons	Males	Females	Persons	Males	Females	Persons	Males	Females
1	2	3	4	5	6	7	8	9	10	11	12	13	14
Osmanabad ..	Muslim	80,308	41,525	38,783	32,499	18,311	14,188	41,120	20,969	20,151	6,689	2,245	4,444
	0—1	*3,036*	1,471	1,565	*2,997*	1,449	1,548	*39*	22	17	..	..	..
	1—5	*11,636*	5,787	5,849	*10,761*	5,393	5,368	*866*	393	473	*9*	1	8
	5—10	*10,166*	5,094	5,072	*8,138*	4,281	3,857	*1,975*	797	1,178	*53*	16	37
	10—15	*9,255*	4,753	4,502	*5,896*	3,474	2,422	*3,257*	1,243	2,014	*102*	36	66
	15—20	*7,048*	3,539	3,509	*2,029*	1,583	446	*4,868*	1,900	2,968	*151*	56	95
	20—30	*13,647*	7,042	6,605	*1,764*	1,407	357	*11,133*	5,407	5,726	*750*	228	522
	30—40	*10,516*	5,612	4,904	*486*	385	101	*8,716*	4,777	3,939	*1,314*	450	864
	40—50	*7,187*	3'939	3,228	*245*	211	34	*5,401*	3,303	2,098	*1,541*	445	1,096
	50—60	*4,198*	2,319	1,879	*81*	49	32	*2,814*	1,824	990	*1,303*	446	857
	60 and over	*3,619*	1,949	1,670	*102*	79	23	*2,051*	1,303	748	*1,466*	567	899
	Jain	2,744	1,424	1,320	918	543	375	1,498	766	732	328	115	213
	0—1	*97*	52	45	*96*	52	44	*1*	..	1	..	..	..
	1—5	*335*	173	162	*299*	155	144	*31*	16	15	*5*	2	3
	5—10	*345*	178	167	*224*	121	103	*119*	57	62	*2*	..	2
	10—15	*311*	152	159	*148*	88	60	*153*	63	90	*10*	1	9
	15—20	*249*	112	137	*61*	50	11	*171*	58	113	*17*	4	13
	20—30	*490*	240	250	*52*	44	8	*387*	182	205	*51*	14	37
	30—40	*363*	192	171	*19*	17	2	*271*	156	115	*73*	19	54
	40—50	*265*	149	116	*12*	11	1	*186*	108	78	*67*	30	37
	50—60	*180*	104	76	*6*	5	1	*114*	78	36	*60*	21	39
	60 and over	*109*	72	37	*1*	..	1	*65*	48	17	*43*	24	19
	Tribal	11,299	6,032	5,267	4,525	2,472	2,053	5,708	3,146	2,562	1,066	414	652
	0—1	*605*	322	283	*599*	318	281	*1*	1	..	*5*	3	2
	1—5	*1,883*	952	931	*1,783*	909	874	*79*	43	36	*21*	..	21
	5—10	*1,395*	747	648	*1,107*	608	499	*280*	138	142	*8*	1	7
	10—15	*1,130*	575	555	*640*	377	263	*479*	197	282	*11*	1	10
	15—20	*813*	403	410	*175*	131	44	*619*	267	352	*19*	5	14
	20—30	*1,763*	942	821	*137*	83	54	*1,527*	815	712	*99*	44	55
	30—40	*1,518*	792	726	*45*	24	21	*1,276*	690	586	*197*	78	119
	40—50	*1,026*	589	437	*17*	9	8	*774*	500	274	*235*	80	155
	50—60	*637*	396	241	*11*	6	5	*411*	294	117	*215*	96	119
	60 and over	*529*	314	215	*11*	7	4	*262*	201	61	*256*	106	150

TABLE VII.

Age, Sex and Civil Condition Part II.—Districts.

District	Religion and Age	POPULATION			UNMARRIED			MARRIED			WIDOWED		
		Persons	Males	Females	Persons	Males	Females	Persons	Males	Females	Persons	Males	Females
1	2	3	4	5	6	7	8	9	10	11	12	13	14
Raichur ..	All Religions	937,535	473,161	464,374	379,532	225,579	153,953	448,036	222,574	225,462	109,967	25,008	84,959
	0—1	22,959	10,738	12,221	22,785	10,695	12,090	168	43	125	6	..	6
	1—5	113,230	54,164	59,066	107,230	52,430	54,800	5,350	1,629	3,721	650	105	545
	5—10	117,516	59,813	57,703	98,673	54,361	44,312	17,380	5,206	12,174	1,463	246	1,217
	10—15	106,812	55,735	51,077	75,736	47,286	28,450	28,754	7,856	20,898	2,322	593	1,729
	15—20	84,439	43,529	49,910	29,458	24,247	5,211	51,899	18,452	33,447	3,082	830	2,252
	20—30	181,300	89,787	91,513	29,407	24,630	4,777	138,401	62,408	75,993	13,492	2,749	10,743
	30—40	141,312	73,849	67,463	10,057	7,810	2,247	107,834	61,217	46,617	23,421	4,822	18,599
	40—50	86,990	45,996	40,994	3,401	2,218	1,183	58,154	38,185	19,969	25,435	5,593	19,842
	50—60	50,177	24,166	26,011	1,728	1,207	521	26,585	17,933	8,652	21,864	5,026	16,838
	60 and over	32,800	15,384	17,416	1,057	695	362	13,511	9,645	3,866	18,232	5,044	13,188
	Hindu (Brahmanic) . ..	708,167	357,673	350,494	279,698	170,989	108,709	339,978	167,331	172,647	88,491	19,353	69,138
	0—1	17,236	7,921	9,315	17,116	7,891	9,225	115	30	85	5	..	5
	1—5	83,351	39,829	43,522	79,086	38,886	40,200	3,698	863	2,835	567	80	487
	5—10	87,539	44,267	43,272	73,365	41,329	32,036	12,909	2,745	10,164	1,265	193	1,072
	10—15	79,496	41,866	37,630	55,653	35,985	19,668	22,042	5,400	16,642	1,801	481	1,320
	15—20	63,697	38,071	30,626	21,558	18,414	3,144	39,519	13,972	25,547	2,620	685	1,935
	20—30	137,128	68,255	68,873	21,764	19,448	2,316	104,513	46,702	57,811	10,851	2,105	8,746
	30—30	107,507	56,336	51,171	7,211	6,136	1,075	81,441	46,548	34,893	18,855	3,652	15,203
	40—50	66,662	35,155	31,507	1,990	1,456	534	44,484	29,431	15,053	20,188	4,268	15,920
	50—60	39,256	18,728	20,528	1,147	882	265	20,509	13,925	6,584	17,600	3,921	13,679
	60 and over	26,295	12,245	14,050	808	562	246	10,748	7,715	3,033	14,739	3,968	10,771
	Adi Hindu	112,992	55,726	57,266	51,852	27,899	23,953	51,659	25,488	26,171	9,481	2,339	7,142
	0—1	2,776	1,356	1,420	2,751	1,350	1,401	25	6	19	..	..	..
	1—5	14,959	7,250	7,709	14,449	6,999	7,450	463	245	218	47	6	41
	5—10	15,158	7,467	7,691	13,317	6,897	6,420	1,716	547	1,169	125	23	102
	10—15	13,807	6,792	7,015	10,026	5,696	4,330	3,421	1,034	2,387	360	62	298
	15—20	10,448	5,056	5,392	3,820	2,697	1,123	6,353	2,293	4,060	275	66	209
	20—30	21,860	10,222	11,638	4,272	2,551	1,721	16,398	7,427	8,971	1,190	244	946
	30—40	16,261	8,164	8,097	1,867	1,042	825	12,328	6,656	5,672	2,066	466	1,600
	40—50	9,789	5,261	4,528	813	393	420	6,634	4,305	2,329	2,342	563	1,779
	50—60	5,130	2,672	2,458	377	210	167	2,956	1,972	984	1,797	490	1,307
	60 and over	2,804	1,486	1,318	160	64	96	1,365	1,003	362	1,279	419	860

TABLE VII.

Age, Sex and Civil Condition Part II.—Districts.

District	Religion and Age	POPULATION			UNMARRIED			MARRIED			WIDOWED		
		Persons	Males	Females	Persons	Males	Females	Persons	Males	Females	Persons	Males	Females
1	2	3	4	5	6	7	8	9	10	11	12	13	14
Raichur ..	Muslim	95,699	48,756	46,943	39,295	21,352	17,943	46,587	24,997	21,590	9,817	2,407	7,410
	0—1	*2,443*	1,214	1,229	*2,418*	1,207	1,211	*25*	7	18	..	..	..
	1—5	*11,867*	5,678	6,189	*10,800*	5,190	5,610	*1,045*	476	569	*22*	12	10
	5—10	*12,471*	6,510	5,961	*9,969*	4,647	5,322	*2,438*	1,835	603	*64*	28	36
	10—15	*10,777*	5,614	5,163	*8,114*	4,827	3,787	*2,556*	1,256	1,300	*107*	31	76
	15—20	*8,287*	4,446	3,841	*3,402*	2,602	800	*4,760*	1,793	2,967	*125*	51	74
	20—30	*18,597*	9,435	9,162	*2,931*	2,322	609	*14,493*	6,857	7,636	*1,173*	256	917
	30—40	*14,767*	7,712	7,055	*874*	569	305	*11,875*	6,666	5,209	*2,018*	477	1,541
	40—50	*8,664*	4,610	4,054	*551*	346	205	*5,748*	3,712	2,036	*2,365*	552	1,813
	50—60	*4,784*	2,269	2,515	*172*	95	77	*2,560*	1,696	864	*2,052*	478	1,574
	60 and over	*3,042*	1,268	1,774	*64*	47	17	*1,087*	699	388	*1,891*	522	1,369
	Christian	3,875	2,130	1,745	1,760	1,027	733	1,367	525	842	748	578	170
	0—1	*104*	47	57	*104*	47	57	..	..	..	..	..	..
	1—5	*469*	234	235	*462*	230	232	*3*	1	2	*4*	3	1
	5—10	*545*	296	249	*507*	289	218	*37*	7	30	*1*	..	1
	10—15	*464*	275	189	*374*	245	129	*69*	14	55	*21*	16	5
	15—20	*313*	150	163	*132*	97	35	*154*	32	122	*27*	21	6
	20—30	*722*	343	379	*121*	91	30	*473*	142	331	*128*	110	18
	30—40	*557*	312	245	*38*	17	21	*320*	138	182	*199*	157	42
	40—50	*389*	252	137	*14*	6	8	*181*	99	82	*194*	147	47
	50—60	*198*	132	66	*8*	5	3	*93*	64	29	*97*	63	34
	60 and over	*114*	89	25	..	..	..	*37*	28	9	*77*	61	16
	Tribal	15,800	8,343	7,457	6,516	4,088	2,428	8,005	3,979	4,026	1,279	276	1,003
	0—1	*385*	193	192	*381*	193	188	*3*	..	3	*1*	..	1
	1—5	*2,461*	1,125	1,336	*2,314*	1,078	1,236	*137*	43	94	*10*	4	6
	5—10	*1,701*	1,229	472	*1,426*	1,161	265	*267*	66	201	*8*	2	6
	10—15	*2,180*	1,138	1,042	*1,512*	996	516	*637*	140	497	*31*	2	29
	15—20	*1,621*	758	863	*515*	410	105	*1,074*	342	732	*32*	6	26
	20—30	*2,800*	1,427	1,373	*251*	175	76	*2,414*	1,222	1,192	*135*	30	105
	30—40	*2,076*	1,243	833	*46*	31	15	*1,773*	1,151	622	*257*	61	196
	40—50	*1,379*	657	722	*30*	14	16	*1,041*	594	447	*308*	49	259
	50—60	*718*	319	399	*20*	12	8	*416*	246	170	*282*	61	221
	60 and over	*479*	254	225	*21*	18	3	*243*	175	68	*215*	61	154

TABLE VII.

Age, Sex and Civil Condition Part II.—Districts.

District	Religion and Age	POPULATION			UNMARRIED			MARRIED			WIDOWED		
		Persons	Males	Females	Persons	Males	Females	Persons	Males	Females	Persons	Males	Females
1	2	3	4	5	6	7	8	9	10	11	12	13	14
Bidar ..	**All Religions**	873,615	446,256	427,359	317,618	171,157	146,461	471,962	246,734	225,228	84,035	28,365	55,670
	0—1	*37,291*	14,666	22,625	*36,654*	14,353	22,301	*617*	309	308	*20*	4	16
	1—5	*138,166*	65,760	72,406	*124,162*	58,464	65,698	*13,312*	6,926	6,386	*692*	370	322
	5—10	*103,377*	52,652	50,725	*72,047*	40,251	31,796	*30,057*	11,783	18,274	*1,273*	618	655
	10—15	*91,821*	49,381	42,440	*47,231*	31,200	16,031	*43,097*	17,451	25,646	*1,493*	730	763
	15—20	*74,122*	37,342	36,780	*17,155*	13,550	3,605	*54,900*	22,954	31,946	*2,067*	838	1,229
	20—30	*144,075*	73,408	70,667	*12,639*	9,044	3,595	*123,377*	61,523	61,854	*8,059*	2,841	5,218
	30—40	*113,126*	60,032	53,094	*3,761*	2,060	1,701	*95,057*	53,503	41,554	*14,308*	4,469	9,839
	40—50	*79,002*	43,232	35,770	*1,888*	987	901	*58,045*	36,147	21,898	*19,069*	6,098	12,971
	50—60	*51,767*	28,596	23,171	*1,091*	594	497	*32,660*	22,182	10,528	*18,016*	5,870	12,146
	60 and over	*40,868*	21,187	19,681	*990*	654	336	*20,840*	14,006	6,834	*19,038*	6,527	12,511
	Hindu (Brahmanic) ..	554,768	284,718	270,050	190,842	101,659	89,183	304,977	161,930	143,047	58,949	21,129	37,820
	0—1	*23,686*	9,419	14,267	*23,343*	9,303	14,040	*327*	112	215	*16*	4	12
	1—5	*86,196*	39,023	47,173	*76,781*	34,020	42,761	*8,906*	4,692	4,214	*509*	311	198
	5—10	*61,543*	32,591	28,952	*41,655*	23,661	17,994	*18,923*	8,418	10,510	*965*	517	448
	10—15	*57,399*	31,723	25,676	*27,690*	18,944	8,746	*28,637*	12,208	16,429	*1,072*	571	501
	15—20	*46,550*	23,409	23,141	*9,703*	7,825	1,878	*35,410*	14,939	20,471	*1,437*	645	792
	20—30	*90,532*	46,376	44,156	*7,076*	5,173	1,903	*77,705*	39,022	38,683	*5,751*	2,181	3,570
	30—40	*74,116*	40,065	34,051	*2,254*	1,290	964	*61,506*	35,254	26,252	*10,356*	3,521	6,835
	40—50	*52,907*	28,985	23,922	*1,060*	594	466	*38,271*	23,806	14,465	*13,576*	4,585	8,991
	50—60	*35,119*	19,625	15,494	*663*	386	277	*21,918*	15,062	6,856	*12,538*	4,177	8,361
	60 and over	*26,720*	13,502	13,218	*617*	463	154	*13,374*	8,422	4,952	*12,729*	4,617	8,112
	Adi Hindu	163,143	81,971	81,172	56,426	31,744	24,682	93,203	46,128	47,075	13,514	4,099	9,415
	0—1	*6,010*	2,749	3,261	*5,843*	2,635	3,208	*164*	114	50	*3*	..	3
	1—5	*27,240*	15,092	12,148	*24,458*	13,566	10,892	*2,649*	1,500	1,140	*133*	26	107
	5—10	*21,914*	10,031	11,883	*14,135*	7,885	6,250	*7,558*	2,082	5,476	*221*	64	157
	10—15	*16,588*	8,084	8,504	*7,838*	4,968	2,870	*8,442*	2,994	5,448	*308*	122	186
	15—20	*13,398*	6,129	7,269	*2,011*	1,452	559	*10,944*	4,539	6,405	*443*	138	305
	20—30	*27,731*	13,420	14,311	*1,317*	832	485	*25,060*	12,167	12,893	*1,354*	421	933
	30—40	*21,261*	10,532	10,729	*374*	176	198	*18,675*	9,808	8,867	*2,212*	548	1,664
	40—50	*13,938*	7,753	6,185	*230*	126	104	*10,666*	6,717	3,949	*3,042*	910	2,132
	50—60	*8,458*	4,700	3,758	*120*	49	71	*5,405*	3,644	1,761	*2,933*	1,007	1,926
	60 and over	*6,605*	3,481	3,124	*100*	55	45	*3,640*	2,563	1,077	*2,865*	863	2,002

TABLE VII.

Age, Sex and Civil Condition Part II.—Districts.

District	Religion and Age	POPULATION			UNMARRIED			MARRIED			WIDOWED		
		Persons	Males	Females	Persons	Males	Females	Persons	Males	Females	Persons	Males	Females
1	2	3	4	5	6	7	8	9	10	11	12	13	14
Bidar ..	Muslim	136,309	69,509	66,800	61,548	32,943	28,605	64,596	33,838	30,758	10,165	2,728	7,437
	0—1	6,950	2,172	4,778	6,831	2,091	4,740	118	81	37	1	..	1
	1—5	21,402	9,992	11,410	19,930	9,366	10,564	1,429	595	834	43	31	12
	5—10	17,416	8,818	8,598	14,316	7,733	6,583	3,035	1,057	1,978	65	28	37
	10—15	15,811	8,554	7,257	10,445	6,561	3,884	5,275	1,963	3,312	91	30	61
	15—20	12,540	7,019	5,521	4,907	3,947	960	7,489	3,034	4,455	144	38	106
	20—30	22,202	11,692	10,510	3,117	2,276	841	18,274	9,216	9,058	811	200	611
	30—40	15,685	8,302	7,383	1,009	516	493	13,138	7,441	5,697	1,538	345	1,193
	40—50	10,652	5,597	5,055	529	225	304	7,934	4,846	3,088	2,189	526	1,663
	50—60	7,120	3,687	3,433	240	123	117	4,605	2,962	1,643	2,275	602	1,673
	60 and over	6,531	3,676	2,855	224	105	119	3,299	2,643	656	3,008	928	2,080
	Christian	4,354	2,194	2,160	1,523	784	739	2,501	1,307	1,194	330	103	227
	0—1	144	73	71	144	73	71	..	..	..	..	..	..
	1—5	614	295	319	473	240	233	137	54	83	4	1	3
	5—10	484	234	250	266	134	132	207	94	113	11	6	5
	10—15	436	214	222	214	123	91	209	86	123	13	5	8
	15—20	382	170	212	128	56	72	234	104	130	20	10	10
	20—30	713	372	341	144	74	70	527	288	239	42	10	32
	30—40	555	289	266	66	35	31	425	237	188	64	17	47
	40—50	416	213	203	40	18	22	315	177	138	61	18	43
	50—60	314	136	178	33	22	11	222	96	126	59	18	41
	60 and over	296	198	98	15	9	6	225	171	54	56	18	38
	Tribal	13,787	7,201	6,586	6,810	3,761	3,049	6,069	3,192	2,877	908	248	660
	0—1	441	219	222	434	218	216	7	1	6	..	..	..
	1—5	2,541	1,298	1,243	2,363	1,215	1,148	177	82	95	1	1	..
	5—10	1,876	909	967	1,570	780	790	298	126	172	8	3	5
	10—15	1,463	731	732	980	552	428	478	179	299	5	..	5
	15—20	1,136	548	588	370	241	129	748	302	446	18	5	13
	20—30	2,683	1,440	1,243	959	671	288	1,650	747	903	74	22	52
	30—40	1,343	757	586	49	37	12	1,190	689	501	104	31	73
	40—50	976	614	362	27	22	5	784	540	285	165	43	122
	50—60	676	399	277	30	9	21	468	337	131	178	53	125
	60 and over	652	286	366	28	16	12	269	180	89	355	90	265

TABLE VII.
AGE, SEX & CIVIL CONDITION.

TABLE VII.

Hyderabad City.

Part III.—Cities.

Religion and Age	POPULATION			UNMARRIED			MARRIED			WIDOWED		
	Persons	Males	Females	Persons	Males	Females	Persons	Males	Females	Persons	Males	Females
1	2	3	4	5	6	7	8	9	10	11	12	13
All Religions ..	**466,894**	**247,623**	**219,271**	**178,581**	**108,207**	**70,374**	**215,327**	**118,210**	**97,117**	**72,986**	**21,206**	**51,780**
0—1 ..	*8,614*	4,101	4,423	*8,577*	4,171	4,406	*37*	20	17	..	..	..
1—5 ..	*44,656*	18,759	25,897	*44,190*	18,542	25,648	*434*	206	228	*32*	11	21
5—10 ..	*42,105*	20,289	21,816	*38,617*	19,126	19,491	*3,356*	1,147	2,209	*132*	16	116
10—15 ..	*40,686*	23,831	16,855	*34,338*	22,080	12,258	*6,120*	1,722	4,398	*228*	29	119
15—20 ..	*53,654*	29,773	23,881	*22,166*	18,473	3,693	*29,157*	10,840	18,317	*2,331*	460	1,871
20—30 ..	*98,210*	51,518	46,692	*24,247*	21,048	3,199	*66,002*	28,870	37,132	*7,961*	1,600	6,361
30—40 ..	*69,018*	37,853	31,165	*3,810*	3,076	734	*51,508*	31,002	20,506	*13,700*	3,775	9,925
40—50 ..	*52,895*	29,793	23,102	*1,455*	988	467	*33,663*	23,247	10,416	*17,777*	5,558	12,219
50—60 ..	*35,012*	21,072	13,940	*729*	406	323	*17,856*	15,171	2,685	*16,427*	5,495	10,932
60 and over ..	*22,044*	10,544	11,500	*452*	297	155	*7,194*	5,985	1,209	*14,398*	4,262	10,136
Hindu (Brahmanic)	**172,279**	**90,790**	**81,489**	**73,410**	**42,143**	**31,267**	**78,002**	**43,479**	**34,523**	**20,867**	**5,168**	**15,699**
0—1 ..	*3,230*	1,353	1,877	*3,224*	1,353	1,871	*6*	..	6	..	..	..
1—5 ..	*20,298*	5,959	14,339	*20,130*	5,910	14,220	*153*	45	108	*15*	4	11
5—10 ..	*17,636*	7,216	10,420	*15,366*	6,466	8,900	*2,181*	742	1,439	*89*	8	81
10—15 ..	*17,776*	10,881	6,895	*13,106*	9,827	3,279	*4,526*	1,033	3,493	*144*	21	123
15—20 ..	*19,470*	12,109	7,361	*8,646*	8,096	550	*10,108*	3,682	6,426	*716*	331	385
20—30 ..	*38,169*	22,131	16,038	*9,957*	8,348	1,609	*25,587*	13,093	12,494	*2,625*	690	1,935
30—40 ..	*24,244*	14,373	9,871	*1,479*	1,120	359	*18,436*	12,378	6,058	*4,329*	875	3,454
40—50 ..	*15,659*	8,760	6,899	*779*	562	217	*9,829*	7,059	2,770	*5,051*	1,139	3,912
50—60 ..	*9,466*	4,904	4,562	*422*	263	159	*4,667*	3,572	1,095	*4,377*	1,069	3,308
60 and over ..	*6,331*	3,104	3,227	*301*	198	103	*2,509*	1,875	634	*3,521*	1,031	2,490
Adi-Hindu ..	**79,839**	**41,120**	**38,719**	**19,867**	**12,800**	**7,067**	**30,759**	**17,953**	**12,806**	**29,213**	**10,367**	**18,846**
0—1 ..	*1,351*	732	619	*1,334*	719	615	*17*	13	4	..	..	..
1—5 ..	*6,104*	3,360	2,744	*5,958*	3,277	2,681	*139*	80	59	*7*	3	4
5—10 ..	*5,722*	3,284	2,438	*5,007*	3,065	1,942	*689*	213	476	*26*	6	20
10—15 ..	*4,198*	2,893	1,305	*3,658*	2,520	1,138	*493*	368	125	*47*	5	42
15—20 ..	*6,526*	2,785	3,741	*1,686*	1,467	219	*3,569*	1,280	2,289	*1,271*	38	1,233
20—30 ..	*14,623*	6,867	7,756	*1,607*	1,395	212	*9,954*	5,258	4,696	*3,062*	214	2,848
30—40 ..	*14,295*	7,356	6,939	*346*	249	97	*8,785*	5,307	3,478	*5,164*	1,800	3,364
40—50 ..	*11,548*	6,441	5,107	*157*	66	91	*4,348*	3,121	1,227	*7,043*	3,254	3,789
50—60 ..	*8,624*	4,789	3,835	*88*	24	64	*1,833*	1,496	337	*6,703*	3,269	3,434
60 and over ..	*6,848*	2,613	4,235	*26*	18	8	*932*	817	115	*5,890*	1,778	4,112
Arya ..	**382**	**196**	**186**	**96**	**52**	**44**	**259**	**133**	**126**	**27**	**11**	**16**
0—1 ..	*25*	13	12	*25*	13	12	..	..	..	..	..	..
1—5 ..	*42*	32	10	*40*	30	10	*2*	2	..	..	..	..
5—10 ..	*14*	2	12	*12*	2	10	*2*	..	2	..	..	..
10—15 ..	*13*	2	11	*12*	2	10	*1*	..	1	..	..	..
15—20 ..	*8*	4	4	*2*	2	..	*5*	1	4	*1*	1	..
20—30 ..	*13*	4	9	..	..	..	*8*	2	6	*5*	2	3
30—40 ..	*48*	25	23	*1*	..	1	*43*	25	18	*4*	..	4
40—50 ..	*72*	39	33	*2*	1	1	*64*	36	28	*6*	2	4
50—60 ..	*65*	29	36	*2*	2	..	*57*	24	33	*6*	3	3
60 and over ..	*82*	46	36	..	..	..	*77*	43	34	*5*	3	2
Brahmo ..	**77**	**44**	**33**	**20**	**10**	**10**	**43**	**30**	**13**	**14**	**4**	**10**
0—1 ..	*1*	..	1	*1*	..	1	..	..	..	..	..	..
1—5 ..	*9*	3	6	*9*	3	6	..	..	..	..	..	..
5—10 ..	*5*	3	2	*2*	2	..	*3*	1	2	..	..	..
10—15 ..	*5*	3	2	*2*	1	1	*3*	2	1	..	..	..
15—20 ..	*8*	3	5	*2*	1	1	*5*	2	3	*1*	..	1
20—30 ..	*17*	8	9	*1*	..	1	*11*	8	3	*5*	..	3
30—40 ..	*12*	9	3	..	..	..	*7*	6	1	*5*	3	2
40—50 ..	*18*	15	3	*3*	3	..	*12*	11	1	*3*	1	2
50—60 ..	*2*	..	2	..	..	..	*2*	..	2	..	..	..
60 and over ..	..	..	..	..	..	..	..	..	..	..	..	..
Jain ..	**312**	**194**	**118**	**113**	**80**	**33**	**131**	**84**	**47**	**68**	**30**	**38**
0—1 ..	*8*	3	5	*8*	3	5	..	..	..	..	..	..
1—5 ..	*23*	11	12	*18*	11	7	*5*	..	5	..	..	..
5—10 ..	*23*	21	2	*18*	18	..	*5*	3	2	..	..	..
10—15 ..	*23*	18	5	*16*	16	..	*7*	2	5	..	..	..
15—20 ..	*26*	15	11	*15*	10	5	*11*	5	6	..	..	..
20—30 ..	*54*	33	21	*23*	10	13	*26*	20	6	*5*	3	2
30—40 ..	*48*	35	13	*9*	7	2	*33*	26	7	*6*	2	4
40—50 ..	*43*	23	20	*6*	5	1	*20*	14	6	*17*	4	13
50—60 ..	*33*	16	17	..	..	..	*13*	8	5	*20*	8	12
60 and over ..	*31*	19	12	..	..	..	*11*	6	5	*20*	13	7
Sikh ..	**1,002**	**690**	**312**	**447**	**315**	**132**	**503**	**353**	**150**	**52**	**22**	**30**
0—1 ..	*13*	10	3	*13*	10	3	..	..	..	..	..	..
1—5 ..	*76*	52	24	*73*	49	24	*3*	3	..	..	..	..
5—10 ..	*63*	35	28	*58*	33	25	*5*	2	3	..	..	..
10—15 ..	*95*	33	62	*77*	29	48	*18*	4	14	..	..	..
15—20 ..	*154*	114	40	*77*	69	8	*76*	45	31	*1*	..	1
20—30 ..	*314*	237	77	*124*	110	14	*182*	126	56	*8*	1	7
30—40 ..	*139*	100	39	*25*	15	10	*106*	81	25	*8*	4	4
40—50 ..	*86*	65	21	..	..	..	*75*	58	17	*11*	7	4
50—60 ..	*31*	21	10	..	..	..	*19*	16	3	*12*	5	7
60 and over ..	*31*	23	8	..	..	..	*19*	18	1	*12*	5	7

TABLE VII.

Part III.—Cities.

Hyderabad City.

Religion and Age	POPULATION			UNMARRIED			MARRIED			WIDOWED		
	Persons	Males	Females	Persons	Males	Females	Persons	Males	Females	Persons	Males	Females
1	2	3	4	5	6	7	8	9	10	11	12	13
Muslim ..	192,343	103,095	89,248	73,594	45,954	27,640	97,630	52,164	45,466	21,119	4,977	6,142
0—1 ..	3,468	1,806	1,662	3,460	1,800	1,660	8	6	2	..	..	..
1—5 ..	15,912	8,091	7,821	15,826	8,042	7,784	77	45	32	9	4	5
5—10 ..	16,764	8,865	7,899	16,396	8,740	7,656	355	123	232	13	2	11
10—15 ..	16,365	8,806	7,559	15,460	8,582	6,878	873	222	651	32	2	30
15—20 ..	25,262	13,548	11,714	10,407	7,983	2,424	14,540	5,483	9,057	315	82	233
20—30 ..	40,320	19,197	21,123	10,019	9,074	945	28,218	9,487	18,731	2,083	636	1,447
30—40 ..	27,572	14,880	12,692	1,448	1,327	121	22,175	12,528	9,647	3,949	1,025	2,924
40—50 ..	23,293	13,170	10,123	344	261	83	17,616	11,844	5,772	5,333	1,065	4,268
50—60 ..	15,658	10,641	5,017	151	91	60	10,530	9,518	1,012	4,977	1,032	3,945
60 and over ..	7,729	4,091	3,638	83	54	29	3,238	2,908	330	4,408	1,129	3,279
Christian ..	16,123	9,217	6,906	9,534	5,969	3,565	5,238	2,701	2,537	1,351	547	804
0—1 ..	424	230	194	418	229	189	6	1	5	..	..	..
1—5 ..	1,775	1,022	753	1,745	1,008	737	29	14	15	1	..	1
5—10 ..	1,504	659	845	1,449	621	828	53	38	15	2	..	2
10—15 ..	1,860	1,031	829	1,755	974	781	103	57	46	2	..	2
15—20 ..	1,829	1,007	822	1,184	758	426	624	242	382	21	7	14
20—30 ..	3,966	2,633	1,333	2,300	1,943	357	1,524	649	875	142	41	101
30—40 ..	1,686	700	986	451	323	128	1,039	323	716	196	54	142
40—50 ..	1,463	925	538	139	74	65	1,074	774	300	250	77	173
50—60 ..	806	468	338	60	21	39	469	354	115	277	93	184
60 and over ..	810	542	268	33	18	15	317	249	68	460	275	185
Zoroastrian ..	1,092	548	544	533	300	233	467	218	249	92	30	62
0—1 ..	20	9	11	20	9	11	..	..	..	..	..	..
1—5 ..	84	39	45	83	38	45	1	1	..	..	..	..
5—10 ..	82	58	24	75	55	20	7	3	4	..	..	..
10—15 ..	112	52	60	98	48	50	14	4	10	..	..	..
15—20 ..	104	41	63	84	36	48	20	5	15	..	..	..
20—30 ..	174	93	81	98	60	38	71	30	41	5	3	2
30—40 ..	164	75	89	41	28	13	117	45	72	6	2	4
40—50 ..	142	71	71	21	14	7	104	53	51	17	4	13
50—60 ..	116	54	62	4	3	1	87	43	44	25	8	17
60 and over ..	94	56	38	9	9	..	46	34	12	39	13	26
Buddhist ..	38	20	18	12	5	7	23	15	8	3	..	3
0—1 ..	..	..	..	..	..	..	..	..	..	..	..	..
1—5 ..	7	4	3	6	3	3	1	1	..	..	..	..
5—10 ..	2	1	1	..	..	..	2	1	1	..	..	..
10—15 ..	4	2	2	2	1	1	2	1	1	..	..	..
15—20 ..	3	1	2	1	..	1	2	1	1	..	..	..
20—30 ..	11	7	4	3	1	2	8	6	2	..	..	..
30—40 ..	3	1	2	..	..	..	3	1	2	..	..	..
40—50 ..	5	3	2	..	..	..	3	3	..	2	..	2
50—60 ..	3	1	2	..	..	..	2	1	1	1	..	1
60 and over ..	..	..	..	..	..	..	..	..	..	..	..	..
Jew ..	27	11	16	10	4	6	15	6	9	2	1	1
0—1 ..	..	..	..	..	..	..	..	..	..	..	..	..
1—5 ..	3	1	2	3	1	2	..	..	..	..	..	..
5—10 ..	..	..	..	..	..	..	..	..	..	..	..	..
10—15 ..	3	1	2	1	..	1	2	1	1	..	..	..
15—20 ..	3	1	2	..	..	..	3	1	2	..	..	..
20—30 ..	5	2	3	2	1	1	3	1	2	..	..	..
30—40 ..	11	5	6	4	2	2	7	3	4	..	..	..
40—50 ..	1	..	1	..	..	..	..	..	..	1	..	1
50—60 ..	1	1	..	..	..	..	..	..	..	1	1	..
60 and over ..	..	..	..	..	..	..	..	..	..	..	..	..
Tribal ..	3,380	1,698	1,682	945	575	370	2,257	1,074	1,183	178	49	129
0—1 ..	74	35	39	74	35	39	..	..	..	..	..	..
1—5 ..	323	185	138	299	170	129	24	15	9	..	..	..
5—10 ..	290	145	145	234	124	110	54	21	33	2	..	2
10—15 ..	232	109	123	151	80	71	78	28	50	3	1	2
15—20 ..	261	145	116	62	51	11	194	93	101	5	1	4
20—30 ..	544	306	238	113	106	7	410	190	220	21	10	11
30—40 ..	796	294	502	6	5	1	757	279	478	33	10	23
40—50 ..	565	281	284	4	2	2	518	274	244	43	5	38
50—60 ..	207	148	59	2	2	..	177	139	38	28	7	21
60 and over ..	88	50	38	..	..	..	45	35	10	43	15	28

TABLE VII.

Part III.—Cities.

Warangal City.

Religion and Age	POPULATION			UNMARRIED			MARRIED			WIDOWED		
	Persons	Males	Females	Persons	Males	Females	Persons	Males	Females	Persons	Males	Females
1	2	3	4	5	6	7	8	9	10	11	12	13
All Religions ..	62,119	33,326	28,793	23,931	12,757	11,174	32,384	18,606	13,778	5,804	1,963	3,841
0—1 ..	*1,176*	572	604	*1,176*	572	604	..	..	..	..	..	..
1—5 ..	*6,663*	2,895	3,768	*6,476*	2,771	3,705	*183*	123	60	*4*	1	3
5—10 ..	*7,748*	3,212	4,536	*6,395*	3,004	3,391	*1,272*	202	1,070	*81*	6	75
10—15 ..	*8,042*	3,698	4,344	*4,601*	2,358	2,243	*3,339*	1,327	2,012	*102*	13	89
15—20 ..	*7,411*	3,756	3,655	*1,846*	1,110	736	*5,386*	2,626	2,760	*179*	20	159
20—30 ..	*12,091*	6.905	5,186	*1,358*	958	400	*10,156*	5,864	4,292	*577*	83	494
30—40 ..	*6,484*	3,710	2,774	*519*	470	49	*4,939*	2,903	2,036	*1,026*	337	689
40—50 ..	*5,389*	3,594	1,795	*721*	700	21	*3,355*	2,402	953	*1,313*	492	821
50—60 ..	*4,028*	2,872	1,156	*498*	488	10	*2,163*	1,762	401	*1,367*	622	745
60 and over ..	*3,087*	2,112	975	*341*	326	15	*1,591*	1,397	194	*1,155*	389	766
Hindu (Brahmanic)	35,199	18,926	16,273	11,998	6,076	5,922	20,281	12,398	7,883	2,920	452	2,468
0—1 ..	*678*	333	345	*678*	333	345	..	..	..	..	..	..
1—5 ..	*3,865*	1,490	2,375	*3,824*	1,490	2,334	*41*	..	41	..	..	..
5—10 ..	*4,085*	1,726	2,359	*3,532*	1,709	1,823	*534*	17	517	*19*	..	19
10—15 ..	*4,425*	2,648	1,777	*2,294*	1,438	856	*2,093*	1,204	889	*38*	6	32
15—20 ..	*4,769*	2,914	1,855	*768*	555	213	*3,906*	2,344	1,562	*95*	15	80
20—30 ..	*8,477*	5,146	3,331	*721*	403	318	*7,407*	4,705	2,702	*349*	38	311
30—40 ..	*3,652*	1,968	1,684	*108*	87	21	*3,006*	1,803	1,203	*538*	78	460
40—50 ..	*2,430*	1,273	1,157	*32*	30	2	*1,757*	1,152	605	*641*	91	550
50—60 ..	*1,521*	781	740	*19*	18	1	*912*	665	247	*590*	98	492
60 and over ..	*1,297*	647	650	*22*	13	9	*625*	508	117	*650*	126	524
Adi-Hindu ..	11,336	5,812	5,524	4,740	2,508	2,232	4,853	2,142	2,711	1,743	1,162	581
0—1 ..	*208*	96	112	*208*	96	112	..	..	..	..	..	..
1—5 ..	*1,098*	448	650	*1,074*	436	638	*24*	12	12	..	..	..
5—10 ..	*1,855*	410	1,445	*1,259*	370	889	*544*	39	505	*52*	1	51
10—15 ..	*1,522*	330	1,192	*812*	264	548	*654*	63	591	*56*	3	53
15—20 ..	*691*	223	468	*96*	83	13	*526*	139	387	*69*	1	68
20—30 ..	*1,172*	390	782	*109*	96	13	*928*	264	664	*135*	30	105
30—40 ..	*1,248*	854	394	*239*	233	6	*709*	388	321	*300*	233	67
40—50 ..	*1,247*	1,015	232	*363*	357	6	*529*	384	145	*355*	274	81
50—60 ..	*1,321*	1,176	145	*369*	365	4	*470*	412	58	*482*	399	83
60 and over ..	*974*	870	104	*211*	208	3	*469*	441	28	*294*	221	73
Sikh ..	114	72	42	56	38	18	51	32	19	7	2	5
0—1 ..	*2*	1	1	*2*	1	1	..	..	..	..	..	..
1—5 ..	*9*	5	4	*9*	5	4	..	..	..	..	..	..
5—10 ..	*12*	8	4	*12*	8	4	..	..	..	..	..	..
10—15 ..	*16*	9	7	*14*	8	6	*2*	1	1	..	..	..
15—20 ..	*15*	10	5	*11*	8	3	*4*	2	2	..	..	..
20—30 ..	*21*	13	8	*7*	7	..	*14*	6	8	..	..	..
30—40 ..	*9*	6	3	*1*	1	..	*8*	5	3	..	..	..
40—50 ..	*8*	6	2	..	..	..	*8*	6	2	..	..	..
50—60 ..	*8*	4	4	..	..	..	*5*	3	2	*3*	1	2
60 and over ..	*14*	10	4	..	..	..	*10*	9	1	*4*	1	3
Muslim ..	14,460	8,003	6,457	6,641	3,849	2,792	6,753	3,817	2,936	1,066	337	729
0—1 ..	*265*	123	142	*265*	123	142	..	..	..	..	..	..
1—5 ..	*1,534*	851	683	*1,414*	741	673	*116*	109	7	*4*	1	3
5—10 ..	*1,688*	988	700	*1,500*	845	655	*178*	138	40	*10*	5	5
10—15 ..	*1,944*	650	1,294	*1,374*	597	777	*562*	49	513	*8*	4	4
15—20 ..	*1,819*	570	1,249	*906*	441	465	*899*	125	774	*14*	4	10
20—30 ..	*2,232*	1,280	952	*483*	436	47	*1,663*	830	833	*86*	14	72
30—40 ..	*1,453*	825	628	*164*	147	17	*1,113*	655	458	*176*	23	153
40—50 ..	*1,627*	1,260	367	*321*	311	10	*1,003*	823	180	*303*	126	177
50—60 ..	*1,125*	883	242	*107*	104	3	*743*	658	85	*275*	121	154
60 and over ..	*773*	573	200	*107*	104	3	*476*	430	46	*190*	39	151
Christian ..	748	357	391	391	221	170	318	131	187	39	5	34
0—1 ..	*14*	14	..	*14*	14	..	..	..	..	..	..	..
1—5 ..	*127*	85	42	*125*	83	42	*2*	2	..	..	..	..
5—10 ..	*76*	59	17	*61*	52	9	*15*	7	8	..	..	..
10—15 ..	*106*	45	61	*82*	35	47	*24*	10	14	..	..	..
15—20 ..	*96*	28	68	*60*	19	41	*35*	9	26	*1*	..	1
20—30 ..	*140*	47	93	*34*	12	22	*105*	35	70	*1*	..	1
30—40 ..	*75*	26	49	*6*	2	4	*65*	23	42	*4*	1	3
40—50 ..	*53*	23	30	*5*	2	3	*39*	21	18	*9*	..	9
50—60 ..	*38*	20	18	*3*	1	2	*24*	17	7	*11*	2	9
60 and over ..	*23*	10	13	*1*	1	..	*9*	7	2	*13*	2	11

TABLE VII.

Part III.—Cities.

Warangal City.

Religion and Age	POPULATION			UNMARRIED			MARRIED			WIDOWED		
	Persons	Males	Females	Persons	Males	Females	Persons	Males	Females	Persons	Males	Females
1	2	3	4	5	6	7	8	9	10	11	12	13
Zoroastrian ..	7	7	..	1	1	..	6	6	..	..	..	..
0—1 ..	..	..	..	..	..	..	..	..	..	..	..	..
1—5 ..	..	..	..	..	..	..	..	..	..	..	..	..
5—10 ..	1	1	..	..	..	..	1	1	..	..	..	..
10—15 ..	1	1	..	1	1	..	..	..	..	..	..	..
15—20 ..	..	..	..	..	..	..	..	..	..	..	..	..
20—30 ..	1	1	..	..	..	..	1	1	..	..	..	..
30—40 ..	2	2	..	..	..	..	2	2	..	..	..	..
40—50 ..	1	1	..	..	..	..	1	1	..	..	..	..
50—60 ..	1	1	..	..	..	..	1	1	..	..	..	..
60 and over ..	..	..	..	..	..	..	..	..	..	..	..	..
Tribal ..	255	149	106	104	64	40	122	80	42	29	5	24
0—1 ..	9	5	4	9	5	4	..	..	..	..	..	..
1—5 ..	30	16	14	30	16	14	..	..	..	..	..	..
5—10 ..	31	20	11	31	20	11	..	..	..	..	..	..
10—15 ..	28	15	13	24	15	9	4	..	4	..	..	..
15—20 ..	21	11	10	5	4	1	16	7	9	..	..	..
20—30 ..	48	28	20	4	4	..	38	23	15	6	1	5
30—40 ..	45	29	16	1	..	1	36	27	9	8	2	6
40—50 ..	23	16	7	..	..		18	15	3	5	1	4
50—60 ..	14	7	7	..	..	..	8	6	2	6	1	5
60 and over ..	6	2	4	..	..	..	2	2	..	4	..	4

TABLE VII.
AGE, SEX & CIVIL CONDITION.

Aurangabad City.

TABLE VII.

Part III.—Cities.

Religion and Age	POPULATION			UNMARRIED			MARRIED			WIDOWED		
	Persons	Males	Females	Persons	Males	Females	Persons	Males	Females	Persons	Males	Females
1	2	3	4	5	6	7	8	9	10	11	12	13
All Religions	**36,870**	**19,622**	**17,248**	**12,825**	**8,111**	**4,714**	**20,546**	**10,661**	**9,885**	**3,499**	**850**	**2,649**
0— 1	*735*	346	389	*735*	346	389	..	..	..	..	..	..
1— 5	*2,987*	1,490	1,497	*2,968*	1,490	1,478	*19*	..	19	..	..	..
5—10	*3,138*	1,569	1,569	*2,787*	1,488	1,299	*346*	78	268	*5*	3	2
10—15	*3,812*	2,154	1,658	*2,225*	1,358	867	*1,575*	791	784	*12*	5	7
15—20	*5,876*	3,118	2,758	*1,427*	1,188	239	*4,400*	1,913	2,487	*49*	17	32
20—30	*8,743*	4,908	3,835	*1,502*	1,360	142	*7,003*	3,479	3,524	*238*	69	169
30—40	*4,907*	2,756	2,151	*647*	622	25	*3,612*	1,971	1,641	*648*	163	485
40—50	*3,052*	1,628	1,424	*252*	160	92	*1,953*	1,272	681	*847*	196	651
50—60	*1,953*	927	1,026	*134*	26	108	*992*	722	270	*827*	179	648
60 and over	*1,667*	726	941	*148*	73	75	*646*	435	211	*873*	218	655
Hindu (Brahmanic)	**15,520**	**8,372**	**7,148**	**5,395**	**3,574**	**1,821**	**8,469**	**4,369**	**4,100**	**1,656**	**429**	**1,227**
0— 1	*327*	166	161	*327*	166	161	..	..	..	..	..	..
1— 5	*1,319*	670	649	*1,305*	670	635	*14*	..	14	..	..	..
5—10	*1,364*	709	655	*1,161*	647	514	*200*	60	140	*3*	2	1
10—15	*1,294*	687	607	*871*	566	305	*417*	119	298	*6*	2	4
15—20	*3,194*	1,442	1,752	*749*	622	127	*2,423*	818	1,610	*22*	7	15
20—30	*3,393*	2,163	1,230	*697*	632	65	*2,561*	1,494	1,067	*135*	37	98
30—40	*1,903*	1,133	770	*222*	215	7	*1,398*	852	546	*283*	66	217
40—50	*1,288*	675	613	*29*	24	5	*834*	554	280	*425*	97	328
50—60	*813*	423	390	*15*	13	2	*405*	305	100	*393*	105	288
60 and over	*625*	304	321	*19*	19	..	*217*	172	45	*389*	113	276
Adi-Hindu	**3,212**	**1,494**	**1,718**	**985**	**629**	**356**	**1,957**	**827**	**1,130**	**270**	**38**	**232**
0— 1	*60*	31	29	*60*	31	20	..	..	..	..	..	..
1— 5	*243*	136	107	*240*	136	104	*3*	..	3	..	..	..
5—10	*224*	126	98	*177*	114	63	*45*	11	34	*2*	1	1
10—15	*426*	105	321	*138*	82	56	*286*	22	264	*2*	1	1
15—20	*383*	76	307	*36*	28	8	*342*	46	296	*5*	2	3
20—30	*659*	394	265	*34*	20	14	*597*	372	225	*28*	2	26
30—40	*445*	274	171	*105*	101	4	*302*	169	133	*38*	4	34
40—50	*395*	246	149	*143*	115	28	*187*	119	68	*65*	12	53
50—60	*196*	63	133	*50*	..	50	*81*	55	26	*65*	8	57
60 and over	*181*	43	138	*2*	2	..	*114*	33	81	*65*	8	57
Arya	**145**	**60**	**85**	**31**	**15**	**16**	**89**	**39**	**50**	**25**	**6**	**19**
0— 1	*2*	1	1	*2*	1	1	..	..	..	..	..	..
1— 5	*14*	10	4	*14*	10	4	..	..	..	..	..	..
5—10	*14*	5	9	*9*	2	7	*5*	3	2	..	..	..
10—15	*17*	8	9	*3*	2	1	*13*	6	7	*1*	..	1
15—20	*11*	7	4	*2*	..	2	*9*	7	2	..	..	..
20—30	*26*	14	12	*1*	..	1	*23*	13	10	*2*	1	1
30—40	*12*	3	9	..	..	..	*7*	1	6	*5*	2	3
40—50	*20*	5	15	..	..	..	*13*	2	11	*7*	3	4
50—60	*15*	3	12	..	..	..	*10*	3	7	*5*	..	5
60 and over	*14*	4	10	..	..	..	*9*	4	5	*5*	..	5
Brahmo	**2**	**1**	**1**	..	..	..	**2**	**1**	**1**	..	..	..
0— 1	..	..	..	..	..	..	..	..	..	..	..	..
1— 5	..	..	..	..	..	..	..	..	..	..	..	..
5—10	..	..	..	..	..	..	..	..	..	..	..	..
10—15	..	..	..	..	..	..	..	..	..	..	..	..
15—20	..	..	..	..	..	..	..	..	..	..	..	..
20—30	*2*	1	1	..	..	..	*2*	1	1	..	..	..
30—40	..	..	..	..	..	..	..	..	..	..	..	..
40—50	..	..	..	..	..	..	..	..	..	..	..	..
50—60	..	..	..	..	..	..	..	..	..	..	..	..
60 and over	..	..	..	..	..	..	..	..	..	..	..	..
Jain	**361**	**215**	**146**	**88**	**63**	**25**	**232**	**135**	**97**	**41**	**17**	**24**
0— 1	*8*	5	3	*8*	5	3	..	..	..	..	..	..
1— 5	*29*	13	16	*29*	13	16	..	..	..	..	..	..
5—10	*23*	16	7	*17*	13	4	*6*	3	3	..	..	..
10—15	*25*	18	7	*15*	13	2	*10*	5	5	..	..	..
15—20	*40*	24	16	*9*	9	..	*29*	14	15	*2*	1	1
20—30	*95*	52	43	*6*	6	..	*85*	45	40	*4*	1	3
30—40	*70*	46	24	*4*	4	..	*58*	38	20	*8*	4	4
40—50	*33*	17	16	..	..	..	*20*	12	8	*13*	5	8
50—60	*21*	13	8	..	..	..	*12*	9	3	*9*	4	5
60 and over	*17*	11	6	..	..	..	*12*	9	3	*5*	2	3

TABLE VII.

Part III.—Cities.

Aurangabad City.

Religion and Age	POPULATION			UNMARRIED			MARRIED			WIDOWED		
	Persons	Males	Females	Persons	Males	Females	Persons	Males	Females	Persons	Males	Females
1	2	3	4	5	6	7	8	9	10	11	12	13
Sikh ..	**374**	**296**	**78**	**132**	**115**	**17**	**196**	**148**	**48**	**46**	**33**	**13**
0— 1 ..	4	3	1	4	3	1	..	..	..	..	..	..
1— 5 ..	50	46	4	48	46	2	2	..	2	..	..	..
5—10 ..	28	21	7	23	20	3	5	1	4	..	..	..
10—15 ..	40	30	10	27	20	7	13	10	3	..	..	..
15—20 ..	41	25	16	17	13	4	23	11	12	1	1	..
20—30 ..	79	61	18	12	12	..	62	46	16	5	3	2
30—40 ..	55	43	12	1	1	..	44	38	6	10	4	6
40—50 ..	43	35	8	..	..	..	28	24	4	15	11	4
50—60 ..	23	22	1	..	..	..	16	15	1	7	7	..
60 and over ..	11	10	1	..	..	..	3	3	..	8	7	1
Muslim ..	**16,104**	**8,567**	**7,537**	**5,859**	**3,535**	**2,324**	**8,883**	**4,744**	**4,139**	**1,362**	**288**	**1,074**
0— 1 ..	315	135	180	315	135	180	..	..	..	..	..	..
1— 5 ..	1,290	592	698	1,290	592	698	..	..	..	..	..	..
5—10 ..	1,451	677	774	1,370	677	693	81	..	81	..	..	..
10—15 ..	1,884	1,196	688	1,154	665	489	727	529	198	3	2	1
15—20 ..	1,994	1,351	643	548	450	98	1,428	895	533	18	6	12
20—30 ..	4,302	2,070	2,232	691	629	62	3,548	1,417	2,131	63	24	39
30—40 ..	2,103	1,191	912	315	301	14	1,545	842	703	243	48	195
40—50 ..	1,144	621	523	30	21	9	818	533	285	296	67	229
50—60 ..	814	389	425	19	13	6	453	322	131	342	54	288
60 and over ..	807	345	462	127	52	75	283	206	77	397	87	310
Christian ..	**788**	**440**	**348**	**205**	**104**	**101**	**502**	**303**	**199**	**81**	**33**	**48**
0— 1 ..	..	..	..	..	..	..	..	..	..	..	..	..
1— 5 ..	2	1	1	2	1	1	..	..	..	..	..	..
5—10 ..	1	1	..	1	1	..	..	..	..	..	..	..
10—15 ..	101	100	1	..	..	..	101	100	1	..	..	..
15—20 ..	175	175	..	50	50	..	125	125	..	..	..	..
20—30 ..	128	127	1	52	52	..	76	75	1	..	..	..
30—40 ..	255	34	221	..	..	..	198	1	197	57	33	24
40—50 ..	75	2	73	50	..	50	2	2	..	23	..	23
50—60 ..	51	..	51	50	..	50	..	..	..	1	..	1
60 and over ..	..	..	..	..	..	..	..	..	..	..	..	..
Zoroastrian ..	**197**	**101**	**96**	**90**	**49**	**41**	**99**	**50**	**49**	**8**	**2**	**6**
0— 1 ..	9	3	6	9	3	6	..	..	..	..	..	..
1— 5 ..	26	12	14	26	12	14	..	..	..	..	..	..
5—10 ..	29	10	19	25	10	15	4	..	4	..	..	..
10—15 ..	19	5	14	11	5	6	8	..	8	..	..	..
15—20 ..	23	14	9	12	12	..	11	2	9	..	..	..
20—30 ..	24	12	12	7	7	..	17	5	12	..	..	..
30—40 ..	31	20	11	..	..	..	27	18	9	4	2	2
40—50 ..	17	12	5	..	..	..	17	12	5	..	..	..
50—60 ..	8	5	3	..	..	..	7	5	2	1	..	1
60 and over ..	11	8	3	..	..	..	8	8	..	3	..	3
Tribal ..	**167**	**76**	**91**	**40**	**27**	**13**	**117**	**45**	**72**	**10**	**4**	**6**
0— 1 ..	10	2	8	10	2	8	..	..	..	..	..	..
1— 5 ..	14	10	4	14	10	4	..	..	..	..	..	..
5—10 ..	4	4	..	4	4	..	..	..	..	..	..	..
10—15 ..	6	5	1	6	5	1	..	..	..	..	..	..
15—20 ..	15	4	11	4	4	..	10	..	10	1	..	1
20—30 ..	35	14	21	2	2	..	32	11	21	1	1	..
30—40 ..	33	12	21	..	..	..	33	12	21	..	..	..
40—50 ..	37	15	22	..	..	..	34	14	20	3	1	2
50—60 ..	12	9	3	..	..	..	8	8	..	4	1	3
60 and over ..	1	1	..	..	..	..	..	..	..	1	1	..

TABLE VII.

Part III.—Cities.

Gulbarga City.

Religion and Age	POPULATION			UNMARRIED			MARRIED			WIDOWED		
	Persons	Males	Females	Persons	Males	Females	Persons	Males	Females	Persons	Males	Females
1	2	3	4	5	6	7	8	9	10	11	12	13
All Religions ..	41,083	21,567	19,516	16,467	10,008	6,459	20,210	10,669	9,541	4,406	890	3,516
0— 1 ..	*1,215*	632	583	*1,187*	621	566	*21*	8	13	*7*	3	4
1— 5 ..	*5,580*	2,485	3,095	*5,265*	2,328	2,937	*280*	150	130	*35*	7	28
5—10 ..	*4,480*	2,586	1,894	*3,929*	2,368	1,561	*513*	210	303	*38*	8	30
10—15 ..	*3,616*	2,367	1,249	*2,685*	2,072	613	*898*	281	617	*33*	14	19
15—20 ..	*4,030*	2,012	2,018	*1,573*	1,299	274	*2,330*	694	1,636	*127*	19	108
20—30 ..	*8,470*	4,141	4,329	*1,335*	1,074	261	*6,611*	2,952	3,659	*524*	115	409
30—40 ..	*5,745*	3,197	2,548	*216*	145	71	*4,727*	2,889	1,838	*802*	163	639
40—50 ..	*3,717*	2,064	1,653	*75*	51	24	*2,644*	1,865	779	*998*	148	850
50—60 ..	*2,347*	1,172	1,175	*111*	27	84	*1,342*	981	361	*894*	164	730
60 and over ..	*1,883*	911	972	*91*	23	68	*844*	639	205	*948*	249	699
Hindu (Brahmanic)	17,509	9,465	8,044	6,529	4,214	2,315	8,775	4,777	3,998	2,205	474	1,731
0— 1 ..	*496*	256	240	*496*	256	240	..	..	..	..	..	..
1— 5 ..	*1,725*	886	839	*1,725*	886	839	..	..	..	..	..	..
5—10 ..	*1,854*	1,034	820	*1,613*	948	665	*238*	85	153	*3*	1	2
10—15 ..	*1,798*	1,049	749	*1,267*	879	388	*518*	165	353	*13*	5	8
15—20 ..	*1,960*	981	979	*738*	635	103	*1,134*	338	796	*88*	8	80
20—30 ..	*3,807*	1,985	1,822	*583*	503	80	*2,950*	1,429	1,521	*274*	53	221
30—40 ..	*2,531*	1,507	1,024	*64*	64	..	*2,055*	1,353	702	*412*	90	322
40—50 ..	*1,610*	901	709	*24*	24	..	*1,074*	784	290	*512*	93	419
50—60 ..	*948*	487	461	*12*	12	..	*494*	374	120	*442*	101	341
60 and over ..	*780*	379	401	*7*	7	..	*312*	249	63	*461*	123	338
Adi-Hindu ..	3,428	1,715	1,713	1,240	746	494	1,860	908	952	328	61	267
0— 1 ..	*101*	60	41	*101*	60	41	..	..	..	..	..	..
1— 5 ..	*415*	240	175	*387*	224	163	*26*	16	10	*2*	..	2
5—10 ..	*388*	215	173	*336*	215	121	*48*	..	48	*4*	..	4
10—15 ..	*315*	169	146	*223*	153	70	*87*	15	72	*5*	1	4
15—20 ..	*204*	66	138	*55*	48	7	*141*	16	125	*8*	2	6
20—30 ..	*569*	153	416	*74*	33	41	*458*	111	347	*37*	9	28
30—40 ..	*614*	282	332	*47*	7	40	*499*	264	235	*68*	11	57
40—50 ..	*392*	260	132	*9*	2	7	*315*	249	66	*68*	9	59
50—60 ..	*252*	157	95	*3*	1	2	*181*	146	35	*68*	10	58
60 and over ..	*178*	113	65	*5*	3	2	*105*	91	14	*68*	19	40
Jain ..	181	88	93	69	37	32	93	44	49	19	7	12
0— 1 ..	*7*	3	4	*4*	1	3	*2*	1	1	*1*	1	..
1— 5 ..	*15*	4	11	*15*	4	11	..	..	..	..	..	..
5—10 ..	*19*	10	9	*17*	9	8	*2*	1	1	..	..	..
10—15 ..	*18*	6	12	*13*	6	7	*5*	..	5	..	..	..
15—20 ..	*23*	11	12	*8*	6	2	*14*	5	9	*1*	..	1
20—30 ..	*46*	25	21	*9*	9	..	*32*	13	19	*5*	3	2
30—40 ..	*25*	16	9	*1*	1	..	*21*	13	8	*3*	2	1
40—50 ..	*15*	10	5	*1*	1	..	*11*	8	3	*3*	1	2
50—60 ..	*7*	2	5	..	..	..	*5*	2	3	*2*	..	2
60 and over ..	*6*	1	5	*1*	..	1	*1*	1	..	*4*	..	4
Sikh ..	4	4	..	2	2	..	1	1	..	1	1	..
0— 1 ..	..	..	..	..	..	..	..	..	..	..	..	..
1— 5 ..	..	..	..	..	..	..	..	..	..	..	..	..
5—10 ..	..	..	..	..	..	..	..	..	..	..	..	..
10—15 ..	*1*	1	..	*1*	1	..	..	..	..	..	..	..
15—20 ..	*1*	1	..	..	..	..	*1*	1	..	..	..	..
20—30 ..	..	..	..	..	..	..	..	..	..	*1*	1	..
30—40 ..	*1*	1	..	..	..	..	..	..	..	..	..	..
40—50 ..	*1*	1	..	*1*	1	..	..	..	..	..	..	..
50—60 ..	..	..	..	..	..	..	..	..	..	..	..	..
60 and over ..	..	..	..	..	..	..	..	..	..	..	..	..
Muslim ..	19,792	10,228	9,564	8,528	4,978	3,550	9,442	4,925	4,517	1,822	325	1,497
0— 1 ..	*607*	310	297	*583*	302	281	*19*	7	12	*5*	1	4
1— 5 ..	*3,406*	1,347	2,059	*3,123*	1,207	1,916	*252*	134	118	*31*	6	25
5—10 ..	*2,194*	1,322	872	*1,939*	1,192	747	*225*	124	101	*30*	6	24
10—15 ..	*1,453*	1,133	320	*1,156*	1,029	127	*286*	100	186	*11*	4	7
15—20 ..	*1,825*	947	878	*763*	607	156	*1,035*	333	702	*27*	7	20
20—30 ..	*4,016*	1,963	2,053	*658*	523	135	*3,157*	1,397	1,760	*201*	43	158
30—40 ..	*2,555*	1,380	1,175	*94*	68	26	*2,148*	1,257	891	*313*	55	258
40—50 ..	*1,683*	886	797	*38*	23	15	*1,236*	820	416	*409*	43	366
50—60 ..	*1,138*	524	614	*96*	14	82	*660*	457	203	*382*	53	329
60 and over ..	*915*	416	499	*78*	13	65	*424*	296	128	*413*	107	306

TABLE VII.

Part III.—Cities.

Gulbarga City.

Religion and Age	POPULATION			UNMARRIED			MARRIED			WIDOWED		
	Persons	Males	Females	Persons	Males	Females	Persons	Males	Females	Persons	Males	Females
1	2	8	4	5	6	7	8	9	10	11	12	18
Christian ..	**145**	**50**	**95**	**90**	**25**	**65**	**27**	**6**	**21**	**28**	**19**	**9**
0— 1 ..	*4*	3	1	*3*	2	1	..	..	..	*1*	1	..
1— 5 ..	*15*	6	9	*14*	6	8	..	..	..	*1*	..	1
5—10 ..	*25*	5	20	*24*	4	20	..	..	..	*1*	1	..
10—15 ..	*30*	8	22	*25*	4	21	*1*	..	1	*4*	4	..
15—20 ..	*16*	5	11	*8*	2	6	*5*	1	4	*3*	2	1
20—30 ..	*26*	11	15	*8*	4	4	*12*	1	11	*6*	6	..
30—40 ..	*15*	8	7	*7*	3	4	*3*	1	2	*5*	4	1
40—50 ..	*11*	3	8	*1*	..	1	*5*	2	3	*5*	1	4
50—60 ..	*1*	1	..	..	..	..	*1*	1	..	..	..	..
60 and over ..	*2*	..	2	..	..	..	..	..	..	*2*	..	2
Zoroastrian ..	**16**	**9**	**7**	**5**	**2**	**3**	**9**	**5**	**4**	**2**	**2**	..
0— 1 ..	..	..	..	..	..	..	..	..	..	..	..	..
1— 5 ..	*2*	..	2	..	..	..	*2*	..	2	..	..	..
5—10 ..	..	..	..	..	..	..	..	..	..	..	..	..
10—15 ..	*1*	1	..	..	..	..	*1*	1	..	..	..	..
15—20 ..	..	..	..	..	..	..	..	..	..	..	..	..
20—30 ..	*4*	2	2	*2*	1	1	*1*	..	1	*1*	1	..
30—40 ..	*3*	2	1	*2*	1	1	*1*	1	..	..	..	..
40—50 ..	*4*	2	2	*1*	..	1	*2*	1	1	*1*	1	..
50—60 ..	*1*	1	..	..	..	..	*1*	1	..	..	..	..
60 and over ..	*1*	1	..	..	..	..	*1*	1	..	..	..	..
Tribal ..	**8**	**8**	..	**4**	**4**	..	**3**	**3**	..	**1**	**1**	..
0— 1 ..	..	..	..	..	..	..	..	..	..	..	..	..
1— 5 ..	*2*	2	..	*1*	1	..	..	..	..	*1*	1	..
5—10 ..	..	..	..	..	..	..	..	..	..	..	..	..
10—15 ..	..	..	..	..	..	..	..	..	..	..	..	..
15—20 ..	*1*	1	..	*1*	1	..	..	..	..	..	..	..
20—30 ..	*2*	2	..	*1*	1	..	*1*	1	..	..	..	..
30—40 ..	*1*	1	..	*1*	1	..	..	..	..	..	..	..
40—50 ..	*1*	1	..	..	..	..	*1*	1	..	..	..	..
50—60 ..	..	..	..	..	..	..	..	..	..	..	..	..
60 and over ..	*1*	1	..	..	..	..	*1*	1	..	..	..	..

Table VIII.

AGE, SEX AND CIVIL CONDITION FOR SELECTED CASTES, RACES AND TRIBES

NOTE :— 1. This table does not deal with the whole population; but with certain castes, races and tribes for which details cannot be obtained from the Imperial Table VII. The selection of a caste is either based on account of its numerical strength or its local importance.

2. Figures are given here for the State as a whole and for the two natural divisions, viz., Telangana (including Hyderabad City) and Marathwara.

3. The age-periods as shown in this table are as obtained from the actual returns in the Enumeration Books and hence cannot collaborate with the age-periods in the Imperial Table VII, which have been smoothed into quinary groups.

4. The attention of the reader is drawn to the Imperial Table XVII (Fly-leaf) for those castes which have been grouped into one familiar caste name.

TABLE VIII.
AGE, SEX & CIVIL CONDITION FOR SELECTED CASTES, RACES & TRIBES.

TABLE
Age, Sex and Civil Condition for selected

S. No.	Caste, Race and Tribe	Locality	Sex	Population dealt with	UNMARRIED						
					Total	0—6	7—13	14—16	17—23	24—43	44 and over
1	2	3	4	5	6	7	8	9	10	11	12
	BRAHMANIC HINDU.										
1	Balija ..	*Hyderabad State	Males ..	21,514	9,298	1,983	2,192	1,530	1,510	1,026	1,057
			Females .	17,786	6,164	2,051	1,792	1,288	438	385	210
2	Bender (Bedar) ..	Hyderabad State .	Males ..	119,307	60,458	19,404	20,157	12,747	3,561	2,915	1,674
			Females .	18,467	35,591	14,110	13,369	7,317	505	219	71
		Telangana ..	Males ..	*1,264*	*530*	270	126	64	34	30	6
			Females .	*950*	*235*	122	88	16	14	..	..
		Marathwara ..	Males ..	*118,043*	*59,928*	19,134	20,081	12,683	3,527	2,885	1,668
			Females .	*117,517*	*35,356*	13,988	13,286	7,301	491	219	71
3	Bhat (Bhatraj) ..	Hyderabad State .	Males ..	9,522	3,647	1,245	1,185	476	389	280	72
			Females .	7,748	2,565	1,808	528	113	53	35	28
		Telangana ..	Males ..	*6,948*	*2,619*	871	846	352	318	172	60
			Females .	*5,543*	*1,990*	1,563	267	65	38	29	28
		Marathwara ..	Males ..	*2,574*	*1,028*	374	330	124	71	108	12
			Females .	*2,205*	*575*	245	261	48	15	6	..
4	Bhoi (Besta) ..	Hyderabad State .	Males ..	141,869	53,329	16,347	14,188	10,082	6,669	3,242	2,801
			Females .	143,404	39,811	16,652	14,924	4,024	2,596	1,126	489
		Telangana ..	Males ..	*62,389*	*25,427*	8,383	6,592	4,228	2,869	1,837	1,518
			Females .	*64,793*	*17,433*	7,204	5,055	2,774	1,261	778	366
		Marathwara ..	Males ..	*79,480*	*27,902*	7,964	7,596	5,854	3,800	1,405	1,288
			Females .	*78,611*	*22,378*	9,448	9,869	1,250	1,335	358	123
5	Bogam ..	Hyderabad State .	Males ..	12,535	5,277	1,322	1,159	1,170	917	367	342
			Females .	14,397	7,595	1,188	1,891	1,364	1,350	1,362	440
		Telangana ..	Males ..	*7,116*	*3,260*	571	723	801	796	168	201
			Females .	*9,930*	*5,716*	857	982	1,099	1,200	1,247	331
		Marathwara ..	Males ..	*5,419*	*2,017*	751	436	369	121	199	141
			Females .	*4,467*	*1,879*	331	909	265	150	115	109
6	Brahman ..	Hyderabad State .	Males ..	196,654	77,259	28,649	20,877	12,593	7,483	5,276	2,381
			Females .	179,814	60,727	24,335	18,039	11,195	4,120	1,807	1,231
		Telangana ..	Males ..	*75,153*	*29,517*	12,149	8,806	3,123	3,005	1,855	579
			Females .	*68,506*	*24,489*	10,106	7,046	4,815	1,558	442	522
		Marathwara ..	Males ..	*121,501*	*47,742*	16,500	12,071	9,470	4,478	3,421	1,802
			Females .	*111,308*	*36,238*	14,229	10,993	6,380	2,502	1,365	709
7	Burud (Medari) ..	Hyderabad State .	Males ..	19,054	6,241	1,763	1,356	1,053	988	542	539
			Females .	15,723	4,881	1,840	1,246	888	362	266	279
		Telangana ..	Males ..	*12,148*	*4,044*	902	870	814	557	437	464
			Females .	*10,233*	*3,213*	1,020	673	694	331	238	262
		Marathwara ..	Males ..	*6,906*	*2,197*	861	486	239	431	105	75
			Females .	*5,490*	*1,668*	820	573	104	81	38	17
8	Darzi (Simpi) ..	Hyderabad State..	Males ..	32,220	11,231	3,697	3,690	1,639	939	753	513
			Females .	31,411	10,840	5,591	3,069	1,286	380	291	223
		Telangana ..	Males ..	*20,256*	*7,021*	2,360	2,099	1,028	499	349	86
			Females .	*20,614*	*6,501*	3,283	1,929	960	155	137	87
		Marathwara ..	Males ..	*11,964*	*4,210*	1,837	991	611	440	404	427
			Females .	*10,797*	*4,339*	2,358	1,140	326	225	154	136
9	Dhobi (Chakala) ..	Hyderabad State .	Males ..	138,790	58,889	14,312	20,036	11,503	8,527	3,577	934
			Females .	130,702	40,823	16,120	14,109	7,580	1,851	869	294
		Telangana ..	Males ..	*109,857*	*46,933*	10,686	15,079	10,210	7,549	2,784	625
			Females .	*102,852*	*32,145*	12,178	10,218	7,247	1,635	652	215
		Marathwara ..	Males ..	*28,933*	*11,956*	3,626	4,957	1,298	978	798	309
			Females .	*27,850*	*8,678*	3,942	3,891	338	216	217	79
10	Erakala (Kaikadi)	†Hyderabad State .	Males ..	5,049	2,723	1,042	1,081	282	165	136	17
			Females .	4,937	2,480	1,074	1,108	181	79	29	9

VIII.

Castes, Races and Tribes.

TABLE VIII.
AGE, SEX & CIVIL CONDITION FOR SELECTED CASTES, RACES & TRIBES.

MARRIED							WIDOWED						
Total	0—6	7—13	14—16	17—23	24—43	44 and over	Total	0—6	7—13	14—16	17—23	24—43	44 and over
13	14	15	16	17	18	19	20	21	22	23	24	25	26
9,649	123	306	819	1,693	3,461	3,247	2,567	6	69	219	295	756	1,222
7,584	116	539	1,482	1,766	1,818	1,863	4,038	9	153	216	353	1,235	2,072
47,546	698	1,284	2,120	4,817	20,869	17,758	11,303	34	98	326	621	3,549	6,675
62,422	298	7,717	8,784	9,870	18,642	17,111	20,454	35	435	843	1,083	6,526	11,532
632	40	62	66	66	202	196	*102*	..	..	..	4	36	62
509	7	57	40	189	113	108	*206*	..	..	..	9	48	154
46,914	658	1,222	2,054	4,751	20,667	17,562	*11,201*	34	98	326	617	3,513	6,613
61,913	291	7,660	8,744	9,681	18,529	17,008	*20,248*	35	435	848	1,074	6,483	11,378
4,791	59	321	443	710	1,681	1,577	1,084	..	11	34	140	224	675
4,488	62	334	424	1,079	1,778	811	695	..	6	19	53	175	442
3,501	23	186	268	501	1,262	1,261	*828*	..	5	18	121	159	525
3,234	33	276	296	879	1,273	477	*319*	..	6	14	51	53	195
1,290	36	135	175	209	419	316	*256*	..	6	16	19	65	150
1,254	29	58	128	200	505	384	*376*	..	..	5	2	122	247
68,528	339	2,864	4,280	8,517	27,657	24,871	20,012	119	293	483	1,057	5,515	12,545
75,509	623	6,579	7,949	14,301	27,255	18,802	28,084	170	369	579	649	8,243	18,074
29,152	144	1,150	1,750	4,409	11,023	10,676	*7,810*	101	127	256	471	2,736	4,119
33,008	246	3,670	4,377	8,059	10,299	6,357	*14,352*	94	177	283	243	4,441	9,114
39,376	195	1,714	2,530	4,108	16,634	14,195	*12,202*	18	106	227	586	2,779	8,426
42,501	377	2,909	3,572	6,242	16,956	12,445	*13,732*	76	192	296	406	3,802	8,960
5,727	56	253	459	716	2,377	1,866	1,531	..	12	43	272	455	749
6,039	33	246	698	779	1,357	2,926	763	..	..	6	37	165	555
3,137	31	145	209	401	1,388	963	*719*	..	5	12	132	184	386
3,749	15	101	247	428	764	2,194	*465*	..	..	..	10	112	343
2,590	25	108	250	315	989	908	*812*	..	7	31	140	271	363
2,290	18	145	451	331	593	732	*298*	..	..	6	27	53	212
100,482	144	374	1,008	9,252	56,538	33,166	18,913	23	82	223	1,164	5,509	11,912
99,526	368	4,337	14,603	17,057	37,738	25,423	19,561	90	439	663	1,908	6,536	9,925
37,612	60	176	545	3,092	20,844	12,895	*8,024*	10	26	89	275	2,208	5,416
35,811	208	2,158	5,166	7,971	11,356	8,952	*8,206*	33	75	197	375	3,286	5,240
62,870	84	198	468	6,160	35,694	20,271	*10,889*	13	56	184	889	3,301	6,496
63,715	160	2,179	9,437	9,086	26,382	16,471	*11,355*	57	364	466	1,533	4,250	4,685
10,539	193	348	777	2,620	4,282	2,319	2,274	11	46	142	189	721	1,165
8,713	375	763	1,004	2,561	2,940	1,070	2,129	5	44	42	150	706	1,182
6,624	·88	236	398	1,556	2,617	1,739	*1,480*	2	16	92	116	495	759
5,632	176	491	582	1 503	2,010	870	*1,388*	3	10	81	114	456	774
3,915	110	112	384	1,064	1,665	580	*794*	9	30	50	73	226	406
3,081	199	272	422	1,058	980	200	*741*	2	34	11	36	250	408
16,574	156	554	827	2,586	7,378	5,073	4,415	11	31	269	468	1,193	2,443
16,489	482	2,181	1,857	2,928	6,388	2,653	4,082	34	74	105	297	1,296	2,276
10,586	81	294	370	1,738	4,371	3,782	*2,649*	8	8	129	201	687	1,671
11,306	193	1,542	1,215	2,137	4,484	1,785	*2,807*	20	50	80	192	815	1,650
5,988	125	260	457	848	3,007	1,291	*1,766*	8	23	140	267	556	772
5,183	289	689	642	791	1,954	868	*1,275*	14	24	25	105	481	626
68,470	797	3,422	4,718	12,786	27,277	19,470	11,431	31	279	428	1,813	2,899	5,981
72,810	1,313	8,564	10,721	15,895	25,842	10,475	17,069	133	283	397	1,195	6,422	8,639
54,054	436	2,539	3,687	9,837	21,318	16,237	*8,870*	18	181	274	1,811	2,369	4,717
58,125	918	6,834	9,105	11,433	21,207	8,628	*12,582*	113	213	344	954	4,852	6,106
14,416	361	888	1,031	2,949	5,959	3,233	*2,561*	13	98	154	502	530	1,264
14,685	395	1,730	1,616	4,462	4,635	1,847	*4,487*	20	70	53	241	1,570	2,533
2,082	..	8	29	109	1,064	872	244	..	..	..	2	58	184
2,050	..	27	107	359	1,039	518	407	..	..	5	2 3	89	290

TABLE

TABLE VIII.

AGE, SEX & CIVIL CONDITION FOR SELECTED CASTES, RACES & TRIBES

Age, Sex and Civil Condition for selected

S. No.	Caste, Race and Tribe	Locality	Sex	Population dealt with	UNMARRIED						
					Total	0—6	7—13	14—16	17—23	24—43	44 and over
1	2	3	4	5	6	7	8	9	10	11	12
11	Gosain (Gosavi)	Hyderabad State ..	Males ..	17,147	9,461	2,319	2,656	1,520	1,776	568	622
			Females .	12,080	4,188	2,711	997	157	209	68	46
		Telangana ..	Males ..	*509*	*200*	59	46	35	26	11	23
			Females .	*494*	*175*	78	71	16	3	3	4
		Marathwara ..	Males ..	*16,638*	*9,261*	2,260	2,610	1,485	1,750	557	599
			Females .	*11,586*	*4,013*	2,638	926	141	206	65	42
12	Gujrat (Gurjar)	Hyderabad State ..	Males ..	4,893	1,832	830	566	275	108	47	6
			Females .	3,170	912	640	231	34	7	..	..
		Telangana ..	Males ..	*626*	*238*	125	84	34	25	15	5
			Females .	*336*	*158*	75	55	24	4	..	..
		Marathwara ..	Males ..	*4,267*	*1,594*	705	532	241	83	32	1
			Females .	*2,834*	*754*	565	176	10	3	..	..
13	Gurav (Tambli) ..	Hyderabad State .	Males ..	15,676	6,192	2,616	1,099	1,033	600	491	353
			Females .	14,734	3,944	1,982	1,098	802	49	13	..
		Telangana ..	Males ..	*3,710*	*961*	208	204	239	70	185	60
			Females .	*3,875*	*1,161*	650	275	228	8	..	..
		Marathwara ..	Males ..	*11,966*	*5,231*	2,418	895	794	580	306	293
			Females .	*10,859*	*2,783*	1,332	823	574	41	13	..
14	Hajjam(Mangala)	Hyderabad State .	Males ..	83,855	37,406	13,098	11,807	5,881	4,426	1,549	645
			Females .	75,890	25,752	14,111	7,400	1,817	1,428	710	286
		Telangana ..	Males ..	*51,094*	*21,511*	7,842	6,541	3,829	2,333	663	303
			Females .	*45,821*	*14,335*	8,125	4,368	725	628	356	133
		Marathwara ..	Males ..	*32,761*	*15,895*	5,256	5,266	2,052	2,093	886	342
			Females .	*30,069*	*11,417*	5,986	3,032	1,092	800	354	153
15	Hatkar ..	Hyderabad State .	Males ..	24,337	10,328	3,818	3,814	1,117	901	526	152
			Females .	20,831	5,353	3,063	1,768	383	111	25	3
		Telangana ..	Males ..	*2,685*	*1,071*	566	400	69	21	4	11
			Females .	*2,306*	*728*	484	208	48	21	19	8
		Marathwara ..	Males ..	*21,652*	*9,257*	3,252	3,414	1,048	880	522	141
			Females .	*18,525*	*4,625*	2,629	1,560	340	90	6	..
16	Julahi (Sale, Devang).	Hyderabad State .	Males ..	211,803	79,223	38,499	23,105	8,458	4,674	3,107	1,380
			Females	195,078	66,792	35,820	25,408	2,347	1,300	1,144	773
		Telangana ..	Males ..	*159,117*	*60,735*	26,482	20,422	7,125	3,583	2,204	919
			Females .	*147,727*	*53,955*	26,466	23,128	1,669	1,050	961	681
		Marathwara ..	Males ..	*52,686*	*18,488*	12,017	2,683	1,333	1,091	908	461
			Females .	*47,351*	*12,837*	9,354	2,280	678	250	183	92
17	Kalal (Eadiga, Goundla).	Hyderabad State ..	Males ..	220,637	86,116	40,426	17,359	10,226	8,688	5,111	4,306
			Females .	206,199	68,539	41,782	19,911	3,935	1,753	796	362
		Telangana ..	Males ..	*192,011*	*73,994*	36,922	14,015	7,884	7,408	3,971	3,794
			Females .	*181,330*	*60,553*	38,335	16,885	2,997	1,437	686	263
		Marathwara ..	Males ..	*28,626*	*12,122*	3,504	3,344	2,342	1,280	1,140	512
			Females .	*24,869*	*7,986*	3,447	3,026	938	316	160	99
18	Kapu (Kunbi) ..	Hyderabad State .	Males ..	490,183	190,620	57,807	65,165	34,680	15,448	12,258	5,262
			Females .	452,737	336,317	65,621	54,887	6,251	5,326	2,923	1,309
		Telangana ..	Males	*412,094*	*162,576*	44,107	57,722	32,206	13,782	10,558	4,206
			Females	*381,949*	*110,393*	52,245	46,225	4,746	3,739	2,209	1,229
		Marathwara ..	Males ..	*78,089*	*28,044*	13,700	7,443	2,474	1,666	1,705	1,056
			Females .	*70,788*	*25,924*	13,376	8,662	1,505	1,587	714	80
19	Kasab (Aray, Katik)	Hyderabad State .	Males ..	42,801	16,980	7,711	5,125	2,442	1,398	200	104
			Females .	38,364	14,838	7,388	4,744	2,379	129	136	62
		Telangana ..	Males ..	*34,218*	*13,549*	5,549	3,979	2,399	1,361	170	91
			Females .	*31,343*	*11,867*	6,015	3,404	2,302	65	59	22
		Marathwara ..	Males ..	*8,583*	*3,431*	2,162	1,146	43	37	80	18
			Females .	*7,021*	*2,971*	1,373	1,340	77	64	77	40

TABLE VIII.

AGE, SEX & CIVIL CONDITION FOR SELECTED CASTES, RACES & TRIBES.

MARRIED							WIDOWED						
Total	0—6	7—13	14—16	17—23	24—43	44 and over	Total	0—6	7—13	14—16	17—23	24—43	44 and over
13	14	15	16	17	18	19	20	21	22	23	24	25	26
6,461	..	17	116	209	1,738	4,381	1,225	..	..	..	55	328	842
6,567	1	50	390	650	1,945	3,531	1,325	..	8	39	93	446	739
249	..	7	2	19	189	32	60	..	..	..	4	12	44
209	1	14	51	56	60	27	110	..	..	9	1	76	24
6,212	..	10	114	190	1,549	4,349	1,165	..	..	..	51	316	798
6,358	..	36	339	594	1,885	3,504	1,215	..	8	30	92	370	715
2,573	12	36	298	348	961	918	488	..	3	24	38	147	276
1,754	27	200	235	350	709	233	504	1	1	5	11	136	350
366	8	22	25	43	150	118	22	..	..	..	4	7	11
158	15	19	41	35	31	17	20	..		..	1	9	10
2,207	4	14	273	305	811	800	466	..	3	24	34	140	265
1,596	12	181	194	315	678	216	484	1	1	5	10	127	340
8,286	82	254	1,385	1,278	2,070	3,217	1,198	9	46	97	214	508	324
8,040	92	455	824	2,098	3,197	1,374	2,750	39	51	123	327	816	1,394
2,532	28	78	954	380	719	373	217	..	4	26	24	66	7
2,199	35	157	365	432	782	428	515	3	4	14	12	157	325
5,754	54	176	431	898	1,851	2,344	981	9	42	71	190	442	227
5,841	57	298	459	1,666	2,415	946	2,235	36	47	109	315	659	1,069
40,978	776	2,445	3,385	8,526	15,900	9,946	5,471	51	73	122	340	1,618	3,267
41,024	1,483	6,283	5,771	7,049	13,758	6,680	9,114	73	158	388	692	2,973	4,830
26,440	474	1,419	1,949	4,698	10,267	7,633	3,143	28	21	35	161	920	1,978
26,226	863	4,201	3,863	4,657	8,544	4,098	5,260	28	71	241	375	1,820	2,725
14,538	302	1,026	1,436	3,828	5,633	2,313	2,328	23	52	87	179	698	1,289
14,798	620	2,082	1,908	2,392	5,214	2,582	3,854	45	87	147	317	1,153	2,105
12,520	145	395	1,599	2,105	4,409	3,867	1,489	..	14	25	78	536	836
12,598	298	1,965	1,660	2,688	4,312	1,675	2,880	..	27	98	164	381	2,210
1,471	6	59	164	286	500	456	143	..	5	6	2	18	112
1,277	14	91	181	236	475	280	301	..	10	20	10	97	164
11,049	139	336	1,435	1,819	3,909	3,411	1,346	..	9	19	76	518	724
11,321	284	1,874	1,479	2,452	3,837	1,395	2,579	..	17	78	154	284	2,046
112,426	1,313	4,969	7,713	24,757	45,961	27,713	20,154	198	363	477	730	7,472	10,914
98,909	2,104	10,663	13,739	19,346	41,674	11,383	29,377	113	326	845	1,174	9,088	17,831
83,397	553	3,533	6,216	21,293	30,209	21,593	14,985	140	281	365	580	5,853	7,757
72,873	1,458	9,091	10,033	14,206	30,765	7,320	20,899	82	254	680	1,001	6,666	12,216
29,029	760	1,436	1,497	3,464	15,752	6,120	5,169	49	82	112	150	1,619	3,157
26,036	646	1,572	3,706	5,140	10,909	4,063	8,478	31	72	165	173	2,422	5,615
118,654	1,292	6,106	8,897	18,110	49,208	35,041	15,867	74	252	430	797	5,193	9,121
104,057	2,607	14,974	13,949	17,631	43,040	11,856	33,603	337	552	789	1,761	10,999	19,165
104,770	707	4,987	7,302	15,445	43,252	33,077	13,247	14	119	233	647	4,398	7,836
90,223	1,566	12,269	11,046	15,535	39,790	10,017	30,554	213	287	553	1,279	10,126	18,096
13,884	585	1,119	1,595	2,665	5,956	1,964	2,620	60	133	197	150	795	1,285
13,834	1,041	2,705	2,903	2,096	3,250	1,839	3,049	124	265	236	482	873	1,069
252,443	3,760	12,840	22,840	34,872	108,548	69,583	47,120	1,154	1,435	1,676	3,304	11,658	27,893
238,055	4,515	33,723	30,778	42,452	83,192	43,395	78,365	527	1,402	1,676	4,298	26,019	44,443
209,935	2,616	8,321	16,959	27,679	93,254	61,106	39,583	1,047	1,278	1,421	2,848	9,554	23,435
201,752	3,473	30,980	28,063	35,046	68,731	35,459	69,804	884	1,067	1,419	3,665	23,341	39,928
42,508	1,144	4,519	5,881	7,193	15,294	8,477	7,537	107	157	255	456	2,104	4,458
36,303	1,042	2,743	2,715	7,406	14,461	7,936	8,561	143	335	257	638	2,678	4,515
21,822	86	399	940	4,811	10,700	4,886	3,999	3	15	34	130	771	3,046
16,342	179	530	4,177	2,293	6,060	3,103	7,184	9	30	58	199	917	5,971
17,267	66	342	699	3,708	8,708	3,744	3,402	1	3	12	112	531	2,743
13,331	131	403	3,209	1,757	5,578	2,253	6,145	3	24	40	139	647	5,292
4,555	20	57	241	1,103	1,992	1,142	597	2	12	22	18	240	303
3,011	48	127	968	536	482	850	1,039	6	6	18	60	270	679

TABLE VIII.
AGE, SEX & CIVIL CONDITION FOR SELECTED CASTES, RACES & TRIBES.

TABLE

Age, Sex and Civil Condition for selected

S. No.	Caste, Race and Tribe	Locality	Sex	Population dealt with	UNMARRIED						
					Total	0—6	7—13	14—16	17—23	24—43	44 and over
1	2	3	4	5	6	7	8	9	10	11	12
20	Kasar (Kanchari)	Hyderabad State .	Males ..	19,036	7,119	2,620	2,152	1,162	506	382	297
			Females ..	16,694	5,675	2,769	2,037	314	320	149	86
		Telangana ..	Males ..	*8,927*	*3,665*	1,549	1,146	751	113	77	29
			Females ..	*7,465*	*2,404*	1,254	1,069	47	20	5	..
		Marathwara ..	Males ..	*10,109*	*3,454*	1,071	1,006	411	393	305	268
			Females ..	*9,229*	*3,271*	1,515	968	267	291	144	86
21	Khumbhar (Kummari).	Hyderabad State .	Males ..	80,919	31,976	14,225	9,564	3,239	2,484	1,758	706
			Females ..	73,229	23,162	14,142	6,494	826	828	625	247
		Telangana ..	Males ..	*48,872*	*18,943*	7,854	5,837	2,380	1,700	1,154	518
			Females ..	*42,571*	*12,346*	7,626	3,472	494	386	257	111
		Marathwara ..	Males ..	*32,047*	*13,033*	6,371	4,227	859	784	604	188
			Females ..	*30,658*	*10,816*	6,516	3,022	332	442	368	136
22	Koli ..	Hyderabad State	Males ..	29,264	13,425	5,605	5,130	1,060	839	501	290
			Females ..	23,208	6,466	4,098	1,921	243	101	87	16
		Telangana ..	Males ..	*8,930*	*4,177*	1,696	1,869	327	227	42	16
			Females ..	*4,361*	*995*	648	321	21	3	2	..
		Marathwara ..	Males ..	*20,334*	*9,248*	8,909	8,261	733	612	459	274
			Females ..	*18,847*	*5,471*	8,450	1,600	222	98	85	16
23	Komati (Vaishya)	Hyderabad State .	Males ..	163,432	64,258	24,674	17,598	8,984	6,745	4,449	1,808
			Females ..	145,479	41,064	22,312	13,609	4,094	656	324	69
		Telangana ..	Males ..	*119,131*	*49,218*	18,715	13,492	7,267	5,227	8,232	1,285
			Females ..	*105,529*	*29,989*	16,748	9,705	2,946	382	184	24
		Marathwara ..	Males ..	*44,301*	*15,040*	5,959	4,106	1,717	1,518	1,217	523
			Females ..	*39,950*	*11,075*	5,564	3,904	1,148	274	140	45
24	Kshatriya (Rajput)	Hyderabad State..	Males ..	46,256	20,096	9,305	5,409	2,481	1,362	1,101	438
			Females ..	42,178	14,635	8,711	4,154	792	344	481	153
		Telangana ..	Males ..	*15,976*	*7,230*	3,192	1,811	1,402	511	252	62
			Females ..	*13,697*	*4,625*	2,851	1,520	136	32	77	9
		Marathwara ..	Males ..	*30,280*	*12,866*	6,113	3,598	1,079	851	849	376
			Females ..	*28,481*	*10,010*	5,860	2,684	656	312	404	144
25	Kurma ..	Hyderabad State .	Males ..	89,646	37,447	15,801	11,439	7,115	1,344	898	850
			Females ..	83,672	28,833	13,630	12,046	1,732	697	498	230
		Telangana ..	Males ..	*85,415*	*35,548*	14,888	10,912	6,845	1,271	855	827
			Females ..	*78,600*	*26,584*	12,653	11,339	1,465	518	388	226
		Marathwara ..	Males ..	*4,231*	*1,899*	963	527	270	73	43	23
			Females ..	*5,072*	*2,249*	977	707	267	179	115	4
26	Lingayat ..	Hyderabad State .	Males ..	397,604	194,467	57,434	66,300	38,233	16,799	11,075	4,626
			Females ..	391,285	163,150	59,665	64,557	24,293	7,458	4,485	2,692
		Telangana ..	Males ..	*37,150*	*14,888*	5,818	3,926	1,514	2,138	994	498
			Females ..	*35,676*	*12,699*	6,557	3,785	1,472	326	299	260
		Marathwara ..	Males ..	*360,454*	*179,579*	51,616	62,874	36,719	14,661	10,081	4,128
			Females ..	*355,559*	*150,451*	58,108	60,772	22,821	7,132	4,186	2,432
27	Lohar(Kammari).	Hyderabad State..	Males ..	51,365	20,179	8,163	5,753	3,638	1,397	912	316
			Females ..	42,095	12,458	6,419	4,195	1,089	425	246	84
		Telangana ..	Males ..	*33,874*	*13,429*	5,431	4,462	2,149	813	444	180
			Females	*28,151*	*8,463*	4,674	2,835	548	220	144	42
		Marathwara ..	Males ..	*17,491*	*6,750*	2,732	1,291	1,489	584	468	186
			Females ..	*13,944*	*3,995*	1,745	1,360	541	205	102	42
28	Mali ..	Hyderabad State .	Males ..	51,611	20,807	9,622	5,931	3,406	851	761	236
			Females ..	50,997	18,172	9,598	5,870	1,895	394	259	156
		Telangana ..	Males ..	*2,183*	*889*	399	288	174	22	6	..
			Females ..	*1,983*	*660*	283	210	94	78	..	..
		Marathwara ..	Males ..	*49,428*	*19,918*	9,228	5,643	3,282	829	755	286
			Females ..	*49,014*	*17,512*	9,315	5,660	1,801	321	259	156

MARRIED							WIDOWED						
Total	0—6	7—13	14—16	17—23	24—43	44 and over	Total	0—6	7—13	14—16	17—23	24—43	44 and over
13	14	15	16	17	18	19	20	21	22	23	24	25	26
9,920	190	728	697	993	3,804	3,508	1,997	9	13	71	139	702	1,063
8,244	273	772	868	880	3,320	2,131	2,775	11	18	41	131	742	1,832
4,516	10	59	82	180	2,324	1,861	*746*	..	..	2	17	344	383
3,841	75	180	246	814	1,860	1,166	*1,220*	..	6	14	11	212	977
5,404	180	669	615	813	1,480	1,647	*1,251*	9	13	69	122	358	680
4,403	198	592	622	566	1,460	965	*1,555*	11	12	27	120	580	855
42,875	956	2,543	3,135	5,624	19,267	11,350	6,068	29	48	65	187	1,395	4,344
37,442	807	3,760	4,334	6,758	15,049	6,734	12,625	67	239	253	607	3,532	7,927
26,215	219	1,458	1,973	3,815	11,390	7,360	*3,714*	8	18	33	115	799	2,741
22,223	431	2,278	3,122	4,685	8,211	3,496	*8,002*	40	171	187	446	2,349	4,809
16,660	737	1,085	1,162	1,809	7,877	3,990	*2,354*	21	30	32	72	596	1,608
15,219	376	1,482	1,212	2,073	6,838	3,238	*4,623*	27	68	66	161	1,183	3,118
13,959	70	907	1,198	2,652	6,735	2,397	1,880	19	54	71	108	621	1,007
13,174	503	1,764	1,933	2,470	4,323	2,181	3,568	45	66	70	203	1,263	1,921
4,365	11	148	251	605	2,031	1,319	*388*	..	4	10	33	87	254
2,888	35	320	391	617	1,133	392	*478*	..	..	2	2	174	300
9,594	59	759	947	2,047	4,704	1,078	*1,492*	19	50	61	75	534	753
10,286	468	1,444	1,542	1,858	3,190	1,789	*3,090*	45	66	68	201	1,089	1,621
83,001	1,942	6,839	8,942	21,087	23,376	20,815	16,173	59	180	397	876	5,024	9,637
71,282	3,239	12,682	11,670	12,093	20,646	10,952	33,133	278	992	914	3,672	11,206	16,071
59,131	934	4,651	6,511	16,967	15,015	15,058	*10,782*	7	52	116	349	8,251	7,007
51,155	2,103	9,989	9,084	7,942	14,043	7,994	*24,385*	223	860	702	2,243	8,684	11,673
23,870	1,008	2,188	2,431	4,120	8,361	5,762	*5,391*	52	128	281	527	1,778	2,630
20,127	1,136	2,693	2,586	4,151	6,603	2,958	*8,748*	55	132	212	1,429	2,522	4,398
22,920	299	1,225	1,469	3,257	10,304	6,366	3,240	44	44	121	166	859	2,006
21,153	364	2,059	3,047	4,853	7,167	3,663	6,390	38	94	180	369	1,500	4,209
7,688	96	150	369	918	3,717	2,438	*1,058*	..	1	3	17	372	665
6,543	132	305	259	1,871	2,659	1,317	*2,529*	6	16	12	65	638	1,792
15,232	203	1,075	1,160	2,339	6,587	3,928	*2,182*	44	43	118	149	487	1,341
14,610	232	1,754	2,788	2,982	4,508	2,346	*3,861*	32	78	168	304	862	2,417
41,164	273	2,054	2,622	5,581	19,772	10,862	11,035	114	236	397	470	2,919	6,899
39,231	503	4,439	4,355	6,421	15,241	8,272	15,608	144	338	419	565	4,222	9,920
39,203	186	1,877	2,482	5,227	19,087	10,344	*10,664*	112	220	344	448	2,823	6,722
36,980	382	4,285	4,126	5,990	14,459	7,738	*15,036*	143	321	407	545	3,948	9,672
1,961	87	177	140	354	685	518	*371*	2	16	53	27	96	177
2,251	121	154	229	431	782	534	*572*	1	17	12	20	274	248
171,127	2,125	6,902	7,497	17,847	79,548	57,208	32,010	152	292	457	904	6,996	23,209
169,566	5,357	15,375	16,763	30,683	71,620	29,768	58,519	351	505	834	1,785	17,872	37,172
19,238	231	971	1,462	2,826	8,053	5,695	*3,024*	2	27	32	141	889	1,983
17,595	476	1,709	1,542	2,712	6,916	4,240	*5,382*	38	54	174	393	1,339	3,384
151,889	1,894	5,931	6,035	15,021	71,495	51,518	*28,986*	150	265	425	763	6,107	21,276
151,971	4,881	13,666	15,221	27,971	64,704	25,528	*53,137*	813	451	660	1,392	16,533	33,788
24,390	324	959	1,245	2,694	11,577	7,591	6,796	40	93	246	299	1,691	4,427
21,854	680	2,333	2,077	4,493	7,357	4,914	7,783	54	128	231	513	2,157	4,700
15,639	182	426	677	1,886	7,767	4,801	*4,806*	20	24	124	154	1,067	3,417
14,494	380	1,352	1,485	3,574	4,711	2,902	*5,194*	26	65	120	321	1,417	3,245
8,751	192	538	568	858	3,810	2,790	*1,990*	20	69	122	145	624	1,010
7,360	300	981	592	919	2,646	1,922	*2,589*	28	68	111	192	740	1,455
24,054	658	1,192	2,181	3,674	10,233	6,116	6,750	17	38	155	295	1,770	4,475
25,443	1,211	2,760	3,765	4,252	8,086	5,369	7,382	23	140	248	329	2,055	4,587
1,022	12	100	150	188	358	214	*272*	..	..	..	18	44	210
1,035	25	169	214	261	213	158	*288*	..	8	7	20	73	180
23,032	646	1,092	2,031	3,486	9,875	5,902	*6,478*	17	38	155	277	1,726	4,265
24,408	1,186	2,591	3,551	3,091	7,873	5,216	*7,094*	23	132	241	309	1,982	4,407

TABLE VIII.

AGE, SEX & CIVIL CONDITION FOR SELECTED CASTES, RACES & TRIBES.

TABLE

Age, Sex and Civil Condition for selected

Srl. No.	Caste, Race and Tribe	Locality	Sex	Population dealt with	UNMARRIED						
					Total	0—6	7—13	14—16	17—23	24—43	44 and over
1	2	3	4	5	6	7	8	9	10	11	12
29	Maratha ..	Hyderabad State .	Males ..	751,082	393,516	11,017	82,606	51,322	35,847	19,880	8,844
			Females ..	740,476	234,892	123,170	65,112	30,183	7,750	6,207	2,470
		Telangana ..	Males ..	*34,437*	*14,464*	5,687	4,679	1,560	1,232	851	455
			Females ..	*36,079*	*13,038*	7,458	3,010	1,787	499	250	39
		Marathwara ..	Males ..	*716,645*	*299,052*	109,330	77,927	49,762	34,615	19,029	8,389
			Females ..	*704,397*	*221,854*	115,717	62,102	28,396	7,251	5,957	2,431
30	Marwari ..	Hyderabad State .	Males ..	34,572	11,983	5,722	3,122	2,313	632	124	70
			Females ..	27,739	8,891	5,716	2,430	609	93	43	..
		Telangana ..	Males ..	*6,250*	*2,265*	1,078	665	482	35	5	..
			Females ..	*6,003*	*2,150*	1,444	483	212	7	4	..
		Marathwara ..	Males ..	*28,322*	*9,718*	4,644	2,457	1,831	597	119	70
			Females ..	*21,736*	*6,741*	4,272	1,947	397	86	39	..
31	Panchal ..	Hyderabad State .	Males ..	35,707	13,513	3,835	3,512	2,691	1,555	1,716	204
			Females ..	34,167	12,022	4,914	3,369	2,300	714	549	176
		Telangana ..	Males	*747*	*298*	164	74	26	16	8	10
			Females ..	*340*	*90*	39	25	24	2	..	..
		Marathwara ..	Males ..	*34,960*	*13,215*	3,671	3,438	2,665	1,530	1,708	194
			Females ..	*33,827*	*11,932*	4,875	3,344	2,276	712	549	176
32	Perka ..	*Hyderabad State.	Males ..	25,723	10,517	2,495	4,069	1,974	760	969	250
			Females ..	25,781	6,946	2,590	2,396	1,208	315	266	171
33	Rangrez (Rangari)	Hyderabad State .	Males ..	14,875	5,072	2,521	1,398	391	341	274	147
			Females ..	11,876	3,946	2,325	860	368	152	187	54
		Telangana ..	Males ..	*4,439*	*1,389*	641	444	128	91	60	25
			Females ..	*3,904*	*1,039*	549	303	127	27	22	11
		Marathwara ..	Males ..	*10,436*	*3,683*	1,880	954	263	250	214	122
			Females ..	*7,972*	*2,907*	1,776	557	241	125	165	48
34	Satani (Ayyawar)	Hyderabad State .	Males ..	30,365	12,532	5,349	3,363	2,138	801	486	395
			Females ..	24,031	10,384	4,685	2,892	1,834	484	359	130
		Telangana ..	Males ..	*28,327*	*11,692*	5,116	3,099	2,033	700	393	351
			Females ..	*22,301*	*9,744*	4,351	2,098	1,802	449	321	123
		Marathwara ..	Males ..	*2,038*	*840*	233	264	105	101	93	44
			Females ..	*1,730*	*640*	334	194	32	35	38	7
35	Sunar (Ausala, Kamsala).	Hyderabad State .	Males ..	72,550	26,088	12,748	7,482	2,613	1,947	1,027	271
			Females ..	65,341	23,523	13,675	6,623	1,352	1,027	671	175
		Telangana ..	Males ..	*47,586*	*17,298*	8,279	5,117	1,874	1,352	542	134
			Females ..	*42,031*	*14,864*	8,805	3,726	1,007	736	460	121
		Marathwara ..	Males ..	*24,964*	*8,790*	4,469	2,365	739	595	485	137
			Females ..	*23,310*	*8,659*	4,870	2,897	345	291	202	54
36	Sutar (Bade, Wadia).	Hyderabad State .	Males ..	58,274	22,711	8,327	7,074	2,947	2,233	1,347	783
			Females ..	52,076	17,643	9,145	5,685	1,248	778	569	218
		Telangana ..	Males ..	*41,999*	*15,850*	6,397	4,927	1,885	1,268	847	531
			Females ..	*38,273*	*13,784*	6,998	4,957	870	492	841	126
		Marathwara ..	Males ..	*16,275*	*6,861*	1,930	2,147	1,062	970	500	252
			Females ..	*13,803*	*3,859*	2,147	728	378	286	228	92
37	Telaga (Mutrasi, Munnur).	Hyderabad State .	Males ..	448,805	186,229	79,834	58,658	20,177	14,544	10,455	2,561
			Females ..	517,385	169,324	98,432	43,715	9,964	6,690	5,420	5,103
		Telangana ..	Males ..	*399,813*	*166,106*	71,320	52,770	17,940	12,940	8,985	2,151
			Females ..	*460,061*	*150,182*	89,415	36,936	7,496	6,268	5,132	4,985
		Marathwara ..	Males ..	*48,992*	*20,123*	8,514	5,888	2,237	1,604	1,470	410
			Females ..	*57,324*	*19,142*	9,017	6,779	2,468	422	288	168
38	Teli (Gandla) ..	Hyderabad State .	Males ..	38,773	15,282	7,618	4,160	1,360	1,046	833	265
			Females ..	34,382	11,531	7,516	2,736	710	296	157	116
		Telangana ..	Males ..	*13,423*	*5,609*	3,203	1,720	353	168	133	32
			Females ..	*11,952*	*4,242*	2,938	903	220	112	45	24
		Marathwara ..	Males ..	*25,350*	*9,673*	4,415	2,440	1,007	878	700	238
			Females ..	*22,430*	*7,289*	4,578	1,833	490	184	112	92

VIII.

Castes, Races and Tribes.

TABLE VIII.

AGE, SEX & CIVIL CONDITION FOR SELECTED CASTES, RACES & TRIBES.

MARRIED							WIDOWED						
Total	0—6	7—13	14—16	17—23	24—43	44 and over	Total	0—6	7—13	14—16	17—23	24—43	44 and over
13	14	15	16	17	18	19	20	21	22	23	24	25	26
379,343	2,760	17,632	27,159	45,939	195,726	90,127	58,223	738	1,191	2,028	2,354	20,225	31,687
400,255	13,285	46,881	51,260	72,516	163,823	52,490	105,329	903	1,393	2,100	4,625	32,574	63,734
16,766	145	1,408	1,674	2,771	6,512	4,256	3,207	11	65	43	142	951	1,995
16,186	271	1,433	2,551	3,687	4,410	3 834	*6,855*	64	108	108	360	2,427	3 788
362,577	2,615	16,224	25,485	48,168	189,214	85,871	*55,016*	727	1,126	1,985	2,212	19,274	29,692
384,069	13,014	45,448	48,709	68,829	159,413	48 656	*98,474*	839	1,285	1,992	4,265	30,147	59,946
19,535	488	2,582	2,475	3,583	6,554	3,853	3,054	8	51	81	182	650	2,082
15,374	462	2,987	2,417	2,838	4,668	2,002	3,474	42	100	74	237	1,282	1,739
3,686	160	258	210	596	1,543	919	*299*	1	7	10	17	93	171
3,067	85	501	608	574	859	440	*786*	..	9	18	66	318	375
15,849	828	2,324	2,165	2,987	5,011	3,034	*2,755*	7	44	71	165	557	1,911
12,307	877	2,486	1,809	2,264	3,809	1,562	*2,688*	42	91	56	171	964	1,364
18,041	469	619	2,063	3,686	6,295	4,909	4,153	8	12	52	184	438	3,459
14,719	367	814	1,910	2,849	6,166	2,613	7,426	21	73	191	254	2,285	4,602
369	1	12	29	144	124	59	*80*	..	..	..	6	20	54
164	1	24	32	33	51	23	*86*	4	12	15	11	20	24
17,672	468	607	2,034	3,542	6,171	4,850	*4,073*	8	12	52	178	418	3,405
14,555	366	790	1,878	2,816	6,115	2,590	*7,340*	17	61	176	248	2,265	4,578
12,685	180	155	1,152	1,955	4,426	4,817	2,521	7	36	32	48	231	2,167
11,507	272	544	1,086	1,486	4,749	3,370	7,328	5	136	229	183	1,381	5,394
8,621	168	385	513	925	4,257	2,373	1,182	14	18	25	40	335	750
6,514	277	493	817	1,093	2,672	1,162	1,416	12	46	85	168	450	655
2,733	15	138	147	257	1,416	760	*317*	..	8	10	10	105	184
2,428	52	264	358	454	795	505	*437*	10	13	12	34	134	234
5,888	153	247	366	668	2,841	1,613	*865*	14	10	15	80	230	566
4,086	225	229	459	639	1,877	657	*979*	2	33	73	134	316	421
14,833	101	363	2,641	2,405	4,819	4,504	3,000	19	65	180	359	1,027	1,350
10,740	105	425	2,923	3,248	2,686	1,353	2,907	22	69	237	385	1,061	1,133
13,786	82	285	2,554	2,278	4,517	4,070	*2,849*	19	64	179	341	980	1,266
9,846	88	345	2,824	3,097	2,894	1,098	*2,711*	19	61	228	359	998	1,051
1,047	19	78	87	127	302	434	*151*	..	1	1	18	47	84
894	17	80	99	151	292	255	*196*	8	8	14	26	63	82
38,553	650	2,759	3,268	7,739	13,255	10,882	7,909	35	40	247	358	2,855	4,374
32,230	1,006	4,731	4,582	6,078	10,231	5,602	9,588	60	168	326	692	3,235	5,107
25,098	241	1,850	1,716	4,688	9,214	7,889	*5,190*	12	18	187	154	2,132	2,737
20,855	566	3,259	2,963	4,106	6,903	3,058	*6,312*	33	104	212	459	2,080	3,424
13,455	409	1,409	1,552	3,051	4,041	2,093	*2,719*	28	22	110	204	728	1,687
11,375	440	1,472	1,619	1,972	3,328	2,544	*3,276*	27	64	114	288	1,155	1,683
29,478	383	1,710	2,600	4,932	11,047	8,806	6,085	40	73	105	225	2,269	3,373
26,544	510	3,621	4,031	4,594	8,521	5,267	7,889	55	150	231	593	2,657	4,203
21,792	245	1,064	1,548	3,884	8,592	6,459	*4,357*	24	39	57	118	1,724	2,400
19,142	305	2,949	2,648	3,209	6,650	3,381	*5,347*	35	77	182	409	2,055	2,589
7,686	138	646	1,052	1,048	2,455	2,347	*1,728*	16	84	48	112	545	978
7,402	205	672	1,383	1,385	1,871	1,886	*2,542*	20	78	49	184	602	1,614
228,850	2,860	8,955	14,288	32,197	108,682	61,868	33,726	164	393	689	1,877	9,133	21,470
257,635	4,393	26,139	30,075	53,533	106,340	37,155	90,426	439	1,303	1,829	6,143	30,915	49,797
203,813	2,343	8,170	12,561	28,540	96,323	55,876	*29,894*	107	325	594	1,659	8,304	18,905
225,834	3,581	23,615	26,372	47,277	92,808	32,096	*84,045*	320	1,078	1,646	5,862	28,558	46,581
25,037	517	785	1,727	3,657	12,359	5,992	*3,832*	57	68	95	218	829	2,565
31,801	812	2,524	3,708	6,256	18,447	5,059	*6,381*	119	225	183	281	2,857	3,216
20,533	615	1,205	1,524	3,017	8,883	5,289	2,958	33	93	99	278	896	1,559
17,976	806	2,156	2,264	3,317	5,951	3,482	4,875	47	137	149	273	1,350	2,919
6,848	76	214	366	984	3,545	1,663	*996*	10	15	24	128	296	493
6,245	107	567	691	1,053	2,409	1,418	*1,465*	19	28	43	78	369	928
13,685	539	991	1,158	2,033	5,338	3,626	*1,992*	23	78	75	150	600	1,066
11,731	699	1,589	1,573	2,264	3,542	2,064	*3,410*	28	109	106	195	981	1,991

TABLE VIII.

AGE, SEX & CIVIL CONDITION FOR SELECTED CASTES, RACES & TRIBES

TABLE

Age, Sex and Civil Condition for selected

S. No.	Caste, Race and Tribe	Locality	Sex	Population dealt with	UNMARRIED						
					Tota	0—6	7—13	14—16	17—23	24—43	44 and over
1	2	3	4	5	6	7	8	9	10	11	12
39	Uppara. ..	Hyderabad State .	Males ..	39,623	16,000	7,693	5,351	1,213	998	563	182
			Females	39,869	15,010	8,987	4,675	638	489	171	50
		Telangana ..	Males ..	15,717	6,481	3,274	2,212	418	329	179	69
			Females .	13,567	5,376	3,538	1,516	130	161	20	11
		Marathwara ..	Males ..	23,906	9,519	4,419	3,139	795	669	384	113
			Females .	26,302	9,634	5,449	3,159	508	328	151	39
40	Velama ..	Hyderabad State..	Males	26,217	9,514	4,328	3,150	1,046	557	236	197
			Females .	25,771	9,109	4,025	3,455	726	565	278	60
41	Viswabrahman ..	Hyderabad State .	Males ..	14,293	5,615	2,086	2,288	541	410	171	119
			Females .	12,449	4,846	2,563	1,561	650	52	20	..
		Telangana ..	Males ..	13,367	5,305	1,981	2,213	508	391	110	102
			Females .	11,876	4,582	2,482	1,496	572	22	10	..
		Marathwara ..	Males ..	926	310	105	75	33	19	61	17
			Females .	573	264	81	65	78	30	10	..
42	Waddar	Hyderabad State .	Males ..	70,085	30,629	12,915	9,584	3,718	2,700	1,219	493
			Females .	67,997	23,607	9,884	8,912	3,363	771	485	192
		Telangana ..	Males ..	46,885	20,812	8,536	6,963	2,585	1,865	582	281
			Females .	47,061	17,585	7,568	6,274	2,864	513	246	120
		Marathwara ..	Males ..	23,200	9,817	4,379	2,621	1,133	835	637	212
			Females ..	20,936	6,022	2,316	2,638	499	258	239	72
43	Wanjari (Banjari).	Hyderabad State .	Males ..	38,965	15,976	5,524	3,260	3,604	1,842	976	770
			Females .	31,971	11,354	5,269	3,579	1,753	391	196	166
		Telangana ..	Males ..	21,797	8,068	2,655	1,702	1,646	1,179	451	435
			Females ..	18,943	6,948	3,019	2,219	1,283	236	135	106
		Marathwara ..	Males ..	17,168	7,908	2,869	1,558	1,958	663	525	335
			Females ..	13,028	4,406	2,250	1,360	520	155	61	60
44	Yadava (Golla, Gowli, Dhangar, Ahir).	Hyderabad State .	Males ..	471,464	171,183	74,024	52,758	25,128	11,263	5,409	2,601
			Females .	456,940	157,994	72,413	51,590	16,380	9,749	5,574	2,288
		Telangana ..	Males ..	261,307	95,729	38,807	32,005	14,569	5,308	3,243	1,797
			Females ..	249,269	86,616	36,568	32,087	9,013	4,610	2,971	1,872
		Marathwara ..	Males ..	210,157	75,454	35,217	20,753	10,559	5,955	2,166	804
			Females .	207,671	71,378	25,850	19,503	7,867	5,139	2,603	916
	ADI HINDU.										
1	Dher (Mala, Mahar)	Hyderabad State .	Males ..	552,632	245,597	83,166	69,378	37,290	31,623	17,775	6,365
			Females	523,907	175,467	82,997	52,512	22,930	8,948	5,322	2,758
		Telangana ..	Males ..	252,085	119,978	34,598	30,795	10,848	17,342	12,484	4,911
			Females ..	229,637	85,169	39,389	24,161	12,433	4,512	3,061	1,613
		Marathwara ..	Males ..	300,547	125,619	48,568	38,583	17,442	14,281	5,291	1,454
			Females ..	294,270	90,298	43,608	28,351	10,497	4,436	2,261	1,145
2	Madiga (Chambhar, Mang, Mochi)	Hyderabad State .	Males ..	639,197	282,495	75,447	85,404	59,625	30,094	22,371	9,554
			Females .	641,895	240,180	94,834	72,851	34,342	17,686	12,809	7,658
		Telangana ..	Males ..	386,574	176,116	46,854	54,175	36,482	19,231	14,890	4,484
			Females ..	386,106	156,483	57,590	40,117	23,792	12,423	8,729	4,832
		Marathwara ..	Males ..	252,623	106,379	28,593	31,229	23,143	10,863	7,481	5,070
			Females .	255,789	83,697	37,244	23,734	10,550	5,263	4,080	2,826
	TRIBALS.										
1	Bhil	† Hyderabad State	Males ..	7,551	3,261	1,240	1,309	287	243	143	39
			Females ..	7,501	2,322	1,145	724	255	93	64	41
2	Chenchu ..	*Hyderabad State..	Males ..	1,090	451	187	146	62	18	24	14
			Females .	1,174	428	175	125	50	39	21	18
3	Erakala (Kaikadi and Korwah) ..	Hyderabad State .	Males ..	32,002	13,262	5,270	3,674	2,594	855	589	280
			Females ..	27,170	9,216	4,161	2,684	1,264	719	265	123
		Telangana ..	Males ..	20,771	8,608	4,125	1,834	1,792	423	294	140
			Females ..	16,956	6,120	3,065	1,587	881	384	132	71
		Marathwara ..	Males ..	11,231	4,654	1,145	1,840	802	432	295	140
			Females ..	10,214	3,096	1,096	1,097	383	335	188	52

TABLE VIII.

AGE, SEX & CIVIL CONDITION FOR SELECTED CASTES, RACES & TRIBES.

MARRIED							WIDOWED						
Total	0—6	7—13	14—16	17—23	24—43	44 and over	Total	0—6	7—13	14—16	17—23	24—43	44 and over
13	14	15	16	17	18	19	20	21	22	23	24	25	26
20,892	80	515	912	2,666	9,868	6,851	2,731	4	9	59	122	666	1,871
17,292	155	822	1,329	2,945	7,299	4,742	7,567	13	106	164	351	1,646	5,287
8,329	15	186	388	1,061	3,908	2,776	*907*	..	3	17	58	232	597
6,050	47	405	605	1,143	1,946	1,904	*2,141*	2	36	54	136	481	1,432
12,563	65	329	529	1,605	5,960	4,075	*1,824*	4	6	42	64	484	1,274
11,242	108	417	724	1,802	5,358	2,838	*5,426*	11	70	110	215	1,165	3,855
14,214	147	494	1,739	3,914	4,528	3,392	2,489	21	60	95	155	752	1,406
12,788	182	1,024	1,493	2,556	5,256	2,277	3,874	28	74	85	199	1,086	2,402
7,374	17	180	249	674	4,111	2,143	1,304	4	41	58	34	333	834
5,530	16	423	677	877	2,399	1,138	2,073	11	191	144	135	282	1,310
6,903	13	141	233	607	3,892	2,017	*1,159*	4	21	33	15	308	778
5,290	12	395	649	776	2,330	1,128	*2,004*	11	179	138	123	265	1,288
471	4	39	16	67	219	126	*145*	..	20	25	19	25	56
240	4	28	28	101	69	10	*69*	..	12	6	12	17	22
33,474	1,077	2,478	2,660	5,387	13,660	8,212	5,982	52	248	328	652	2,027	2,675
32,478	919	2,873	4,405	6,457	12,369	5,455	11,912	56	331	430	886	3,729	6,480
22,052	578	1,219	1,834	3,380	9,555	5,991	*4,021*	31	177	236	476	1,389	1,712
22,254	580	2,047	2,628	4,068	8,709	4,222	*7,222*	40	266	294	686	1,995	3,941
11,422	504	1,259	1,326	2,007	4,105	2,221	*1,961*	21	71	92	176	638	968
10,224	339	826	1,777	2,389	3,660	1,233	*4,690*	16	65	186	200	1,734	2,539
18,592	13	489	700	3,709	7,344	6,337	4,397	42	86	164	207	987	2,911
15,705	157	1,551	2,229	2,129	6,180	3,459	4,912	43	144	253	294	1,332	2,846
11,246	5	332	430	1,887	4,329	4,263	*2,483*	81	57	115	114	488	1,678
9,128	69	998	1,583	1,269	3,210	1,999	*2,867*	30	61	159	188	820	1,609
7,346	8	157	270	1,822	3,015	2,074	*1,914*	11	29	49	93	499	1,288
6,577	88	338	646	860	2,970	1,460	*2,045*	13	83	94	106	512	1,237
230,422	4,372	13,624	17,385	32,668	97,376	64,997	69,859	650	2,834	4,600	7,180	22,687	31,908
223,424	7,761	23,839	25,165	32,953	79,640	54,066	75,522	890	3,911	4,744	8,211	25,758	32,008
125,953	1,651	6,069	8,573	18,078	55,153	36,429	*39,625*	440	2,200	3,229	5,262	12,225	16,269
122,597	4,939	14,605	14,666	20 287	40,780	27,320	*40,056*	501	2,524	3,217	4,217	18,120	16,477
104,469	2,721	7,553	8,812	14,590	42,228	28,568	*30,234*	210	634	1,871	1,918	10,462	15,630
100,827	2,822	9,231	10,499	12,666	38,860	26,746	*35,466*	389	1,387	1,527	3,994	12,638	15,581
258,584	3,087	14,807	21,460	36,347	117,412	65,471	48,451	658	1,624	6,213	8,777	13,106	18,073
255,150	5,244	17,205	29,577	53,215	102,239	47,670	93,290	537	2,343	6,593	7,894	25,780	50,143
107,846	968	5,575	10,865	14,897	50,388	25,138	*24,261*	261	766	3,215	5,274	6,249	8,496
101,807	1,960	6,463	9,641	17,604	46,259	19,880	*42,661*	334	804	3,709	4,225	12,275	21,314
150,738	2,124	9,282	10,595	21,450	67,024	40,818	*24,190*	397	858	2,998	8,508	6,857	9,577
153,343	3,284	10,742	19,936	35,611	55,980	27,790	*50,629*	203	1,539	2,884	8,669	18,505	28,829
291,814	3,080	9,207	18,384	43,365	130,774	87,004	64,888	1,199	2,003	4,262	6,916	18,266	32,242
306,936	3,542	22,437	43,906	64,811	113,868	58,372	94,779	1,550	3,535	7,566	8,450	28,423	45,255
166.567	2,589	5,021	10,588	20,807	80,206	47,456	*43,891*	924	1,440	3,714	5,752	11,218	20,848
181,668	2,663	17,571	28,824	38,871	63,147	31,092	*47,955*	1,174	2,582	4,309	6,050	12,758	21,087
125,247	541	4,186	7,846	22,558	50,568	39,548	*20,997*	275	568	548	1,164	7,048	11,399
125,268	879	4,866	15,582	25,940	50,721	27,280	*46,824*	876	953	8,257	2,400	15,670	24,168
4,039	208	278	302	584	1,590	1,077	251	1	8	9	14	78	141
4,093	119	582	470	1,045	1,164	713	1,086	7	17	14	69	296	683
519	5	12	21	74	265	142	120	..	..	1	2	40	77
543	10	54	92	115	167	105	203	..	5	17	37	66	78
14,068	151	451	901	2,765	5,851	3,949	4,672	..	17	53	290	1,496	2,816
12,740	250	922	1,141	2,496	6,078	1,853	5,214	17	39	146	410	1,574	3,028
9,408	100	273	346	1,874	3,901	2,714	*2,755*	..	8	26	143	889	1,689
7,789	173	656	808	1,229	4,011	917	*3,047*	8	19	71	237	906	1,806
4,660	51	178	355	891	1,950	1,235	*1,917*	..	9	27	147	607	1,127
4,951	77	266	338	1,267	2,067	936	*2,167*	9	20	75	178	668	1,222

TABLE VIII.

AGE, SEX & CIVIL CONDITION FOR SELECTED CASTES, RACES & TRIBES.

TABLE

Age, Sex and Civil Condition for selected

S. No.	Caste, Race and Tribe	Locality	Sex	Population dealt with	UNMARRIED						
					Total	0—6	7—13	14—16	17—23	24—43	44 and over
1	2	3	4	5	6	7	8	9	10	11	12
4	Gond ..	Hyderabad State .	Males ..	57,048	27,025	9,483	7,493	4,761	2,147	2,546	595
			Females .	56,232	20,566	5,735	6,871	3,594	2,097	1,954	315
		Telangana ..	Males ..	*55,075*	*26,209*	9,161	7,276	4,650	2,081	2,499	542
			Females .	*54,755*	*20,080*	5,420	6,792	3,569	2,066	1,929	304
		Marathwara ..	Males ..	*1,973*	*816*	322	217	111	66	47	58
			Females .	*1,477*	*486*	315	79	25	31	25	11
5	Koya ..	*Hyderabad State..	Males ..	18,217	7,976	1,524	2,604	1,260	970	842	776
			Females .	15,421	4,769	2,149	1,010	1,053	233	196	128
6	Lambada (Banjari).	Hyderabad State .	Males ..	153,856	72,176	23,101	19,222	11,664	9,095	5,345	3,749
			Females ..	146,610	60,118	24,181	17,972	7,246	7,868	1,879	972
		Telangana ..	Males ..	*103,592*	*50,714*	18,989	13,161	7,969	5,208	3,907	1,480
			Females .	*98,831*	*39,657*	15,439	10,548	5,228	6,630	1,813	499
		Marathwara ..	Males ..	*50,264*	*21,462*	4,112	6,061	3,095	3,887	1,438	2,269
			Females .	*47,779*	*20,461*	8,742	7,424	2,018	1,238	566	473
	CHRISTIAN.										
1	Indian Christian..	Hyderabad State .	Males ..	74,988	34,424	14,870	9,494	4,478	3,685	1,541	356
			Females .	70,397	25,577	13,045	7,611	2,531	1,387	837	166
		Telangana ..	Males ..	*62,447*	*29,276*	12,691	7,709	4,060	3,315	1,297	204
			Females .	*58,341*	*21,120*	10,702	6,406	1,958	1,261	683	115
		Marathwara ..	Males ..	*12,541*	*5,148*	2,179	1,785	418	370	244	152
			Females ..	*12,056*	*4,457*	2,343	1,205	578	126	154	51

* Telangana only † Marathwara only.

VIII.

Castes, Races and Tribes.

TABLE VIII.

AGE, SEX & CIVIL CONDITION FOR SELECTED CASTES, RACES & TRIBES.

MARRIED							WIDOWED						
Total	0—6	7—13	14—16	17—23	24—43	44 and over	Total	0—6	7—13	14—16	17—23	24—43	44 and over
13	14	15	16	17	18	19	20	21	22	23	24	25	26
25,674	535	1,127	2,196	3,510	9,666	8,640	4,349	37	123	340	470	1,295	2,084
23,931	612	1,695	2,272	4,134	9,877	5,341	11,735	20	151	366	530	2,409	8,259
24,709	496	1,044	2,077	3,341	9,317	8,434	*4,157*	35	128	327	438	1,246	1,988
23,154	571	1,680	2,194	3,982	9,626	5,151	*11,521*	18	146	345	489	2,349	8,174
965	39	83	119	169	349	206	*192*	2	..	13	32	49	96
777	41	65	78	152	251	190	*214*	2	5	21	41	60	85
8,592	7	506	689	1,709	3,337	2,344	1,649	39	146	82	177	393	812
8,228	96	869	969	1,398	2,683	2,213	2,424	9	81	61	188	620	1,465
69,166	982	3,857	5,328	13,787	28,740	16,472	12,514	91	214	226	565	4,064	7,354
67,541	2,424	6,095	7,566	11,966	26,202	13,288	18,951	100	320	564	956	6,017	10,994
46,384	604	2,410	2,909	9,190	20,541	10,730	*6,494*	30	45	77	273	2,272	3,797
46,218	856	2,835	3,486	8,847	20,141	10,058	*12,956*	51	107	284	574	4,005	7,985
22,782	378	1,447	2,419	4,597	8,199	5,742	*6,020*	61	169	149	292	1,792	3,557
21,323	1,568	3,260	4,080	8,119	6,061	3,283	*5,995*	49	213	280	382	2,012	3,059
37,454	402	1,414	1,927	4,906	19,309	9,496	3,110	14	21	38	76	746	2,215
35,969	438	2,502	3,056	7,986	16,745	5,242	8,851	29	63	128	380	2,676	5,575
30,654	282	1,050	1,489	3,980	15,675	8,228	*2,517*	8	11	22	42	553	1,881
29,808	307	2,034	2,442	6,917	13,934	4,174	*7,413*	23	51	106	322	2,814	4,597
6,800	120	364	438	976	3,634	1,268	*593*	6	10	16	34	198	384
6,161	131	468	614	1,060	2,811	1,068	*1,438*	6	12	22	58	362	978

Table IX.

INFIRMITIES

PART I.—DISTRIBUTION BY AGE.

PART II.—DISTRIBUTION BY DISTRICTS.

1. The infirmities recorded at the Census were insanity, deaf-mutism, blindness and leprosy.

2. The table is divided into two parts—Part I shows the distribution of the persons afflicted according to age, and Part II their distribution according to locality.

3. None was returned as suffering from more than one infirmity.

TABLE IX.

Infirmities. Part I.—Distribution by Age.

Age	Population afflicted			Insane			Deaf-mute			Blind			Leper		
	Persons	Males	Females	Persons	Males	Females	Persons	Males	Females	Persons	Males	Females	Persons	Males	Females
1	2	3	4	5	6	7	8	9	10	11	12	13	14	15	16
Total	22,196	12,656	9,540	2,200	1,337	863	3,742	2,209	1,533	12,516	6,480	6,036	3,738	2,630	1,108
0—1	*13*	9	4	..	..	..	..	..	..	*13*	9	4	..	..	..
1—2	*65*	43	22	*9*	5	4	*6*	4	2	*50*	34	16	..	..	..
2—3	*122*	62	60	*6*	3	3	*15*	10	5	*92*	46	46	*9*	3	6
3—4	*190*	108	82	*19*	8	11	*46*	23	23	*116*	73	43	*9*	4	5
4—5	*263*	151	112	*33*	25	8	*71*	50	21	*149*	70	79	*10*	6	4
Total 0—5	653	373	280	67	41	26	138	87	51	420	232	188	28	13	15
5—10	*1,189*	688	501	*141*	86	55	*288*	169	119	*687*	882	805	*73*	51	22
10—15	*1,457*	828	629	*190*	111	79	*342*	194	148	*798*	442	856	*127*	81	46
15—20	*1,585*	934	651	*230*	142	88	*322*	205	117	*852*	468	384	*181*	119	62
20—25	*1,765*	1,047	718	*245*	149	96	*329*	197	132	*886*	489	397	*305*	212	93
25—30	*1,820*	1,129	691	*273*	175	98	*330*	201	129	*905*	529	376	*312*	224	88
30—35	*1,855*	1,054	801	*229*	134	95	*325*	178	147	*916*	473	443	*385*	269	116
35—40	*1,471*	850	621	*165*	106	59	*230*	145	85	*750*	369	381	*326*	230	96
40—45	*1,916*	1,119	797	*196*	120	76	*304*	173	131	*938*	482	456	*478*	344	134
45—50	*1,374*	818	556	*102*	68	34	*193*	122	71	*742*	384	358	*337*	244	93
50—55	*1,671*	946	725	*99*	66	33	*239*	136	103	*963*	480	483	*370*	264	106
55—60	*955*	538	417	*48*	25	23	*121*	75	46	*619*	308	311	*167*	130	37
60—65	*1,724*	913	811	*90*	55	35	*225*	132	93	*1,098*	512	586	*311*	214	97
65—70	*781*	424	357	*57*	29	28	*108*	59	49	*490*	250	240	*126*	86	40
70 and over	*1,980*	995	985	*68*	30	38	*248*	136	112	*1,452*	680	772	*212*	149	63

Infirmities. Part II.—Distribution by Districts.

DISTRICT	Population afflicted			Insane			Deaf-mute			Blind			Leper		
	Persons	Males	Females	Persons	Males	Females	Persons	Males	Females	Persons	Males	Females	Persons	Males	Females
1	2	3	4	5	6	7	8	9	10	11	12	13	14	15	16
Hyderabad State ..	22,196	12,656	9,540	2,200	1,337	863	3,742	2,209	1,533	12,516	6,480	6,036	3,738	2,630	1,108
1. Hyderabad City	*675*	458	217	*287*	221	66	*158*	100	58	*172*	99	73	*58*	38	20
2. Atraf-i-Balda ..	*779*	449	330	*102*	56	46	*146*	88	58	*427*	238	189	*104*	67	37
3. Warangal ..	*1,105*	634	471	*168*	92	76	*255*	162	93	*525*	274	251	*157*	106	51
4. Karimnagar ..	*2,423*	1485	938	*268*	160	108	*476*	263	213	*1,067*	609	458	*612*	453	159
5. Adilabad ..	*575*	295	280	*63*	38	25	*156*	85	71	*268*	115	153	*88*	57	31
6. Medak ..	*1,352*	701	651	*234*	130	104	*125*	76	49	*742*	328	414	*251*	167	84
7. Nizamabad ..	*1,171*	686	485	*146*	87	59	*148*	80	68	*531*	273	258	*346*	246	100
8. Mahbubnagar ..	*1,663*	922	741	*164*	104	60	*327*	191	136	*954*	480	474	*218*	147	71
9. Nalgonda ..	*1,517*	821	696	*213*	128	85	*324*	189	135	*747*	357	390	*233*	147	86
10. Aurangabad ..	*1,957*	1098	859	*93*	52	41	*251*	167	84	*1,413*	724	689	*200*	155	45
11. Bir ..	*1,164*	699	465	*49*	31	18	*124*	82	42	*825*	465	360	*166*	121	45
12. Nander ..	*418*	205	213	*22*	13	9	*64*	43	21	*278*	114	164	*54*	35	19
13. Parbhani ..	*1,807*	1 006	801	*84*	51	33	*211*	109	102	*1,353*	730	623	*159*	116	43
14. Gulbarga ..	*1,690*	967	723	*65*	32	33	*315*	185	130	*971*	509	462	*339*	241	98
15. Osmanabad ..	*1,586*	944	642	*76*	40	36	*181*	114	67	*856*	445	411	*473*	345	128
16. Raichur ..	*962*	536	426	*103*	58	45	*246*	139	107	*510*	280	230	*103*	59	44
17. Bidar ..	*1,352*	750	602	*63*	44	19	*235*	136	99	*877*	440	437	*177*	130	47

Table X.

OCCUPATION OR MEANS OF LIVELIHOOD

Note :—1. In this table the occupations have been arranged in 4 classes, 12 sub-classes, 55 orders and 195 groups and figures are given for the whole population of the State and districts also.

2. Figures are given for Earners and Working Dependents only for each occupational group. It also shows for each group, the number of persons who follow it as a subsidiary means of livelihood to any other principal occupation. Persons who are totally dependent are shown on the top for the State and as well as for the districts but no attempt has been made to distribute their numbers among the different occupations.

3. " Working Dependents " means those persons of either sex who, working part or whole time, help to augment the source of the family income, living under his or her principal Earner.

4. Group 160 has been split into 160 and 160a, showing His Exalted Highness the Nizam's State servants in the former and other Indian and foreign servants in the latter category.

5. No distinction is made of figures in regard to Prisoners undergoing rigorous and other kind of imprisonment as their details have not been forthcoming and these have been shown as " working dependents " under the corresponding group.

6. The following groups which are blank for the State are omitted from the table :—

Order	Group	Occupation	
1	9	Cultivation of	Cinchona.
,,	10	Do	Cocoanut.
,,	11	Do	Coffee.
,,	12	Do	Ganja
,,	14	Do	Rubber.
,,	15	Do	Tea.
3	29	Exploitation of	Gold.
,,	31	Do	Lead, silver and Zinc.
,,	32	Do	Manganese.
,,	33	Do	Tin and Wolfram.
,,	34	Do	Other metallic minerals.
4	36	Do	Petroleum.
5	44	Jute pressing, ginning and Weaving.	
11	79	Manufacture of Opium.	
15	93	Transport—Ship, boat aeroplane builders.	
18	101	Persons concerned with aerodromes and aeroplanes.	
19	102	Ship owners, boat owners and their employees, etc.	
,,	103	Persons 'other than labourers' employed in harbours, docks, rivers, canals, etc.	
41	155	Navy.	
42	156	Air Force.	

TABLE X.

Occupation or Means of Livelihood.

	HYDERABAD STATE Males	HYDERABAD STATE Females	HYDERABAD CITY Males	HYDERABAD CITY Females	ATRAF-I-BALDA Males	ATRAF-I-BALDA Females
Total Earners	3,262,208	1,561,674	160,848	34,498	129,233	79,207
Total Working Dependents	987,432	991,220	48,082	47,714	46,066	53,176
Total Non-working Dependents	3,120,370	4,313,242	38,693	137,059	78,676	113,303
Total Population	7,370,010	7,066,138	247,623	219,271	253,975	245,686

Serial No.	Occupation	HYDERABAD STATE: Total earners showing occupation as Principal		Total working dependents		Total following occupation as subsidiary		HYDERABAD CITY: Total earners showing occupation as Principal		Total working dependents		Total following occupation as subsidiary		ATRAF-I-BALDA: Total earners showing occupation as Principal		Total working dependents		Total following occupation as subsidiary	
		Males	Females	Males	Females	Males	Females	Males	Females	Males	Females	Males	Females	Males	Females	Males	Females	Males	Females
	1	2	3	4	5	6	7	8	9	10	11	12	13	14	15	16	17	18	19
1	TOTAL WORKERS	3,262,208	1,561,674	987,412	991,220	616,751	348,984	160,848	34,498	48,082	47,714	13,984	2,226	129,333	79,207	46,066	53,176	25,881	10,836
2	A.—Production of raw Materials ..	1,850,887	982,131	512,243	558,945	342,188	199,300	14,805	2,812	5,866	8,218	3,989	280	77,448	53,182	23,102	33,081	15,828	6,457
3	I.—Exploitation of Animals and vegetation	1,887,462	979,181	505,218	553,687	338,751	197,770	14,361	2,812	5,866	8,218	3,963	280	77,448	53,182	23,102	33,081	15,828	6,457
4	1. Pasture and Agriculture.	1,785,442	958,011	489,090	543,524	328,829	190,439	14,205	2,784	5,061	8,117	3,567	280	74,940	52,738	21,708	32,640	15,415	6,287
5	(a) Cultivation ..	1,558,371	877,074	427,798	473,700	290,629	162,095	8,306	1,102	2,518	3,064	1,927	243	69,954	50,493	19,502	30,323	14,383	6,242
6	(G.1) Non-cultivating proprietors taking rent in money or kind ..	228,280	90,417	68,419	53,577	40,584	23,222	8,840	430	602	1,118	571	121	14,805	3,960	5,092	2,922	3,271	1,443
7	(G.2) Estate Agents and Managers of owners ..	4,367	2	979	26	731	..	589	2	376	26	295	..	110	..	72	..	18	..
8	(G.3) Estate Agents and Managers of Government	3,596	..	962	..	389	..	255	..	237	..	141	..	49	..	36	..	20	..
9	(G.4) Rent Collectors, clerks, etc. ..	7,409	..	1,753	..	1,169	..	1,769	..	712	..	372	..	275	..	110	..	65	..
10	(G.5) Cultivating owners ..	370,863	210,786	146,099	128,084	101,773	42,586	549	146	279	221	141	18	24,532	11,866	5,490	9,155	4,483	2,030
11	(G.6) Tenant cultivators ..	264,521	112,856	69,812	44,705	30,174	22,914	790	112	101	227	271	4	8,236	5,535	3,174	3,519	2,383	1,096
12	(G.7) Agricultural labourers	479,335	463,018	139,774	237,308	86,859	73,373	514	412	211	1,472	136	100	21,947	29,132	5,528	14,727	4,093	1,673
13	(b.) Cultivation of special crops, fruit, etc. ..	20,500	14,992	7,374	13,611	4,801	4,865	1,066	436	348	1,074	212	26	2,288	388	912	260	347	7
14	(G.13) Pan-Vine ..	1,794	638	779	853	504	321	45	2	37	28	11	1	361	65	233	37	114	5
15	(G.16) Market Gardeners, flower, fruit growers, etc.	18,706	14,354	6,595	12,758	4,297	4,544	1,021	434	311	1,046	201	25	1,927	323	679	232	233	2
16	(c.) Forestry	22,947	5,080	6,451	4,864	5,263	1,263	773	239	346	932	154	10	669	115	284	49	87	8
17	(G.17) Forest officers rangers, guards, etc. ..	433	..	137	..	17	..	123	..	21	..	..	..	57	..	39	..	15	..
18	(G.18) Wood-cutters and charcoal burners ..	21,181	4,669	5,784	4,474	4,864	1,106	509	222	229	871	82	3	612	115	245	49	72	8
19	(G-19) Collectors of forest produce.	703	208	174	229	160	88	72	17	18	61	33	7	..	..	..	..	..	..
20	(G.20) Collectors of lac ..	610	203	356	161	222	69	69	..	78	..	39	..	..	..	..	..	..	..
21	(d) Stock raising ..	180,863	60,349	46,874	50,792	27,482	22,049	3,954	904	1,790	2,992	1,256	..	1,843	1,741	890	1,967	563	29
22	(G.21) Cattle and buffalo breeders and keepers ..	22,751	9,404	7,368	7,816	4,421	2,969	2,514	772	1,132	2,691	825	..	439	247	380	102	118	10

23	(G.22) Breeders of transport animals	1,431	11	542	1	726	..	399	1	262	1	182	..	17	..	12	..	10	..
24	(G.23) Herdsmen, shepherds and breeders of other animals	156,681	50,934	38,944	42,975	22,835	19,080	1,041	221	396	300	249	..	1,387	1,494	498	1,865	435	16
25	(e) Raising of small animals and insects ..	2,761	516	593	557	646	167	106	13	59	55	18	1	186	21	120	32	85	4
26	(G.24) Birds, bees, etc. ..	1,651	319	383	314	411	92	79	12	42	25	15	1	176	21	112	32	79	4
27	(G.25) Silk worms ..	615	133	126	171	152	36	21	..	14	17	3	..	10	..	8	..	6	..
28	(G.26) Lac cultivation ..	495	64	84	72	73	39	6	1	3	13	..	..	..	..	..	..	..	..
29	2. Fishing and hunting ..	52,020	21,170	16,128	10,163	9,930	7,331	356	28	805	101	396	..	2,508	424	1,394	441	413	170
30	(G.27) Fishing and pearling	33,578	14,864	8,228	7,473	5,365	3,951	204	26	524	79	247	..	1,954	83	775	211	222	11
31	(G.28) Hunting ..	18,442	6,306	7,900	2,590	4,565	3,380	152	2	281	22	149	..	554	341	619	230	191	159
32	II. Exploitation of Minerals	13,425	2,950	7,025	5,258	3,437	1,530	244	..	..	..	26	..	..	..	..	..	..	..
33	3. Metallic minerals ..	385	38	222	132	22	1	17	..	..	..	4	..	..	..	..	..	..	..
34	(G.30) Iron	385	38	222	132	22	1	17	..	..	..	4	..	..	..	..	..	..	..
35	4. Non-Metallic minerals .	13,040	2,912	6,803	5,126	3,415	1,529	227	..	..	..	22	..	..	..	..	..	..	..
36	(G.35) Coal	6,832	2,230	3,696	4,013	3,146	1,419	46	..	..	..	10	..	..	..	..	..	..	..
37	(G.37) Building materials (including stone, materials for cement manufacture and clays)	5,657	648	2,977	1,033	246	102	171	..	..	..	8	..	..	..	..	..	..	..
38	(G.38) Mica	153	11	47	36	20	7	7	..	..	..	1	..	..	..	..	..	..	..
39	(G.40) Salt, saltpetre and other saline substances ..	398	23	83	44	3	1	3	..	..	..	3	..	..	..	..	..	..	..
40.	**B.—Preparation and supply of material substances.**	899,824	350,220	301,941	262,169	188,603	100,054	62,833	8,620	15,206	15,422	6,307	341	33,078	18,789	14,213	15,080	5,334	3,346
41	III. Industry ..	359,044	140,729	124,053	91,381	76,531	37,763	16,978	2,999	4,571	3,899	2,001	115	13,223	6,213	5,628	6,264	2,339	1,717
42	5. Textiles	99,427	43,852	29,466	21,318	18,962	9,931	909	182	570	409	205	8	4,439	1,981	1,880	2,180	1,230	646
43	(G.42) Cotton ginning, cleaning and Pressing ..	7,059	4,188	3,195	3,338	2,014	840	126	26	89	71	42	2	213	167	121	132	41	43
44	(G.43) Cotton spinning, seizing and weaving ..	78,949	34,092	18,990	13,941	13,853	7,693	227	45	118	87	47	2	545	273	259	286	183	95
45	(G.45) Rope, twine, string and other fibres ..	5,455	1,908	1,797	1,446	1,007	514	49	9	27	16	16	..	1,563	682	556	916	430	216
46	(G.46) Wool carding spinning and weaving ..	9,151	2,045	3,461	1,639	1,686	633	18	3	5	4	3	..	1,969	784	872	765	545	276
47	(G.47) Silk spinning and weaving	881	375	552	348	141	84	51	11	26	18	7	..	..	..	..	..	..	..
48	(G.48) Hair (Horse-hair) etc.	72	16	26	30	36	11	5	1	17	9	3	..	..	..	..	..	..	..
49	(G.49) Dyeing, bleaching, printing, preparation and sponging of textiles ..	2,483	480	1,261	462	641	124	332	66	201	151	52	8	149	75	72	81	31	16
50	(G.50) Lace, crepe, embroideries, fringes, etc., and insufficiently described textiles.	377	148	184	119	84	32	101	21	87	53	35	1	..	..	..	..	..	..
51	6. Hides, skips and hard materials from the animal kingdom.	5,507	1,097	2,817	779	1,451	225	241	47	94	53	15	..	135	67	100	125	26	12
52	(G.51) Working in leather .	5,229	1,069	2,690	741	1,421	225	196	39	53	31	12	..	135	67	100	125	26	12
53	(G.52) Furriers and persons occupied with feathers and bristles; brush makers ..	78	7	45	14	3	..	37	7	29	14	..	..	..	..	..	..	..	..
54	(G.53) Bone, Ivory horn shell, etc., workers (except buttons)	200	21	82	24	27	..	8	1	12	8	3	..	..	..	..	..	..	..
55	7. Wood	28,388	9,985	8,831	5,630	6,723	2,852	1,981	277	386	355	145	8	848	334	282	292	131	95
56	(G.54) Sawyers ..	908	39	337	123	113	3	97	19	118	89	21	1	24	10	11	16	5	2
57	(G.55) Carpenters, turners and joiners, etc. ..	18,964	3,223	5,743	2,758	4,603	1,422	982	94	127	90	101	1	596	188	180	102	107	57

TABLE X.

Occupation or Means of Livelihood.

	HYDERABAD STATE Males	HYDERABAD STATE Females	HYDERABAD CITY Males	HYDERABAD CITY Females	ATRAF-I-BALDA Males	ATRAF-I-BALDA Females
Total Earners	3,262,208	1,561,674	160,848	34,498	129,288	79,207
Total Working Dependents	987,432	991,220	48,082	47,714	46,066	53,176
Total Non-working Dependents	3,120,370	4,513,242	38,693	137,059	78,676	113,303
Total Population	7,370,010	7,066,138	247,623	219,271	253,975	245,686

Serial No.	Occupation	HYDERABAD STATE: Total earners showing occupation as principal — Males	Females	Total working dependents — Males	Females	Total following occupation as subsidiary — Males	Females	HYDERABAD CITY: Total earners showing occupation as principal — Males	Females	Total working dependents — Males	Females	Total following occupation as subsidiary — Males	Females	ATRAF-I-BALDA: Total earners showing occupation as principal — Males	Females	Total working dependents — Males	Females	Total following occupation as subsidiary — Males	Females
	1	2	3	4	5	6	7	8	9	10	11	12	13	14	15	16	17	18	19
58	(G.56) Basket-makers and other industries of woody materials, including leaves and thatchers and builders working with bamboo, reeds or similar materials ..	8,511	6,723	2,751	2,749	2,007	1,427	902	167	141	176	23	6	228	136	91	174	19	36
59	8. Metals	22,346	6,485	7,827	3,190	5,474	2,019	962	105	339	132	111	1	495	233	307	208	79	40
60	(G.57) Smelting, forging and rolling of iron and other metals	139	2	53	3	21	..	15	2	14	3	..	..	..	..	..	..	..	..
61	(G.58) Makers of arms, guns, etc. ..	55	..	31	..	8	..	12	..	10	..	2	..	40	..	21	..	6	..
62	(G.59) Black-smiths, other workers in iron, makers of implements	13,817	3,879	4,801	2,192	3,808	1,425	532	76	171	94	70	1	264	188	81	97	57	29
63	(G.60) Workers in brass, copper and bell metals ..	7,439	2,514	2,496	892	1,423	556	196	15	79	18	14	..	191	95	105	111	16	11
64	(G.61) Workers in other metals (except precious) ..	765	90	410	102	195	38	76	12	29	16	6	..	..	..	..	..	..	..
65	(G.62) Workers in mints, die-sinkers, etc ..	131	..	36	1	19	..	131	..	36	1	19	..	..	..	..	..	..	..
66	9. Ceramics	20,233	10,845	5,379	7,476	3,837	2,800	350	170	141	92	72	8	446	291	166	252	33	22
67	(G.63) Potters and makers of earthen ware ..	18,190	10,353	4,897	7,146	3,247	2,707	179	135	34	26	25	1	306	226	125	239	28	16
68	(G.64) Brick and tile makers	1,656	472	362	291	518	90	127	25	35	27	18	4	120	65	27	13	..	6
69	(G.65) Other workers in ceramics	387	20	120	39	77	3	53	10	72	39	29	3	20	..	14	..	5	..
70	10. Chemical products properly so-called and analogous	8,076	3,905	2,690	4,135	1,440	1,741	180	20	77	56	40	1	89	33	33	18	34	10
71	(G.66) Manufacture of matches, fireworks and other explosives ..	218	37	104	54	29	9	69	11	48	36	17	1	18	8	15	6	4	4
72	(G.67) Manufacture of aerated and mineral waters and ice	147	11	38	18	20	..	62	9	12	18	11	..	5	1	4	..	2	..

TABLE X.
OCCUPATION OR MEANS OF LIVELIHOOD.

73	(G.68) Manufacture and refining of vegetable oils ..	7,272	3,596	2,406	3,915	1,328	1,720	37	..	14	2	12	..	64	24	11	12	28	6
74	(G.69) Manufacture and refining of mineral oils ..	84	10	15	16	5	..	10	..	3	..	..	..	2	..	3	..	..	..
75	(G.70) Others ..	355	251	127	132	58	12	2	..	..	..	..	..	..	..	..	..	..	..
76	11. Food Industries ..	13,057	4,155	4,259	3,429	2,537	930	3,194	487	681	640	344	44	613	330	238	293	87	96
77	(G.71) Rice pounders and huskers and flour grinders	451	583	193	536	73	128	31	16	38	140	7	1	74	58	10	36	1	18
78	(G.72) Grain Parchers, etc.	38	102	12	93	1	25	15	2	9	12	1	1	..	..	..	..	..	..
79	(G.73) Butchers ..	4,902	1,232	1,437	615	757	185	941	19	109	51	59	2	181	94	32	38	25	16
80	(G.74) Makers of sugar, molasses and gur ..	202	104	41	100	26	16	99	16	21	13	12	..	..	..	..	..	..	..
81	(G.75) Sweetmeat and condiment makers ..	1,156	647	390	626	276	225	466	115	107	137	38	36	57	28	16	18	10	9
82	(G.76) Toddy drawers ..	3,520	621	1,422	772	850	158	179	34	27	18	18	..	235	117	142	168	44	49
83	(G.77) Brewers and distillers	546	68	153	68	72	7	245	49	51	39	22	2	18	..	12	..	1	..
84	(G.78) Manufacturers of tobacco	2,080	788	588	608	479	185	1,175	235	312	228	184	2	48	33	21	33	6	4
85	(G.80) Manufacturers of Ganja.	67	2	9	..	..	..	16	..	3	..	..	..	..	..	..	..	..	..
86	(G.81) Others ..	86	8	14	11	3	1	27	1	4	2	3	..	..	..	..	..	..	..
87	12. Industries of dress and toilet	125,804	48,006	51,674	36,136	28,495	12,905	5,898	840	1,379	1,262	388	11	5,226	2,412	2,061	2,285	513	674
88	(G.82) Boot, shoe, sandal and clog makers ..	40,841	8,871	12,435	11,467	11,724	3,376	1,242	248	279	304	76	3	1,061	432	488	499	128	199
89	(G.83) Tailors, milliners, dress makers and darners .	18,923	8,365	6,348	7,218	3,727	2,669	1,245	211	216	343	149	3	1,240	575	662	690	97	198
90	(G.84) Embroiderers, hatmakers and makers of other articles of wear ..	709	235	282	273	52	118	69	2	12	6	5	4	336	168	97	164	29	80
91	(G.85) Washing and cleaning	44,030	26,492	25,274	12,918	7,950	5,193	1,323	264	399	307	91	1	1,317	1,083	444	842	158	187
92	(G.86) Barbers, hair dressers and wigmakers ..	21,021	4,023	7,300	4,236	5,016	1,549	1,490	115	461	299	51	..	1,166	134	368	69	91	10
93	(G.87) Other industries connected with the toilet ..	280	20	35	24	26	..	29	..	12	3	16	..	106	20	7	21	10	..
94	13. Furniture industries ..	550	22	126	54	69	4	88	16	24	20	18	1	14	6	5	6	3	3
95	(G.88) Cabinet-makers, carriage painters, etc. ..	455	20	120	50	69	4	71	14	20	16	18	1	14	6	5	6	3	8
96	(G.89) Upholsterers, tentmakers, etc.	55	2	6	4	..	..	12	2	4	4	..	..	..	..	..	..	..	..
97	14. Building industries ..	10,641	2,807	3,466	3,421	2,443	1,477	761	142	122	146	79	2	130	76	40	25	27	12
98	(G.90) Lime burners cement workers: excavators and well sinkers; stone cutters and dressers; brick layers and masons; builders (other than buildings made of bamboo and similar materials) painters decorators of houses, tilers, plumbers, etc., ...	10,641	2,807	3,466	3,421	2,443	1,477	761	142	122	146	79	2	13	76	40	25	27	12
99	15. Construction of means of transport	2,085	38	586	37	411	9	710	3	183	18	213	5	131	31	73	16	42	4
100	(G.91) Persons engaged in making, assembling or repairing motor vehicles or cycles	697	..	175	..	161	..	391	..	87	..	112	..	44	..	14	..	10	..
101	(G.92) Carriage, cart, palki, etc., makers and wheelwrights	1,388	38	411	37	250	9	319	3	96	18	101	5	87	31	59	16	32	4
102	16. Production and transmission of physical force ..	214	..	29	3	21	..	168	..	26	3	17	..	6	..	..	..	..	..

TABLE X

Occupation or Means of Livelihood.

	HYDERABAD STATE Males	HYDERABAD STATE Females	HYDERABAD CITY Males	HYDERABAD CITY Females	ATRAF-I-BALDA Males	ATRAF-I-BALDA Females
Total Earners	3,262,208	1,561,674	160,848	34,498	129,238	79,207
Total Working Dependents	987,432	991,220	48,082	47,714	46,066	58,176
Total Non-working Dependents	3,120,370	4,513,242	38,693	137,059	78,676	118,303
Total Population	7,370,010	7,066,138	247,623	219,271	253,975	245,686

Serial No.	Occupation	HYDERABAD STATE: Total earners showing occupation as principal — Males	Females	Total working dependents — Males	Females	Total following occupation as subsidiary — Males	Females	HYDERABAD CITY: Total earners showing occupation as principal — Males	Females	Total working dependents — Males	Females	Total following occupation as subsidiary — Males	Females	ATRAF-I-BALDA: Total earners showing occupation as principal — Males	Females	Total working dependents — Males	Females	Total following occupation as subsidiary — Males	Females
	1	2	3	4	5	6	7	8	9	10	11	12	13	14	15	16	17	18	19
103	(G.94) Heat, light, electricity, motive power, etc., Gas works and electric light and power ..	214	..	29	3	21	..	168	..	26	3	17	..	6	..	..	..	..	..
104	17. Miscellaneous and undefined industries. ..	22,721	9,532	6,908	5,773	4,668	2,870	2,032	710	549	713	354	26	651	419	548	564	134	108
105	(G.95) Printers, engravers, book-binders, etc. ..	658	..	184	..	157	..	376	..	105	..	71	..	12	..	4	..	3	..
106	(G.96) Makers of musical instruments ..	75	..	16	..	15	..	29	..	8	..	12	..	..	..	..	..	..	..
107	(G.97) Makers of clocks and surgical or scientific instruments, etc... ..	504	..	79	..	33	..	397	..	39	..	21	..	4	..	..	..	..	..
108	(G.98) Makers of jewellery and ornaments ..	16,414	7,263	5,000	4,132	3,970	2,508	441	88	192	98	140	11	368	186	354	398	69	34
109	(G.99) Other miscellaneous and undefined industries, toy making taxidermy, etc.	1,084	963	293	890	125	280	240	212	72	239	39	9	125	132	70	84	20	26
110	(G. 100) Scavenging ..	3,991	1,306	1,322	744	368	82	549	410	133	376	71	6	142	101	120	82	42	43
111	IV. Transport ..	146,588	48,047	59,750	51,811	23,800	20,782	20,841	3,101	3,809	5,515	317	17	1,095	830	311	306	129	186
112	19. Transport by water ..	5,410	624	2,987	981	1,285	526	123	17	19	28	3	..	12	6	4	2	1	..
113	(G.104) Labourers employed on harbours, docks, rivers and canals ..	5,410	624	2,987	981	1,285	526	123	17	19	28	3	17	12	6	4	2	1	..
114	20. Transport by Road ..	95,793	33,642	38,963	27,568	13,021	7,657	13,491	3,005	2,820	3,006	238	17	770	533	224	178	74	147
115	(G.105) Persons (other than labourers) employed on the construction and maintenance of roads and bridges .	1,068	37	319	20	108	2	269	..	112	..	15	..	74	37	17	18	4	2
116	(G.106) Labourers employed on roads and bridges ..	54,140	29,493	27,260	23,646	8,227	6,833	3,976	1,907	445	1,663	19	17	115	410	31	87	12	132
117	(G.107) Owners, managers and employees (excluding personal servants) connected with mechanically driven vehicles (including trams)	1,579	380	405	556	469	163	112	19	27	36	..	..	23	..	14	..	..	..

118	(G. 108) Owners, managers, employees (excluding personal servants) connected with other vehicles	25,100	2,399	6,971	1,896	2,887	307	5,719	990	1,455	722	146	..	69	72	28	56	5	10
119	(G.109) Palki, etc., bearers and owners	5,802	254	1,367	410	812	65	396	57	119	264	27	..	283	..	70	...	28	..
120	(G.110) Pack elephant, camel, mule, ass and bullock owners and drivers	4,115	1,010	1,456	698	682	284	49	..	20	..	4	..	25	..	10	..	..	..
121	(G.111) Porters and messengers	8,971	60	1,184	842	886	3	2,970	32	642	321	27	..	181	14	54	17	25	3
122	21. Transport by rail	42,795	13,766	16,909	23,228	9,089	12,599	6,600	65	404	2,449	72	..	278	201	64	126	49	39
123	(G.112) Railway employees of all kinds other than porters and coolies	7,976	188	1,167	352	642	54	4,674	35	293	129	27	..	127	..	34	..	14	..
124	(G.113) Labourers employed on railway construction and maintenance and coolies and porters employed on railway premises	34,819	13,578	15,742	22,876	8,447	12,545	1,926	30	111	2,820	45	..	146	201	30	126	35	39
125	22. Post Office, Telegraph and Telephone services	2,590	15	891	34	405	..	627	14	66	32	4	..	40	..	19	..	5	..
126	(G.114) Post office, Telegraph and Telephone services	2,590	15	891	34	405	..	627	14	66	32	4	..	40	..	19	..	5	..
127	V. Trade	394,192	161,444	118,138	118,977	88,272	41,509	25,014	2,520	7,326	6,008	3,989	209	18,760	11,746	8,274	8,510	2,866	1,443
128	23. Banks, establishments of credit, exchange and insurance	14,069	2,036	2,985	755	2,207	291	1,242	124	481	128	237	5	209	13	153	7	115	16
129	(G.115) Bank managers, money-lenders, exchange & insurance agents, money-changers and brokers and their employees	14,069	2,036	2,985	755	2,207	291	1,242	124	481	128	237	5	209	13	153	7	115	16
130	24. Brokerage commission and export	1,137	84	166	20	129	..	861	84	143	20	99	..	16	..	12	..	14	..
131	(G.116) Brokers, commission agents, commercial travellers, warehouse owners and employees	1,137	84	166	20	129	..	861	84	143	220	99	..	16	..	12	..	14	..
132	25. Trade in Textiles	20,025	5,725	7,123	5,690	3,379	1,005	1,415	141	396	207	201	6	1,227	418	866	385	392	55
133	(G.117) Trade in piece-goods, wool, cotton, silk, hair and other textiles	20,025	5,725	7,123	5,690	3,379	1,005	1,415	141	396	207	201	6	1,227	418	866	385	392	55
134	26. Trade in skins, leather, and furs.	3,893	1,567	1,717	1,488	960	288	463	16	181	95	67	2	606	885	389	582	123	84
135	(G.118) Trade in skins, leather, furs, feathers, horn, etc., and the articles made from these	3,893	1,567	1,717	1,488	960	288	463	16	181	95	67	2	606	885	389	582	123	84
136	27. Trade in Wood	4,541	1,303	1,496	1,464	972	806	1,900	205	829	516	523	39	250	367	165	290	34	82
137	(G.119) Trade in wood (not fire-wood)	2,134	279	1,018	448	587	71	1,093	90	602	227	431	13	124	68	110	115	32	82
138	(G.120) Trade in barks	660	324	97	249	92	79	245	25	34	39	27	9	..	18	..	20	..	10
139	(G.121) Trade in bamboos and canes	1,228	309	234	471	229	83	598	49	162	163	55	12	12	..	..	..	..	..
140	(G.122) Trade in thatches and other forest produce	519	391	147	296	64	73	54	41	31	87	10	5	114	286	55	155	2	40
141	28. Trade in metals	1,438	509	449	428	188	78	268	27	61	55	29	..	55	31	33	20	20	..
142	(G.123) Trade in metals, machinery, knives, tools, etc.	1,438	509	449	428	188	78	268	27	61	55	29	..	55	31	33	20	20	..
143	29. Trade in pottery, bricks and tiles	4,205	4,739	1,247	4,971	548	1,389	422	44	70	365	46	..	1,010	785	353	872	118	131

TABLE X.

Occupation or Means of Livelihood.

	HYDERABAD STATE Males	HYDERABAD STATE Females	HYDERABAD CITY Males	HYDERABAD CITY Females	ATRAF-I-BALDA Males	ATRAF-I-BALDA Females
Total Earners	3,262,208	1,561,674	160,848	34,498	129,233	79,207
Total Working Dependents	987,432	991,220	48,082	47,714	46,066	53,176
Total Non-working Dependents	3,120,370	4,513,242	38,693	137,059	78,676	113,303
Total Population	7,370,010	7,066,138	247,623	219,271	253,975	245,686

Serial Number	Occupation	HYDERABAD STATE: Total earners showing occupation as principal		Total working dependents		Total following occupation as subsidiary		HYDERABAD CITY: Total earners showing occupation as principal		Total working dependents		Total following occupation as subsidiary		ATRAF-I-BALDA: Total earners showing occupation as principal		Total working dependents		Total following occupation as subsidiary	
		Males	Females	Males	Females	Males	Females	Males	Females	Males	Females	Males	Females	Males	Females	Males	Females	Males	Females
	1	2	3	4	5	6	7	8	9	10	11	12	13	14	15	16	17	18	19
144	(G.124) Trade in pottery, bricks and tiles ..	4,205	4,739	1,247	4,971	548	1,389	422	44	70	365	46	..	1,010	78	353	872	118	131
145	30. Trade in chemical products	736	34	103	26	47	..	343	34	54	22	38	..	14	..	6	..	1	..
146	(G.125) Drugs, dyes, paints, petroleum, explosives, etc.	736	34	103	26	47	..	343	34	54	22	38	..	14	..	6	..	1	..
147	31. Hotels, cafes, restaurants, etc.	76,798	45,451	21,049	21,795	19,944	10,636	2,585	176	686	411	412	31	716	668	470	688	111	83
148	(G.126) Vendors of wine, liquors, aerated waters and ice.	74,133	44,641	20,305	21,062	19,255	10,371	1,799	98	533	261	331	21	277	452	190	363	32	48
149	(G.127) Owners and managers of hotels, cook shops, sarais, etc., (and employees)	1,815	373	512	271	467	208	595	58	123	111	69	3	310	71	153	39	44	15
150	(G.128) Hawkers of drink and food stuffs ..	850	437	232	462	222	57	191	20	30	39	12	7	129	145	118	286	35	20
151	32. Other trade in food stuffs	79,830	37,616	28,407	34,097	15,990	8,106	6,028	779	1,251	1,338	641	55	5,844	2,285	2,398	2,055	974	273
152	(G.129) Grain and pulse dealers	35,256	7,274	12,068	8,428	6,109	1,446	2,763	188	332	216	240	10	3,385	693	1,043	875	522	121
153	(G.130) Dealers in sweetmeats, sugar and spices ..	3,505	2,455	1,246	2,734	672	798	697	69	193	257	59	12	897	543	213	396	61	45
154	(G.131) Dealers in dairy product, eggs and poultry.	15,577	25,214	5,871	19,866	3,900	507	686	373	285	658	128	18	806	969	682	656	270	52
155	(G.132) Dealers in animals for food	1,516	114	363	153	93	47	387	17	86	29	32	..	271	52	182	83	41	40
156	(G.133) Dealers in fodder for animals	765	80	254	49	142	3	210	26	37	24	49	..	36	..	19	..	6	..
157	(G.134) Dealers in other food stuffs	16,860	1,602	6,931	2,152	3,956	490	185	5	60	3	15	..	120	..	62	..	18	..
158	(G.135) Dealers in tobacco.	5,684	877	1,565	678	1,020	244	889	101	192	114	101	15	214	28	157	45	56	15
159	(G.136) Dealers in opium .	272	..	36	18	26	..	135	..	27	18	5	..	..	..	..	..	..	..
160	(G.137) Dealers in ganja ..	395	..	73	19	12	..	126	..	30	19	12	..	25	..	10	..	..	..
161	33. Trade in clothing and toilet articles	8,269	1,484	2,303	1,417	1,161	250	1,184	118	289	165	110	10	423	210	260	237	34	50

15*

162	(G.138) Trade in ready-made clothing and other article of dress and the toilet (hats, umbrellas, socks, ready-made shoes, perfumes, etc.)	8,269	1,484	2,303	1,417	1,161	250	1,184	118	289	165	110	10	423	210	260	237	34	50
163	34. Trade in furniture ..	2,436	711	677	1,094	350	299	596	58	73	55	37	..	49	5	22	3	6	..
164	(G.139) Trade in furniture, carpet, curtains and bedding	1,117	95	273	63	167	12	386	31	43	20	21	..	15	..	4	..	..	..
165	(G.140) Hardware, cooking utensils, porcelain crockery, glass-ware bottles, articles for gardening, etc. ..	1,319	616	404	1,031	183	287	212	27	30	35	16	..	34	5	18	3	6	..
166	35. Trade in building materials	2,614	122	890	336	242	58	244	14	62	40	36	..	64	2	46	3	11	..
167	(G.141) Trade in building materials(other than bricks, tiles and woody materials).	2,614	122	890	336	242	58	244	14	62	40	36	..	64	2	46	3	11	..
168	36. Trade in means of transport	7,689	508	2,086	544	1,041	167	868	49	213	89	70	5	778	5	396	18	102	12
169	(G.142) Dealers and hirers in mechanical transport motors, cycles, etc. ..	1,008	8	277	10	206	2	341	6	89	9	20	2	120	..	65	..	32	..
170	(G.143) Dealers and hirers in other carriages, carts, boats, etc.	4,696	437	1,316	484	595	145	493	43	94	76	38	3	482	5	243	18	40	12
171	(G.144) Dealers and hirers of elephants, camels, horses, cattle, asses, mules, etc. .	1,985	58	493	50	240	20	29	..	30	4	12	..	176	..	88	..	30	..
172	37. Trade in fuel ..	16,917	9,266	6,219	7,321	4,097	2,808	753	79	214	540	152	5	2,686	2,845	843	956	360	329
173	(G.145) Delears in firewood, charcoal, coal, cowdung, etc.	16,917	9,266	6,219	7,321	4,097	2,808	753	79	214	540	152	5	2,686	2,845	843	956	360	329
174	38. Trade in articles of luxury and those pertaining to letters and the arts and sciences	8,444	4,669	3,382	6,336	1,594	1,273	4,003	213	1,370	785	745	14	406	1,381	253	1,642	69	112
175	(G.146) Dealers in precious stones, jewellery (real and imitation) clocks, optical instruments, etc. ..	2,049	144	700	209	285	3	944	81	278	123	134	3	6	..	2	..	..	..
176	(G.147) Dealers in common bangles, bead necklaces, fans, small articles, toys, hunting and fishing tackle, flowers, etc.	3,318	4,464	1,642	6,048	706	1,266	528	76	290	593	101	7	236	1,381	118	1,642	27	112
177	(G.148) Publishers, booksellers, stationers, dealers in music, pictures, musical instruments and curiosities	3,077	61	1,040	79	603	4	2,531	56	802	69	510	4	164	..	133	..	42	..
178	39. Trade of other sorts ..	141,151	45,025	37,839	31,194	35,423	14,605	1,757	359	953	1,177	546	37	4,407	1,846	1,609	752	382	216
179	(G.149) Dealers in rags, stable refuse, etc. ..	528	108	357	108	48	20	24	41	18	37	7	3	265	41	280	30	20	17
180	(G.150) General store-keepers and shop-keepers, otherwise unspecified ..	138,379	43,755	36,500	30,700	34,904	13,705	1,245	299	721	1,116	449	29	3,703	1,764	983	655	323	186
181	(G.151) Itinerant traders, pedlars, and hawkers (of other than food, etc.) ..	1,646	1,745	721	360	400	878	379	15	142	20	59	5	125	23	184	45	19	11
182	(G.152) Other trades (including farmers of pound, tools and markets) ..	598	22	261	26	71	2	109	4	72	4	31	..	314	18	162	22	20	2
183	C. Public Administration and Liberal Arts ..	163,197	23,826	57,978	22,126	24,126	6,015	42,638	5,120	13,021	5,015	2,533	215	5,357	814	1,528	862	1,571	188
184	VI. Public Force ..	39,421	1,209	9,510	2,457	2,340	151	17,066	440	2,297	691	35	..	1,723	..	140	..	11	..

TABLE X.

Occupation or Means of Livelihood.

	Hyderabad State Males	Hyderabad State Females	Hyderabad City Males	Hyderabad City Females	Atraf-i-Balda Males	Atraf-i-Balda Females
Total Earners	3,262,208	1,561,674	160,848	34,498	129,233	79,207
Total Working Dependents	987,432	991,220	48,082	47,714	46,066	53,176
Total Non-working Dependents	3,120,370	4,513,242	38,693	137,059	78,676	113,303
Total Population	7,370,010	7,066,138	247,623	219,271	253,975	245,686

Serial No.	Occupation	Hyderabad State: Total earners showing occupation as principal		Total working dependents		Total following occupation as subsidiary		Hyderabad City: Total earners showing occupation as principal		Total working dependents		Total following occupation as subsidiary		Atraf-i-Balda: Total earners showing occupation as principal		Total working dependents		Total following occupation as subsidiary	
		Males	Females	Males	Females	Males	Females	Males	Females	Males	Females	Males	Females	Males	Females	Males	Females	Males	Females
	1	2	3	4	5	6	7	8	9	10	11	12	13	14	15	16	17	18	19
185	40. Army	20,518	358	4,235	602	1,326	39	12,932	174	1,325	237	32	..	82	..	21	..	..	..
186	(G.153) Imperial Army ..	3,651	5	413	12	17	..	1,895	5	322	4	..	..	..	..	..	..	..	..
187	(G.154) *State Army* ..	16,867	348	3,822	590	1,309	39	11,087	169	1,003	233	32	..	82	..	21	..	..	..
188	43. Police	19,003	856	5,275	1,855	714	112	4,134	266	972	454	3	..	1,641	..	119	..	11	..
189	(G.157) Police.. ..	12,079	562	3,392	941	327	23	3,898	266	876	454	3	..	462	..	96	..	..	..
190	(G.158) Village watchmen .	6,924	294	1,883	1,114	587	89	236	..	96	..	..	..	1,179	..	23	..	11	..
191	VII. Public administration .	58,465	3,331	20,198	3,625	7,220	236	15,984	1,010	6,365	1,996	1,201	16	1,206	26	430	79	1,126	..
192	44. Public administration .	58,465	3,331	20,198	3,625	7,220	236	15,984	1,010	6,365	1,996	1,201	16	1,206	26	430	79	1,126	..
193	(G.159) Imperial service ..	1,279	19	544	6	29	..	1,193	16	521	4	29	..	..	..	..	..	..	..
194	(G.160) State service ..	28,498	1,179	13,151	2,253	2,504	53	13,805	410	5,395	1,586	1,066	11	693	13	258	32	361	..
195	(G.160a)Service of other Indian and foreign States .	42	..	5	2	..	..	22	..	4	..	..	..	..	..	..	..	..	..
196	(G.161) Municipal and other local (not village) service..	6,905	1,334	2,123	1,084	1,329	142	846	584	399	406	101	5	146	13	52	47	120	..
197	(G.162) Village officials and servants other than watchmen	21,741	799	4,375	280	3,358	41	118	..	46	..	5	..	367	..	120	..	645	..
198	VIII-Professions and Liberal Arts	65,311	19,286	28,270	10,044	14,566	5,628	9,588	3,670	4,359	2,328	1,297	199	2,428	788	958	783	434	188
199	45. Religion	39,087	11,288	18,998	10,649	8,892	3,741	1,457	709	932	339	243	2	492	146	245	106	104	16

No.	Occupation																		
200	(G.163) Priests, ministers etc.	35,573	10,150	18,129	10,066	8,308	3,606	832	406	509	159	142	2	236	78	124	74	65	16
201	(G.164) Monks, nuns, religious mendicants ..	382	40	59	18	33	..	115	38	36	18	18	..	..	..	..	..	..	..
202	(G.165) Other religious workers	1,072	400	181	111	227	10	217	171	142	70	39	..	15	16	14	14	10	..
203	(G.166) Servants in religious edifices, burial and burning grounds, pilgrim conductors, circumcisors, etc.	2,060	698	629	454	324	125	293	94	185	92	44	..	241	52	107	18	29	..
204	46. Law	4,372	88	1,135	15	617	..	702	19	236	12	83	..	59	..	28	..	6	..
205	(G.167) Lawyers of all kind including Qazis,Law Agents and Mukhtiars ..	3,870	88	977	15	561	..	530	19	172	12	54	..	25	..	15	..	..	..
206	(G.168) Lawyers' clerks, petition-writers, etc. ..	502	..	158	..	56	..	172	..	64	..	29	..	34	..	13	..	6	..
207	47. Medicine	5,624	2,526	1,793	2,014	1,263	640	2,186	1,067	866	838	384	47	275	230	145	305	57	117
208	(G.169) Registered medical practitioners including oculists	1,270	291	452	130	237	22	1,034	232	396	99	194	14	45	8	32	4	10	..
209	(G.170) Other persons practising the healing arts without being registered ..	3,060	242	517	76	691	24	699	169	112	55	101	10	139	26	66	18	29	8
210	(G.171) Dentists ..	110	9	27	..	17	..	72	9	24	..	12	..	..	..	..	..	..	..
211	(G. 172) Midwives, vaccinators, compounders, nurses, masseures, etc. ..	1,112	1,984	784	1,808	315	594	336	657	321	684	74	23	89	196	47	283	18	109
212	(G.173) Veterinary surgeons	72	..	13	..	3	..	45	..	13	..	3	..	2	..	..	..	..	..
213	48. Instruction ..	6,794	2,064	2,200	1,437	1,107	374	1,861	839	858	710	153	38	1,411	297	440	176	214	49
214	(G.174) Professors and teachers of all kinds ..	5,833	1,986	1,771	1,307	1,007	353	1,500	808	633	606	114	24	1,249	286	386	162	194	45
215	(G.175) Clerks and servants connected with education .	961	78	429	130	100	21	352	36	225	104	39	14	102	11	54	14	20	4
216	49. Letters, arts and science (other than 44) ..	9,434	3,320	4,144	1,920	2,687	873	3,382	1,036	1,467	429	434	112	191	115	100	196	53	6
217	(G.176) Public scribes, stenographers, etc. . ..	276	14	117	10	52	3	183	14	96	10	46	3	16	..	14	..	..	..
218	(G.177) Architects, surveyors, engineers, and their employees (not being State servants)	334	..	105	..	29	..	304	..	102	..	28	..	3	..	..	..	..	..
219	(G.178) Authors, editors, journalists and photographers	1,273	12	469	5	152	..	1,096	12	439	5	119	..	2	..	4	..	..	..

TABLE X.

Occupation or Means of Livelihood.

	HYDERABAD STATE Males	HYDERABAD STATE Females	HYDERABAD CITY Males	HYDERABAD CITY Females	ATRAF-I-BALDA Males	ATRAF-I-BALDA Females
Total Earners	3,262,208	1,561,674	160,848	84,498	129,233	79,207
Total Working Dependents	987,412	991,220	48,082	47,714	46,066	53,176
Total Non-working Dependents	3,120,390	4,513,242	38,693	137,059	78,676	113,303
Total Population	7,370,010	7,066,138	247,623	219,271	253,975	245,686

Serial No.	Occupation	HYDERABAD STATE						HYDERABAD CITY						ATRAF-I-BALDA					
		Total earners showing occupation as principal		Total working dependents		Total following occupation as subsidiary		Total earners showing occupation as principal		Total working dependents		Total following occupation as subsidiary		Total earners showing occupation as principal		Total working dependents		Total following occupation as subsidiary	
		Males	Females	Males	Females	Males	Females	Males	Females	Males	Females	Males	Females	Males	Females	Males	Females	Males	Females
	1	2	3	4	5	6	7	8	9	10	11	12	13	14	15	16	17	18	19
220	(G.179) Artists, sculptors and image-makers ..	980	110	411	119	156	40	240	4	76	2	20	1	..	..	..	..	..	..
221	(G.180) Scientists (astronomers, botanists, etc.) ..	128	..	36	..	19	..	106	..	32	..	14	..	..	..	..	..	..	
222	(G.181) Horoscope casters, astrologers, fortune tellers, wizards, witches and mediums	2,047	1,600	1,304	537	1,084	341	556	414	275	122	60	25	128	18	34	12	33	..
223	(G.182) Musicians (composers and performers other than military) actors, dancers, etc.	1,822	1,151	906	903	769	355	229	346	76	119	25	72	35	97	46	184	20	6
224	(G.183) Managers and employees of places of public entertainments, race courses, societies and clubs ..	623	10	322	37	114	5	527	10	294	37	95	5	7	..	2	..	..	..
225	(G.184) Conjurors, acrobats, recitors, exhibitors of curiosities and wild animals, etc.	1,051	423	474	318	362	120	141	236	77	134	27	6	..	..	..	..	..	..
226	**D. Miscellaneous** ..	**348,300**	**205,497**	**115,270**	**147,980**	**61,834**	**43,615**	**40,572**	**17,946**	**13,989**	**19,059**	**1,157**	**1,390**	**13,350**	**6,422**	**7,223**	**4,153**	**3,148**	**845**
227	IX. Persons living on their income	12,012	3,341	3,135	3,205	830	278	6,545	1,906	1,136	2,178	206	31	3,978	1,020	1,507	705	514	220
228	50. Persons living principally on their income ..	12,012	3,341	3,135	3,205	830	278	6,545	1,906	1,136	2,178	206	31	3,978	1,020	1,507	705	514	229

TABLE X.

OCCUPATION OR MEANS OF LIVELIHOOD.

229	(G.185) Proprietors (other than of agricultural land) fund and scholarships holders and pensioners ..	12,012	3,341	3,135	3,205	830	278	6,545	1,906	1,136	2,178	206	31	3,978	1,020	1,507	705	514	229
230	X. Domestic service ..	214,425	112,347	65,016	82,791	37,876	21,888	18,878	10,291	5,292	7,844	512	605	6,635	2,579	3,790	1,495	1,206	238
231	51. Domestic service ..	214,425	112,347	65,016	82,791	37,876	21,888	18,878	10,291	5,292	7,844	512	605	6,635	2,579	3,790	1,495	1,206	238
232	(G.186) Private motor drivers and cleaners ..	4,326	95	1,415	86	429	36	2,520	..	1,087	46	200	21	247	..	63	..	101	..
233	(G.187) Other domestic service	210,099	112,252	63,601	82,705	37,447	21,852	16,358	10,291	4,205	7,798	308	584	6,388	2,579	3,727	1,495	1,105	238
234	XI. Insufficiently defined occupations	65,879	35,987	31,027	38,122	12,743	12,258	10,413	2,900	4,997	6,271	161	391	800	695	293	570	419	181
235	52. General terms which do not indicate a definite occupation	65,879	35,987	31,027	38,122	12,743	12,258	10,413	2,900	4,997	6,271	161	391	800	695	293	570	419	181
236	(G.188) Manufacturers, business men and contractors, otherwise unspecified ..	7,069	1,337	2,129	1,550	1,021	1,144	2,579	43	1,346	27	52	6	130	140	45	200	32	62
237	(G. 189) Cashiers, accountants, bookkeepers, clerks and other employees in unspecified offices and ware-houses and shops ..	3,516	242	1,353	120	292	26	1,945	242	672	112	36	20	20	..	10	..	3	..
238	(G.190) Mechanics, otherwise unspecified ..	1,021	..	354	..	69	..	145	..	210	..	20	..	5	..	4	..	..	..
239	(G.191) Labourers and workmen otherwise unspecified	54,273	34,408	27,191	36,452	11,361	11,084	5,744	2,615	2,769	6,132	53	365	645	555	234	370	384	69
240	XII. Unproductive ..	55,984	53,822	16,092	23,862	10,385	9,191	4,736	2,849	2,504	2,766	278	363	1,987	2,128	1,633	1,383	1,009	252
241	53. Inmates of jails asylums and alms-houses ..	..	..	3,877	665	..	..	..	..	1,359	81	..	..	..	..	19	..	..	..
242	(G.192) Inmates of jails, asylums and alms-houses .	..	..	3,877	665	..	..	..	..	1,359	81	..	..	..	..	19	..	..	..
243	54. Beggars, vagrants and prostitutes	54,103	52,907	11,279	22,657	9,763	9,139	3,461	2,613	683	2,558	213	333	1,772	1,706	1,238	1,080	456	234
244	(G.193) Beggars and vagrants	52,889	48,154	10,594	18,058	9,686	8,402	3,295	1,961	641	2,161	213	262	1,562	1,029	1,093	586	420	120
245	(G.194) Procurers and prostitutes	1,214	4,796	685	4,599	81	737	166	652	42	397	..	71	210	677	145	444	36	114
246	55. Other unclassified non-productive industries ..	1,881	705	936	540	629	52	1,275	236	522	127	65	30	165	422	376	353	553	18
247	(G.195) Other unclassified non-productive industries .	1,881	705	936	540	629	52	1,275	236	522	127	65	30	165	422	376	353	553	18

TABLE X.

Occupation or Means of Livelihood.

	WARANGAL Males	WARANGAL Females	KARIMNAGAR Males	KARIMNAGAR Females	ADILABAD Males	ADILABAD Females
Total Earners ..	305,604	145,426	325,497	181,455	162,467	100,230
Total Working Dependents ..	40,345	23,531	40,094	39,503	40,402	32,484
Total Non-working Dependents ..	229,870	372,917	268,825	386,031	186,785	239,562
Total Population ..	515,819	541,874	634,416	606,989	389,754	372,276

Serial No.	Occupation	WARANGAL: Total earners showing occupation as principal, Males	Females	Total working dependents, Males	Females	Total following occupation as subsidiary, Males	Females	KARIMNAGAR: Total earners showing occupation as principal, Males	Females	Total working dependents, Males	Females	Total following occupation as subsidiary, Males	Females	ADILABAD: Total earners showing occupation as principal, Males	Females	Total working dependents, Males	Females	Total following occupation as subsidiary, Males	Females
	1	20	21	22	23	24	25	26	27	28	29	30	31	32	33	34	35	36	37
1	TOTAL WORKERS. ..	305,604	145,426	40,345	23,531	64,466	21,359	325,497	181,455	40,094	39,503	59,857	44,815	162,467	100,230	40,402	32,484	29,781	14,331
2	A. Production of Raw Materials ..	209,396	103,045	29,998	16,016	39,345	14,226	186,776	118,942	19,893	24,538	34,730	28,790	92,145	57,736	22,355	17,501	13,411	7,146
3	I-Exploitation of Animals and Vegetation ..	202,429	101,027	26,522	12,337	36,322	12,930	186,776	118,942	19,893	24,538	34,730	28,790	90,810	57,381	21,936	16,941	13,256	6,986
4	1. Pasture and Agriculture .	197,227	94,656	26,183	11,850	34,906	11,624	177,463	115,741	18,138	23,807	32,912	27,493	84,657	55,819	18,971	16,057	12,538	6,785
5	(a) Cultivation ..	170,824	86,190	20,809	9,167	31,266	9,867	148,359	106,056	13,846	20,175	27,481	24,093	74,317	51,072	15,973	13,881	11,794	6,599
6	(G.1) Non-cultivating proprietors taking rent in money or kind ..	38,215	10,750	5,581	1,285	8,689	2,184	15,818	6,592	1,080	7,914	749	8,836	11,185	5,400	2,366	1,388	2,656	861
7	(G.2) Estate Agents and Managers of owners ..	160	..	35	..	22	..	15	..	10	..	4	..	18	..	..	..	3	..
8	(G.3) Estate Agents and Managers of Government ..	372	..	186	..	90	..	76	..	32	..	10	..	49	..	10	..	3	..
9	(G.4) Rent Collectors, clerks, etc.	645	..	332	..	140	..	123	..	46	..	21	..	264	..	39	..	24	..
10	(G.5) Cultivating owners ..	48,962	9,718	7,433	1,765	9,598	2,876	78,916	45,874	6,590	9,037	23,496	10,265	28,066	20,366	8,636	5,590	4,226	3,081
11	(G.6) Tenant cultivators ..	25,793	10,327	4,768	3,528	7,079	3,290	21,390	5,163	803	870	1,889	701	10,150	2,301	2,909	748	2,390	655
12	(G.7) Agricultural labourers.	56,677	55,409	2,474	2,589	5,653	1,517	32,021	48,427	5,835	2,354	1,812	4,291	24,585	23,005	2,013	6,151	2,492	2,002
13	(b) Cultivation of special crops, fruits, etc. ..	579	4,055	280	920	280	632	1,866	1,354	444	1,040	646	1,096	143	79	101	35	32	81
14	(G.13) Pan-Vine ..	43	20	35	19	13	4	40	28	5	16	18	24	25	..	5	5	4	6
15	(G.16) Market gardeners, flower, fruit growers, etc. ..	536	4,035	245	901	267	628	1,826	1,326	439	1,024	628	1,072	118	79	96	30	28	25
16	(c.) Forestry	955	274	636	243	269	84	3,704	166	885	39	1,302	54	732	231	171	204	136	82
17	(G.17) Forest officers, rangers, guards, etc. ..	26	..	13	..	..	..	30	..	6	..	..	..	54	..	22	..	..	..
18	(G.18) Wood-cutters and charcoal burners ..	516	120	368	145	129	19	3,750	166	864	39	1,268	54	687	181	189	162	128	27

TABLE X. OCCUPATION OR MEANS OF LIVELIHOOD

19	(G.19) Collectors of forest produce.	101	52	45	28	30	10	..	..	..	..	..	..	26	20	10	18	..	3
20	(G.20) Collectors of lac ..	312	102	210	70	110	55	14	..	15	..	34	..	15	30	..	24	8	2
21	(d.)— Stock raising ..	23,360	3,978	4,253	1,400	2,860	971	23,376	8,150	2,943	2,550	3,463	2,242	9,282	4,309	2,704	1,820	426	90
22	(G.21) Cattle and buffaloe breeders and keepers ..	1,020	..	503	136	422	115	2,415	2,468	162	548	87	931	620	242	202	287	145	28
23	(G.22) Breeders of transport animals	383	..	142	..	410	..	..	..	..	..	..	..	48	..	12	..	28	..
24	(G.23) Herdsmen, shepherds and breeders of other animals	21,957	3,978	3,608	1,264	2,028	856	20,961	5,682	2,781	2,002	3,376	1,311	8,614	4,067	2,400	1,533	253	67
25	(e) Raising of small animals and insects	1,500	150	205	120	231	70	68	15	20	3	20	8	183	128	22	117	150	33
26	(G.24) Birds, bees, etc. ..	885	95	129	62	133	38	60	15	20	3	20	8	124	72	10	68	110	19
27	(G.25) Silk worms ..	326	38	36	27	57	5	8	..	..	..	..	..	59	51	12	49	40	14
28	(G.26) Lac cultivation ..	298	17	40	31	51	27	..	..	..	..	..	..	..	5	..	..	..	..
29	2. Fishing and Hunting ..	5,202	6,371	339	487	1,416	1,806	9,313	3,201	1,755	731	1,818	1,297	6,158	1,562	2,965	884	718	201
30	(G.27) Fishing and pearling .	2,600	2,762	187	263	767	1,052	8,639	2,935	1,416	664	1,660	907	2,892	1,881	1,320	473	321	65
31	(G.28) Hunting ..	2,602	3,609	152	224	649	254	674	266	339	67	158	390	3,261	381	1,645	411	397	136
32	II. Exploitation of Minerals	6,967	2,018	3,476	3,679	3,023	1,296	..	..	..	..	..	..	1,335	355	419	560	155	160
33	3. Metallic minerals ..	20	3	6	..	2	..	..	..	..	..	..	..	75	..	30	61	..	..
34	(G.30) Iron	20	3	6	..	2	..	..	..	..	..	..	..	75	..	30	61	..	..
35	4. Non-metallic minerals ..	6,947	2,015	3,470	3,679	3,021	1,296	..	..	..	..	..	..	1,260	355	389	499	155	160
36	(G.35) Coal	5,856	1,975	3,332	3,619	2,997	1,291	..	..	..	..	..	..	905	242	354	382	129	125
37	(G.37) Building materials (including stone, materials for cement manufacture and clays)	1,045	40	120	60	18	5	..	..	..	..	..	..	326	110	27	115	26	35
38	(G.38) Mica	26	..	18	..	6	..	..	..	..	..	..	..	29	3	8	2	..	..
39	(G.40) Salt, saltpetre and other saline substances ..	20	..	..	..	..	..	..	..	..	..	..	..	..	..	..	..	..	..
40	B.—Preparation and supply of material substances	71,590	23,147	8,597	4,727	20,972	3,635	108,733	49,271	17,341	12,080	22,621	14,161	49,969	29,946	11,283	11,658	12,747	6,577
41	III. Industry	30,181	14,063	6,085	3,941	10,308	2,730	66,468	20,840	12,061	8,291	14,816	8,428	17,567	6,054	2,749	1,796	2,804	1,096
42	5. Textiles ..	8,143	4,049	1,900	817	2,161	499	26,530	9,627	6,804	1,202	5,816	3,284	4,723	2,039	843	487	473	262
43	(G.42) Cotton ginning, cleaning and pressing ..	2,186	1,098	670	242	1,020	104	330	15	100	10	37	29	260	54	32	31	29	4
44	(G.43) Cotton spinning, sizing and weaving ..	4,841	2,420	1,160	385	1,009	252	22,122	9,226	5,878	1,177	5,240	3,201	4,210	1,897	754	426	379	246
45	(G.45) Rope, twine, string and other fibres ..	843	526	72	186	82	140	1,225	246	363	7	156	24	167	88	41	30	39	12
46	(G.46) Wool carding, spinning and weaving ..	125	..	40	..	20	..	2,583	140	431	8	272	30	14	..	3	..	2	..
47	(G.47) Silk spinning and weaving.	110	5	24	4	30	3	..	..	..	..	..	..	..	..	..	..	..	..
48	(G.48) Hair (Horse-hair, etc.)	..	..	..	..	..	..	..	..	..	..	..	..	..	..	..	..	..	..

TABLE X.

Occupation or Means of Livelihood.

	WARANGAL Males	WARANGAL Females	KARIMNAGAR Males	KARIMNAGAR Females	ADILABAD Males	ADILABAD Females
Total Earners	305,604	145,426	325,497	181,455	162,467	100,230
Total Working Dependents	40,345	23,531	40,094	39,503	40,402	32,484
Total Non-working Dependents	229,870	372,917	268,825	386,031	186,785	239,562
Total Population	575,819	541,874	634,416	606,989	389,754	372,276

Serial No.	Occupation	WARANGAL: Total earners showing occupation as principal		WARANGAL: Total working dependents		WARANGAL: Total following occupation as subsidiary		KARIMNAGAR: Total earners showing occupation as principal		KARIMNAGAR: Total working dependents		KARIMNAGAR: Total following occupation as subsidiary		ADILABAD: Total earners showing occupation as principal		ADILABAD: Total working dependents		ADILABAD: Total following occupation as subsidiary	
		Males	Females	Males	Females	Males	Females	Males	Females	Males	Females	Males	Females	Males	Females	Males	Females	Males	Females
	1	20	21	22	23	24	25	26	27	28	29	30	31	32	33	34	35	36	37
49	(G.49) Dyeing, bleaching, printing, preparation and sponging of textiles ..	38	..	24	..	..	..	270	..	32	..	111	..	69	..	13	..	24	..
50	(G.50) Lace, crepe, embroideries, fringes, etc., and insufficiently described textiles	..	..	..	..	..	..	..	..	..	..	..	..	3	..	..	..	..	..
51	6. Hides, skins and hard materials from the animal kingdom	342	114	124	67	106	28	96	..	..	..	..	..	..	..	..	..	..	..
52	(G.51) Working in leather ..	322	108	110	55	106	28	96	..	..	..	..	..	..	..	..	..	..	..
53	(G.52) Furriers and persons occupied with feathers and bristles ; brush makers ..	..	..	..	..	..	..	..	..	..	..	..	..	..	..	..	..	..	..
54	(G.53) Bone, ivory, horn, shell, etc., workers (except buttons)	20	6	14	12	..	..	..	..	..	..	..	..	..	..	..	..	..	..
55	7. Wood	4,866	1,991	832	397	1,086	462	3,048	1,354	532	507	457	473	1,574	722	347	281	551	252
56	(G.54) Sawyers ..	140	..	18	..	..	..	23	..	..	..	..	..	80	..	27	..	14	..
57	(G.55) Carpenters, turners and joiners, etc. ..	2,821	405	431	108	530	225	2,714	423	407	366	253	229	1,102	218	242	226	430	158
58	(G.56) Basket-makers and other industries of woody materials, including leaves and thatchers and builders working with bamboo, reeds or similar materials ..	1,905	1,586	383	289	556	237	306	931	125	231	204	244	392	504	78	55	107	99
59	8. Metals	2,900	828	605	348	1,387	347	4,628	2,547	559	513	1,104	600	1,305	956	214	80	215	132
60	(G.57) Smelting, forging and rolling of iron and other metals	..	..	..	..	..	..	..	..	..	..	..	..	4	..	..	..	..	
61	(G.58) Makers of arms, guns, etc.	..	..	..	..	..	..	..	..	..	..	..	..	..	..	..	..	..	..

No.	Occupation	1	2	3	4	5	6	7	8	9	10	11	12	13	14	15	16	17	18
62	(G.59) Blacksmiths, other workers in iron, makers of implements	2,562	623	407	206	1,064	158	1,685	653	271	319	553	356	1,090	885	187	20	184	91
63	(G.60) Workers in brass, copper and bell metals	286	145	145	79	306	164	2,993	1,894	288	194	551	244	211	71	27	10	31	41
64	(G.61) Workers in other metals (except precious metals)	112	60	53	63	17	25	..	..	..	..	..	..	..	..	..	..	..	..
65	(G.62) Workers in mints, dye-sinkers, etc	..	..	..	..	..	..	..	..	..	..	..	..	..	..	..	..	..	..
66	9. Ceramics	2,851	2,103	307	634	369	369	1,185	1,282	140	623	547	295	853	574	83	176	14	..
67	(G.63) Potters and makers of earthen ware	2,449	1,988	247	565	158	342	1,105	1,253	118	620	511	275	252	504	57	149	12	..
68	(G.64) Brick and tile makers	280	115	50	69	176	27	80	27	22	3	36	20	101	70	26	27	2	..
69	(G.65) Other workers in ceramics	122	..	10	..	35	..	..	..	..	..	..	..	..	..	..	..	..	..
70	10. Chemical products properly so-called and analogous	162	24	72	24	7	4	169	221	50	..	38	12	372	12	30	6	44	2
71	(G.66) Manufacture of matches, fireworks and other explosives	65	14	29	12	3	4	4	..	..	..	..	..	6	..	..	..	1	..
72	(G.67) Manufacture of aerated and mineral waters and ice	18	..	3	..	2	..	..	..	..	..	..	..	18	..	3	..	2	..
73	(G.68) Manufacture and refining of vegetable oils	43	..	18	..	2	..	..	..	..	..	..	..	340	12	25	6	40	2
74	(G.69) Manufacture and refining of mineral oils	4	..	2	..	..	..	..	..	..	..	..	..	3	..	..	..	..	..
75	(G.70) Others	32	10	20	12	..	..	165	221	50	..	38	12	5	..	2	..	1	..
76	11. Food Industries	1,385	595	388	327	420	150	822	542	132	163	298	158	537	39	95	6	74	19
77	(G.71) Rice pounders and huskers and flour grinders	163	279	70	190	45	32	4	28	3	4	..	11	..	18	..	3	..	4
78	(G.72) Grain Parchers, etc.	..	..	..	..	..	..	..	4	..	..	..	..	..	4	..	..	..	..
79	(G.73) Butchers	369	14	66	3	6	..	567	455	85	146	235	119	117	..	34	..	..	..
80	(G.74) Makers of sugar, molasses and gur	..	..	..	..	..	..	..	3	..	..	..	..	12	2	3	..	2	..
81	(G.75) Sweetmeat and condiment makers	179	84	42	24	86	46	40	12	14	1	18	..	40	..	10	..	5	..
82	(G.76) Toddy drawers	245	43	100	51	120	32	149	27	15	8	21	10	316	..	45	..	55	..
83	(G.77) Brewers and distillers.	42	10	10	5	20	2	13	..	..	..	..	..	17	..	..	..	..	..
84	(G.78) Manufacturers of tobacco	337	165	100	54	143	38	49	13	15	4	24	18	30	15	3	3	12	15
85	(G.80) Manufacturers of Ganja	..	..	..	..	..	..	..	..	..	..	..	..	2	..	..	..	..	..
86	(G.81) Others	..	..	..	..	..	..	..	..	..	..	..	..	3	..	..	..	..	..
87	12. Industries of dress and toilet	7,163	3,661	1,136	1,181	3,727	696	22,436	11,227	2,036	4,110	5,715	2,739	6,938	1,506	985	641	1,328	389
88	(G.82) Boot, shoe, sandal and clog makers	1,847	928	284	296	1,011	230	10,217	1,673	123	1,832	2,863	715	2,883	262	426	115	877	84
89	(G.83) Tailors, milliners, dress-makers and darners	1,862	1,431	289	294	825	211	1,865	826	142	418	472	147	262	225	24	194	36	239
90	(G.84) Embroiderers, hat-makers and makers of other articles of wear	12	13	24	12	10	6	..	..	..	..	..	..	..	..	..	..	..	..
91	(G.85) Washing and cleaning	1,667	1,236	332	364	857	214	8,075	8,001	1,280	1,587	1,802	1,636	2,546	903	395	280	280	63

TABLE X.

Occupation or Means of Livelihood.

District		Males	Females
WARANGAL	Total Earners	305,604	145,426
	Total Working Dependents	40,345	23,531
	Total Non-working Dependents	229,870	372,917
	Total Population	575,819	541,874
KARIMNAGAR	Total Earners	325,497	181,455
	Total Working Dependents	40,094	39,503
	Total Non-working Dependents	268,825	386,031
	Total Population	634,416	606,989
ADILABAD	Total Earners	162,467	100,230
	Total Working Dependents	40,402	32,484
	Total Non-working Dependents	186,785	239,562
	Total Population	389,754	372,276

Serial No.	Occupation	WARANGAL: Total earners showing occupation as principal, Males	Females	WARANGAL: Total working dependents, Males	Females	WARANGAL: Total following occupation as subsidiary, Males	Females	KARIMNAGAR: Total earners showing occupation as principal, Males	Females	KARIMNAGAR: Total working dependents, Males	Females	KARIMNAGAR: Total following occupation as subsidiary, Males	Females	ADILABAD: Total earners showing occupation as principal, Males	Females	ADILABAD: Total working dependents, Males	Females	ADILABAD: Total following occupation as subsidiary, Males	Females
	1	20	21	22	23	24	25	26	27	28	29	30	31	32	33	34	35	36	37
92	(G.86) Barbers, hair dressers and wig-makers ..	1,751	53	207	215	1,024	15	2,279	727	511	273	578	241	1,247	116	140	52	135	8
93	(G.87) Other industries connected with toilet ..	24	..	..	..	..	..	..	..	..	..	..	..	..	..	..	..	..	..
94	13. Furniture industries ..	14	..	12	..	2	..	10	..	..	..	..	..	6	..	..	..	..	2
95	(G. 88) Cabinet-makers carriage painters, etc. ..	14	..	12	..	2	..	10	..	..	..	..	..	6	..	..	..	..	..
96	(G.89) Upholsterers, tent makers, etc. ..	..	..	..	..	..	..	..	..	..	..	..	..	..	..	..	..	..	2
97	14. Building industries ..	749	24	247	29	74	14	498	46	47	..	12	32	901	50	10	30	8	2
98	(G.90) Lime burners, cement workers; Excavators and well sinkers; stone cutters and dressers. brick layers and masons; builders (other than buildings made of bamboo and similar materials) painters decorators of houses, tilers, plumbers, etc.	749	24	247	29	74	14	498	46	47	..	12	32	901	50	10	30	8	2
99	15. Construction of means of transport	83	..	52	..	27	..	24	..	3	..	5	..	39	..	10	..	15	..
100	(G.91) Persons engaged in making, assembling or repairing motor vehicles or cycles	37	..	20	..	15	..	2	..	..	..	..	..	12	..	6	..	3	..
101	(G.92) Carriage, cart, palki, etc. makers and wheel-wrights	46	..	32	..	12	..	22	..	3	..	5	..	27	..	4	..	12	..
102	16. Production and transmission of physical force ..	..	..	..	..	..	..	..	..	..	..	..	..	..	..	..	..	..	..
103	(G.94) Heat, light, electricity, motive power, etc. Gas works and electric light and power ..	..	..	..	..	..	..	..	..	..	..	..	..	..	..	..	..	..	..

TABLE X.

OCCUPATION OR MEANS OF LIVELIHOOD.

104	17. Miscellaneous and undefined industries ..	1,573	674	320	117	942	170	7,027	2,994	1,738	1,088	824	885	819	156	132	139	82	18
105	(G.95) Printers, engravers, book binders, etc. ..	135	..	41	..	70	..	3	..	..	..	..	..	12	..	4	..	2	..
106	(G.96) Makers of musical instruments	12	..	3	..	..	..	5	..	..	..	..	..	3	..	..	..	3	..
107	(G.97) Makers of clocks and surgical or scientific instruments, etc.	8	..	14	..	..	..	4	..	..	..	..	..	..	..	..	..	..	..
108	(G.98) Makers of jewellery and ornaments ..	1,019	564	246	67	822	170	4,370	2,339	812	1,076	702	885	620	135	108	121	59	18
109	(G.99) Other miscellaneous and undefined industries (toy making, taxidermy, etc.)	124	..	16	..	50	..	334	148	38	..	..	..	31	..	..	..	..	..
110	(G.100) Scavenging ..	275	110	..	50	..	..	2,311	507	888	7	122	..	153	21	20	18	18	..
111	IV. Transport	8,416	1,675	561	42	1,177	55	11,470	3,717	1,263	845	876	1,274	3,201	738	1,613	425	1,045	288
112	19. Transport by water ..	20	..	..	..	..	..	246	..	55	..	130	..	159	58	30	15	20	5
113	(G.104) Labourers employed on harbours, docks, rivers and canals	20	..	..	..	..	..	246	..	55	..	130	..	159	58	30	15	20	5
114	20. Transport by Road ..	6,823	439	238	27	555	25	7,626	1,534	1,014	397	646	441	1,826	359	201	152	738	52
115	(G.105) Persons (other than labourers) employed on the construction and maintenance of roads and bridges .	40	..	3	..	10	..	24	..	8	..	12	..	14	..	2	..	1	..
116	(G.106) Labourers employed on roads and bridges ..	3,675	384	113	13	182	15	3,155	1,347	359	376	234	409	648	310	89	105	292	36
117	(G.107) Owners, managers & employees (excluding personal servants) connected with mechanically driven vehicles (including trams) .	112	..	16	..	107	..	10	..	5	..	3	..	6	7	..	..	..	..
118	(G.108) Owners, managers, employees (excluding personal servants) connected with other vehicles ..	2,654	55	69	14	99	10	1,158	187	37	21	19	32	932	21	52	36	397	10
119	(G.109) Palki, etc., bearers and owners	272	..	32	..	132	..	2,861	..	459	..	181	..	96	6	14	8	27	4
120	(G.110) Pack elephant, camel mule, ass and bullock, owners and drivers ..	..	..	..	..	..	..	70	..	36	..	25	..	125	15	40	3	18	2
121	(G.111) Porters and messengers	70	..	5	..	25	..	348	..	110	..	172	..	5	..	4	..	3	..
122	21. Transport by Rail ..	1,308	1,286	300	15	560	30	3,512	2,183	166	448	100	833	1,080	321	1,334	258	260	231
123	(G.112) Railway employees of all kind other than coolies	1,072	18	172	5	320	4	118	13	25	2	32	10	157	1	24	18	10	..
124	(G.113) Labourers employed on railway construction and maintenance and coolies and porters employed on Railway premises ..	236	1,218	128	10	240	26	3,394	2,170	141	446	68	823	928	320	1,310	240	250	231
125	22. Post Office, Telegraph and Telephone services ..	265	..	23	..	62	..	86	..	28	..	..	..	136	..	48	..	27	..
126	(G.114) Post office, Telegraph and Telephone services	265	..	23	..	62	..	86	..	28	..	..	..	136	..	48	..	27	..
127	V. Trade	32,993	7,409	1,951	744	9,487	841	30,795	15,714	4,017	2,944	6,979	4,459	29,201	23,154	6,921	9,487	8,898	4,293

TABLE X.

Occupation or Means of Livelihood.

	WARANGAL Males	WARANGAL Females	KARIMNAGAR Males	KARIMNAGAR Females	ADILABAD Males	ADILABAD Females
Total Earners	305,604	145,426	325,497	181,455	162,467	100,280
Total Working Dependents	40,345	23,531	40,094	39,503	40,402	32,484
Total Non-working Dependents	229,870	372,917	268,825	386,031	186,785	239,562
Total Population	575,819	541,874	634,416	606,989	389,754	372,276

Serial No.	Occupation	WARANGAL: Total earners showing occupation as principal — Males	Females	Total working dependents — Males	Females	Total following occupation as subsidiary — Males	Females	KARIMNAGAR: Total earners showing occupation as principal — Males	Females	Total working dependents — Males	Females	Total following occupation as subsidiary — Males	Females	ADILABAD: Total earners showing occupation as principal — Males	Females	Total working dependents — Males	Females	Total following occupation as subsidiary — Males	Females
	1	20	21	22	23	24	25	26	27	28	20	30	31	32	33	34	35	36	37
128	23. Banks, establishments of credit, exchange and insurance	141	..	4	..	30	..	140	..	26	..	18	..	128	29	46	12	23	12
129	(G.115) Bank managers, money lenders, exchange and insurance agents, money changers and brokers and their employees ..	141	..	4	..	30	..	140	..	26	..	18	..	128	29	46	12	23	12
130	24. Brokerage, commission and export	24	..	..	..	..	..	..	..	..	..	..	..	51	..	..	..	..	..
131	(G.116) Brokers, commission agents, commercial travellers, warehouse owners and employees	24	..	..	..	..	..	..	..	..	..	..	..	51	..	..	..	..	..
132	25. Trade in Textiles ..	695	232	130	35	386	..	1,265	316	26	12	21	5	707	315	328	210	163	40
133	(G.117) Trade in piece goods, wool, cotton, silk, hair and other textiles ..	695	232	130	35	386	..	1,265	316	26	12	21	5	707	315	328	210	163	40
134	26. Trade in skins, leather and furs	463	5	120	..	472	..	26	..	3	..	..	..	310	112	125	76	72	24
135	(G.118) Trade in skins, leather, furs, feathers, horn, etc., and the articles made from these	463	5	120	..	472	..	26	..	3	..	..	..	310	112	125	76	72	24
136	27. Trade in Wood ..	436	135	12	41	169	35	30	58	..	32	3	6	600	101	211	152	121	46
137	(G.119) Trade in wood (not fire-wood)	8	..	..	..	10	..	..	..	..	..	..	..	376	29	180	18	66	5
138	(G.120) Trade in barks ..	120	65	..	13	34	2	15	20	..	15	..	..	55	40	10	75	13	18
139	(G.121) Trade in bamboos and canes	256	46	12	14	110	15	10	24	..	14	..	4	151	28	18	49	24	20
140	(G.122) Trade in thatches and other forest produce ..	52	24	..	14	15	18	5	14	..	3	3	2	18	4	3	10	18	3
141	28. Trade in metals ..	24	..	2	..	30	..	27	4	8	..	2	..	15	12	4	3	3	1

42	(G.123) Trade in metals, machinery, knives, tools, etc. ..	24	..	2	..	30	..	27	4	8	..	2	..	15	12	4	3	3	1
143	29. Trade in pottery, bricks and tiles	112	336	..	125	18	25	339	736	75	416	137	311	18	39	28	137	4	14
144	(G.124) Trade in pottery, bricks and tiles ..	112	336	..	125	18	25	339	736	75	416	137	311	18	39	28	137	4	14
145	30. Trade in chemical products	15	..	..	..	..	..	18	..	..	..	..	..	5	..	..	..	1	..
146	(G.125) Drugs, dyes, paints petroleum, explosives, etc. ..	15	..	..	..	..	..	18	..	..	..	..	..	5	..	..	..	1	..
147	31. Hotels, cafes, restaurants, etc.	13,079	2,955	866	65	2,950	302	13,105	7,736	1,887	1,532	2,889	2,151	4,091	6,478	1,337	2,260	1,582	660
148	(G.126) Vendors of wine, liquors, aerated waters and ice	12,486	2,738	825	42	2,627	141	12,974	7,704	1,877	1,528	2,831	2,148	3,936	6,450	1,315	2,251	1,557	654
149	(G.127) Owners and managers of hotels, cook shops sarais, etc., (and employees)	272	163	25	14	213	143	101	..	10	..	35	..	137	10	2	7	20	2
150	(G.128) Hawkers of drink and food stuffs ..	321	54	16	9	110	18	30	32	..	4	23	3	18	18	20	2	5	4
151	32. Other trade in food stuffs	3,117	540	258	41	982	161	7,570	4,471	787	501	1,676	521	2,032	3,884	1,257	2,914	508	676
152	(G.129) Grain and pulse dealers	828	245	136	5	382	42	1,386	692	150	62	210	30	1,285	342	960	97	372	34
153	(G.130) Dealers in sweetmeats, sugar and spices ..	130	136	10	24	55	59	37	24	..	1	15	3	155	17	72	4	30	8
154	(G.131) Dealers in dairy product, eggs and poultry ..	472	..	36	..	146	..	4,568	3,607	296	438	897	472	372	3,498	185	2,809	76	619
155	(G.132) Dealers in animals for food	120	..	4	..	3	..	21	..	..	..	..	..	18	..	..	..	..	..
156	(G.133) Dealers in fodder for animals	50	..	..	..	..	..	13	..	..	..	..	..	27	..	..	..	30	..
157	(G.134) Dealers in other food stuffs	1,375	159	52	12	349	60	1,290	27	318	..	515	..	40	..	10	..	..	..
158	(G.135) Dealers in tobacco .	132	..	20	..	47	..	176	31	23	..	18	16	127	27	24	4	..	15
159	(G.136) Dealers in opium ..	15	..	..	..	..	..	34	..	..	..	21	..	5	..	4	..	..	..
160	(G.137) Dealers in ganja ..	..	..	..	..	..	..	35	..	..	..	..	..	3	..	2	..	..	..
161	33. Trade in clothing and toilet articles ..	175	53	2	28	140	14	758	32	136	11	232	18	695	..	386	3	212	..
162	(G.138) Trade in ready-made clothing and other articles of dress and the toilet (hats, umbrellas, socks, ready-made shoes, perfumes, etc.)	175	53	2	28	140	14	758	32	136	11	232	18	695	..	386	3	212	..
163	34. Trade in furniture ..	61	..	..	..	52	..	35	..	..	..	4	..	10	40	8	75	..	12
164	(G.139) Trade in furniture carpets, curtains and bedding	25	..	..	..	25	..	15	..	..	..	..	..	10	..	8	..	..	..
165	(G.140) Hardware, cooking utensils, porcelain crockery, glassware bottles, articles for gardening, etc. ..	36	..	..	..	27	..	20	..	..	..	..	..	..	40	..	75	..	12
166	35. Trade in building materials	45	5	..	..	47	..	50	14	..	..	..	8	40	..	5	..	1	..
167	(G.141) Trade in building materials (other than brick, tiles and woody materials).	45	5	..	..	47	..	50	14	..	..	..	8	40	..	5	..	1	..
168	36. Trade in means of transport	738	24	38	1	820	12	143	18	10	3	19	14	163	8	81	4	25	..

TABLE X.

Occupation or Means of Livelihood.

	WARANGAL Males	WARANGAL Females	KARIMNAGAR Males	KARIMNAGAR Females	ADILABAD Males	ADILABAD Females
Total Earners	305,604	145,426	325,497	181,455	162,467	100,230
Total Working Dependents	40,345	23,531	40,094	39,503	40.402	32,484
Total Non-working Dependents	229,870	372,917	268,825	386,031	186,785	289,562
Total Population	575,819	541,874	364,416	606,989	389,754	372,276

Serial No.	Occupation	WARANGAL						KARIMNAGAR						ADILABAD					
		Total earners showing occupation as principal		Total working dependents		Total following occupation as subsidiary		Total earners showing occupation as principal		Total working dependents		Total following occupation as subsidiary		Total earners showing occupation as principal		Total working dependents		Total following occupation as subsidiary	
		Males	Females	Males	Females	Males	Females	Males	Females	Males	Females	Males	Females	Males	Females	Males	Females	Males	Females
	1	20	21	22	23	24	25	26	27	28	29	30	31	32	33	34	35	36	37
169	(G.142) Dealers and hirers, in mechanical transport motors, cycles, etc. ..	56	..	5	..	76	..	16	..	..	..	..	..	24	..	10	..	5	..
170	(G.143) Dealers and hirers in other carriages, carts, boas, etc	477	24	3	1	124	12	127	18	10	3	19	14	110	8	8	4	16	..
171	(G.144) Dealers and hirers of elephants, camels, horses, cattle, asses, mules, etc.	205	..	30	..	120	..	..	..	..	..	..	..	29	..	13	..	4	..
172	37. Trade in fuel	376	345	..	62	110	45	34	246	10	76	..	45	5,967	3,365	1,650	1,505	1,895	1,469
173	(G.145) Dealers in firewood, charcoal, coal, cowdung, etc.	376	345	..	62	110	45	34	246	10	76	..	45	5,967	3,365	1,650	1,505	1,895	1,469
174	38. Trade in articles of luxury and those pertaining to letters and the arts and sciences	81	440	35	67	75	23	83	167	10	49	3	31	35	362	34	178	19	64
175	(G.146) Dealers in precious stones, jewellery (real and imitation) clocks, optical instruments, etc ..	8	..	..	..	..	..	12	..	1	..	..	..	..	..	..	..	..	..
176	(G.147) Dealers in common bangles, bead necklaces, fans, small articles, toys hunting, and fishing, tackle, flowers, etc. ..	40	440	35	67	65	23	49	167	6	49	..	31	27	362	32	178	15	64
177	(G.148) Publishers, booksellers, stationers, dealers in music, pictures, musical instruments and curiosities	33	..	..	..	10	..	22	..	3	..	3	..	8	..	2	..	4	..
178	39. Trade of other sorts ..	13,411	2,339	484	279	3,706	224	7,182	1,916	1,039	312	1,975	1,349	14,334	8,409	1,471	1,908	4,269	1,275
179	(G.149) Dealers in rags, stable refuse and etc ..	..	..	..	..	..	..	2	3	..	..	..	..	7	..	..	..	..	..
180	(G.150) General store-keepers and shop keepers, otherwise unspecified ..	13,347	2,339	484	279	3,706	224	7,149	1,913	1,035	312	1,944	1,349	14,305	8,409	1,456	1,908	4,265	1,275

TABLE X.
OCCUPATION OR MEANS OF LIVELIHOOD.

No.	Occupation																		
181	(G.151) Itinerant traders, pedlars and hawkers (of other than food, etc.)	40	..	..	..	..	..	28	..	4	..	31	..	20	..	15	..	4	..
182	(G.152) Other trades (including farmers of pounds, tools and markets)	24	..	..	..	..	..	3	..	..	..	..	..	2	..	..	..	..	..
183	**C. Public Administration and Liberal Arts**	8,423	2,454	793	209	1,516	611	5,206	1,718	584	873	721	463	6,866	1,167	2,082	471	1,101	227
184	VI. Public Force	836	105	136	3	..	62	386	19	102	60	32	..	1,108	16	714	40	136	..
185	40. Army	162	51	70	..	..	22	10	..	5	..	14	..	269	..	222	..	26	..
186	(G.153) Imperial Army	..	..	..	..	..	..	..	..	..	..	..	..	..	..	..	..	..	..
187	(G.154) State Army	162	51	70	..	..	22	10	..	5	..	14	..	269	..	222	..	26	..
188	43. Police	674	54	66	3	..	40	376	19	97	60	18	..	839	16	492	40	110	..
189	(G.157) Police.	385	20	60	3	..	..	243	10	86	31	..	..	639	16	390	40	110	..
190	(G.158) Village watchmen	289	34	6	..	..	40	133	9	11	29	18	..	200	..	102	..	..	..
191	VII. Public Administration	3,152	..	141	..	262	..	2,376	159	31	224	109	16	2,733	557	1,024	150	453	73
192	44. Public Administration	3,152	..	141	..	262	..	2,376	159	31	224	109	16	2,733	357	1,024	150	453	73
193	(G.159) Imperial service	4	..	..	..	..	..	..	..	..	..	..	..	4	1	..	2	..	..
194	(G.160) State service	988	..	43	..	156	..	2,099	135	29	185	75	16	2,504	335	992	46	218	..
195	(G.160 a) Service of other Indian and foreign States	2	..	..	..	..	..	..	..	..	..	..	..	1	..	..	2	..	..
196	(G.161) Municipal and other local (not village) service	473	..	42	..	81	..	234	24	2	39	15	..	118	221	14	100	20	73
197	(G.162) Village officials and servants other than watchmen	1,685	..	56	..	25	..	43	..	..	..	19	..	106	..	18	..	220	..
198	VIII. Profession and Liberal Arts	4,435	2,349	516	206	1,254	549	2,444	1,540	451	589	580	447	3,025	594	344	281	512	154
199	45. Religion	2,981	1,669	362	150	721	319	1,625	1,142	255	525	359	351	2,373	370	158	117	388	112
200	(G.163) Priests, ministers, etc.	2,909	1,366	349	127	665	297	1,534	910	255	486	324	289	2,262	346	92	107	351	104
201	(G.164) Monks, nuns, religious mendicants	..	..	..	..	..	..	..	..	..	..	..	..	30	..	20	..	15	..
202	(G.165) Other religious workers	..	..	..	..	..	..	5	177	..	13	..	10	2	..	..	..	..	..
203	(G.166) Servants in religious edifices, burial and burning grounds, pilgrim conductors, circumcisers, etc.	22	303	13	23	56	22	86	55	..	26	35	52	79	24	46	10	22	8
204	46. Law	80	6	10	..	6	..	68	..	..	..	28	..	84	..	25	..	40	..
205	(G.167) Lawyers of all kinds including Qazis, Law Agents and Mukhtiars	56	6	10	..	6	..	54	..	..	..	18	..	66	..	15	..	37	..
206	(G.168) Lawyers' clerks petition-writers, etc.	24	..	..	..	..	..	14	..	..	..	10	..	18	..	10	..	3	..
207	47. Medicine	680	186	45	27	93	149	207	106	34	1	65	1	187	48	21	4	6	..
208	(G.169) Registered medical practitioners including oculists	30	3	2	..	14	..	11	4	..	..	1	..	5	4	..	..	..	..

TABLE X.

Occupation or Means of Livelihood.

	WARANGAL			KARIMNAGAR			ADILABAD		
		Males	Females		Males	Females		Males	Females
Total Earners		305,604	145,426		325,497	181,455		162,467	100,230
Total Working Dependents		40,345	23,531		40,094	39,503		40,402	32,484
Total Non-working Dependents		229,870	372,917		268,825	386,031		186,785	239,562
Total Population		575,819	541,874		634,416	606,989		389,754	372,276

Serial No.	Occupation	WARANGAL						KARIMNAGAR						ADILABAD					
		Total earners showing occupation as principal		Total working dependents		Total following occupation as subsidiary		Total earners showing occupation as principal		Total working dependents		Total following occupation as subsidiary		Total earners showing occupation as principal		Total working dependents		Total following occupation as subsidiary	
		Males	Females	Males	Females	Males	Females	Males	Females	Males	Females	Males	Females	Males	Females	Males	Females	Males	Females
	1	20	21	22	23	24	25	26	27	28	29	30	31	32	33	34	35	36	37
209	(G.170) Other persons practising the healing arts without being registered ..	543	12	16	..	69	4	83	20	10	1	21	1	150	6	7	..	3	..
210	(G.171) Dentists ..	2	..	..	..	..	..	..	..	..	..	..	..	1	..	..	..	..	..
211	(G.172) Midwives, vaccinaters, compounders, nurses, masseurs, etc. ..	94	171	27	27	10	145	112	82	24	..	40	..	29	38	14	4	3	..
212	(G.173) Veterinary Surgeons.	2	..	..	..	..	..	1	..	..	..	..	..	2	..	..	..	..	..
213	48. Instruction ..	537	276	56	10	102	66	211	56	10	..	33	..	148	114	47	88	27	12
214	(G.174) Professors and teachers of all kinds ..	513	276	56	10	99	66	187	56	2	..	33	..	89	114	19	88	9	12
215	(G.175) Clerks and servants connected with education .	24	..	..	..	3	..	21	..	8	..	..	..	51	.	28	..	18	..
216	49. Letters, arts and sciences (other than 44) ..	207	212	43	19	332	15	333	236	152	63	95	95	238	62	93	72	51	30
217	(G.176) Public scribes, stenographers, etc. ..	5	..	..	..	..	..	..	..	..	.	..	..	2	..	..	..	..	..
218	(G.177) Architects, surveyors, engineets, and their employees (not being State servants)	1	..	..	..	..	..	..	..	..	..	..	..	..	..	..	..	..	..
219	(G.178) Authors, editors, journalists and photographers	..	..	..	..	8	..	4	..	.	..	..	..	6	..	..	..	..	..
220	(G.179) Artists, sculptors and image-makers ..	6	12	..	..	..	..	..	26	..	..	..	13	34	..	5	..	..	..
221	(G.180) Scientists (astronomers, botanists,) etc. ..	8	..	4	..	2	..	..	.	..	..	..	..	..	..	..	..	..	..
222	(G.181) Horoscope casters, astrologers, fortune tellers, wizards, witches and mediums	150	100	24	2	300	15	92	180	3	63	42	..	153	20	65	24	18	15

223	(G.182) Musicians (composers and performers other than military) actors, dancers, etc. ..	16	100	10	17	11	..	232	80	146	..	88	92	27	40	20	80	19	14
224	(G.183) Managers and employees of places of public entertainments, race courses, societies, and clubs. ..	9	..	3	..	..	..	..	..	..	..	..	..	2	..	..	..	4	..
225	(G.184) Conjurors, acrobats, recitors, exhibitors of curiosities and wild animals, etc.	12	..	2	..	5	..	5	..	3	..	15	..	14	2	8	18	10	1
226	**D. Miscellaneous** ..	16,195	16,780	957	2,579	2,633	2,887	24,782	11,524	2,276	2,012	1,735	1,401	13,487	11,381	4,682	2,854	2,522	1,281
227	IX. Persons living on their income	257	211	8	39	24	..	49	11	..	..	1	10	175	39	61	20	15	2
228	50. Persons living principally on their income ..	257	211	8	39	24	..	49	11	..	..	1	10	175	39	61	20	15	2
229	(G.185) Proprietors (other than of agricultural land), fund and scholarship holders and pensioners ..	257	211	8	39	24	..	49	11	..	..	1	10	175	39	61	20	15	2
230	X. Domestic service ..	11,029	5,539	508	944	1,855	550	10,020	7,860	1,226	919	1,174	449	8,468	5,394	2,879	617	1,574	117
231	51. Domestic service ..	11,029	5,539	508	944	1,855	550	10,020	7,866	1,226	919	1,174	449	8,468	5,394	2,879	617	1,574	117
232	(G.186) Private motor drivers and cleaners ..	315	15	19	..	15	..	34	..	..	..	..	..	62	..	10	..	..	..
233	(G 187) Other domestic service	10,714	5,524	489	944	1,840	550	18,986	7,866	1,226	919	1,174	449	8,406	5,394	2,869	617	1,574	117
234	XI. Insufficiently defined occupations	412	4,892	..	215	..	1,112	365	708	409	313	147	230	1,591	2,084	634	1,432	158	252
235	52. General terms which do not indicate a definite occupation	412	4,892	..	215	..	1,112	365	708	409	313	147	230	1,591	2,084	634	1,432	158	252
236	(G.188) Manufacturers, businessmen and contractors otherwise unspecified ..	50	..	..	100	..	476	165	..	30	..	27	..	158	177	151	322	78	45
237	(G.189) Cashiers, accountants, book-keepers, clerks and other employees in unspecified offices and warehouses and shops ..	47	..	..	..	..	..	124	..	212	..	76	..	144	..	30	..	18	..
238	(G.190) Mechanics otherwise unspecified ..	13	..	..	..	..	..	6	..	..	..	..	..	483	..	83	..	20	..
239	(G.191) Labourers and workmen otherwise unspecified .	302	4,892	..	115	..	636	70	708	187	313	44	230	846	1,907	370	1,110	42	207
240	XII. Unproductive ..	4,497	6,138	446	1,381	754	1,225	5,848	2,944	641	780	413	712	3,253	3,864	1,108	785	775	910
241	53. Inmates of jails, asylums and alms houses ..	..	..	176	86	..	..	..	..	33	..	..	..	..	..	75	18	..	..
242	(G.192) Inmates of jails, asylums and alms houses ..	..	..	176	86	..	..	..	..	33	..	..	..	..	..	75	18	..	..
243	54. Beggars, vagrants and prostitutes	4,886	6,188	270	1,295	754	1,225	5,281	2,734	60[illegible]	753	413	712	3,253	3,864	1,033	767	775	910
244	(G.193) Beggars and vagrants	4,326	5,953	212	919	741	1,085	5,260	2,524	587	753	413	712	3,231	3,636	863	726	775	910
245	(G.194) Procurers and prostitutes	60	185	58	376	13	140	21	210	15	..	..	..	22	228	170	41	..	..
246	55. Other unclassified nonproductive industries ..	111	..	..	..	..	..	67	43	6	27	..	..	..	..	..	..	..	..
247	(G.195) Other unclassified non-productive industries .	111	..	..	..	..	..	67	43	6	27	..	..	..	..	..	..	..	..

TABLE X.

Occupation or Means of Livelihood.

MEDAK	Males	Females
Total Earners	203,377	104,867
Total Working Dependents	65,236	58,304
Total Non-working Dependents.. ..	104,862	202,019
Total Population	373,475	365,190

NIZAMABAD	Males	Females
Total Earners	140,434	76,739
Total Working Dependents ..	51,584	53,503
Total Non-working Dependents ..	121,538	179,427
Total Population	318,556	309,669

MAHBUBNAGAR	Males	Females
Total Earners	244,014	117,658
Total Working Dependents ..	46,398	41,078
Total Non-working Dependents ..	203,649	318,829
Total Population	494,061	477,555

Serial No.	Occupation	MEDAK: Total earners showing occupation as principal		MEDAK: Total working dependents		MEDAK: Total following occupation as subsidiary		NIZAMABAD: Total earners showing occupation as principal		NIZAMABAD: Total working dependents		NIZAMABAD: Total following occupation as subsidiary		MAHBUBNAGAR: Total earners showing occupation as principal		MAHBUBNAGAR: Total working dependents		MAHBUBNAGAR: Total following occupation as subsidiary	
		Males	Females	Males	Females	Males	Females	Males	Females	Males	Females	Males	Females	Males	Females	Males	Females	Males	Females
	1	38	39	40	41	42	43	44	45	46	47	48	49	50	51	52	53	54	55
1	TOTAL WORKERS. ..	203,377	104,867	65,236	58,304	31,180	20,333	140,434	76,739	51,584	53,503	38,441	19,287	244,014	117,653	46,398	41,073	35,329	22,718
2	A. Production of Raw Materials	96,357	41,798	21,789	28,925	10,073	12,091	84,570	47,330	26,269	31,255	20,732	12,583	126,491	73,105	24,690	13,651	20,464	12,970
3	I-Exploitation of Animals and Vegetation ..	96,357	41,798	21,789	28,925	10,073	12,091	84,570	47,330	26,269	31,255	20,732	12,583	126,491	73,105	24,690	13,651	20,464	12,970
4	1. Pasture and Agriculture .	92,189	38,602	21,537	28,417	9,901	11,985	76,998	46,798	24,419	31,095	19,608	12,293	122,135	71,279	23,392	12,811	19,899	12,163
5	(a) Cultivation ..	77,958	36,311	20,410	26,306	9,209	11,402	67,605	43,728	21,209	29,001	16,641	9,398	107,351	63,810	19,550	7,831	16,580	9,491
6	(G.1) Non-cultivating proprietors taking rent in money or kind ..	2,279	2,684	1,198	1,597	352	471	8,411	4,100	3,378	3,577	1,773	1,575	17,320	5,705	3,060	692	2,526	313
7	(G.2) Estate Agents and Managers of owners ..	25	..	18	..	3	..	18	..	6	..	12	..	411	..	116	..	26	..
8	(G.3) Estate Agents and Managers of Government..	132	..	20	..	1	..	56	..	22	..	10	..	230	..	73	..	5	..
9	(G.4) Rent Collectors, clerks, etc.	46	..	23	..	8	..	230	..	43	..	18	..	194	..	12	..	18	..
10	(G.5) Cultivating owners ..	55,141	8,490	6,144	6,447	3,018	1,204	19,580	8,417	5,655	11,776	5,569	2,654	43,327	8,527	9,079	2,561	9,028	1,109
11	(G.6) Tenant cultivators ..	6,514	1,448	562	1,661	413	184	26,247	3,960	10,113	4,618	6,173	2,028	9,317	6,865	1,058	2,501	1,460	712
12	(G.7) Agricultural labourers.	13,821	23,680	12,445	10,601	5,414	9,543	13,063	27,251	1,992	9,030	3,086	3,141	36,543	42,713	6,161	2,077	3,517	7,357
13	(b) Cultivation of special crops, fruits, etc. ..	166	49	72	31	49	15	290	66	142	78	325	20	766	239	177	280	164	120
14	(G.13) Pan-Vine ..	18	8	14	12	8	4	..	6	..	8	..	..	156	23	20	49	31	21
15	(G.16) Market Gardeners, flower, fruit growers, etc. ..	153	41	58	19	41	11	290	60	142	70	325	20	610	216	157	231	183	99
16	(c.) Forestry	324	147	67	148	20	27	325	138	34	50	365	16	3,068	607	468	977	271	195
17	(G.17) Forest officers, rangers, guards, etc. ..	27	..	4	..	..	..	14	..	6	..	..	..	35	..	8	..	..	..
18	(G.18) Wood-cutters and charcoal burners ..	249	132	51	148	18	27	287	138	17	50	358	16	2,840	530	405	871	234	163

TABLE X.

OCCUPATION OR MEANS OF LIVELIHOOD.

19	(G.19) Collectors of forest produce.	15	..	4	..	..	..	14	..	3	..	10	..	43	21	25	39	10	20
20	(G.20) Collectors of lac ..	33	15	8	..	2	..	10	..	8	..	2	..	150	56	30	67	27	12
21	(d.)—Stock raising ..	13,683	2,079	955	1,927	623	541	8,733	2,842	3,021	1,941	2,274	2,848	10,516	6,530	3,089	3,605	2,786	2,334
22	(G.21) Cattle and buffaloe breeders and keepers ..	1,052	479	135	326	116	41	1,399	725	652	306	247	201	626	186	232	259	296	182
23	(G.22) Breeders of transport animals	28	..	10	..	..	..	..	..	..	..	..	..	71	10	20	..	..	..
24	(G.23) Herdsmen, shepherds and breeders of other animals	12,603	1,600	810	1,601	507	500	7,334	2,117	2,369	1,635	2,027	2,647	9,819	6,334	2,837	3,846	2,490	2,152
25	(e) Raising of small animals and insects	58	16	33	5	..	..	45	24	13	25	3	11	484	93	99	118	98	28
26	(G.24) Birds, bees, etc. ..	37	4	24	3	..	..	15	4	3	3	1	2	162	43	21	46	39	3
27	(G.25) Silk worms ..	9	8	2	..	..	..	18	12	4	14	2	5	128	21	50	58	41	12
28	(G.26) Lac cultivation ..	12	4	7	2	..	..	12	8	6	8	..	4	144	29	28	14	18	8
29	2. Fishing and Hunting ..	4,168	3,196	252	508	172	106	7,572	532	1,850	160	1,124	290	4,356	1,826	1,298	840	565	807
30	(G.27) Fishing and pearling	3,916	3,096	179	450	121	106	3,366	471	760	114	532	204	3,650	1,512	1,044	642	460	707
31	(G.28) Hunting ..	252	100	73	58	51	..	4,206	61	1,090	46	592	86	706	314	254	198	105	100
32	II. Exploitation of Minerals	..	..	..	..	..	..	..	..	..	..	..	..	..	..	..	..	..	..
33	3. Metallic minerals ..	..	..	..	..	..	..	..	..	..	..	..	..	..	..	..	..	..	..
34	(G.30) Iron	..	..	..	..	..	..	..	..	..	..	..	..	..	..	..	..	..	..
35	4. Non-metallic minerals ..	..	..	..	..	..	..	..	..	..	..	..	..	..	..	..	..	..	..
36	(G.35) Coal	..	..	..	..	..	..	..	..	..	..	..	..	..	..	..	..	..	..
37	(G.37) Building materials (including stone, materials for cement manufacture and clays)	..	..	..	..	..	..	..	..	..	..	..	..	..	..	..	..	..	..
38	(G.38) Mica, ...	..	..	..	..	..	..	..	..	..	..	..	..	..	..	..	..	..	..
39	(G.40) Salt, saltpetre and other saline substances ..	..	..	..	..	..	..	..	..	..	..	..	..	..	..	..	..	..	..
40	B.—Preparation and supply of material substances	70,543	30,761	34,905	18,283	18,290	4,715	41,975	21,639	16,042	17,204	11,772	5,405	61,710	21,162	13,416	11,863	5,940	6,946
41	III. Industry	30,166	12,748	13,947	10,783	6,763	2,080	17,720	6,740	7,177	5,054	6,332	2,349	24,740	6,845	4,640	3,521	700	976
42	5. Textiles	4,895	3,466	1,159	403	788	209	4,186	3,319	1,579	1,427	1,011	1,137	10,602	2,828	2,255	1,142	160	209
43	(G.42) Cotton ginning, cleaning and Pressing ..	340	154	210	71	99	15	295	260	138	27	58	45	40	10	14	11	1	..
44	(G.43) Cotton spinning, sizing and weaving ..	3,788	3,106	394	299	633	142	3,650	2,853	1,823	1,819	893	1,047	8,306	2,287	1,575	834	98	156
45	(G.45) Rope, twine, string and other fibres ..	280	16	260	5	18	25	70	57	32	14	18	12	36	9	15	12	..	..
46	(G.46) Wool carding spinning and weaving ..	126	50	36	..	..	..	72	18	8	2	4	..	1,872	482	467	150	38	41
47	(G.47) Silk spinning and weaving.	180	72	210	17	18	16	8	4	2	4	4	..	280	74	163	122	21	12
48	(G.48) Hair (Horse-hair) etc.	..	..	..	..	..	..	3	1	3	..	..	..	..	..	..	..	..	..

TABLE X.

Occupation or Means of Livelihood.

	MEDAK			
			Males	Females
Total Earners			203,377	104,867
Total Working Dependents			65,236	58,304
Total Non-working Dependents			104,862	202,010
Total Population			373,475	305,190

	NIZAMABAD			
			Males	Females
Total Earners			140,434	76,739
Total Working Dependents			51,584	53,503
Total Non-working Dependents			121,538	179,427
Total Population			313,556	309,669

	MAHBUBNAGAR			
			Males	Females
Total Earners			244,014	117,653
Total Working Dependents			46,398	41,073
Total Non-working Dependents			203,649	318,829
Total Population			494,061	477,555

Serial No.	Occupation	MEDAK						NIZAMABAD						MAHBUBNAGAR					
		Total earners showinig occupation as principal		Total working dependents		Total following occupation as subsidiary		Total earners showing occupation as principal		Total working dependents		Total following occupation as subsidiary		Total earners showing occupation as principal		Total working dependents		Total following occupation as subsidiary	
		Males	Females	Males	Females	Males	Females	Males	Females	Males	Females	Males	Females	Males	Females	Males	Females	Males	Females
	1	38	39	40	41	42	43	44	45	46	47	48	49	50	51	52	53	54	55
49	(G.49) Dyeing, bleaching, printing, preparation and sponging of textiles ..	163	..	49	..	20	..	110	120	71	58	30	32	63	16	21	13	2	..
50	(G.50) Lace, crepe, embroideries, fringes, etc., and insufficiently described textiles	18	68	..	11	..	11	8	6	2	3	4	1	5	..	..	..	..	..
51	6. Hides, skins and hard materials from the animal kingdom	121	59	63	31	26	14	..	..	..	..	..	..	32	12	6	11	16	..
52	(G.51) Working in leather ..	108	51	60	27	25	14	..	..	..	..	..	..	28	6	6	11	16	..
53	(G.52) Furriers and persons occupied with feathers and bristles ; brush makers ..	3	..	..	..	..	..	..	..	..	..	..	..	..	..	..	..	..	..
54	(G.53) Bone, ivory, horn, shell, etc., workers (except buttons)	10	8	3	4	1	..	..	..	..	..	..	..	4	6	..	..	..	..
55	7. Wood	2,661	484	1,000	531	581	79	1,004	434	707	579	574	190	1,895	581	356	647	100	76
56	(G.54) Sawyers ..	52	..	..	..	18	..	28	10	7	10	12	..	55	..	12	8	21	..
57	(G.55) Carpenters, turners and joiners, etc. ..	1,760	367	640	292	279	41	781	106	514	330	127	27	1,078	182	185	255	42	17
58	(G.56) Basket-makers and other industries of woody materials, including leaves and thatchers and builders working with bamboo, reeds or similar materials ..	849	117	360	239	284	38	195	318	186	239	135	163	762	399	159	384	37	59
59	8. Metals	519	101	560	82	314	29	298	27	109	90	175	34	1,056	242	162	173	52	46
60	(G.57) Smelting, forging and rolling of iron and other metals	..	..	..	..	..	..	..	..	..	..	..	..	3	..	..	..	..	..
61	(G.58) Makers of arms, guns, etc.	..	..	..	..	..	..	..	..	..	..	..	..	..	..	..	..	..	..

TABLE X.
OCCUPATION OR MEANS OF LIVELIHOOD.

62	(G.59) Black-smiths other workers in iron, makers of implements ..	312	75	400	33	139	13	276	27	95	90	170	34	855	214	138	122	40	34
63	(G.60) Workers in brass, copper and bell metals ..	207	26	160	49	175	16	22	..	14	..	5	..	184	26	22	51	12	12
64	(G.61) Workers in other metals, (except precious) .	..	..	..	..	..	..	..	..	..	..	..	..	14	..	2	..	..	..
65	(G.62) Workers in mints, die-sinkers, etc.	..	..	..	..	..	..	..	..	..	..	..	..	..	..	..	..	..	..
66	9. Ceramics ..	1,391	588	298	1,049	339	397	1,916	581	582	501	516	60	1,581	865	271	369	32	66
67	(G.63) Potters and makers of earthen ware ..	1,300	567	277	1,080	291	397	1,876	581	568	501	446	60	1,458	865	257	369	31	66
68	(G.64) Brick and tile workers	76	21	21	19	18	..	40	..	14	..	70	..	123	..	14	..	1	..
69	(G.65) Other workers in ceramics	15	..	..	..	..	..	..	..	..	..	..	..	..	..	..	..	..	..
70	10. Chemical products properly so-called and analogous	1,795	619	641	1,270	290	161	138	19	16	60	5	54	287	45	44	48	35	18
71	(G.66) Manufacture of matches, fireworks and other explosives ..	3	..	..	..	..	..	..	..	..	..	..	..	2	..	..	..	..	..
72	(G.67) Manufacture of aerated and mineral waters and ice	2	..	..	..	..	..	..	..	..	..	..	..	5	..	..	..	..	..
73	(G.68) Manufacture and refining of vegetable oils ..	1,787	619	641	1,270	290	161	138	19	16	60	5	54	280	45	44	48	35	18
74	(G.69) Manufacture and refining of mineral oils ..	3	..	..	..	..	..	..	..	..	..	..	..	..	..	..	..	..	..
75	(G.70) Others	..	..	..	..	..	..	..	..	..	..	..	..	..	..	..	..	..	..
76	11. Food Industries ..	1,278	276	496	488	270	37	488	200	211	208	84	..	1,389	484	263	330	98	180
77	(G.71) Rice pounders and huskers and flour grinders .	..	24	..	13	..	1	..	24	..	18	..	..	..	48	..	57	..	29
78	(G.72) Grain parchers, etc. ..	..	6	..	8	..	2	..	6	..	8	..	..	..	16	..	14	..	5
79	(G.73) Butchers ..	272	3	106	22	..	..	212	14	91	19	..	..	845	110	126	24	39	7
80	(G.74) Makers of sugar, molasses and gur ..	15	..	..	10	..	..	..	3	..	5	..	..	7	24	..	18	..	..
81	(G.75) Sweet-meat and condiment makers ..	..	5	..	18	..	..	5	105	4	107	20	..	12	89	4	76	2	41
82	(G.76) Toddy drawers ..	947	220	378	395	260	27	210	25	99	14	54	..	452	143	104	112	27	36
83	(G.77) Brewers and distillers.	18	6	12	12	..	3	15	3	3	12	2	..	14	..	..	..	..	..
84	(G.78) Manufacturers of tobacco	25	12	..	10	10	4	40	18	10	25	8	..	51	59	29	38	30	21
85	(G.80) Manufacturers of ganja	1	..	..	..	..	..	5	2	4	..	..	..	3	..	..	..	..	..
86	(G.81) Others ..	..	..	..	..	..	..	1	..	..	..	..	..	5	..	..	..	..	..
87	12. Industries of dress and toilet	17,058	7,018	9,534	6,526	4,100	1,071	7,218	1,407	3,257	1,199	3,057	237	5,740	1,427	818	554	60	342
88	(G.82) Boot, shoe, sandal and clog makers ..	6,695	2,011	4,080	3,984	2,711	360	4,067	181	1,451	277	1,534	81	805	213	181	69	10	28
89	(G.83) Tailors, milliners, dress makers and darners ..	1,580	705	922	912	308	215	189	269	164	396	94	22	1,345	346	201	137	10	31
90	(G.84) Embroiderers, hat-makers and makers of other articles of wear ..	20	12	11	20	..	1	3	..	2	..	..	..	7	..	..	..	..	..
91	(G.85) Washing and cleaning	6,758	4,275	3,676	1,442	880	475	1,628	887	1,241	343	758	108	2,631	581	315	190	30	168

TABLE X.

Occupation or Means of Livelihood.

	MEDAK Males	MEDAK Females	NIZAMABAD Males	NIZAMABAD Females	MAHBUBNAGAR Males	MAHBUBNAGAR Females
Total Earners	203,377	104,867	140,434	76,739	244,014	117,653
Total Working Dependents	65,236	58,304	51,584	53,503	46,398	41,073
Total Non-working Dependents	104,862	202,019	121,538	179,427	203,649	318,829
Total Population	373,475	365,190	313,556	309,669	494,061	477,555

Serial No.	Occupation	MEDAK: Total earners showing occupation as principal		Total working dependents		Total following occupation as subsidiary		NIZAMABAD: Total earners showing occupation as principal		Total working dependents		Total following occupation as subsidiary		MAHBUBNAGAR: Total earners showing occupation as principal		Total working dependents		Total following occupation as subsidiary	
		Males	Females	Males	Females	Males	Females	Males	Females	Males	Females	Males	Females	Males	Females	Males	Females	Males	Females
	1	38	39	40	41	42	43	44	45	46	47	48	49	50	51	52	53	54	55
92	(G.86) Barbers, hair dressers and wig-makers ..	2,005	15	895	168	201	20	1,362	70	399	183	671	31	952	287	171	158	10	115
93	(G.87) Other industries connected with toilet ..	..	..	..	..	..	..	4	..	..	..	..	..	..	..	..	..	..	..
94	13. Furniture Industries ..	75	..	26	28	12	..	17	..	..	..	..	..	77	..	10	..	10	..
95	(G.88) Cabinet-makers carriage painters, etc ..	75	..	26	28	12	..	3	..	..	..	..	..	66	..	10	..	10	..
96	(G.89) Upholsterers, tent makers, etc. ..	..	..	..	..	..	..	14	..	..	..	..	..	11	..	..	..	..	..
97	14. Building Industries ..	124	11	34	27	23	..	1,226	123	485	572	448	307	760	75	186	89	56	20
98	(G.90) Lime burners, cement workers ; Excavators and well sinkers; stone cutters and dressers; Brick layers and masons ; Builders (other than buildings made of bamboo and similar materials) painters, decorators of houses, tilers, plumbers, etc.	124	11	34	27	23	..	1,226	123	485	572	448	307	760	75	186	89	56	20
99	15. Construction of means of transport	61	..	9	..	9	..	27	..	19	..	7	..	56	..	20	..	5	..
100	(G.91) Persons engaged in making, assembling or repairing motor vehicles or cycles	12	..	3	..	2	..	7	..	4	..	1	..	8	..	2	..	1	..
101	(G.92) Carriage, cart, palki, etc. makers and wheelwrights	49	..	6	..	7	..	20	..	15	..	6	..	48	..	18	..	4	..
102	16. Production and transmission of physical force ..	2	..	..	..	..	..	..	..	..	..	..	..	27	..	3	..	4	..
103	(G.94) Heat, light, electricity, motive power, etc., Gas works and electric light and power ..	2	..	..	..	..	..	..	..	..	..	..	..	27	..	3	..	4	..

No.	Occupation																		
104	17. Miscellaneous and undefined industries ..	186	126	127	298	41	83	1,222	630	212	418	455	330	1,288	286	246	149	72	60
105	(G.95) Printers, engravers, book binders, etc. ..	3	..	..	..	..	..	3	..	..	..	1	..	6	..	2	..	8	..
106	(G.96) Makers of musical instruments	4	..	..	..	..	..	1	..	..	..	..	..	2	..	..	..	..	..
107	(G.97) Makers of clocks and surgical or scientific instruments, etc.	4	..	..	..	..	..	4	..	..	..	4	..	12	..	2	..	2	..
108	(G.98) Makers of jewellery and ornaments ..	148	112	127	261	41	72	1,164	603	202	362	450	330	1,177	262	205	110	68	39
109	(G.99) Other miscellaneous and undefined industries (toy making, taxi dermy, etc.)	..	14	..	37	..	11	..	..	..	..	..	..	5	24	10	39	4	21
110	(G.100) Scavenging ..	27	..	..	..	..	..	50	27	10	56	..	..	36	..	27	..	..	..
111	IV. Transport	10,780	2,215	9,965	3,769	3,765	572	6,168	2,123	1,892	927	1,514	464	12,729	3,291	3,985	4,672	872	930
112	19. Transport by water ..	..	..	..	..	..	..	..	..	..	..	..	..	1,037	261	365	295	14	136
113	(G.104) Labourers employed on harbours, docks, rivers and canals	..	..	..	..	..	..	..	..	..	..	..	..	1,037	261	365	295	14	136
114	20. Transport by Road ..	7,215	1,991	8,346	3,483	3,250	460	4,777	1,013	1,250	675	1,078	235	11,238	2,915	3,453	4,233	304	755
115	(G.105) Persons (other than labourers) employed on the construction and maintenance of roads and bridges .	39	..	13	..	4	..	28	..	10	..	..	..	139	..	35	..	..	..
116	(G.106) Labourers employed on roads and bridges ..	6,065	1,812	7,618	3,268	2,720	417	2,418	400	625	399	418	101	7,986	2,761	2,840	3,923	407	683
117	(G.107) Owners, managers & employees (excluding personal servants) connected with mechanically driven vehicles (including trams) .	52	4	1	3	14	2	20	..	5	..	15	..	144	2	..	14	10	..
118	(G.108) Owners, managers, employees (excluding personal servants) connected with other vehicles ..	329	59	347	74	190	18	629	48	227	49	394	11	2,183	92	220	153	181	26
119	(G.109) Palki, etc., bearers and owners	221	41	110	12	128	..	54	..	18	..	24	..	249	4	138	31	115	17
120	(G.110) Pack elephant, camel, mule, ass and bullock, owners and drivers ..	484	75	127	126	139	28	1,581	568	365	227	227	123	407	56	175	112	128	29
121	(G.111) Porters and messengers	25	..	130	..	55	..	47	..	..	..	..	..	70	..	45	..	18	..
122	21. Transport by Rail ..	3,400	224	1,588	286	511	112	1,363	1,110	628	252	433	229	379	115	145	144	51	39
123	(G.112) Railway employees of all kind other than coolies	159	8	78	3	2	..	150	10	75	52	75	29	48	3	18	8	..	..
124	(G.113) Labourers employed on railway construction and maintenance and coolies and porters employed on Railway premises ..	3,250	216	1,510	283	509	112	1,213	1,100	553	200	358	200	331	112	127	136	51	39
125	22. Post Office, Telegraph and Telephone services ..	156	..	31	..	4	..	28	..	14	..	3	..	75	..	22	..	3	..
126	(G.114) Post office, Telegraph and Telephone services	156	..	31	..	4	..	28	..	14	..	8	..	75	..	22	..	8	..
127	V. Trade	29,597	15,798	10,993	3,781	7,762	2,063	18,087	12,776	6,973	11,223	3,926	2,592	24,241	11,026	4,791	3,670	4,868	5,040

TABLE X.

Occupation or Means of Livelihood.

	MEDAK Males	MEDAK Females	NIZAMABAD Males	NIZAMABAD Females	MAHBUBNAGAR Males	MAHBUBNAGAR Females
Total Earners	203,377	104,867	140,484	76,739	244,014	117,653
Total Working Dependents	65,236	58,304	51,584	53,503	46,398	41,073
Total Non-working Dependents	104,862	202,019	121,538	179,427	203,649	318,829
Total Population	373,475	365,190	313,536	309,669	494,061	477,555

Serial No.	Occupation	MEDAK: Total earners showing occupation as principal — Males	Females	Total working dependents — Males	Females	Total following occupation as subsidiary — Males	Females	NIZAMABAD: Total earners showing occupation as principal — Males	Females	Total working dependents — Males	Females	Total following occupation as subsidiary — Males	Females	MAHBUBNAGAR: Total earners showing occupation as principal — Males	Females	Total working dependents — Males	Females	Total following occupation as subsidiary — Males	Females
	1	38	39	40	41	42	43	44	45	46	47	48	49	50	51	52	53	54	55
128	23. Banks, establishments of credit, exchange and insurance	515	51	4	..	14	22	49	..	20	..	18	..	968	441	41	49	30	36
129	(G.115) Bank managers, money lenders, exchange and insurance agents, money changers and brokers and their employees ..	515	51	4	..	14	22	49	..	20	..	18	..	968	441	41	49	30	36
130	24. Brokerage commission and export	8	..	..	..	..	..	12	..	..	..	..	..	3	..	..	..	..	..
131	(G.116) Brokers, commission agents, commercial travellers, warehouse owners and employees	8	..	..	..	..	..	12	..	..	..	..	..	3	..	..	..	..	..
132	25. Trade in Textiles ..	298	49	45	16	20	7	345	126	210	77	47	24	53	61	..	20	..	3
133	(G.117) Trade in piece goods, wool, cotton, silk, hair and other textiles ..	298	49	45	16	20	7	345	126	210	77	47	24	53	61	..	20	..	3
134	26. Trade in skins, leather and furs	316	63	58	28	14	8	127	..	40	..	20	..	151	33	72	21	22	6
135	(G.118) Trade in skins, leather, furs, feathers, horn, etc., and the articles made from these	316	63	58	28	14	8	127	..	40	..	20	..	151	33	72	21	22	6
136	27. Trade in wood ..	65	27	27	16	10	2	35	79	22	44	20	38	462	150	88	71	51	30
137	(G.119) Trade in wood (not fire-wood)	..	..	..	..	..	..	..	..	..	..	..	..	361	78	81	34	41	17
138	(G.120) Trade in barks ..	39	18	15	7	6	2	8	59	4	20	6	30	49	52	2	14	3	4
139	(G.121) Trade in bamboos and canes	21	9	8	9	4	..	27	12	18	18	14	5	22	6	..	2	..	7
140	(G.122) Trade in thatches and other forest produce .	5	..	4	..	..	..	..	8	..	6	..	3	30	14	5	21	7	2
141	28. Trade in metals ..	168	31	14	18	10	4	49	51	18	20	24	10	21	4	5	..	3	..

TABLE X.

OCCUPATION OR MEANS OF LIVELIHOOD.

142	(G.123) Trade in metals, machinery, knives, tools, etc.	168	31	14	18	10	4	40	51	18	20	24	10	21	4	5	..	8	..
143	29. Trade in pottery, bricks and tiles	274	384	210	191	46	59	30	372	14	486	18	179	61	136	17	58	..	71
144	(G.124) Trade in pottery, bricks and tiles ..	274	384	210	191	46	59	30	372	14	486	18	179	61	136	17	58	..	71
145	30. Trade in chemical products	15	..	..	..	..	..	..	..	..	..	..	..	3	..	..	..	..	..
146	(G.125) Drugs, dyes, paints, petroleum, explosives, etc.	15	..	..	..	..	..	..	..	..	..	..	..	3	..	..	..	..	..
147	31. Hotels, cafes, restaurants, etc.	10,671	5,838	4,408	909	2,610	307	4,642	2,484	2,001	2,521	1,105	618	6,922	5,056	2,346	1,907	2,280	3,094
148	(G.126) Vendors of wine, liquors, aerated waters and ice	10,636	5,785	4,405	891	2,610	306	4,564	2,483	1,971	2,521	1,083	618	6,872	5,027	2,346	1,897	2,275	3,092
149	(G.127) Owners and managers of hotels, cook shops, sarais, etc. (and employees)	30	..	..	..	..	..	54	..	20	..	12	..	17	8	..	3	3	2
150	(G.128) Hawkers of drink and food stuffs ..	5	53	3	18	..	1	24	..	10	..	10	..	33	21	..	7	2	..
151	32. Other trade in food stuffs	1,012	560	230	292	252	131	1,045	5,816	841	1,871	162	854	1,472	2,596	833	440	1,114	618
152	(G.129) Grain and pulse dealers	116	153	134	22	125	..	620	110	470	56	55	20	2,008	260	185	27	26	39
153	(G.130) Dealers in sweetmeats, sugar and spices ..	124	71	..	14	..	13	5	70	8	39	..	30	47	53	12	39	2	22
154	(G.131) Dealers in dairy product, eggs and poultry ..	441	399	76	215	120	118	226	5,591	189	1,751	76	789	1,467	1,899	489	281	822	395
155	(G.132) Dealers in animals for food	224	..	6	..	..	..	17	5	4	..	1	..	71	16	15	..	18	..
156	(G.133) Dealers in fodder for animals	16	..	16	..	..	..	2	..	..	..	..	..	15	..	..	17	..	3
157	(G.134) Dealers in other food stuffs	55	..	4	..	..	..	160	40	170	25	30	13	382	213	20	61	58	101
158	(G.135) Dealers in tobacco .	31	27	..	41	7	18	12	..	..	..	..	..	469	153	112	24	198	53
159	(G.136) Dealers in opium ..	2	..	..	..	..	..	2	..	..	..	..	..	2	..	..	..	..	..
160	(G.137) Dealers in ganja ..	3	..	..	..	..	..	1	..	..	..	..	..	16	..	..	..	..	..
161	33. Trade in clothing and toilet articles ..	329	5	5	20	2	..	141	13	10	23	8	4	503	162	211	201	136	78
162	(G.138) Trade in ready-made clothing and other articles of dress and the toilet (hats, umbrellas, socks, ready-made shoes, perfumes, etc.)	329	5	5	20	2	..	141	15	10	23	8	4	503	162	211	201	136	78
163	34. Trade in furniture ..	129	13	28	21	10	7	4	..	..	..	..	..	398	199	168	97	86	32
164	(G.139) Trade in furniture, carpets, curtains and bedding	21	..	24	..	10	..	..	..	..	..	..	..	321	64	108	43	66	12
165	(G.140) Hardware, cooking utensils, porcelain crockery, glassware bottles, articles for gardening, etc. ..	108	13	4	21	..	7	4	..	..	..	..	..	77	135	60	54	20	40
166	35. Trade in building materials	12	..	..	..	..	..	55	29	30	36	10	21	21	..	..	..	..	..
167	(G.141) Trade in building materials (other than bricks, tiles and woody materials)	12	..	..	..	..	..	55	29	30	36	10	21	21	..	..	..	..	..
168	36. Trade in means of transport	346	14	1	28	20	7	77	..	40	..	17	..	424	103	68	102	22	31

TABLE X.

Occupation or Means of Livelihood.

District	Item	Males	Females
MEDAK	Total Earners	203,377	104,867
	Total Working Dependents	65,236	58,304
	Total Non-working Dependents	104,862	202,019
	Total Population	373,475	365,190
NIZAMABAD	Total Earners	140,434	76,739
	Total Working Dependents	51,584	53,503
	Total Non-working Dependents	121,538	179,427
	Total Population	313,556	309,669
MAHBUBNAGAR	Total Earners	244,014	117,653
	Total Working Dependents	46,398	41,073
	Total Non-working Dependents	203,649	318,829
	Total Population	494,061	477,555

Serial No.	Occupation	MEDAK						NIZAMABAD						MAHBUBNAGAR					
		Total earners showing occupation as principal		Total working dependents		Total following occupation as subsidiary		Total earners showing occupation as principal		Total working dependents		Total following occupation as subsidiary		Total earners showing occupation as principal		Total working dependants		Total following occupation as subsidiary	
		Males	Females	Males	Females	Males	Females	Males	Females	Males	Females	Males	Females	Males	Females	Males	Females	Males	Females
	1	38	39	40	41	42	43	44	45	46	47	48	49	50	51	52	53	54	55
169	(G.142) Dealers and hirers, in mechanical transport motors, cycles, etc. ..	8	..	..	..	2	..	15	..	10	..	3	..	8	..	..	..	2	..
170	(G.143) Dealers and hirers in other carriages, carts, boats, etc.	311	14	1	28	18	7	54	..	22	..	12	..	246	59	41	73	17	24
171	(G.144.) Dealers and hirers of elephants, camels, horses, cattle, asses, mules, etc.	27	..	..	..	..	..	8	..	8	..	2	..	170	44	27	29	3	7
172	37. Trade in fuel ..	264	30	31	64	5	17	320	117	130	150	21	54	681	301	156	273	277	104
173	(G.145) Dealers in firewood, charcoal, coal, cowdung, etc.	264	30	31	64	5	17	320	117	130	150	21	54	681	301	156	273	277	104
174	38. Trade in articles of luxury and those pertaining to letters and the arts and sciences	159	111	22	77	5	23	126	129	102	386	135	210	698	244	198	153	79	138
175	(G.146) Dealers in precious stones jewellery (real and imitation) clocks, optical instruments, etc ..	27	..	..	..	2	..	..	..	..	..	..	..	387	22	140	7	59	..
176	(G.147) Dealers in common bangles bead necklaces, fans, small articles, toys hunting, and fishing tackle, flowers, etc. ..	120	111	22	77	3	23	124	129	102	386	130	210	303	222	58	146	20	138
177	(G.148) Publishers, booksellers, stationers, dealers in music, pictures, musical instruments and curiosities	8	..	..	..	..	..	2	..	..	..	5	..	8	..	..	..	..	..
178	39. Trade of other sorts ..	15,016	8,532	5,904	2,101	4,744	1,449	11,030	3,558	3,495	5,609	2,321	585	8,310	1,540	588	269	268	784
179	(G.149) Dealers in rags, stable refuse and etc. ..	..	..	..	..	..	..	..	..	..	..	..	..	7	..	..	..	..	..
180	(G.150) General store-keepers and shop-keepers, otherwise unspecified ..	14,998	8,532	5,904	2,101	4,744	1,449	11,030	3,558	3,495	5,609	2,321	585	8,267	1,540	567	269	267	784

TABLE X.

OCCUPATION OR MEANS OF LIVELIHOOD.

181	(G.151) Itinerant traders, pedlars and hawkers (of other than food, etc.) ..	15	..	..	..	..	..	..	..	..	..	..	..	23	..	18	..	1	..
182	(G.152) Other trades (including farmers of pounds, tools and markets) ..	3	..	..	..	..	..	..	..	..	..	..	..	11	..	3	..	..	..
183	**C. Public Administration and Liberal Arts**	6,259	1,274	1,100	704	547	474	3,456	238	3,262	626	250	23	6,838	942	1,681	390	828	284
184	VI. Public Force ..	2,001	16	382	35	138	..	1,106	82	240	58	66	6	1,910	27	133	..	414	6
185	40. Army	1,041	..	162	..	137	..	601	7	125	43	36	6	419	..	33	..	242	..
186	(G.153) Imperial Army ..	..	..	..	..	..	..	..	..	..	..	..	..	..	..	..	..	..	..
187	(G.154) State Army ..	1,041	..	162	..	137	..	601	7	125	43	36	6	419	..	33	..	242	..
188	43. Police	960	16	220	35	1	..	505	75	115	10	30	..	1,500	27	100	..	172	6
189	(G.157) Police	803	16	165	35	1	..	505	75	115	10	10	..	1,055	27	100	..	..	6
190	(G.158) Village watchmen ..	157	..	55	..	..	..	..	..	..	..	20	..	445	..	..	..	172	..
191	VII. Public Administration .	1,524	..	245	67	4	..	1,310	10	2,755	471	138	8	1,904	203	295	78	42	..
192	44. Public Administration .	1,524	..	245	67	4	..	1,310	10	2,755	471	138	8	1,904	203	295	78	42	..
193	(G.159) Imperail serviec ..	..	..	..	..	..	..	..	..	..	..	..	..	..	..	..	..	..	..
194	(G.160) State service ..	1,345	..	225	7	..	..	1,242	10	2,741	271	107	8	1,708	123	277	64	21	..
195	(G.160 *a*) Service of other Indian and foreign States..	..	..	..	..	..	..	..	..	..	..	..	..	1	..	..	..	..	..
196	(G.161) Municipal and other local (not village) service..	27	..	8	60	..	..	15	..	4	200	21	..	122	80	15	14	..	..
197	(G.162) Village officials and servants other than watchmen	152	..	12	..	4	..	53	..	10	..	10	..	73	..	3	..	21	..
198	VIII. Professions and Liberal Arts	2,734	1,238	473	602	405	474	1,040	146	267	102	46	9	3,015	712	1,253	312	372	278
199	45. Religion	2,057	664	378	363	265	340	315	46	157	29	42	..	2,268	562	1,188	236	272	193
200	(G.163) Priests, ministers, etc.	2,001	664	358	363	265	340	268	46	140	29	42	..	2,212	538	1,189	200	270	186
201	(G.164) Monks, nuns, religious mendicants ..	8	..	..	..	..	..	5	..	3	..	..	..	1	..	..	..	..	..
202	(G.165) Other religious workers	3	..	..	..	..	..	17	..	..	..	..	..	2	..	..	..	..	..
203	(G.166) Servants in religious edifices, burial and burning grounds, pilgrim conductors, circumcisers, etc.	43	..	20	..	..	..	30	..	14	..	..	..	58	24	1	36	2	7
204	46. Law	84	..	..	..	8	..	215	..	5	..	..	..	298	5	17	3	10	..
205	(G.167) Lawyers of all kinds including Qazis, Law Agents and Mukhtiars ..	79	..	..	..	8	..	201	..	..	..	..	..	283	5	11	3	8	..
206	(G.168) Lawyers' clerks petition-writers, etc. ..	5	..	..	..	..	..	14	..	5	..	..	..	15	..	6	..	2	..
207	47. Medicine	226	46	45	24	40	18	111	37	7	20	..	5	90	84	15	28	22	37
208	(G.169) Registered medical practitioners including oculists	6	4	..	..	..	..	4	1	..	2	..	..	8	2	1	2	..	..

TABLE X.

Occupation or Means of Livelihood.

District		Males	Females
MEDAK	Total Earners	208,377	104,867
	Total Working Dependents	65,236	58,304
	Total Non-working Dependents	104,862	202,019
	Total Population	373,475	365,190
NIZAMABAD	Total Earners	140,434	76,739
	Total Working Dependents	51,584	53,503
	Total Non-working Dependents	121,538	179,427
	Total Population	313,556	309,669
MAHBUBNAGAR	Total Earners	244,014	117,653
	Total Working Dependents	46,396	41,073
	Total Non-working Dependents	203,649	318,829
	Total Population	494,061	477,555

Serial No.	Occupation	MEDAK						NIZAMABAD						MAHBUBNAGAR					
		Total earners showing occupation as principal		Total working dependents		Total following occupation as subsidiary		Total earners showing occupation as principal		Total working dependents		Total following occupation as subsidiary		Total earners showing occupation as principal		Total working dependents		Total following occupation as subsidiary	
		Males	Females	Males	Females	Males	Females	Males	Females	Males	Females	Males	Females	Males	Females	Males	Females	Males	Females
	1	38	39	40	41	42	43	44	45	46	47	48	49	50	51	52	53	54	55
209	(G.170) Other persons practising the healing arts without being registered ..	101	2	..	..	20	..	92	..	1	..	..	..	27	..	..	..	8	..
210	(G.171) Dentists ..	2	..	..	..	1	..	..	..	..	..	..	..	2	..	..	..	..	..
211	(G.172) Midwives, vaccinators, compounders, nurses, masseurs, etc. ..	115	40	45	24	19	18	15	36	6	18	..	5	51	82	14	26	14	37
212	(G.173) Veterinary Surgeons.	2	..	..	..	..	..	..	..	..	..	..	..	2	..	..	..	..	..
213	48. Instruction ..	151	28	50	22	50	28	233	34	61	27	4	4	294	36	40	29	56	27
214	(G. 174) Professors and teachers of all kinds ..	131	28	49	22	50	28	213	34	61	27	4	4	273	34	23	29	50	27
215	(G.175) Clerks and servants connected with education .	20	..	1	..	..	..	20	..	..	..	..	..	21	2	17	..	6	..
216	49. Letters, arts and sciences (other than 44) ..	216	..	..	193	42	88	166	29	37	26	..	..	65	25	42	10	12	21
217	(G.176) Public scribes stenographers, etc. ..	3	520	..	..	..	..	..	..	..	..	..	..	2	..	..	..	1	..
218	(G.177) Architects, surveyors, engineers, and their employees (not being State servants)	2	..	..	..	..	..	..	..	..	..	..	..	2	..	..	..	..	..
219	(G.178) Authors, editors, journalists and photographers	11	..	..	..	..	..	14	..	3	..	..	..	18	..	..	..	3	..
220	(G.179) Artists, sculptors and image-makers ..	30	..	..	..	8	..	..	..	..	..	..	..	5	..	10	..	4	..
221	(G.180) Scientists (astronomers, botanists, etc,) ..	..	..	..	..	..	..	..	..	..	..	..	..	..	..	..	..	..	..
222	(G.181) Horoscope casters, astrologers, fortune tellers, wizards, witches and mediums	118	464	..	175	20	77	53	15	12	8	..	..	24	16	9	4	..	6

TABLE X.
OCCUPATION OR MEANS OF LIVELIHOOD.

223	(G.182) Musicians (composers and performers other than military) actors, dancers, etc. ..	24	5	..	3	6	4	75	8	16	10	..	..	12	4	8	2	1	..
224	(G.183) Managers and employees of places of public entertainments, race courses, societies, clubs. ..	4	..	..	..	..	..	..	..	..	..	..	..	2	..	..	..	..	..
225	(G.184) Conjurors, acrobats, reciters, exhibitors of curiosities and wild animals, etc.	24	51	..	15	8	7	24	6	6	8	..	..	5	5	20	10	8	15
226	D. Miscellaneous. ..	30,218	31,034	7,442	10,392	2,270	3,053	10,433	7,532	6,011	4,418	5,687	1,276	48,975	22,444	6,611	15,169	8,097	2,518
227	IX. Persons living on their income	99	37	13	20	3	..	16	3	4	..	..	..	101	1	..	..	30	..
228	50. Persons living principally on their income ..	90	37	13	29	3	..	16	3	4	..	..	..	101	1	..	..	30	..
229	(G.185) Proprietors (other than of agricultural land), fund and scholarships holders and pensioners ..	99	37	13	29	3	..	16	3	4	..	..	..	101	1	..	..	30	
230	X Domestic service ..	19,261	18,551	3,918	5,215	209	1,367	7,618	6,460	4,871	3,059	4,795	623	40,291	12,123	4,442	13,188	6,561	1,062
231	51. Domestic service ..	19,261	18,551	3,918	5,215	209	1,367	7,618	6,460	4,871	3,059	4,705	623	40,291	12,123	4,442	13,188	6,561	1,062
232	(G.186) Private motor drivers and cleaners ..	132	..	27	..	..	..	..	..	..	..	..	..	63	3	10	2	..	..
233	(G.187) Other domestic service	19,129	18,551	3,891	5,215	209	1,367	7,618	6,460	4,871	3,059	4,795	623	40,228	12,120	4,432	13,186	6,561	1,062
234	XI. Insufficiently defined occupations	8,495	2,706	2,984	4,549	1,928	1,531	1,732	412	598	679	295	303	1,686	949	1,938	1,218	743	387
235	52. General terms which do not indicate a definite occupation	8,495	2,706	2,984	4,549	1,928	1,531	1,732	412	598	679	295	303	1,686	949	1,938	1,218	743	387
236	(G.188) Manufacturers, businessmen and contractors otherwise unspecified ..	271	..	11	..	5	18	53	..	67	..	38	..	120	..	16	15	..	82
237	(G.189) Cashiers, accountants, book-keepers, clerks and other employees in unspecified offices and warehouses and shops ..	54	..	34	8	1	6	20	..	48	..	21	..	134	..	..	..	31	..
238	(G.190) Mechanics otherwise unspecified ..	32	..	..	..	4	..	10	..	..	..	..	..	55	..	5	..	..	..
239	(G.191) Labourers and workmen otherwise unspecified .	8,138	2,706	2,939	4,541	1,918	1,512	1,649	412	483	679	236	303	1,377	949	1,017	1,203	712	355
240	XII. Unproductive ..	2,363	9,740	527	599	40	155	1,067	657	538	680	597	350	6,897	9,371	231	763	763	1,069
241	53. Inmates of jails, asylums and alms houses ..	..	..	77	15	..	..	..	..	20	..	..	..	..	..	41	5	..	..
242	(G.192) Inmates of jails, asylums and alms houses..	..	..	77	15	..	..	..	..	20	..	..	..	..	..	41	5	..	..
243	54. Beggars, vagrants, prostitutes	2,363	9,740	450	584	40	155	1,067	657	518	680	597	350	6,897	9,371	190	758	763	1,069
244	(G.193) Beggars and vagrants	2,340	9,358	433	450	37	140	1,051	377	502	531	597	350	6,845	9,009	190	653	743	993
245	(G.194) Procurers and prostitutes	23	382	17	134	3	15	16	280	16	149	..	..	52	362	..	105	20	76
246	55. Other unclassified nonproductive industries ..	..	..	..	..	..	..	..	..	..	..	..	..	..	..	..	..	..	..
247	(G.195) Other unclassified non-productive industries .	..	..	..	..	..	..	..	..	..	..	..	..	..	..	..	..	..	..

TABLE X.

Occupation or Means of Livelihood.

District		Males	Females
NALGONDA	Total Earners	261,723	153,980
	Total Working Dependents	68,829	60,428
	Total Nonworking Dependents	250,345	338,104
	Total Population	580,897	552,512
AURANGABAD	Total Earners	174,305	70,779
	Total Working Dependents	73,982	67,233
	Total Non-working Dependents	232,211	326,283
	Total Population	480,498	464,295
BIR	Total Earners	121,679	61,970
	Total Working Dependents	66,480	68,298
	Total Non-working Dependents	137,237	178,026
	Total Population	325,396	308,294

Serial No.	Occupation	NALGONDA						AURANGABAD						BIR					
		Total earners showing occupation as principal		Total working dependents		Total following occupation as subsidiary		Total earners showing occupation as principal		Total working dependents		Total following occupation as subsidiary		Total earners showing occupation as principal		Total working dependents		Total following occupation as subsidiary	
		Males	Females	Males	Females	Males	Females	Males	Females	Males	Females	Males	Females	Males	Females	Males	Females	Males	Females
	1	56	57	58	59	60	61	62	63	64	65	66	67	68	69	70	71	72	73
1	TOTAL WORKERS. ..	261,723	153,980	68,829	60,428	48,400	32,707	174,305	70,779	73,982	67,233	31,217	16,087	121,679	61,970	66,480	68,298	35,046	26,506
2	A. Production of Raw Materials	152,104	91,190	27,373	30,892	29,814	20,703	99,367	401,070	34,951	40,128	15,813	7,359	80,834	40,326	48,736	47,638	22,993	16,215
3	I-Exploitation of Animals and Vegetation ..	152,104	91,190	27,373	30,892	29,814	20,703	99,242	40,052	34,912	40,109	15,813	7,359	80,834	40,326	48,736	47,638	22,993	16,215
4	1. Pasture and Agriculture .	150,154	90,742	26,891	30,172	29,121	20,532	98,704	39,325	34,654	39,426	15,655	7,149	97,754	40,182	48,182	47,425	22,625	16,133
5	(a) Cultivation ..	114,519	81,084	21,995	22,567	23,654	17,211	92,778	35,618	30,488	37,136	14,685	6,082	73,853	35,712	44,911	45,198	21,014	14,735
6	(G.1) Non-cultivating proprietors taking rent in money or kind ..	10,288	5,007	1,728	1,228	2,299	1,410	14,845	5,997	4,366	3,008	2,189	1,060	5,398	557	3,891	4,236	1,517	239
7	(G.2) Estate Agents and Managers of owners ..	18	..	3	..	12	..	246	..	15	..	39	..	56	..	3	..	12	..
8	(G.3) Estate Agents and Managers of Government..	186	..	92	..	15	..	351	..	54	..	18	..	124	..	21	..	8	..
9	(G.4) Rent Collectors, clerks, etc.	231	..	50	..	30	..	698	..	70	..	120	..	398	..	32	..	37	..
10	(G.5) Cultivating owners ..	48,575	16,125	7,812	3,184	6,688	4,687	24,877	5,912	7,987	6,142	3,487	1,410	23,362	15,066	21,889	20,875	3,221	3,726
11	(G.6) Tenant cultivators ..	24,991	18,011	7,468	3,048	5,835	3,780	20,429	8,386	7,655	6,123	3,752	1,318	15,077	1,883	6,787	2,807	3,533	2,009
12	(G.7) Agricultural labourers.	30,230	41,941	4,847	15,112	8,775	7,325	31,887	15,318	10,341	21,863	5,080	2,299	29,438	21,206	12,288	17,275	12,686	8,161
13	(b) Cultivation of special crops and fruit growers ..	565	222	232	413	115	58	890	244	691	274	368	198	524	200	155	306	127	80
14	(G.13) Pan-Vine ..	40	10	34	32	12	7	121	35	14	68	36	14	55	28	2	22	14	4
15	(G.16) Market Gardeners, flower, fruits, etc. ..	525	212	198	381	103	46	769	209	677	206	332	184	469	172	153	284	113	76
16	(c.) Forestry	2,654	112	250	57	380	75	1,705	648	335	432	426	314	698	301	363	272	335	141
17	(G.17) Forest officers, rangers, guards, etc. ..	24	..	10	..	2	..	20	..	2	..	..	..	5	..	..	..	..	..
18	(G.18) Wood-cutters and charcoal burners ..	2,584	112	215	..	373	75	1,532	610	306	376	385	281	693	301	363	272	335	141

TABLE X.
OCCUPATION OR MEANS OF LIVELIHOOD.

No.	Occupation																		
19	(G.19) Collectors of forest produce.	39	..	18	..	5	..	153	38	27	56	41	33	..	..	..	..	..	..
20	(G.20) Collectors of lac ..	7	..	7	..	..	..	..	..	..	..	..	..	..	..	..	..	..	..
21	(d)—Stock raising ..	32,406	9,314	4,403	7,121	4,964	3,190	3,293	2,802	3,135	1,577	176	555	4,679	969	2,753	1,654	1,149	1,177
22 23	(G.21) Cattle and buffaloe-breeders and keepers ..	341	70	185	116	120	20	384	362	163	389	25	52	765	142	556	187	106	68
	(G.22) Breeders of transport animals	54	..	10	..	15	..	76	..	12	..	20	..	..	..	..	..	..	..
24	(G.23) Herdsmen, shepherds and breeders of other animals	32,011	9,244	4,208	7,005	4,829	3,170	2,833	2,440	2,960	1,188	131	503	3,914	827	2,197	1,467	1,043	1,114
25	(e) Raising of small animals and insects	10	10	11	14	8	3	38	18	5	6	..	..	..	..	..	..	..	..
26	(G.24) Birds, bees, etc. ..	10	10	11	14	8	3	23	15	5	6	..	..	..	..	..	..	..	..
27	(G.25) Silk worms ..	..	..	..	..	..	..	15	3	..	..	..	..	..	..	..	..	..	..
28	(G.26) Lac cultivation ..	..	..	..	..	..	..	..	..	..	..	..	..	..	..	..	..	..	..
29	2. Fishing and Hunting ..	1,950	448	482	720	693	171	538	727	258	684	158	210	1,080	144	554	213	368	82
30	(G.27) Fishing and pearling .	1,568	360	94	620	131	121	278	476	110	445	142	167	428	139	24	203	167	78
31	(G.28) Hunting ..	382	88	388	100	562	50	260	251	148	239	16	43	652	5	343	10	201	4
32	II. Exploitation of Minerals	..	..	..	..	..	..	125	18	39	19	..	..	..	..	..	..	..	..
33	3. Metallic minerals ..	..	..	..	..	..	..	..	..	..	..	..	..	..	..	..	..	..	..
34	(G.30) Iron	..	..	..	..	..	..	..	..	..	..	..	..	..	..	..	..	..	..
35	4. Non-metallic minerals ..	..	..	..	..	..	..	125	18	39	19	..	..	..	..	..	..	..	..
36	(G.35) Coal	..	..	..	..	..	..	..	..	..	..	..	..	..	..	..	..	..	..
37	(G.37) Building materials (including stone, materials for cement manufacture and clays)	..	..	..	..	..	..	5	..	..	4	..	..	..	..	..	..	..	..
38	(G.38) Mica	..	..	..	..	..	..	4	..	2	3	..	..	..	..	..	..	..	..
39	(G.40) Salt, saltpetre and other saline substances ..	..	..	..	..	..	..	116	18	37	12	..	..	..	..	..	..	..	..
40	B.—Preparation and supply of material substances	75,998	34,207	34,407	15,891	13,695	7,120	36,308	17,136	21,405	13,102	6,552	3,924	26,870	12,425	9,381	9,404	8,347	6,367
41	III. Industry	38,190	17,588	22,018	6,837	5,994	3,062	10,406	5,278	7,258	3,883	2,833	1,430	6,538	2,006	4,176	2,802	1,763	1,804
42	5. Textiles	8,812	7,363	2,505	2,438	1,408	956	1,397	594	1,585	696	665	341	1,166	368	687	785	388	332
43	(G.42) Cotton ginning, cleaning and pressing ..	491	1,005	386	276	75	56	286	131	324	162	98	42	245	54	146	133	169	21
44	(G.43) Cotton spinning, sizing and weaving ..	7,841	6,210	1,829	2,010	1,187	833	896	387	624	474	397	282	500	234	444	548	109	271
45	(G.45) Rope, twine, string and other fibres ..	177	31	86	73	32	24	56	22	33	10	12	5	78	20	21	10	13	5
46	(G.46) Wool carding spinning and weaving ..	85	72	90	42	70	26	78	31	195	32	36	7	155	8	39	14	64	3
47	(G.47) Silk spinning and weaving.	24	12	30	8	11	7	..	..	..	..	..	..	18	6	5	18	4	4
48	(G.48) Hair (Horse-hair), etc.	5	..	4	..	2	..	..	..	..	..	..	..	..	14	..	21	..	11

TABLE X.

Occupation or Means of Livelihood.

	NALGONDA Males	NALGONDA Females	AURANGABAD Males	AURANGABAD Females	BIR Males	BIR Females
Total Earners	261,723	163,980	174,305	70,779	121,679	61,970
Total Working Dependents	68,829	60,428	73,982	67,233	66,480	68,298
Total Non-working Dependents	250,345	338,104	232,211	326,283	137,237	178,026
Total Population	580,879	532,512	480,495	464,295	325,396	308,294

Serial No.	Occupation	NALGONDA						AURANGABAD						BIR					
		Total earners showing occupation as principal		Total working dependents		Total following occupations as subsidiary		Total earners showing occupation as principal		Total working dependents		Total following occupation as subsidiary		Total earners showing occupation as principal		Total working dependents		Total following occupation as subsidiary	
		Males	Females	Males	Females	Males	Females	Males	Females	Males	Females	Males	Females	Males	Females	Males	Females	Males	Females
	1	56	57	58	59	60	61	62	63	64	65	66	67	68	69	70	71	72	73
49	(G.49) Dyeing, bleaching, printing, preparation and sponging of textiles ..	171	33	78	20	31	10	45	15	392	16	110	4	146	32	32	17	19	14
50	(G.50) Lace, crepe, embroideries, fringes, etc., and insufficiently described textiles	18	..	2	..	..	..	36	8	17	2	12	1	24	..	..	24	5	3
51	6. Hides, skins and hard materials from the animal kingdom	1,089	215	1,500	110	619	29	360	292	136	90	110	42	..	..	..	..	..	..
52	(G.51) Working in leather ..	1,979	215	1,484	110	618	29	340	292	128	90	110	42	..	..	..	..	..	..
53	(G.52) Furriers and persons occupied with feathers and bristles ; brush makers ..	7	..	12	..	1	..	..	..	..	..	..	..	..	..	..	..	..	..
54	(G.53) Bone, ivory, horn shell, etc., workers (except buttons)	3	..	4	..	..	..	20	..	8	..	..	..	..	..	..	..	..	..
55	7. Wood	2,880	964	719	180	362	106	1,121	297	347	295	354	107	562	181	386	166	93	143
56	(G.54) Sawyers ..	10	..	..	..	10	..	40	..	..	..	..	..	..	..	..	..	..	..
57	(G.55) Carpenters, turners and joiners, etc. ..	2,886	264	500	64	268	117	510	100	331	223	343	59	362	108	298	147	86	140
58	(G.56) Basket-makers and other industries of woody materials, including leaves and thatchers and builders working with bamboo, reeds or similar materials ..	784	700	210	116	84	79	571	188	16	72	11	48	200	73	88	19	7	8
59	8. Metals	2,846	96	811	19	239	59	637	158	226	73	168	28	691	149	680	155	248	296
60	(G.57) Smelting, forging and rolling of iron and other metals	..	..	..	..	..	..	5	..	2	..	..	..	..	..	..	..	..	..
61	(G.58) Makers of arms, guns, etc.	..	..	..	..	..	..	3	..	..	..	..	..	..	..	..	..	..	..

TABLE X.
OCCUPATION OR MEANS OF LIVELIHOOD.

62	(G.59) Black-smiths, other workers in iron, makers of implements ..	1,606	75	446	9	239	57	567	134	205	61	148	22	412	134	608	120	234	283
63	(G.60) Workers in brass, copper and bell metals ..	1,240	18	365	10	..	2	44	24	14	12	18	6	279	15	72	35	14	13
64	(G.61) Workers in other metals, (except precious metals)	..	..	..	..	..	..	18	..	5	..	2	..	..	..	..	..	..	..
65	(G.62) Workers in mints, die sinkers, etc	..	..	..	..	..	..	..	..	..	..	..	..	..	..	..	..	..	..
66	9. Ceramics ..	2,837	1,085	979	572	635	396	591	1,051	446	365	280	208	469	124	262	137	114	133
67	(G.63) Potters and makers of earthen ware ..	2,700	1,077	923	572	615	396	534	981	434	365	224	208	469	124	262	137	114	133
68	(G.64) Brick and tile makers.	180	8	56	..	20	..	57	60	12	..	56	..	..	..	..	..	..	..
69	(G.65) Other workers in ceramics	7	..	..	..	..	..	..	10	..	..	..	..	..	..	..	..	..	..
70	10. Chemical products properly so-called and analogous	184	129	36	28	75	15	336	64	92	12	15	2	679	330	386	367	168	211
71	(G.66) Manufacture of matches, fireworks and other explosives ..	4	..	2	..	..	..	17	..	5	..	3	..	4	..	2	..	1	..
72	(G.67) Manufacture of aerated and mineral waters and ice	3	..	..	..	..	..	8	..	2	..	1	..	8	..	6	..	..	..
73	(G.68) Manufacture and refining of vegetable oils ..	173	129	34	28	75	15	266	64	65	12	11	2	632	330	378	367	167	211
74	(G.69) Manufacture and refining of mineral oils ..	..	..	..	..	..	..	..	..	..	..	..	..	20	..	..	..	..	..
75	(G.70) Others	4	..	..	..	..	..	45	..	20	..	..	..	15	..	..	..	..	..
76	11. Food Industries ..	1,161	290	992	144	430	35	788	348	251	267	155	69	113	75	70	48	30	14
77	(G.71) Rice pounders and huskers and flour grinders .	5	..	3	..	2	..	108	16	37	14	18	19	..	11	..	3	..	1
78	(G.72) Grain parchers, etc...	..	6	..	14	..	3	5	8	3	7	..	6	..	4	..	2	..	..
79	(G.73) Butchers ..	262	161	369	62	85	25	441	203	140	102	115	5	73	18	47	15	23	2
80	(G.74) Makers of sugar, molasses and gur ..	18	16	14	16	10	8	15	18	..	14	..	3	..	..	..	..	..	..
81	(G.75) Sweet meat and condiment makers ..	230	51	146	24	75	4	49	4	14	15	2	3	..	21	..	14	..	5
82	(G.76) Toddy drawers ..	485	6	304	3	210	2	54	6	18	3	3	2	20	..	18	..	5	..
83	(G.77) Brewers and distillers.	101	..	53	..	27	..	..	..	..	..	..	..	14	..	..	..	..	..
84	(G.78) Manufacturers of tobacco ..	53	50	13	25	21	13	112	93	31	112	17	31	6	21	5	14	2	6
85	(G.80) Manufacturers of Ganja	2	..	..	..	..	..	4	..	2	..	..	..	..	..	..	..	..	..
86	(G.81) Others ..	5	..	..	..	..	..	..	..	..	..	..	..	..	..	..	..	..	..
87	12. Industries of dress and toilet	13,680	6,344	13,507	3,066	1,717	1,186	3,504	1,518	3,575	1,599	726	352	2,314	604	1,299	934	618	508
88	(G.82) Boot, shoe, sandal and clog makers ..	846	287	554	160	54	..	869	311	875	619	200	197	1,160	336	681	295	339	228
89	(G.83) Tailors, milliners, dress makers and darners ..	1,287	959	357	378	97	124	873	507	380	307	106	90	143	91	54	161	11	112
90	(G.84) Embroiderers, hat-makers and makers of other articles of wear ..	..	..	..	..	..	..	16	..	2	..	..	..	..	..	..	..	..	..
91	(G.85) Washing and cleaning	9,359	593	11,820	2,309	851	872	841	607	1,785	498	276	19	212	50	215	333	152	98

TABLE X.

Occupation or Means of Livelihood.

	NALGONDA Males	NALGONDA Females	AURANGABAD Males	AURANGABAD Females	BIR Males	BIR Females
Total Earners	261,723	153,980	174,305	70,779	121,679	61,970
Total Working Dependents	68,829	60,428	73,962	67,233	66,480	68,298
Total Non-working Dependents	250,345	338,104	232,211	326,283	137,237	178,026
Total Population	580,897	552,512	480,498	464,295	325,396	308,294

Serial No.	Occupation	NALGONDA: Total earners showing occupation as principal — Males	Females	Total working dependents — Males	Females	Total following occupation as subsidiary — Males	Females	AURANGABAD: Total earners showing occupation as principal — Males	Females	Total working dependents — Males	Females	Total following occupation as subsidiary — Males	Females	BIR: Total earners showing occupation as principal — Males	Females	Total working dependents — Males	Females	Total following occupation as subsidiary — Males	Females
	1	56	57	58	59	60	61	62	63	64	65	66	67	68	69	70	71	72	73
92	(G.86) Barbers, hair dressers and wig-makers ..	2,238	505	1,246	219	715	190	965	155	533	175	144	46	793	127	349	145	116	135
93	(G.87) Other industries connected with toilet ..	..	..	..	..	..	..	..	..	..	..	..	..	..	..	..	..	..	..
94	13. Furniture industries ..	56	..	23	..	12	..	24	..	4	..	..	..	..	..	..	..	..	..
95	(G.88) Cabinet-makers carriage painters, etc ..	56	..	23	..	12	..	21	..	4	..	..	..	..	..	..	..	..	..
96	(G.89) Upholsterers, tent makers, etc. ..	..	..	..	..	..	..	3	..	..	..	..	..	..	..	..	..	..	..
97	14. Building industries ..	1,124	204	265	103	140	1	348	432	41	325	17	215	293	25	285	80	20	..
98	(G.90) Lime burners, cement workers ; excavators and well sinkers ; stone cutters and dressers ; brick layers and masons ; builders (other than buildings made of bamboo and similar materials) painters decorators of houses, tilers, plumbers, etc.	1,124	204	265	103	140	1	348	432	41	325	17	215	293	25	285	80	20	..
99	15. Construction of means of transport	11	..	9	..	..	..	202	..	46	..	21	..	96	..	38	..	12	..
100	(G.91) Persons engaged in making, assembling or repairing motor vehicles or cycles	3	..	2	..	..	..	38	..	15	..	3	..	18	..	..	..	..	..
101	(G.92) Carriage, cart, palki, etc., makers and wheelwrights	8	..	7	..	..	..	164	..	31	..	18	..	78	..	38	..	12	..
102	16. Production and transmission of physical force ..	..	..	..	..	..	..	5	..	..	..	..	..	..	..	..	..	..	..
103	(G.94) Heat, light, electricity, motive power, etc. Gas works and electric light and power ..	..	..	..	..	..	..	5	..	..	..	..	..	..	..	..	..	..	..

104	17. Miscellaneous and undefined industries ..	2,610	901	672	177	357	169	1,038	462	509	161	322	66	155	150	88	130	77	107
105	(G.95) Printers, engravers, book binders, etc. ..	15	..	8	..	2	..	18	..	2	..	..	..	4	..	2	..	..	..
106	(G.96) Makers of musical instruments	2	..	3	..	..	..	3	..	..	..	..	..	..	..	..	..	..	..
107	(G.97) Makers of clocks and surgical or scientific instruments, etc.	2	..	3	..	..	..	22	..	4	..	4	..	3	..	..	..	..	..
108	(G.98) Makers of jewellery and ornaments ..	2,581	826	658	102	355	153	602	306	419	59	203	38	148	150	81	130	77	107
109	(G.99) Other miscellaneous and undefined industries (toymaking, taxidermy, etc.)	..	25	..	15	..	16	51	76	..	..	..	..	..	..	..	..	..	..
110	(G.100) Scavenging ..	10	50	..	60	..	..	337	80	84	102	115	33	..	..	..	..	..	..
111	IV. Transport	7,136	912	3,525	1,285	1,300	601	10,202	6,006	5,150	891	992	375	890	89	416	550	144	21
112	19. Transport by water ..	3,025	162	1,945	70	985	22	166	27	42	56	5	..	..	..	..	..	..	..
113	(G.104) Labourers employed on harbours, docks, rivers and canals	3,025	162	1,945	70	985	22	166	27	42	56	5	..	..	..	..	..	..	..
114	20. Transport by Road ..	4,021	646	1,324	368	270	248	7,293	5,139	4,717	575	962	255	631	80	339	38	123	21
115	(G.105) Persons (other than labourers) employed on the construction and maintenance of roads and bridges .	17	..	14	..	5	..	85	..	24	..	11	..	7	..	..	..	..	..
116	(G.106) Labourers employed on roads and bridges ..	2,912	496	601	358	106	208	6,030	4,924	4,230	301	745	186	167	33	138	373	27	7
117	(G.107) Owners, managers and employees (excluding personal servants) connected with mechanically driven vehicles (including trams)	..	..	..	..	..	..	270	..	56	..	71	..	13	..	2	..	4	..
118	(G.108) Owners, managers, employees (excluding personal servants) connected with other vehicles ..	1,092	150	579	10	109	40	285	..	74	..	31	..	378	41	149	..	67	..
119	(G.109) Palki, etc., bearers and owners	..	..	110	..	30	..	126	52	140	60	28	18	52	6	50	25	25	14
120	(G.110) Pack elephant, camel mule, ass and bullock, owners and drivers ..	..	..	20	..	20	..	398	140	151	210	66	51	..	..	..	..	..	..
121	(G.111) Porters and messengers	..	..	..	..	..	..	99	23	42	4	10	..	14	..	..	..	..	..
122	21. Transport by Rail ..	60	104	251	847	95	331	2,586	840	346	260	23	120	228	9	60	152	17	..
123	(G.112) Railway employees of all kind other than coolies	46	14	15	7	5	1	406	25	74	36	5	2	18	9	8	1	..	..
124	(G.113) Labourers employed on railway construction and maintenance and coolies and porters employed on railway premises ..	14	90	236	840	90	330	2,180	815	272	224	18	118	210	..	52	151	17	..
125	22. Post Office, Telegraph and Telephone services ..	30	..	5	..	..	..	157	..	45	..	2	..	31	..	17	..	4	..
126	(G.114) Post office, Telegraph and Telephone services	30	..	5	..	..	..	157	..	45	..	2	..	31	..	17	..	4	..
127	V. Trade	30,672	15,707	8,864	7,769	6,401	3,457	15,700	5,852	8,997	8,328	2,727	2,119	19,442	10,330	4,739	6,052	6,440	4,542

TABLE X.

Occupation or Means of Livelihood.

Serial No.	Occupation	NALGONDA						AURANGABAD						BIR					
		Total Earners .. .. .. Total Working Dependents .. Total Non-working Dependents .. Total Population				Males 261,723 68,829 250,345 580,897	Females 153,980 60,428 338,104 552,512	Total Earners .. .. Total Working Dependents .. Total Non-working Dependents Total Population ..				Males 174,305 73,982 232,211 480,498	Females 70,779 67,233 326,283 464,295	Total Earners .. Total Working Dependents .. Total Non-working Dependents Total Population ..				Males 121,679 66,480 137,237 325,396	Females 61,970 68,298 178,026 308,294
		Total Earners showing occupation as principal		Total working dependents		Total following occupation as subsidiary		Total earners showing occupation as principal		Total working dependents		Total following occupation as subsidiary		Total earners showing occupation as principal		Total working dependents		Total following occupation as subsidiary	
		Males	Females	Males	Females	Males	Females	Males	Females	Males	Females	Males	Females	Males	Females	Males	Females	Males	Females
	1	56	57	58	59	60	61	62	63	64	65	66	67	68	69	70	71	72	73
128	23. Banks, establishments of credit, exchange and insurance	450	60	160	..	128	6	1,452	252	504	87	321	38	708	321	353	156	149	72
129	(G.115) Bank managers, money lenders, exchange and insurance agents, money changers and brokers and their employees ..	450	60	160	..	128	6	1,452	252	504	87	321	38	708	321	353	156	149	72
130	24. Brokerage commission and export	..	..	..	..	..	..	56	..	..	..	13	..	26	..	..	..	..	..
131	(G.116) Brokers, commission agents, commercial travellers, warehouse owners and employees	..	..	..	..	..	..	56	..	..	..	13	..	26	..	..	..	..	..
132	25. Trade in Textiles ..	1,612	826	415	431	222	105	642	210	322	328	80	39	651	315	362	384	74	86
133	(G.117) Trade in piece-goods wool, cotton, silk, hair and other textiles ..	1,612	826	415	431	222	105	642	210	322	328	80	39	651	315	362	484	74	86
134	26. Trade in skins, leather and furs	250	201	120	122	..	70	172	64	96	84	28	26	105	53	72	184	21	31
135	(G.118) Trade in skins, leather, furs, feathers, horn etc., and the articles made from these	250	201	120	122	..	70	172	64	96	84	28	26	105	53	72	184	21	31
136	27. Trade in Wood ..	27	3	9	12	12	4	156	32	27	61	13	6	93	20	16	31	4	8
137	(G.119) Trade in wood (not fire-wood)	5	..	3	..	..	..	38	13	2	36	..	4	18	..	9	..	2	..
138	(G.120) Trade in barks ..	4	3	..	4	..	1	27	9	13	14	3	..	24	..	7	..	..	..
139	(G.121) Trade in bamboos and canes	18	..	6	8	12	3	38	10	4	11	8	2	37	20	..	31	2	8
140	(G.122) Trade in thatches and other forest produce .	..	..	..	..	..	..	53	..	8	..	2	..	14	..	..	..	..	..
141	28. Trade in metals ..	28	16	20	2	16	4	121	72	62	76	16	14	484	241	179	206	23	41

142	(G.123) Trade in metals, machinery, knives, tools, etc.	28	16	20	2	16	4	121	72	62	76	1	14	484	242	179	206	23	41
143	29. Trade in pottery, bricks and tiles	1,079	562	125	137	54	38	54	168	7	240	..	55	345	489	142	506	33	184
144	(G.124) Trade in pottery, bricks and tiles ..	1,079	562	125	137	54	38	54	168	7	249	..	55	345	489	142	506	33	184
145	30. Trade in chemical products	55	..	2	..	..	..	120	..	18	..	3	..	16	..	2	..	..	..
146	(G.125) Drugs, dyes, paints petroleum, explosives, etc.	55	..	2	..	..	..	120	..	18	..	3	..	16	..	2	..	..	..
147	31. Hotels, cafes, restaurants, etc.	12,720	9,842	3,890	4,976	4,410	1,707	868	1,043	281	606	68	142	1,558	599	194	701	21	477
148	(G.126) Vendors of wine, liquors, aerated waters and ice	12,720	9,842	3,890	4,976	4,410	1,707	702	1,043	185	606	24	142	1,537	575	187	670	21	460
149	(G. 127) Owners and managers of hotels, cook shops sarais, etc., (and employees)	..	..	..	..	..	..	97	..	81	..	16	..	18	24	7	31	..	17
150	(G.128) Hawkers of drink and foodstuffs ..	..	..	..	..	..	..	64	..	15	..	23	..	8	..	..	..	..	..
151	32. Other trade in foodstuffs	1,195	1,252	527	451	342	402	4,784	2,541	2,291	3,539	386	498	7,016	2,421	1,446	2,064	1,279	1,153
152	(G.129) Grain and pulse dealers ..	681	345	270	182	136	102	1,902	267	260	349	70	36	2,899	264	342	415	562	98
153	(G.130) Dealers in sweetmeats, sugar and spices ..	65	212	20	45	10	..	71	163	20	141	5	84	68	371	21	486	17	155
154	(G.131) Dealers in dairy product, eggs and poultry ..	291	647	163	224	164	300	378	1,699	298	2,805	140	207	485	1,600	161	849	28	823
155	(G.132) Dealers in animals for food	25	..	18	..	3	..	42	..	5	..	..	..	84	21	20	32	..	7
156	(G.133) Dealers in fodder for animals	8	48	4	..	2	..	18	..	..	..	..	..	167	..	140	..	55	..
157	(G. 134) Dealers in other food stuffs	55	..	15	..	10	..	2,221	167	1,691	128	153	40	2,985	116	640	215	516	51
158	(G.135) Dealers in tobacco .	60	..	31	..	17	..	120	240	17	116	18	71	301	49	115	67	71	18
159	(G.136) Dealers in opium ..	2	..	..	..	..	..	18	..	..	..	..	..	12	..	3	..	..	..
160	(G.137) Dealers in ganja ..	8	..	6	..	..	..	14	..	..	..	..	..	20	..	4	..	..	..
161	33. Trade in clothing and toilet articles	741	322	11	79	2	22	586	122	140	128	38	18	384	127	264	148	68	11
162	(G.138) Trade in ready-made clothing and other articles of dress and the toilet (hats, umbrellas, socks, ready-made shoes, perfumes, etc.)	741	322	11	79	2	22	586	122	140	128	38	18	384	127	264	148	68	11
163	34. Trade in furniture ..	328	41	73	39	60	2	102	64	40	138	15	56	155	60	43	137	26	41
164	(G.139) Trade in furniture carpets, curtains and bedding	110	..	20	..	28	..	12	..	2	..	..	..	70	..	33	..	10	..
165	(G.140) Hardware, cooking utensils, porcelain crockery, glassware bottles, articles for gardening, etc. ..	218	41	53	39	32	2	90	64	38	138	15	56	85	60	10	137	16	41
166	35. Trade in building materials	400	..	166	..	18	..	152	50	56	64	1	14	127	..	5	90	..	15
167	(G.141) Trade in building .. materials (other than bricks tiles and woody materials)	400	..	166	..	18	..	152	50	56	64	1	14	127	..	5	90	..	15
168	36. Trade in means of transport	1,207	140	325	57	67	..	472	69	169	98	38	53	846	15	285	51	138	17

TABLE X.

Occupation or Means of Livelihood.

	NALGONDA Males	NALGONDA Females	AURANGABAD Males	AURANGABAD Females	BIR Males	BIR Females
Total Earners ..	261,723	153,980	174,305	70,779	121,679	61,970
Total Working Dependents ..	68,829	60,428	73,982	67,233	66,480	68,298
Total Non-working Dependents ..	250,345	338,104	232,211	326,283	137,237	178,026
Total Population ..	580,897	552,512	480,498	464,295	325,396	308,294

Serial No.	Occupation	NALGONDA: Total earners showing occupation as principal		Total working dependents		Total following occupation as subsidiary		AURANGABAD: Total earners showing occupation as principal		Total working dependents		Total following occupation as subsidiary		BIR: Total earners showing occupation as principal		Total working dependents		Total following occupation as subsidiary	
		Males	Females	Males	Females	Males	Females	Males	Females	Males	Females	Males	Females	Males	Females	Males	Females	Males	Females
	1	56	57	58	59	60	61	62	63	64	65	66	67	68	69	70	71	72	73
169	(G.142) Dealers and hirers, in mechanical transport, motors, cycles, etc. ..	54	..	5	..	7	..	60	2	15	1	3	..	62	..	12	..	18	..
170	(G.143) Dealers and hirers in other carriages, carts, boats, etc.	306	140	110	57	31	..	384	53	151	80	26	40	485	15	216	51	89	17
171	(G.144) Dealers and hirers of elephants, camels, horses, cattle, asses, mules, etc.	847	..	210	..	29	..	28	14	3	17	4	13	299	..	57	..	26	..
172	37. Trade in fuel ..	328	165	156	132	27	..	141	145	26	166	7	37	161	77	44	168	20	91
173	(G.145) Dealers in firewood, charcoal, coal, cowdung, etc.	328	165	156	132	27	..	141	145	26	166	7	37	161	77	44	168	20	91
174	38. Trade in articles of luxury and those pertaining to letters and the arts and sciences	201	173	42	196	20	40	89	66	29	81	9	27	131	254	60	495	81	140
175	(G.146) Dealers in precious stones jewellery (real and imitation) clocks, optical instruments, etc. ..	69	..	10	..	10	..	8	..	..	..	..	..	18	3	..	..	..	..
176	(G.147) Dealers in common bangles bead necklaces, fans, small articles ,toys hunting and fishing, tackle flowers, etc. ..	130	173	32	196	10	40	46	66	18	81	3	27	86	251	57	495	81	140
177	(G.148) Publishers, booksellers, stationers, dealers in music, pictures, musical instruments and curiosities	2	..	..	..	..	..	35	..	11	..	4	..	27	..	3	..	..	..
178	39. Trade of other sorts ..	10,051	2,104	2,823	1,135	1,025	1,057	5,738	954	4,929	2,623	1,701	1,096	6,636	5,388	1,322	631	4,513	2,175
179	(G.149) Dealers in rags, stable refuse, etc. ..	20	..	..	..	..	..	55	..	4	..	..	..	54	..	31	..	17	..
180	(G.150) General store-keepers and shop keepers, otherwise unspecified ..	10,015	2,104	2,823	1,135	1,025	1,057	5,610	954	4,872	2,623	1,683	1,096	6,092	3,785	1,061	574	4,356	1,406

TABLE X.
OCCUPATION OR MEANS OF LIVELIHOOD.

No.	Occupation																		
181	(G.151) Itinerant traders, pedlars and hawkers (of other than food etc.) ..	12	..	..	..	..	..	49	..	53	..	18	..	420	1,553	210	57	125	769
182	(G.152) Other trades (including farmers of pounds, tools and markets) ..	4	..	..	..	..	..	24	..	..	..	..	..	70	..	20	..	15	..
183	**C. Public Administration and Liberal Arts** ..	6,356	1,933	2,954	1,010	918	553	16,071	3,403	7,448	3,292	3,457	929	4,071	751	3,386	1,409	1,908	385
184	VI. Public Force ..	1,644	..	1,399	200	384	..	4,785	269	1,563	485	321	25	525	..	362	8	16	..
185	40. Army	565	..	470	125	374	..	3,324	66	1,108	89	208	..	40	..	62	..	..	..
186	(G.153) Imperial Army ..	56	..	..	..	..	..	1,700	..	91	8	17	..	..	..	..	..	..	..
187	(G.154) State Army ..	509	..	470	125	374	..	1,624	66	1,017	81	191	..	40	..	62	..	..	..
188	43. Police	1,079	..	929	75	10	..	1,461	203	455	396	113	25	485	..	300	8	16	..
189	(G.157) Police	779	..	529	75	10	..	599	71	210	86	62	5	361	..	113	8	5	..
190	(G.158) Village watchmen ..	300	..	400	..	..	..	862	132	245	360	51	20	124	..	187	..	11	..
191	VII. Public Administration	543	10	155	..	26	..	6,024	889	2,987	109	1,257	31	953	..	1,089	23	340	..
192	44. Public Administration .	5	10	155	..	26	..	6,024	889	2,987	109	1,257	31	953	..	1,089	23	340	..
193	(G.159) Imperial service ..	3	..	..	..	..	..	64	..	18	..	..	..	..	..	..	..	..	..
194	(G.160) State service ..	418	10	155	..	26	..	775	92	1,860	19	142	5	159	..	96	6	28	..
195	(G.160a) Service of other Indian and foreign States..	2	..	..	..	..	..	4	..	..	..	..	..	..	..	..	..	..	..
196	(G.161) Municipal and other local (not village) service..	87	..	..	..	..	..	1,888	275	244	39	253	16	368	..	391	5	145	..
197	(G.162) Village officials and servants other than watchmen	33	..	..	..	..	..	3,293	522	856	51	862	10	426	..	602	12	172	..
198	VIII. Professions and Liberal Arts	4,169	1,923	1,400	810	508	553	5,262	2,245	2,898	2,698	1,879	873	2,593	751	1,935	1,378	1,552	385
199	45. Religion	3,682	1,641	1,291	606	408	433	3,269	1,428	2,068	2,152	869	460	1,704	670	1,328	1,279	1,406	353
200	(G.163) Priests, ministers, etc	3,649	1,620	1,287	594	404	433	2,769	1,345	2,048	2,050	669	428	1,678	670	1,314	1,279	1,394	353
201	(G.164) Monks, nuns, religious mendicants ..	..	..	..	..	..	..	37	..	..	..	..	..	..	..	..	..	..	..
202	(G.165) Other religious workers	8	..	3	..	..	..	306	20	8	14	172	..	..	..	..	..	..	..
203	(G.166) Servants in religious edifices, burial and burning grounds, pilgrim conductors, circumcisers, etc.	25	21	1	12	4	..	157	63	12	88	28	32	26	..	14	..	12	..
204	46. Law	63	..	..	..	5	..	262	6	78	..	56	..	405	..	180	..	45	..
205	(G.167) Lawyers of all kinds including Qazis, Law Agents and Mukhtiars ..	53	..	..	..	5	..	249	6	54	..	52	..	399	..	178	..	45	..
206	(G.168) Lawyers' clerks petition-writers, etc. ..	10	..	..	..	..	..	13	..	24	..	4	..	6	..	2	..	..	..
207	47. Medicine	66	143	16	144	9	20	163	162	88	206	68	119	67	15	8	22	15	..
208	(G.169) Registered medical practitoiners including oculists	9	8	..	..	..	..	23	3	8	..	2	..	7	1	..	2	1	..

TABLE X.

Occupation or Means of Livelihood.

	NALGONDA			
			Males	Females
Total Earners	..	..	264,723	153,080
Total Working Dependents		..	68,829	60,428
Total Non-working Dependents		..	250,345	338,104
Total Population	..	..	580 897	552,512

	AURANGABAD	
	Males	Females
Total Earners	174,305	70,779
Total Working dependents	74,982	67,223
Total Non-working Dependents	232,211	326,283
Total Population	480,498	464,295

	BIR	
	Males	Females
Total Earners	121,679	61,970
Total Working Dependents	66,480	68,298
Total Non-working Dependents	137,237	178,026
Total Population	326,396	308,294

Serial No.	Occupation	NALGONDA: Total Earners showing occupation as principal — Males	Females	Total working dependents — Males	Females	Total following occupations as subsidiary — Males	Females	AURANGABAD: Total earners showing occupation as principal — Males	Females	Total working dependents — Males	Females	Total following occupations as subsidiary — Males	Females	BIR: Total earners showing occupation as principal — Males	Females	Total working dependents — Males	Females	Total following occupation as subsidiary — Males	Females
	1	56	57	58	59	60	61	62	63	64	65	66	67	68	69	70	71	72	73
209	(G.170) Other persons practising the healing arts without being registered ..	47	..	..	..	7	..	83	7	39	..	53	..	46	..	8	..	12	..
210	(G.171) Dentists ..	1	..	..	..	..	..	6	..	..	..	1	..	..	..	..	..	..	..
211	(G.172) Midwives, vaccinators, compounders, nurses, masseurs, etc. ..	8	135	16	144	2	20	49	152	41	206	12	119	14	14	..	20	2	..
212	(G.173) Veterinary Surgeons	1	..	..	..	..	..	2	..	..	..	..	..	..	..	..	..	..	..
213	48. Instruction ..	78	39	18	3	12	1	334	145	80	211	70	76	137	4	119	28	29	1
214	(G. 174) Professors and teachers of all kinds ..	57	39	18	3	12	1	268	141	53	205	60	76	114	4	104	28	25	1
215	(G.175) Clerks and servants connected with education .	21	..	..	..	..	..	66	4	27	6	10	..	23	..	15	..	4	..
216	49. Letters arts and sciences (other than 44) ..	280	100	80	57	74	99	1,234	504	584	129	816	218	280	62	300	49	57	31
217	(G.176) Public scribes stenographers, etc. ..	..	..	..	..	..	..	14	..	2	..	2	..	..	..	..	..	..	..
218	(G.177) Architects, surveyors, engineers, and their employees (not being State servants)	..	..	..	..	..	..	8	..	1	..	1	..	..	..	..	..	..	..
219	(G.178) Authors, editors, journalists and photographers ..	8	..	..	..	..	..	24	..	4	..	13	..	5	..	..	..	..	..
220	(G.179) Artists, sculptors and image-makers ..	10	5	..	1	..	..	32	..	21	..	17	..	58	12	64	9	12	11
221	(G.180) Scientists (astronomers, botanists,) etc. ..	..	..	..	..	..	..	5	..	..	..	2	..	..	..	..	..	..	..
222	(G.181) Horoscope casters, astrologers, fortune tellers, wizards, witches and mediums	18	83	8	20	12	88	595	216	250	81	220	89	178	8	174	7	27	8

No.	Occupation																		
223	(G.182) Musicians (composers and performers other than military) actors, dancers, etc. ..	236	2	32	3	6	1	415	245	281	68	477	73	16	40	28	29	14	14
224	(G.183) Managers and employees of places of public entertainments, race courses, societies, and clubs. ..	..	..	..	..	..	..	16	..	3	..	8	..	4	..	..	..	..	..
225	(G.184) Conjurors, acrobats, reciters, exhibitors of curiosities and wild animals, etc.	13	10	40	33	56	10	125	43	22	30	76	56	24	2	34	4	4	8
226	**D. Miscellaneous** ..	**27,265**	**26,650**	**4,095**	**12,635**	**3,973**	**4,331**	**22,559**	**10,170**	**10,178**	**10,711**	**5,395**	**3,875**	**9,904**	**8,468**	**4,977**	**9,847**	**1,798**	**3,089**
227	IX. Persons living on their income	36	2	10	..	..	..	210	45	18	10	15	4	20	..	4	3	..	..
228	50. Persons living principally on their income ..	36	2	10	..	..	..	210	45	18	10	15	4	20	..	4	3	..	..
229	(G.185) Proprietors (other than of agricultural land), fund and scholarships holders and pensioners ..	36	2	10	..	..	..	210	45	18	10	15	4	20	..	4	3	..	..
230	X. Domestic service ..	19,448	14,524	2,658	3,992	2,444	2,257	8,003	4,576	2,510	3,621	1,985	1,367	6,836	6,310	3,970	7,757	1,627	2,824
231	51. Domestic service ..	19,448	14,524	2,658	3,992	2,444	2,257	8,003	4,576	2,510	3,621	1,985	1,367	6,836	6,310	3,970	7,757	1,627	2,824
232	(G.186) Private motor drivers and cleaners ..	16	..	21	..	..	..	276	10	5	..	..	..	13	..	2	..	3	..
233	(G.187) Other domestic service	19,432	14,524	2,637	3,992	2,444	2,257	7,727	4,566	2,505	3,621	1,985	1,367	6,823	6,310	3,968	7,757	1,624	2,824
234	XI. Insufficiently defined occupations	2,200	9,353	672	7,636	391	1,847	10,214	3,057	4,955	3,603	1,673	1,024	1,129	1,200	523	678	7	..
235	52. General terms which do not indicate a definite occupation	2,200	9,353	672	7,636	391	1,847	10,214	3,057	4,955	3,603	1,673	1,024	1,129	1,200	523	678	7	..
236	(G.188) Manufacturers businessmen and contractors otherwise unspecified ..	307	..	..	..	..	..	282	46	20	68	211	28	156	39	..	..	..	..
237	(G.189) Cashiers, accountants, book-keepers, clerks and other employees in unspecified offices and warehouses and shops ..	..	..	..	..	..	..	78	..	16	..	14	..	78	..	..	..	..	..
238	(G.190) Mechanics otherwise unspecified ..	15	..	4	..	..	..	75	..	5	..	8	..	12	..	..	..	..	..
239	(G.191) Labourers and workmen otherwise unspecified	1,878	9,353	668	7,636	391	1,847	9,779	3,011	4,914	3,535	1,440	996	883	1,161	523	678	7	..
240	XII. Unproductive ..	5,581	2,771	755	1,007	1,188	227	4,132	2,492	2,695	3,477	1,722	1,480	1,919	958	480	1,409	164	265
241	53. Inmates of jails, asylums and alms houses ..	..	..	212	..	..	..	..	..	1,098	357	..	..	..	..	68	..	..	..
212	(G.192) Inmates of jails, asylums and alms houses..	..	..	212	..	..	..	..	..	1,098	357	..	..	..	..	68	..	..	..
243	54. Beggars, vagrants, prostitutes	5,581	2,771	543	1,007	1,188	227	4,075	2,492	1,587	3,120	1,722	1,480	1,919	958	412	1,409	164	265
244	(G.193) Beggars and vagrants	5,371	2,105	532	186	1,188	227	3,919	2,374	1,570	2,892	1,722	1,327	1,897	816	412	1,362	164	265
245	(G.194) Procurers and prostitutes	210	666	11	821	..	..	156	118	17	228	..	153	22	142	..	47	..	..
246	55. Other unclassified non-productive industries ..	..	..	..	..	..	..	57	..	15	..	..	..	..	..	..	..	..	..
247	(G.195) Other unclassified non-productive industries.	..	..	..	..	..	..	57	..	15	..	..	..	..	..	..	..	..	..

TABLE X.

Occupation or Means of Livelihood.

NANDER	Males	Females
Total Earners	136,610	54,992
Total Working Dependents	52,348	64,277
Total Non-working Dependents	178,212	235,642
Total population	367,170	354,911

PARBHANI	Males	Females
Total Earners	145,134	79,566
Total Working Dependents	50,855	34,677
Total Non-working Dependents	238,788	304,740
Total Population	434,777	418,983

GULBARGA	Males	Females
Total Earners	209,540	104,235
Total Working Dependents	97,175	102,288
Total Non-working Dependents	314,972	396,798
Total Population	612,687	603,321

Serial No.	Occupation	NANDER						PARBHANI						GULBARGA					
		Total earners showing occupation as principal		Total working dependents		Total following occupation as subsidiary		Total earners showing occupation as principal		Total working dependents		Total following occupation as subsidiary		Total earners showing occupation as principal		Total working dependents		Total following occupation as subsidiary	
		Males	Females	Males	Females	Males	Females	Males	Females	Males	Females	Males	Females	Males	Females	Males	Females	Males	Females
	1	74	75	76	77	78	79	80	81	82	83	84	85	86	87	88	89	90	91
1	TOTAL WORKERS. ..	136,610	54,992	52,348	64,277	37,519	19,074	145,134	79,566	50,855	34,677	39,789	13,646	209,540	104,235	97,175	102,288	35,482	16,441
2	A. Production of Raw Materials	76,303	35,146	22,111	32,080	21,364	10,352	97,402	57,116	32,607	19,814	28,947	7,493	121,648	82,432	60,378	68,080	22,495	11,520
3	I-Exploitation of Animals and Vegetation ..	76,225	35,141	22,080	32,064	21,364	10,352	97,384	57,116	32,587	19,808	28,947	7,498	117,599	81,899	57,569	67,092	22,268	11,447
4	1. Pasture and Agriculture .	75,274	34,358	21,881	30,743	21,095	9,879	96,226	56,963	31,175	18,601	28,495	7,408	116,754	81,450	56,893	67,004	22,139	11,445
5	(a) Cultivation ..	64,202	31,214	19,361	26,803	20,223	8,800	88,936	52,623	28,557	13,984	27,176	6,077	101,717	76,087	49,045	61,201	20,085	10,128
6	(G.1) Non-cultivating proprietors taking rent in money or kind ..	9,942	4,998	2,005	6,050	3,020	1,133	15,280	6,181	4,853	3,548	9,509	825	20,637	4,033	16,445	3,970	4,331	865
7	(G.2) Estate Agents and Managers of owners ..	29	..	..	..	..	..	28	..	4	..	16	..	386	..	56	..	2	..
8	(G.3) Estate Agents and Managers of Government..	163	..	7	..	4	..	216	..	51	..	27	..	249	..	20	..	..	..
9	(G.4) Rent Collectors, clerks, etc.	386	..	19	..	21	..	412	..	89	..	56	..	432	..	60	..	68	..
10	(G.5) Cultivating owners ..	21,839	1,655	6,125	4,367	5,125	602	25,370	6,054	6,976	2,936	3,428	2,291	44,348	18,543	18,752	10,019	7,265	2,061
11	(G.6) Tenant cultivators ..	5,334	1,538	2,706	1,950	2,095	268	24,788	21,893	4,017	4,267	3,573	1,572	15,323	10,023	5,589	6,421	3,219	1,197
12	(G.7) Agricultural labourers.	26,509	23,023	7,599	14,436	9,958	6,707	22,842	18,495	12,567	3,283	10,572	1,389	20,347	43,488	8,114	4,791	5,200	6,000
13	(b) Cultivation of special crops and fruit growers, etc.	1,116	698	297	479	235	323	691	210	170	1,137	418	367	3,863	2,049	1,337	2,191	529	359
14	(G.13) Pan-Vine ..	289	38	56	84	75	21	66	16	..	72	10	30	216	37	253	168	107	44
15	(G.16) Market Gardeners, flower, fruits, etc. ..	827	660	241	395	160	302	625	200	170	1,065	403	337	3,647	2,012	1,084	2,028	422	315
16	(c) Forestry	821	44	56	89	28	16	145	120	21	81	57	21	4,892	1,485	2,047	845	1,036	229
17	(G.17) Forest officers, rangers, guards, etc. ..	4	..	..	..	..	..	2	..	..	..	..	..	26	..	6	..	..	..
18	(G.18) Wood-cutters and charcoal burners ..	298	44	56	89	28	16	143	120	21	81	57	21	4,677	1,375	2,017	818	1,005	214

TABLE X.
OCCUPATION OR MEANS OF LIVELIHOOD.

19	(G.19) Collectors of forest produce.	24	..	..	..	..	..	..	..	..	..	..	..	189	60	24	27	31	15
20	(G.20) Collectors of lac ..	..	..	..	..	..	..	..	..	..	..	..	..	..	..	..	..	..	..
21	(d.)—Stock raising ..	9,550	2,387	2,168	3,331	582	738	6,433	8,986	2,425	3,378	843	936	6,282	1,879	4,464	2,767	489	734
22	(G.21) Cattle and buffalo-breeders and keepers ..	1,962	148	357	318	63	132	1,862	203	420	389	386	73	2,742	378	809	202	55	87
23	(G.22) Breeders of transport animals	88	..	29	..	27	..	36	..	..	..	14	..	53	..	5	..	3	..
24	(G.23) Herdsmen, shepherds and breeders of other animals	7,500	2,239	1,777	3,013	492	601	4,535	3,783	2,005	2,989	443	863	3,487	1,501	3,650	2,565	431	697
25	(e) Raising of small animals and insects	85	10	4	41	27	7	21	18	2	21	6	7	..	..	..	..	..	..
26	(G.24) Birds, bees, etc ..	51	10	4	31	22	7	11	18	2	21	4	7	..	..	..	..	..	..
27	(G.25) Silk worms ..	18	..	..	6	3	..	3	..	..	..	..	..	..	..	..	..	..	..
28	(G.26) Lac cultivation ..	16	..	..	4	2	..	7	..	..	..	2	..	..	..	..	..	..	..
29	2. Fishing and Hunting ..	951	788	199	1,321	269	473	1,158	153	1,412	1,207	452	85	845	449	676	88	129	2
30	(G.27) Fishing and pearling	702	388	98	1,123	186	352	338	103	271	1,141	195	62	682	390	289	86	86	2
31	(G.28) Hunting ..	249	400	101	198	83	121	820	50	1,141	66	257	23	163	59	387	2	43	..
32	II. Exploitation of Minerals	78	5	31	16	..	..	18	..	20	6	..	..	4,049	533	2,809	908	227	73
33	3. Metallic minerals ..	..	..	..	..	..	..	..	..	..	..	..	..	267	32	178	69	15	1
34	(G.30) Iron	..	..	..	..	..	..	..	..	..	..	..	..	267	32	178	69	15	1
35	4. Non-metallic minerals ..	78	5	31	16	..	..	18	..	20	6	..	..	3,782	501	2,631	839	212	72
36	(G.35) Coal	..	..	..	..	..	..	..	..	..	..	..	..	25	13	10	12	10	3
37	(G.37) Building materials (including stone, materials for cement manufacture and clays)	20	2	12	4	..	..	6	..	4	..	..	..	3,675	481	2,617	810	189	62
38	(G.38) Mica	8	1	3	2	..	..	3	..	2	3	..	..	39	7	2	11	13	7
39	(G.40) Salt, saltpetre and other saline substances ..	14	2	16	10	..	..	9	..	14	3	..	..	43	..	2	3	..	..
40	B.—Preparation and supply of material substances	39,642	12,285	16,994	18,648	9,025	3,931	32,332	17,005	11,126	9,028	8,046	4,851	50,013	14,489	23,095	23,946	9,792	3,947
41	III. Industry	14,212	4,962	6,863	9,361	2,845	2,182	12,770	4,637	4,929	8,832	4,718	1,848	13,847	6,645	5,323	2,446	2,006	544
42	5. Textiles	3,856	881	2,192	2,454	857	524	2,639	890	913	1,364	1,104	337	3,136	2,756	964	568	363	110
43	(G.42) Cotton ginning, cleaning and pressing ..	305	241	202	862	110	132	395	166	241	325	3	56	436	143	151	176	63	31
44	(G.43) Cotton spinning, sizing and weaving ..	2,590	320	1,578	1,186	400	239	1,978	733	651	1,039	1,009	281	2,037	2,497	472	285	200	57
45	(G.45) Rope, twine, string and other fibres ..	215	73	77	86	115	26	126	..	23	..	2	..	144	31	88	22	22	7
46	(G.46) Wool carding spinning and weaving ..	289	83	156	161	72	64	..	..	..	..	..	..	272	49	141	66	39	12
47	(G.47) Silk spinning and weaving.	56	36	50	62	14	12	..	..	..	..	..	..	54	13	18	7	12	2
48	(G.48) Hair (Horse-hair,) etc.	..	..	..	..	..	..	..	..	..	..	..	..	13	..	..	..	..	..

TABLE X.

Occupation or Means of Livelihood.

	NANDER Males	NANDER Females	PARBHANI Males	PARBHANI Females	GULBARGA Males	GULBARGA Females
Total Earners	136,610	54,992	145,134	79,566	209,540	104,235
Total Working Dependents	52,348	64,277	50,855	34,677	97,175	102,288
Total Non-working Dependents	178,212	235,642	238,788	304,740	314,972	396,798
Total Population	367,170	354,911	434,777	418,953	612,687	603,321

Serial No.	Occupation	NANDER: Total earners showing occupation as principal, Males	Females	Total working dependents, Males	Females	Total following occupation as subsidiary, Males	Females	PARBHANI: Total earners showing occupation as principal, Males	Females	Total working dependents, Males	Females	Total following occupation as subsidiary, Males	Females	GULBARGA: Total earners showing occupation as principal, Males	Females	Total working dependents, Males	Females	Total following occupation as subsidiary, Males	Females
	1	74	75	76	77	78	79	80	81	82	83	84	85	86	87	88	89	90	91
49	(G.49) Dyeing, bleaching, printing, preparation and sponging of textiles ..	306	102	88	85	136	44	140	..	28	..	..	..	141	21	82	12	27	1
50	(G.50) Lace, crepe, embroideries, fringes, etc., and insufficiently described textiles	55	24	41	12	10	7	..	..	..	..	..	..	39	..	12	..	..	..
51	6. Hides, skins and hard materials from the animal kingdom	157	59	24	36	11	8	549	..	184	..	147	..	325	..	84	..	48	..
52	(G.51) Working in leather ..	140	59	24	36	11	8	549	..	184	..	147	..	296	..	63	..	41	..
53	(G.52) Furriers and persons occupied with feathers and bristles; brush makers ..	3	..	..	..	..	..	..	..	..	..	..	..	..	..	..	..	..	..
54	(G.53) Bone, ivory, horn shell, etc., workers (except buttons)	14	..	..	..	..	..	..	..	..	..	..	..	29	..	21	..	7	..
55	7. Wood	1,731	756	550	248	309	73	1,423	168	567	40	993	26	551	316	318	104	163	41
56	(G.54) Sawyers ..	72	..	14	..	2	..	15	..	10	..	..	..	56	..	29	..	10	..
57	(G.55) Carpenters, turners and joiners, etc. ..	1,358	159	437	125	264	44	1,208	63	506	16	975	18	381	41	171	..	126	..
58	(G.56) Basket-makers and other industries of woody materials, including leaves and thatchers and builders working with bamboo, reeds or similar materials ..	301	597	99	123	43	29	205	105	51	24	18	8	114	275	118	104	27	41
59	8. Metals	1,465	426	238	622	162	243	789	58	286	23	268	2	1,246	179	890	83	122	24
60	(G.57) Smelting, forging and rolling of iron and other metals	5	..	..	..	..	..	12	..	..	..	..	..	6	..	1	..	..	..
61	(G.58) Makers of arms, guns, etc.	..	..	..	..	..	..	..	..	..	..	..	..	..	..	..	..	..	..

No.	Occupation																		
62	(G.59) Black-smiths, other workers in iron, makers of implements ..	1,186	352	162	522	105	243	474	48	219	18	235	2	850	145	767	62	94	17
63	(G.60) Workers in brass, copper and bell metals ..	198	74	54	100	27	..	231	10	67	10	33	..	282	16	100	8	28	5
64	(G.61) workers in other metals, (except precious metals)	76	..	22	..	30	..	72	..	..	..	..	..	99	18	22	18	5	2
65	(G.62) Workers in mints, die sinkers, etc ..	..	..	..	..	..	..	..	..	..	..	..	..	..	..	..	..	..	..
66	9. Ceramics ..	1,579	542	324	915	141	233	1.950	481	370	208	289	196	1,089	250	296	180	90	45
67	(G.63) Potters and makers of earthen ware ..	1,380	482	264	805	104	203	1,860	481	368	208	263	196	856	229	276	157	63	42
68	(G.64) Brick and tile makers	172	60	39	110	37	30	80	..	11	..	23	..	162	21	20	23	22	8
69	(G.65) Other workers in ceramics	18	..	21	..	..	..	10	..	..	..	3	..	70	..	..	..	5	..
70	10. Chemical products properly so-called and analogous	988	333	237	722	45	163	1,557	1,028	289	884	188	917	329	701	85	216	31	90
71	(G.66) Manufacture of matches, fireworks and other explosives ..	4	..	..	..	..	..	..	..	..	..	..	..	3	4	1	..	..	..
72	(G.67) Manufacture of ærated and mineral waters and ice	6	..	..	..	..	..	..	..	..	..	..	..	4	1	2	..	2	..
73	(G.68) Manufacture and refining and vegetable oils ..	954	313	237	602	45	163	1,505	1,028	268	884	171	917	289	690	73	204	27	90
74	(G.69) Manufacture and refining of mineral oils ..	13	..	..	..	..	..	..	..	..	..	..	..	12	6	3	12	..	..
75	(G.70) Others	11	20	..	120	..	..	52	..	21	..	17	..	16	..	6	..	2	..
76	11. Food Industries ..	322	140	114	127	15	18	53	60	21	51	7	21	590	117	154	101	88	30
77	(G.71) Rice pounders and huskers and flour grinders	66	19	32	13	..	..	..	5	..	3	..	..	..	12	..	14	..	5
78	(G.72) Grain parchers, etc.	18	11	..	12	..	..	..	4	..	2	..	..	..	8	..	5	..	2
79	(G.73) Butchers ..	131	86	52	88	13	2	53	14	21	18	7	2	215	41	64	27	55	3
80	(G.74) Makers of sugar, molasses and gur ..	..	4	..	..	..	..	..	..	..	..	..	..	18	..	..	..	..	..
81	(G.75) Sweet meat and condiment makers ..	30	3	10	..	..	..	..	36	..	18	..	15	24	28	8	32	12	16
82	(G.76) Toddy drawers ..	32	..	10	..	..	..	..	..	..	..	..	..	145	..	51	..	16	..
83	(G.77) Brewers and distillers	5	..	2	..	..	..	..	..	..	..	..	..	32	..	7	..	..	..
84	(G.78) Manufacturers of tobacco	21	17	4	14	2	16	..	8	..	7	..	3	84	23	21	17	5	4
85	(G.80) Manufacturers of Ganja	3	..	..	..	..	..	..	..	..	..	..	..	18	..	..	..	..	..
86	(G.81) Others ..	16	..	4	..	..	..	..	2	..	3	..	1	24	5	3	6	..	..
87	12. Industries of dress and toilet	3,289	1,536	3,045	3,306	1,150	779	2,935	1,272	2,012	1,004	1,244	308	5,726	1,059	1,299	803	848	108
88	(G.82) Boot, shoe, sandal and clog makers ..	906	125	560	670	210	..	728	659	915	469	376	136	1,862	361	278	224	353	22
89	(G.83) Tailors, milliners, dress makers and darners ..	573	551	419	888	382	309	590	65	481	212	271	61	904	428	212	202	152	31
90	(G.84) Embroiderers, hat-makers and makers of other articles of wear ..	24	..	3	..	..	..	..	..	..	..	..	..	66	16	34	22	5	7
91	(G.85) Washing and cleaning	1,139	530	1,615	836	252	229	923	339	340	288	344	77	2,088	698	519	223	181	27

TABLE X.

Occupation or Means of Livelihood.

	NANDER	Males	Females
Total Earners		136,610	54,992
Total Working Dependents		52,348	64,277
Total Non-Working Dependents		178,212	235,642
Total Population		367,170	354,911

	PARBHANI	Males	Females
Total Earners		145,134	79,566
Total Working Dependents		50,855	34,677
Total Non-working Dependents		238,788	304,743
Total Population		434,777	418,983

	GULBARGA	Males	Females
Total Earners		209,540	104,235
Total Working Dependents		97,175	102,288
Total Non-working Dependents		314,972	396,798
Total Population		612,687	603,321

Serial No.	Occupation	NANDER: Total earners showing occupation as principal		NANDER: Total working dependents		NANDER: Total following occupation as subsidiary		PARBHANI: Total earners showing occupation as principal		PARBHANI: Total working dependents		PARBHANI: Total following occupation as subsidiary		GULBARGA: Total earners showing occupation as principal		GULBARGA: Total working dependents		GULBARGA: Total following occupation as subsidiary	
		Males	Females	Males	Females	Males	Females	Males	Females	Males	Females	Males	Females	Males	Females	Males	Females	Males	Females
	1	74	75	76	77	78	79	80	81	82	83	84	85	86	87	88	89	90	91
92	(G.86) Barbers, hair dressers and wig-makers ..	647	330	448	912	306	241	685	209	267	35	253	34	806	156	256	132	157	21
93	(G.87) Other industries connected with toilet ..	..	..	..	..	..	..	..	..	..	..	..	..	..	..	..	..	..	..
94	13. Furniture industries ..	31	..	2	..	..	..	12	..	..	..	..	..	24	..	4	..	2	..
95	(G.88) Cabinet-makers carriage painters, etc ..	25	..	2	..	..	..	12	..	..	..	..	..	21	..	3	..	2	..
96	(G.89) Upholsterers, tent makers, etc. ..	6	..	..	..	..	..	..	..	..	..	..	..	3	..	1	..	..	..
97	14. Building industries ..	84	75	24	625	5	75	238	30	38	44	227	20	1,229	370	586	132	98	23
98	(G.90) Lime burners, cement workers ; Excavators and well sinkers ; stone cutters and dressers ; Brick layers and masons ; Builders (other than buildings made of bamboo and similar materials) painters decorators of houses, tilers, plumbers, etc.	84	75	24	625	5	75	238	30	88	44	227	29	1,229	376	586	132	98	23
99	15. Construction of means of transport	88	..	4	..	..	..	70	..	22	..	2	..	195	4	31	3	80	..
100	(G.91) Persons engaged in making, assembling or repairing motor vehicles or cycles	19	..	2	..	..	..	16	..	4	..	..	..	32	..	4	..	12	..
101	(G.92) Carriage, cart, palki, etc. makers and wheelwrights	69	..	2	..	..	..	54	..	18	..	2	..	163	4	27	3	18	..
102	16. Production and transmission of physical force ..	.	..	..	..	..	..	..	..	..	..	..	..	6	..	..	..	..	..
103	(G.94) Heat, light, electricity, motive power, etc. Gas works and electric light and power ..	..	..	..	..	..	..	..	..	..	..	..	..	6	..	..	..	..	..

TABLE X.
OCCUPATION OR MEANS OF LIVELIHOOD.

No.	Occupation																		
104	17. Miscellaneous and undefined industries ..	652	214	109	306	150	66	555	632	188	214	249	12	1,401	287	612	256	128	73
105	(G.95) Printers, engravers, book binders, etc. ..	15	..	..	..	..	..	2	..	..	..	..	..	18	..	4	..	2	..
106	(G.96) Makers of musical instruments	2	..	..	..	..	..	..	..	..	..	.	..	3	..	..	..	..	..
107	(G.97) Makers of clocks and surgical or scientific instruments, etc.	3	..	..	..	..	..	8	..	..	..	..	..	12	..	5	..	1	..
108	(G.98) Makers of jewellery and ornaments ..	539	111	82	200	150	30	531	576	170	207	242	12	1,278	221	558	205	117	33
109	(G.99) Other miscellaneous and undefined industries (toy making) taxidermy, etc.	41	108	12	106	..	36	19	56	18	7	7	..	51	66	20	51	3	40
110	(G.100) Scavenging ..	52	..	15	..	..	..	..	..	..	..	..	..	39	..	25	..	..	..
111	IV. Transport	5,208	1,756	1,229	2,890	608	207	8,449	9,711	3,797	2,638	865	1,423	7,462	1,421	7,719	3,728	2,785	2,923
112	19. Transport by water ..	..	..	..	..	..	..	..	..	..	..	..	..	395	..	426	160	145	182
113	(G.104) Labourers employed on harbours, docks, rivers and canals	..	..	..	..	..	..	..	..	..	..	..	..	395	..	426	160	145	182
114	20. Transport by road ..	4,750	1,558	983	2,638	454	156	5,131	8,163	2,348	1,947	404	1,153	4,717	264	5,828	1,152	1,739	1,076
115	(G.105) Persons (other than labourers) employed on the construction and maintenance of roads and bridges .	56	..	10	..	3	..	18	..	6	..	3	..	76	..	22	..	13	..
116	(G.106) Labourers employed on roads and bridges ..	3,611	1,337	698	2,556	257	55	3,548	7,892	1,860	1,914	148	1,054	2,205	253	3,775	650	1,534	1,062
117	(G. 107) Owners, managers and employees (excluding personal servants) connected with mechanically driven vehicles (including trams)	46	26	12	39	5	18	871	..	194	..	175	..	158	..	20	..	19	..
118	(G.108) Owners, managers, employees (excluding personal servants) connected with other vehicles ..	962	195	184	43	171	83	1,067	27	259	3	75	31	1,581	11	1,485	502	155	14
119	(G.109) Palki, etc., bearers and owners	..	..	..	..	..	..	56	88	22	10	3	12	341	..	46	..	18	..
120	(G.110) Pack elephant, camel, mule, ass and bullock, owners and drivers ..	75	..	29	..	18	..	71	156	7	20	..	56	320	..	360	..	..	..
121	(G.111) Porters and messengers	..	..	..	..	..	..	..	..	..	..	..	..	36	..	120	..	..	..
122	21. Transport by rail ..	289	198	268	252	139	51	3,156	1,548	1,422	691	448	270	2,170	1,157	1,414	2,416	871	1,665
123	(G.112) Railway employees of all kind other than coolies	76	2	25	18	13	..	145	21	78	33	33	7	156	7	78	10	24	..
124	(G.113) Labourers employed on railway construction and maintenance and coolies and porters employed on railway premises ..	213	196	243	234	126	51	3,011	1,527	1,344	658	415	263	2,014	1,150	1,336	2,406	847	1,665
125	22. Post Office, Telegraph and Telephone services ..	164	..	28	..	15	..	162	..	27	..	13	..	180	..	51	..	30	..
126	(G.114) Post office, Telegraph and Telephone services	164	..	28	..	15	..	162	..	27	..	13	..	180	..	51	..	30	..
127	V. Trade	20,197	5,567	8,902	6,397	5,572	1,542	11,113	2,657	2,400	2,558	2,463	1,580	26,704	6,423	10,053	17,772	5,001	480

TABLE X.

Occupation or Means of Livelihood.

	NANDER Males	NANDER Females	PARBHANI Males	PARBHANI Females	GULBARGA Males	GULBARGA Females
Total Earners	186,610	54,992	145,134	79,566	209,540	104,235
Total Working Dependents	52,348	64,277	50,855	34,677	97,175	102,288
Total Non-Working Dependents	178,212	235,642	238,788	304,740	314,972	396,798
Total Population	367,170	354,911	434,777	418,983	612,687	603,321

Serial No.	Occupation	NANDER						PARBHANI						GULBARGA					
		Total earners showing occupation as principal		Total working dependents		Total following occupation as subsidiary		Total earners showing occupation as principal		Total working dependents		Total following occupation as subsidiary		Total earners showing occupation as principal		Total working dependents		Total following occupation as subsidiary	
		Males	Females	Males	Females	Males	Females	Males	Females	Males	Females	Males	Females	Males	Females	Males	Females	Males	Females
	1	74	75	76	77	78	79	80	81	82	83	84	85	86	87	88	89	90	91
128	23. Banks, establishments of credit, exchange and insurance	2,101	36	73	3	53	..	1,436	37	45	5	207	10	1,444	140	235	199	148	29
129	(G.115) Bank managers, money lenders, exchange and insurance agents, money changers and brokers and their employees ..	2,101	36	73	3	53	..	1,436	37	45	5	207	10	1,444	140	235	199	148	29
130	24. Brokerage commission and export	41	..	9	..	3	..	12	..	..	..	..	..	27	..	2	..	..	..
131	(G.116) Brokers, commission agents, commercial travellers, warehouse owners and employees	41	..	9	..	3	..	12	..	..	..	..	..	27	..	2	..	..	..
132	25. Trade in Textiles ..	765	143	324	265	143	38	1,892	341	845	302	262	117	3,346	836	821	1,039	410	24
133	(G.117) Trade in piece goods wool, cotton, silk, hair and other textiles ..	765	143	324	265	143	38	1,892	341	845	302	262	117	3,346	836	821	1,039	410	24
134	26. Trade in skins, leather and furs	189	48	21	39	7	..	27	..	28	26	..	..	262	..	84	..	43	..
135	(G.118) Trade in skins, leather, furs, feathers, horn etc., and the articles made from these , ...	189	48	21	39	7	..	27	..	28	26	..	..	262	..	84	..	43	..
136	27. Trade in wood ..	174	47	41	48	7	4	6	14	..	39	..	3	57	16	6	40	..	..
137	(G.119) Trade in wood (not fire-wood)	15	..	..	..	..	..	2	..	..	..	..	..	19	..	2	..	..	..
138	(G.120) Trade in barks ..	5	..	..	..	..	..	4	6	..	12	..	2	24	..	4	..	..	..
139	(G.121) Trade in bamboos and canes	8	47	2	48	..	4	..	8	..	27	..	1	8	16	..	40	..	..
140	(G.122) Trade in thatches and other forest produce .	146	..	39	..	7	..	..	..	..	..	..	..	6	..	..	..	..	..
141	28. Trade in metals ..	62	16	13	18	5	..	50	4	22	10	7	4	27	..	3	..	..	..

No.	Occupation	1	2	3	4	5	6	7	8	9	10	11	12	13	14	15	16	17	18
142	(G.122) Trade in metals, machinery, knives, tools, etc.	62	16	13	18	5	..	50	4	22	10	7	4	27	..	3	..	..	..
143	29. Trade in pottery, bricks and tiles	150	135	70	187	36	52	21	186	4	395	..	111	140	35	39	163	17	28
144	(G.124) Trade in pottery, bricks and tiles ..	150	135	70	187	36	52	21	186	4	395	..	111	140	35	39	163	17	28
145	30. Trade in chemical products	51	..	10	..	..	..	18	..	2	..	1	..	30	..	5	..	3	..
146	(G.125) Drugs, dyes, paints, petroleum, explosives, etc.	51	..	10	..	..	..	18	..	2	..	1	..	30	..	5	..	3	..
147	31. Hotels, cafes, restaurants etc.	716	320	140	1,006	86	106	603	222	166	502	197	204	2,192	459	1,144	2,073	565	73
148	(G.126) Vendors of wine, liquors, aerated waters and ice	677	320	111	1,006	86	106	591	205	166	461	197	204	2,105	459	1,109	2,073	522	73
149	(G.127) Owners and managers of hotels, cook shops, sarais, etc., and employees	33	..	15	..	..	..	10	..	..	..	..	..	63	..	29	..	41	..
150	(G.128) Hawkers of drink and food stuffs ..	6	..	14	..	..	..	2	17	..	41	..	..	24	..	6	..	2	..
151	32. Other trade in food stuffs	3,465	2,352	2,219	3,032	638	538	3,225	836	720	698	668	604	10,491	3,072	5,371	6,661	3,021	144
152	(G.129) Grain and pulse dealers	762	127	393	51	185	40	1,636	215	392	119	203	172	5,565	914	2,392	2,121	1,264	30
153	(G.130) Dealers in sweetmeats, sugar and spices	22	137	18	147	..	68	15	146	2	122	..	188	541	125	358	499	319	10
154	(G.131) Dealers in dairy product, eggs and poultry ..	2,175	1,980	1,686	2,722	408	366	288	394	46	337	20	228	2,017	1,506	992	2,933	411	46
155	(G.132) Dealers in animals for food	17	..	..	..	..	..	16	..	2	..	..	..	31	..	5	..	..	..
156	(G.133) Dealers in fodder for animals	21	..	5	..	..	..	27	..	..	..	..	..	70	..	28	..	..	..
157	(G.134) Dealers in other food stuffs	427	108	167	112	45	64	808	81	210	120	355	16	1,228	306	1,178	841	810	35
158	(G.135) Dealers in tobacco .	13	..	..	..	..	..	415	..	66	..	90	..	999	221	416	267	217	28
159	(G.136) Dealers in opium ..	8	..	..	..	..	..	4	..	..	..	..	..	11	..	2	..	..	..
160	(G.137) Dealers in ganja ..	20	..	..	..	..	..	16	..	2	..	..	..	29	..	..	..	..	..
161	33. Trade in clothing and toilet articles ..	150	35	101	26	20	10	129	18	11	22	2	..	1,861	260	419	315	156	15
162	(G.138) Trade in ready-made clothing and other articles of dress and the toilet (hats, umbrellas, socks, ready-made shoes, perfumes, etc.)	150	35	101	26	20	10	129	18	11	22	2	..	1,861	260	419	315	156	15
163	34. Trade in furniture ..	182	44	71	168	20	51	64	29	15	58	3	16	224	18	114	124	29	19
164	(G.139) Trade in furniture, carpets, curtains and bedding	47	..	10	..	..	..	15	..	1	..	..	..	44	..	20	..	7	..
165	(G.140) Hardware, cooking utensils porcelain crockery, glassware bottles, articles for gardening, etc. ..	135	44	61	168	20	51	49	29	14	58	3	16	180	18	94	124	22	16
166	35. Trade in building materials	36	8	8	12	..	..	28	..	5	..	1	..	844	..	362	91	78	..
167	(G.141) Trade in building materials (other than brick tiles and woody materials)	36	8	8	12	..	..	28	..	5	..	1	..	844	..	362	91	78	..
168	36. Trade in means of transport	502	24	255	10	21	12	177	4	20	8	28	..	298	12	101	48	65	..

TABLE X.

Occupation or Means of Livelihood.

	NANDER	Males	Females
Total Earners		136,610	54,092
Total Working Dependents		52,348	64,277
Total Non-working Dependents		178,212	235,642
Total Population		367,170	354,911

	PARBHANI	Males	Females
Total Earners		145,134	79,566
Total Working Dependents		50,835	34,677
Total Non-working Dependents		238,788	304,740
Total Population		434,777	418,983

	GULBARGA	Males	Females
Total Earners		209,540	104,235
Total Working Dependents		97,175	102,288
Total Non-working Dependents		314,972	396,798
Total Population		612,687	603,321

Serial No.	Occupation	Nander: Total earners showing occupation as principal, Males	Females	Nander: Total working dependents, Males	Females	Nander: Total following occupation as subsidiary, Males	Females	Parbhani: Total earners showing occupation as principal, Males	Females	Parbhani: Total working dependents, Males	Females	Parbhani: Total following occupation as subsidiary, Males	Females	Gulbarga: Total earners showing occupation as principal, Males	Females	Gulbarga: Total working dependents, Males	Females	Gulbarga: Total following occupation as subsidiary, Males	Females
	1	74	75	76	77	78	79	80	81	82	83	84	85	86	87	88	89	90	91
169	(G.142) Dealers and hirers, in mechanical transport motors, cycles, etc. ..	38	..	16	..	2	..	14	..	2	..	7	..	84	..	21	..	19	..
170	(G.143) Dealers and hirers in other carriages, carts, boats, etc.	401	24	212	10	19	12	168	4	18	8	21	..	199	12	80	48	46	..
171	(G.144) Dealers and hirers of elephants, camels, horses, cattle, asses, mules, etc	63	..	27	..	..	..	..	..	..	..	..	..	15	..	..	..	..	..
172	37. Trade in fuel ..	606	151	230	288	71	61	845	399	299	206	177	120	1,001	235	437	1,498	120	38
173	(G.145) Dealers in firewood charcoal, coal, cowdung, etc.	606	151	230	288	71	61	845	399	299	206	177	120	1,001	235	437	1,498	120	38
174	38. Trade in articles of luxury and those pertaining to letters and the arts and sciences	203	36	94	199	20	36	36	39	8	119	2	48	932	290	540	348	93	55
175	(G.146) Dealers in precious stones jewellery (real and imitation) clocks, optical instruments, etc ..	28	..	..	..	..	..	1	..	1	..	..	..	503	30	244	40	59	..
176	(G.147) Dealers in common bangles, bead necklaces, fans, small articles, toys hunting and fishing, tackle, flowers, etc. ..	140	36	82	199	17	36	27	39	4	119	2	48	381	260	264	298	18	55
177	(G.148) Publishers, booksellers, stationers, dealers in music, pictures, musical instruments and curiosities																		
178	39. Trade of other sorts ..	35	..	12	..	3	..	8	..	3	..	..	..	98	..	32	10	16	..
179	(G.149) Dealers in rags, stable refuse, etc. ..	10,804	2,172	5,223	1,096	4,442	634	2,544	528	210	168	908	343	3,528	1,050	370	5,173	253	55
		24	..	8	..	..	..	4	..	..	..	..	..	19	..	..	..	..	..
180	(G.150) General store-keepers and shop keepers, otherwise unspecified ..	10,748	2,168	5,151	1,037	4,380	618	2,496	528	210	168	905	343	3,354	1,048	352	5,117	251	55

181	(G.151) Itinerant traders, pedlars and hawkers (of other than food, etc.) ..	29	4	64	59	60	16	41	..	..	..	3	..	149	2	18	56	2	..
182	(G.152) Other trades (including farmers of pounds, tools and markets) ..	3	..	..	..	2	..	3	..	..	..	..	..	6	..	..	..	..	..
183	C. Public Administration and Liberal Arts ..	7,958	518	2,808	2,232	2,334	262	5,629	578	2,193	503	1,661	274	17,454	1,595	5,274	1,667	943	242
184	VI. Public Force ..	1,455	116	307	739	810	25	522	89	226	..	180	..	2,705	75	689	120	138	26
185	40. Army	199	40	98	70	174	9	122	..	26	..	76	..	505	15	389	38	38	2
186	(G.153) Imperial Army ..	..	..	..	..	..	..	..	..	..	..	..	..	..	..	..	..	..	..
187	(G.154) State Army ..	199	40	98	70	174	9	122	..	26	..	76	..	505	15	389	38	38	2
188	43. Police	1,256	76	269	669	142	16	400	39	200	..	104	..	2,200	60	300	82	100	24
189	(G.157) Police	356	15	199	17	42	..	363	27	81	..	6	..	645	14	112	24	51	12
190	(G.158) Village watchmen ..	900	61	70	652	100	16	37	12	119	..	98	..	1,555	46	188	58	49	12
191	VII. Public Administration .	3,848	45	678	..	981	4	1,965	16	872	129	309	27	6,737	363	1,094	243	588	58
192	44. Public Administration .	3,848	45	678	..	981	4	1,965	16	872	129	309	27	6,377	363	1,094	243	588	58
193	(G.159) Imperial service ..	..	..	..	..	..	..	..	..	..	..	..	..	3	..	1	..	..	..
194	(G.160) State service ..	500	13	199	..	174	..	297	4	126	14	31	6	826	13	342	12	27	7
195	(G.160 a) Service of other Indian and foreign States..	1	..	..	..	..	..	..	..	..	..	..	..	2	..	..	..	..	..
196	(G.161) Municipal and other local (not village) service..	891	32	134	..	395	4	172	4	148	31	26	8	421	101	284	125	66	36
197	(G.162) Village officials and servants other than watchmen	2,366	..	345	..	412	..	1,496	8	598	84	252	13	5,485	249	467	106	495	15
198	VIII-Profession and Liberal Arts	2,655	357	1,763	1,498	1,037	233	8,142	523	1,095	874	1,172	247	8,012	1,157	3,491	1,304	217	158
199	45. Religion	1,559	208	1,093	1,336	672	147	1,618	485	554	307	284	245	5,825	663	2,697	639	74	55
200	(G.163) Priests, ministers, etc.	1,490	198	1,064	1,330	655	147	1,541	485	519	307	250	245	5,025	593	2,680	599	74	55
201	(G.164) Monks, nuns, religious mendicants ..	2	..	..	..	..	..	..	..	..	..	..	..	157	2	..	..	..	..
202	(G.165) Other religious workers	16	..	..	..	..	..	20	..	14	..	6	..	272	16	..	..	..	..
203	(G.166) Servants in religious edifices, burial and burning grounds, pilgrim conductors, circumcisers, etc.	11	10	29	6	17	..	57	..	21	..	28	..	371	52	17	40	..	..
204	46. Law	227	25	58	..	55	..	544	..	96	..	54	..	382	21	206	..	53	..
205	(G.167) Lawyers of all kinds including Qazis, Law Agents and Mukhtiars ..	207	25	58	..	55	..	504	..	94	..	54	..	326	21	174	..	53	..
206	(G.168) Lawyers' clerks petition-writers, etc. ..	20	..	..	..	..	..	40	..	2	..	..	..	56	..	32	..	..	..
207	47. Medicine	230	30	169	126	59	58	505	84	164	4	361	2	230	187	77	158	20	23
208	(G.169) Registered medical practitioners including oculists	30	5	..	10	9	8	15	2	4	2	..	..	13	7	7	6	2	..

TABLE X.

Occupation or Means of Livelihood.

NANDER	Males	Females
Total Earners ..	136,610	54,992
Total Working Dependents ..	52,348	64,277
Total Non-Working Dependents ..	178,212	235,642
Total Population ..	367,170	354,911

PARBHANI	Males	Females
Total Earners ..	145,134	79,566
Total Woking Dependents ..	50,855	34,677
Total Non-working Dependents	238,788	304,740
Total Population ..	434,777	418,983

GULBARGA	Males	Females
Total Earners ..	209,540	104,235
Total Working Dependents ..	97,175	102,288
Total Non-working Dependents	314,972	396,798
Total Population ..	612,687	603,321

Serial No.	Occupation	NANDER: Total earners showing occupation as principal, Males	Females	NANDER: Total working dependents, Males	Females	NANDER: Total following occupation as subsidiary, Males	Females	PARBHANI: Total earners showing occupation as principal, Males	Females	PARBHANI: Total working dependents, Males	Females	PARBHANI: Total following occupation as subsidiary, Males	Females	GULBARGA: Total earners showing occupation as principal, Males	Females	GULBARGA: Total working dependents, Males	Females	GULBARGA: Total following occupation as subsidiary, Males	Females
	1	74	75	76	77	78	79	80	81	82	83	84	85	86	87	88	89	90	91
209	(G.170) Other persons practising the healing arts without being registered ..	140	..	25	..	26	..	484	..	129	..	292	..	166	..	47	..	10	..
210	(G.171) Dentists ..	3	..	..	..	1	..	6	..	..	..	..	..	8	..	2	..	1	..
211	(G.172) Midwives, vaccinators, compounders, nurses, masseurs, etc. ..	54	25	144	116	23	50	58	32	31	2	60	2	40	180	21	152	7	23
212	(G.173) Veterinary Surgeons.	3	..	..	..	..	..	2	..	..	..	..	..	3	..	..	..	..	..
213	48. Instruction ..	264	20	117	15	23	18	211	4	181	3	270	..	291	27	26	33	33	19
214	(G. 174) Professors and teachers of all kinds ..	224	20	107	15	23	18	191	4	159	3	270	..	236	22	26	33	33	19
215	(G.175) Clerks and servants connected with education .	40	..	10	..	..	..	20	..	22	..	..	..	55	5	..	..	..	..
216	49. Letters arts and sciences (other than 44) ..	375	74	326	16	228	10	204	..	100	..	203	..	1,284	250	485	474	37	61
217	(G.176) Public scribes, stenographers, etc. ..	2	..	..	..	..	..	3	..	..	..	1	..	24	..	3	..	..	..
218	(G.177) Architects, surveyors, engineers, and their employees (not being State servants)	2	..	..	..	..	..	2	..	..	..	..	..	6	..	2	..	..	..
219	(G.178) Authors, editors, journalists and photographers	12	..	2	..	3	..	12	..	2	..	1	..	38	..	12	..	..	..
220	(G.179) Artists, sculptors and image-makers ..	31	14	15	6	8	4	64	..	25	..	16	..	323	37	140	94	14	2
221	(G.180) Scientists (astronomers, botanists, etc.) ..	1	..	..	..	..	..	1	..	..	..	..	..	4	..	..	..	..	..
222	(G.181) Horoscope casters, astrologers, fortune tellers, wizards, witches and mediums	238	38	248	1	142	2	46	..	29	..	53	..	351	72	110	39	22	..

No.	Occupation																		
223	(G.182) Musicians (composers and performers other than military) actors, dancers, etc. ..	52	16	34	8	51	2	31	..	26	..	17	..	161	100	45	304	1	43
224	(G.183) Managers and employees of places of public entertainments, race courses, societies, clubs. ..	14	..	2	..	..	..	2	..	2	..	2	..	18	..	12	..	..	..
225	(G.184) Conjurors, acrobats, recitors, exhibitors of curiosities and wild animals, etc.	28	6	25	1	24	2	43	..	16	..	113	..	359	50	161	37	..	16
226	D. Miscellaneous ..	12,707	7,043	10,435	11,317	4,796	4,529	9,771	4,867	4,929	5,332	1,135	1,028	20,425	5,719	8,428	8,675	2,252	932
227	IX. Persons living on their income	36	2	20	2	..	..	26	1	18	3	..	..	277	50	144	200	8	..
228	50. Persons living principally on their income ..	36	2	20	2	..	..	26	1	18	3	..	..	277	50	144	200	8	..
229	(G.185) Proprietors (other than of agricultural land), fund and scholarships holders and pensioners ..	36	2	20	2	..	..	26	1	18	3	..	..	277	50	144	200	8	..
230	X. Domestic service ..	5,463	4,697	5,354	6,555	1,511	2,585	6,149	2,104	3,956	4,911	383	366	14,084	3,517	5,158	4,896	1,878	443
231	51. Domestic service ..	5,463	4,697	5,354	6,555	1,511	2,585	6,149	2,104	3,956	4,911	383	366	14,084	3,517	5,158	4,896	1,878	443
232	(G.186) Private motor drivers and cleaners ..	73	12	16	..	11	3	16	..	12	3	..	2	254	27	39	14	48	..
233	(G.187) Other domestic service	5,390	4,685	5,338	6,555	1,500	2,582	6,133	2,104	3,944	4,908	383	364	13,830	3,490	5,119	4,882	1,830	443
234	XI. Insufficiently defined occupations	6,061	2,073	4,421	3,969	2,572	1,810	1,740	605	302	112	271	394	2,505	392	1,760	997	210	372
235	52. General terms which do not indicate a definite occupation	6,061	2,073	4,421	3,969	2,572	1,810	1,740	605	302	112	271	394	2,505	392	1,760	997	210	372
236	(G.188) Manufacturers, businessmen and contractors otherwise unspecified ..	1,395	165	75	80	266	123	118	152	..	21	23	118	510	50	176	282	41	40
237	(G.189) Cashiers, accountants, book-keepers, clerks and other employees in unspecified offices and warehouses and shops ..	412	..	160	..	37	..	46	..	12	..	..	..	162	..	39	..	12	..
238	(G.190) Mechanics otherwise unspecified ..	53	..	..	..	..	..	3	..	..	..	..	..	85	..	22	..	..	..
239	(G.191) Labourers and workmen otherwise unspecified.	4,201	1,908	4,186	3,889	2,669	1,687	1,573	453	290	91	248	276	1,748	342	1,523	715	157	332
240	XII. Unproductive ..	1,147	271	640	791	713	134	1,856	2,157	653	306	481	268	3,559	1,760	1,366	2,582	161	117
241	53. Inmates of jails, asylums and alms houses ..	..	..	72	20	..	..	..	..	153	18	..	..	..	..	249	36	..	..
242	(G.192) Inmates of jails, asylums and alms houses ..	..	..	72	20	..	..	..	..	153	18	..	..	..	..	249	36	..	..
243	54. Beggars, vagrants, prostitutes	1,147	271	568	771	713	134	1,850	2,157	500	288	481	268	3,487	1,760	1,100	2,513	161	117
244	(G.193) Beggars and vagrants	1,086	250	555	441	713	100	1,838	2,056	453	206	481	260	3,306	1,366	989	1,636	157	51
245	(G.194) Procurers and prostitutes	61	21	13	330	..	34	12	101	47	82	..	8	131	394	111	877	4	66
246	55. Other unclassified non-productive industries ..	..	..	..	..	..	..	6	..	..	..	..	..	122	..	17	33	..	..
247	(G.195) Other unclassified non-productive industries..	..	..	..	..	..	..	6	..	..	..	..	..	122	..	17	33	..	..

TABLE X.

Occupation or Means of Livelihood.

	OSMANABAD Males	OSMANABAD Females	RAICHUR Males	RAICHUR Females	BIDAR Males	BIDAR Females
Total Earners	160,152	51,955	192.057	81,402	189,534	62,720
Total Working Dependents	72,739	74,795	67,366	96,258	59,431	73,688
Total Non-Working Dependents	124,598	206,829	213,738	286,719	197,291	290,956
Total Population	357,489	333,579	473,161	464,374	446,256	427,359

Serial No.	Occupation	OSMANABAD						RAICHUR						BIDAR					
		Total earners showing occupation as principal		Total working dependents		Total following occupation as subsidiary		Total earners showing occupation as principal		Total working dependents		Total following occupation as subsidiary		Total earners showing occupation as principal		Total working dependents		Total following occupation as subsidiary	
		Males	Females	Males	Females	Males	Females	Males	Females	Males	Females	Males	Females	Males	Females	Males	Females	Males	Females
	1	92	93	94	95	96	97	98	99	100	101	102	103	104	105	106	107	108	109
1	TOTAL WORKERS ..	160,152	51,955	72,799	74,795	30,865	25,174	192,057	81,402	67,366	96,253	28,238	21,416	189,534	62,720	59,431	73,683	31,274	21,278
2	A. Production of Raw Materials	98,970	34,554	40,104	43,596	13,209	12,579	123,833	59,978	38,715	61,310	16,502	12,325	112,438	43,369	33,306	42,302	12,479	6,211
3	I-Exploitation of Animals and Vegetation ..	98,764	34,554	40,096	43,567	13,209	12,579	123,430	59,957	38,492	61,269	16,496	12,324	112,438	43,369	33,306	42,302	12,479	6,211
4	1. Pasture and Agriculture .	98,265	34,472	39,909	43,354	13,152	12,459	120,974	58,893	37,592	60,267	16,203	12,260	109,528	43,194	32,504	41,739	11,590	4,264
5	(a.) Cultivation ..	89,884	32,266	36,038	37,251	11,357	11,888	106,723	50,024	33,118	50,958	12,084	6,619	101,085	40,680	30,459	38,864	10,520	3,725
6	(G.1) Non-cultivating proprietors taking rent in money or kind ..	10,245	2,756	3,215	3,370	2,569	938	18,156	15,561	5,474	5,761	2,272	360	12,116	5,706	3,235	1,013	1,241	588
7	(G.2) Estate Agents and Managers of owners ..	6	..	..	..	..	..	463	..	20	..	5	..	1,789	..	245	..	262	..
8	(G.3) Estate Agents and Managers of Government..	139	..	7	..	11	..	597	..	15	..	6	..	343	..	79	..	20	..
9	(G.4) Rent Collectors, clerks, etc.	287	..	19	..	28	..	429	..	32	..	55	..	595	..	56	..	88	..
10	(G.5) Cultivating owners ..	21,572	7,223	8,023	8,945	4,621	1,874	27,015	18,786	9,884	20,824	4,762	1,819	34,837	8,014	9,345	4,231	3,627	789
11	(G.6) Tenant cultivators ..	14,283	1,828	4,199	5,427	2,250	845	19,361	4,807	2,962	3,994	2,522	2,005	16,498	8,776	5,446	3,006	1,837	646
12	(G.7) Agricultural labourers.	43,352	20,459	20,575	19,509	1,878	7,731	40,702	10,870	14,731	20,374	3,062	2,435	34,907	18,184	12,053	29,714	3,445	1,702
13	(b.) Cultivation of special crops, fruits, etc. ..	3,386	810	1,419	1,933	628	643	1,718	3,551	428	2,706	232	781	583	336	169	445	99	114
14	(G.13) Pan-Vine ..	68	194	21	38	12	63	256	128	50	195	39	73	..	..	..	..	..	..
15	(G.16) Market Gardeners, flower & fruit growers, etc.	3,318	616	1,398	1,895	616	580	1,462	3,423	378	2,511	193	708	583	336	169	445	99	114
16	(c.) Forestry	663	47	227	213	86	..	669	139	176	119	183	24	560	317	85	114	128	17
17	(G. 17) Forest officers, rangers, guards, etc. ..	3	..	..	..	..	..	3	..	..	..	..	..	..	..	..	..	..	..
18	(G.18) Wood-cutters and charcoal burners ..	660	47	227	213	86	..	680	139	176	119	183	24	560	317	85	114	128	17

TABLE X.

OCCUPATION OR MEANS OF LIVELIHOOD.

19	(G.19) Collectors of forest produce.	..	..	..	..	..	..	27	..	..	..	..	..	..	..	..	..	..	..
20	(G.20) Collectors of lac ..	..	..	..	..	..	..	..	..	..	..	..	..	..	..	..	..	..	..
21	(d.)—Stock raising ..	4,314	1,340	2,225	3,957	1,081	428	11,864	5,179	3,870	6,489	3,104	4,836	7,295	1,861	1,791	2,316	843	408
22	(G.21) Cattle and buffaloc-breeders and keepers ..	487	267	216	311	25	22	2,731	1,938	639	949	1,009	951	1,392	782	555	300	876	113
23	(G.22) Breeders of transport animals	..	..	..	..	..	..	178	..	28	..	17	..	..	..	..	..	..	..
24	(G.23) Herdsmen, shepherds and breeders of other animals	3,827	1,082	2,009	3,646	1,056	406	8,955	3,246	3,208	5,540	2,078	3,882	5,903	1,079	1,236	2,016	467	295
25	(e.) Raising of small animals and insects	18	..	..	..	..	..	..	..	..	..	..	..	..	..	..	..	..	..
26	(G.24) Birds, bees etc. ..	18	..	..	..	..	..	..	..	..	..	..	..	..	..	..	..	..	..
27	(G.25) Silk-worms ..	..	..	..	..	..	..	..	..	..	..	..	..	..	..	..	..	..	..
28	(G.26) Lac cultivation ..	..	..	..	..	..	..	..	..	..	..	..	..	..	..	..	..	..	..
29	2. Fishing and Hunting ..	409	82	187	213	57	120	2,456	1,064	900	1,002	293	64	2,915	175	802	563	889	1,947
30	(G.27) Fishing and pearling	300	68	130	100	20	65	1,370	844	716	488	48	41	691	30	104	1	60	11
31	(G.28) Hunting ..	199	14	57	113	37	55	1,086	220	184	134	245	23	2,224	145	698	552	829	1,936
32	II. Exploitation of Minerals	206	..	8	29	..	..	403	21	228	41	6	1	..	..	..	..	..	..
33	3. Metallic minerals ..	..	..	..	..	..	..	6	3	8	2	1	..	..	..	..	..	..	..
34	(G.30) Iron	..	..	..	..	..	..	6	3	8	2	1	..	..	..	..	..	..	..
35	4. Non-metallic minerals ..	206	..	8	29	..	..	397	18	215	39	5	1	..	..	..	..	..	..
36	(G.35) Coal	..	..	..	..	..	..	..	..	..	..	..	..	..	..	..	..	..	..
37	(G.37) Building materials (including stone, materials for cement manufacture and clays)	75	..	2	13	..	..	328	15	195	27	5	..	..	..	..	..	..	..
38	(G.38) Mica	16	..	..	2	..	..	21	..	12	10	..	..	..	..	..	..	..	..
39	(G.40) Salt, saltpetre and other saline substances ..	115	..	6	14	..	..	48	3	8	2	..	1	..	..	..	..	..	..
40	**B.—Preparation and supply of material substances**	44,079	11,669	17,737	19,735	9,976	10,120	49,258	17,469	22,166	29,220	10,000	8,819	44,893	10,200	14,607	16,878	9,137	6,749
41	III. Industry	10,896	3,836	5,722	4,839	3,405	2,014	17,875	6,189	5,728	6,906	3,290	2,438	15,237	4,086	5,158	6,976	3,614	2,941
42	5. Textiles	3,519	1,032	1,504	1,179	1,289	571	6,743	1,404	1,425	1,885	711	292	3,752	1,044	581	1,882	338	214
43	(G.42) Cotton ginning, cleaning and pressing ..	137	184	17	292	89	169	560	318	282	272	110	20	324	160	72	240	20	71
44	(G.43) Cotton spinning, sizing and weaving ..	2,300	652	572	688	809	270	5,418	848	986	1,381	382	194	2,601	754	373	1,517	288	125
45	(G.45) Rope, twine, string and other fibres ..	68	72	30	41	11	15	147	24	22	18	34	3	211	..	51	..	7	..
46	(G.46) Wool carding spinning and weaving ..	924	144	842	158	418	117	284	51	76	112	89	39	385	180	60	125	14	18
47	(G.47) Silk spinning and weaving.	12	..	5	..	..	..	88	142	19	88	20	28	..	..	..	..	..	..
48	(G.48) Hair (Horse-hair), etc.	..	..	..	..	..	..	46	..	2	..	31	..	..	..	..	..	..	..

TABLE X.

Occupation or Means of Livelihood.

	OSMANABAD	Males	Females	RAICHUR	Males	Females	BIDAR	Males	Females
	Total Earners	160,152	51,955	Total Earners	192,057	81,402	Total Earners	189,534	62,730
	Total Working Dependents	72,739	74,795	Total Working Dependents	67,366	96,253	Total Working Dependents	59,431	73,683
	Total Non-working Dependents	124,598	206,829	Total Non-working Dependents	213,738	286,719	Total Non-working Dependents	197,291	290,956
	Total Population	357,489	333,579	Total Population	473,161	464,374	Total Population	446,256	427,359

Serial No.	Occupation	OSMANABAD: Total earners showing occupation as principal		Total working dependents		Total following occupation as subsidiary		RAICHUR: Total earners showing occupation as principal		Total working dependents		Total following occupation as subsidiary		BIDAR: Total earners showing occupation as principal		Total working dependents		Total following occupation as subsidiary	
		Males	Females	Males	Females	Males	Females	Males	Females	Males	Females	Males	Females	Males	Females	Males	Females	Males	Females
	1	92	93	94	95	96	97	98	99	100	101	102	103	104	105	106	107	108	109
49	(G.49) Dyeing, bleaching, printing, preparation and sponging of textiles ..	69	..	38	..	12	..	130	..	15	..	27	..	141	..	25	..	9	..
50	(G.50) Lace, crepe, embroideries, fringes, etc., and insufficiently described textiles	..	..	..	..	..	..	70	21	23	14	18	8	..	..	..	..	..	..
51	6. Hides, skins and hard materials from the animal kingdom	264	78	115	62	53	16	761	120	281	129	220	40	135	34	106	65	54	36
52	(G.51) Working in leather ..	251	78	115	62	53	16	691	120	257	129	202	40	98	34	106	65	54	36
53	(G.52) Furriers and persons occupied with feathers and bristles; brush makers ..	..	..	..	..	..	..	18	..	4	..	2	..	10	..	..	..	..	..
54	(G.53) Bone, ivory, horn shell, etc., workers (except buttons)	13	..	..	..	..	..	52	..	20	..	16	..	27	..	..	..	..	..
55	7. Wood	1,396	467	1,008	357	457	306	381	228	202	306	133	71	466	431	292	258	284	254
56	(G.54) Sawyers ..	150	..	76	..	..	..	40	..	15	..	..	..	26	..	..	..	..	..
57	(G.55) Carpenters, turners and joiners, etc. ..	607	109	400	50	76	40	299	101	126	155	119	51	324	289	248	209	177	208
58	(G.56) Basket-makers and other industries of woody materials, including leaves and thatchers and builders working with bamboo, reeds or similar materials ..	639	358	532	307	381	266	42	127	61	153	14	20	116	142	44	44	57	51
59	8. Metals	537	146	406	135	260	49	616	133	457	191	262	38	1,356	104	1,078	313	308	51
60	(G.57) Smelting, forging and rolling of iron and other metals	28	..	14	..	..	..	46	..	21	..	17	..	15	..	1	..	4	..
61	(G.58) Makers of arms, guns, etc.	..	..	..	..	..	..	..	..	..	..	..	..	..	..	..	..	..	..

TABLE X.

OCCUPATION OR MEANS OF LIVELIHOOD.

No.	Occupation	1	2	3	4	5	6	7	8	9	10	11	12	13	14	15	16	17	18
62	(G.59) Black-smiths, other workers in iron, makers of implements ..	337	146	206	105	160	28	333	98	108	161	93	26	577	56	330	158	223	31
63	(G.60) Workers in brass, copper and bell metals ..	84	..	12	20	5	10	155	35	313	80	134	12	636	48	659	155	59	20
64	(G.61) Workers in other metals, (except precious metals)	88	..	174	10	95	11	82	..	15	..	18	..	128	..	88	..	22	..
65	(G.62) Workers in mints, die-sinkers, etc	..	..	..	..	..	..	48	..	..	..	30	..	60	..	15	..	4	..
66	9 Ceramics ..	425	263	298	321	29	50	400	254	78	343	135	93	802	341	329	739	232	229
67	(G.63) Potters and makers of earthen ware ..	425	263	298	321	29	50	309	254	78	340	105	93	722	341	311	739	228	229
68	(G.64) Brick and tile makers																		
69	(G.65) Other workers in ceramics	..	..	..	..	..	..	52	..	..	..	..	..	20	..	3	..	..	..
70	10. Chemical products properly so-called and analogous	333	158	403	140	101	22	261	88	108	112	109	26	217	81	91	172	215	33
71	(G.66) Manufacture of matches, fireworks and other explosives ..	..	..	..	..	..	..	14	..	2	..	..	..	..	..	..	..	..	..
72	(G.67) Manufacture of aerated and mineral waters and ice	..	..	..	..	..	..	8	..	6	..	..	..	..	..	..	..	..	..
73	(G.68) Manufacture and refining of vegetable oils ..	333	158	403	140	101	22	224	84	88	108	109	26	207	81	91	172	210	33
74	(G.69) Manufacture and refining of mineral oils ..	..	..	..	..	..	..	7	4	4	4	..	..	10	..	..	..	5	..
75	(G.70) Others	..	..	..	..	..	..	8	..	8	..	..	..	..	..	..	..	..	..
76	11. Food Industries ..	46	31	18	63	9	18	265	76	114	126	112	44	63	56	26	88	16	18
77	(G.71) Rice pounders and huskers and flour grinders .	..	18	..	22	..	5	..	6	..	6	..	2	..	6	..	..	..	..
78	(G.72) Grain Parchers, etc.	..	8	..	6	..	2	..	12	..	3	..	4	..	3	..	..	..	..
79	(G.73) Butchers ..	46	..	18	..	9	..	94	..	55	..	70	..	53	..	16	..	16	..
80	(G.74) Makers of sugar, molasses and gur ..	..	..	..	..	..	..	18	3	3	6	2	2	..	15	..	18	..	3
81	(G.75) Sweetmeat and condiment makers ..	..	5	..	35	..	11	24	41	15	93	8	31	..	20	..	14	..	8
82	(G.76) Toddy drawers ..	..	..	..	..	..	..	60	..	21	..	17	..	..	..	..	..	..	..
83	(G.77) Brewers and distillers	..	..	..	..	..	..	12	..	3	..	..	..	..	..	..	..	..	..
84	(G.78) Manufacturers of tobacco	..	..	..	..	..	..	39	14	14	18	15	5	10	12	10	6	..	7
85	(G.80) Manufacturers of ganja	..	..	..	..	..	..	13	..	..	..	..	..	..	..	..	..	..	..
86	(G.81) Others ..	..	..	..	..	..	..	5	..	3	..	..	..	..	..	..	..	..	..
87	12. Industries of dress and toilet	3,417	1,337	1,044	2,242	726	788	6,485	2,481	2,485	2,382	842	915	7,217	1,695	2,182	3,042	1,736	1,742
88	(G.82) Boot, shoe, sandal and clog makers ..	1,061	374	283	477	161	369	971	109	395	56	175	..	3,645	361	657	1,121	646	709
89	(G.83) Tailors, milliners, dress makers and darners ..	1,051	319	339	551	186	210	3,078	510	1081	663	256	301	877	347	405	472	275	365
90	(G.84) Embroiderers, hat-makers and makers of other articles of wear ..	14	..	2	..	..	..	55	8	14	12	3	2	87	16	81	37	..	18
91	(G.85) Washing & cleaning..	697	332	140	800	200	133	1,283	1,682	612	1,417	368	526	1,548	431	637	859	470	365

TABLE X.

Occupation or Means of Livelihood.

	OSMANABAD		RAICHUR		BIDAR	
	Males	Females	Males	Females	Males	Females
Total Earners	160,152	51,955	192,057	81,402	189,534	62,720
Total Working Dependents	72,739	74,795	67,366	96,253	59,431	73,683
Total Non-Working Dependents	124,598	206,829	213,738	286,719	197,291	290,956
Total Population	357,489	333,579	473,161	464,374	446,256	427,359

Serial No.	Occupation	OSMANABAD: Total earners showing occupation as principal, Males	Females	Total working dependents, Males	Females	Total following occupation as subsidiary, Males	Females	RAICHUR: Total earners showing occupation as principal, Males	Females	Total working dependents, Males	Females	Total following occupation as subsidiary, Males	Females	BIDAR: Total earners showing occupation as principal, Males	Females	Total working dependents, Males	Females	Total following occupation as subsidiary, Males	Females
	1	92	93	94	95	96	97	98	99	100	101	102	103	104	105	106	107	108	109
92	(G.86) Barbers, hair dressers and wig-makers ..	578	312	280	414	170	76	1,036	172	383	234	40	86	1,021	540	386	553	345	285
93	(G.87) Other industries connected with toilet ..	16	..	..	..	..	..	62	..	..	..	..	..	39	..	16	..	..	..
94	13. Furniture industries ..	57	..	5	..	..	..	33	..	6	..	10	..	17	..	5	..	..	..
95	(G.88) Cabinet-makers, carriage painters, etc ..	57	..	5	..	..	..	27	..	5	..	10	..	17	..	5	..	..	..
96	(G.89) Upholsterers, tent makers, etc. ..	..	..	..	..	..	..	6	..	1	..	..	..	..	..	..	..	..	..
97	14. Building industries ..	497	130	487	162	375	104	1,134	843	322	332	500	578	545	145	227	200	334	43
98	(G.90) Lime burners, cement workers; excavators and well sinkers; stone cutters and dressers, brick layers and masons; builders (other than buildings made of bamboo and similar materials) painters, decorators of houses, tilers, plumbers, etc.	497	130	487	162	375	104	1,134	843	322	332	500	578	545	145	227	200	334	43
99	15. Construction of means of transport	81	..	20	..	3	..	116	..	27	..	18	..	95	..	20	..	2	..
100	(G.91) Persons engaged in making, assembling or repairing motor vehicles or cycles	12	..	2	..	..	..	31	..	8	..	2	..	15	..	2	..	..	..
101	(G.92) Carriage, cart, palki, etc., makers and wheelwrights	69	..	18	..	3	..	85	..	19	..	16	..	80	..	18	..	2	..
102	16. Production and transmission of physical force ..	..	..	..	..	..	..	..	..	..	..	..	..	..	..	..	..	..	..
103	(G.94) Heat, light, electricity, motive power, etc. Gas works and electric [illegible] power ..	..	..	..	..	..	..	..	..	..	..	..	..	..	..	..	..	..	..

104	17. Miscellaneous and undefined industries ..	324	174	414	178	103	90	671	562	223	598	238	341	572	155	221	272	145	321
105	(G.95) Printers, engravers, book binders, etc. ..	2	..	2	..	..	..	24	..	10	..	3	..	5	..	..	..	..	..
106	(G.96) Makers of musical instruments	1	..	1	..	..	..	6	..	1	..	..	..	2	..	..	..	..	..
107	(G.97) Makers of clocks and surgical or scientific instruments, etc.	6	..	7	..	..	..	14	..	3	..	1	..	6	..	2	..	..	..
108	(G.98) Makers of jewellery and ornaments ..	300	148	300	108	103	64	609	522	204	430	284	316	519	114	201	192	148	251
109	(G.99) Other miscellaneous and undefined industries (toymaking) taxidermy, etc.	15	26	14	70	..	26	18	40	5	162	..	25	30	41	18	80	2	70
110	(G.100) Scavenging ..	..	..	..	..	..	..	..	..	..	..	..	..	10	..	..	..	..	..
111	IV. Transport	13,191	2,684	4,932	9,917	2,498	5,959	11,271	5,223	6,019	8,712	2,699	3,648	8,084	2,555	4,064	4,699	2,214	1,844
112	19. Transport by water ..	85	51	22	269	8	160	142	42	79	86	24	21	..	..	..	..	..	..
113	(G.104) Labourers employed on harbours, docks, rivers and canals	85	51	22	269	8	160	142	42	79	86	24	21	..	..	..	..	..	..
114	20. Transport by road ..	3,440	887	1,023	1,431	303	312	8,178	4,021	3,998	6,468	1,214	2,141	3,866	1,095	912	440	169	168
115	(G.105) Persons (other than labourers) employed on the construction and maintenance of roads and bridges .	78	..	22	..	14	..	76	..	21	2	13	..	28	..	..	..	..	..
116	(G.106) Labourers employed on roads and bridges ..	2,625	576	624	982	225	172	3,836	3,928	2,607	6,418	798	2,122	1,168	723	607	260	108	157
117	(G.107) Owners, managers & employees (excluding personal servants) connected with mechanically driven vehicles (including trams)	180	311	27	449	16	140	49	11	12	15	30	3	31	..	14	..	..	..
118	(G.108) Owners, managers, employees (excluding personal servants) connected with other vehicles ..	515	..	335	..	45	..	3,652	82	1,219	38	338	16	1,895	372	252	180	15	6
119	(G.109) Palki, etc., bearers and owners	..	..	..	..	..	..	51	..	..	..	..	..	744	..	39	..	46	..
120	(G.110) Pack elephant, camel, mule, ass and bullock, owners and drivers ..	..	..	..	..	..	..	450	..	116	..	37	..	..	..	..	..	..	..
121	(G.111) Porters and messengers	42	..	15	..	8	..	64	..	18	..	8	..	..	..	..	..	..	..
122	21. Transport by rail ..	9,545	1,746	3,487	8,217	1,987	5,487	2,696	1,159	1,903	2,156	1,431	1,481	4,141	1,460	3,129	4,259	2,042	1,681
123	(G.112) Railway employees of all kind other than coolies	94	10	14	14	19	..	284	3	88	16	32	1	246	9	68	..	31	..
124	(G.113) Labourers employed on railway construction and maintenance and coolies and porters employed on railway premises ..	9,451	1,736	3,474	8,208	1,968	5,487	2,412	1,156	1,815	2,140	1,399	1,480	3,895	1,451	3,061	4,259	2,011	1,681
125	22. Post Office, Telegraph and Telephone services ..	121	..	400	..	200	..	255	1	44	2	30	..	77	..	23	..	8	..
126	(G.114) Post office, Telegraph and Telephone services	121	..	400	..	200	..	255	1	44	2	30	..	77	..	23	..	8	..
127	V. Trade	19,992	5,149	7,083	4,979	4,078	2,147	20,112	6,057	10,419	13,602	4,011	2,738	21,572	3,559	5,385	5,208	3,309	1,964

TABLE X.

Occupation or Means of Livelihood.

OSMANABAD

	Males	Females
Total Earners	160,152	51,955
Total Working Dependents	72,739	74,795
Total Non-Working Dependents	124,598	206,829
Total Population	357,489	333,579

Serial No.	Occupation	Total earners showing occupation as principal — Males	Total earners showing occupation as principal — Females	Total working dependents — Males	Total working dependents — Females	Total following occupation as subsidiary — Males	Total following occupation as subsidiary — Females
	1	92	93	94	95	96	97
128	23. Banks, establishments of credit, exchange and insurance	808	255	634	16	481	13
129	(G.115) Bank managers, money lenders, exchange and insurance agents, money changers and brokers and their employees	808	255	634	16	481	13
130	24. Brokerage commission and export	..	..	..	..	..	..
131	(G.116) Brokers, commission agents, commercial travellers, warehouse owners and employees	..	..	..	..	..	..
132	25. Trade in Textiles	1,262	316	323	162	184	73
133	(G.117) Trade in piece goods wool, cotton, silk, hair and other textiles	1,262	316	323	162	184	73
134	26. Trade in skins, leather and furs	..	..	..	..	..	..
135	(G.118) Trade in skins, leather, furs, feathers, horn, etc., and the articles made from these	..	..	..	..	..	..
136	27. Trade in Wood	..	18	..	24	..	..
137	(G.119) Trade in wood (not fire-wood)	..	..	..	..	..	..
138	(G.120) Trade in barks	..	..	..	..	..	..
139	(G.121) Trade in bamboos and canes	..	18	..	24	..	..
140	(G.122) Trade in thatches and other forest produce	..	..	..	..	..	..
141	28. Trade in metals	3	..	2	..	..	..

RAICHUR

	Males	Females
Total Earners	192,057	81,402
Total Working Dependents	67,366	96,253
Total Non-working Dependents	213,738	286,719
Total Population	473,161	464,374

Serial No.	Occupation	Total earners showing occupation as principal — Males	Total earners showing occupation as principal — Females	Total working dependents — Males	Total working dependents — Females	Total following occupation as subsidiary — Males	Total following occupation as subsidiary — Females
	1	98	99	100	101	102	103
128	23. Banks, establishments of credit, exchange and insurance	415	38	26	58	115	11
129	(G.115) Bank managers, money lenders, exchange and insurance agents, money changers and brokers and their employees	415	38	26	58	115	11
130	24. Brokerage commission and export	..	..	..	..	..	..
131	(G.116) Brokers, commission agents, commercial travellers, warehouse owners and employees	..	..	..	..	..	..
132	25. Trade in Textiles	2,985	963	1,494	1,565	702	351
133	(G.117) Trade in piece goods wool, cotton, silk, hair and other textiles	2,985	963	1,494	1,565	702	351
134	26. Trade in skins, leather and furs	163	54	121	132	39	19
135	(G.118) Trade in skins, leather, furs, feathers, horn, etc., and the articles made from these	163	54	121	132	39	19
136	27. Trade in Wood	57	18	16	17	..	..
137	(G.119) Trade in wood (not fire-wood)	30	..	14	..	..	..
138	(G.120) Trade in barks	17	6	..	12	..	..
139	(G.121) Trade in bamboos and canes	6	12	..	5	..	..
140	(G.122) Trade in thatches and other forest produce	4	..	2	..	..	..
141	28. Trade in metals	26	..	3	..	..	..

BIDAR

	Males	Females
Total Earners	189,534	62,730
Total Working Dependents	59,481	73,683
Total Non-working Dependents	197,291	290,956
Total Population	446,256	427,359

Serial No.	Occupation	Total earners showing occupation as principal — Males	Total earners showing occupation as principal — Females	Total working dependents — Males	Total working dependents — Females	Total following occupation as subsidiary — Males	Total following occupation as subsidiary — Females
	1	104	105	106	107	108	109
128	23. Banks, establishments of credit, exchange and insurance	1,863	239	180	35	120	21
129	(G.115) Bank managers, money lenders, exchange and insurance agents, money changers and brokers and their employees	1,863	239	180	35	120	21
130	24. Brokerage commission and export	..	..	..	..	..	..
131	(G.116) Brokers, commission agents, commercial travellers, warehouse owners and employees	..	..	..	..	..	..
132	25. Trade in Textiles	865	117	216	152	72	32
133	(G.117) Trade in piece goods wool, cotton, silk, hair and other textiles	865	117	216	152	72	32
134	26. Trade in skins, leather and furs	263	33	187	99	32	18
135	(G.118) Trade in skins, leather, furs, feathers, horn, etc., and the articles made from these	263	33	187	99	32	18
136	27. Trade in Wood	103	13	27	30	5	3
137	(G.119) Trade in wood (not fire-wood)	45	6	15	18	5	..
138	(G.120) Trade in barks	24	3	8	4	..	1
139	(G.121) Trade in bamboos and canes	16	4	4	8	..	2
140	(G.122) Trade in thatches and other forest produce	18	..	..	..	..	..
141	28. Trade in metals	15	..	..	..	..	..

142	(G.123) Trade in metals, machinery, knives, tools, etc. ..	3	..	2	..	..	..	26	..	3	..	..	..	15	..	..	..	..	..
143	29. Trade in pottery, bricks and tiles	16	177	29	189	8	41	98	136	26	359	15	28	36	19	38	136	..	12
144	(G.124) Trade in pottery, bricks and tiles ..	16	177	29	189	8	41	98	136	26	359	15	28	36	19	38	136	..	12
145	30. Trade in chemical products	5	..	..	..	..	..	18	..	4	..	..	..	10	..	..	4	..	..
146	(G.125) Drugs, dyes, paints petroleum, explosives, etc.	5	..	..	..	..	..	18	..	4	..	..	..	10	..	..	4	..	..
147	31. Hotels, cafes, restaurants, etc.	380	107	180	119	28	20	1,186	1,003	698	1,151	454	449	769	465	355	368	181	217
148	(G.126) Vendors of wine, liquors, aerated waters and ice	362	99	160	88	28	16	1,150	962	671	1,103	440	433	745	398	355	325	181	207
149	(G.127) Owners and managers of hotels, cook shops, sarais, etc., (and employees)	18	..	20	..	..	..	39	13	27	38	14	16	24	26	..	28	..	10
150	(G.128) Hawkers of drink and food stuffs ..	..	8	..	31	..	4	..	28	..	10	..	..	..	41	..	15	..	..
151	32. Other trade in food stuff	4,356	958	2,818	1,520	1,250	460	8,977	2,290	3,500	5,567	1,523	688	5,211	873	1,654	1,104	574	315
152	(G.129) Grain and pulse dealer	1,865	461	1,341	670	580	248	4,895	1,633	2,442	2,748	962	321	2,670	365	826	418	215	102
153	(G.130) Dealers in sweetmeat , sugar and spice	360	143	149	163	56	28	160	85	70	193	22	32	116	85	50	164	21	30
154	(G.131) Dealers in dairy product, egg and poultry ..	159	295	76	498	28	168	282	464	69	2,527	33	291	374	203	192	168	193	126
155	(G.132) Dealers in animal for food	18	..	..	..	..	..	56	..	..	..	..	..	98	3	16	9	..	..
156	(G.133) Dealers in fodder for animal	24	..	3	..	..	..	40	..	2	..	..	..	21	6	..	8	..	..
157	(G.134) Dealers in other food stuffs	1,899	59	1,249	189	586	16	1,796	108	518	99	321	44	1,884	211	567	347	145	48
158	(G.135) Dealers in tobacco .	15	..	..	..	..	..	1,695	..	392	..	181	..	16	..	..	..	..	..
159	(G.136) Dealers in opium ..	4	..	..	..	..	..	14	..	..	..	..	..	4	..	..	..	..	..
160	(G.137) Dealers in ganja ..	12	..	..	..	..	..	39	..	7	..	..	..	28	..	3	..	..	..
161	33. Trade in clothing and toilet, articles ..	60	..	27	..	4	..	26	..	14	..	..	..	34	5	17	12	2	..
162	(G.138) Trade in ready-made clothing and other article of dress and the toilet (hats, umbrellas, socks, ready-made shoes , perfumes, etc.)	60	..	27	..	4	..	26	..	14	..	..	..	34	5	17	12	2	..
163	34. Trade in furniture ..	24	63	10	98	2	20	33	41	4	32	..	8	40	36	8	40	..	15
164	(G.139) Trade in furniture carpets, curtain and bedding	3	..	..	..	..	..	7	..	..	..	..	..	16	..	..	..	..	..
165	(G.140) Hardware, cooking utensil, porcelain crockery, glass ware bottle, articles for gardening, etc. ..	21	63	10	98	2	20	26	41	4	32	..	8	24	36	8	49	..	15
166	35. Trade in building material	12	..	2	..	..	..	18	..	2	..	..	..	466	..	141	..	39	..
167	(G.141) Trade in building material (other than brick tile and woody material)	12	..	2	..	..	..	18	..	2	..	..	..	466	..	141	..	39	..
168	36. Trade in means of transport	136	..	31	..	7	..	292	..	49	..	68	..	227	18	54	27	24	4

TABLE X.

Occupation or Means of Livelihood.

	OSMANABAD Males	OSMANABAD Females	RAICHUR Males	RAICHUR Females	BIDAR Males	BIDAR Females
Total Earners	160,152	51,955	192.057	81,402	189,534	62,730
Total Working Dependents	72,739	74,795	67.366	96,253	59,431	73,683
Total Non-working Dependents	124,508	206,829	213,738	286,719	197,291	290,956
Total Population	357,489	333,579	473,161	464,374	446,256	427,359

Serial No.	Occupation	OSMANABAD						RAICHUR						BIDAR					
		Total earners showing occupation as principal		Total working dependents		Total following occupation as subsidiary		Total earners showing occupation as principal		Total working dependents		Total following occupation as subsidiary		Total earners showing occupation as principal		Total working dependents		Total following occupation as subsidiary	
		Males	Females	Males	Females	Males	Females	Males	Females	Males	Females	Males	Females	Males	Females	Males	Females	Males	Females
	1	92	93	94	95	96	97	98	99	100	101	102	103	104	105	106	107	108	109
169	(G.142) Dealers and hirers, in mechanical transport motors, cycles, etc. ..	16	..	..	..	..	..	68	..	21	..	7	..	24	..	6	..	3	..
170	(G.143) Dealers and hirers in other carriages, carts, boats, etc.	120	..	31	..	7	..	190	..	28	..	51	..	148	18	48	27	21	4
171	(G.144) Dealers and hirers of elephants, camels, horses cattle, asses, mules, etc.	..	..	..	..	..	..	34	..	..	..	10	..	55	..	..	..	..	..
172	37. Trade in fuel ..	2,480	683	1,890	1,121	821	372	156	62	77	88	20	14	118	21	26	28	14	7
173	(G.145) Dealers in firewood charcoal, coal, cowdung, etc.	2,480	683	1,890	1,121	821	372	156	62	77	88	20	14	118	21	26	28	14	7
174	38. Trade in articles of luxury and those pertaining to letters and the arts and sciences	186	49	89	168	26	28	365	313	215	491	26	69	710	402	281	902	187	215
175	(G.146) Dealers in precious stones jewellery (real and imitation) clocks, optical instruments, etc ..	..	..	..	..	..	..	5	2	3	6	2	..	33	6	21	33	17	..
176	(G.147) Dealers in common bangles bead necklaces, fans, small articles, toys hunting and fishing, tackle, flowers, etc. ..	170	49	89	168	26	28	312	311	185	485	21	69	640	391	248	869	167	215
177	(G.148) Publishers, booksellers stationers, dealers in music, pictures, musical instruments and curiosities	16	..	..	..	..	..	48	..	27	..	3	..	37	5	12	..	3	..
178	39. Trade of other sorts ..	10,264	2,528	1,048	1,562	1,262	1,120	5,297	1,139	4,170	4,142	1,049	1,101	10,842	1,318	2,201	2,257	2,059	1,105
179	(G.149) Dealers in rags, stable refuse and, etc. ..	..	..	..	..	..	..	16	18	..	41	..	..	31	..	16	..	4	..
180	(G.150) General store-keepers and shop keepers, otherwise unspecified ..	10,063	2,434	1,040	1,463	1,202	1,059	5,167	1,062	4,168	4,077	1,028	1,085	10,790	1,318	2,178	2,257	2,055	1,105

181 (G.151) Itinerant traders, pedlars, and hawkers (of other than food, etc.) ..	201	89	8	99	60	61	102	59	2	24	18	16	11	..	8	..	..	..
182 (G.152) Other trades (including farmers of pounds, tools and markets) ..	..	..	..	..	..	..	12	..	..	..	3	..	10	..	4	..	..	..
183 C. Public Administration and Liberal Arts ..	5,679	220	3,978	367	1,186	103	8,085	404	2,481	1,451	983	250	6,851	697	3,405	1,045	1,669	532
184 VI. Public Force ..	382	5	141	18	16	1	571	..	358	..	97	..	687	..	261	5	40	..
185 40. Army	..	..	..	..	..	..	60	..	58	..	29	..	87	..	61	..	40	..
186 (G.153) Imperial Army ..	..	..	..	..	..	..	..	..	..	..	..	..	..	..	..	..	..	..
187 (G.154) State Army ..	..	..	..	..	..	..	60	..	58	..	29	..	87	..	61	..	40	..
188 43. Police	382	5	141	18	16	1	511	..	300	..	68	..	600	..	200	5	..	..
189 (G.157) Police... ..	280	5	56	3	6	..	381	..	158	..	21	..	325	..	46	5	..	..
190 (G.158) Village watchmen ..	102	..	85	15	10	1	130	..	142	..	47	..	275	..	154	..	..	..
191 VII. Public Administration .	2,101	6	918	50	134	2	4,047	26	805	4	156	..	2,058	11	314	2	94	1
192 44. Public Administration .	2,101	6	918	50	134	2	4,047	26	805	4	156	..	2,058	11	314	2	94	1
193 (G.159) Imperial service ..	..	..	..	..	..	..	8	2	4	..	..	..	..	..	..	..	..	..
194 (G.160) State service ..	395	3	147	11	41	..	365	10	142	..	26	..	289	8	115	..	15	..
195 (G.160a) Service of other Indian and foreign States..	..	..	..	..	..	..	7	..	1	..	..	..	..	..	..	..	..	..
196 (G.161) Municipal and other local (not village) service..	262	..	126	18	27	..	465	..	212	..	37	..	370	..	48	..	22	..
197 (G.162) Village officials and servants other than watchmen	1,444	3	645	21	66	2	3,202	14	446	4	93	..	1,399	3	151	2	57	1
198 VIII-Professions and Liberal Arts	3,196	209	2,919	299	1,036	100	3,467	378	1,318	1,447	730	250	4,106	686	2,830	1,038	1,535	531
199 45. Religion	2,518	68	2,592	211	874	66	1,781	171	1,189	1,259	572	206	3,613	646	2,610	935	1,339	448
200 (G.163) Priests, ministers, etc.	2,118	68	2,486	181	848	66	1,641	171	1,106	1,207	551	202	3,413	646	2,600	914	1,339	448
201 (G.164) Monks, nuns, religious mendicants ..	..	..	..	..	..	..	15	..	..	..	..	..	12	..	..	..	..	..
202 (G.165) Other religious workers	72	..	..	..	..	..	53	..	..	..	..	..	64	..	..	..	..	..
203 (G.166) Servants in religious edifices, burial and burning grounds, pilgrim conductors, circumcisors, etc.	328	..	106	30	26	..	72	..	33	52	21	4	124	..	10	21	..	..
204 46. Law	294	..	76	..	46	..	321	6	15	..	10	..	284	..	105	..	112	..
205 (G.167) Lawyers of all kinds including Qazis, Law Agents and Mukhtiars ..	273	..	76	..	46	..	303	6	15	..	10	..	262	..	105	..	110	..
206 (G.168) Lawyers' clerks, petition-writers, etc. ..	21	..	..	..	..	..	18	..	..	..	..	..	22	..	..	..	2	..
207 47. Medicine	72	54	47	22	18	12	224	77	18	52	14	15	45	20	28	33	32	17
208 (G.169) Registered medical practitioners including oculists	2	3	1	..	..	..	14	3	1	3	2	..	5	1	..	..	3	..

TABLE X.

Occupation or Means of Livelihood.

OSMANABAD	Males	Females
Total Earners	160,152	51,955
Total Working Dependents ..	72,739	74,7[illegible]5
Total Non-Working Dependents ..	124,398	206,829
Total Population	357,489	333,379

RAICHUR	Males	Females
Total Earners ..	192,057	81,402
Total Working Dependents ..	67,366	96,253
Total Non-working Dependents	213,738	286,719
Total Population ..	473,161	464,374

BIDAR	Males	Females
Total Earners ..	189,534	62,720
Total Working Dependents ..	59,431	73,683
Total Non-working Dependents	197,291	290,956
Total Population ..	446,256	427,359

Serial No.	Occupation	OSMANABAD: Total earners showing occupation as principal, Males	Females	Total working dependents, Males	Females	Total following occupation as subsidiary, Males	Females	RAICHUR: Total earners showing occupation as principal, Males	Females	Total working dependents, Males	Females	Total following occupation as subsidiary, Males	Females	BIDAR: Total earners showing occupation as principal, Male	Females	Total working dependents, Males	Females	Total following occupation as subsidiary, Males	Females
	1	92	93	94	95	96	97	98	99	100	101	102	103	104	105	106	107	108	109
209	(G.170) Other persons practising the healing arts without being registered ..	56	..	37	2	4	1	170	..	12	..	11	..	34	..	8	..	22	..
210	(G.171) Dentists ..	2	..	..	..	..	..	4	..	1	..	1	..	1	..	..	..	..	..
211	(G.172) Midwives, vaccinaters, compounders, nurses, masseurs, etc. ..	10	51	9	20	14	11	33	74	4	49	..	15	5	19	20	33	8	17
212	(G.173) Veterinary surgeons	2	..	..	..	..	..	3	..	..	..	..	..	..	..	..	..	..	..
213	48. Instruction ..	52	69	64	36	14	14	505	56	35	24	15	7	81	20	3	22	2	14
214	(G. 174) Professors and teachers of all kinds ..	50	65	44	36	14	14	459	40	33	20	15	7	70	20	3	20	2	11
215	(G.175) Clerks and servants connected with education .	2	4	20	..	..	..	46	16	2	4	..	..	11	..	..	2	..	3
216	49. Letters arts and sciences (other than 44) ..	260	18	140	30	84	8	636	68	111	112	119	22	83	..	84	48	50	57
217	(G.176) Public scribes, stenographers, etc ..	4	..	..	..	..	..	18	..	2	..	2	..	..	..	..	..	..	..
218	(G.177) Architects, surveyors, engineers, and their employees (not being State servants)	2	..	..	..	..	..	2	..	..	..	..	..	..	..	..	..	..	..
219	(G.178) Authors, editors, journalists and photographers	8	..	2	..	2	..	21	..	1	..	8	..	4	..	..	..	..	..
220	(G.179) Artists, sculpters and image-makers ..	58	..	24	..	22	..	68	..	11	..	21	..	21	..	20	7	8	9
221	(G.180) Scientists (astronomers, botanists), etc. ..	..	..	..	..	..	..	3	..	..	..	1	..	..	..	..	..	..	..
222	(G.181) Horoscope casters, astrologers, fortune tellers, wizards, witches and mediums	41	..	12	..	20	..	188	6	35	12	51	..	23	..	16	17	14	21

TABLE X.
OCCUPATION OR MEANS OF LIVELIHOOD.

No.	Occupation																		
223	(G.182) Musicians (composers and performers other than military) actors, dancers, etc. ..	55	12	71	15	25	6	176	58	40	90	32	20	30	..	32	21	26	18
224	(G.183) Managers and employees of places of public entertainments, race courses, societies, clubs. ..	2	..	..	..	2	..	16	..	4	..	3	..	..	..	..	..	..	..
225	(G.184) Conjurors, acrobats, recitors, exhibitors of curiosities and wild animals, etc.	90	6	31	15	13	2	144	6	18	10	6	2	5	..	16	3	2	9
226	**D. Miscellaneous** ..	**11,424**	**5,512**	**10,920**	**11,097**	**6,494**	**2,372**	**10,881**	**3,551**	**4,004**	**4,272**	**753**	**1,022**	**25,352**	**8,454**	**8,113**	**13,458**	**7,989**	**7,786**
227	IX. Persons living on their income	27	2	26	6	3	1	82	2	68	4	8	1	78	9	103	6	8	..
228	50. Persons living principally on their income ..	27	2	26	6	3	1	82	2	68	4	8	1	78	9	103	6	8	..
229	(G.185) Proprietors (other than of agricultural land), fund and scholarships holders and pensioners ..	27	2	26	6	3	1	82	2	68	4	8	1	78	9	103	6	8	..
230	X. Domestic service ..	5,627	2,575	7,627	7,104	4,582	1,144	5,411	1,746	2,436	2,323	371	492	12,204	3,495	4,421	8,351	5,119	5,404
231	51. Domestic service ..	5,627	2,375	7,027	7,104	4,582	1,144	5,411	1,746	2,486	2,323	371	492	12,204	3,495	4,421	8,351	5,119	5,404
232	(G.186) Private motor drivers and cleaners ..	18	..	..	..	..	..	266	28	104	21	42	10	21	..	..	..	..	..
233	(G.187) Other domestic service	5,609	2,575	7,627	7,104	4,582	1,144	5,145	1,718	2,332	2,302	329	482	12,183	3,495	4,421	8,351	5,119	5,404
234	XI. Insufficiently defined occupations	3,333	1,351	2,584	2,208	1,333	251	3,020	309	936	612	270	362	10,183	2,306	3,021	3,060	2,165	1,861
235	52. General terms which do not indicate a definite occupation	3,333	1,351	2,584	2,208	1,333	251	3,020	309	936	612	270	362	10,183	2,306	3,021	3,060	2,165	1,861
236	(G.188) Manufacturers, businessmen and contractors otherwise unspecified ..	149	57	99	..	116	..	448	152	72	275	67	125	183	316	21	160	65	80
237	(G.189) Cashiers, accountants, book-keepers, clerks and other employees in unspecified offices and warehouses and shops ..	81	..	15	..	24	..	120	..	63	..	16	..	41	..	12	..	3	..
238	(G.190) Mechanics other wise unspecified ..	20	..	4	..	3	..	42	..	15	..	13	..	17	..	2	..	1	..
239	(G.191) Labourers and workmen otherwise unspecified .	3,083	1,294	2,466	2,208	1,190	251	2,415	157	786	337	174	237	9,942	1,990	2,986	2,900	2,096	1,781
240	XII. Unproductive ..	2,437	1,584	683	1,779	576	976	2,368	1,494	564	1,333	104	167	2,887	2,644	568	2,041	697	521
241	53. Inmates of jails, asylums and alms houses ..	..	..	53	..	..	.	..	..	164	25	..	..	..	..	13	4	..	..
242	(G.192) Inmates of jails, asylums and alms houses ..	..	..	53	..	..	..	..	..	164	25	..	..	..	..	13	4	..	..
243	54. Beggars, vagrants, prostitutes	2,437	1,580	630	1,779	576	972	2,292	1,494	400	1,308	104	167	2,885	2,644	535	2,037	607	521
244	(G.193) Beggars and vagrants	2,409	1,484	623	1,628	572	972	2,268	1,370	400	1,033	104	107	2,885	2,486	539	1,895	696	521
245	(G.194) Procurers and prostitutes	28	96	7	151	4	..	24	124	..	275	..	60	..	158	16	142	1	..
246	55. Other unclassified non-productive industries ..	..	4	..	..	..	4	76	..	..	..	..	..	2	..	..	..	..	..
247	(G.195) Other unclassified non-productive industries	..	4	..	..	..	4	76	..	..	..	..	..	2	..	..	..	..	..

Table XI.

OCCUPATION BY CASTE, TRIBE AND RACE.

Note :—1. The selection and grouping of castes of this table follow the tables, XVII, VIII and XIV ; but only more important castes have been shown here.

2. Figures in columns 9 and 10 , 13 and 14 , 15 and 16 are intended to throw light on the extent to which traditional caste occupations are followed ; while columns 11 and 12 show how far castes have retained their traditional avocations as subsidiary means of livelihood beside other functions. The figures in column 17 onwards are for actual workers (i. e. earners and working dependents) and are exclusive of the figures shown in columns 9,10,13, and 14 as following traditional occupations. Asterisks have been placed in those columns which are affected by this arrangement.

TABLE XI.
OCCUPATION BY SELECTED CASTE, TRIBE & RACE.

TABLE
Occupation by Selected

S. No.	Caste, Tribe and Race	Traditional occupation	Population dealt with						Number of earners whose traditional caste occupation was returned as their			
			Earners		Working Dependents		Non-working Dependents		Principal means of livelihood		Subsidiary means of livelihood	
			Males	Females	Males	Females	Males	Females	Males	Females	Males	Females
	1	2	3	4	5	6	7	8	9	10	11	12
	HINDU (Brahmanic)											
1	Bedar (Bendar)	Fishermen and hunters	23,801	27,552	8,159	10,013	87,347	80,902	9,331	20,150	3,293	5,043
2	Bhoi (Besta)	Do	67,290	35,550	13,965	13,417	60,614	94,437	30,770	28,680	5,508	7,038
3	Brahman	Priests	68,996	16,792	15,732	15,294	111,926	147,728	12,795	16,337	10,803	24,487
4	Burud (Medari)	Basket makers	3,227	4,278	1,257	1,886	14,570	10,059	2,030	3,866	100	323
5	Darzi (Simpi)	Tailors	19,466	9,507	3,312	5,466	9,442	16,438	5,660	8,437	369	2,965
6	Dhobi (Chakala)	Washermen	65,769	55,036	13,931	16,340	59,090	59,326	48,786	38,752	2,461	24,069
7	Hajjam (Mangala)	Barbers	30,878	20,575	10,440	9,485	42,537	45,830	18,260	12,440	673	6,502
8	Hatkar	Cultivators	8,081	3,970	3,375	5,368	12,881	11,493	6,746	2,816	196	2,599
9	Julahi (Sale, Devang)	Weavers	139,797	60,863	30,695	27,301	41,311	106,914	110,293	52,274	2,063	13,007
10	Kalal (Eadiga, Goundla)	Toddy drawers and liquor sellors	105,326	70,295	33,000	30,904	82,311	105,000	80,232	65,163	1,624	18,195
11	Kapu (Kunbi)	Cultivators	218,815	63,807	128,156	64,789	143,212	324,141	133,391	37,545	3,519	35,661
12	Kasab (Aray, Katika)	Butchers	8,560	5,794	2,996	2,667	31,245	29,903	5,318	4,028	391	1,171
13	Kasar (Kanchari)	Brass and Copper smiths	2,807	2,718	1,429	2,037	14,800	11,939	2,428	2,214	93	191
14	Kumbhar (Kummari)	Potters	36,292	27,065	10,339	9,696	34,288	36,468	28,871	16,935	363	6,565
15	Koli	Cultivators	14,087	9,613	7,600	3,458	7,577	10,137	7,210	363	115	10,545
16	Komati	Traders	63,210	30,101	23,056	22,584	77,166	92,794	54,721	26,325	1,639	14,001
17	Kshatriya (Rajput)	Soldiers	18,881	8,206	5,470	6,271	21,905	27,701	9,531	7,534	98	2,813
18	Kurma	Cultivators	23,087	14,723	12,905	5,970	53,654	62,979	19,921	9,345	133	3,680
19	Lingayat	Traders	150,875	62,350	32,495	44,394	214,734	284,491	109,293	41,019	2,369	27,514
20	Lohar (Kammari)	Black-smiths	20,638	8,879	10,004	6,590	20,723	26,626	18,331	6,192	671	3,714
21	Mali	Gardeners	14,340	18,531	8,009	13,758	29,262	18,708	12,961	15,492	93	1,967
22	Maratha	Cultivators	245,300	197,183	175,983	184,211	329,799	359,082	237,309	157,392	4,214	63,926
23	Panchal	Artisans	12,484	9,976	5,120	12,598	18,103	11,593	12,191	9,892	61	291
24	Perka	Carriers	10,495	7,611	2,232	2,280	12,996	15,890	7,174	2,510	28	1,086
25	Rangrez (Rangari)	Dyers and weavers	3,174	2,281	1,391	3,779	10,310	5,866	2,369	1,973	122	1155
26	Satani (Ayyawar)	Religious beggars	13,824	3,859	4,104	6,392	12,437	13,780	13,024	3,560	495	537
27	Sunar (Ausala, Kamsala)	Goldsmiths	29,599	16,843	9,632	11,365	33,319	37,133	23,470	12,858	5,719	6,101
28	Sutar (Wadla, Bade).	Carpenters	25,711	12,889	7,142	9,144	25,421	30,543	19,228	10,721	5,097	4,968
29	Telaga, (Munnur and Mutrasi)	Cultivators	184,664	93,458	48,474	70,064	215,667	353,863	146,291	82,612	30,891	9,772
30	Teli (Gandla)	Oil mongers	18,707	15,440	3,706	7,021	16,260	11,921	16,308	13,256	1,777	2,007
31	Uppara (Govandi)	Masons	16,071	10,343	4,223	5,452	19,329	24,074	12,391	7,699	1,627	2,298
32	Velama	Cultivators	10,704	8,622	2,451	4,289	18,062	12,860	6,041	6,535	3,639	2,766
33	Viswabrahman	Artisans	6,870	1,661	2,031	1,629	5,392	9,159	3,321	1,520	2,813	812
34	Waddar	Earth diggers and stone breakers	31,156	19,690	8,950	8,616	29,079	39,691	25,338	14,536	2,846	4,028
35	Wanjari (Banjara)	Cultivators	16,391	11,061	4,196	9,120	18,378	11,790	9,999	8,407	9,005	5,208
36	Yadava (Golla, Gowli, Dhangar)	Cowherds and shepherds	239,405	155,266	84,254	116,111	147,805	185,563	201,511	144,822	38,446	19,729
	ADI-HINDU.											
37	Dher (Mala, Mahar)	Menial service	124,417	71,382	92,269	91,744	335,946	360,781	81,583	14,089	34,304	31,035
38	Madiga (Chambhar Mochi, Mang)	Do and tanners	131,173	82,281	106,791	92,804	401,238	466,810	86,551	36,276	38,656	20,961
	TRIBAL.											
39	Bhil	Hunters	4,340	2,447	1,771	3,881	1,440	1,223	585	1,640	418	8
40	Chenchu	Do	733	241	200	196	157	737	198	210	4	10
41	Erakala (Kaikadi)	Sooth sayers and basket makers	12,069	8,159	5,075	7,676	14,858	11,335	8,338	5,360	822	751
42	Gond	Cultivators	20,964	15,877	8,219	16,831	27,865	23,524	15,282	10,080	6,435	4,888
43	Lambadi (Banjari)	Carriers	36,690	44,118	18,638	22,889	98,528	79,653	5,760	26,812	8,414	6,838
44	**Muslim**	..	396,080	117,389	165,035	87,482	230,320	538,360	..	..	..	..
	CHRISTIAN.											
45	Anglo-Indian	..	1,177	428	322	226	689	528	..	..	..	..
46	Europeans and Allied Races.	..	1,911	7	6	13	351	339	..	..	..	..
47	Indian Christian	..	22,998	16,209	8,249	10,265	43,741	48,923	..	..	..	..

XI.

TABLE XI.

Caste, Tribe and Race.

OCCUPATION BY SELECTED CASTE, TRIBE & RACE.

Number of dependents following their traditional occupation		No. of actual workers returning their traditional occupation as their principal means of livelihood who had some subsidiary occupation		RECORDED PRINCIPAL OCCUPATION OF ACTUAL WORKERS — I. Exploitation of Animals and Vegetation											
				Income from rent of land		Cultivators of all kinds		Agents, managers of landed estates, planters, forest officers, their clerks, etc.		Field Labourers, wood cutters, etc.		Raisers of Live stock, milkmen and herdsmen		Fishing and hunting	
Males	Females	Males	Females	Males	Females	Males	Females	Males	Females	Males	Females	Males	Females	Males	Females
13	14	15	16	17	18	19	20	21	22	23	24	25	26	27	28
6,526	9,160	1,124	121	1,034	104	2,260	1,891	83	2	3,741	2,209	1,239	621	*	*
8,852	10,101	2,561	226	519	289	13,952	800	98	28	14,188	4,987	1,068	122	*	*
6,202	14,801	1,763	2	5,609	1,551	13,398	2,294	970	326	477	1,354	892	126	..	..
820	732	244	11	21	6	250	18	..	..	369	466	236	2	..	..
1,865	2,688	568	25	176	447	805	302	28	3	228	1,089	172	5	15	1
4,674	16,522	286	260	1,144	299	6,205	1,874	391	4	5,647	8,545	1,017	144	447	104
5,922	3,210	2,029	206	578	276	3,980	1,001	180	..	2,734	8,280	411	82	38	33
1,427	1,820	171	625	77	366	*	*	50	8	670	1,200	419	91	16	8
29,049	10,418	302	12	1,491	812	5,963	1,620	53	7	6,673	15,775	1,926	146	213	32
13,128	15,121	768	210	2,601	1,166	13,092	3,577	717	..	13,352	5,072	2,893	701	278	5
83,554	16,432	1,564	1,254	6,707	4,616	*	5,193	5,196	73	65,100	38,506	9,452	2,747	78	276
2,138	1,315	265	28	69	43	683	292	4	..	1,061	1,716	142	42	..	..
1,205	1,570	85	14	83	8	49	112	4	..	53	62	13	10	8	23
3,725	9,534	924	502	837	190	3,531	1,480	38	..	2,107	5,298	734	107	87	..
2,030	134	268	347	1,042	180	*	*	610	35	5,057	8,359	1,437	172	297	185
13,109	19,267	1,002	1,341	2,757	608	5,509	1,220	210	18	556	1,544	553	47	..	..
2,392	3,456	1,893	..	1,814	776	2,342	386	568	10	671	713	368	101	45	..
8,208	3,887	1,361	361	461	219	*	*	137	11	1,415	4,170	1,775	382	28	8
12,256	33,102	3,169	1,401	7,306	1,147	20,166	6,677	1,293	383	6,682	15,857	2,080	928	..	..
8,364	4,702	241	153	379	279	1,385	539	21	..	680	2,274	..	188	..	..
4,562	10,143	359	210	1,224	219	*	*	231	68	853	1,025	80	27	79	42
113,113	178,827	4,508	3,512	4,145	1,888	*	*	1,705	447	27,550	28,265	3,993	1,430	359	32
4,756	12,283	312	285	42	18	165	80	8	..	199	83	1	5	..	..
1,000	1,601	121	25	64	317	633	393	106	7	1,305	3,420	286	140	8	17
689	3,120	61	126	85	24	268	118	15	..	332	152	5	..	5	..
3,661	5,331	201	54	94	38	286	30	67	..	80	290	75	10	..	..
5,633	9,101	593	83	813	472	3,171	60	93	..	626	2,667	354	56	..	..
4,558	5,418	816	26	494	376	2,378	70	137	..	2,681	2,234	314	99	..	..
14,560	18,126	3,063	1,198	4,798	2,783	*	*	1,213	29	29,702	34,754	6,520	2,068	1,786	47
2,028	5,013	721	56	270	158	1,204	20	94	..	657	1,297	41	18	8	..
2,434	2,707	124	25	162	240	1,123	25	180	..	1,443	2,733	248	135	42	..
1,100	2,515	316	253	946	229	*	*	86	..	2,375	1,871	593	75	81	..
1,322	1,075	83	68	164	14	1,685	5	80	..	595	286	82	12	..	..
5,539	5,261	120	253	186	195	2,042	3	13	..	1,870	4,037	384	416	28	..
1,447	5,590	221	117	1,019	214	*	*	250	8	1,986	2,116	1,044	66	112	54
39,361	55,881	923	563	5,892	2,491	23,468	740	324	..	17,209	41,404	*	*	105	..
43,610	15,765	265	110	8,092	905	15,532	18,478	157	..	35,969	74,236	689	863	595	127
49,597	42,646	112	53	2,778	824	24,813	15,150	212	..	39,470	46,191	1,702	768	2,800	238
1,875	2,187	..	..	81	..	315	104	..	..	846	1,016	172	85	*	*
102	104	..	..	..	..	219	32	..	..	104	91	180	..	*	*
4,649	6,340	53	..	97	12	709	586	..	..	1,453	2,114	186	46	65	28
6,520	13,712	36	..	805	328	*	*	..	..	2,964	6,278	822	420	546	37
2,004	11,399	516	2	1,120	1,087	14,575	4,920	33	..	12,721	13,020	7,171	3,459	242	47
..	..	..	..	33,174	15,351	112,179	100,013	8,877	1,513	53,018	28,390	10,409	4,211	2,756	516
..	..	..	..	2	..	..	..	4	..	..	..	8	..	..	..
..	..	..	..	..	..	..	..	2	..	..	..	..	..	..	..
..	..	..	..	1,287	1,541	7,234	9,427	1,068	88	9,995	4,995	756	756	44	..

TABLE XI.

OCCUPATION BY SELECTED CASTE, TRIBE & RACE.

TABLE

Occupation by Selected

S. No.	Caste, Tribe & Race	Traditional occupation	RECORDED												PRINCIPAL	
			II. Exploitation of Minerals				III. Industry				IV. Transport				V. Trade	
			Owners managers, clerks, etc.		Labourers		Owners, managers, clerks, etc.		Artisans, and other workmen		Owners, managers, officers, etc.		Labourers, boatmen, carters, palki bearers			
			Males	Females	Males	Females	Males	Females	Males	Female	Males	Females	Males	Females	Males	Females
	1	2	29	30	31	32		34	35	36	37	38	39	40	41	42
	H NDU(Brahmanic)															
1	Bedar (Bendar) ..	Fishermen and Hunters ..	..	..	330	989	..	..	253	136	..	..	489	..	402	67
2	Bhoi (Bes ..	Do ..	..	..	470	179	44	..	164	111	105	..	1,485	275	930	924
3	Brahman ..	Priests ..	357	..	63	145	1,435	2	1,240	846	294	..	284	186	6,764	395
4	urud (Medar) ..	Basket makers ..	..	..	180	332	..	..	*83	*	..	..	18	..	193	87
5	Darzi (Simpi) ..	Tailors ..	..	..	182	540	442	..	*367	*	..	..	132	42	11,230	244
6	Dhobi (Chakala) ..	Washermen ..	..	..	921	472	*3	..	*160	*	13	..	551	156	274	106
7	Hajjam (Mangala) ..	Barbers ..	..	..	681	129	*21	..	*46	*	9	..	254	15	442	253
8	Hatkar ..	Cultivators ..	..	..	313	1,093	..	..	281	350	89	..	20	..	214	63
9	Julahi (Sale, Devang)..	Weavers ..	..	..	331	490	1,449	..	*589	*	116	..	340	16	5,080	1,002
10	Kalal (Ediga, Gound Goundla). ..	Toddy drawers and liquor sellers ..	4	..	1,035	1,764	7	..	*206	*	200	..	574	61	*655	3,799
11	Kapu (Kunbi) ..	Cultivators ..	57	..	3,899	289	215	..	881	1,991	228	..	2,158	325	9,489	1,758
12	Kasab (Aray, Khatik).	Butehers ..	..	..	170	53	..	..	*	*	..	..	9	11	1,108	293
13	Kasar (Kanchari) ..	Brass and copper smiths ..	..	..	91	634	..	..	*	*	9	..	31	43	156	14
14	Kumbhar (Kummari)	Potters ..	..	..	130	404	5	..	*	*	19	..	320	162	2,050	449
15	Koli ..	Cultivators ..	..	..	487	294	5	..	338	104	..	..	527	68	944	388
16	Komati ..	Traders ..	107	..	176	55	140	..	899	955	47	..	379	152	*	*
17	Kshatriya (Rajput) .	Soldiers ..	55	..	97	449	68	..	512	345	109	..	193	94	1,256	72
18	Kurma ..	Cultivators ..	..	..	416	734	212	..	144	304	3	..	148	17	891	152
19	Lingayat ..	Traders ..	1	..	1,015	928	176	..	1,177	588	236	..	636	109	*	*
20	Lohar (Kammari) ..	Black-smiths ..	..	..	294	56	*2	..	*	*	..	..	327	12	240	175
21	Mali ..	Gardeners ..	..	..	266	3,690	5	..	110	2	6	..	151	1	180	151
22	Maratha ..	Cultivators ..	12	..	2,050	2	823	..	451	367	165	..	2,419	917	5,905	1,267
23	Panchal ..	Artisans ..	..	..	2	139	*	..	*	*	..	..	13	..	39	3
24	Perka ..	Carriers ..	..	..	110	1	199	..	286	350	..	..	*	*	346	127
25	Rangrez (Rangari) .	Dyers and weavers ..	..	..	6	..	*	..	*337	*	..	..	115	12	107	66
26	Satani (Ayyawar) ..	Religious beggars ..	..	..	45	147	..	..	33	20	..	..	101	..	3	51
27	Sunar (Ausala, Kamsala).	Goldsmiths ..	9	..	722	479	..	..	*	*	2	..	243	22	1,030	299
28	Sutar (Wadla, Bade).	Carpenters ..	2	..	444	295	..	..	*4	*	2	..	118	151	627	142
29	Telaga, (Munnur and Mutrasi)	Cultivators ..	30	..	3,889	3,513	1,324	..	510	1,411	32	..	1,972	564	4,667	2,058
30	Teli (Gandla) ..	Oil mongers ..	..	..	37	165	..	..	*34	*	..	..	46	..	*558	608
31	Uppara (Govandi) ..	Masons ..	..	..	77	488	..	..	*	*	..	..	274	..	190	156
32	Velama ..	Cultivators ..	11	..	98	143	58	..	24	37	..	..	36	1	450	88
33	Vishwabrahman ..	Artisans ..	..	..	56	14	..	..	*16	*	3	..	48	30	215	..
34	Waddar ..	Earth diggers and stone breakers) ..	..	..	1,036	1,209	..	..	*	*	236	..	378	20	252	115
35	Wanjari (Banjara) ..	Cultivators ..	..	..	208	306	..	..	695	13	..	..	270	30	1,228	419
36	Yadava (Golla, Gowli, Dhangar. ..	Cow herds and shepherds ..	..	..	4,691	1,347	..	..	5,375	1,066	33	..	2,532	138	2,935	2,087
	ADI-HINDU.															
37	Dher (Mala, Mahar) .	Menial service) ..	..	..	4,928	5,450	16	13	761	941	474	..	1,171	2,461	1,920	1,631
38	Madiga (Chambhar Mochi, Mang).	Do tanners ..	..	..	4,196	3,435	24	19	*..	*	382	..	1,235	471	3,654	1,600
	TRIBAL.															
39	Bhil ..	Hunters ..	..	..	193	176	..	..	75	37	..	..	62	6	20	13
40	Chenchu ..	Do ..	..	..	..	..	..	..	..	..	..	..	30	..	..	..
41	Erakal (Kaikadi) ..	Sooth sayers and basket makers) ..	..	..	254	47	..	..	*	99	..	..	16	55	410	211
42	Gond ..	Cultivators ..	..	..	640	160	..	..	54	5	..	..	221	13	170	495
43	Lambadi (Banjari) ..	Carriers ..	..	..	2,825	1,305	..	..	140	55	..	..	*..	*	1,649	554
44	**Muslim** ..	..	686	84	10,883	2,941	3,845	985	46,454	4,027	2,318	160	6,898	626	55,312	5,822
	CHRISTIAN.															
45	Anglo-Indian ..	.. ..	1	..	20	16	27	..	..	51	46	..	165	67	171	22
46	Europeans and Allied Races ..	.. ..	13	..	..	..	13	..	..	2	5	..	..	..	36	3
47	Indian Christian ..	.. ..	49		598	898	258	8	1,281	202	408	108	348	348	402	302

XI.. Caste, Tribe and Race.

TABLE XI.

OCCUPATION BY SELECTED CASTE, TRIBE & RACE.

OCCUPATION OF ACTUAL WORKERS

VI. Public Force				VII. Public Adminstration				VIII. Professions and Liberal Arts						IX. Persons living on their own income		X Domestic service		XI. Insufficiently described occupations				XII Unproductive	
Commissioned, & Gazetted officers		Others		Gazetted officers		Others		Religious		Lawyers, doctors, teachers		Others						Contractors, clerks, cashiers, etc., otherwise unspecified		Labourers, unspecified		Beggars, vagrants prostitutes criminals & inmates of jail & asylum, etc.	
Males	Females	Males	Females	Males	Females	Males	Females	Males	Females	Males	Females	Males	Females	Males	Females	Males	Females	Males	Females	Males	Females	Males	Females
43	44	45	46	47	48	49	50	51	52	53	54	55	56	57	58	59	60	61	62	63	64	65	66
..	..	40	..	..	..	576	3	41	..	..	..	18	16	1	18	3,380	341	..	16	228	1	1,988	1,751
..	..	79	..	..	..	391	9	..	5	14	31	84	18	4	50	6,097	898	54	15	559	277	1,328	1,168
11	..	814	..	138	3	7,432	51	*	*	5,036	679	2,668	67	2,547	537	7,917	348	1,176	73	1,141	424	5,048	2,041
..	..	..	28	..	..	..	..	..	..	15	..	22	1	6	54	68	44	2	..	8	30	163	48
..	..	83	..	..	..	80	..	50	10	7	..	120	29	47	62	791	484	59	10	84	77	205	553
..	..	185	7	..	..	58	6	338	27	37	11	590	87	182	38	3,069	1,099	132	50	2,994	344	1,882	2,729
..	..	199	..	..	..	77	7	685	27	58	32	497	316	962	83	3,393	1,942	9	68	403	208	1,389	1,708
..	..	..	5	10	..	30	..	32	20	95	5	..	6	45	4	478	443	..	..	65	286	379	754
..	..	73	7	..	..	86	10	530	24	83	1	221	12	459	104	2,329	1,609	127	45	648	836	2,370	2,924
..	..	222	..	3	..	50	..	389	27	166	..	401	161	871	574	3,706	1,533	226	94	907	465	2,411	1,896
10	..	502	..	26	..	1,922	2	319	30	392	63	927	116	2,172	571	8,361	4,283	1,625	80	2,308	1,390	7,708	12,810
..	..	..	..	..	..	15	..	..	10	6	..	26	28	5	10	314	208	112	10	32	..	344	402
..	..	..	..	..	..	19	..	..	..	5	..	..	..	..	20	56	29	..	..	5	..	21	16
..	..	..	..	..	..	93	4	225	17	29	..	78	29	58	58	1,107	783	1,126	5	179	168	1,287	1,138
..	..	..	15	..	..	225	1	57	12	44	..	20	19	37	27	423	483	21	1	107	727	769	1,504
..	..	..	..	..	..	105	..	288	13	129	13	139	67	177	161	2,630	845	934	13	2,491	531	710	851
*	..	*	*	17	..	909	6	106	14	125	7	116	26	490	40	1,217	102	404	1	328	143	623	232
..	..	11	..	..	..	162	..	249	..	63	..	136	101	206	133	531	649	7	8	37	180	1,331	893
..	..	52	..	4	..	347	2	1,665	126	422	37	515	90	727	2	4,847	1,811	625	43	2,459	489	8,890	3,406
..	..	..	..	..	..	5	4	30	3	..	..	15	125	18	15	145	385	8	17	..	260	398	293
..	..	24	..	14	..	898	..	..	1	..	..	1	7	44	391	628	198	..	16	32	89	..	732
7	..	1,468	66	..	..	..	5	452	302	198	..	337	692	712	2	6,856	4,078	1,060	100	2,600	1,303	7,654	9,012
..	..	..	..	..	..	34	..	3	..	..	2	..	..	48	3	9	24	..	..	1	..	93	42
..	..	10	..	..	..	..	..	..	1	..	..	228	..	13	1	274	164	..	9	34	90	656	743
..	..	..	..	..	..	..	..	..	..	..	..	7	..	7	..	76	180	7	21	51	29	89	320
..	..	18	..	..	..	32	..	*	*	15	..	98	..	9	..	182	362	6	..	59	6	*40	*347
..	..	68	..	..	..	68	..	381	11	164	27	765	7	23	8	831	821	109	7	198	630	458	683
..	..	16	290	..	..	37	..	180	83	13	5	71	10	22	31	666	802	88	..	104	330	669	476
8	..	970	..	6	..	783	..	74	37	113	4	1,220	45	224	108	2,006	4,014	1,483	13	1,976	..	6,981	11,836
..	..	..	..	..	..	19	..	12	1	5	..	21	..	5	1	555	464	48	..	161	988	312	477
..	..	..	..	..	..	2	..	29	..	12	..	40	5	1	47	851	274	14	4	13	129	768	1,203
3	..	..	..	2	..	92	..	2	12	72	4	3	24	71	6	510	617	28	2	6	16	517	736
..	..	..	..	..	..	38	..	34	..	36	..	72	5	3	..	375	16	156	..	231	361	399	2
..	..	..	..	..	..	325	..	300	27	14	..	90	34	6	76	434	276	50	2	102	295	1,483	1,804
..	..	..	..	..	..	37	..	37	180	10	..	95	4	144	79	525	651	540	3	198	1,407	739	634
..	..	119	138	..	..	585	..	249	164	55	11	402	33	102	385	6,490	4,513	932	15	694	1,115	10,595	15,527
..	..	604	19	..	..	213	530	501	318	48	24	78	84	668	98	*..	*..	128	..	3,876	6,027	15,073	21,067
..	..	212	5	..	..	283	85	1,040	84	123	23	69	109	1,125	58	*..	*..	149	..	4,548	5,545	13,051	22,058
..	..	4	..	..	..	84	1	16	5	..	..	..	..	51	20	151	30	1	..	13	81	1,567	877
..	..	..	..	..	..	..	..	..	..	..	..	..	..	..	..	50	..	..	..	..	..	50	..
..	..	4	8	..	..	6	..	..	17	..	..	*	*	20	..	162	316	..	..	312	113	463	483
..	..	..	..	..	..	..	1	3	10	..	..	..	..	243	..	867	122	3	..	116	214	427	888
..	..	16	..	..	..	28	..	40	80	2	..	323	171	404	..	2,070	849	29	..	250	470	3,926	2,729
459	..	53,829	320	1604	31	57,023	1565	2,743	522	8,899	517	4,582	947	8,206	3891	45,793	19,802	13,407	1188	6,283	1,810	11,478	10,189
4	..	442	1	4	21	126	87	6	11	8	12	40	13	43	13	315	216	13	..	..	68	54	61
17	..	1,734	..	22	2	48	..	4	5	14	8	2	..	5	..	..	..	2	..	..	..	..	..
17	..	560	40	56	6	576	52	640	644	450	468	639	740	1,150	143	2,007	3,107	93	83	157	257	1,154	2,257

Table XIII.

LITERACY BY RELIGION AND AGE.

1. This table corresponds with the Table VIII of 1921, except that the lowest age group has been divided into 0–5 and 5–10, classifying the first group under "illiterates." It consists of three parts, Part I gives the statistics for the whole State and for all religions; Part II distributes the literates for the total district populaton and by main religions; Part III gives similar figures for the cities.

2. "Literate" in the Census means that all those persons who know how to read and write an ordinary letter and the number of persons shown as literates are those for vernaculars which include English and Urdu literates.

3. For the first time separate figures for Urdu literates are shown along with English figures.

4. The details for Christians by sect and race are shown below:—

Race and Sect	Total Strength		Literates		Illiterates		Literate in English		Literate in Urdu	
	Males	Females	Males	Females	Males	Females	Males	Females	Males	Females
1	2	3	4	5	6	7	8	9	10	11
1. Europeans ..	2,268	359	2,206	322	62	37	2,204	321	9	..
2. Anglo-Indians .	2,188	1,182	1,973	1,015	215	167	1,953	997	198	35
3. Indian Christians ..	74,988	70,397	10,695	5,483	64,293	64,914	4,231	2,121	3,478	542
(i) Roman Catholics.	10,185	8,927	3,050	1,096	7,085	7,831	1,220	655	799	210
(ii) Syrians ..	12	5	8	2	4	3	6	2	..	..
*(iii) Others ..	64,841	61,465	7,637	4,385	57,204	57,080	3,005	1,464	2,679	332
Total Christians	**79,444**	**71,938**	**14,874**	**6,820**	**64,570**	**65,118**	**8,388**	**3,439**	**3,685**	**577**

* Others include all Protestants as Anglican-communion, Baptist, Methodist, Wesleyan, Presbyterian, Church of England, etc.

TABLE XIII.

Literacy by Religion and Age.—Part I— State Summary.

Religion and Age	POPULATION									LITERATE IN ENGLISH			LITERATE IN URDU		
	Total			Literate			Illiterate								
	Persons	Males	Females	Persons	Males	Females	Persons	Males	Females	Persons	Males	Females	Persons	Males	Females
1	2	3	4	5	6	7	8	9	10	11	12	13	14	15	16
All Religions	14,436,148	7,370,010	7,066,138	595,633	527,594	68,039	13,840,515	6,842,416	6,998,099	72,846	65,329	7,517	192,039	159,794	32,245
0—5	2,428,219	1,158,829	1,269,390	..	..	..	2,428,219	1,158,829	1,269,390	..	..	..	..	..	..
5—10	1,758,013	914,853	843,160	42,835	35,827	7,508	1,715,178	879,326	835,652	3,704	2,869	835	9,479	7,126	2,353
10—15	1,575,481	827,213	748,268	68,163	58,801	9,362	1,507,318	768,412	738,906	7,640	6,445	1,195	18,881	15,720	3,161
15—20	1,294,390	638,789	655,601	100,258	87,270	12,979	1,194,132	551,510	642,622	12,303	10,955	1,348	30,280	26,332	3,948
20 and over ..	7,380,045	3,830,326	3,540,719	384,377	346,187	38,190	6,995,668	3,484,139	3,511,529	49,199	45,060	4,139	133,399	110,616	22,783
Hindu (Brahmanic) ..	9,699,615	4,948,408	4,751,207	391,317	355,358	35,959	9,308,298	4,593,050	4,715,248	38,872	36,699	2,173	78,418	64,859	13,559
0—5	1,589,804	747,870	841,984	..	..	..	1,589,804	747,870	841,934	..	..	..	..	..	..
5—10	1,170,888	610,169	560,719	27,020	23,181	3,839	1,143,868	586,988	556,880	1,187	966	221	2,753	2,399	354
10—15	1,064,485	559,251	505,284	45,316	40,859	4,457	1,019,169	518,392	500,777	3,603	3,250	353	7,091	6,584	507
15—20	872,670	431,572	441,098	69,669	62,440	7,229	803,001	369,132	433,869	6,459	6,048	411	13,165	12,362	803
20 and over ..	5,001,768	2,599,546	2,402,222	249,312	228,878	20,434	4,752,456	2,370,668	2,381,788	27,623	26,435	1,188	55,409	43,514	11,895
Adi Hindu	2,473,230	1,252,651	1,220,579	13,880	12,148	1,732	2,459,350	1,240,50	1,218,847	1,174	1,097	77	2,472	2,283	189
0—5	449,914	221,140	228,774	..	..	..	449,914	221,140	228,774	..	..	..	..	..	..
5—10	305,760	157,591	148,169	1,325	1,076	249	304,435	156,515	147,920	100	93	7	235	216	19
10—15	264,014	137,882	126,132	1,726	1,454	272	262,288	136,428	125,860	153	144	9	272	247	25
15—20	212,404	101,139	111,265	2,322	2,002	820	210,082	99,187	110,945	232	216	16	415	379	36
20 and over ..	1,241,138	634,899	606,239	8,507	7,616	891	1,232,631	627,283	605,348	689	644	45	1,550	1,441	109
Arya	3,700	1,896	1,804	295	213	82	3,405	1,683	1,722	47	33	14	67	53	14
0—5	691	345	346	..	..	..	691	345	346	..	..	..	..	..	..
5—10	375	205	170	37	25	12	338	180	158	8	4	4	4	1	3
10—15	379	229	150	29	22	7	350	207	143	3	1	2	4	4	..
15—20	284	142	142	36	24	12	248	118	130	7	6	1	10	7	3
20 and over ..	1,971	975	996	193	142	51	1,778	833	945	29	22	7	49	41	8
Brahmo	182	98	84	122	75	47	60	23	37	107	65	42	45	34	11
0—5	15	8	7	..	..	..	15	8	7	..	..	..	..	..	..
5—10	7	2	5	7	2	5	..	..	..	5	2	3	4	2	2
10—15	7	4	3	7	4	3	..	..	..	7	4	3	7	4	3
15—20	17	7	10	16	6	10	1	1	..	16	6	10	8	4	4
20 and over ..	136	77	59	92	63	29	44	14	30	79	53	26	26	24	2
Jain	21,543	11,456	10,087	3,684	3,131	553	17,859	8,325	9,534	243	215	28	413	374	39
0—5	3,307	1,642	1,665	..	..	..	3,307	1,642	1,665	..	..	..	..	..	..
5—10	2,553	1,383	1,170	323	254	69	2,230	1,129	1,101	14	12	2	35	30	5
10—15	2,277	1,151	1,126	486	381	105	1,791	770	1,021	47	42	5	59	54	5
15—20	1,986	1,022	964	587	481	106	1,399	541	858	58	50	8	73	67	6
20 and over ..	11,430	6,258	5,162	2,288	2,015	273	9,132	6,243	4,889	124	111	13	246	223	23

TABLE XIII.
LITERACY BY RELIGION & AGE.

Religion and Age																
Sikh ..	..	5,178	3,064	2,114	1,580	1,378	202	3,598	1,686	1,912	241	205	36	531	496	35
0—5 ..	..	*750*	392	358	..	..	..	*750*	392	358	..	..	..	..	..	..
5—10 ..	..	*502*	262	240	*67*	48	19	*435*	214	221	*7*	4	8	*22*	18	4
10—15 ..	..	*506*	237	269	*76*	54	22	*430*	183	247	*10*	9	1	*27*	22	5
15—20 ..	..	*512*	288	224	*233*	205	28	*279*	83	196	*32*	29	3	*120*	116	4
20 and over	..	*2,908*	1,885	1,023	*1,204*	1,071	133	*1,704*	814	890	*192*	168	29	*362*	340	22
Muslim ..	..	1,534,666	791,435	743,231	158,859	137,410	21,449	1,375,807	654,025	721,782	19,275	17,982	1,293	104,980	87,403	17,577
0—5 ..	..	*248,998*	122,035	126,963	..	..	..	*248,998*	122,035	126,963	..	..	..	..	..	..
5—10 ..	..	*182,954*	93,048	87,906	*10,320*	7,982	2,388	*172,634*	87,116	85,518	*881*	737	144	*6,079*	4,217	1,862
10—15 ..	..	*164,680*	86,439	78,241	*16,141*	12,877	3,264	*148,539*	73,562	74,977	*2,131*	1,883	248	*10,683*	8,175	2,508
15—20 ..	..	*147,168*	75,384	71,784	*23,436*	19,539	3,897	*123,732*	55,845	67,887	*3,442*	3,163	279	*15,044*	12,098	2,951
20 and over	..	*790,866*	412,529	378,337	*108,962*	97,002	11,000	*681,904*	315,467	366,437	*12,821*	12,199	622	*73,174*	62,918	10,256
Christian ..	..	151,382	79,444	71,938	21,694	14,874	6,820	129,688	64,570	65,118	11,827	8,388	3,439	4,262	3,685	577
0—5 ..	..	*24,851*	12,208	12,643	..	..	..	*24,851*	12,208	12,643	..	..	..	..	..	..
5—10 ..	..	*17,624*	9,303	8,319	*3,254*	2,490	764	*14,370*	6,815	7,555	*1,412*	1,003	409	*254*	202	52
10—15 ..	..	*16,506*	9,187	7,319	*3,773*	2,713	1,060	*12,733*	6,474	6,259	*1,564*	1,050	514	*639*	564	75
15—20 ..	..	*14,087*	7,376	6,711	*3,297*	2,134	1,163	*10,790*	5,242	5,548	*1,920*	1,368	552	*1,327*	1,230	97
20 and over	..	*78,314*	41,368	36,946	*11,370*	7,537	3,833	*66,944*	33,881	33,113	*6,931*	4,967	1,964	*2,042*	1,689	353
Zoroastrian ..	..	1,784	937	847	1,485	808	677	299	129	170	913	529	384	550	383	167
0—5 ..	..	*204*	107	97	..	..	..	*204*	107	97	..	..	..	..	..	..
5—10 ..	..	*120*	78	42	*109*	67	12	*11*	11	..	*79*	37	42	*49*	28	21
10—15 ..	..	*154*	69	85	*132*	66	96	*22*	3	19	*107*	47	60	*63*	35	28
15—20 ..	..	*158*	58	100	*142*	50	92	*16*	8	8	*120*	52	68	*66*	34	32
20 and over	..	*1,148*	625	523	*1,102*	625	477	*46*	..	46	*607*	393	214	*372*	286	86
Buddhist ..	..	52	26	26	26	19	7	26	7	19	21	18	3	..	..	..
0—5 ..	..	*7*	4	3	..	..	..	*7*	4	3	..	..	..	..	..	..
5—10 ..	..	*2*	1	1	..	..	..	*2*	1	1	..	..	..	..	..	..
10—15 ..	..	*5*	3	2	*1*	1	..	*4*	2	2	..	..	..	..	..	..
15—20 ..	..	*6*	2	4	*3*	2	1	*3*	..	3	*2*	2	..	..	..	..
20 and over	..	*32*	16	16	*22*	16	6	*10*	..	10	*19*	16	3	..	..	..
Jew ..	..	27	11	16	19	9	10	8	2	6	2	2	..	..	..	..
0—5 ..	..	*3*	1	2	..	..	..	*3*	1	2	..	..	..	..	..	..
5—10 ..	..	..	..	..	..	..	..		..		..	..	..	..	..	..
10—15 ..	..	*3*	1	2	*2*	1	1	*1*	..	1	..	..	..	..	..	..
15—20 ..	..	*3*	1	2	*3*	1	2	..	..	..	..	..	..	..	..	..
20 and over	..	*18*	8	10	*14*	7	7	*4*	1	3	*2*	2	..	..	..	..
Tribal ..	..	544,789	280,584	264,205	2,672	2,171	501	542,117	278,413	263,704	124	96	28	301	224	77
0—5 ..	..	*109,675*	53,077	56,598	..	..	..	*109,675*	53,077	56,598	..	..	..	..	..	..
5—10 ..	..	*77,228*	40,809	36,419	*373*	252	121	*76,855*	40,557	36,298	*11*	11	..	*44*	13	31
10—15 ..	..	*62,465*	32,760	29,705	*474*	369	105	*61,991*	32,391	29,600	*15*	15	..	*36*	31	5
15—20 ..	..	*45,095*	21,798	23,297	*514*	395	119	*44,581*	21,403	23,178	*15*	15	..	*52*	40	12
20 and over	..	*250,326*	132,140	118,186	*1,311*	1,155	156	*249,015*	130,985	118,030	*83*	55	28	*169*	140	29

TABLE XIII.

Literacy by Religion and Age.—Part II—Districts.

District	Religion and Age	POPULATION									Literate in English			Literate in Urdu		
		Total			Literate			Illiterate								
		Persons	Males	Females	Persons	Males	Females	Persons	Males	Females	Persons	Males	Females	Persons	Males	Females
1	2	3	4	5	6	7	8	9	10	11	12	13	14	15	16	17
Atrafi-i-Balda	**All Religions.**	499,661	253,975	245,686	21,080	19,843	1,237	478,581	234,132	244,449	1,512	1,324	188	4,932	4,461	481
	0—5 ..	*88,798*	43,456	45,342	..	..	..	*88,798*	43,456	45,342	..	..	..	..	..	..
	5—10 ..	*62,029*	33,324	28,705	*1,477*	1,349	128	*60,552*	31,975	28,577	*102*	61	41	*273*	232	41
	10—15 ..	*50,969*	27,819	23,150	*2,045*	1,877	168	*48,924*	25,942	22,982	*141*	113	28	*480*	410	70
	15—20 ..	*37,764*	18,258	19,506	*3,246*	3,029	217	*34,518*	15,229	19,289	*240*	208	32	*947*	862	85
	20 and over ..	*260,101*	131,118	128,983	*14,312*	13,588	724	*245,789*	117,530	128,259	*1,029*	942	87	*3,242*	2,957	285
	Hindu (Brahmanic)	333,919	169,509	164,410	16,334	15,656	678	317,585	153,853	163,732	735	706	29	1,600	1,569	31
	0—5 ..	*58,194*	28,959	29,235	..	..	..	*58,194*	28,959	29,235	..	..	..	..	..	..
	5—10 ..	*42,644*	23,125	19,519	*1,174*	1,106	68	*41,470*	22,019	19,451	*32*	28	4	*48*	44	4
	10—15 ..	*34,734*	19,253	15,481	*1,600*	1,510	90	*33,134*	17,743	15,391	*66*	60	6	*119*	114	5
	15—20 ..	*24,333*	12,208	12,125	*2,689*	2,562	127	*21,644*	9,646	11,998	*117*	110	7	*269*	263	6
	20 and over .	*174,014*	85,964	88,050	*10,871*	10,478	393	*163,143*	75,486	87,657	*520*	508	12	*1,164*	1,148	16
	Adi-Hindu ..	98,366	50,243	48,123	159	133	26	98,207	50,110	48,097	20	20	..	43	32	11
	0—5 ..	*19,388*	9,171	10,217	..	..	..	*19,388*	9,171	10,217	..	..	..	..	..	..
	5—10 ..	*13,164*	6,886	6,278	*7*	5	2	*13,157*	6,881	6,276	..	..	..	*2*	2	..
	10—15 ..	*10,158*	5,862	4,296	*12*	9	3	*10,146*	5,853	4,293	*1*	1	..	*3*	2	1
	15—20 ..	*7,030*	3,220	3,810	*19*	16	3	*7,011*	3,204	3,807	*3*	3	..	*16*	15	1
	20 and over ..	*48,626*	25,104	23,522	*121*	103	18	*48,505*	25,001	23,504	*16*	16	..	*22*	13	9
	Muslim ..	50,412	25,417	24,995	4,238	3,817	421	46,174	21,600	24,574	310	291	19	2,941	2,605	336
	0—5 ..	*7,533*	3,568	3,965	..	..	..	*7,533*	3,568	3,965	..	..	..	..	..	..
	5—10 ..	*3,771*	2,021	1,750	*253*	213	40	*3,518*	1,808	1,710	*13*	12	1	*196*	168	28
	10—15 ..	*3,960*	1,583	2,377	*388*	328	60	*3,572*	1,255	2,317	*23*	20	3	*297*	247	50
	15—20 ..	*4,895*	2,087	2,808	*500*	428	72	*4,395*	1,659	2,736	*50*	46	4	*355*	293	62
	20 and over ..	*30,253*	16,158	14,095	*3,097*	2,848	249	*27,156*	13,310	13,846	*224*	213	11	*2,093*	1,897	196
	Christian ..	3,154	1,573	1,581	243	148	95	2,911	1,425	1,486	97	61	36	9	6	3
	0—5 ..	*577*	259	318	..	..	..	*577*	259	318	..	..	..	..	..	..
	5—10 ..	*413*	203	210	*22*	6	16	*391*	197	194	*6*	1	5	*1*	1	..
	10—15 ..	*377*	186	191	*27*	12	15	*350*	174	176	*10*	5	5	*3*	1	2
	15—20 ..	*258*	109	149	*26*	11	15	*232*	98	184	*10*	5	5	..	..	..
	20 and over ..	*1,529*	816	713	*168*	119	49	*1,361*	697	664	*71*	50	21	*5*	4	1

TABLE XIII.

Literacy by Religion and Age.—Part II—Districts.

District	Religion and Age	POPULATION Total Persons	Total Males	Total Females	Literate Persons	Literate Males	Literate Females	Illiterate Persons	Illiterate Males	Illiterate Females	Literate in English Persons	Literate in English Males	Literate in English Females	Literate in Urdu Persons	Literate in Urdu Males	Literate in Urdu Females
1	2	3	4	5	6	7	8	9	10	11	12	13	14	15	16	17
Warangal	**All Religions.**	1,117,693	575,819	541,874	46,664	43,121	3,543	1,071,029	532,698	538,331	4,234	4,096	138	9,184	8,236	948
	0—5 ..	*184,088*	89,262	94,826	..	..	..	*184,088*	89,262	94,826	..	..	..	..	..	..
	5—10 ..	*142,556*	72,643	69,913	*4,514*	4,158	356	*138,042*	68,485	69,557	*604*	599	5	*550*	441	109
	10—15 ..	*122,725*	64,312	58,413	*6,299*	5,839	460	*116,426*	58,473	57,953	*838*	832	6	*1,055*	887	168
	15—20 ..	*100,558*	50,512	50,046	*7,577*	7,056	521	*92,981*	43,456	49,525	*696*	679	17	*1,438*	1,246	192
	20 and over ..	*567,766*	299,090	268,676	*28,274*	26,068	2,206	*539,492*	273,022	266,470	*2,096*	1,986	110	*6,141*	5,662	479
	Hindu (Brahmanic).	705,102	362,125	342,977	33,359	31,499	1,860	671,743	330,626	341,117	2,020	1,968	52	4,255	4,152	103
	0—5 ..	*109,673*	52,831	56,842	..	..	..	*109,673*	52,831	56,842	..	..	..	..	..	..
	5—10 ..	*89,431*	44,871	44,560	*2,592*	2,420	172	*86,839*	42,451	44,388	*52*	30	2	*182*	173	9
	10—15 ..	*77,303*	40,654	36,649	*4,036*	3,887	199	*73,267*	36,817	36,450	*244*	246	4	*513*	498	15
	15—20 ..	*64,071*	33,021	31,050	*6,159*	5,950	200	*57,912*	27,071	30,841	*359*	350	9	*751*	787	14
	20 and over ..	*364,624*	190,748	173,876	*20,572*	19,292	1,280	*344,052*	171,456	172,596	*1,365*	1,328	37	*2,809*	2,744	65
	Adi-Hindu ..	175,687	90,922	84,765	694	531	163	174,993	90,391	84,602	29	28	1	41	39	2
	0—5 ..	*32,286*	15,615	16,671	..	..	..	*32,286*	15,615	16,671	..	..	..	..	..	..
	5—10 ..	*21,114*	10,906	10,208	*48*	25	23	*21,066*	10,881	10,185	..	..	..	..	..	..
	10—15 ..	*18,295*	9,511	8,784	*74*	47	27	*18,221*	9,464	8,757	*2*	2	..	*4*	3	1
	15—20 ..	*15,272*	7,364	7,908	*80*	62	18	*15,192*	7,302	7.890	*7*	7	..	*5*	5	..
	20 and over ..	*88,720*	47,526	41,194	*492*	397	95	*88,228*	47,129	41,099	*20*	19	1	*32*	31	1
	Muslim ..	67,820	36,176	31,644	8,034	7,021	1,013	59,786	29,155	30,631	805	785	20	4,618	3,816	802
	0—5 ..	*10,481*	5,529	4,952	..	..	..	*10,481*	5,529	4,952	..	..	..	..	..	..
	5—10 ..	*8,759*	4,616	4,148	*462*	349	113	*8,297*	4,267	4,030	*25*	24	1	*316*	218	98
	10—15 ..	*8,248*	3,987	4,261	*677*	514	163	*7,571*	3,473	4,098	*49*	47	2	*475*	328	147
	15—20 ..	*6,918*	3,161	3,757	*1,031*	816	215	*5,887*	2,345	3,542	*84*	81	3	*652*	481	171
	20 and over ..	*33,414*	18,883	14,531	*5,864*	5,342	522	*27,550*	13,541	14,009	*647*	633	14	*3,175*	2,789	386
	Christian ..	28,952	14,955	13,997	4,044	3,603	441	24,908	11,352	13,556	1.371	1,309	62	214	188	26
	0—5 ..	*5,092*	2,531	2,561	..	..	..	*5,092*	2,531	2,561	..	..	..	..	..	..
	5—10 ..	*3,404*	1,729	1,675	*1,883*	1,338	45	*2,021*	391	1,630	*527*	525	2	*52*	50	2
	10—15 ..	*2,992*	1,675	1,317	*1,449*	1,388	66	*1,543*	292	1,251	*542*	542	..	*55*	52	3
	15—20 ..	*2,409*	1,266	1,143	*223*	157	66	*2,186*	1,109	1,077	*245*	240	5	*16*	14	2
	20 and over ..	*15,055*	7,754	7,301	*989*	725	264	*14,066*	7,029	7,037	*57*	2	55	*91*	72	19
	Tribal . ..	139,499	71,305	68,194	348	299	49	139,151	71,006	68,145	9	6	3	57	41	16
	0—5 ..	*26,471*	12,715	13,756	..	..	..	*26,471*	12,715	13,756	..	..	..	..	..	..
	5—10 ..	*19,782*	10,486	9,296	*17*	15	2	*19,765*	10,471	9,294	..	..	..	..	..	..
	10—15 ..	*15,819*	8,446	7,373	*46*	42	4	*15,773*	8,404	7,369	*1*	1	..	*8*	6	2
	15—20 ..	*11,824*	5,664	6,160	*56*	46	10	*11,768*	5,618	6,150	*1*	1	..	*14*	9	5
	20 and over ..	*65,603*	33,994	31,609	*229*	196	33	*65,374*	33,798	31,576	*7*	4	3	*35*	26	9

TABLE XIII.

Literacy by Religion and Age.—Part II— Districts.

District	Religion and Age	POPULATION									Literate in English			Literate in Urdu		
		Total			Literate			Illiterate								
		Persons	Males	Females	Persons	Males	Females	Persons	Males	Females	Persons	Males	Females	Persons	Males	Females
1	2	3	4	5	6	7	8	9	10	11	12	13	14	15	16	17
Karimnagar	**All Religions.**	**1,241,405**	**634,416**	**606,989**	**26,153**	**23,563**	**2,590**	**1,215,252**	**610,853**	**604,399**	**1,059**	**983**	**76**	**6,203**	**4,865**	**1,338**
	0—5 ..	*223,611*	100,008	123,603	..	..	..	*223,611*	100,008	123,603	..	..	..	..	..	..
	5—10 ..	*137,284*	82,321	54,963	*1,386*	1,164	222	*135,898*	81,157	54,741	*88*	83	5	*323*	283	40
	10—15 ..	*138,056*	74,026	64,030	*2,272*	2,025	247	*135,784*	72,001	63,783	*174*	162	12	*515*	450	65
	15—20 ..	*117,634*	58,380	59,254	*4,597*	4,042	555	*113,037*	54,338	58,699	*249*	233	16	*815*	742	73
	20 and over ..	*624,820*	319,681	305,139	*17,898*	16,332	1,566	*606,922*	303,349	303,573	*548*	505	43	*4,550*	3,390	1,160
	Hindu (Brahmanic).	**933,527**	**476,884**	**456,643**	**19,048**	**17,224**	**1,824**	**914,479**	**459,660**	**454,819**	**542**	**527**	**15**	**2,915**	**1,886**	**1,029**
	0—5 ..	*164,731*	70,750	93,981	..	..	..	*164,731*	70,750	93,981	..	..	..	..	..	..
	5—10 ..	*97,927*	61,687	36,290	*891*	751	140	*97,036*	60,886	36,150	*42*	41	1	*107*	102	5
	10—15 ..	*105,062*	56,915	48,147	*1,505*	1,383	122	*103,557*	55,532	48,025	*81*	75	6	*200*	192	8
	15—20 ..	*89,703*	44,584	45,119	*3,584*	3,185	399	*86,119*	41,399	44,720	*150*	146	4	*342*	337	5
	20 and over ..	*476,104*	242,998	233,106	*13,068*	11,905	1,163	*463,036*	231,093	231,943	*269*	265	4	*2,266*	1,255	1,011
	Adi-Hindu ..	**227,274**	**116,291**	**110,983**	**542**	**464**	**78**	**226,732**	**115,827**	**110,905**	**31**	**31**	..	**50**	**50**	..
	0—5 ..	*45,055*	22,386	22,669	..	..	..	*45,055*	22,386	22,669	..	..	..	..	..	..
	5—10 ..	*29,052*	15,457	13,595	*59*	52	7	*28,993*	15,405	13,588	*6*	6	..	*4*	4	..
	10—15 ..	*23,452*	12,118	11,334	*126*	117	9	*23,326*	12,001	11,325	*15*	15	..	*16*	16	..
	15—20 ..	*20,431*	10,022	10,409	*121*	111	10	*20,310*	9,911	10,399	*9*	9	..	*21*	21	..
	20 and over ..	*109,284*	56,308	52,976	*236*	184	52	*109,048*	56,124	52,924	*1*	1	..	*9*	9	..
	Muslim ..	**55,802**	**28,256**	**27,546**	**5,859**	**5,428**	**431**	**49,943**	**22,828**	**27,115**	**316**	**304**	**12**	**3,221**	**2,912**	**309**
	0—5 ..	*9,483*	4,751	4,732	..	..	..	*9,483*	4,751	4,732	..	..	..	..	..	..
	5—10 ..	*7,276*	3,720	3,556	*346*	301	45	*6,930*	3,419	3,511	*17*	17	..	*212*	177	35
	10—15 ..	*6,571*	3,389	3,182	*502*	428	74	*6,069*	2,961	3,108	*37*	36	1	*301*	244	57
	15—20 ..	*5,018*	2,419	2,599	*763*	673	90	*4,255*	1,746	2,509	*59*	56	3	*451*	383	68
	20 and over ..	*27,454*	13,977	13,477	*4,248*	4,026	222	*23,206*	9,951	13,255	*203*	195	8	*2,257*	2,108	149
	Christian ..	**13,622**	**7,188**	**6,434**	**525**	**314**	**211**	**13,097**	**6,874**	**6,223**	**170**	**121**	**49**	**16**	**16**	..
	0—5 ..	*2,219*	1,106	1,113	..	..	..	*2,219*	1,106	1,113	..	..	..	..	..	..
	5—10 ..	*1,678*	887	791	*76*	53	23	*1,602*	834	768	*23*	19	4	..	..	..
	10—15 ..	*1,645*	907	738	*120*	87	33	*1,525*	820	705	*41*	36	5	..	..	..
	15—20 ..	*1,422*	763	659	*95*	49	46	*1,327*	714	613	*31*	22	9	..	..	..
	20 and over ..	*6,658*	3,525	3,133	*234*	125	109	*6,424*	3,400	3,024	*75*	44	31	*16*	16	..
	Tribal ..	**10,394**	**5,384**	**5,010**	**30**	**17**	**13**	**10,364**	**5,367**	**4,997**	..	..	..	**3**	**3**	..
	0—5 ..	*1,939*	919	1,020	..	..	..	*1,939*	919	1,020	..	..	..	..	..	..
	5—10 ..	*1,298*	582	716	*5*	..	5	*1,293*	582	711	..	..	..	..	..	..
	10—15 ..	*1,244*	646	598	*4*	1	3	*1,240*	645	595	..	..	..	..	..	..
	15—20 ..	*999*	563	436	*6*	4	2	*993*	559	484	..	..	..	*1*	1	..
	20 and over ..	*4,914*	2,674	2,240	*15*	12	3	*4,899*	2,662	2,237	..	..	..	*2*	2	..

TABLE XIII.

Literacy by Religion and Age.—Part II-- Districts.

District	Religion and Age	POPULATION									Literate in English			Literate in Urdu		
		Total			Literate			Illiterate								
		Persons	Males	Females	Persons	Males	Females	Persons	Males	Females	Persons	Males	Females	Persons	Males	Females
1	2	3	4	5	6	7	8	9	10	11	12	13	14	15	16	17
Adilabad	**All Religions**	762,030	389,754	372,276	18,144	16,621	1,523	743,886	373,133	370,753	992	886	106	4,291	3,500	791
	0—5 ..	*141,754*	68,436	73,318	..	..	..	*141,754*	68,436	73,318	..	..	..	..	..	..
	5—10 ..	*99,627*	53,549	46,078	*749*	593	156	*98,878*	52,956	45,922	*18*	12	6	*164*	140	24
	10—15 ..	*83,810*	44,943	38,867	*1,947*	1,741	206	*81,863*	43,202	38,661	*61*	52	9	*424*	394	30
	15—20 ..	*66,092*	32,136	33,956	*2,428*	2,146	282	*63,664*	29,990	33,674	*219*	196	23	*576*	525	51
	20 and over ..	*370,747*	190,690	180,057	*13,020*	12,141	879	*357,727*	178,549	179,178	*694*	626	68	*3,127*	2,441	686
	Hindu (Brahmanic) .	491,088	252,021	239,067	13,511	12,446	1,065	477,577	239,575	238,002	697	609	88	2,668	2,069	599
	0—5 ..	*88,192*	42,784	45,408	..	..	..	*88,192*	42,784	45,408	..	..	..	..	..	..
	5—10 ..	*63,081*	34,742	28,339	*529*	439	90	*62,552*	34,303	28,249	*10*	6	4	*71*	70	1
	10—15 ..	*54,766*	29,427	25,339	*1,487*	1,366	121	*53,279*	28,061	25,218	*28*	21	7	*231*	229	2
	15—20 ..	*43,567*	21,075	22,492	*1,819*	1,632	187	*41,748*	19,443	22,305	*169*	150	19	*304*	286	18
	20 and over ..	*241,482*	123,993	117,489	*9,676*	9,009	667	*231,806*	114,984	116,822	*490*	432	58	*2,062*	1,484	578
	Adi-Hindu ..	115,554	57,843	57,711	256	233	23	115,298	57,610	57,683	8	7	1	16	16	..
	0—5 ..	*23,286*	10,931	12,355	..	..	..	*23,286*	10,931	12,355	..	..	..	..	..	..
	5—10 ..	*15,097*	8,029	7,068	*9*	7	2	*15,088*	8,022	7,066	..	..	..	..	..	..
	10—15 ..	*12,247*	6,455	5,792	*42*	39	3	*12,205*	6,416	5,789	..	..	..	*4*	4	..
	15—20 ..	*9,825*	4,865	4,960	*70*	64	6	*9,755*	4,801	4,954	*2*	2	..	*5*	5	..
	20 and over	*55,099*	27,563	27,536	*135*	123	12	*54,964*	27,440	27,524	*6*	5	1	*7*	7	..
	Muslim ..	45,821	24,030	21,791	3,869	3,613	256	41,952	20,417	21,535	245	244	1	1,573	1,385	188
	0—5 ..	*7,865*	3,896	3,969	..	..	..	*7,865*	3,896	3,969	..	..	..	..	..	..
	5—10 ..	*6,393*	2,931	3,462	*155*	117	38	*6,238*	2,814	3,424	*6*	5	1	*90*	67	28
	10—15 ..	*5,099*	2,787	2,312	*311*	278	33	*4,788*	2,514	2,274	*28*	28	..	*184*	156	28
	15—20 ..	*4,261*	2,243	2,018	*431*	387	44	*3,830*	1,856	1,974	*39*	39	..	*262*	229	33
	20 and over ..	*22,203*	12,173	10,030	*2,972*	2,836	136	*19,231*	9,337	9,894	*172*	172	..	*1,037*	933	104
	Christian ..	4,244	2,092	2,152	172	105	67	4,072	1,987	2,085	40	24	16	21	17	4
	0—5 ..	*880*	413	467	..	..	..	*880*	413	467	..	..	..	..	..	..
	5—10 ..	*439*	264	175	*18*	12	6	*421*	252	169	*1*	..	1	*1*	1	..
	10—15 ..	*382*	214	168	*32*	21	11	*350*	193	157	*4*	2	2	*2*	2	..
	15—20 ..	*348*	169	179	*29*	16	13	*319*	153	166	*9*	5	4	*3*	3	..
	20 and over ..	*2,195*	1,032	1,163	*93*	56	37	*2,102*	976	1,126	*26*	17	9	*15*	11	4
	Tribal ..	104,807	53,513	51,294	242	155	87	104,565	53,358	51,207	2	2	..	13	13	..
	0—5 ..	*21,429*	10,869	11,060	..	..	..	*21,429*	10,869	11,060	..	..	..	..	..	..
	5—10 ..	*14,562*	7,558	7,004	*31*	14	17	*14,531*	7,544	6,987	*1*	1	..	*2*	2	..
	10—15 ..	*11,259*	6,031	5,228	*57*	30	27	*11,202*	6,001	5,201	*1*	1	..	*3*	3	..
	15—20 ..	*8,048*	3,765	4,283	*57*	32	25	*7,991*	3,733	4,258	..	..	..	*2*	2	..
	20 and over ..	*49,509*	25,790	23,719	*97*	79	18	*49,412*	25,711	23,701	..	..	..	*6*	6	..

TABLE XIII.

Literacy by Religion and Age.—Part II— Districts.

District	Religion and Age	POPULATION									Literate in English			Literate in Urud		
		Total			Literate			Illiterate								
		Persons	Males	Females	Persons	Males	Females	Persons	Males	Females	Persons	Males	Females	Persons	Males	Females
1	2	3	4	5	6	7	8	9	10	11	12	13	14	15	16	17
Medak	**All Religions.**	**738,665**	**373,475**	**365,190**	**22,520**	**20,786**	**1,734**	**716,145**	**352,689**	**363,456**	**1,157**	**1,027**	**130**	**4,572**	**3,958**	**614**
	0—5 ..	*128,763*	58,818	69,945	..	..	..	*128,763*	58,818	69,945	..	..	..	..	..	..
	5—10 ..	*83,485*	41,369	42,116	*1,199*	987	212	*82,286*	40,382	41,904	*79*	60	19	*292*	242	50
	10—15 ..	*76,726*	34,891	41,835	*2,581*	2,299	282	*74,145*	32,592	41,553	*182*	150	32	*464*	416	48
	15—20 ..	*67,722*	31,380	36,342	*3,804*	3,497	307	*63,918*	27,883	36,035	*225*	199	26	*622*	574	48
	20 and over ..	*381,969*	207,017	174,952	*14,936*	14,003	933	*367,033*	193,014	174,019	*671*	618	53	*3,194*	2,726	468
	Hindu (Brahmanic).	**508,690**	**256,911**	**251,779**	**16,290**	**15,621**	**669**	**492,400**	**241,290**	**251,110**	**304**	**299**	**5**	**1,733**	**1,584**	**146**
	0—5 ..	*89,506*	40,287	49,219	..	..	..	*89,506*	40,287	49,219	..	..	..	..	..	..
	5—10 ..	*62,183*	30,644	31,539	*692*	612	80	*61,491*	30,032	31,459	*9*	9	..	*98*	97	1
	10—15 ..	*51,556*	21,864	29,692	*1,747*	1,672	75	*49,809*	20,192	29,617	*29*	28	1	*199*	198	1
	15—20 ..	*46,089*	20,441	25,648	*2,811*	2,675	136	*43,278*	17,766	25,512	*55*	52	3	*250*	249	1
	20 and over ..	*259,356*	143,675	115,681	*11,040*	10,662	378	*248,316*	133,013	115,303	*211*	210	1	*1,186*	1,040	146
	Adi-Hindu .	**133,599**	**67,943**	**65,656**	**95**	**49**	**46**	**133,504**	**67,894**	**65,610**	**3**	**2**	**1**	**7**	**5**	**2**
	0—5 ..	*23,975*	11,614	12,361	..	..	..	*23,975*	11,614	12,361	..	..	..	..	..	..
	5—10 ..	*13,010*	6,419	6,591	*12*	2	10	*12,998*	6,417	6,581	..	..	..	..	..	..
	10—15 ..	*14,456*	7,065	7,391	*14*	2	12	*14,442*	7,063	7,379	..	..	..	*1*	..	1
	15—20 ..	*12,312*	5,801	6,511	*20*	10	10	*12,292*	5,791	6,501	*1*	..	1	*2*	1	1
	20 and over ..	*69,846*	37,044	32,802	*49*	35	14	*69,797*	37,009	32,788	*2*	2	..	*4*	4	..
	Muslim ..	**71,518**	**35,396**	**36,122**	**4,597**	**4,085**	**512**	**66,921**	**31,311**	**35,610**	**495**	**482**	**13**	**2,715**	**2,308**	**407**
	0—5 ..	*11,835*	5,182	6,653	..	..	..	*11,835*	5,182	6,653	..	..	..	..	..	..
	5—10 ..	*5,580*	2,819	2,761	*290*	237	53	*5,290*	2,582	2,708	*27*	26	1	*178*	139	39
	10—15 ..	*7,962*	4,333	3,629	*401*	358	43	*7,561*	3,975	3,586	*64*	62	2	*226*	200	26
	15—20 ..	*6,814*	3,693	3,121	*608*	562	46	*6,206*	3,131	3,075	*88*	86	2	*341*	309	32
	20 and over ..	*39,327*	19,369	19,958	*3,298*	2,028	370	*36,029*	16,441	19,588	*316*	308	8	*1,970*	1,660	310
	Christian ..	**19,662**	**10,488**	**9,174**	**1,462**	**966**	**496**	**18,200**	**9,522**	**8,678**	**352**	**241**	**111**	**114**	**58**	**56**
	0—5 ..	*2,493*	1,251	1,242	..	..	..	*2,493*	1,251	1,242	..	..	..	..	..	..
	5—10 ..	*2,131*	1,177	954	*202*	133	69	*1,929*	1,044	885	*42*	24	18	*16*	6	10
	10—15 ..	*2,214*	1,365	849	*408*	256	152	*1,806*	1,109	697	*88*	59	29	*37*	17	20
	15—20 ..	*2,076*	1,218	858	*351*	238	113	*1,725*	980	745	*81*	61	20	*26*	12	14
	20 and over ..	*10,748*	5,477	5,271	*501*	339	162	*10,247*	5,138	5,109	*141*	97	44	*35*	23	12
	Tribal ..	**4,570**	**2,396**	**2,174**	**31**	**24**	**7**	**4,539**	**2,372**	**2,167**	**3**	**3**	..	**7**	**7**	..
	0—5 ..	*883*	454	429	..	..	..	*883*	454	429	..	..	..	..	..	..
	5—10 ..	*550*	290	260	*3*	3	..	*547*	287	260	*1*	1	..	..	..	..
	10—15 ..	*508*	259	249	*4*	4	..	*504*	255	249	*1*	1	..	*1*	1	..
	15—20 ..	*359*	188	171	*8*	6	2	*351*	182	169	..	..	..	*3*	3	..
	20 and over ..	*2,270*	1,205	1,065	*16*	11	5	*2,254*	1,194	1,060	*1*	1	..	*3*	3	..

TABLE XIII.

Literacy by Religion and Age.—Part II— Districts.

District	Religion and Age	POPULATION									Literate in English			Literate in Urdu		
		Total			Literate			Illiterate								
		Persons	Males	Females	Persons	Males	Females	Persons	Males	Females	Persons	Males	Females	Persons	Males	Females
1	2	3	4	5	6	7	8	9	10	11	12	13	14	15	16	17
Nizamabad	**All Religions.**	623,225	313,556	309,669	19,060	18,011	1,049	604,165	295,545	308,620	598	562	36	3,422	3,118	304
	0—5 ..	*100,462*	49,586	50,926	..	..	..	*100,462*	49,536	50,926	..	..	..	..	..	..
	5—10 ..	*73,247*	37,848	35,399	*823*	715	108	*72,424*	37,133	35,291	*60*	55	5	*254*	212	42
	10—15 ..	*64,874*	33,100	31,774	*1,773*	1,658	115	*63,101*	31,442	31,659	*68*	58	10	*344*	301	43
	15—20 ..	*56,236*	26,285	29,951	*3,644*	3,443	201	*52,592*	22,842	29,750	*96*	88	8	*600*	545	55
	20 and over ..	*328,406*	166,787	161,619	*12,820*	12,195	625	*315,586*	154,592	160,994	*374*	361	13	*2,224*	2,060	164
	Hindu (Brahmanic)	439,962	220,875	219,087	14,957	14,313	644	425,005	206,562	218,443	234	229	5	1,154	1,144	10
	0—5 ..	*67,345*	32,872	34,473	..	..	..	*67,345*	32,872	34,473	..	..	..	..	..	..
	5—10 ..	*52,641*	26,908	25,733	*430*	378	52	*52,211*	26,530	25,681	*3*	3	..	*53*	53	..
	10—15 ..	*46,801*	23,726	23,075	*1,320*	1,267	53	*45,481*	22,459	23,022	*20*	20	..	*109*	108	1
	15—20 ..	*40,468*	19,064	21,404	*2,938*	2,811	127	*37,530*	16,253	21,277	*44*	43	1	*192*	189	3
	20 and over ..	*232,707*	118,305	114,402	*10,269*	9,857	412	*222,438*	108,448	113,990	*167*	163	4	*800*	794	6
	Adi -Hindu .	103,061	51,751	51,310	119	91	28	102,942	51,660	51,282	4	4	..	11	11	..
	0—5 ..	*18,489*	8,819	9,670	..	..	..	*18,489*	8,819	9,670	..	..	..	..	..	..
	5—10 ..	*11,614*	6,236	5,378	*10*	7	3	*11,604*	6,229	5,375	..	..	..	*2*	2	..
	10—15 ..	*10,349*	5,351	4,998	*18*	14	4	*10,331*	5,337	4,994	*1*	1	..	*2*	2	..
	15—20 ..	*9,372*	4,161	5,211	*23*	18	5	*9,349*	4,143	5,206	*2*	2	..	*2*	2	..
	20 and over ..	*53,237*	27,184	26,053	*68*	52	16	*53,169*	27,132	26,037	*1*	1	..	*5*	5	..
	Muslim ..	48,769	24,761	24,008	3,340	3,031	309	45,429	21,730	23,699	181	176	5	2,177	1,883	294
	0—5 ..	*9,214*	5,143	4,071	..	..	..	*9,214*	5,143	4,071	..	..	..	..	..	..
	5—10 ..	*5,398*	2,742	2,656	*261*	215	46	*5,137*	2,527	2,610	*6*	4	2	*191*	149	42
	10—15 ..	*4,484*	2,310	2,174	*339*	294	45	*4,145*	2,016	2,129	*17*	15	2	*225*	183	42
	15—20 ..	*3,889*	1,825	2,064	*597*	543	54	*3,292*	1,282	2,010	*36*	35	1	*397*	345	52
	20 and over ..	*25,784*	12,741	13,043	*2,143*	1,979	164	*23,641*	10,762	12,879	*122*	122	..	*1,364*	1,206	158
	Christian ..	13,856	7,128	6,728	536	493	43	13,320	6,635	6,685	179	153	26	79	79	..
	0—5 ..	*2,052*	1,026	1,026	..	..	..	*2,052*	1,026	1,026	..	..	..	..	..	..
	5—10 ..	*1,416*	792	624	*110*	105	5	*1,306*	687	619	*51*	48	3	*8*	8	..
	10—15 ..	*1,444*	735	709	*78*	68	10	*1,366*	667	699	*30*	22	8	*8*	8	..
	15—20 ..	*1,080*	531	549	*61*	52	9	*1,019*	479	540	*14*	8	6	*9*	9	..
	20 and over ..	*7,864*	4,044	3,820	*287*	268	19	*7,577*	3,776	3,801	*84*	75	9	*54*	54	..
	Tribal ..	17,358	8,925	8,433	47	42	5	17,311	8,883	8,428	..	..	..	2	2	..
	0—5 ..	*3,327*	1,660	1,667	..	..	..	*3,327*	1,660	1,667	..	..	..	..	..	..
	5—10 ..	*2,161*	1,163	998	*2*	2	..	*2,159*	1,161	998	..	..	..	*1*	1	..
	10—15 ..	*1,776*	969	807	*10*	10	..	*1,766*	959	807	..	..	..	..	..	..
	15—20 ..	*1,411*	695	716	*12*	12	..	*1,399*	683	716	..	..	..	..	..	..
	20 and over ..	*8,683*	4,488	4,245	*23*	18	5	*8,660*	4,420	4,240	..	..	..	*1*	1	..

TABLE XIII.

Literacy by Religion and Age.—Part II—Districts.

District	Religion and Age	POPULATION									Literate in English			Literate in Urdu		
		Total			Literate			Illiterate								
		Persons	Males	Females	Persons	Males	Females	Persons	Males	Females	Persons	Males	Females	Persons	Males	Females
1	2	3	4	5	6	7	8	9	10	11	12	13	14	15	16	17
Mahbubnagar	**All Religions.**	971,616	494,061	477,555	30,760	29,491	1,269	940,856	464,570	476,286	835	800	35	6,455	5,762	693
	0—5 ..	*167,765*	81,741	86,024	..	..	..	*167,765*	81,741	86,024	..	..	..	..	..	..
	5—10 ..	*119,405*	59,362	60,043	*1,563*	1,435	128	*117,842*	57,927	59,915	*36*	36	..	*537*	517	20
	10—15 ..	*106,725*	54,454	52,271	*3,203*	3,072	131	*103,522*	51,382	52,140	*84*	82	2	*1,287*	1,249	38
	15—20 ..	*89,684*	43,147	46,537	*4,958*	4,726	232	*84,726*	38,421	46,305	*192*	185	7	*1,556*	1,524	32
	20 and over ..	*488,037*	255,357	232,680	*21,036*	20,258	778	*467,001*	235,099	231,902	*523*	497	26	*3,075*	2,472	603
	Hindu (Brahmanic)	637,927	323,041	314,886	16,533	15,694	839	621,394	307,347	314,047	388	382	6	2,277	1,760	517
	0—5 ..	*107,502*	51,726	55,776	..	..	..	*107,502*	51,726	55,776	..	..	..	..	..	..
	5—10 ..	*75,866*	36,382	39,484	*798*	740	58	*75,068*	35,642	39,426	*15*	15	..	*106*	106	..
	10—15 ..	*68,617*	34,447	34,170	*1,690*	1,625	65	*66,927*	32,822	34,105	*30*	30	..	*222*	221	1
	15—20 ..	*59,880*	28,913	30,967	*3,219*	3,046	173	*56,661*	25,867	30,794	*100*	98	2	*343*	337	6
	20 and over ..	*326,062*	171,573	154,489	*10,826*	10,283	543	*315,236*	161,290	153,946	*243*	239	4	*1,606*	1,096	510
	Adi-Hindu ..	197,784	100,913	96,871	160	130	30	197,624	100,783	96,841	4	4	..	5	5	..
	0—5 ..	*35,822*	17,778	18,044	..	..	..	*35,822*	17,778	18,044	..	..	..	..	..	..
	5—10 ..	*24,855*	12,783	12,072	*5*	2	3	*24,850*	12,781	12,069	..	..	..	..	..	..
	10—15 ..	*22,122*	11,430	10,692	*17*	11	6	*22,105*	11,419	10,686	..	..	..	..	..	..
	15—20 ..	*17,732*	8,390	9,342	*17*	10	7	*17,715*	8,380	9,335	..	..	..	..	..	..
	20 and over ..	*97,253*	50,532	46,721	*121*	107	14	*97,132*	50,425	46,707	*4*	4	..	*5*	5	..
	Muslim ..	84,604	43,281	41,323	13,081	12,789	292	71,523	30,492	41,031	353	350	3	4,144	3,977	167
	0—5 ..	*13,343*	6,682	6,661	..	..	..	*13,343*	6,682	6,661	..	..	..	..	..	..
	5—10 ..	*11,162*	5,974	5,188	*628*	569	59	*10,534*	5,405	5,129	*16*	16	..	*428*	410	18
	10—15 ..	*10,097*	5,888	4,709	*1,353*	1,306	47	*8,744*	4,082	4,662	*48*	48	..	*1,061*	1,026	35
	15—20 ..	*7,878*	3,767	4,111	*1,570*	1,540	30	*6,308*	2,227	4,081	*76*	76	..	*1,210*	1,186	24
	20 and over ..	*42,124*	21,470	20,654	*9,530*	9,374	156	*32,594*	12,096	20,498	*213*	210	3	*1,445*	1,355	90
	Christian ..	2,705	1,410	1,295	295	195	100	2,410	1,215	1,195	90	64	26	28	19	9
	0—5 ..	*523*	268	255	..	..	..	*523*	268	255	..	..	..	..	..	..
	5—10 ..	*367*	190	177	*19*	11	8	*348*	179	169	*5*	5	..	*3*	1	2
	10—15 ..	*308*	156	152	*25*	13	12	*283*	143	140	*6*	4	2	*4*	2	2
	15—20 ..	*228*	113	115	*49*	28	21	*179*	85	94	*16*	11	5	*3*	1	2
	20 and over ..	*1,279*	683	596	*202*	143	59	*1,077*	540	537	*63*	44	19	*18*	15	3
	Tribal ..	47,881	25,049	22,832	669	666	3	47,212	24,383	22,829	..	..	..	1	1	..
	0—5 ..	*10,449*	5,217	5,232	..	..	..	*10,449*	5,217	5,232	..	..	..	..	..	..
	5—10 ..	*7,077*	3,991	3,086	*112*	112	..	*6,965*	3,879	3,086	..	..	..	..	..	..
	10—15 ..	*5,526*	3,007	2,519	*117*	117	..	*5,409*	2,890	2,519	..	..	..	..	..	..
	15—20 ..	*3,912*	1,940	1,972	*99*	99	..	*3,813*	1,841	1,972	..	..	..	..	..	..
	20 and over ..	*20,917*	10,894	10,023	*341*	338	3	*20,576*	10,556	10,020	..	..	..	*1*	1	..

TABLE XIII.

Literacy by Religion and Age.—Part II— Districts.

District	Religion and Age	POPULATION									Literate in English			Literate in Urdu		
		Total			Literate			Illiterate								
		Persons	Males	Females	Persons	Males	Females	Persons	Males	Females	Persons	Males	Females	Persons	Males	Females
1	2	3	4	5	6	7	8	9	10	11	12	13	14	15	16	17
Nalgonda	**All Religions.**	1,133,409	580,897	552,512	30,017	28,136	1,881	1,103,392	552,761	550,631	832	694	138	5,689	5,237	452
	0—5 ..	*194,185*	94,975	99,210	..	..	..	*194,185*	94,975	99,210	..	..	..	..	..	..
	5—10 ..	*147,732*	76,174	71,558	*1,725*	1,457	268	*146,007*	74,717	71,290	*91*	78	13	*336*	277	59
	10—15 ..	*130,205*	70,399	59,806	*2,712*	2,396	316	*127,493*	68,003	59,490	*159*	131	28	*572*	495	77
	15—20 ..	*104,454*	52,080	52,374	*4,890*	4,587	303	*99,564*	47,498	52,071	*178*	150	28	*972*	893	79
	20 and over ..	*556,833*	287,269	269,564	*20,690*	19,696	994	*536,143*	267,573	268,570	*404*	335	69	*3,809*	3,572	237
	Hindu (Brahmanic) .	780,440	399,249	381,191	22,034	21,128	906	758,406	378,121	380,285	200	189	11	2,352	2,297	55
	0—5 ..	*130,408*	63,059	67,349	..	..	..	*130,408*	63,059	67,349	..	..	..	..	..	..
	5—10 ..	*102,084*	52,200	49,884	*1,205*	1,051	154	*100,879*	51,149	49,730	*35*	35	..	*140*	132	8
	10—15 ..	*90,497*	48,993	41,504	*1,914*	1,769	145	*88,583*	47,224	41,359	*58*	57	1	*264*	257	7
	15—20 ..	*73,121*	36,453	36,668	*3,749*	3,629	120	*69,372*	32,824	36,548	*69*	68	1	*458*	448	10
	20 and over ..	*384,330*	198,544	183,786	*15,166*	14,679	487	*369,164*	183,865	185,299	*38*	29	9	*1,490*	1,460	30
	Adi-Hindu ..	208,980	106,897	102,083	536	459	77	208,444	106,438	102,006	34	24	10	64	58	6
	0—5 ..	*38,069*	18,474	19,595	..	..	..	*38,069*	18,474	19,595	..	..	..	..	..	..
	5—10 ..	*26,058*	13,607	12,451	*41*	38	3	*26,017*	13,569	12,448	..	..	..	..	..	..
	10—15 ..	*23,010*	12,049	10,361	*61*	50	11	*22,949*	12,599	10,350	..	..	..	*2*	2	..
	15—20 ..	*18,876*	9,390	9,486	*106*	74	32	*18,770*	9,316	9,454	*5*	3	2	*15*	13	2
	20 and over ..	*102,967*	52,777	50,190	*328*	297	31	*102,639*	52,480	50,159	*29*	21	8	*47*	43	4
	Muslim ..	62,233	31,842	30,391	6,330	5,798	532	55,903	26,044	29,859	337	305	32	3,217	2,841	376
	0—5 ..	*10,155*	5,694	4,461	..	..	..	*10,155*	5,694	4,461	..	..	..	..	..	..
	5—10 ..	*7,538*	4,074	3,464	*327*	262	65	*7,211*	3,812	3,399	*15*	13	2	*194*	145	49
	10—15 ..	*6,435*	3,386	3,049	*525*	437	88	*5,910*	2,949	2,961	*37*	31	6	*300*	234	66
	15—20 ..	*5,242*	2,737	2,505	*874*	781	93	*4,368*	1,956	2,412	*61*	52	9	*492*	428	64
	20 and over ..	*32,863*	15,951	16,912	*4,604*	4,318	286	*28,259*	11,633	16,626	*224*	209	15	*2,231*	2,084	197
	Christian ..	23,689	12,324	11,365	881	528	353	22,808	11,796	11,012	216	131	85	46	31	15
	0—5 ..	*3,968*	1,972	1,996	..	..	..	*3,968*	1,972	1,996	..	..	..	..	..	..
	5—10 ..	*3,210*	1,708	1,502	*130*	84	46	*3,080*	1,624	1,456	*34*	23	11	*2*	..	2
	10—15 ..	*2,740*	1,463	1,277	*179*	109	70	*2,561*	1,354	1,207	*54*	33	21	*6*	2	4
	15—20 ..	*2,169*	1,045	1,124	*122*	65	57	*2,047*	980	1,067	*37*	21	16	*7*	4	3
	20 and over ..	*11,602*	6,136	5,466	*450*	270	180	*11,152*	5,866	5,286	*91*	54	37	*31*	25	6
	Tribal ..	57,549	30,321	27,228	158	156	2	57,391	30,165	27,226	45	45	..	10	10	..
	0—5 ..	*11,508*	5,740	5,768	..	..	..	*11,508*	5,740	5,768	..	..	..	..	..	..
	5—10 ..	*8,799*	4,561	4,238	*21*	21	..	*8,778*	4,540	4,238	*7*	7	..	..	..	..
	10—15 ..	*7,480*	3,887	3,593	*26*	26	..	*7,454*	3,861	3,593	*10*	10	..	..	..	..
	15—20 ..	*5,011*	2,439	2,572	*28*	28	..	*4,983*	2,411	2,572	*6*	6	..	..	..	..
	20 and over ..	*24,751*	13,694	11,057	*83*	81	2	*24,668*	13,613	11,055	*22*	22	..	*10*	10	..

TABLE XIII.

Literacy by Religion and Age.—Part II—Districts.

District	Religion and Age	POPULATION									Literate in English			Literate in Urdu		
		Total			Literate			Illiterate								
		Persons	Males	Females	Persons	Males	Females	Persons	Males	Females	Persons	Males	Females	Persons	Males	Females
1	2	3	4	5	6	7	8	9	10	11	12	13	14	15	16	17
Aurangabad	All Religions	944,793	480,498	464,295	52,684	45,656	7,028	892,109	434,842	457,267	4,662	4,366	296	14,896	11,481	3,415
	0—5 ..	154,922	78,123	76,799	..	..	..	154,922	78,123	76,799	..	..	..	..	..	..
	5—10 ..	120,491	62,636	57,855	4,192	3,436	756	116,299	59,200	57,099	188	175	13	1,186	1,030	156
	10—15 ..	106,672	54,727	51,945	6,419	5,412	1,007	100,253	49,315	50,938	839	816	23	2,314	2,083	231
	15—20 ..	87,004	41,359	45,645	8,314	7,317	997	78,690	34,042	44,648	1,174	1,111	63	2,908	2,410	498
	20 and over ..	475,704	243,653	232,051	33,759	29,491	4,268	441,945	214,162	227,788	2,461	2,264	197	8,488	5,958	2,530
	Hindu (Brahmanic).	641,214	325,257	315,957	37,519	32,502	5,017	603,695	292,755	310,940	2,128	1,957	171	6,971	4,682	2,289
	0—5 ..	103,102	52,510	50,592	..	..	..	103,102	52,510	50,592	..	..	..	..	..	..
	5—10 ..	80,346	41,519	38,827	2,925	2,420	505	77,421	39,099	38,322	118	115	3	304	292	12
	10—15 ..	71,054	36,795	34,259	4,084	3,426	658	66,970	33,369	33,601	310	305	5	1,079	1,057	22
	15—20 ..	58,810	27,681	31,129	5,322	4,747	575	53,488	22,934	30,554	556	514	42	1,259	1,039	220
	20 and over ..	327,902	166,752	161,150	25,188	21,900	3,270	302,714	144,843	157,871	1,144	1,023	121	4,329	2,294	2,035
	Adi-Hindu ..	140,336	70,323	70,013	2,108	1,919	189	138,228	68,404	69,824	42	39	3	397	377	20
	0—5 ..	24,627	12,261	12,366	..	..	..	24,627	12,261	12,366	..	..	..	..	..	..
	5—10 ..	17,600	8,768	8,832	216	188	28	17,384	8,580	8,804	2	2	..	62	62	..
	10—15 ..	15,906	7,676	8,230	242	218	24	15,664	7,458	8,206	2	2	..	54	52	2
	15—20 ..	12,344	5,511	6,833	302	275	27	12,042	5,236	6,806	7	6	1	66	63	3
	20 and over ..	69,859	36,107	33,752	1,348	1,238	110	68,511	34,869	33,642	31	29	2	215	200	15
	Muslim ..	124,441	65,065	59,376	10,603	9,292	1,311	113,838	55,773	58,065	2,045	1,998	47	7,207	6,164	1,043
	0—5 ..	20,004	10,186	9,818	..	..	..	20,004	10,186	9,818	..	..	..	..	..	..
	5—10 ..	17,219	9,462	7,757	872	689	183	16,347	8,773	7,574	52	45	7	768	630	138
	10—15 ..	15,214	7,845	7,369	1,801	1,542	259	13,413	6,303	7,110	488	475	13	1,126	923	203
	15—20 ..	12,225	6,345	5,880	2,307	1,990	317	9,918	4,355	5,563	528	519	9	1,536	1,266	270
	20 and over ..	59,779	31,227	28,552	5,623	5,071	552	54,156	26,156	28,000	977	959	18	3,777	3,345	432
	Jain ..	5,313	2,906	2,407	756	649	107	4,557	2,257	2,300	88	85	3	85	69	16
	0—5 ..	770	387	383	..	..	..	770	387	383	..	..	..	..	..	..
	5—10 ..	574	322	252	56	44	12	518	278	240	..	..	..	14	11	3
	10—15 ..	590	308	282	116	101	15	474	207	267	17	17	..	15	14	1
	15—20 ..	503	250	253	150	132	18	353	118	235	27	26	1	16	14	2
	20 and over ..	2,876	1,639	1,237	434	372	62	2,442	1,267	1,175	44	42	2	40	30	10
	Christian ..	10,576	5,393	5,183	888	659	229	9,688	4,734	4,954	357	285	72	228	181	47
	0—5 ..	1,787	883	904	..	..	..	1,787	883	904	..	..	..	..	..	..
	5—10 ..	1,499	757	742	101	75	26	1,398	682	716	16	13	3	38	35	3
	10—15 ..	1,352	732	620	110	84	26	1,242	648	594	21	16	5	38	35	3
	15—20 ..	1,017	564	453	118	91	27	899	473	426	55	45	10	29	26	3
	20 and over ..	4,921	2,457	2,464	559	409	150	4,362	2,048	2,314	265	211	54	123	85	38
	Tribal ..	22,137	11,066	11,071	336	267	69	21,801	10,799	11,002	2	2	..	8	8	..
	0—5 ..	3,928	1,807	2,121	..	..	..	3,928	1,807	2,121	..	..	..	..	..	..
	5—10 ..	3,436	1,778	1,658	5	5	..	3,431	1,778	1,658	..	..	..	..	..	..
	10—15 ..	2,786	1,341	1,445	19	18	1	2,767	1,323	1,444	1	1	..	2	2	..
	15—20 ..	2,076	989	1,087	34	21	18	2,042	968	1,074	1	1	..	2	2	..
	20 and over ..	9,911	5,151	4,760	278	228	55	9,633	4,928	4,705	..	..	..	4	4	..

TABLE XIII.

Literacy by Religion and Age.—Part II—Districts.

District.	Religion and Age	POPULATION									Literate in English			Literate in Urdu		
		Total			Literate			Illiterate								
		Persons	Males	Females	Persons	Males	Females	Persons	Males	Females	Persons	Males	Females	Persons	Males	Females
1	2	3	4	5	6	7	8	9	10	11	12	13	14	15	16	17
Bir	**All Religions.**	633,690	325,396	308,294	15,781	14,381	1,400	617,909	311.015	306,894	670	649	21	3,806	3,130	676
	0—5 ..	106,703	49,813	56,890	..	..	..	106,703	49,813	56,890	..	..	..	..	..	..
	5—10 ..	72,752	38,584	34,168	814	702	112	71,938	37,882	34,056	39	38	1	229	195	34
	10—15 ..	69,249	37,106	32,143	2,453	2,209	244	66,796	34,897	31,899	91	87	4	436	395	41
	15—20 ..	55,340	26,342	28,998	2,998	2,756	242	52,342	23,586	28,756	123	117	6	537	496	41
	20 and over	329,646	173,551	156,095	9.516	8,714	802	320,130	164,837	155,298	417	407	10	2,604	2,044	560
	Hindu (Brahmanic).	473,445	243,844	229,601	12,999	11,872	1,127	460,446	231,972	228,474	504	483	21	2,237	1,700	537
	0—5 ..	77,342	35,389	41,953	..	..	..	77,342	35,389	41,953	..	..	..	..	..	..
	5—10 ..	53,522	28,491	25,031	598	538	60	52,924	27,953	24,971	31	30	1	99	98	1
	10—15 ..	50,548	26,711	23,837	2,039	1,849	190	48,509	24,862	23,647	61	57	4	148	185	13
	15—20 ..	42,075	20,170	21,905	2,464	2,283	181	39,611	17,887	21,724	92	86	6	193	187	6
	20 and over ..	249,958	133,083	116,875	7,898	7,202	696	242,060	125,881	116,179	320	310	10	1,797	1,280	517
	Adi-Hindu .	95,051	47,701	47,350	118	68	50	94,933	47,633	47,300	4	4	..	12	9	3
	0—5 ..	17,647	8,747	8,900	..	..	..	17,647	8,747	8,900	..	..	..	..	..	..
	5—10 ..	10,901	5,378	5,523	11	5	6	10,890	5,373	5,517	..	..	..	..	..	..
	10—15 ..	11,632	6,470	5,162	19	8	11	11,613	6,462	5,151	..	..	..	1	1	..
	15—20 ..	7,811	3,356	4,455	32	18	14	7,779	3,338	4,441	..	..	..	3	3	..
	20 and over ..	47,060	23,750	23,310	56	37	19	47,004	23,713	23,291	4	4	..	8	5	3
	Muslim ..	53,421	27,691	25,730	2,114	1,951	163	51,307	25,740	25,567	154	154	..	1,513	1,377	136
	0—5 ..	9,289	4,371	4,918	..	..	..	9,289	4,371	4,918	..	..	..	..	..	..
	5—10 ..	6,722	3,706	3,016	179	140	39	6,543	3,566	2,977	8	8	..	129	96	33
	10—15 ..	5,803	3,302	2,501	352	321	31	5,451	2,981	2,470	29	29	..	284	256	28
	15—20 ..	4,445	2,340	2,105	426	387	39	4,019	1,953	2,066	29	29	..	331	296	35
	20 and over ..	27,162	13,972	13,190	1,157	1,108	54	26,005	12,869	13,136	88	88	..	769	729	40
	Jain ..	3,183	1,728	1,455	493	453	40	2,690	1,275	1,415	8	8	..	44	44	..
	0—5 ..	409	224	185	..	..	..	409	224	185	..	..	..	..	..	..
	5—10 ..	415	265	150	23	16	7	392	249	143	..	..	..	..	..	..
	10—15 ..	283	147	136	37	28	9	246	119	127	1	1	..	1	1	..
	15—20 ..	299	183	116	72	66	6	227	117	110	2	2	..	3	3	..
	20 and over ..	1,777	909	868	361	343	18	1,416	566	850	5	5	..	10	10	..
	Tribal ..	8,280	4,273	4,007	..	..	..	8,280	4,273	4,007	..	..	..	..	..	..
	0—5 ..	1,973	1,064	909	..	..	..	1,973	1,064	909	..	..	..	..	..	..
	5—10 ..	1,148	725	423	..	..	..	1,148	725	423	..	..	..	..	..	..
	10—15 ..	958	463	495	..	..	..	958	463	495	..	..	..	..	..	..
	15—20 ..	682	277	405	..	..	..	682	277	405	..	..	..	..	..	..
	20 and over ..	3,519	1,744	1,775	..	..	..	3,519	1,744	1,775	..	..	..	30	30	..

TABLE XIII.

Literacy by Religion and Age.— Part II —Districts.

District	Religion and Age	POPULATION									Literate in English			Literate in Urdu		
		Total			Literate			Illiterate								
		Persons	Males	Females	Persons	Males	Females	Persons	Males	Females	Persons	Males	Females	Persons	Males	Females
1	2	3	4	5	6	7	8	9	10	11	12	13	14	15	16	17
Nander	**All Religions**	722,081	367,170	354,911	19,297	18,236	1,061	702,784	348,934	353,850	1,297	1,261	36	3,850	3,597	253
	0—5 ..	115,017	57,428	57,589	..	..	..	115,017	57,428	57,589	..	..	..	..	..	..
	5—10 ..	90,159	47,756	42,403	906	783	123	89,253	46,973	42,280	26	24	2	205	176	29
	10—15 ..	77,995	41,202	36,793	2,467	2,347	120	75,528	38,855	36,673	82	80	2	368	339	29
	15—20 ..	64,123	31,652	32,471	2,989	2,794	195	61,134	28,858	32,276	246	238	8	673	623	50
	20 and over ..	374,787	189,132	185,655	12,935	12,312	623	361,852	176,820	185,032	943	919	24	2,604	2,459	145
	Hindu (Brahmanic)	479,445	244,003	235,442	13,678	13,163	515	465,767	230,840	234,927	538	523	15	1,598	1,577	21
	0—5 ..	72,508	36,706	35,802	..	..	..	72,508	36,706	35,802	..	..	..	..	..	..
	5—10 ..	58,477	31,252	27,225	578	526	52	57,899	30,726	27,173	14	13	1	61	59	2
	10—15 ..	52,005	27,334	24,671	2,005	1,946	59	50,000	25,388	24,612	45	43	2	161	157	4
	15—20 ..	42,167	20,463	21,704	2,101	2,009	92	40,066	18,454	21,612	105	99	6	299	296	3
	20 and over ..	254,288	128,248	126,040	8,994	8,682	312	245,294	119,566	125,728	374	368	6	1,077	1,065	12
	Adi-Hindu ..	141,820	71,492	70,328	139	85	54	141,681	71,407	70,274	4	1	3	17	8	9
	0—5 ..	24,168	12,274	11,894	..	..	..	24,168	12,274	11,894	..	..	..	..	..	..
	5—10 ..	18,359	9,619	8,740	12	6	6	18,347	9,613	8,734	..	..	..	1	1	..
	10—15 ..	15,222	7,800	7,422	17	11	6	15,205	7,789	7,416	..	..	..	..	..	..
	15—20 ..	12,742	6,317	6,425	30	13	17	12,712	6,304	6,408	1	..	1	4	1	3
	20 and over ..	71,329	35,482	35,847	80	55	25	71,249	35,427	35,822	3	1	2	12	6	6
	Muslim ..	81,155	41,667	39,488	4,803	4,440	363	76,362	37,237	39,125	633	633	..	2,173	1,950	223
	0—5 ..	14,333	6,457	7,876	..	..	..	14,333	6,457	7,876	..	..	..	..	..	..
	5—10 ..	10,719	5,546	5,173	264	221	43	10,455	5,325	5,130	8	8	..	141	114	27
	10—15 ..	8,658	5,020	3,638	403	357	46	8,255	4,663	3,592	33	33	..	202	177	25
	15—20 ..	7,630	4,142	3,488	788	714	74	6,842	3,428	3,414	129	129	..	360	316	44
	20 and over ..	39,815	20,502	19,313	3,348	3,148	200	36,477	17,364	19,113	463	463	..	1,470	1,343	127
	Jain ..	1,085	556	529	76	71	5	1,009	485	524	7	7	..	16	16	..
	0—5 ..	181	113	68	..	..	..	181	113	68	..	..	..	..	..	..
	5—10 ..	138	73	65	9	9	..	129	64	65	..	..	..	1	1	..
	10—15 ..	126	60	66	13	12	1	113	48	65	1	1	..	2	2	..
	15—20 ..	104	44	60	15	13	2	89	31	58	1	1	..	3	3	..
	20 and over ..	536	266	270	39	37	2	497	229	268	5	5	..	10	10	..
	Sikh ..	1,588	869	719	441	380	61	1,147	489	658	115	97	18	46	46	..
	0—5 ..	222	85	137	..	..	..	222	85	137	..	..	..	..	..	..
	5—10 ..	153	76	77	21	16	5	132	60	72	4	3	1	1	1	..
	10—15 ..	141	66	75	18	16	2	123	50	73	3	3	..	3	3	..
	15—20 ..	122	63	59	40	36	4	82	27	55	10	9	1	7	7	..
	20 and over ..	950	579	371	362	312	50	588	267	321	98	82	16	35	35	..
	Tribal ..	16,369	8,231	8,138	58	10	48	16,311	8,221	8,090	..	..	..	..	..	..
	0—5 ..	3,482	1,730	1,752	..	..	..	3,482	1,730	1,752	..	..	..	..	..	..
	5—10 ..	2,243	1,148	1,095	20	3	17	2,223	1,145	1,078	..	..	..	..	..	..
	10—15 ..	1,773	883	890	8	3	5	1,765	880	885	..	..	..	..	..	..
	15—20 ..	1,289	592	697	3	1	2	1,286	591	695	..	..	..	..	..	..
	20 and over ..	7,582	3,878	3,704	27	3	24	7,555	3,875	3,680	..	..	..	..	..	..

TABLE XIII.

Literacy by Religion and Age.—Part II—Districts.

District.	Religion and Age	POPULATION — Total — Persons	Total — Males	Total — Females	Literate — Persons	Literate — Males	Literate — Females	Illiterate — Persons	Illiterate — Males	Illiterate — Females	Literate in English — Persons	Literate in English — Males	Literate in English — Females	Literate in Urdu — Persons	Literate in Urdu — Males	Literate in Urdu — Females
1	2	3	4	5	6	7	8	9	10	11	12	13	14	15	16	17
Parbhani	**All Religions.**	853,760	434,777	418,983	32,637	28,987	3,650	821,123	405,790	415,333	1,139	1,093	46	7,093	5,806	1,287
	0—5 ..	*147,211*	68,353	78,858	..	..	..	*147,211*	68,353	78,858	..	..	..	..	..	..
	5—10 ..	*113,918*	58,473	55,445	*3,037*	2,543	494	*110,881*	55,930	54,951	*93*	86	7	*556*	449	107
	10—15 ..	*100,765*	51,783	48,982	*3,089*	2,301	788	*97,676*	49,482	48,194	*96*	91	5	*614*	514	100
	15—20 ..	*72,843*	35,609	37,234	*4,438*	3,627	811	*68,405*	31,982	36,423	*142*	136	6	*858*	753	105
	20 and over ..	*419,023*	220,559	198,464	*22,073*	20,516	1,557	*396,950*	200,043	196,907	*808*	780	28	*5,065*	4,090	975
	Hindu (Brahmanic).	589,258	301,611	287,647	24,499	21,913	2,586	564,759	279,698	285,061	828	803	25	3,294	2,528	766
	0—5 ..	*96,272*	44,308	51,964	..	..	..	*96,272*	44,308	51,964	..	..	..	..	..	..
	5—10 ..	*78,024*	40,380	37,644	*2,152*	1,808	344	*75,872*	38,572	37,300	*77*	72	5	*196*	175	21
	10—15 ..	*71,193*	37,211	33,982	*2,235*	1,625	610	*68,958*	35,586	33,372	*76*	73	3	*252*	237	15
	15—20 ..	*51,162*	25,069	26,093	*3,332*	2,720	612	*47,830*	22,349	25,481	*97*	94	3	*383*	373	10
	20 and over ..	*292,607*	154,643	137,964	*16,780*	15,760	1,020	*275,827*	138,883	136,944	*578*	564	14	*2,463*	1,743	720
	Adi-Hindu ..	153,030	76,344	76,686	1,157	1,032	125	151,873	75,312	76,561	9	9	..	91	87	4
	0—5 ..	*29,305*	13,517	15,788	..	..	..	*29,305*	13,517	15,788	..	..	..	..	..	..
	5—10 ..	*21,258*	11,195	10,063	*233*	211	22	*21,025*	10,984	10,041	*3*	3	..	*13*	13	..
	10—15 ..	*18,173*	9,293	8,880	*218*	194	24	*17,955*	9,099	8,856	*1*	1	..	*12*	12	..
	15—20 ..	*12,896*	6,447	6,449	*166*	147	19	*12,730*	6,300	6,430	*2*	2	..	*13*	13	..
	20 and over ..	*71,398*	35,892	35,506	*540*	480	60	*70,858*	35,412	35,446	*3*	3	..	*53*	49	4
	Muslim ..	88,425	45,332	43,093	5,754	5,110	644	82,671	40,222	42,449	282	274	8	3,665	3,148	517
	0—5 ..	*16,255*	8,358	7,897	..	..	..	*16,255*	8,358	7,897	..	..	..	..	..	..
	5—10 ..	*10,970*	5,331	5,639	*514*	416	98	*10,456*	4,915	5,541	*13*	11	2	*345*	259	86
	10—15 ..	*8,671*	4,074	4,597	*500*	398	102	*8,171*	3,676	4,495	*17*	16	1	*346*	261	85
	15—20 ..	*7,087*	3,333	3,754	*767*	655	112	*6,320*	2,078	3,642	*37*	37	..	*454*	359	95
	20 and over ..	*45,442*	24,236	21,206	*3,973*	3,641	332	*41,469*	20,595	20,874	*215*	210	5	*2,520*	2,269	21
	Jain ..	3,685	1,924	1,761	774	645	129	2,911	1,279	1,632	20	7	13	43	43	..
	0—5 ..	*637*	290	347	..	..	..	*637*	290	347	..	..	..	..	..	..
	5—10 ..	*482*	243	239	*90*	76	14	*392*	167	225	..	..	..	*2*	2	..
	10—15 ..	*437*	222	215	*85*	59	26	*352*	163	189	*2*	1	1	*4*	4	..
	15—20 ..	*372*	184	188	*107*	74	33	*265*	110	155	*6*	3	3	*8*	8	..
	0 and over ..	*1,757*	985	772	*492*	436	56	*1,265*	549	716	*12*	3	9	*29*	29	..
	Tribal ..	17,580	8,648	8,932	78	67	11	17,502	8,581	8,921	..	..	..	..	..	..
	0—5 ..	*4,390*	1,690	2,700	..	..	..	*4,390*	1,690	2,700	..	..	..	..	..	..
	5—10 ..	*2,967*	1,218	1,749	*5*	5	..	*2,962*	1,213	1,749	..	..	..	..	..	..
	10—15 ..	*2,066*	864	1,202	*18*	13	5	*2,048*	851	1,197	..	..	..	..	..	..
	15—20 ..	*1,189*	515	674	*21*	16	5	*1,168*	499	669	..	..	..	..	..	..
	20 and over ..	*6,968*	4,361	2,607	*34*	33	1	*6,934*	4,828	2,606	..	..	..	..	..	..

TABLE XIII.

Leteracy by Religion and Age.—Part II— Districts.

District.	Religion and Age	POPULATION									Literate in English			Literate in Urdu		
		Total			Literate			Illiterate								
		Persons	Males	Females	Persons	Males	Females	Persons	Males	Females	Persons	Males	Females	Persons	Males	Females
1	2	3	4	5	6	7	8	9	10	11	12	13	14	15	16	17
Gulbarga	**All Religions.**	1,225,008	621,687	603,321	39,851	33,873	5,978	1,185,157	587,814	597,343	1,937	1,579	358	9,926	8,568	1,358
	0—5 ..	190,796	91,993	98,803	..	..	..	190,796	91,993	98,803	..	..	..	..	..	..
	5—10 ..	146,342	74,670	71,672	3,295	2,409	886	143,047	72,261	70,786	149	103	46	651	460	191
	10—15 ..	129,572	68,599	60,973	4,547	3,840	707	125,025	64,759	60,266	290	236	54	1,172	962	210
	15—20 ..	104,008	51,550	52,458	6,052	5,263	789	97,956	46,287	51,669	208	166	42	1,591	1,411	180
	20 and over ..	654,290	334,875	319,415	25,957	22,361	3,596	628,333	312,514	315,819	1,290	1,074	216	6,512	5,735	777
	Hindu (Brahmanic)	785,929	398,524	387,405	29,070	24,519	4,551	756,859	374,005	382,854	1,020	753	267	4,296	3,772	524
	0—5 ..	113,795	53,882	59,913	..	..	..	113,795	53,882	59,913	..	..	..	..	..	..
	5—10 ..	90,906	45,242	45,664	2,410	1,694	716	88,496	43,548	44,948	91	53	38	224	128	101
	10—15 ..	82,999	43,648	39,351	3,343	2,848	495	79,656	40,800	38,856	204	159	45	559	472	87
	15—20 ..	67,441	33,452	33,989	4,496	3,924	572	62,945	29,528	33,417	79	53	26	782	722	60
	20 and over ..	430,788	222,300	208,488	18,821	16,053	2,768	411,967	206,247	205,720	646	488	158	2,731	2,455	276
	Adi-Hindu ..	194,810	98,250	96,560	391	294	97	194,419	97,956	96,463	12	11	1	43	33	10
	0—5 ..	35,136	17,529	17,607	..	..	..	35,136	17,529	17,607	..	..	..	..	..	..
	5—10 ..	23,992	12,898	11,094	40	23	17	23,952	12,875	11,077	..	..	..	..	..	..
	10—15 ..	19,989	10,833	9,156	62	45	17	19,927	10,788	9,139	..	..	..	7	4	3
	15—20 ..	14,873	7,331	7,542	83	61	22	14,790	7,270	7,520	2	2	..	9	9	..
	20 and over ..	100,820	49,659	51,161	206	165	41	100,614	49,494	51,120	10	9	1	27	20	7
	Muslim ..	195,586	99,636	95,950	9,403	8,296	1,107	186,183	91,340	94,843	763	716	47	5,524	4,704	820
	0—5 ..	32,394	16,007	16,387	..	..	..	32,394	16,007	16,387	..	..	..	..	..	..
	5—10 ..	24,630	12,819	11,811	698	571	127	23,932	12,248	11,684	34	29	5	421	331	90
	10—15 ..	21,270	11,308	9,962	1,003	847	156	20,267	10,461	9,806	67	62	5	597	477	120
	15—20 ..	17,729	8,740	8,989	1,348	1,194	154	16,381	7,546	8,835	112	104	8	791	672	119
	20 and over ..	99,563	50,762	48,801	6,354	5,684	670	93,209	45,078	48,131	550	521	29	3,715	3,224	491
	Jain ..	1,948	1,013	935	456	379	77	1,492	634	858	33	31	2	38	37	1
	0—5 ..	337	183	154	..	..	..	337	383	154	..	..	..	..	..	..
	5—10 ..	251	126	125	45	29	16	206	97	109	2	2	..	3	3	..
	10—15 ..	221	103	118	64	49	15	157	54	103	8	7	1	3	3	..
	15—20 ..	148	75	73	58	49	9	90	26	64	4	3	1	3	3	..
	20 and over ..	991	526	465	289	252	37	702	274	428	19	19	..	29	28	1
	Christian ..	5,645	2,861	2,784	287	229	58	5,358	2,632	2,726	105	64	41	7	7	..
	0—5 ..	946	485	461	..	..	..	946	485	461	..	..	..	..	..	..
	5—10 ..	662	352	310	65	60	5	597	292	305	22	19	3	1	1	..
	10—15 ..	491	194	297	34	29	5	457	165	292	10	7	3	2	2	..
	15—20 ..	515	238	277	19	10	9	496	228	268	9	2	7	..		..
	20 and over ..	3,031	1,592	1,439	169	130	39	2,862	1,462	1,400	64	36	28	4	4	..
	Tribal ..	40,468	21,061	19,407	107	64	43	40,361	20,997	19,364	4	4	..	18	15	3
	0—5 ..	8,075	3,856	4,219	..	..	..	8,075	3,856	4,219	..	..	..	..	..	..
	5—10 ..	5,836	3,203	2,633	17	12	5	5,819	3,191	2,628	..	..	..	2	2	..
	10—15 ..	4,540	2,481	2,059	18	9	9	4,522	2,477	2,050	1	1	..	4	4	..
	15—20 ..	3,236	1,693	1,543	29	16	13	3,207	1,672	1,580	2	2	..	6	5	1
	20 and over ..	18,781	9,828	8,953	43	27	16	18,738	9,801	8,987	1	1	..	6	4	2

TABLE XIII.

Literacy by Religion and Age.—Part II—Districts.

District	Religion and Age	POPULATION									Literate in English			Literate in Urdu		
		Total			Literate			Illiterate								
		Persons	Males	Females	Persons	Males	Females	Persons	Males	Females	Persons	Males	Females	Persons	Males	Females
1	2	3	4	5	6	7	8	9	10	11	12	13	14	15	16	17
Osmanabad	**All Religions.**	691,068	357,489	333,579	16,832	15,123	1,709	674,236	342,366	331,870	969	923	46	2,781	2,313	468
	0—5 ..	119,110	58,580	60,530	..	..	..	119,110	58,580	60,580	..	..	..	..	..	..
	5—10 ..	85,887	43,378	42,509	1,501	1,309	192	84,386	42,069	42,317	48	45	3	170	124	46
	10—15 ..	77,831	40,909	36,922	1,677	1,381	296	76,154	39,528	36,626	108	99	9	353	259	94
	15—20 ..	58,731	29,458	29,273	3,041	2,683	358	55,690	26,775	28,915	318	307	11	574	457	117
	20 and over ..	349,509	185,164	164,345	10,613	9,750	863	338,896	175,414	163,482	495	472	23	1,684	1,473	211
	Hindu (Brahmanic).	464,455	241,373	223,082	14,015	13,150	865	450,440	224,223	226,217	762	737	25	1,198	1,118	80
	0—5 ..	77,237	38,303	38,934	..	..	..	77,237	38,303	38,934	..	..	..	..	..	..
	5—10 ..	57,038	28,702	28,336	1,207	1,111	96	55,831	27,591	28,240	36	35	1	54	52	2
	10—15 ..	52,679	27,803	24,876	1,139	1,020	119	51,540	26,783	24,757	78	77	1	125	117	8
	15—20 ..	40,066	20,389	19,677	2,256	2,108	148	37,810	18,281	19,529	274	269	5	252	233	19
	20 and over ..	237,435	126,176	111,259	9,413	8,911	502	228,022	113,265	114,757	374	356	18	767	716	51
	Adi-Hindu ..	131,904	66,921	64,983	461	348	113	131,443	66,573	64,870	16	13	3	67	52	15
	0—5 ..	24,220	11,484	12,736	..	..	..	24,220	11,484	12,786	..	..	..	..	..	..
	5—10 ..	16,892	8,628	8,264	44	33	11	16,848	8,595	8,253	..	..	..	3	3	..
	10—15 ..	14,412	7,602	6,810	64	43	21	14,348	7,559	6,789	1	..	1	12	8	4
	15—20 ..	10,516	4,994	5,522	111	82	29	10,405	4,912	5,493	4	4	..	20	15	5
	20 and over ..	65,864	34,218	31,651	242	190	52	65,622	34,023	31,599	11	9	2	32	26	6
	Muslim ..	80,308	41,525	38,783	1,813	1,221	592	78,495	40,304	38,191	179	162	17	1,495	1,135	360
	0—5 ..	14,672	7,258	7,414	..	..	..	14,672	7,258	7,414	..	..	..	..	..	..
	5—10 ..	10,166	5,094	5,072	209	141	68	9,957	4,953	5,004	12	10	2	112	69	48
	10—15 ..	9,255	4,753	4,502	394	271	123	8,861	4,482	4,379	29	22	7	214	133	81
	15—20 ..	7,048	3,539	3,509	560	410	150	6,488	3,129	3,359	38	32	6	297	207	90
	20 and over ..	39,167	20,881	18,286	650	399	251	38,517	20,482	18,035	100	98	2	872	726	146
	Jain ..	2,744	1,424	1,320	358	304	54	2,386	1,120	1,266	25	25	..	46	46	..
	0—5 ..	432	225	207	..	..	..	432	225	207	..	..	..	..	..	..
	5—10 ..	345	178	167	21	14	7	324	164	160	2	2	..	..	..	..
	10—15 ..	311	152	159	54	40	14	257	112	145	4	4	..	8	8	..
	15—20 ..	249	112	137	75	62	13	174	50	124	7	7	..	13	13	..
	20 and over ..	1,407	757	650	208	188	20	1,199	569	630	12	12	..	25	25	..
	Tribal ..	11,299	6,032	5,267	86	27	59	11,213	6,005	5,208	4	3	1	17	6	11
	0—5 ..	2,488	1,274	1,214	..	..	..	2,488	1,274	1,214	..	..	..	..	..	..
	5—10 ..	1,395	747	648	8	1	7	1,387	746	641	..	..	..	1	..	1
	10—15 ..	1,130	575	555	20	5	15	1,110	570	540	..	..	..	2	1	1
	15—20 ..	813	403	410	19	6	13	794	397	397	1	1	..	4	1	8
	20 and over ..	5,473	3,033	2,440	39	15	24	5,434	3,018	2,416	3	2	1	10	4	6

TABLE XIII.

Literacy by Religion and Age.—Part II— Districts.

District	Religion and Age	POPULATION									Literate in English			Literate in Urdu		
		Total			Literate			Illiterate								
		Persons	Males	Females	Persons	Males	Females	Persons	Males	Females	Persons	Males	Females	Persons	Males	Females
1	2	3	4	5	6	7	8	9	10	11	12	13	14	15	16	17
Raichur	**All Religions.**	937,535	473,161	464,374	44,986	40,532	4,454	892,549	432,629	459,920	3,093	2,873	220	13,494	11,309	2,185
	0—5 ..	136,189	64,902	71,287	..	..	..	136,189	64,902	71287	..	..	..	..	..	..
	5—10 ..	117,516	59,813	57,703	4,839	4,018	821	112,677	55,795	56,882	180	137	43	984	704	280
	10—15 ..	106,812	53,735	51,077	6,670	5,831	839	100,142	49,904	50,238	353	304	49	1.407	1,158	249
	15—20 ..	84,439	43,529	40,910	8,992	8,186	806	75,447	35,343	40,104	594	547	47	1,926	1,708	218
	20 and over ..	492,579	249,182	243,397	24,485	22,497	1,988	468,094	226,685	241,409	1,966	1,885	81	9,177	7.739	1,438
	Hindu (Brahmanic) .	708,167	357,673	350,494	32,023	28,998	3,025	676,144	328,675	347,469	1,868	1,717	151	6,617	5,451	1,166
	0—5 ..	100,587	47750	52,837	..	..	..	100,587	47,750	52,837	..	..	..	..	..	..
	5—10 ..	87,539	44267	43,272	3,725	3,180	545	83,814	41,087	42,727	86	55	31	337	259	78
	10—15 ..	79,496	41866	37,630	5,310	4,688	622	74,186	37,178	37,008	212	175	37	692	586	106
	15—20 ..	63,697	33,071	30,626	7,252	6,654	598	56,445	26,417	30,028	373	340	33	1,054	979	75
	20 and over ..	376,848	190,719	186,129	15,736	14,476	1,260	361,112	176,243	184,869	1,197	1,147	50	4,534	3,627	907
	Adi-Hindu ..	112,992	55,726	57,266	1,902	1,821	81	111,090	53,905	57,185	164	162	2	452	448	4
	0—5 ..	17,735	8,606	9,129	..	..	..	17,735	8,606	9,129	..	..	..	..	..	..
	5—10 ..	15,158	7,467	7,691	148	133	15	15,010	7,334	7,676	6	6	..	39	39	..
	10—15 ..	13,807	6,792	7,015	237	220	17	13,570	6,372	6,998	22	22	..	36	36	..
	15—20 ..	10,448	5,056	5,392	357	343	14	10,091	4,713	5,378	46	45	1	69	67	2
	20 and over ..	55,844	27,805	28,039	1,160	1,125	35	54,684	26,680	28,004	90	89	1	308	306	2
	Muslim ..	95,699	48,756	46,943	9,780	8,641	1,139	85,919	40,115	45,804	728	705	23	6,280	5,269	1,011
	0—5 ..	14,310	6,892	7,418	..	..	..	14,310	6,892	7,418	..	..	..	..	..	..
	5—10 ..	12,471	6,510	5,961	795	575	220	11,676	5,935	5,741	47	41	6	594	393	201
	10—15 ..	10,777	5,614	5,163	960	793	167	9,817	4,821	4,996	88	82	6	659	517	142
	15—20 ..	8,287	4,446	3,841	1,206	1,046	160	7,081	3,400	3,681	129	125	4	787	646	141
	20 and over ..	49,854	25,294	24,560	6,819	6,227	592	43,035	19,067	23,968	464	457	7	4,240	3,718	527
	Christian ..	3,875	2,130	1,745	763	671	92	3,112	1,459	1,653	328	285	43	104	100	4
	0—5 ..	573	281	292	..	..	..	573	281	292	..	..	..	..	..	..
	5—10 ..	545	296	249	112	94	18	433	202	231	41	35	6	10	9	1
	10—15 ..	464	275	189	92	77	15	372	198	174	31	25	6	13	12	1
	15—20 ..	313	150	163	106	90	16	207	60	147	45	36	9	12	12	..
	20 and over ..	1,980	1,128	852	453	410	43	1,527	718	809	211	189	22	69	67	2
	Tribal ..	15,800	8,343	7,457	144	123	21	15,656	8,220	7,436	5	4	1	41	41	..
	0—5 ..	2,846	1,318	1,528	..	..	..	2,846	1,318	1,528	..	..	..	..	..	..
	5—10 ..	1,701	1,229	472	17	12	5	1,684	1,217	467	..	..	..	4	4	..
	10—15 ..	2,180	1,138	1,042	22	20	2	2,158	1,118	1,040	..	..	..	7	7	..
	15—20 ..	1,621	758	863	22	19	3	1,599	739	800	1	1	1	4	4	..
	20 and over ..	7,452	3,900	3,552	83	72	11	7,369	3,828	35,41	4	3		26	26	..

TABLE XIII.

Literacy by Religion and Age.—Part II— Districts.

District	Religion and Age	POPULATION									Literate in English			Literate in Urdu		
		Total			Literate			Illiterate								
		Persons	Males	Females	Persons	Males	Females	Persons	Males	Females	Persons	Males	Females	Persons	Males	Females
1	2	3	4	5	6	7	8	9	10	11	12	13	14	15	16	17
Bidar	**All Religions.**	873,615	446,256	427,359	22,097	20,000	2,097	851,518	426,256	425,262	1,255	1,034	221	6,028	5,431	597
	0—5 ..	*175,457*	80,426	95,031	..	..	..	*175,457*	80,426	95,031	..	..	..	..	..	..
	5—10 ..	*103,377*	52,652	50,725	*2,116*	1,881	235	*101,261*	50,771	50,490	*147*	133	14	*876*	803	73
	10—15 ..	*91,821*	49,381	42,440	*1,668*	1,270	398	*90,153*	48,111	42,042	*267*	235	32	*1,266*	1,141	125
	15—20 ..	*74,122*	37,342	36,780	*5,958*	5,493	465	*68,164*	31,849	36,315	*244*	203	41	*1,339*	1,198	141
	20 and over ..	*428,838*	226,455	202,383	*12,355*	11,356	999	*416,483*	215,099	201,384	*597*	463	134	*2,547*	2,289	258
	Hindu (Brahmanic) ..	554,768	284,718	270,050	15,386	14,682	704	539,382	270,036	269,346	517	495	22	2,255	2,181	74
	0—5 ..	*109,882*	48,442	61,440	..	..	..	*109,882*	48,442	61,440	..	..	..	..	..	..
	5—10 ..	*61,543*	32,591	28,952	*1,197*	1,083	114	*60,346*	31,508	28,838	*56*	53	3	*213*	205	8
	10—15 ..	*57,399*	31,723	25,676	*2,278*	2,121	157	*55,121*	29,602	25,519	*118*	113	5	*476*	465	11
	15—20 ..	*46,550*	23,409	23,141	*4,325*	4,164	161	*42,225*	19,245	22,980	*108*	102	6	*583*	566	17
	20 and over ..	*279,394*	148,553	130,841	*7,586*	7,314	272	*271,808*	141,239	130,569	*235*	227	8	*983*	945	38
	Adi-Hindu ..	163,143	81,971	81,172	579	442	137	162,564	81,529	81,035	147	142	5	87	73	14
	0—5 ..	*33,250*	17,841	15,409	..	..	..	*33,250*	17,841	15,409	..	..	..	..	..	..
	5—10 ..	*21,914*	10,031	11,883	*112*	80	32	*21,802*	9,951	11,851	*50*	48	2	*10*	6	4
	10—15 ..	*16,588*	8,084	8,504	*118*	94	24	*16,470*	7,990	8,480	*59*	58	1	*10*	6	4
	15—20 ..	*13,398*	6,129	7,269	*90*	72	18	*13,308*	6,057	7,251	*24*	24	..	*12*	9	3
	20 and over ..	*77,993*	39,886	38,107	*259*	196	63	*77,734*	39,690	38,044	*14*	12	2	*55*	52	3
	Muslim ..	136,309	69,509	66,800	5,240	4,562	678	131,069	64,947	66,122	391	372	19	3,632	3,161	471
	0—5 ..	*28,352*	12,164	16,188	..	..	..	*28,352*	12,164	16,188	..	..	..	..	..	..
	5—10 ..	*17,416*	8,818	8,598	*762*	695	67	*16,654*	8,123	8,531	*31*	30	1	*653*	592	61
	10—15 ..	*15,811*	8,554	7,257	*1,049*	893	156	*14,762*	7,661	7,101	*66*	62	4	*776*	668	108
	15—20 ..	*12,540*	7,019	5,521	*1,085*	897	188	*11,455*	6,122	5,333	*76*	71	5	*729*	617	112
	20 and over ..	*62,190*	32,954	29,236	*2,344*	2,077	267	*59,846*	30,877	28,969	*218*	209	9	*1,474*	1,284	190
	Christian ..	4,354	2,194	2,160	656	115	541	3,698	2,079	1,619	200	25	175	50	12	38
	0—5 ..	*758*	368	390	..	..	..	*758*	368	390	..	..	..	..	..	..
	5—10 ..	*484*	234	250	*33*	12	21	*451*	222	229	*10*	2	8	..	..	..
	10—15 ..	*436*	214	222	*79*	23	56	*357*	191	166	*24*	2	22	*3*	1	2
	15—20 ..	*382*	170	212	*120*	30	90	*262*	140	122	*36*	6	30	*13*	4	9
	20 and over ..	*2,294*	1,208	1,086	*424*	50	374	*1,870*	1,158	712	*130*	15	115	*34*	7	27
	Tribal ..	13,787	7,201	6,586	30	30	..	13,757	7,171	6,586	..	..	..	4	4	..
	0—5 ..	*2,982*	1,517	1,465	..	..	..	*2,982*	1,517	1,465	..	..	..	..	..	..
	5—10 ..	*1,876*	909	967	*5*	5	..	*1,871*	904	967	..	..	..	..	..	..
	10—15 ..	*1,463*	731	732	*6*	6	..	*1,457*	725	732	..	..	..	*1*	1	..
	15—20 ..	*1,136*	548	588	*8*	8	..	*1,128*	540	588	..	..	..	*2*	2	..
	20 and over ..	*6,330*	3,496	2,834	*11*	11	..	*6,319*	3,485	2,834	..	..	..	*1*	1	..

TABLE XIII.

Literacy by Religion and Age—Part III.—Hyderabad City.

RELIGION AND AGE	POPULATION									Literate in English			Literate in Urdu		
	Total			Literate			Illiterate								
	Persons	Males	Females	Persons	Males	Females	Persons	Males	Females	Persons	Males	Females	Persons	Males	Females
1	2	3	4	5	6	7	8	9	10	11	12	13	14	15	16
All Religions ..	**466,894**	**247,623**	**219,271**	**137,070**	**111,234**	**25,836**	**329,824**	**136,389**	**193,435**	**46,605**	**41,179**	**5,426**	**85,407**	**69,022**	**16,385**
0—5	*53,270*	22,950	30,320	..	..	..	*53,270*	22,950	30,320	..	..	..	..	..	..
5—10	*42,105*	20,289	21,816	*8,556*	6,287	2,269	*33,549*	14,002	19,547	*1,756*	1,144	612	*1,893*	841	1,052
10—15	*40,686*	23,831	16,855	*14,388*	11,338	3,050	*26,298*	12,493	13,805	*3,807*	2,917	890	*5,810*	4,267	1,543
15—20	*53,654*	29,773	23,881	*22,303*	16,613	5,690	*31,351*	13,160	18,191	*7,159*	6,192	967	*12,348*	10,365	1,983
20 and over ..	*277,179*	150,780	126,399	*91,823*	76,996	14,827	*185,356*	73,784	111,572	*33,883*	30,926	2,957	*65,356*	53,549	11,807
Hindu (Brahmanic) ..	**172,279**	**90,790**	**81,489**	**60,062**	**50,978**	**9,084**	**112,217**	**39,812**	**72,405**	***25,587***	**24,322**	**1,265**	**30,998**	**25,398**	**5,609**
0—5	*23,528*	7,312	16,216	..	..	..	*23,528*	7,312	16,216	..	..	..	..	..	..
5—10	*17,636*	7,216	10,420	*3,817*	3,224	593	*13,819*	3,992	9,827	*480*	353	127	*460*	359	101
10—15	*17,776*	10,881	6,895	*7,529*	6,852	677	*10,247*	4,029	6,218	*1,943*	1,717	226	*1,742*	1,541	201
15—20	*19,470*	12,109	7,361	*11,153*	8,341	2,812	*8,317*	3,768	4,549	*3,712*	3,474	238	*5,451*	5,121	330
20 and over ..	*93,869*	53,272	40,597	*37,563*	32,561	5,002	*56,306*	20,711	35,595	*19,452*	18,778	674	*23,345*	18,368	4,977
Adi Hindu ..	**79,839**	**41,120**	**38,719**	**4,464**	**4,049**	**415**	**75,375**	**37,071**	**38,304**	***643***	**596**	**47**	**1,069**	**980**	**89**
0—5	*7,455*	4,092	3,363	..	..	..	*7,455*	4,092	3,363	..	..	..	..	..	..
5—10	*5,722*	3,284	2,438	*318*	259	59	*5,404*	3,025	2,379	*33*	28	5	*99*	84	15
10—15	*4,198*	2,893	1,305	*385*	332	53	*3,813*	2,561	1,252	*49*	42	7	*108*	99	9
15—20	*6,526*	2,785	3,741	*695*	626	69	*5,831*	2,159	3,672	*117*	107	10	*153*	137	16
20 and over ..	*55,938*	28,066	27,872	*3,066*	2,832	234	*52,872*	25,234	27,638	*444*	419	25	*709*	660	49
Arya	**382**	**196**	**186**	**53**	**43**	**10**	**329**	**153**	**176**	***32***	**20**	**12**	**43**	**37**	**6**
0—5	*67*	45	22	..	..	..	*67*	45	22	..	..	..	..	..	..
5—10	*14*	2	12	*3*	2	1	*11*	..	11	*2*	1	1	..	..	..
10—15	*13*	2	11	*3*	2	1	*10*	..	10	*2*	1	1	*2*	1	1
15—20	*8*	4	4	*6*	2	4	*2*	2	..	*5*	2	3	*2*	1	1
20 and over ..	*280*	143	137	*41*	37	4	*239*	106	133	*23*	16	7	*39*	35	4
Brahmo	**77**	**44**	**33**	**48**	**38**	**10**	**29**	**6**	**23**	***35***	**30**	**5**	**30**	**30**	..
0—5	*10*	3	7	..	..	..	*10*	3	7	..	..	..	..	..	..
5—10	*5*	3	2	*3*	2	1	*2*	1	1	*1*	1	..	*2*	2	..
10—15	*5*	3	2	*4*	2	2	*1*	1	..	*2*	2	..	*2*	2	..
15—20	*8*	3	5	*5*	2	3	*3*	1	2	*4*	2	2	*2*	2	..
20 and over ..	*49*	32	17	*36*	32	4	*13*	..	13	*28*	25	3	*24*	24	..

TABLE XIII.

Literacy by Religion and Age.—Part III—Hyderabad City.

RELIGION AND AGE	POPULATION									Literate in English			Literate in Urdu		
	Total			Literate			Illiterate								
	Persons	Males	Females	Persons	Males	Females	Persons	Males	Females	Persons	Males	Females	Persons	Males	Females
1	2	3	4	5	6	7	8	9	10	11	12	13	14	15	16
Jain	312	194	118	175	151	24	137	43	94	45	43	2	105	105	..
0—5	31	14	17	..	..	..	31	14	17	..	..	..	..	..	..
5—10	23	21	2	20	19	1	3	2	1	..	..	..	12	12	..
10—15	23	18	5	18	17	1	5	1	4	11	10	1	15	15	..
15—20	26	15	11	18	15	2	8	..	8	9	8	1	14	14	..
20 and over ..	209	126	83	119	100	19	90	26	64	25	25	..	64	64	..
Sikh	1,002	690	312	369	310	59	633	380	253	123	105	18	319	303	16
0—5	89	62	27	..	..	..	89	62	27	..	..	..	..	..	..
5—10	63	35	28	14	9	5	49	26	23	3	1	2	8	5	3
10—15	95	33	62	9	3	6	86	30	56	4	3	1	5	2	3
15—20	154	114	40	62	55	7	92	59	33	22	20	2	56	54	2
20 and over ..	601	446	155	284	243	41	317	203	114	94	81	13	250	242	8
Muslim	192,343	103,095	89,248	60,001	48,315	11,686	132,342	54,780	77,562	11,058	10,031	1,027	48,885	38,768	10,117
0—5	19,380	9,897	9,483	..	..	..	19,380	9,897	9,483	..	..	..	..	..	..
5—10	16,764	8,865	7,899	3,305	2,221	1,084	13,459	6,644	6,815	551	438	113	1,111	260	851
10—15	16,365	8,806	7,559	5,183	3,517	1,666	11,182	5,289	5,893	1,011	815	196	3,410	2,115	1,265
15—20	25,262	13,548	11,714	8,575	6,516	2,059	16,687	7,032	9,655	1,871	1,046	225	5,599	4,060	1,539
20 and over ..	114,572	61,970	52,598	42,938	36,061	6,877	71,634	25,918	45,716	7,625	7,132	493	38,765	32,303	6,462
Christian	16,123	9,217	6,906	10,575	6,604	3,971	5,548	2,613	2,935	8,322	5,625	2,697	3,346	2,971	375
0—5	2,199	1,252	947	..	..	..	2,199	1,252	947	..	..	..	..	..	..
5—10	1,504	659	845	953	483	470	551	176	375	634	289	345	122	90	32
10—15	1,860	1,031	829	1,121	541	580	739	490	249	703	297	406	468	430	38
15—20	1,829	1,007	822	1,656	1,000	656	173	7	166	1,332	906	426	1,009	945	64
20 and over ..	8,731	5,268	3,463	6,845	4,580	2,265	1,886	688	1,198	5,653	4,133	1,520	1,747	1,506	241

TABLE XIII.

Literacy by Religion and Age.—Part III.—Hyderabad City.

RELIGION AND AGE	POPULATION									Literate in English			Literate in Urdu		
	Total			Literate			Illiterate								
	Persons	Males	Females	Persons	Males	Females	Persons	Males	Females	Persons	Males	Females	Persons	Males	Females
1	2	3	4	5	6	7	8	9	10	11	12	13	14	15	16
Zoroastrian	1,092	548	544	984	508	476	108	40	68	695	368	327	492	366	126
0—5	44	20	24	..	..	..	44	20	24	..	..	..	..	..	..
5—10	82	58	24	78	56	22	4	2	2	50	31	19	44	24	20
10—15	112	52	60	110	50	60	2	2	..	82	30	52	50	26	24
15—20	104	41	63	96	33	63	8	8	..	83	23	60	48	20	28
20 and over ..	750	377	373	700	369	331	0	8	42	480	284	166	350	296	54
Buddhist	38	20	18	24	17	7	14	3	11	13	10	3	..	..	..
0—5	4	1	3	..	..	..	4	1	3	..	..	..	..	..	..
5—10	2	1	1	..	..	..	2	1	1	..	..	..	..	..	..
10—15	4	2	2	1	1	..	3	1	2	..	..	..	..	..	..
15—20	3	1	2	2	1	1	1	..	1	1	1	..	..	..	..
20 and over ..	25	15	10	21	15	6	4	..	4	12	9	3	..	..	..
Jew	27	11	16	19	9	10	8	2	6	2	2	..	..	..	..
0—5	3	1	2	..	..	..	3	1	2	..	..	..	..	..	..
5—10	..	..	..	..	..	..	..	..	..	..	..	..	..	..	..
10—15	3	1	2	2	1	1	1	..	1	..	..	..	..	..	..
15—20	3	1	2	3	1	2	..	..	..	..	..	..	..	..	..
20 and over ..	18	8	10	14	7	7	4	1	3	2	2	..	..	..	..
Tribal	3,380	1,698	1,682	296	212	84	3,084	1,486	1,598	50	27	23	120	73	47
0—5	460	251	209	..	..	..	460	251	209	..	..	..	..	..	..
5—10	290	145	145	45	12	33	245	133	112	2	2	..	35	5	30
10—15	232	109	123	23	20	3	209	89	120	..	..	..	8	6	2
15—20	261	145	116	31	20	11	230	125	105	3	3	..	14	11	3
20 and over ..	2,137	1,048	1,089	197	160	37	1,940	888	1,052	45	22	23	63	51	12

TABLE XIII.

Literacy by Religion and Age.—Part III.—Warangal City.

RELIGION AND AGE	POPULATION									Literate in English			Literate in Urdu		
	Total			Literate			Illiterate								
	Persons	Males	Females	Persons	Males	Females	Persons	Males	Females	Persons	Males	Females	Persons	Males	Females
1	2	3	4	5	6	7	8	9	10	11	12	13	14	15	16
All Religions ..	62,119	33,326	28,793	10,962	9,199	1,763	51,157	24,127	27,030	1,732	1,626	106	3,943	3,257	686
0—5	*7,837*	3,465	4,372	..	..	..	*7,837*	3,465	4,372	..	..	..	..	..	..
5—10	*7,748*	3,212	4,536	*678*	499	179	*7,070*	2,713	4,357	*45*	37	8	*266*	183	83
10—15	*8,042*	3,698	4,344	*1,329*	1,086	243	*6,713*	2,612	4,101	*203*	192	11	*526*	392	134
15—20	*7,411*	3,756	3,655	*1,786*	1,507	279	*5,625*	2,249	3,376	*315*	301	14	*667*	519	148
20 and over ..	*31,081*	19,195	11,886	*7,169*	6,107	1,062	*23,912*	13,088	10,824	*1,169*	1,096	73	*2,484*	2,163	321
Hindu (Brahmanic) ..	35,199	18,926	16,273	7,261	6,460	801	27,938	12,466	15,472	1,348	1,316	32	1,710	1,652	58
0—5	*4,543*	1,823	2,720	..	..	..	*4,543*	1,823	2,720	..	..	..	..	..	..
5—10	*4,085*	1,726	2,359	*377*	301	76	*3,708*	1,425	2,283	*34*	31	3	*58*	52	6
10—15	*4,425*	2,648	1,777	*861*	782	79	*3,564*	1,866	1,698	*170*	166	4	*208*	200	8
15—20	*4,769*	2,914	1,855	*1,204*	1,119	85	*3,565*	1,795	1,770	*249*	244	5	*301*	292	9
20 and over ..	*17,377*	9,815	7,562	*4,819*	4,258	561	*12,558*	5,557	7,001	*895*	875	20	*1,143*	1,108	35
Adi Hindu ..	11,336	5,812	5,524	294	189	105	11,042	5,623	5,419	11	11	..	55	55	..
0—5	*1,304*	542	762	..	..	..	*1,304*	542	762	..	..	..	..	..	..
5—10	*1,855*	410	1,445	*26*	14	12	*1,829*	396	1,433	..	..	..	..	..	..
10—15	*1,522*	330	1,192	*46*	27	19	*1,476*	303	1,173	*1*	1	..	*2*	2	..
15—20	*691*	223	468	*51*	38	13	*640*	185	455	*3*	3	..	*4*	4	..
20 and over ..	*5,964*	4,307	1,657	*171*	110	61	*5,793*	4,197	1,596	*7*	7	..	*49*	49	..
Sikh	114	72	42	46	44	2	68	28	40	3	3	..	12	12	..
0—5	*11*	6	5	..	..	..	*11*	6	5	..	..	..	..	..	..
5—10	*12*	8	4	*1*	1	..	*11*	7	4	..	..	..	..	..	..
10—15	*16*	9	7	*2*	2	..	*14*	7	7	..	..	..	*1*	1	..
15—20	*15*	10	5	*7*	6	1	*8*	4	4	..	..	..	*3*	3	..
20 and over ..	*60*	39	21	*36*	35	1	*24*	4	20	*3*	3	..	*8*	8	..

TABLE XIII.

Literacy by Religion and Age.—Part III.—Warangal City.

RELIGION AND AGE	POPULATION									Literate in English			Literate in Urdu		
	Total			Literate			Illiterate								
	Persons	Males	Females	Persons	Males	Females	Persons	Males	Females	Persons	Males	Females	Persons	Males	Females
1	2	3	4	5	6	7	8	9	10	11	12	13	14	15	16
Muslim	14,460	8,003	6,457	3,016	2,292	724	11,444	5,711	5,733	238	222	16	2,139	1,526	613
0—5	*1,799*	974	825	..	..	..	*1,799*	974	825	..	..	..	..	..	..
5—10	*1,688*	988	700	*244*	164	80	*1,444*	824	620	..	..	..	*207*	131	76
10—15	*1,944*	650	1,294	*375*	241	134	*1,569*	409	1,160	*14*	13	1	*314*	189	125
15—20	*1,819*	570	1,249	*484*	316	168	*1,335*	254	1,081	*44*	40	4	*358*	220	138
20 and over ..	*7,210*	4,821	2,389	*1,913*	1,571	342	*5,297*	3,250	2,047	*180*	169	11	*1,260*	986	274
Christian	748	357	391	328	197	131	420	160	260	129	74	55	22	8	14
0—5	*141*	99	42	..	..	..	*141*	99	42	..	..	..	..	..	..
5—10	*76*	59	17	*29*	18	11	*47*	41	6	*11*	6	5	*1*	..	1
10—15	*106*	45	61	*44*	33	11	*62*	12	50	*18*	12	6	*1*	..	1
15—20	*96*	28	68	*38*	26	12	*58*	2	56	*19*	14	5	*1*	..	1
20 and over ..	*329*	126	203	*217*	120	97	*112*	6	106	*81*	42	39	*19*	8	11
Zoroastrian ..	7	7	..	4	4	..	3	3	..	3	..	3	3	3	..
0—5	..	..	..	..	..	..	..	..	..	..	..	..	..	..	..
5—10	*1*	1	..	..	..	..	*1*	1	..	..	..	..	..	..	..
10—15	*1*	1	..	..	..	..	*1*	1	..	..	..	..	..	..	..
15—20	..	..	..	..	..	..	..	..	..	..	..	..	..	..	..
20 and over ..	*5*	5	..	*4*	4	..	*1*	1	..	*3*	..	3	*3*	3	..
Tribal	255	149	106	13	13	..	242	136	106	..	..	..	2	1	1
0—5	*39*	21	18	..	..	..	*39*	21	18	..	..	..	..	..	..
5—10	*31*	20	11	*1*	1	..	*30*	19	11	..	..	..	..	..	..
10—15	*28*	15	13	*1*	1	..	*27*	14	13	..	..	..	..	..	..
15—20	*21*	11	10	*2*	2	..	*19*	9	10	..	..	..	..	..	..
20 and over ..	*136*	82	54	*9*	9	..	*127*	73	54	..	..	..	*2*	1	1

TABLE XIII.

Literacy by Religion and Age.— Part III—Aurangabad City.

RELIGION AND AGE	POPULATION									Literate in English			Literate in Urdu		
	Total			Literate			Illiterate								
	Persons	Males	Females	Persons	Males	Females	Persons	Males	Females	Persons	Males	Females	Persons	Males	Females
1	2	3	4	5	6	7	8	9	10	11	12	13	14	15	16
All Religions ..	36,870	19,622	17,248	12,127	10,855	1,272	24,743	8,767	15,976	2,592	2,475	117	6,046	5,503	543
0—5	*3,722*	1,836	1,886	..	..	..	*3,722*	1,836	1,886	..	..	..	..	..	..
5—10	*3,138*	1,569	1,569	*1,170*	1,042	128	*1,968*	527	1,441	*90*	80	10	*718*	663	55
10—15	*3,812*	2,154	1,658	*1,655*	1,496	159	*2,157*	658	1,499	*500*	485	15	*873*	792	81
15—20	*5,876*	3,118	2,758	*2,176*	1,967	209	*3,700*	1,151	2,549	*580*	561	19	*1,079*	938	141
20 and over ..	*20,322*	10,945	9,377	*7,126*	6,350	776	*13,196*	4,595	8,601	*1,422*	1,349	73	*3,376*	3,110	266
Hindu (Brahmanic) ..	15,520	8,372	7,148	4,452	4,057	395	11,068	4,315	6,753	944	920	24	790	754	36
0—5	*1,646*	836	810	..	..	..	*1,646*	836	810	..	..	..	..	..	..
5—10	*1,364*	709	655	*365*	315	50	*999*	394	605	*40*	38	2	*159*	155	4
10—15	*1,294*	687	607	*489*	435	54	*805*	252	553	*110*	108	2	*132*	127	5
15—20	*3,194*	1,442	1,752	*649*	599	50	*2,545*	843	1,702	*193*	190	3	*82*	80	2
20 and over ..	*8,022*	4,698	3,324	*2,949*	2,708	241	*5,073*	1,990	3,083	*601*	584	17	*417*	392	25
Adi Hindu ..	3,212	1,494	1,718	421	390	31	2,791	1,104	1,687	45	43	2	177	174	3
0—5	*303*	167	136	..	..	..	*303*	167	136	..	..	..	..	..	..
5—10	*224*	126	98	*63*	58	5	*161*	68	93	*2*	2	..	*49*	49	..
10—15	*426*	105	321	*42*	36	6	*384*	69	315	*1*	1	..	*27*	27	..
15—20	*383*	76	307	*57*	52	5	*326*	24	302	*8*	7	1	*2*	2	..
20 and over ..	*1,876*	1,020	856	*259*	244	15	*1,617*	776	841	*34*	33	1	*99*	96	3
Jain	361	215	146	156	137	19	205	78	127	56	56	..	23	22	1
0—5	*37*	18	19	..	..	..	*37*	18	19	..	..	..	..	..	..
5—10	*23*	16	7	*11*	6	5	*12*	10	2	..	..	..	*6*	6	..
10—15	*25*	18	7	*13*	11	2	*12*	7	5	*10*	10	..	*5*	5	..
15—20	*40*	24	16	*14*	13	1	*26*	11	15	*10*	10	..	*3*	3	..
20 and over ..	*236*	139	97	*118*	107	11	*118*	32	86	*36*	36	..	*9*	8	1

TABLE XIII.

Literacy by Religion and Age.—Part III—Aurangabad City.

RELIGION AND AGE	POPULATION									Literate in English			Literate in Urdu		
	Total			Literate			Illiterate								
	Persons	Males	Females	Persons	Males	Females	Persons	Males	Females	Persons	Males	Females	Persons	Males	Females
1	2	3	4	5	6	7	8	9	10	11	12	13	14	15	16
Sikh	**374**	**296**	**78**	**154**	**148**	**6**	**220**	**148**	**72**	**19**	**19**	..	**105**	**105**	..
0—5	*54*	49	5	..	..	..	*54*	49	5	..	..	..	..	..	..
5—10	*28*	21	7	*10*	10	..	*18*	11	7	..	..	..	*9*	9	..
10—15	*40*	30	10	*10*	10	..	*30*	20	10	*2*	2	..	*7*	7	..
15—20	*41*	25	16	*18*	15	3	*23*	10	13	*3*	3	..	*39*	39	..
20 and over ..	*211*	171	40	*116*	113	3	*95*	58	37	*14*	14	..	*50*	50	..
Muslim	**16,104**	**8,567**	**7,537**	**6,331**	**5,713**	**618**	**9,773**	**2,854**	**6,919**	**1,244**	**1,214**	**30**	**4,717**	**4,259**	**458**
0—5	*1,605*	727	878	..	..	..	*1,605*	727	878	..	..	..	..	..	..
5—10	*1,451*	677	774	*700*	644	56	*751*	33	718	*34*	30	4	*452*	406	46
10—15	*1,884*	1,196	688	*1,046*	962	84	*838*	234	604	*363*	355	8	*660*	590	70
15—20	*1,994*	1,351	643	*1,266*	1,122	144	*728*	229	409	*318*	312	6	*916*	783	133
20 and over ..	*9,170*	4,616	4,554	*3,319*	2,985	334	*5,851*	1,681	4,220	*529*	517	12	*2,689*	2,480	209
Christian	**788**	**440**	**348**	**479**	**339**	**140**	**309**	**101**	**208**	**245**	**200**	**45**	**161**	**137**	**24**
0—5	*2*	1	1	..	..	..	*2*	1	1	..	..	..	..	..	..
5—10	*1*	1	..	..	..	..	*1*	1	..	*11*	8	3	*28*	25	3
10—15	*101*	100	1	*39*	39	..	*62*	61	1	*11*	8	3	*25*	22	3
15—20	*175*	175	..	*156*	156	..	*19*	19	..	*38*	33	5	*21*	18	3
20 and over ..	*509*	168	340	*284*	144	140	*225*	19	206	*185*	151	34	*87*	72	15
Zoroastrian ..	**197**	**101**	**96**	**134**	**71**	**63**	**63**	**30**	**33**	**39**	**23**	**16**	**73**	**52**	**21**
0—5	*35*	15	20	..	..	..	*35*	15	20	..	..	..	..	..	..
5—10	*29*	10	19	*21*	9	12	*8*	1	7	*3*	2	1	*15*	13	2
10—15	*19*	5	14	*16*	8	18	*3*	2	1	*3*	1	2	*17*	14	3
15—20	*23*	14	9	*16*	10	6	*7*	4	3	*10*	6	4	*16*	13	3
20 and over ..	*91*	57	34	*81*	49	32	*10*	8	2	*23*	14	9	*25*	12	13

TABLE XIII.

Literacy by Religion and Age Part III—Gulbarga City.

RELIGION AND AGE	POPULATION									Literate in English			Literate in Urdu		
	Total			Literate			Illiterate								
	Persons	Males	Females	Persons	Males	Females	Persons	Males	Females	Persons	Males	Females	Persons	Males	Females
1	2	3	4	5	6	7	8	9	10	11	12	13	14	15	16
All Religions ..	**41,083**	**21,567**	**19,516**	**6,220**	**5,525**	**695**	**34,863**	**16,042**	**18,821**	**994**	**927**	**67**	**2,988**	**2,597**	**391**
0—5	*6,795*	3,117	3,678	..	..	..	*6,795*	3,117	3,678	..	..	..	..	..	..
5—10	*4,480*	2,586	1,894	*450*	377	73	*4,030*	2,209	1,821	*55*	48	7	*232*	187	45
10—15	*3,616*	2,367	1,249	*737*	650	87	*2,879*	1,717	1,162	*100*	93	7	*360*	308	52
15—20	*4,030*	2,012	2,018	*1,024*	922	102	*3,006*	1,090	1,916	*193*	179	14	*500*	446	54
20 and over ..	*22,162*	11,485	10,677	*4,009*	3,576	433	*18,153*	7,909	10,244	*646*	607	39	*1,896*	1,656	240
Hindu (Brahmanic) ..	**17,509**	**9,465**	**8,044**	**3,636**	**3,363**	**273**	**13,873**	**6,102**	**7,771**	**505**	**485**	**20**	**996**	**954**	**42**
0—5	*2,221*	1,142	1,079	..	..	..	*2,221*	1,142	1,079	..	..	..	..	..	..
5—10	*1,854*	1,034	820	*264*	241	23	*1,590*	793	797	*31*	30	1	*79*	76	3
10—15	*1,798*	1,049	749	*485*	452	33	*1,313*	597	716	*60*	58	2	*158*	154	4
15—20	*1,960*	981	979	*715*	675	40	*1,245*	306	939	*127*	121	6	*224*	218	6
20 and over ..	*9,676*	5,259	4,417	*2,172*	1,995	177	*7,504*	3,264	4,240	*287*	276	11	*535*	506	29
Adi Hindu ..	**3,428**	**1,715**	**1,713**	**18**	**18**	..	**3,410**	**1,697**	**1,713**	**1**	**1**	..	**2**	**2**	..
0—5	*516*	300	216	..	..	..	*516*	300	216	..	..	..	..	..	..
5—10	*388*	215	173	..	..	..	*388*	215	173	..	..	..	..	..	..
10—15	*315*	169	146	*2*	2	..	*313*	167	146	..	..	..	..	..	..
15—20	*204*	66	138	*3*	3	..	*201*	63	138	..	..	..	*1*	1	..
20 and over ..	*2,005*	965	1,040	*13*	13	..	*1,992*	952	1,040	*1*	1	..	*1*	1	..
Jain	**181**	**88**	**93**	**74**	**60**	**14**	**107**	**28**	**79**	**6**	**6**	..	**4**	**4**	..
0—5	*22*	7	15	..	..	..	*22*	7	15	..	..	..	..	..	..
5—10	*19*	10	9	*6*	6	..	*13*	4	9	*1*	1	..	*1*	1	..
10—15	*18*	6	12	*6*	6	..	*12*	..	12	*1*	1	..	*1*	1	..
15—20	*23*	11	12	*11*	8	3	*12*	3	9	*1*	1	..	*1*	1	..
20 and over ..	*99*	54	45	*51*	40	11	*48*	14	34	*3*	3	..	*1*	1	..

Literacy by Religion and Age.—Part III.—Gulbarga City.

RELIGION AND AGE	POPULATION									Literate in English			Literate in Urdu		
	Total			Literate			Illiterate								
	Persons	Males	Females	Persons	Males	Females	Persons	Males	Females	Persons	Males	Females	Persons	Males	Females
1	2	3	4	5	6	7	8	9	10	11	12	13	14	15	16
Sikh	4	4	..	3	3	..	1	1	..	..	..	..	3	3	..
0—5	..	..	..	..	..	..	..	..	..	..	..	..	..	..	..
5—10	..	..	..	..	..	..	..	..	..	..	..	..	..	..	..
10—15	*1*	1	..	..	..	..	*1*	1	..	..	..	..	..	..	..
15—20	*1*	1	..	*1*	1	..	..	..	..	..	..	..	*1*	1	..
20 and over ..	*2*	2	..	*2*	2	..	..	..	..	..	..	..	*2*	2	..
Muslim	19,792	10,228	9,564	2,431	2,052	379	17,361	8,176	9,185	448	418	30	1,981	1,632	349
0—5	*4,013*	1,657	2,356	..	..	..	*4,013*	1,657	2,356	..	..	..	..	..	..
5—10	*2,194*	1,322	872	*178*	130	48	*2,016*	1,192	824	*22*	17	5	*152*	110	42
10—15	*1,453*	1,133	320	*241*	189	52	*1,212*	944	268	*38*	33	5	*201*	153	49
15—20	*1,825*	947	878	*287*	233	54	*1,538*	714	824	*61*	56	5	*273*	225	48
20 and over ..	*10,307*	5,169	5,138	*1,725*	1,500	225	*8,582*	3,669	4,913	*327*	312	15	*1,355*	1,144	211
Christian	145	50	95	49	23	26	96	27	69	31	15	16	..	..	..
0—5	*19*	9	10	..	..	..	*19*	9	10	..	..	..	..	..	..
5—10	*25*	5	20	*2*	..	2	*23*	5	18	*1*	..	1	..	..	..
10—15	*30*	8	22	*3*	1	2	*27*	7	20	*1*	1	..	..	..	..
15—20	*16*	5	11	*7*	2	5	*9*	3	6	*4*	1	3	..	..	..
20 and over ..	*55*	23	32	*37*	20	17	*18*	3	15	*25*	13	12	..	..	..
Zoroastrian ..	16	9	7	8	5	3	8	4	4	3	2	1	2	2	..
0—5	*2*	..	2	..	..	..	*2*	..	2	..	..	..	..	..	..
5—10	..	..	..	..	..	..	..	..	..	..	..	..	..	..	..
10—15	*1*	1	..	..	..	..	*1*	1	..	..	..	..	..	..	..
15—20	..	..	..	..	..	..	..	..	..	..	..	..	..	..	..
20 and over	*13*	8	5	*8*	5	3	*5*	3	2	*3*	2	1	*2*	2	..
Tribal	8	8	..	1	1	..	7	7	..	..	..	..	..	..	..
0—5	*2*	2	..	..	..	..	*2*	2	..	..	..	..	..	..	..
5—10	..	..	..	..	..	..	..	..	..	..	..	..	..	..	..
10—15	..	..	..	..	..	..	..	..	..	..	..	..	..	..	..
15—20	*1*	1	..	..	..	..	*1*	1	..	..	..	..	..	..	..
20 and over	*5*	5	..	*1*	1	..	*4*	4	..	..	..	..	..	..	..

Table XIV.

LITERACY BY SELECTED CASTES, RACES AND TRIBES.

1. This table repeats the statistics given in the preceding one in respect of literacy with the difference that whereas in the Table XIII the whole population with all the literates is distributed by age and religion, it is here treated with partial population as only certiain selected castes, etc., are taken.

2. The selection and grouping of castes is governed by the same principle as followed in Tables VIII and XVII.

3. As this table contains only such literates as are aged 7 and over and also for the reason that certain minor castes are left out, the totals for Hindu, Adi Hindu, and Tribal will differ from the Table XIII.

TABLE XIV.

Literacy by Selected Castes, Races and Tribes

Caste, Race and Tribe with Locality		POPULATION AGED SEVEN AND OVER									LITERATES IN ENGLIS			LITERATES IN URDU		
		Total Strength			Literates			Illiterates								
		Persons	Males	Females	Persons	Males	Females	Persons	Males	Females	Persons	Males	Females	Persons	Males	Females
1		2	3	4	5	6	7	8	9	10	11	12	13	14	15	16
HINDU (Brahmanic)																
1. **Balija** ..	*State ..	35,012	19,402	15,610	1,687	1,561	126	33,325	17,841	15,484	92	80	12	183	166	17
2. **Bender** ..	State ..	203,195	99,171	104,024	437	387	50	202,758	98,784	103,974	13	13	..	42	41	1
	Telangana ..	1,775	954	821	146	127	19	1,629	827	802	2	2	..	4	4	..
	Marathwara	201,420	98,217	103,208	291	260	31	201,129	97,957	103,172	11	11	..	38	37	1
3. **Bhat** ..	State ..	14,096	8,218	5,878	2,213	1,874	339	11,883	6,344	5,539	56	53	3	59	58	1
	Telangana ..	10,001	6,054	3,947	1,832	1,524	308	8,169	4,530	3,639	44	41	3	32	32	..
	Marathwara	4,095	2,164	1,931	381	350	31	3,714	1,814	1,900	12	12	..	27	26	1
4. **Bhoi** ..	State ..	251,023	125,064	125,959	1,515	1,450	65	249,508	123,614	125,894	54	47	7	74	72	2
	Telangana ..	111,010	53,761	57,249	887	849	38	110,123	52,012	57,211	48	41	7	68	66	2
	Marathwara	140,013	71,303	68,710	628	601	27	139,385	70,702	68,683	6	6	..	6	6	..
5. **Bogam** ..	State ..	24,323	11,147	13,176	1,440	1,224	216	22,883	9,923	12,960	109	107	2	119	119	..
	Telangana ..	15,572	6,514	9,058	1,162	1,009	153	14,410	5,505	8,905	109	107	2	105	105	..
	Marathwara	8,751	4,633	4,118	278	215	63	8,473	4,418	4,055	..	..	..	14	14	..
6. **Brahman** ..	State ..	322,859	167,838	155,021	129,957	117,663	12,294	192,902	50,175	142,727	12,921	11,890	1,031	21,894	21,353	541
	Telangana ..	121,093	62,934	58,159	57,972	52,291	5,681	63,121	10,643	52,478	8,092	7,427	665	13,354	12,960	394
	Marathwara	201,766	104,904	96,862	71,985	65,372	6,613	129,781	39,532	90,249	4,829	4,463	366	8,540	8,393	147
7. **Burud** ..	State ..	30,590	17,087	13,503	351	323	28	30,239	16,764	13,475	14	14	..	12	12	..
	Telangana ..	20,195	11,161	9,034	216	201	15	19,979	10,960	9,019	14	14	..	2	2	..
	Marathwara	10,395	5,926	4,469	135	122	13	10,260	5,804	4,456	..	..	..	10	10	..
8. **Darzi** ..	State ..	53,660	28,356	25,304	3,038	2,865	173	50,622	25,491	25,131	121	114	7	343	317	26
	Telangana ..	35,030	17,862	17,168	1,968	1,886	82	33,062	15,976	17,086	107	102	5	184	176	8
	Marathwara	18,630	10,494	8,136	1,070	979	91	17,560	9,515	8,045	14	12	2	159	141	18
9. **Dhobi** ..	State ..	236,786	123,650	113,136	2,084	1,989	95	234,702	121,661	113,041	81	79	2	100	94	6
	Telangana ..	188,360	98,717	89,643	1,498	1,423	75	186,862	97,294	89,568	61	61	..	44	38	6
	Marathwara	48,426	24,933	23,493	586	566	20	47,840	24,367	23,473	20	18	2	56	56	..
10. **Erakala** ..	†State ..	7,870	4,007	3,863	244	233	11	7,626	3,774	3,852	..	..	..	1	1	..

TABLE XIV.

Literacy by Selected Castes, Races and Tribes

Caste, Race and Tribe with Locality		POPULATION AGED SEVEN AND OVER									LITERATES IN ENGLISH			LITERATES IN URDU		
		Total Strength			Literates			Illiterates								
		Persons	Males	Females	Persons	Males	Females	Persons	Males	Females	Persons	Males	Females	Persons	Males	Females
1		2	3	4	5	6	7	8	9	10	11	12	13	14	15	16
HINDU (Brahmanic).																
11. Gosain ..	State ..	24,196	14,828	9,368	2,807	2,651	156	21,389	12,177	9,212	61	58	3	108	105	3
	Telangana ..	865	450	415	164	137	27	701	318	388	48	45	3	25	25	..
	Marathwara	23,331	14,378	8,953	2,643	2,514	129	20,688	11,864	8,824	13	13	..	83	80	3
12. Gujarati ..	State ..	6,553	4,051	2,502	2,424	2,205	219	4,129	1,846	2,283	180	175	5	193	178	15
	Telangana ..	739	493	246	306	252	54	433	241	192	108	104	4	61	61	..
	Marathwara	5,814	3,558	2,256	2,118	1,953	165	3,696	1,605	2,091	72	71	1	132	117	15
13. Gurav ..	State ..	25,590	12,969	12,621	1,467	1,301	166	24,123	11,668	12,455	20	20	..	8	8	..
	Telangana ..	6,666	3,479	3,187	491	460	31	6,175	3,019	3,156	16	16	1	1	1	..
	Marathwara	18,924	9,490	9,434	976	841	135	17,948	8,649	9,299	4	4	..	7	7	..
14. Hajjam ..	State ..	130,153	69,930	60,223	2,441	2,312	129	127,712	67,618	60,094	141	125	16	253	233	20
	Telangana ..	79,555	42,750	36,805	957	935	22	78,598	41,815	36,783	86	81	5	165	161	4
	Marathwara	50,598	27,180	23,418	1,484	1,377	107	49,114	25,803	23,311	55	44	11	88	72	16
15. Hatkar ..	State ..	37,844	20,374	17,470	1,101	694	407	36,743	19,680	17,063	25	25	..	183	180	3
	Telangana ..	3,971	2,113	1,858	267	261	6	3,704	1,852	1,852	15	15	..	61	61	..
	Marathwara	33,873	18,261	15,612	834	433	401	33,039	17,828	15,211	10	10	..	122	119	3
16. Julahi ..	State ..	328,834	171,793	157,041	7,562	7,043	519	321,272	164,750	156,522	169	157	12	890	863	27
	Telangana ..	251,654	131,933	119,721	5,916	5,529	387	245,738	126,404	119,334	110	98	12	612	602	10
	Marathwara	77,180	39,860	37,320	1,646	1,514	132	75,534	38,346	37,188	59	59	..	278	261	17
17. Kalal ..	State ..	340,318	178,845	161,473	7,158	6,480	678	333,160	172,365	160,795	239	232	7	559	554	5
	Telangana ..	295,584	154,368	141,216	5,949	5,428	521	289,635	148,940	140,695	175	168	7	425	423	2
	Marathwara	44,734	24,477	20,257	1,209	1,052	157	43,525	23,425	20,100	64	64	..	134	131	3
18. Kapu ..	State ..	809,536	427,462	382,074	30,299	27,304	2,995	779,237	400,158	379,079	2,400	2,126	274	5,325	5,002	323
	Telangana ..	690,171	364,324	325,847	23,219	21,335	1,884	666,952	342,989	323,963	1,393	1,298	95	3,268	3,123	145
	Marathwara	119,365	63,138	56,227	7,080	5,969	1,111	112,285	57,169	55,116	1,007	828	179	2,057	1,879	178
19. Kasab ..	State ..	65,789	35,001	30,788	687	631	56	65,102	34,370	30,732	7	7	..	31	26	5
	Telangana ..	53,796	28,602	25,194	523	479	44	53,273	28,123	25,150	5	5	..	18	16	2
	Marathwara	11,993	6,399	5,594	164	152	12	11,829	6,247	5,582	2	2	..	13	10	3

TABLE XIV.

Literacy by Selected Castes, Races and Tribes

Caste, Race and Tribe with Locality		POPULATION AGED SEVEN AND OVER									LITERATES IN ENGLISH			LITERATES IN URDU		
		Total Strength			Literates			Illiterates								
		Persons	Males	Females	Persons	Males	Females	Persons	Males	Females	Persons	Males	Females	Persons	Males	Females
1		2	3	4	5	6	7	8	9	10	11	12	13	14	15	16
HINDU (Brahmanic).																
20. Kasar ..	State	29,858	16,217	13,641	1,111	959	152	28,747	15,258	13,489	128	127	1	20	20	..
	Telangana ..	13,504	7,368	6,136	471	439	32	13,033	6,929	6,104	122	122	..	2	2	..
	Marathwara	16,354	8,849	7,505	640	520	120	15,714	8,329	7,385	6	5	1	18	18	..
21. Kayasth ..	State ..	3,994	2,267	1,727	1,605	1,310	295	2,389	957	1,432	767	710	57	1,421	1,180	241
	Telangana	2,894	1,674	1,220	1,210	990	220	1,684	684	1,000	646	601	45	1,090	909	180
	Marathwara	1,100	593	507	395	320	75	705	273	432	121	109	12	331	271	60
22. Khatri ..	State ..	3,771	2,081	1,690	1,015	839	176	2,756	1,242	1,514	226	208	18	685	651	34
	Telangana	2,266	1,237	1,029	740	639	101	1,526	598	928	151	136	15	613	590	23
	Marathwara	1,505	844	661	275	200	75	1,230	644	586	75	72	3	72	61	11
23. Kumbhar ..	State ..	123,922	65,709	58,213	1,600	1,466	134	122,322	64,243	58,079	133	123	10	253	251	2
	Telangana ..	75,265	40,791	34,474	668	613	55	74,597	40,178	34,419	58	48	10	85	83	2
	Marathwara	48,657	24,918	23,739	932	853	79	47,725	24,065	23,660	75	75	..	168	168	..
24. Koli ..	State ..	42,132	23,570	18,562	644	570	74	41,488	23,000	18,488	..	..	..	95	82	13
	Telangana ..	10,901	7,223	3,678	187	163	24	10,714	7,060	3,654	..	..	..	..	..	..
	Marathwara	31,231	16,347	14,884	457	407	50	30,774	15,940	14,834	..	..	..	95	82	13
25. Komati ..	State ..	256,407	136,757	119,650	37,398	35,334	2,064	219,009	101,423	117,586	1,230	1,066	164	1,424	1,319	105
	Telangana ..	185,930	99,475	86,455	30,531	29,150	1,381	155,399	70,325	85,074	907	772	135	932	877	55
	Marathwara	70,477	37,282	33,195	6,867	6,184	683	63,610	31,098	32,512	323	294	29	492	442	50
26. Kshatriya ..	State ..	69,673	36,608	33,065	7,850	6,820	1,030	61,823	29,788	32,035	743	660	83	1,738	1,581	157
	Telangana ..	23,396	12,688	10,708	4,339	3,667	672	19,057	9,021	10,036	445	384	61	919	829	90
	Marathwara	46,277	23,920	22,357	3,511	3,153	358	42,766	20,767	21,999	298	276	22	819	752	67
27. Kurma ..	State ..	142,853	73,458	69,395	2,062	1,908	154	140,791	71,550	69,241	46	36	10	16	16	..
	Telangana ..	135,701	70,279	65,422	1,831	1,704	127	133,870	68,575	65,295	46	36	10	16	16	..
	Marathwara .	7,152	3,179	3,973	231	204	27	6,921	2,975	3,946	..	..	..	..	..	..
28. Lingayat ..	State ..	663,755	337,893	325,862	32,290	29,607	2,683	631,465	308,286	323,179	2,140	2,012	128	2,737	2,617	120
	Telangana ..	59,704	31,099	28,605	6,528	6,112	416	53,176	24,987	28,189	628	587	41	196	195	1
	Marathwara	604,051	306,794	297,257	25,762	23,495	2,267	578,289	283,299	294,990	1,512	1,425	87	2,541	2,422	119

TABLE XIV.

Literacy by Selected Castes, Races and Tribes

Caste, Race and Tribe with Locality		POPULATION AGED SEVEN AND OVER: Total Strength: Persons	Total Strength: Males	Total Strength: Females	Literates: Persons	Literates: Males	Literates: Females	Illiterates: Persons	Illiterates: Males	Illiterates: Females	LITERATES IN ENGLISH: Persons	Males	Females	LITERATES IN URDU: Persons	Males	Females
1		2	3	4	5	6	7	8	9	10	11	12	13	14	15	16
HINDU (Brahmanic)																
29. Lohar ..	State ..	77,780	42,838	34,942	4,618	4,368	250	73,162	38,470	34,692	163	156	7	512	499	13
	Telangana ..	*51,362*	28,291	23,071	*3,187*	3,081	106	*48,175*	25,210	22,965	*45*	39	6	*68*	68	..
	Marathwara	*26,418*	14,547	11,871	*1,431*	1,287	144	*24,987*	13,260	11,727	*118*	117	1	*444*	431	13
30. Mali ..	State ..	81,479	41,314	40,165	1,728	1,548	180	79,751	39,766	39,985	1	1	..	31	31	..
	Telangana ..	*3,447*	1,772	1,675	*392*	338	54	*3,055*	1,434	1,621	..	..	..	*18*	18	..
	Marathwara	*78,032*	39,542	38,490	*1,336*	1,210	126	*76,696*	38,332	38,364	*1*	1	..	*13*	13	..
31. Maratha ..	State ..	1,235,685	632,567	603,118	21,087	18,873	2,214	1,214,598	613,694	600,904	1,643	1,525	118	2,825	2,645	180
	Telangana ..	*56,885*	28,594	28,291	*4,027*	3,662	365	*52,858*	24,932	27,926	*592*	543	49	*894*	823	71
	Marathwara	*1,178,800*	603,973	574,827	*17,060*	15,211	1,849	*1,161,740*	588,762	572,978	*1,051*	982	69	*1,931*	1,822	109
32. Marwari ..	State ..	49,873	28,354	21,519	7,053	6,617	436	42,820	21,737	21,083	441	422	19	1,217	1,037	180
	Telangana ..	*9,485*	5,011	4,474	*3,186*	2,976	210	*6,299*	2,035	4,264	*160*	146	14	*175*	104	71
	Marathwara .	*40,388*	23,343	17,045	*3,867*	3,641	226	*36,521*	19,702	16,819	*281*	276	5	*1,042*	933	109
33. Panchal ..	*State ..	60,260	31,395	28,865	1,643	1,323	320	58,617	30,072	28,545	299	297	2	358	346	12
	Telangana ..	*878*	582	296	*152*	141	11	*726*	441	285	*13*	13	..	*55*	55	..
	Marathwara	*59,382*	30,813	28,569	*1,491*	1,182	309	*57,891*	29,631	28,260	*286*	284	2	*303*	291	12
34. Perka ..	*State ..	45,955	23,041	22,914	220	212	8	45,735	22,829	22,906	..	..	..	..	..	..
35. Rangrez ..	State ..	21,434	12,172	9,262	1,482	1,130	352	19,952	11,042	8,910	127	117	10	158	147	11
	Telangana ..	*7,076*	3,783	3,293	*244*	221	23	*6,832*	3,562	3,270	*24*	20	4	*4*	4	..
	Marathwara	*14,358*	8,389	5,969	*1,238*	909	329	*13,120*	7,480	5,640	*103*	97	6	*154*	143	11
36. Satani ..	State ..	44,115	24,896	19,219	3,864	3,426	438	40,251	21,470	18,781	85	78	7	187	181	6
	Telangana ..	*40,953*	23,110	17,843	*3,533*	3,156	377	*37,420*	19,954	17,466	*58*	54	4	*94*	93	1
	Marathwara .	*3,162*	1,786	1,376	*331*	270	61	*2,831*	1,516	1,315	*27*	24	3	*93*	88	5
37. Sunar ..	State ..	109,717	59,117	50,600	12,166	11,180	986	97,551	47,937	49,614	161	130	31	653	613	40
	Telangana ..	*71,681*	39,054	32,627	*9,563*	8,762	801	*62,118*	30,292	31,826	*120*	101	19	*436*	417	19
	Marathwara	*38,036*	20,063	17,973	*2,603*	2,418	185	*35,433*	17,645	17,788	*41*	29	12	*217*	196	21

TABLE XIV.

Literacy by Selected Castes, Races and Tribes

Caste, Race and Tribe with Locality		POPULATION AGED SEVEN AND OVER									LITERATES IN ENGLISH			LITERATES IN URDU		
		Total Strength			Literates			Illiterates								
		Persons	Males	Females	Persons	Males	Females	Persons	Males	Females	Persons	Males	Females	Persons	Males	Females
1		2	3	4	5	6	7	8	9	10	11	12	13	14	15	16
HINDU (Brahmanic)																
38. Sutar ..	State ..	91,890	49,524	42,366	3,142	2,745	397	88,748	46,779	41,969	49	48	1	147	142	5
	Telangana ..	66,268	35,333	30,935	2,457	2,155	302	63,811	33,178	30,633	49	48	1	118	114	4
	Marathwara	25,622	14,191	11,431	685	590	95	24,937	13,601	11,336	..	..	..	29	28	1
39. Telaga ..	State ..	780,068	365,947	414,121	16,942	15,385	1,557	763,126	350,562	412,564	2,934	2,799	135	3,971	3,757	214
	Telangana ..	692,788	326,043	366,745	15,196	14,049	1,147	677,592	311,994	365,598	2,540	2,439	101	2,685	2,598	87
	Marathwara	87,280	39,904	47,376	1,746	1,336	410	85,534	38,568	46,966	394	360	34	1,286	1,159	127
40. Teli ..	State ..	56,520	30,507	26,013	3,619	3,468	151	52,901	27,039	25,862	129	116	13	431	415	16
	Telangana ..	19,022	10,134	8,888	1,348	1,270	78	17,674	8,864	8,810	94	85	9	282	272	10
	Marathwara	37,498	20,373	17,125	2,271	2,198	73	35,227	18,175	17,052	35	31	4	149	143	6
41. Uppara ..	State ..	62,560	31,846	30,714	457	393	64	62,103	31,453	30,650	38	33	5	22	22	..
	Telangana ..	22,408	12,428	9,980	318	274	44	22,090	12,154	9,936	37	32	5	12	12	..
	Marathwara	40,152	19,418	20,734	139	119	20	40,013	19,299	20,714	1	1	..	10	10	..
42. Velama ..	*State ..	43,257	21,721	21,536	6,250	5,876	374	37,007	15,845	21,162	485	468	17	292	277	15
43. Vellala ..	State ..	3,461	1,813	1,648	2,048	1,611	437	1,413	202	1,211	1,387	1,089	298	505	465	40
	Telangana ..	3,340	1,731	1,609	1,955	1,535	420	1,385	196	1,189	1,310	1,019	291	460	423	37
	Marathwara	121	82	39	93	76	17	28	6	22	77	70	7	45	42	3
44. Vishwabrahman	State ..	22,045	12,186	9,859	2,130	2,025	105	19,915	10,161	9,754	70	69	1	38	38	..
	Telangana ..	20,740	11,369	9,371	2,000	1,900	100	18,740	9,469	9,271	56	55	1	33	33	..
	Marathwara .	1,305	817	488	130	125	5	1,175	692	483	14	14	..	5	5	..
45. Waddar ..	State ..	113,179	56,041	57,138	604	551	53	112,575	55,490	57,085	6	6	..	6	6	..
	Telangana ..	76,618	37,745	38,873	500	461	39	76,118	37,284	38,834	6	6	..	6	6	..
	Marathwara	36,561	18,296	18,265	104	90	14	36,457	18,206	18,251	..	..	..	..	..	..
46. Wanjari ..	State ..	59,888	33,386	26,502	1,168	1,043	125	58,720	32,343	26,377	35	35	..	74	74	..
	Telangana ..	34,931	19,106	15,825	620	562	58	34,311	18,544	15,767	14	14	..	14	14	..
	Marathwara	24,957	14,280	10,677	548	481	67	24,409	13,799	10,610	21	21	..	60	60	..
47. Yadava ..	State ..	768,294	392,418	375,876	7,086	6,434	652	761,208	385,984	375,224	448	388	60	664	619	45
	Telangana ..	427,675	220,409	207,266	3,845	3,708	187	423,830	216,701	207,129	220	198	22	183	159	24
	Marathwara	340,619	172,009	168,610	3,241	2,726	515	337,378	169,283	168,095	228	190	38	481	460	21

TABLE XIV.

Literacy by Selected Castes, Races and Tribes

Caste, Race and Tribe with Locality		POPULATION AGED SEVEN AND OVER									LITERATES IN ENGLISH			LITERATES IN URDU		
		Total Strength			Literates			Illiterates								
		Persons	Males	Females	Persons	Males	Females	Persons	Males	Females	Persons	Males	Females	Persons	Males	Females
1		2	3	4	5	6	7	8	9	10	11	12	13	14	15	16
ADI-HINDU.																
1. Dher ..	State ..	900,850	465,721	435,129	6,102	5,303	799	894,748	460,418	434,330	361	331	30	1,170	1,078	92
	Telangana ..	*404,217*	216,263	187,954	*3,258*	2,813	445	*400,959*	213,450	187,509	*246*	222	24	*575*	522	53
	Marathwara	*496,633*	249,458	247,175	*2,844*	2,490	354	*493,789*	246,968	246,821	*115*	109	6	*595*	556	39
2. Madiga ..	State ..	1,101,440	559,471	541,969	6,270	5,618	652	1,095,170	553,853	541,317	403	365	38	835	762	73
	Telangana ..	*660,936*	336,257	324,679	*3,045*	2,687	358	*657,891*	333,570	324,321	*283*	253	30	*458*	417	41
	Marathwara	*440,504*	223,214	217,290	*3,225*	2,931	294	*437,279*	220,283	216,996	*120*	112	8	*377*	345	32
TRIBAL.																
1. Bhil ..	†State ..	12,332	6,102	6,230	15	15	..	12,317	6,087	6,230	..	..	..	1	1	..
2. Chenchu ..	*State ..	1,887	898	989	8	8	..	1,879	890	989	..	..	..	..	..	..
3. Erakala ..	State ..	49,323	26,581	22,742	974	838	136	48,349	25,743	22,606	10	10	..	57	48	9
	Telangana ..	*29,716*	16,546	13,170	*31*	29	2	*29,685*	16,517	13,168	*10*	10	..	*18*	12	6
	Marathwara	*19,607*	10,035	9,572	*943*	809	134	*18,664*	9,226	9,438	..	..	..	*39*	36	3
4. Gond ..	State ..	96,858	46,993	49,865	631	457	174	96,227	46,536	49,691	85	63	22	170	147	23
	Telangana ..	*94,129*	45,383	48,746	*601*	436	165	*93,528*	44,947	48,581	*71*	51	20	*135*	120	15
	Marathwara	*2,729*	1,610	1,119	*30*	21	9	*2,699*	1,589	1,110	*14*	12	2	*35*	27	8
5. Koya ..	*State ..	29,814	16,647	13,167	32	32	..	29,782	16,615	13,167	4	4	..	18	15	3
6. Lambada ..	State ..	249,587	129,682	119,905	1,674	1,560	114	247,913	128,122	119,791	23	19	4	61	45	16
	Telangana ..	*166,454*	83,969	82,485	*1,080*	1,006	74	*165,374*	82,963	82,411	*22*	18	4	*38*	25	13
	Marathwara	*83,133*	45,718	37,420	*594*	554	40	*82,539*	45,159	37,380	*1*	1	..	*23*	20	3
7. Pardhi ..	State ..	5,992	3,223	2,769	128	95	33	5,864	3,128	2,736	..	..	..	15	13	2
	Telangana ..	*4,988*	2,678	2,810	*35*	30	5	*4,953*	2,648	2,305	..	..	..	*15*	13	2
	Marathwara	*1,004*	545	450	*93*	65	28	*911*	480	481	..	..	..	..	..	..

TABLE XIV.

Literacy by Selected Castes, Races and Tribes

Caste, Race and Tribe with Locality	POPULATION AGED SEVEN AND OVER									LITERATES IN ENGLISH			LITERATES IN URDU		
	Total Strength			Literates			Illiterates								
	Persons	Males	Females	Persons	Males	Females	Persons	Males	Females	Persons	Males	Females	Persons	Males	Females
1	2	3	4	5	6	7	8	9	10	11	12	13	14	15	16
CHRISTIAN.															
1. Indian Christian State ..	116,587	59,702	56,885	15,190	10,017	5,173	101,397	49,685	51,712	6,200	4,110	2,090	8,020	7,478	542
Telangana ..	*96,775*	49,466	47,309	*12,399*	8,281	4,168	*84,376*	41,235	43,141	*5,207*	3,445	1,762	*7,635*	7,187	448
Marathwara	*19,812*	10,286	9,576	*2,791*	1,786	1,005	*17,021*	8,450	8,571	*993*	665	328	*385*	291	94
2. Anglo-Indian . State	2,967	1,957	1,010	2,925	1,937	988	42	20	22	2,711	1,826	885	233	198	35
Telangana ..	*2,729*	1,817	912	*2,705*	1,805	900	*24*	12	12	*2,501*	1,702	799	*203*	172	31
Marathwara	*238*	140	98	*220*	132	88	*18*	8	10	*210*	124	86	*30*	26	4

N.B. * Caste found only in Telangana.
Do † do Marathwara.

Table XV—Part I.

LANGUAGE.

Note I. The name of individual dialects returned, have been grouped under languages to which they belong and are shown below :—

S. No.	Dialect	Language	Persons	Males	Females
1	Pardesi ..	Eastern Hindi ..	540	315	225
2	Koya ..	Gondi ..	13,149	7,633	5,516
3	Ghisadi ..	Gujarati ..	356	187	169
4	Khatri ..	Do ..	1,064	753	311
5	Nagari ..	Do ..	944	630	314
6	Parsi Gujarati ..	Do ..	908	540	468
7	Are ..	Marathi ..	510	291	219
8	Goanese ..	Do ..	48	24	24
9	Konkani ..	Do ..	144	60	84
10	Panchali ..	Do ..	7	5	2
11	Marwari ..	Rajasthani ..	51,886	28,017	23,869
12	Cutchi ..	Sindhi ..	754	469	285
13	Bondili ..	Western Hindi ..	168	87	81
14	Hindi ..	Do ..	45,997	25,491	20,506
15	Hindusthani ..	Do ..	19,884	9,599	10,285
16	Lodhi ..	Do ..	309	161	148
17	Banjari ..	Lambadi ..	4,953	2,938	2,015
18	Kaikadi ..	Erakala ..	2,812	1,085	1,727
19	Korvi ..	Do ..	3,315	2,151	1,164
20	Wadari ..	Telugu ..	6,473	3,355	3,118
21	Chenchu ..	Do ..	1,869	875	994

2. Details of the number of speakers included under " others " are the following :—

S. No.	Language	Persons	Males	Females
	" A " Vernaculars of India. ..	**2,764**	**1,745**	**1,019**
1	Assamese	2	2	..
2	Baluchi	15	12	3
3	Bengali	195	105	90
4	Burmese	20	16	4
5	Eastern Hindi	540	315	225
6	Kashmiri	12	7	5
7	Kolhati	421	202	219
8	Malayalam	270	176	94
9	Oriya	55	35	20
10	Pashto	320	264	56
11	Sanskrit	96	86	10
12	Sindhi	764	495	269
13	Language not returned	54	30	24
	" B " Vernaculars of Asia. ..	**314**	**178**	**136**
1	Armenian	7	6	1
2	Chinese	12	8	4
3	Japanese	1	1	..
4	Persian	282	156	126
5	Sinhalese	3	3	..
6	Turkish	9	4	6
	" C " European Languages.	**251**	**165**	**86**
1	Danish	6	4	2
2	French	64	44	20
3	German	11	8	3
4	Greek	7	6	1
5	Italian	42	23	19
6	Irish	17	16	1
7	Portuguese	92	52	40
8	Spanish	6	6	..
9	Welsh	6	6	..

TABLE XV. PART I.

Language.

Language	Population			Hyderabad City			Atraf-i-Balda			Warangal		
	Persons	Males	Females	Persons	Males	Females	Persons	Males	Females	Persons	Males	Females
1	2	3	4	5	6	7	8	9	10	11	12	13
TOTAL	**14,436,148**	**7,370,010**	**7,066,138**	**466,894**	**247,623**	**219,271**	**499,661**	**253,975**	**245,686**	**1,117,693**	**575,819**	**541,874**
"A" VERNACULARS OF INDIA	**14,418,595**	**7,357,576**	**7,061,019**	**455,035**	**239,293**	**215,742**	**499,424**	**253,851**	**245,573**	**1,116,765**	**575,243**	**541,522**
(a) Vernaculars of the State	14,225,694	7,252,729	6,972,965	412,942	214,192	198,750	497,795	253,020	244,775	1,109,543	571,525	538,018
DRAVIDIAN FAMILY	8,700,689	4,432,890	4,267,799	177,167	92,724	84,443	418,142	213,721	204,421	980,634	503,668	476,966
Andhra group	6,972,534	3,544,413	3,428,121	173,357	90,565	82,792	397,612	203,471	194,141	949,488	487,746	461,742
Telugu	6,972,534	3,544,413	3,428,121	173,357	90,565	82,792	397,612	203,471	194,141	949,488	487,746	461,742
Dravida Group	1,652,068	849,522	802,546	3,810	2,159	1,651	20,530	10,250	10,280	6,291	3,307	2,984
Erakala (Kaikadi)	31,974	17,333	14,641	289	188	101	665	369	296	5,931	3,120	2,811
Kanarese	1,620,094	832,189	787,905	3,521	1,971	1,550	19,865	9,881	9,984	360	187	173
Intermediate group	76,087	38,955	37,132	..	..	..	..	..	..	24,855	12,615	12,240
Gondi	76,087	38,955	37,132	..	..	..	..	..	..	24,855	12,615	12,240
INDO-EUROPEAN FAMILY	5,525,005	2,819,839	2,705,166	235,775	121,468	114,307	79,653	39,299	40,354	128,909	67,857	61,052
(Indo-Aryan Branch)	5,525,005	2,819,839	2,705,166	235,775	121,468	114,307	79,653	39,299	40,354	128,909	67,857	61,052
Bhili	9,619	5,072	4,547	..	..	..	..	..	..	..	..	..
Lambadi (Banjari)	214,617	110,570	104,047	387	207	180	5,896	3,077	2,819	54,136	27,420	26,716
Marathi	3,786,838	1,916,549	1,870,289	16,344	8,440	7,904	17,903	7,858	10,045	13,689	7,021	6,668
Pardhi	6,659	3,848	2,811	838	440	398	99	59	40	386	229	157
Urdu (Western Hindi)	1,507,272	783,800	723,472	218,206	112,381	105,825	55,755	28,305	27,450	60,698	33,187	27,511
(b) Other Vernaculars of India	190,134	103,099	87,035	41,290	24,535	16,755	1,629	831	798	7,131	3,653	3,478
DRAVIDIAN FAMILY	29,050	15,598	13,452	18,063	9,937	8,126	648	307	341	4,110	2,027	2,083
Tamil	29,050	15,598	13,452	18,063	9,937	8,126	648	307	341	4,110	2,027	2,083
INDO-EUROPEAN FAMILY	161,084	87,501	73,583	23,227	14,598	8,629	981	524	457	3,021	1,626	1,395
(Indo-Aryan Branch)	161,084	87,501	73,583	23,227	14,598	8,629	981	524	457	3,021	1,626	1,395
Gujarati	33,915	18,069	15,846	5,626	3,113	2,513	283	159	124	367	187	180
Panjabi	4,560	3,630	930	2,928	2,627	301	2	2	..	66	40	26
Rajasthani	56,251	30,464	25,787	8,439	4,979	3,460	589	308	281	1,016	530	486
Western Hindi	66,358	35,338	31,020	6,234	3,879	2,355	107	55	52	1,572	869	703
(c) Others	2,764	1,745	1,019	800	563	237	..	..	..	91	65	26
"B" VERNACULARS OF ASIATIC COUNTRIES AND AFRICA.	**3,486**	**2,110**	**1,376**	**2,132**	**1,214**	**918**	**25**	**14**	**11**	**61**	**33**	**28**
(a) Semitic Family	3,172	1,932	1,240	1,855	1,065	790	25	14	11	61	33	28
Arabic	3,172	1,932	1,240	1,855	1,065	790	25	14	11	61	33	28
(b) Others	314	178	136	277	149	128	..	..	..	..	..	..
"C" EUROPEAN LANGUAGES.	**14,070**	**10,327**	**3,743**	**9,730**	**7,119**	**2,611**	**212**	**110**	**102**	**867**	**543**	**324**
(a) *Teutonic group*	13,819	10,162	3,657	9,517	6,985	2,532	212	110	102	865	541	324
English	13,819	10,162	3,657	9,517	6,985	2,532	212	110	102	865	541	324
(b) Others	251	165	86	213	134	79	..	..	..	2	2	..

TABLE XV. PART I.

Language.

Language	Karimnagar Persons	Karimnagar Males	Karimnagar Females	Adilabad Persons	Adilabad Males	Adilabad Females	Medak Persons	Medak Males	Medak Females	Nizamabad Persons	Nizamabad Males	Nizamabad Females
1	14	15	16	17	18	19	20	21	22	23	24	25
TOTAL	**1,241,405**	**634,416**	**606,989**	**762,030**	**389,754**	**372,276**	**738,665**	**373,475**	**365,190**	**623,225**	**313,556**	**309,669**
"A" VERNACULARS OF INDIA ..	**1,241,247**	**634,302**	**606,945**	**761,333**	**389,261**	**372,072**	*738,337*	*373,214*	*365,123*	*623,148*	*313,514*	*309,634*
(a) Vernaculars of the State	*1,239,772*	633,539	606,233	*754,125*	385,510	368,615	*733,751*	370,767	362,984	*619,136*	311,382	307,754
DRAVIDIAN FAMILY	*1,170,104*	596,384	573,720	*526,638*	269,789	256,849	*645,630*	325,768	319,862	*551,762*	276,746	275,016
Andhra Group	*1,168,062*	595,267	572,795	*463,558*	237,130	226,428	*639,350*	322,599	316,751	*545,188*	273,585	271,603
Telugu	*1,168,062*	595,267	572,795	*463,558*	237,130	226,428	*639,350*	322,599	316,751	*545,188*	273,585	271,603
Dravida Group	*1,022*	564	458	*13,999*	7,411	6,588	*6,280*	3,160	3,111	*6,574*	3,161	3,413
Erakala (Kaikadi)	*724*	402	322	*3,595*	1,862	1,733	*984*	452	532	*813*	453	360
Kanarese	*298*	162	136	*10,404*	5,549	4,855	*5,296*	2,717	2,579	*5,761*	2,708	3,053
Intermediate Group	*1,020*	558	467	*49,081*	25,248	23,833	..	..	..	..	..	..
Gondi	*1,020*	558	467	*49,081*	25,248	23,833	..	..	..	..	..	..
INDO-EUROPEAN FAMILY	*69,668*	37,155	32,513	*227,487*	115,721	111,766	*88,121*	44,999	43,122	*67,374*	34,636	32,738
(Indo-Aryan Branch)	*69,668*	37,155	32,513	*227,487*	115,721	111,766	*88,121*	44,999	43,122	*67,374*	34,636	32,738
Bhili	..	..	..	..	..	..	..	..	..	..	..	..
Lambadi (Banjari)	*7,224*	3,859	3,365	*26,276*	14,164	12,112	*3,292*	1,779	1,513	*13,196*	6,772	6,424
Marathi	*9,554*	5,018	4,536	*159,509*	79,555	79,954	*8,549*	4,036	4,513	*8,365*	3,969	4,396
Pardhi	..	..	..	..	..	..	*135*	90	45	*83*	43	40
Urdu (Western Hindi)	*52,890*	28,278	24,612	*41,702*	22,002	19,700	*76,145*	39,094	37,051	*45,730*	23,852	21,878
(b) Other Vernaculars of India	**1,430**	739	691	**6,705**	3,493	3,212	**4,556**	2,427	2,120	**4,009**	2,129	1,880
DRAVIDIAN FAMILY	*286*	139	147	*1,896*	1,001	895	*1,171*	576	595	*353*	159	194
Tamil	*286*	139	147	*1,896*	1,001	895	*1,171*	576	595	*353*	159	194
INDO-EUROPEAN FAMILY	*1,144*	600	544	*4,809*	2,492	2,317	*3,386*	1,851	1,534	*3,656*	1,970	1,686
(Indo-Aryan Branch)	*1,144*	600	544	*4,809*	2,492	2,317	*3,385*	1,851	1,534	*3,656*	1,970	1,686
Gujarati	*82*	41	41	*2,068*	1,093	975	*668*	385	283	*760*	458	302
Panjabi	*16*	14	2	*270*	143	127	..	..	..	*6*	2	4
Rajasthani	*1,046*	545	501	*1,182*	625	557	*721*	304	417	*837*	497	340
Western Hindi	..	..	..	*1,289*	631	658	*1,996*	1,162	834	*2,053*	1,013	1,040
(c) Others	**45**	24	21	**503**	258	245	**30**	20	10	**3**	3	
"B" VERNACULARS OF ASIATIC COUNTRIES AND AFRICA.	20	10	10	51	49	2	43	33	10	31	21	10
(a) Semitic Family	*18*	9	9	*51*	49	2	*41*	31	10	*31*	21	10
Arabic	*18*	9	9	*51*	49	2	*41*	31	10	*31*	21	10
(b) Others	**2**	1	1	..	..	..	**2**	2	..	..	..	..
"C" EUROPEAN LANGUAGES. ..	138	104	34	646	444	202	285	228	57	*46*	21	25
(a) *Teutonic Group*	*138*	104	34	*646*	444	202	*285*	228	57	*46*	21	25
English	*138*	104	34	*646*	444	202	*285*	228	57	*46*	21	25
(b) Others	..	..	..	..	..	..	..	..	..	..	..	..

TABLE XV. PART I.

Language.

Language	Mahbubnagar			Nalgonda			Aurangabad			Bir			Nander		
	Persons	Males	Females	Persons	Males	Females	Persons	Males	Females	Persons	Males	Females	Persons	Males	Females
1	26	27	28	29	30	31	32	33	34	35	36	37	38	39	40
TOTAL	971,616	494,061	477,555	1,113,409	580,897	552,512	944,793	480,498	464,295	633,690	325,396	308,294	722,081	367,170	354,911
"A" VERNACULARS OF INDIA ..	971,231	493,740	477,491	1,133,174	580,730	552,444	943,751	479,680	464,071	633,478	325,277	308,201	721,956	367,083	354,873
(a) Vernaculars of the State ..	*969,029*	492,557	476,472	*1,130,785*	579,483	551,302	*903,214*	459,463	443,751	*622,491*	318,732	303,759	*705,935*	357,825	348,110
DRAVIDIAN FAMILY	*848,685*	431,342	417,343	*1,034,374*	529,975	504,399	*23,923*	12,598	11,325	*7,486*	4,400	2,996	*161,368*	82,451	78,917
Andhra Group	*821,902*	418,628	403,274	*1,029,506*	527,440	502,066	*16,452*	8,465	7,987	*4,609*	2,437	2,172	*120,477*	60,965	59,512
Telugu	*821,902*	418,628	403,274	*1,029,506*	527,440	502,066	*16,452*	8,465	7,987	*4,609*	2,437	2,172	*120,477*	60,965	59,512
Dravida Group	*26,783*	12,714	14,069	*4,868*	2,535	2,333	*6,445*	3,648	2,797	*2,772*	1,990	778	*40,891*	21,486	19,405
Erakala (Kaikadi) ..	*6,533*	3,238	3,295	*3,918*	2,006	1,912	*108*	76	32	*517*	248	269	*2,736*	1,651	1,085
Kanarese	*20,250*	9,476	10,774	*960*	529	421	*6,337*	3,572	2,765	*2,255*	1,751	504	*38,155*	19,835	18,320
Intermediate Group ..	..	..	..	..	..	..	*1,026*	485	541	*105*	54	51	..	..	..
Gondi	..	..	..	..	..	..	*1,026*	485	541	*105*	54	51	..	..	..
INDO-EUROPEAN FAMILY ..	*120,344*	61,215	59,129	*96,411*	49,508	46,903	*879,291*	446,865	432,426	*615,005*	314,242	300,763	*544,567*	275,374	269,193
(Indo-Aryan Branch) ..	*120,344*	61,215	59,129	*96,411*	49,508	46,903	*879,291*	446,865	432,426	*615,005*	314,242	300,763	*544,567*	275,374	269,193
Bhili	..	..	..	..	..	..	*8,385*	4,384	4,001	*303*	182	121	*636*	346	290
Lambadi (Banjari) ..	*32,592*	16,658	15,934	*31,123*	16,243	14,880	*2,246*	865	1,381	*5,254*	2,465	2,789	*7,003*	3,703	3,300
Marathi	*12,187*	6,502	5,685	*3,646*	1,943	1,703	*740,614*	373,626	366,988	*552,642*	278,862	273,780	*450,621*	226,700	223,921
Pardhi	*289*	240	49	..	..	..	*2,414*	1,492	922	*135*	84	51	*1,022*	517	505
Urdu (Western Hindi) ..	*75,276*	37,815	37,461	*61,642*	31,322	30,320	*125,632*	66,498	59,134	*56,671*	32,649	24,022	*85,285*	44,108	41,177
(b) Other Vernaculars of India ..	**2,202**	1,183	1,019	**2,389**	1,247	1,142	**40,300**	20,046	20,254	**10,707**	6,880	4,827	**15,959**	9,213	6,746
DRAVIDIAN FAMILY ..	*424*	231	193	*490*	274	216	*192*	150	42	*44*	23	21	*363*	193	170
Tamil	*424*	231	193	*490*	274	216	*192*	150	42	*44*	23	21	*363*	193	170
INDO-EUROPEAN FAMILY ..	*1,778*	952	826	*1,899*	973	926	*40,108*	19,896	20,212	*10,663*	6,357	4,306	*15,596*	9,020	6,576
(Indo-Aryan Branch) ..	*1,778*	952	826	*1,899*	973	926	*40,108*	19,896	20,212	*10,663*	6,357	4,306	*15,596*	9,020	6,576
Gujarati	*183*	115	68	*10*	7	3	*10,990*	5,596	5,394	*2,481*	1,263	1,218	*1,314*	867	447
Panjabi	..	..	..	..	..	..	*428*	272	156	*40*	22	18	*104*	92	12
Rajasthani	*1,227*	615	612	*543*	269	274	*10,009*	4,465	5,544	*4,763*	3,200	1,563	*4,592*	2,734	1,858
Western Hindi	*368*	222	146	*1,347*	697	640	*18,681*	9,563	9,118	*3,379*	1,872	1,507	*9,586*	5,827	4,259
(c) Others	..	..	..	..	..	..	**237**	171	66	**280**	165	115	**62**	45	17
"B" VERNACULARS OF ASIATIC COUNTRIES AND AFRICA.	38	33	5	11	6	5	348	194	154	198	105	93	54	32	22
(a) Semitic Family ..	*38*	33	5	*11*	6	5	*343*	191	152	*198*	105	93	*50*	28	22
Arabic	*38*	33	5	*11*	6	5	*343*	191	152	*198*	105	93	*50*	28	22
(b) Others	..	..	..	..	..	..	5	3	2	..	..	..	4	4	..
"C" EUROPEAN LANGUAGES.	*347*	288	59	224	161	63	694	624	70	14	14	..	71	55	16
(a) *Teutonic Group* ..	*347*	288	59	*224*	161	63	*663*	598	65	*14*	14	..	*71*	55	16
English	*347*	288	59	*224*	161	63	*663*	598	65	*14*	14	..	*71*	55	16
(b) Others	..	..	..	..	..	..	*31*	26	5	..	..	..	..	..	..

TABLE XV. PART I.

Language.

Language	Parbhani			Gulbarga			Osmanabad			Raichur			Bidar		
	Persons	Males	Females	Persons	Males	Females	Persons	Males	Females	Persons	Males	Females	Persons	Males	Females
1	41	42	43	44	45	46	47	48	49	50	51	52	53	54	55
TOTAL	853,760	434,777	418,983	1,225,008	621,687	603,321	691,068	357,489	333,579	937,535	473,161	464,374	873,615	446,256	427,359
"A" VERNACULARS OF INDIA ..	853,547	434,627	418,920	1,224,753	621,506	603,247	690,952	357,396	333,556	937,059	472,762	464,297	873,405	446,097	427,308
(a) Vernaculars of the State	*833,099*	424,092	409,007	*1,215,928*	617,069	598,859	*677,651*	350,153	327,498	*932,734*	470,229	462,505	*867,764*	443,191	424,573
DRAVIDIAN FAMILY	*19,812*	10,556	9,256	*847,619*	431,076	416,543	*55,556*	28,699	26,857	*836,693*	421,301	415,392	*395,096*	201,602	193,494
Andhra Group	*13,850*	7,397	6,453	*239,796*	110,522	129,274	*17,994*	9,036	8,958	*237,553*	121,113	116,440	*133,780*	68,047	65,733
Telugu	*13,850*	7,397	6,453	*239,796*	110,522	129,274	*17,994*	9,036	8,958	*237,553*	121,113	116,440	*133,780*	68,047	65,733
Dravida Group	*5,962*	3,159	2,803	*607,823*	320,554	287,269	*37,562*	19,663	17,899	*599,140*	300,188	298,952	*261,316*	133,555	127,761
Erakala (Kaikadi)	*51*	35	16	*3,414*	2,378	1,036	*532*	261	271	*630*	319	311	*534*	275	259
Kanarese	*5,911*	3,124	2,787	*604,409*	318,176	286,233	*37,030*	19,402	17,628	*598,510*	299,869	298,641	*260,782*	133,280	127,502
Intermediate Group	..	..	..	..	..	..	..	..	..	..	..	..	..	..	..
Gondi	..	..	..	..	..	..	..	..	..	..	..	..	..	..	..
INDO-EUROPEAN FAMILY	*813,287*	413,536	399,751	*368,309*	185,993	182,316	*622,095*	321,454	300,641	*96,041*	48,928	47,113	*472,668*	241,589	231,079
(Indo-Aryan Branch)	*813,287*	413,536	399,751	*368,309*	185,993	182,316	*622,095*	321,454	300,641	*96,041*	48,928	47,113	*472,668*	241,589	231,079
Bhili	*295*	160	135	..	..	..	..	..	..	..	..	..	..	..	..
Lambadi (Banjari)	*9,243*	4,275	4,968	*3,293*	1,354	1,939	*1,962*	1,287	675	*4,856*	2,292	2,564	*6,638*	4,150	2,488
Marathi	*708,720*	360,075	348,645	*198,950*	100,974	97,976	*546,749*	279,341	267,408	*11,258*	6,149	5,109	*327,538*	166,480	161,058
Pardhi	*633*	281	352	*203*	141	62	*346*	168	178	..	..	..	*76*	64	12
Urdu (Western Hindi)	*94,396*	48,745	45,651	*165,863*	83,524	82,339	*73,038*	40,658	32,380	*79,927*	40,487	39,440	*138,416*	70,895	67,521
(b) Other Vernaculars of India. ..	***20,253***	10,435	9,818	***8,808***	4,423	4,385	***12,959***	7,028	5,931	***4,310***	2,522	1,788	***5,497***	2,815	2,682
DRAVIDIAN FAMILY	*402*	208	194	*278*	173	105	..	..	..	*304*	184	120	*26*	16	10
Tamil	*402*	208	194	*278*	173	105	..	..	..	*304*	184	120	*26*	16	10
INDO-EUROPEAN FAMILY	*19,851*	10,227	9,624	*8,530*	4,250	4,280	*12,959*	7,028	5,931	*4,006*	2,338	1,668	*5,471*	2,799	2,672
(Indo-Aryan Branch)	*19,851*	10,227	9,624	*8,530*	4,250	4,280	*12,959*	7,028	5,931	*4,006*	2,338	1,668	*5,471*	2,799	2,672
Gujarati	*1,383*	793	590	*2,350*	1,278	1,072	*3,026*	1,525	1,501	*1,442*	747	695	*882*	442	440
Panjabi	*216*	160	56	*70*	56	14	*342*	156	186	..	..	..	*72*	44	28
Rajasthani	*9,403*	4,816	4,587	*2,987*	1,196	1,791	*5,205*	3,141	2,064	*1,991*	1,275	716	*1,701*	965	736
Western Hindi	*8,849*	4,458	4,391	*3,123*	1,720	1,403	*4,386*	2,206	2,180	*573*	316	257	*2,816*	1,348	1,468
(c) Others	***195***	100	95	***17***	14	3	***342***	215	127	***15***	11	4	***144***	91	53
"B" VERNACULARS OF ASIATIC COUNTRIES AND AFRICA.	73	56	17	162	115	47	88	74	14	137	114	23	14	7	7
(a) Semitic Family	***73***	56	17	***162***	115	47	***72***	59	13	***133***	112	21	***10***	5	5
Arabic	*73*	56	17	*162*	115	47	*72*	59	13	*133*	112	21	*10*	5	5
(b) Others	..	..	..	..	..	..	16	15	1	4	2	2	4	2	2
"C" EUROPEAN LANGUAGES. ..	140	94	46	93	66	27	28	19	9	339	285	54	196	152	44
(a) *Teutonic Group*	***140***	94	46	***93***	66	27	***28***	19	9	***334***	282	52	***196***	152	44
English	*140*	94	46	*93*	66	27	*28*	19	9	*334*	282	52	*196*	152	44
(b) Others	..	..	..	..	..	..	..	..	..	5	3	2	..	..	..

Hyderabad Census, 1931.

Table XV–Part II.

BILINGUALISM.

THIS table is new and gives for the State and also for the districts the number of persons who use other languages besides their mother-tongue. It is confined to only thirteen important mother-tongues in the State, viz., Telugu, Marathi, Kanarese, Urdu, Bhili, Gondi, Banjari (Lambadi), Erakala (Kaikadi), Gujarati, Rajasthani, Tamil, Arabic and English.

2. Only four important languages, Kanarese, Telugu, Marathi and Urdu have been tabulated for subsidiary tongues. The other subsidiary language-speakers being too insignificant a number have been left out.

TABLE XV—PART II.

BILINGUALISM.

TABLE XV—

Biling

District	Mother Tongue	Number of — Mother Tongue: Persons	Males	Females	Subsidiary — Kanarese: Persons	Males	Females
1	2	3	4	5	6	7	8
HYDERABAD STATE ..	TOTAL	14,355,242	7,325,106	7,030,136	248,489	138 509	109,980
	Telugu	6,972,534	3,544,413	3,428,121	110,941	54,259	56,682
	Marathi	3,786,838	1,916,549	1,870,289	70,627	44,026	26,601
	Kanarese	1,620,094	832,189	787,905	..	..	..
	Urdu	1,507,272	783,800	723,472	56,385	33,522	22,863
	Bhili	9,619	5,072	4,547	..	..	..
	Gondi	76,087	38,955	37,132	12	12	..
	Banjari	214,617	110,570	104,047	6,471	3,791	2,680
	Erakala	31,974	17,333	14,641	792	494	298
	Gujarati	33,915	18,069	15,846	1,074	870	204
	Rajasthani	56,251	30,464	25,787	1,742	1,218	524
	Tamil	29,050	15,598	13,452	255	167	88
	Arabic	3,172	1,932	1,240	..	..	..
	English	13,819	10,162	3,657	190	150	40
1. Hyderabad City ..	Total	455,604	239,831	215,773	1,724	993	731
	Telugu	173,357	90.565	82,792	1,308	757	551
	Marathi	16,344	8,440	7,904	235	120	115
	Kanarese	3,521	1,971	1,550	..	..	..
	Urdu	218,206	112,381	105,825	5	1	4
	Banjari	387	207	180	..	..	..
	Erakala	289	188	101	..	..	..
	Gujarati	5,626	3,113	2,513	..	..	..
	Rajasthani	8,439	4,979	3,460	..	..	..
	Tamil	18,063	9,937	8,126	176	115	61
	Arabic	1,855	1,065	790	..	..	..
	English	9,517	6,985	2,532	..	..	..
2. Atraf-i-Balda ..	Total	499,453	253,859	245,594	2,297	1,653	644
	Telugu	397,612	203,471	194,141	421	300	121
	Marathi	17,903	7,858	10,045	442	322	120
	Kanarese	19,865	9,881	9,984	..	..	..
	Urdu	55,755	28,305	27,450	1,428	1,028	400
	Banjari	5,896	3,077	2,819	6	3	3
	Erakala	665	369	296	..	..	..
	Gujarati	283	159	124	..	..	..
	Rajasthani	589	308	281	..	..	..
	Tamil	648	307	341	..	..	..
	Arabic	25	14	11	..	..	..
	English	212	110	102	..	..	..
3. Warangal ..	Total	1,115,576	574,614	540,962	269	165	104
	Telugu	949,488	487,746	461,742	255	155	100
	Marathi	13,689	7,021	6,668	14	10	4
	Kanarese	360	187	173	..	..	..
	Urdu	60,698	33,187	27,511	..	..	..
	Gondi	24,855	12,615	12,240	..	..	..
	Banjari	54,136	27,420	26,716	..	..	..
	Erakala	5,931	3,120	2,811	..	..	..
	Gujarati	367	187	180	..	..	..
	Rajasthani	1,016	530	486	..	..	..
	Tamil	4,110	2,027	2,083	..	..	..
	Arabic	61	33	28	..	..	..
	English	865	541	324	..	..	..
4. Karimnagar ..	Total	1,241,342	634,377	606,965	13	3	10
	Telugu	1,168,062	595,267	572,795	..	..	..
	Marathi	9,554	5,018	4,536	13	3	10
	Kanarese	298	162	136	..	..	..
	Urdu	52,890	28,278	24,612	..	..	..
	Gondi	1,020	553	467	..	..	..
	Banjari	7,224	3,859	3,365	..	..	..
	Erakala	724	402	322	..	..	..
	Gujarati	82	41	41	..	..	..
	Rajasthani	1,046	545	501	..	..	..
	Tamil	286	139	147	..	..	..
	Arabic	18	9	9	..	..	..
	English	138	104	34	..	..	..

PART II.

ualism.

TABLE XV--PART II.
BILINGUALISM.

PERSONS SPEAKING LANGUAGES.								
Marathi			Telugu			Urdu		
Persons	Males	Females	Persons	Males	Females	Persons	Males	Females
9	10	11	12	13	14	15	16	17
136,397	81,237	55,160	232,359	127,021	105,338	450,773	325,720	125,053
42,714	24,366	18,348	..	..	..	181,490	126,836	54,654
..	..	..	45,714	23,284	22,430	163,629	118,251	45,378
49,155	29,264	19,891	69,689	82,943	36,746	68,438	52,795	15,643
30,953	17,551	13,402	49,899	32,516	17,383	..	..	..
359	282	77	..	..	..	..	..	..
2,561	1,401	1,160	2,291	2,071	220	227	217	10
2,400	1,921	479	46,876	25,184	21,692	7,128	5,512	1,616
228	174	54	9,060	5,556	3,504	552	893	159
1,573	1,030	543	222	142	80	6,989	4,742	2,247
6,174	5,021	1,153	789	547	242	13,045	9,838	3,707
4	2	2	5,973	3,561	2,412	5,037	4,508	529
4	3	1	30	30	..	1,615	1,209	406
272	222	50	1,816	1,187	629	2,623	1,919	704
695	419	276	6,554	3,652	2,902	,462	43,033	22,429
128	74	54	..	..	..	46,689	29,766	16,923
..	..	..	130	106	24	7,726	5,164	2,562
506	316	190	834	488	346	1,626	1,444	182
57	26	31	2,578	1,495	1,083	..	..	..
..	..	..	30	15	15	18	10	8
2	2	..	17	12	5	94	53	41
2	1	1	10	5	5	641	229	412
..	..	..	..	..	..	3,526	2,318	1,208
..	..	..	2,919	1,513	1,406	2,771	2,453	318
..	..	..	..	..	..	1,143	831	312
..	..	..	36	18	18	1,228	765	463
1,750	1,163	587	19,131	10,517	8,614	20,859	19,754	1,105
1,113	899	214	..	..	..	10,201	10,001	200
..	..	..	2,494	1,246	1,248	6,186	5,625	561
337	137	200	613	306	307	3,663	3,541	122
265	107	158	9,321	5,173	4,148	..	..	..
35	20	15	5,679	3,089	2,590	6	5	1
..	..	..	645	450	195	13	10	3
..	..	..	..	..	..	142	98	44
..	..	..	23	14	9	392	239	153
..	..	..	341	229	112	220	207	13
..	..	..	..	..	..	10	7	3
..	..	..	15	10	5	26	21	5
1,265	883	382	45,512	23,932	21,580	14,151	9,294	4,857
1,102	725	377	..	..	..	7,476	4,982	2,494
..	..	..	4,382	3,214	1,168	4,516	2,593	1,923
11	6	5	113	59	54	103	84	19
152	152	..	7,206	4,000	3,206	..	..	..
..	..	..	1,458	1,340	118	..	..	..
..	..	..	23,858	10,494	13,364	..	..	..
..	..	..	5,587	2,820	2,767	17	12	5
..	..	..	24	13	11	72	44	28
..	..	..	42	35	7	616	430	186
..	..	..	1,986	1,415	571	1,091	977	114
..	..	..	9	9	..	29	23	6
..	..	..	847	533	314	231	149	82
2,808	1,570	1,238	6,879	3,501	3,378	1,964	934	1,030
2,780	1,552	1,228	..	..	..	1,015	451	564
..	..	..	1,836	941	895	276	101	175
..	..	..	169	54	115	54	42	12
21	15	6	3,114	1,581	1,533	..	..	..
..	..	..	..	..	..	..	..	..
..	..	..	1,453	729	724	255	130	125
..	..	..	68	38	30	..	..	..
..	..	..	11	5	6	31	15	16
7	3	4	59	34	25	266	144	122
..	..	..	77	29	48	52	41	11
..	..	..	..	..	..	..	..	..
..	..	..	92	90	2	15	10	5

TABLE XV—PART II.
BILINGUALISM.

District	Mother Tongue	NUMBER OF					
		Mother Tongue			Subsidiary		
					Kanarese		
		Persons	Males	Females	Persons	Males	Females
1	2	3	4	5	6	7	8
5. Adilabad ..	Total	759,968	388,722	371,246	1,214	829	385
	Telugu	463,558	237,130	226,428	800	463	337
	Marathi	159,509	79,555	79,954	180	146	34
	Kanarese	10,404	5,549	4,855	..	..	..
	Urdu	41,702	22,002	19,700	204	199	5
	Gondi	49,081	25,248	23,833	12	12	..
	Banjari	26,276	14,164	12,112	14	7	7
	Erakala	3,595	1,862	1,733	..	..	..
	Gujarati	2,068	1,093	975	4	2	2
	Rajasthani	1,182	625	557	..	..	..
	Tamil	1,896	1,001	895	..	..	..
	Arabic	51	49	2	..	..	..
	English	646	444	202	..	..	..
6. Medak	Total	736,502	372,201	364,301	262	192	70
	Telugu	639,350	322,599	316,751	262	192	70
	Marathi	8,549	4,036	4,513	..	..	..
	Kanarese	5,296	2,717	2,579	..	..	..
	Urdu	76,145	39,094	37,051	..	..	..
	Banjari	3,292	1,779	1,513	..	..	..
	Erakala	984	452	532	..	..	..
	Gujarati	668	385	283	..	..	..
	Rajasthani	721	304	417	..	..	..
	Tamil	1,171	576	595	..	..	..
	Arabic	41	31	10	..	..	..
	English	285	228	57	..	..	..
7. Nizamabad ..	Total	621,080	312,495	308,585	2,862	1,672	1,190
	Telugu	545,188	273,585	271,603	1,558	1,010	548
	Marathi	8,365	3,969	4,396	1,175	545	630
	Kanarese	5,761	2,703	3,058	..	..	..
	Urdu	45,730	23,852	21,878	129	117	12
	Banjari	13,196	6,772	6,424	..	..	..
	Erakala	813	453	360	..	..	..
	Gujarati	760	458	302	..	..	..
	Rajasthani	837	497	340	..	..	..
	Tamil	353	159	194	..	..	..
	Arabic	31	21	10	..	..	..
	English	46	21	25	..	..	..
8. Mahbubnagar ..	Total	970,959	493,599	477,360	459	389	70
	Telugu	821,902	418,628	403,274	431	363	68
	Marathi	12,187	6,502	5,685	21	21	..
	Kanarese	20,250	9,476	10,774	..	..	..
	Urdu	75,276	37,815	37,461	..	..	..
	Banjari	32,592	16,658	15,934	..	..	..
	Erakala	6,533	3,238	3,295	..	..	..
	Gujarati	183	115	68	7	5	2
	Rajasthani	1,227	615	612	..	..	..
	Tamil	424	231	193	..	..	..
	Arabic	38	33	5	..	..	..
	English	347	288	59	..	..	..
9. Nalgonda ..	Total	1,132,063	580,200	551,863	282	240	42
	Telugu	1,029,506	527,440	502,066	280	238	42
	Marathi	3,646	1,943	1,703	..	..	..
	Kanarese	950	529	421	..	..	..
	Urdu	61,642	31,322	30,320	..	..	..
	Banjari	31,123	16,243	14,880	..	..	..
	Erakala	3,918	2,006	1,912	..	..	..
	Gujarathi	10	7	3	2	2	..
	Rajasthani	543	269	274	..	..	..
	Tamil	490	274	216	..	..	..
	Arabic	11	6	5	..	..	..
	English	224	161	63	..	..	..

PART II.

ualism.

TABLE XV—PART II.
BILINGUALISM.

PERSONS SPEAKING								
LANGUAGES.								
MARATHI			TELUGU			URDU		
Persons	Males	Females	Persons	Males	Females	Persons	Males	Females
9	10	11	12	13	14	15	16	17
8,070	5,005	3,065	14,045	10,516	3,529	27,824	12,048	15,776
4,040	2,816	1,224	..	..	..	10,803	4,676	6,127
..	..	..	2,379	1,528	851	12,673	4,428	8,245
751	348	403	528	183	345	2,354	1,468	891
1,151	601	550	5,314	3,977	1,337	..	..	..
1,748	890	858	833	731	102	213	205	8
221	215	6	3,760	3,097	663	246	191	55
79	79	..	937	884	53	133	121	12
58	46	12	58	35	23	649	368	281
18	8	10	48	18	30	240	155	85
4	2	2	7	6	1	262	247	15
..	..	..	..	..	..	33	33	..
..	..	..	181	57	124	218	161	57
2,642	2,212	430	4,296	2,853	1,443	7,678	6,031	1,647
2,498	2,078	420	..	..	..	2,540	1,707	833
..	..	..	547	267	280	3,115	2,528	587
..	..	..	169	54	115	1,034	924	110
140	130	10	2,628	1,969	659	..	..	..
..	..	..	521	323	198	135	112	23
..	..	..	81	28	53	..	..	..
..	..	..	55	30	25	304	261	43
..	..	..	74	46	28	212	184	28
..	..	..	129	56	73	184	176	8
..	..	..	..	..	..	13	11	2
4	4	..	92	80	12	141	128	13
2,957	1,885	1,072	9,354	5,214	4,140	41,712	27,109	14,603
2,513	1,535	978	..	..	..	36,705	23,225	13,480
..	..	..	765	391	374	2,284	1,981	303
163	140	23	607	402	205	1,795	1,204	591
192	152	40	4,409	2,410	1,999	..	..	..
19	17	2	2,924	1,627	1,297	345	261	84
15	8	7	354	185	169	12	10	2
1	1	..	39	36	3	329	248	81
51	31	20	7	5	2	182	127	55
..	..	..	211	140	71	54	49	5
..	..	..	..	..	..	..	..	..
3	1	2	38	18	20	6	4	2
141	115	26	7,570	5,395	2,175	29,753	22,653	7,100
106	81	25	..	..	..	19,450	14,519	4,931
..	..	..	2,377	1,360	1,017	4,459	3,591	868
26	26	..	2,394	1,806	588	2,881	2,488	393
3	3	..	869	693	176	..	..	..
..	..	..	1,382	1,103	279	2,466	1,590	876
..	..	..	250	192	58	9	8	1
6	5	1	10	7	3	82	78	4
..	..	..	..	..	..	127	119	8
..	..	..	37	24	13	114	112	2
..	..	..	21	21	..	29	24	5
..	..	..	230	189	41	136	124	12
498	331	167	15,840	12,649	3,191	12,266	10,989	1,277
452	308	144	..	..	..	9,415	8,534	881
..	..	..	371	272	99	1,101	991	110
..	..	..	28	24	4	117	114	3
46	23	23	9,333	8,054	1,279	..	..	..
..	..	..	5,059	3,459	1,600	989	891	98
..	..	..	690	650	40	193	110	83
..	..	..	2	1	1	3	2	1
..	..	..	21	14	7	209	128	81
..	..	..	212	114	98	130	118	12
..	..	..	..	..	..	..	..	..
..	..	..	124	61	63	109	101	8

TABLE XV—

Biling

TABLE XV.—PART II.

BILINGUALISM.

District	Mother Tongue	Mother Tongue: Persons	Mother Tongue: Males	Mother Tongue: Females	Number of Subsidiary — Kanarese: Persons	Kanarese: Males	Kanarese: Females
1	2	3	4	5	6	7	8
10. Aurangabad ..	Total	922,997	468,971	454,026	10,820	6,850	3,970
	Telugu	16,452	8,463	7,987	250	105	145
	Marathi	740,614	373,626	366,988	4,405	3,348	1,057
	Kanarese	6,337	3,572	2,765	..	..	..
	Urdu	125,632	66,498	59,134	6,148	3,386	2,762
	Bhili	8,385	4,384	4,001	..	..	..
	Gondi	1,026	485	541	..	..	..
	Banjari	2,246	865	1,381	..	..	..
	Erakala	108	76	32	..	..	..
	Gujarati	10,990	5,596	5,394	6	6	..
	Rajasthani	10,009	4,465	5,544	11	5	6
	Tamil	192	150	42	..	..	..
	Arabic	343	191	152	..	..	..
	English	663	598	65	..	..	..
11. Bir	Total	629,856	323,253	306,603	3,472	2,595	877
	Telugu	4,609	2,437	2,172	470	244	226
	Marathi	552,642	278,862	273,780	2,886	2,274	612
	Kanarese	2,255	1,751	504	..	..	..
	Urdu	56,671	32,649	24,022	35	25	10
	Bhili	303	182	121	..	..	..
	Gondi	105	54	51	..	..	..
	Banjari	5,254	2,465	2,789	..	..	..
	Erakala	517	248	269	..	..	..
	Gujarati	2,481	1,263	1,218	..	..	..
	Rajasthani	4,763	3,200	1,563	81	52	29
	Tamil	44	23	21	..	..	..
	Arabic	198	105	93	..	..	..
	English	14	14	..	..	..	..
12. Nander ..	Total	711,303	361,185	350,118	15,675	9,951	5,724
	Telugu	120,477	60,965	59,512	6,285	3,563	2,722
	Marathi	450,621	226,700	223,921	8,069	5,717	2,352
	Kanarese	38,155	19,835	18,320	..	..	..
	Urdu	85,285	44,108	41,177	496	295	201
	Bhil	636	346	290	..	..	..
	Banjari	7,003	3,703	3,300	816	367	449
	Erakala	2,736	1,651	1,085	..	..	..
	Gujarati	1,314	867	447	8	8	..
	Rajasthani	4,592	2,734	1,858	..	..	..
	Arabic	50	28	22	..	..	..
	Tamil	363	193	170	..	..	..
	English	71	55	16	1	1	..
13. Parbhani ..	Total	843,867	429,778	414,089	705	260	445
	Telugu	13,850	7,897	6,453	13	7	6
	Marathi	708,720	360,075	348,645	692	253	439
	Kanarese	5,911	3,124	2,787	..	..	..
	Urdu	94,396	48,745	45,651	..	..	..
	Bhili	295	160	135	..	..	..
	Banjari	9,243	4,275	4,968	..	..	..
	Erakala	51	35	16	..	..	..
	Gujarati	1,383	793	590	..	..	..
	Rajasthani	9,403	4,816	4,587	..	..	..
	Arabic	73	56	17	..	..	..
	Tamil	402	208	194	..	..	..
	English	140	94	46	..	..	..
14. Gulbarga ..	Total	1,221,595	619,756	601,839	51,075	27,480	23,595
	Telugu ..	239,796	110,522	129,274	14,999	7,093	7,906
	Marathi	198,950	100,974	97,976	23,082	12,571	10,511
	Kanarese	604,409	318,176	286,233	..	..	..
	Urdu	165,863	83,524	82,339	9,470	5,973	3,497
	Banjari	3,293	1,354	1,939	2,465	1,172	1,293
	Erakala	3,414	2,378	1,036	670	405	265
	Gujarati	2,350	1,278	1,072	131	88	48
	Rajasthani	2,987	1,196	1,791	206	146	60
	Tamil	278	173	105	52	37	15
	Arabic	162	115	47	..	..	..
	English	93	66	27	..	..	..

PART II.

ualism.

TABLE XV—PART II.

BILINGUALISM.

PERSONS SPEAKING

LANGUAGES

Marathi			Telugu			Urdu		
Persons	Males	Females	Persons	Males	Females	Persons	Males	Females
9	10	11	12	13	14	15	16	17
16,427	11,188	5,239	13,100	5,719	7,381	27,541	22,762	4,779
1,116	800	316	..	..	..	4,455	3,461	994
..	..	..	12,188	5,182	7,006	17,105	14,937	2,168
,888	937	951	871	500	371	1,578	1,284	294
,080	4,984	3,096	35	33	2	..	..	..
293	247	46	..	..	..	..	..	..
813	311	302	..	..	..	14	12	2
12	12	..	2	2	..	9	8	1
12	12	..	..	..	..	..	..	..
169	125	44	..	..	..	2,175	1,284	891
4,026	3,552	474	..	..	..	1,816	1,433	383
..	..	..	4	2	2	14	12	2
..	..	..	..	..	..	186	150	36
18	8	10	..	..	..	189	181	8
6,292	3,614	2,678	1,694	915	779	14,916	9,069	5,847
419	307	112	..	..	..	701	591	110
..	..	..	1,512	781	731	12,571	7,022	5,549
377	305	72	42	32	10	547	524	23
3,573	1,956	1,617	96	72	24	..	..	..
66	35	31	..	..	..	..	..	..
..	..	..	..	..	..	..	..	..
115	85	30	..	..	..	139	118	21
103	63	40	32	20	12	1	1	..
815	514	301	..	..	..	619	501	118
819	344	475	..	..	..	235	224	11
..	..	..	8	6	2	2	2	..
..	..	..	..	..	..	95	80	15
5	5	..	4	4	..	6	6	..
15,933	9,366	6,567	23,783	9,923	13,860	16,662	11,618	5,044
8,675	4,428	4,247	..	..	..	3,619	2,575	1,044
..	..	..	14,657	6,841	7,816	6,695	4,332	2,363
3,528	2,655	873	8,160	2,807	5,353	5,194	3,702	1,492
2,834	1,649	1,185	364	151	213	..	..	..
..	..	..	..	..	..	..	..	..
590	444	146	598	120	478	206	194	12
..	..	..	..	..	..	..	..	..
133	43	90	..	..	..	226	197	29
169	143	26	..	..	..	699	598	101
..	..	..	..	..	..	..	..	..
..	..	..	..	..	..	14	12	2
4	4	..	4	4	..	9	8	1
10,299	4,444	5,855	461	419	42	64,070	52,733	11,337
567	236	331	..	..	..	3,154	2,261	893
..	..	..	31	20	11	55,186	46,630	8,556
510	380	130	44	41	3	1,911	1,124	787
8,573	3,347	5,226	386	358	28	..	..	..
..	..	..	..	..	..	..	..	..
241	121	120	..	..	..	1,091	979	112
15	8	7	..	..	..	..	..	..
15	9	6	..	..	..	382	298	84
374	341	33	..	..	..	2,275	1,381	894
..	..	..	..	..	..	..	..	..
..	..	..	..	..	..	19	16	3
4	2	2	..	..	..	52	44	8
31,157	18,485	12,672	3,069	2,065	1,004	45,095	28,511	16,584
2,745	1,670	1,075	..	..	..	9,505	6,291	3,214
..	..	..	474	286	188	20,811	12,302	8,509
25,832	14,638	11,194	..	..	..	12,648	8,143	4,505
1,412	1,150	262	608	350	258	..	..	..
1,063	955	108	1,435	1,038	397	327	264	63
..	..	..	179	133	46	80	68	12
105	72	33	..	..	..	679	567	112
..	..	..	315	225	90	899	773	126
..	..	..	42	27	15	54	42	12
..	..	..	..	..	..	31	20	11
..	..	..	16	6	10	61	41	20

TABLE XV—PART II.

BILINGUALISM.

District	Mother Tongue	NUMBER OF					
		Mother Tongue			Subsidiary		
					Kanarese		
		Persons	Males	Females	Persons	Males	Females
1	2	3	4	5	6	7	8
15. Osmanabad ..	Total ..	685,366	354,729	330,907	18,497	12,935	5,562
	Telugu	17,994	9,036	8,958	1,224	770	454
	Marathi	546,749	279,341	267,408	13,289	8,547	4,742
	Kanarese	37,030	19,402	17,628	..	..	..
	Urdu	73,038	40,658	32,380	3,957	3,593	364
	Banjari	1,962	1,287	675	4	2	
	Erakala	532	261	271	..	..	..
	Gujarati	3,026	1,525	1,501	8	8	..
	Rajasthani	5,205	3,141	2,064	15	15	..
	Arabic	72	59	13	..	..	..
	English	28	19	9	..	..	..
16. Raichur ..	Total	936,938	472,829	464,109	121,758	61,770	59,988
	Telugu	237,553	121,113	116,440	72,715	33,266	39,449
	Marathi	11,258	6,149	5,109	9,061	5,589	3,472
	Kanarese	598,510	299,869	298,641	..	..	..
	Urdu	79,927	40,487	39,440	35,323	19,805	15,518
	Banjari	4,856	2,292	2,564	2,114	1,210	904
	Erakala	630	319	311	122	89	33
	Gujarati	1,442	747	695	883	737	146
	Rajasthani	1,991	1,275	716	1,324	910	414
	Tamil	304	184	120	27	15	12
	Arabic	133	112	21	..	..	..
	English	334	282	52	189	149	40
17. Bidar ..	Total	870,503	444,707	425,796	17,105	10,532	6,573
	Telugu	133,780	68,047	65,733	9,670	5,733	3,937
	Marathi	327,538	166,480	161,058	7,063	4,560	2,503
	Kanarese	260,782	133,280	127,502	..	..	..
	Urdu	138,416	70,895	67,521	190	100	90
	Banjari	6,638	4,150	2,488	52	30	22
	Erakala	534	275	259	..	..	..
	Gujarathi	882	442	440	25	19	6
	Rajasthani	1,701	965	786	105	90	15
	Arabic	10	5	5	..	..	..
	Tamil	26	16	10	..	..	..
	English	196	152	44	..	..	..

PART II.

ualism.

TABLE XV—PART II.

BILINGUALISM.

PERSONS SPEAKING								
LANGUAGES								
MARATHI			TELUGU			URDU		
Persons	Males	Females	Persons	Males	Females	Persons	Males	Females
9	10	11	12	13	14	15	16	17
12,055	7,908	4,147	2,466	1,980	486	4,632	3,552	1,080
724	425	299	..	..	..	680	538	142
..	..	..	308	155	153	1,731	1,171	560
8,055	4,886	3,169	2,077	1,774	303	1,428	1,214	214
2,899	2,292	607	21	19	2	..	..	..
8	4	4	47	28	24	362	284	78
2	2	..	2	2	..	..	..	..
259	210	40	4	3	1	133	112	21
91	72	19	7	4	3	282	219	63
..	..	..	..	..	..	4	2	2
17	17	..	..	..	..	12	12	..
4,524	2,667	1,857	57,144	27,013	30,131	46,004	39,050	6,954
856	525	331	..	..	..	13,925	12,864	1,561
..	..	..	1,263	694	569	3,392	2,394	998
3,234	1,826	1,408	51,863	23,825	28,038	27,283	23,172	4,111
211	122	89	3,461	2,076	1,385	..	..	..
..	..	..	..	..	..	219	191	28
..	..	..	218	142	76	..	..	..
..	..	..	9	7	2	282	228	54
153	140	13	193	152	41	711	547	164
..	..	..	..	..	..	56	44	12
..	..	..	..	..	..	42	28	14
70	54	16	137	117	20	94	82	12
18,884	9,982	8,902	1,461	758	703	10,184	6,580	3,604
12,880	5,907	6,978	..	..	..	1,157	894	263
..	..	..	..	..	..	3,802	2,461	1,341
3,937	2,664	1,273	1,177	588	589	4,222	2,328	1,894
1,344	842	502	156	105	51	..	..	..
96	48	48	128	65	63	315	284	31
..	..	..	..	..	..	..	..	..
10	4	6	..	..	..	240	212	28
466	387	79	..	..	..	358	319	39
4	3	1	..	..	..	..	..	..
..	..	..	..	..	..	..	..	..
147	127	20	..	..	..	90	82	8

Table XVI

RELIGION.

1. The corresponding table for 1921 is Table VI and it classifies the population by main Religions with the change in the omission of the headings, Indo-Aryan. Semitic and Iranian; replacing Muslim for Musalman and Tribal for Animist.

2. On the present occasion, the "depressed class" population has been separately headed as "Adi Hindu" and they have been grouped under "Hindu," according to the general classification.

3. Aryas and Brahmos, whose population, unlike the last time, when it came under the head "others," has now been grouped under the general head "Hindu."

4. Under the Christians, no race or denomination is given as in the last time (Table XV—1921) but they are divided into Roman Catholics, Syrians and others, for which the details are shown below :—

Sect or denomination	Persons	Males	Females
Roman Catholics	21,259	11,591	9,668
Romo—Syrians	..	..	..
Other—Syrians	17	12	5
*Others	130,106	67,841	62,265
Total ..	151,382	79,444	71,938

* Others include all Protestants as Anglican-Communion, Baptist, Methodist, Wesleyan, Presbyterian, Church of England, etc.

TABLE XVI.

Religion.

DISTRICT	TOTAL POPULATION			HINDU — Brahmanic Hindu			HINDU — Adi-Hindu			HINDU — Arya		
	Persons	Males	Females	Persons	Males	Females	Persons	Males	Females	Persons	Males	Females
1	2	3	4	5	6	7	8	9	10	11	12	13
HYDERABAD STATE.	14,436,148	7,370,010	7,066,138	9,699,615	4,948,408	4,751,207	2,473,230	1,252,651	1,220,579	3,700	1,896	1,804
1. Hyderabad City ..	*466,894*	247,628	219,271	*172,279*	90,790	81,489	*79,839*	41,120	38,719	*382*	196	186
2. Atraf-i-Balda	*499,661*	253,975	245,686	*333,919*	169,509	164,410	*98,366*	50,243	48,123	*3*	2	1
3. Warangal	*1,117,693*	575,819	541,874	*705,102*	362,125	342,977	*175,687*	90,922	84,765	*247*	117	130
4. Karimnagar	*1,241,405*	634,416	606,989	*933,527*	476,884	456,643	*227,274*	116,291	110,983	*446*	232	214
5. Adilabad	*762,030*	389,754	372,276	*491,088*	252,021	239,067	*115,554*	57,843	57,711	*64*	29	35
6. Medak	*738,665*	373,475	365,190	*508,690*	256,911	251,779	*133,599*	67,943	65,656	*16*	15	1
7. Nizamabad	*623,225*	313,556	309,669	*439,962*	220,875	219,087	*103,061*	51,751	51,310	*10*	5	5
8. Mahbubnagar ..	*971,616*	494,061	477,555	*637,927*	323,041	314,886	*197,784*	100,913	96,871	*284*	145	139
9. Nalgonda	*1,133,409*	580,897	552,512	*780,440*	399,249	381,191	*208,980*	106,897	102,083	*187*	98	89
10. Aurangabad	*944,793*	480,498	464,295	*641,214*	325,257	315,957	*140,336*	70,323	70,013	*37*	7	30
11. Bir	*633,690*	325,396	308,294	*473,445*	243,844	229,601	*95,051*	47,701	47,350	*222*	109	113
12. Nander	*722,081*	367,170	354,911	*479,445*	244,003	235,442	*141,820*	71,492	70,328	*197*	123	74
13. Parbhani	*853,760*	434,777	418,983	*589,258*	301,611	287,647	*153,030*	76,344	76,686	*1,115*	568	547
14. Gulbarga	*1,225,008*	621,687	603,321	*785,929*	398,524	387,405	*194,810*	98,250	96,560	*208*	116	92
15. Osmanabad	*691,068*	357,489	333,579	*464,455*	241,373	223,082	*131,904*	66,921	64,983	..	..	..
16. Raichur	*937,535*	473,161	464,374	*708,167*	357,673	350,494	*112,992*	55,726	57,266	*77*	31	46
17. Bidar	*873,615*	446,256	427,359	*554,768*	284,718	270,050	*163,143*	81,071	81,172	*205*	103	102

TABLE XVI.

Religion.

DISTRICT	HINDU — Brahmo Persons	HINDU — Brahmo Males	HINDU — Brahmo Females	HINDU — Total Hindu Persons	HINDU — Total Hindu Males	HINDU — Total Hindu Females	Jain Persons	Jain Males	Jain Females	Sikh Persons	Sikh Males	Sikh Females	Muslim Persons	Muslim Males	Muslim Females
1	14	15	16	17	18	19	20	21	22	23	24	25	26	27	28
HYDERABAD STATE.	182	98	84	12,176,727	6,203,053	5,973,674	21,543	11,456	10,087	5,178	3,064	2,114	1,534,666	791,435	743,231
1. Hyderabad City ..	*77*	44	33	*252,577*	132,150	120,427	*312*	194	118	*1,002*	690	312	*192,343*	103,095	89,248
2. Atraf-i-Balda ..	..	..	..	*432,288*	219,754	212,534	*86*	46	40	*52*	26	26	*50,412*	25,417	24,995
3. Warangal ..	..	..	..	*881,036*	453,164	427,872	*63*	13	50	*226*	137	89	*67,820*	36,176	31,644
4. Karimnagar ..	*76*	41	35	*1,161,323*	593,448	567,875	*19*	2	17	*230*	127	103	*55,802*	28,256	27,546
5. Adilabad ..	..	..	..	*606,706*	309,893	296,813	*304*	149	155	*121*	62	59	*45,821*	24,030	21,791
6. Medak ..	..	..	..	*642,305*	324,869	317,436	*522*	285	237	*85*	41	44	*71,518*	35,396	36,122
7. Nizamabad ..	..	..	..	*543,033*	272,631	270,402	*38*	23	15	*129*	67	62	*48,769*	24,761	24,008
8. Mahbubnagar	..	..	..	*835,995*	424,099	411,896	*181*	92	89	*248*	128	120	*84,604*	43,281	41,323
9. Nalgonda ..	..	..	..	*989,607*	506,244	483,363	*191*	92	99	*134*	72	62	*62,233*	31,842	30,391
10. Aurangabad ..	..	..	..	*781,587*	395,587	386,000	*5,313*	2,906	2,407	*492*	356	136	*124,441*	65,065	59,376
11. Bir ..	..	..	..	*568,718*	291,654	277,064	*3,183*	1,728	1,455	*53*	30	23	*53,421*	27,691	25,730
12 Nander ..	..	..	..	*621,462*	315,618	305,844	*1,085*	556	529	*1,588*	869	719	*81,155*	41,667	39,488
13. Parbhani ..	*19*	7	12	*743,422*	378,530	364,892	*3,685*	1,924	1,761	*134*	83	51	*88,425*	45,332	43,093
14. Gulbarga ..	..	..	..	*980,947*	496,890	484,057	*1,948*	1,013	935	*329*	176	153	*195,586*	99,636	95,950
15. Osmanabad ..	..	..	..	*596,359*	308,294	288,065	*2,744*	1,424	1,320	*292*	169	123	*80,308*	41,525	38,783
16. Raichur ..	*10*	6	4	*821,246*	418,436	40',810	*872*	476	396	*14*	6	8	*95,699*	48,756	46,943
17. Bidar ..	..	..	..	*718,116*	366,792	351,324	*997*	583	464	*49*	25	24	*136,309*	69,509	66,800

TABLE XVI.

Religion.

DISTRICT	Christian			Zoroastrian			Buddhist			Jew			Tribal		
	Persons	Males	Females	Persons	Males	Females	Persons	Males	Females	Persons	Males	Females	Persons	Males	Females
1	29	30	31	32	33	34	35	36	37	38	39	40	41	42	43
HYDERABAD STATE.	151,382	79,444	71,938	1,784	937	847	52	26	26	27	11	16	544,789	280,584	264,205
1. Hyderabad City ..	*16,123*	9,217	6,906	*1,092*	548	544	*38*	20	18	*27*	11	16	*3,380*	1,698	1,682
2. Atraf-i-Balda	*3,154*	1,573	1,581	*38*	21	17	..	..	..	..	..	..	*13,631*	7,138	6,498
3. Warangal	*28,952*	14,955	13,997	*97*	69	28	..	..	..	..	..	..	*139,499*	71,305	68,194
4. Karimnagar	*13,622*	7,188	6,434	*13*	10	3	*2*	1	1	..	..	..	*10,394*	5,384	5,010
5. Adilabad	*4,244*	2,092	2,152	*27*	15	12	..	..	..	..	..	..	*104,807*	53,513	51,294
6. Medak	*19,662*	10,488	9,174	*3*	..	3	..	..	..	..	..	..	*4,570*	2,396	2,174
7. Nizamabad	*13,856*	7,128	6,728	*42*	21	21	..	..	..	..	..	..	*17,358*	8,925	8,433
8. Mahbubnagar	*2,705*	1,410	1,295	*2*	2	..	..	..	..	..	..	..	*47,881*	25,049	22,832
9. Nalgonda	*23,689*	12,324	11,365	*6*	2	4	..	..	..	..	..	..	*57,549*	30,321	27,228
10. Aurangabad	*10,576*	5,393	5,183	*247*	125	122	..	..	..	..	..	..	*22,137*	11,066	11,071
11. Bir	*28*	15	13	*7*	5	2	..	..	..	..	..	..	*8,280*	4,273	4,007
12. Nander	*398*	218	180	*24*	11	13	..	..	..	..	..	..	*16,369*	8,231	8,138
13. Parbhani	*436*	216	220	*78*	44	34	..	..	..	..	..	..	*17,580*	8,648	8,932
14. Gulbarga	*5,645*	2,861	2,784	*85*	50	35	..	..	..	..	..	..	*40,468*	21,061	19,407
15. Osmanabad	*63*	42	21	*3*	3	..	..	..	..	..	..	..	*11,299*	6,032	5,267
16. Raichur	*3,875*	2,130	1,745	*19*	10	9	*10*	4	6	..	..	..	*15,800*	8,343	7,457
17. Bidar	*4,354*	2,194	2,160	*1*	1	..	*2*	1	1	..	..	..	*13,787*	7,201	6,586

Table XVII.

CASTE, TRIBE AND RACE.

As last time this table is divided into two parts :—Part I deals with all the castes returned in the alphabetical order and Part II by territorial distribution of principal castes whose number exceeds 5,000. On the present occasion the following are the changes effected :—

Hindus.

(1) Wherever there has been an overlapping of names of a caste, they have been grouped under a common familiar name.

(2) Those castes, who have rigidly been observing their old names and returned as such, though identically same with the similar group, have been kept as they are, *e.g.*, Kurma, Hatkar, Panchal, Vishwabrahman, etc., in order that the purpose of census which is to measure the social facts of a caste may not suffer for want of a separate figure for comparative study.

(3) Of the three new names listed on the present occasion, the one is "Yadava", embracing all the shepherd and cowherd-population. The other is "Adi Hindu", representing all the depressed classes; some minor tribes of primitive religions have been shown as "Tribal unclassified."

(4) Certain castes, *e.g.*, Panchal and Vishwabrahman, who are practically either one or the other from the five artisan classes as Sunars, Lohars, etc., have been retained as such for the same reason as mentioned under para. 2 supra.

(5) A number of minor castes of 1921 did not return, while 4,558 persons (2,529 males and 1,969 females) returned has "*no caste*", and they have been included under "Hindu unclassified" together with thirteen other minor castes whose population fell below 1,000.

Adi-Hindus.

All the minor castes and as well as those who have returned as Adi-Hindu, Adi Andhra, Adi Dravida or Adi Karnatak have been shown as Adi-Hindu minor castes. Separate figures for Dhers (including Mala and Mahar) and Madiga (including Mang, Mochi and Chambhar) have also been given, which is for convenience of comparison with previous figures.

Muslims.

The distinction between a Syed or Sheikh, a Pathan or Moghal being merely nominal, having no intrinsic value, they have been grouped under one head.

The etymological expression of various castes which have been grouped with one another under a familiar name is shown below :—

Urdu	English	Telugu	Marathi	Kanarese
Barai	Carpenter	Wadla	Sutar	Badega.
Burud	Basket maker ..	Medari ..	Burud ..	Buruda.
Beldar ..	Mason ..	Uppara ..	Beldar or Mahadi	Govandi.
Dhobi ..	Washerman ..	Chakala ..	Dhobi ..	Ageseru.
Gowli ..	Cowherd ..	Golla or Yadava	Gowli or Ahir .. or Gopi	Yadava.
Hajjam ..	Barber ..	Mangala ..	Warik ..	Nhavi.
Julahi ..	Weaver ..	Sala or Dewang .	Koshti, Chenewar	Jyandra, Hatgaru
Kasab ..	Butcher ..	Katika ..	Are-Katik or Katika.	Katika.
Kunbi ..	Cultivator ..	Kapu ..	Kunbi ..	Kapu.
Kasar ..	Coppersmith ..	Kanchari ..	Kasar ..	Kanchar.
Kalal ..	Toddy drawer ..	Goundla or Idiga.	Kalal ..	Kalal.
Kumbhar	Potter ..	Kummara or Kummari.	Kumbhar ..	Kumbhar.
Lohar ..	Black smith ..	Kammari ..	Lohar ..	Kambara
Rangrez ..	Dyer ..	Rangari ..	Rangari ..	Rangari or Bhavsagar.
Sunar ..	Gold smith ..	Kamsala or Ausala ..	Sunar ..	Kamsali.
Teli ..	Oil Monger ..	Gandla ..	Teli ..	Ganigaru.

TABLE XVII.—PART I.

Caste, Race and Tribe.

TABLE XVII.—PART I.
CASTE, RACE AND TRIBE.

N.B.—H : Hindu A. H : Adi-Hindu T : Tribal

Serial No.	Caste	Persons	Males	Females
1	2	3	4	5
	POPULATION	14,436,148	7,370,010	7,066,138
1	Adi Hindu (Minor castes unclassified) ..	*115,599*	60,822	54,777
2	Andh (T)	*6,100*	2,800	3,300
3	Anglo-Indian ..	*3,370*	2,188	1,182
4	Armenian	*14*	12	2
5	Arya	*3,700*	1,896	1,804
6	Balija	*39,300*	21,514	17,786
7	Bedar (Bender) ..	*237,774*	119,307	118,467
8	Bhat (Bhatraj) ..	*17,270*	9,522	7,748
9	Bhil (T)	*15,052*	7,551	7,501
10	Bhoi (Besta) ..	*285,273*	141,869	143,404
11	Bogam	*26,932*	12,535	14,397
12	Brahman	*376,468*	196,654	179,814
13	Brahmo	*182*	98	84
14	Buddhist	*52*	26	26
15	Burud	*34,777*	19,054	15,723
16	Chenchu (T)	*2,264*	1,090	1,174
17	Darzi (Simpi) ..	*63,631*	32,220	31,411
18	Dasari	*3,220*	1,693	1,527
19	Dher (Mala, Mahar) (A.H.)	*1,076,539*	552,632	523,907
20	Dhobi (Chakala) ..	*269,492*	138,790	130,702
21	European	*2,613*	2,256	357
22	Erakala (Kaikadi Korwa): (T) ..	*59,172*	32,002	27,170
23	Erakala (Kaikadi) (H) ..	*9,986*	5,049	4,937
24	Ghisadi (T)	*2,171*	1,090	1,081
25	Gond (T)	*113,280*	57,048	56,232
26	Gosain (Gosavi) ..	*29,227*	17,147	12,080
27	Gujarati (Gurjar) ..	*8,063*	4,893	3,170
28	Gurav (Tambli) ..	*30,410*	15,676	14,734
29	Hajjam (Mangala) ..	*159,745*	83,855	75,890
30	Hatkar	*45,168*	24,337	20,831
31	Hindu (Minor cas ..	*17,610*	9,862	7,748
32	Indian Christian ..	*145,385*	74,988	70,397
33	Jain	*21,543*	11,456	10,087
34	Jew	*27*	11	16
35	Julahi (Sale, Dewang Koshti)	*406,881*	211,803	195,078
36	Kalal (Ediga, Goundla) ..	*426,836*	220,637	206,199
37	Kapu (Kunbi) ..	*942,920*	490,183	452,737
	Reddi	*164,372*	*86,609*	*77,763*
	Kapu	*778,548*	*403,574*	*374,974*
38	Kasab (Aray, Khatik) ..	*81,165*	42,801	38,364
39	Kasar (Kanchari) ..	*35,730*	19,036	16,694
40	Kayasth	*4,895*	2,818	2,082
41	Khatri	*4,739*	2,566	2,173
42	Khumbhar (Kummar) ..	*154,148*	80,919	73,229
43	Koli ..	*52,472*	29,264	23,208
44	Komati (Vaishya) ..	*308,911*	163,432	145,479
45	Koya (T)	*33,638*	18,217	15,421
46	Kshatriya (Rajput ..	*88,434*	46,256	42,178
47	Kurma	*173,318*	89,646	83,672
	Kurma Kshatriya ..	*11,076*	*6,304*	*4,772*
	Kurma	*162,242*	*83,342*	*78,900*
48	Lambadi (Banjari) (T) ..	*300,466*	153,856	146,610
49	Lingayat (Jangam) ..	*788,839*	397,604	391,235
50	Lodha	*6,908*	4,033	2,875
51	Lohar (Kammari) ..	*93,460*	51,365	42,095
52	Mali	*102,608*	51,611	50,997
53	Maratha	*1,491,558*	751,082	740,476
54	Marwari	*62,311*	34,572	27,739
55	Madiga (Mochi, Mang, Chambhar) ..	*1,281,092*	639,197	641,895
56	Muslim	*1,534,666*	791,435	743,231
57	Panchal	*69,874*	35,707	34,167
58	Pardhi (H)	*5,466*	2,977	2,489
59	Pardhi (T)	*7,172*	3,833	3,339
60	Patkari	*3,535*	1,949	1,586
61	Perka	*51,504*	25,723	25,781
62	Pichakuntla	*8,957*	5,310	3,647
63	Pindhari (T) ..	*1,246*	671	575
64	Rangrez (Rangari) ..	*26,751*	14,875	11,876
65	Sadhu	*3,493*	2,396	1,097
	Bairagi	*1,356*	*993*	*363*
	Sanyasi	*2,137*	*1,403*	*734*
66	Satani (Ayyawar) ..	*54,396*	30,365	24,031
67	Sikh	*5,178*	3,064	2,114
68	Sunar (Ausala Kamsala) .	*137,891*	72,550	65,341
69	Sutar (Bade, Wadla) ..	*110,350*	58,274	52,076
70	Telaga (Munnur, Mutrasi) .	*966,190*	448,805	517,385
71	Teli (Gandla) ..	*73,155*	38,773	34,382
72	Tribals (Unclasified) ..	*4,228*	2,426	1,802
73	Uppara (Beldar Govandi)	*79,492*	39,623	39,869
74	Velama	*51,988*	26,217	25,771
75	Vellala	*4,485*	2,339	2,146
76	Viramusthi	*7,445*	*4,118*	*3,327*
77	Viswabrahman ..	*26,742*	*14,293*	*12,449*
78	Waddar	*138,082*	70,085	67,997
79	Wanjari (Banjari) (H) ..	*70,936*	38,965	31,971
80	Yadava (Ahir, Golla, Gowli, Dhangar) ..	*928,404*	471,464	456,940
81	Zoroastrian	*1,784*	937	847

TABLE XVII—PART II.

Territorial Distribution of Principal Castes

TABLE XVII.—PART II.
TERRITORIAL DISTRIBUTION OF PRINCIPAL CASTES.

Caste and District	Persons	Males	Females
1	2	3	4
HINDU (Brahmanic).			
1. Balija	39,300	21,514	17,786
Hyderabad City	*2,244*	1,157	1,087
Atraf-i-Balda	*4,610*	2,561	2,049
Warangal	*2,151*	897	1,254
Karimnagar	*11,591*	6,834	4,757
Adilabad	*2,851*	1,630	1,221
Medak	*6,922*	3,535	3,387
Mahbubnagar	*8,931*	4,900	4,031
2. Bendar (Bedar)	237,774	119,307	118,467
Hyderabad City	*1,147*	742	405
Karimnagar	*370*	180	190
Nizamabad	*697*	342	355
Aurangabad	*2,743*	1,504	1,239
Bir	*1,991*	1,045	946
Nander	*323*	171	152
Gulbarga	*81,500*	40,660	40,840
Osmanabad	*1,094*	644	450
Raichur	*143,047*	71,222	71,825
Bidar	*4,862*	2,797	2,065
3. Bhat (Bhatraj)	17,270	9,522	7,748
Hyderabad City	*305*	146	159
Warangal	*1,234*	561	673
Karimnagar	*2,049*	823	1,226
Adilabad	*2,884*	1,812	1,072
Medak	*747*	389	358
Nizamabad	*351*	195	156
Mahbubnagar	*2,570*	1,877	693
Nalgonda	*2,351*	1,145	1,206
Nander	*323*	171	152
Parbhani	*236*	138	98
Gulbarga	*3,042*	1,592	1,450
Osmanabad	*491*	206	285
Raichur	*687*	467	220
4. Bhoi (Besta)	285,273	141,869	143,404
Hyderabad City	*6,053*	3,447	2,606
Atraf-i-Balda	*4,390*	2,525	1,865
Warangal	*15,022*	6,680	8,342
Karimnagar	*18,226*	9,038	9,188
Adilabad	*14,236*	7,668	6,568
Medak	*7,068*	3,312	3,756
Nizamabad	*15,845*	7,405	8,440
Mahbubnagar	*36,430*	16,858	19,572
Nalgonda	*9,912*	5,456	4,456
Aurangabad	*5,859*	2,503	3,356
Bir	*4,711*	2,353	2,358
Nander	*25,743*	13,566	12,177
Parbhani	*3,174*	1,634	1,540
Gulbarga	*35,243*	18,207	17,036
Osmanabad	*11,313*	5,203	6,110
Raichur	*27,186*	13,217	13,969
Bidar	*44,862*	22,797	22,065
5. Bogam (Kasban)	26,932	12,535	14,397
Hyderabad City	*638*	240	398
Atraf-i-Balda	*914*	300	614
Warangal	*903*	202	701
Karimnagar	*3,406*	1,606	1,800
Adilabad	*2,568*	1,193	1,375
Medak	*2,189*	882	1,307
Nizamabad	*941*	376	365
Mahbubnagar	*2,031*	606	1,425
Nalgonda	*3,456*	1,711	1,745
Aurangabad	*107*	50	57
Gulbarga	*6,670*	3,883	2,787
Raichur	*3,109*	1,486	1,623
6. Brahman	376,468	196,654	179,814
Hyderabad City	*20,294*	10,289	10,005
Atraf-i-Balda	*13,198*	6,680	6,518
Warangal	*18,385*	10,104	8,281
Karimnagar	*18,226*	9,038	9,188
labad	*14,557*	7,469	7,068
dak	*12,166*	6,241	5,925
zamabad	*13,691*	7,847	6,844
hbubnagar	*15,932*	8,162	7,770
HINDU (Brahmanic). (*contd.*)			
6. Brahman—(*contd.*)			
Nalgonda	*17,210*	9,828	7,387
Aurangabad	*41,244*	20,733	20,511
Bir	*24,997*	12,613	12,384
Nander	*18,323*	10,190	8,133
Parbhani	*32,022*	16,722	15,300
Gulbarga	*32,832*	17,351	15,481
Osmanabad	*24,986*	12,880	12,106
Raichur	*36,994*	19,146	17,848
Bidar	*21,411*	11,866	9,545
7. Burud (Medari)	34,777	19,054	15,723
Hyderabad City	*2,785*	1,570	1,215
Atraf-i-Balda	*262*	143	119
Warangal	*2,610*	1,699	911
Karimnagar	*2,314*	1,185	1,129
Adilabad	*2,678*	1,538	1,140
Medak	*2,039*	1,091	948
Nizamabad	*6,130*	3,106	3,024
Mahbubnagar	*2,546*	1,367	1,179
Nalgonda	*1,017*	449	568
Aurangabad	*716*	574	142
Bir	*638*	326	312
Nander	*3,841*	1,966	1,875
Parbhani	*495*	250	245
Gulbarga	*2,535*	1,454	1,081
Osmanabad	*2,197*	1,270	927
Raichur	*1,074*	613	461
Bidar	*900*	453	447
8. Darzi (Simpi)	63,631	32,220	31,411
Hyderabad City	*4,106*	2,002	2,104
Atraf-i-Balda	*791*	439	352
Warangal	*4,967*	2,471	2,496
Karimnagar	*10,203*	5,506	4,697
Adilabad	*4,190*	2,096	2,094
Medak	*3,683*	1,873	1,810
Nizamabad	*4,103*	1,407	2,696
Mahbubnagar	*3,813*	1,926	1,887
Nalgonda	*5,014*	2,536	2,478
Aurangabad	*4,612*	2,299	2,313
Bir	*1,443*	717	726
Nander	*3,808*	1,921	1,887
Parbhani	*1,311*	745	566
Gulbarga	*4,529*	2,364	2,165
Osmanabad	*2,376*	1,325	1,051
Raichur	*2,421*	1,364	1,057
Bidar	*2,261*	1,229	1,032
9. Dhobi (Chakala)	269,492	138,790	130,702
Hyderabad	*5,222*	3,002	2,220
Atraf-i-Balda	*10,695*	5,389	5,306
Warangal	*33,277*	17,229	16,048
Karimnagar	*43,341*	21,514	21,827
Adilabad	*13,635*	7,948	5,687
Medak	*19,864*	10,814	9,050
Nizamabad	*14,120*	7,254	6,866
Mahbubnagar	*28,606*	14,541	14,,065
Nalgonda	*43,949*	22,166	21,783
Aurangabad	*6,203*	3,122	3,081
Bir	*2,866*	1,386	1,480
Nander	*4,725*	2,428	2,297
Parbhani	*3,307*	1,891	1,416
Gulbarga	*10,038*	5,180	4,858
Osmanabad	*3,753*	2,360	1,393
Raichur	*18,221*	8,938	9,283
Bidar	*7,670*	3,628	4,042
10. Erakala (Kaikadi) (H.)	9,986	5,049	4,937
Gulbarga	*6,476*	3,319	3,157
Osmanabad	*1,548*	752	796
Bidar	*1,962*	978	984
11. Gosain (Gosavi)	29,227	17,147	12,080
Hyderabad City	*65*	37	28
Karimnagar	*315*	188	127
Adilabad	*568*	253	315
Medak	*55*	31	24

TABLE XVII—PART II.
TERRITORIAL DISTRIBUTION OF PRINCIPAL CASTES.

TABLE XVII—PART II.

Territorial Distribution of Principal Castes.

Caste and District	Persons	Males	Females
1	2	3	4
HINDU (Brahmanic).			
11. Gosain (Gosavi).—(*contd.*)			
Aurangabad ..	4,960	3,008	1,952
Bir ..	4,474	2,685	1,789
Nander ..	5,249	3,015	2,234
Parbhani ..	6,659	3,804	2,855
Gulbarga ..	2,088	1,025	1,063
Osmanabad ..	3,894	2,501	1,393
Bidar ..	900	600	300
12. Gujarati (Gurjar) ..	**8,063**	**4,893**	**3,170**
Hyderabad City ..	536	311	225
Atraf-i-Balda ..	347	270	77
Warangal ..	30	18	12
Adilabad ..	49	27	22
Aurangabad ..	4,746	2,792	1,954
Bir ..	870	680	190
Parbhani ..	334	166	168
Gulbarga ..	744	409	335
Raichur ..	407	220	187
13. Gurav (Tambli) ..	**30,410**	**15,676**	**14,734**
Warangal ..	725	422	303
Karimnagar ..	1,091	598	493
Adilabad ..	366	214	152
Medak ..	337	179	158
Nizamabad ..	1,072	623	449
Mahbubnagar ..	2,695	978	1,717
Nalgonda ..	1,299	696	603
Aurangabad ..	1,335	452	883
Bir ..	2,692	1,447	1,245
Nander ..	4,266	2,136	2,130
Parbhani ..	2,220	1,239	981
Gulbarga ..	6,224	3,310	2,914
Osmanabad ..	3,056	1,854	1,202
Bidar ..	3,032	1,528	1,504
14. Hajjam (Mangala)	**159,745**	**83,855**	**75,890**
Hyderabad City ..	5,650	2,696	2,954
Atraf-i-Balda ..	2,437	1,204	1,233
Warangal ..	14,182	7,858	6,324
Karimanagar ..	16,122	7,831	8,291
Adilabad ..	10,289	5,362	4,927
Medak ..	10,107	5,782	4,325
Nizamabad ..	6,275	3,747	2,528
Mahbubnagar ..	17,127	8,724	8,403
Nalgonda ..	14,726	7,890	6,836
Aurangabad ..	8,682	4,455	4,227
Bir ..	5,122	3,094	2,028
Nander ..	6,608	3,574	3,034
Parbhani ..	5,933	2,994	2,939
Gulbarga ..	11,189	5,450	5,739
Osmanabad ..	4,779	2,758	2,021
Raichur ..	11,885	6,116	5,769
Bidar ..	8,632	4,320	4,312
15. Hatkar ..	**45,168**	**24,337**	**20,831**
Adilabad ..	2,969	1,596	1,373
Nizamabad ..	1,049	599	450
Mahbubnagar ..	973	490	483
Aurangabad ..	4,501	2,514	1,987
Bir ..	6,437	3,195	3,242
Nander ..	7,178	3,936	3,242
Parbhani ..	22,061	12,007	10,054
16. Julahi (Dewang, Sale) .	**406,881**	**211,803**	**195,078**
Hyderabad City ..	2,338	1,256	1,082
Atraf-i-Balda ..	17,671	8,901	8,770
Warangal ..	43,297	23,086	20,211
Karimnagar ..	86,673	43,716	42,957
Adilabad ..	35,228	16,746	18,482
Medak ..	30,708	17,288	13,420
Nizamabad ..	30,074	16,042	14,032
Mahbubnagar ..	21,679	12,549	9,130
Nalgonda ..	39,176	19,533	19,643
Aurangabad ..	6,444	3,487	2,957
Bir ..	8,325	4,591	3,734
Nander ..	16,101	9,132	6,969
Parbhani ..	6,326	3,254	3,072
Gulbarga ..	20,208	10,422	9,786
Osmanabad ..	3,862	1,967	1,895
Raichur ..	26,186	13,206	12,980
Bidar ..	12,585	6,627	5,958
HINDU Brahmanic—(*contd.*)			
17. Kalal (Eadiga, Goundla).	**426,836**	**220,637**	**206,199**
Hyderabad City ..	6,781	3,644	3,137
Atraf-i-Balda ..	32,807	16,773	16,034
Warangal ..	54,574	27,396	27,178
Karimnagar ..	73,127	36,564	36,563
Adilabad ..	19,751	10,169	9,582
Medak ..	38,347	20,475	17,872
Nizamabad ..	17,516	9,826	7,690
Mahbubnagar ..	40,209	21,257	18,952
Nalgonda ..	90,229	45,907	44,322
Aurangabad ..	4,776	2,701	2,075
Bir ..	3,459	1,864	1,595
Nander ..	4,000	2,275	1,725
Parbhani ..	3,740	1,927	1,813
Gulbarga ..	12,244	6,241	6,003
Osmanabad ..	3,844	1,972	1,872
Raichur ..	15,097	8,180	6,917
Bidar ..	6,335	3,466	2,869
18. Kapu (Kunbi) ..	**942,920**	**490,183**	**452,737**
Hyderabad City ..	14,658	7,973	6,685
Atraf-i-Balda ..	56,706	28,459	28,247
Warangal ..	112,046	55,942	56 104
Karimnagar ..	155,466	83,717	71,749
Adilabad ..	85,290	46,527	38,763
Medak ..	74,086	39,085	35,001
Nizamabad ..	71,261	35,255	36,006
Mahbubnagar ..	87,524	45,713	41,811
Nalgonda ..	137,006	69,423	67,583
Aurangabad ..	33,760	17,720	16,040
Bir ..	9,706	5,623	4,083
Nander ..	7,495	4,001	3,494
Gulbarga ..	42,846	22,243	20,603
Osmanabad ..	3,560	2,397	1,163
Raichur ..	48,498	24,470	24,028
Bidar ..	3,012	1,635	1,377
19. Kasab (Aray, Khatik) ..	**81,165**	**42,801**	**38,364**
Hyderabad City ..	2,154	1,067	1,087
Atraf-i-Balda ..	2.656	1,422	1,234
Warangal ..	7,318	3,455	3,863
Karimnagar ..	20,250	10,177	10,073
Adilabad ..	16,309	8,893	7,416
Medak ..	4,308	2,654	1,654
Nizamabad ..	2,173	973	1,200
Mahbubnagar ..	7,109	3,685	3,424
Nalgonda ..	3,284	1,892	1,392
Aurangabad ..	770	428	342
Bir ..	591	300	291
Nander ..	900	500	400
Parbhani ..	7,616	4,049	3,567
Gulbarga ..	3,493	1.958	1,535
Osmanabad ..	956	623	333
Raichur ..	838	480	358
Bidar ..	440	245	195
20. Kasar (Kanchari) ..	**35,730**	**19,036**	**16,694**
Hyderabad City ..	1,915	1,050	865
Warangal ..	2,256	1,297	959
Karimnagar ..	2,553	1,298	1,255
Adilabad ..	2,152	1,097	1,055
Medak ..	1,423	864	559
Nizamabad ..	2,035	1,140	895
Mahbubnagar ..	1,043	645	398
Nalgonda ..	3,015	1,536	1,479
Aurangabad ..	2,566	1,064	1,502
Bir ..	3,206	1,559	1,647
Nander ..	2,802	1,496	1,306
Parbhani ..	2,350	1,513	837
Gulbarga ..	2,352	1,250	1,102
Osmanabad ..	1,853	959	894
Raichur ..	3,368	1,708	1,660
Bidar ..	841	560	281
21. Khumbhar (Kummara)	**154,148**	**80,919**	**73,229**
Hyderabad City ..	1,563	789	774
Atraf-i-Balda ..	6,154	3,052	3,102
Warangal ..	10,917	5,761	5,156
Karimnagar ..	16,756	8,659	8,097
Adilabad ..	10,786	6,688	4,098
Medak ..	8,120	4,821	3,799
Nizamabad ..	6,499	3,485	[illegible]
Mahbubnagar ..	12,142	6,857	5,285
Nalgonda ..	18,506	9,260	9,246

TABLE XVII—PART II.

Territorial Distribution of Principal Castes.

TABLE XVII—PART II.
TERRITORIAL DISTRIBUTION OF PRINCIPAL CASTES

Caste and District	Persons	Males	Females
1	2	3	4
HINDU (Brahmanic).			
21. Khumbhar (Kummara). (contd.)			
Aurangabad	*13,889*	7,403	6,486
Bir	*5,419*	2,993	2,426
Nander	*8,802*	3,832	4,970
Parbhani	*4,786*	2,499	2,287
Gulbarga	*8,351*	4,336	4,015
Osmanabad	*5,963*	3,024	2,939
Raichur	*8,580*	4,258	4,322
Bidar	*6,915*	3,702	3,213
22. Koli	**52,472**	**29,264**	**23,208**
Hyderabad City	*2,259*	1,113	1,146
Warangal	*8,330*	5,873	2,457
Karimnagar	*1,702*	944	758
Aurangabad	*31,935*	16,302	15,633
Bir	*3,046*	1,832	1,214
Parbhani	*5,200*	3,200	2,000
23. Komati (Vaishya)	**308,911**	**163,432**	**145,479**
Hyderabad City	*7,307*	3,660	3,647
Atraf-i-Balda	*14,798*	8,078	6,720
Warangal	*39,162*	20,970	18,192
Karimnagar	*36,017*	17,526	18,491
Adilabad	*12,766*	7,256	5,510
Medak	*28,797*	15,540	13,257
Nizamabad	*20,670*	10,537	10,133
Mahbubnagar	*28,277*	15,427	12.850
Nalgonda	*36,866*	20,137	16,729
Aurangabad	*24,240*	11,967	12,273
Bir	*3,484*	1,905	1,579
Nander	*17,030*	9,959	7,071
Parbhani	*4,266*	2,049	2,217
Gulbarga	*7,943*	4,039	3,904
Osmanabad	*3,913*	2,431	1,482
Raichur	*14,039*	7,271	6,768
Bidar	*9,336*	4,680	4,656
24. Kshatriya (Rajput)	**88.434**	**46,256**	**42,178**
Hyderabad City	*9,716*	5,495	4,221
Atraf-i-Balda	*2,699*	1,228	1,471
Warangal	*1,354*	660	694
Karimnagar	*4,218*	2,115	2,103
Adilabad	*2,021*	1,155	866
Medak	*2,840*	1,428	1,412
Nizamabad	*2,575*	1,410	1,165
Mahbubnagar	*2,494*	1,355	1,139
Nalgonda	*1,756*	1,130	626
Aurangabad	*14,211*	7,653	6,558
Bir	*2,884*	1,827	1,057
Nander	*6,187*	3,293	2,894
Parbhani	*5,303*	2,760	2,543
Gulbarga	*12,313*	6,106	6,207
Osmanabad	*4,698*	2,018	2,680
Raichur	*8,347*	4,153	4,194
Bidar	*4,818*	2,470	2,348
25. Kurma	**173,318**	**89,646**	**83,672**
Hyderabad City	*2,294*	1,072	1,222
Atraf-i-Balda	*17,008*	8,236	8,772
Warangal	*21,724*	12,542	9,182
Karimnagar	*20,311*	10,647	9,664
Adilabad	*7,050*	4,084	2,966
Medak	*26,143*	13,720	12,423
Nizamabad	*14,968*	7,894	7,074
Mahbubnagar	*29,391*	14,797	14,594
Nalgonda	*25,126*	12,423	12,703
Nander	*2,474*	1,144	1,330
Gulbarga	*4,724*	2,038	2,686
Raichur	*2,105*	1,049	1,056
26. Lingayat (Jangam)	**788,839**	**397,604**	**391,235**
Hyderabad City	*1,850*	962	888
Atraf-i-Balda	*8,086*	3,837	4,249
Warangal	*6,672*	3,407	3,265
Karimnagar	*9,572*	4,812	4,760
Adilabad	*9,198*	4,282	4,916
Medak	*9,982*	5,066	4,916
Nizamabad	*5,179*	2,639	2,540
Mahbubnagar	*15,920*	8,338	7,582
HINDU Brahmanic—(contd.)			
26. Lingayat—(contd.)			
Nalgonda	*6,367*	3,807	2,560
Aurangabad	*18,159*	9,677	8,482
Bir	*76,663*	38,887	37,776
Nander	*52,360*	26,740	25,620
Parbhani	*20,688*	10,610	10,078
Gulbarga	*235,940*	118,822	117,118
Osmanabad	*47,274*	21,965	25,309
Raichur	*140,128*	71,208	68,920
Bidar	*124,801*	62,545	62,256
27. Lodha	**6.908**	**4.033**	**2,875**
Hyderabad City	*640*	360	280
Medak	*2,477*	1,344	1,133
Nizamabad	*745*	506	239
Nalgonda	*918*	591	327
Bir	*1,016*	516	500
Nander	*1,112*	716	396
28. Lohar (Kammari)	**93.460**	**51,365**	**42,095**
Hyderabad City	*455*	243	212
Atraf-i-Balda	*4,450*	2,815	1,635
Warangal	*13,341*	9,032	4,309
Karimnagar	*9,572*	4,812	4,760
Adilabad	*5,681*	2,725	2,956
Medak	*7,198*	3,223	3,975
Nizamabad	*5,737*	2,354	3,383
Mahbubnagar	*6,337*	3,248	3,089
Nalgonda	*9,254*	5,422	3,832
Aurangabad	*5,786*	3,147	2,639
Bir	*3,329*	2,102	1,227
Nander	*3,308*	1,876	1,432
Parbhani	*2,920*	1,597	1,323
Gulbarga	*4,447*	2,763	1,684
Osmanabad	*2,377*	1,079	1,298
Raichur	*5,929*	3,240	2,689
Bidar	*3,339*	1,687	1,652
29. Mali	**102,608**	**51.611**	**50,997**
Hyderabad City	*342*	219	123
Adilabad	*3,824*	1,964	1,860
Aurangabad	*33,951*	17,079	16,872
Bir	*12,440*	6,622	5,818
Nander	*5,545*	2,665	2,880
Parbhani	*24,085*	11,833	12,252
Gulbarga	*5,401*	3,027	2,374
Osmanabad	*12,796*	6,024	6,772
Bidar	*4,224*	2,178	2,046
30. Maratha	**1.491.558**	**751,082**	**740,476**
Hyderabad City	*4,164*	2,124	2,040
Atraf-i-Balda	*5,190*	2,674	2,516
Warangal	*7,224*	4,350	2,874
Karimnagar	*9,242*	4,415	4,827
Adilabad	*29,312*	12,841	16,471
Medak	*979*	481	498
Nizamabad	*8,574*	4,532	4,042
Mahbubnagar	*2,199*	996	1,203
Nalgonda	*3,632*	2,024	1,608
Aurangabad	*229,468*	114,009	115,459
Bir	*207,021*	103,495	103,526
Nander	*183,456*	87,014	96,442
Parbhani	*323,962*	163,110	160,852
Gulbarga	*50,637*	25,149	25,488
Osmanabad	*246,490*	130,051	116,439
Raichur	*12,012*	6,073	5,939
Bidar	*167,996*	87,744	80,252
31. Marwari	**62.311**	**34,572**	**27,739**
Hyderabad City	*2,914*	1,458	1,456
Atraf-i-Balda	*474*	264	210
Warangal	*720*	369	351
Karimnagar	*2,700*	1,427	1,273
Adilabad	*1,448*	451	997
Medak	*660*	420	240
Nizamabad	*436*	292	144
Mahbubnagar	*1,338*	732	606
Nalgonda	*1,563*	837	726
Aurangabad	*10,097*	5,579	4,518

TABLE XVII—PART II.

Territorial Distribution of Principal Castes.

Caste and District	Persons	Males	Females
1	2	3	4
HINDU (Brahmanic) *(contd.)*			
31. Marwari—*(contd.)*			
Bir	6,845	3,648	3,197
Nander	3,584	2,386	1,198
Parbhani	11,961	6,379	5,582
Gulbarga	9,282	5,579	3,703
Osmanabad	3,543	2,337	1,206
Raichur	2,637	1,331	1,306
Bidar	2,109	1,083	1,026
32. Panchal	69,874	35,707	34,167
Adilabad	923	672	251
Nalgonda	164	75	89
Aurangabad	7,576	3,451	4,125
Bir	6,213	3,015	3,198
Nander	8,210	4,563	3,647
Gulbarga	14,667	8,129	6,538
Osmanabad	7,784	3,223	4,561
Raichur	9,145	4,650	4,495
Bidar	15,192	7,929	7,263
33. Pardhi	5,466	2,977	2,489
Hyderabad City	448	240	208
Atraf-i-Balda	111	59	52
Warangal	496	308	188
Karimnagar	1,739	920	819
Adilabad	460	245	215
Medak	16	11	5
Nizamabad	174	132	42
Mahbubnagar	366	194	172
Aurangabad	1,520	800	720
Bir	136	68	68
34. Perka	51,504	25,723	25,781
Atraf-i-Balda	1,522	744	778
Warangal	8,078	3,380	4,698
Karimnagar	15,228	7,059	8,169
Adilabad	14,226	7,385	6,841
Medak	3,742	2,360	1,382
Nizamabad	975	583	392
Mahbubnagar	453	312	141
Nalgonda	7,280	3,900	3,380
35. Pichakuntla	8,957	5,310	3,647
Hyderabad City	425	202	223
Atraf-i-Balda	761	370	391
Warangal	224	122	102
Karimnagar	2,629	1,599	1,030
Adilabad	939	688	251
Nizamabad	1,056	631	425
Mahbubnagar	1,200	800	400
Nalgonda	1,723	898	825
36. Rangrez (Rangari)	26,751	14,875	11,876
Hyderabad City	850	450	400
Atraf-i-Balda	846	378	468
Warangal	220	108	112
Karimnagar	724	367	357
Adilabad	1,754	1,192	562
Medak	858	497	361
Nizamabad	2,373	1,063	1,310
Mahbubnagar	251	147	104
Nalgonda	467	237	230
Aurangabad	3,104	1,943	1,161
Bir	1,392	774	618
Nander	1,358	939	419
Parbhani	2,685	1,448	1,237
Gulbarga	2,679	1,390	1,289
Osmanabad	1,105	605	500
Raichur	4,818	2,621	2,197
Bidar	1,267	716	551
37. Satani	54,396	30,365	24,031
Hyderabad City	678	402	276
Atraf-i-Balda	1,273	621	652
Warangal	8,090	4,378	3,712
Karimnagar	11,534	7,115	4,419
Adilabad	14,901	7,876	7,025
Medak	2,632	1,454	1,178
HINDU (Brahmanic) *(contd.)*			
37. Satani—*(contd.)*			
Nizamabad	3,441	1,820	1,621
Mahbubnagar	4,313	2,360	1,953
Nalgonda	3,766	2,301	1,465
Bidar	3,768	2,038	1,730
38. Sunar (Ausala, Kamsala)	137,891	72,550	65,341
Hyderabad City	3,346	1,696	1,650
Atraf-i-Balda	6,302	3,927	2,375
Warangal	12,598	6,452	6,146
Karimnagar	17,446	8,678	8,768
Adilabad	9,552	5,011	4,541
Medak	8,881	4,575	4,306
Nizamabad	7,591	4,318	3,273
Mahbubnagar	9,773	5,232	4,541
Nalgonda	14,128	7,697	6,431
Aurangabad	13,140	6,761	6,379
Bir	4,989	2,622	2,367
Nander	5,636	2,917	2,719
Parbhani	7,049	3,368	3,681
Gulbarga	3,272	1,962	1,310
Osmanabad	4,234	2,414	1,820
Raichur	5,875	2,848	3,027
Bidar	4,079	2,072	2,007
39. Sutar (Bade, Wadla)	110,350	58,274	52,076
Hyderabad City	2,532	1,361	1,171
Atraf-i-Balda	4,417	2,989	1,428
Warangal	5,978	3,118	2,865
Karimnagar	20,404	10,347	10,057
Adilabad	6,914	3,119	3,795
Medak	9,063	4,757	4,306
Nizamabad	7,192	3,550	3,642
Mahbubnagar	9,702	5,202	4,500
Nalgonda	14,070	7,561	6,509
Aurangabad	6,492	3,716	2,776
Bir	1,689	1,037	652
Nander	1,079	601	478
Parbhani	5,136	2,942	2,194
Gulbarga	1,571	884	687
Osmanabad	1,237	612	625
Raichur	8,795	4,411	4,384
Bidar	4,079	2,072	2,007
40. Telaga (Munnur, Mutrasi)	966,190	448,805	517,385
Hyderabad City	29,483	14,543	14,940
Atraf-i-Balda	63,932	30,026	33,906
Warangal	109,504	52,708	56,796
Karimnagar	129,481	65,085	64,396
Adilabad	54,786	24,484	30,302
Medak	130,306	54,717	75,589
Nizamabad	105,013	48,925	56,088
Mahbubnagar	125,719	56,645	69,074
Nalgonda	111,650	52,680	58,970
Aurangabad	13,888	6,828	7,060
Bir	3,312	1,617	1,695
Nander	25,707	12,811	12,896
Parbhani	4,223	2,136	2,087
Gulbarga	22,994	7,055	15,939
Osmanabad	1,668	469	1,199
Raichur	18,553	11,044	7,509
Bidar	15,971	7,082	8,939
41. Teli (Gandla)	73,155	38,773	34,382
Hyderabad City	452	232	220
Atraf-i-Balda	1,448	988	460
Warangal	398	175	223
Karimnagar	6,724	3,760	2,964
Adilabad	6,271	2,888	3,383
Medak	1,599	985	614
Nizamabad	3,564	1,828	1,736
Mahbubnagar	3,036	1,546	1,490
Nalgonda	1,883	1,021	862
Aurangabad	10,130	5,116	5,014
Bir	4,581	2,732	1,849
Nander	5,401	2,962	2,439
Parbhani	6,889	3,624	3,265
Gulbarga	4,749	2,744	2,005
Osmanabad	5,085	2,488	2,597
Raichur	6,740	3,598	3,142
Bidar	4,205	2,086	2,119

TABLE XVII—PART II.

Territorial Distribution of Principal Castes.

Caste and District	Persons	Males	Females
1	2	3	4
HINDU Brahmanic (*contd.*)			
42. Uppara (Beldar) ..	**79,492**	**39,623**	**39,869**
Hyderabad City ..	*1,734*	995	739
Atraf-i-Balda ..	*1,670*	847	823
Warangal ..	*2,706*	1,186	1,520
Karimnagar ..	*7,073*	3,711	3,362
Medak ..	*1,034*	520	514
Nizamabad ..	*1,841*	966	875
Mahbubnagar ..	*10,790*	6,146	4,644
Nalgonda ..	*2,436*	1,346	1,090
Aurangabad ..	*17,243*	8,357	8,886
Bir ..	*2,900*	1,453	1,447
Nander ..	*1,266*	646	620
Gulbarga ..	*6,890*	3,479	3,411
Osmanabad ..	*2,423*	1,336	1,087
Raichur ..	*17,649*	7,762	9,887
Bidar ..	*1,837*	873	964
43. Velama ..	**51,988**	**26,217**	**25,771**
Hyderabad City ..	*36*	15	21
Atraf-i-Balda ..	*1,220*	637	583
Warangal ..	*10,562*	5,280	5,282
Karimnagar ..	*12,324*	6,725	8,599
Adilabad ..	*7,530*	4,115	3,415
Medak ..	*933*	627	306
Nizamabad ..	*4,283*	2,129	2,154
Mahbubnagar ..	*5,720*	2,832	2,888
Nalgonda ..	*6,380*	3,857	2,523
44. Viramushti ..	**7,445**	**4,118**	**3,327**
Atraf-i-Balda ..	*241*	190	51
Warangal ..	*826*	507	319
Karimnagar ..	*1,808*	952	856
Adilabad ..	*1,179*	799	380
Medak ..	*735*	264	471
Nizamabad ..	*1,001*	481	520
Mahbubnagar ..	*412*	222	190
Nalgonda ..	*1,243*	703	540
45. Viswabrahman ..	**26,742**	**14,293**	**12,449**
Hyderabad City ..	*1,265*	668	597
Warangal ..	*9,533*	4,577	4,956
Karimnagar ..	*13,264*	7,513	5,751
Mahbubnagar ..	*898*	506	392
Nalgonda ..	*283*	103	180
Aurangabad ..	*112*	57	55
Bir ..	*442*	229	213
Gulbarga ..	*945*	640	305
46. Waddar ..	**138,082**	**70,085**	**67,997**
Hyderabad City ..	*800*	413	387
Atraf-i-Balda ..	*10,302*	4,787	5,515
Warangal ..	*17,367*	8,290	9,077
Karimnagar ..	*11,133*	5,929	5,204
Adilabad ..	*9,357*	4,390	4,967
Medak ..	*5,887*	3,499	2,388
Nizamabad ..	*11,169*	5,223	5,946
Mahbubnagar ..	*11,029*	5,734	5,295
Nalgonda ..	*16,902*	8,620	8,282
Aurangabad ..	*3,404*	1,703	1,701
Bir ..	*2,401*	1,642	759
Nander ..	*6,071*	3,212	2,859
Parbhani ..	*3,027*	1,521	1,506
Gulbarga ..	*14,466*	7,585	6,881
Osmanabad ..	*3,065*	1,967	1,098
Raichur ..	*11,702*	5,570	6,132
47. Wanjari (Banjari) ..	**70,936**	**38,965**	**31,971**
Warangal ..	*11,775*	5,550	6,225
Karimnagar ..	*5,155*	2,747	2,408
Adilabad ..	*3,242*	2,097	1,145
Medak ..	*3,922*	2,535	1,387
Nizamabad ..	*5,843*	2,963	2,880
Nalgonda ..	*10,803*	5,905	4,898
Parbhani ..	*20,680*	11,619	9,061
Gulbarga ..	*3,261*	1,709	1,552
Osmanabad ..	*6,255*	3,840	2,415
HINDU Brahmanic (*contd.*)			
48. Yadava (Dhangar, Golla, Gowli) ..	**928,404**	**471,464**	**456,940**
Hyderabad City ..	*11,513*	6,868	4,645
Atraf-i-Balda ..	*32,469*	17,106	15,363
Warangal ..	*79,368*	40,909	38,459
Karimnagar ..	*96,518*	48,156	48,362
Adilabad ..	*44,812*	22,499	22,313
Medak ..	*35,705*	18,711	16,994
Nizamabad ..	*29,705*	15,711	13,994
Mahbubnagar ..	*73,812*	37,393	36,419
Nalgonda ..	*106,674*	53,954	52,720
Aurangabad ..	*44,846*	22,140	22,706
Bir ..	*40,600*	20,618	19,982
Nander ..	*29,024*	15,148	13,876
Parbhani ..	*37,048*	17,570	19,478
Gulbarga ..	*85,325*	43,750	41,575
Osmanabad ..	*29,164*	14,840	14,324
Raichur ..	*91,445*	45,496	45,949
Bidar ..	*60,376*	30,595	29,781
ADI-HINDU.			
1. Dher (Mala, Mahar) ..	**1,076,539**	**552,632**	**523,907**
Hyderabad City ..	*52,436*	26,572	25,864
Atraf-i-Balda ..	*22,960*	12,022	10,938
Warangal ..	*55,009*	30,642	24,367
Karimnagar ..	*82,571*	42,494	40,077
Adilabad ..	*56,316*	29,064	27,252
Medak ..	*53,900*	27,900	26,000
Nizamabad ..	*46,113*	23,964	22,149
Mahbubnagar ..	*47,727*	23,080	24,647
Nalgonda ..	*64,690*	36,347	28,343
Aurangabad ..	*97,740*	49,343	48,397
Bir ..	*47,277*	23,483	23,794
Nander ..	*90,800*	43,749	47,051
Parbhani ..	*82,329*	41,961	40,368
Gulbarga ..	*101,404*	54,071	47,333
Osmanabad ..	*72,484*	36,912	35,572
Raichur ..	*19,082*	9,401	9,591
Bidar ..	*83,701*	41,537	42,164
2. Madiga (Mochi, Mang)	**1,281,092**	**639,197**	**641,895**
Hyderabad City ..	*23,953*	12,806	11,147
Atraf-i-Balda ..	*72,722*	36,818	35,904
Warangal ..	*112,293*	55,400	56,893
Karimnagar ..	*125,430*	64,391	61,039
Adilabad ..	*39,273*	18,684	20,589
Medak ..	*78,344*	39,244	39,100
Nizamabad ..	*52,949*	25,589	27,360
Mahbubnagar ..	*127,226*	64,989	62,237
Nalgonda ..	*140,490*	68,653	71,837
Aurangabad ..	*42,001*	20,626	21,375
Bir ..	*42,951*	21,519	21,432
Nander ..	*50,205*	27,339	22,866
Parbhani ..	*58,231*	28,396	29,835
Gulbarga ..	*90,111*	42,446	47,665
Osmanabad ..	*54,524*	27,863	26,661
Raichur ..	*93,411*	45,637	47,774
Bidar ..	*76,978*	38,797	38,181
TRIBAL.			
1. Andh ..	**6,100**	**2,800**	**3,300**
Adilabad ..	*3,600*	1,800	1,800
Aurangabad ..	*2,500*	1,000	1,500
2. Bhil ..	**15,052**	**7,551**	**7,501**
Aurangabad ..	*10,848*	5,376	5,472
Bir ..	*1,292*	691	601
Nander ..	*1,691*	856	835
Parbhani ..	*1,221*	628	593
3. Chenchu ..	**2,264**	**1,090**	**1,174**
Mahbubnagar ..	*2,264*	1,090	1,174

TABLE XVII.—PART II.
TERRITORIAL DISTRIBUTION OF PRINCIPAL CASTES.

TABLE XVII.—PART II.

Territorial Distribution of Principal Castes

Caste and District	Persons	Males	Females
1	2	3	4
TRIBAL—*ontd.*)			
4. Erakala (Kaikadi, Korwah)	**59,172**	**32,002**	**27,170**
Hyderabad City ..	*591*	311	280
Atraf-i-Balda ..	*1,285*	592	693
Warangal	*5,567*	2,770	2,797
Karimnagar	*1,578*	936	642
Adilabad ..	*12,494*	6,932	5,562
Medak	*1,610*	729	881
Nizamabad	*2,528*	1,248	1,280
Mahbubnagar.. ..	*7,065*	3,955	3,110
Nalgonda	*5,009*	3,298	1,711
Bir	*352*	181	171
Nander	*1,428*	775	653
Gulbarga	*11,119*	5,915	5,204
Osmanabad	*2,907*	1,437	1,470
Raichur	*4,335*	2,182	2,158
Bidar	*1,304*	741	563
5. Gond	**113,280**	**57,048**	**56,232**
Warangal	*52,586*	26,215	26,371
Adilabad	*57,244*	28,860	28,384
Aurangabad	*3,246*	1,860	1,386
Bir	*204*	113	91
6. Koya	**33,638**	**18,217**	**15,421**
Warangal	*21,376*	11,936	9.440
Karimnagar	*1.131*	613	518
Adilabad	*9.858*	4,962	4,896
Mahbubnagar.. ..	*1,273*	706	567
7. Lambadi (Banjari) ..	**300,466**	**153,856**	**146,610**
Hyderabad City ..	*1,495*	760	735
Atraf-i-Balda ..	*12,060*	6.886	5,674
Warangal	*54,548*	27,518	27,030
Karimanagar ..	*7,539*	3,754	3,785
Adilabad	*20,553*	10,410	10,143
Medak	*2,726*	1,508	1,218
Nizamabad	*14,770*	7,647	7,123
Mahbubnagar.. ..	*36,602*	18,794	17,808
Nalgonda	*52,130*	26,815	25,315
TRIBAL—(*concld.*)			
7. Lambadi (Banjari) (*contd.*)			
Aurangabad	*4,447*	2,233	2,214
Bir	*6,086*	3,108	2,978
Nander	*13,250*	6,600	6,650
Parbhani	*16,359*	8,020	8,339
Gulbarga	*29,349*	15,146	14,203
Osmanabad	*4,654*	2,551	2,103
Raichur	*11,465*	6,166	5,299
Bidar	*12,433*	6,440	5,993
8. Pardhi	**7,172**	**3,833**	**3,339**
Hyderabad City ..	*1,284*	627	657
Atraf-i-Balda ..	278	153	120
Warangal	*3,366*	•1,831	1,535
Adilabad	*391*	178	213
Medak	*234*	159	75
Nizamabad	*60*	30	30
Aurangabad	*1,096*	597	499
Bir	*180*	94	86
Osmanabad	*238*	144	94
Bidar	*50*	20	30
9. Indian Christian ..	**145,385**	**74,988**	**70,397**
Hyderabad City ..	*11,184*	5,434	5,750
Atraf-i-Balda ..	*3,149*	1,569	1,580
Warangal	*28,782*	14,871	13,911
Karimnagar	*13,595*	7,178	6,417
Adilabad	*4,242*	2,091	2,151
Medak	*19,653*	10,484	9,169
Nizamabad	*13,853*	7,128	6,725
Mahbubnagar.. ..	*2,673*	1,388	1,285
Nalgonda	*23,657*	12,304	11,358
Aurangabad	*10,123*	5,046	5,077
Bir	21	12	9
Nander	*371*	199	172
Parbhani	*269*	129	140
Gulbarga	*5,576*	2,828	2,748
Osmanabad	*34*	20	14
Raichur	*3,849*	2,118	1,736
Bidar	*4,354*	2,194	2,160

Table XVIII.

VARIATION IN POPULATION OF SELECTED TRIBES.

Note :—1. The figures given here are only for 30 years, as it is only since 1901 that certain Tribals were excluded from the Hindus and shown separately, though in 1891 in one place (Age and Sex Table) *Bhils and †Gonds were shown as a sub-head of Hindus, the figures being untrustworthy for comparison have not been shown here.

2. In 1911 certain tribes did not appear at all which was perhaps due to either mixing up of these into other kindred tribes or their inclusion under Hindus.

(*) In 1891 Bhils numbered 470 (235 males and 235 females).

(†) In 1891 Gonds numbered 28,646 (14,635 males and 14,011 females).

TABLE XVIII.

Variation in Population of Selected Tribes.

Tribe and Locality	PERSONS				Variation: + Increase −Decrease			Net variation	MALES				FEMALES			
	1931	1921	1911	1901	1921 to 1931	1911 to 1921	1901 to 1911	1901 to 1931 + Increase − Decrease	1931	1921	1911	1901	1931	1921	1911	1901
1	2	3	4	5	6	7	8	9	10	11	12	13	14	15	16	17
HYDERABAD STATE.																
1 **Andh**	6,100	6,634	2,625	21,863	− 534	+ 4,009	− 19,238	− 15,763	2,800	4,671	1,364	11,390	3,300	1,963	1,261	10,473
2 **Bhil**	15,052	13,723	9,921	9,554	+ 1,329	+ 3,802	+ 367	+ 5,498	7,551	7,470	5,036	4,804	7,501	6,253	4,885	4,757
3 **Chenchu**	2,264	6,121	..	1,259	− 3,857	+ 6,121	− 1,259	+ 1,005	1,090	3,692	..	402	1,174	2,429	..	850
4 **Erakala**	69,158	64,935	2,013	49,970	+ 4,223	+ 62,922	− 47,957	+ 19,188	37,051	34,081	969	25,765	32,107	30,854	1,044	24,205
Erakala (Tribal)	*53,045*	30,385	2,013	33,419	+ 22,660	+ 28,372	− 31,486	+ 19,596	*28,766*	14,937	969	17,631	*24,279*	15,448	1,044	15,818
Korwa (Tribal)	*3,315*	9,756	..	12,305	− 6,441	+ 9,756	− 12,305	− 8,990	*2,151*	6,502	..	5,961	*1,164*	3,254	..	6,844
Kaikadi (Tribal)	*2,812*	..	..	4,216	+ 2,812	..	− 4,216	− 1,404	*1,085*	..	..	2,173	*1,727*	..	..	2,043
Kaikadi (Hindu)	*9,986*	24,794	..	..	− 14,808	+ 24,794	..	+ 9,986	*5,049*	12,642	..	..	*4,937*	12,152	..	..
5 **Gond**	113,280	98,879	124,341	55,761	+ 14,401	− 25,462	+ 68,580	+ 57,519	57,048	48,781	62,583	27,315	56,232	50,098	61,758	28,446
6 **Koya**	33,638	25,029	..	46,714	+ 8,609	+ 25,029	− 46,714	− 13,076	18,217	14,459	..	24,369	15,421	10,570	..	22,345
7 **Lambadi**	371,402	287,405	316,083	172,578	+ 83,997	− 28,678	+143,505	+198,824	192,821	152,871	164,546	90,359	178,581	134,534	151,537	82,219
Lambadi (Tribal)	*291,293*	228,779	142,044	86,271	+ 67,514	+ 81,735	+ 55,773	+ 205,022	*148,498*	118,405	76,703	45,757	*142,795*	105,874	65,341	40,514
Lamani (Tribal)	*4,220*	..	..	86,130	+ 4,220	..	− 86,130	− 81,910	*2,420*	..	..	44,510	*1,800*	..	..	41,620
Banjari (Tribal)	*4,953*	..	..	177	+ 4,953	..	− 177	+ 4,776	*2,938*	..	..	92	*2,015*	..	..	85
Banjari (Hindu)	*70,936*	63,626	174,039	..	+ 7,310	− 110,413	+ 174,039	+ 70,936	*38,965*	34,466	87,843	..	*31,971*	29,160	86,196	..
8 **Pardhi**	12,638	4,466	..	..	+ 8,172	..	..	..	6,810	1,412	..	..	5,828	3,054	..	..
Pardhi (Tribal)	*7,172*	375	..	..	+ 6,797	..	..	..	*3,833*	105	..	..	*3,339*	270	..	..
Pardhi (Hindu)	*5,466*	4,091	..	..	+ 1,375	..	..	..	*2,977*	1,307	..	..	*2,489*	2,784	..	..

Table XIX.

PART A.—EUROPEAN & ALLIED RACES BY RACE & AGE.
PART B.—ANGLO-INDIANS BY AGE.

This table is divided into two parts and gives figures by Race and Age

Part "A" Europeans and Allied Races.

Part "B" Anglo-Indians.

The following are the details for the Allied Races :—

Race or Denomination	Persons	Males	Females
TOTAL	774	506	268
American	106	40	66
Armenian	12	10	2
Australian	16	11	5
Dutch	9	7	2
Europeans Unspecified	290	220	70
French	28	11	17
German	4	3	1
Greek	17	11	6
Irish	172	135	37
Italian	42	28	14
Portuguese	72	29	43
Spanish	6	6	..

Armenians	Persons	Males	Females
All Ages	12	10	2
0–13	1	1	..
14–16	1	1	..
17–23	1	..	1
24–33	3	3	..
34–43	2	2	..
44–53	2	2	..
54 and over	2	1	1

TABLE XIX.

Part A.— European and Allied Races by Race and Age.

DISTRICT	(A) EUROPEAN AND ALLIED RACES (INCLUDING ARMENIANS)																																				
	Total			(a) British Subjects																	(b) Others																
				All Ages			0—13		14—16		17—23		24—33		34—43		44—53		54 and over		All Ages			0—13		14—16		17—23		24—33		34—43		44—53		54 and over	
	Persons	Males	Females	Persons	Males	Females	Males	Females	Males	Females	Males	Females	Males	Females	Males	Females	Males	Females	Males	Females	Persons	Males	Females	Males	Females	Males	Females	Males	Females	Males	Females	Males	Females	Males	Females	Males	Females
1	2	3	4	5	6	7	8	9	10	11	12	13	14	15	16	17	18	19	20	21	22	23	24	25	26	27	28	29	30	31	32	33	34	35	36	37	38
Hyderabad State ..	2,627	2,268	359	1,853	1760	93	29	12	18	6	82	10	1,061	27	153	11	170	15	247	12	774	508	266	95	52	51	39	87	51	129	49	88	33	26	24	32	18
1. Hyderabad City ..	*2,107*	1,894	218	*1,660*	1,600	60	22	9	18	5	24	8	998	18	134	3	161	8	243	9	*447*	294	153	48	36	34	29	59	33	75	25	49	16	10	4	19	10
2. Atraf-i-Balda ..	*3*	3	..	*3*	3	..	..	..	..	..	1	..	1	..	..	..	..	..	1	..	..	..	..	..	..	..	..	..	..	..	..	..	..	..	..	..	..
3. Warangal ..	*15*	6	9	*13*	4	9	..	..	..	..	..	1	3	4	1	3	..	1	..	..	*2*	2	..	..	..	..	..	..	..	1	..	1	..	..	..	..	..
4. Karimnagar ..	*16*	7	9	*16*	7	9	..	..	..	..	..	..	2	2	2	2	2	4	1	1	..	..	..	..	..	..	..	..	..	..	..	..	..	..	..	..	..
5. Adilabad ..	..	..	..	..	..	..	..	..	..	..	..	..	..	..	..	..	..	..	..	..	..	..	..	..	..	..	..	..	..	..	..	..	..	..	..	..	..
6. Medak ..	*9*	4	5	*7*	4	3	..	1	..	..	..	..	2	..	1	..	1	1	..	1	*2*	..	2	..	..	..	..	..	..	..	..	..	1	..	..	..	1
7. Nizamabad ..	*3*	..	3	..	..	..	..	..	..	..	..	..	..	..	..	..	..	..	..	..	*3*	..	3	..	..	..	1	..	..	..	..	..	1	..	1	..	..
8. Mahbubnagar ..	*2*	1	1	*2*	1	1	..	..	..	..	..	..	..	..	..	..	..	1	1	..	..	..	..	..	..	..	..	..	..	..	..	..	..	..	..	..	..
9. Nalgonda ..	*19*	11	8	*11*	8	3	..	..	..	..	4	..	..	1	2	2	2	..	..	..	*8*	3	5	..	1	..	..	1	2	..	1	1	..	..	..	1	1
10. Aurangabad ..	*437*	334	103	*133*	128	5	6	..	..	1	53	..	52	2	13	1	3	..	1	1	*304*	206	98	46	15	17	9	27	15	53	22	36	14	15	18	12	5
11. Bir	*1*	1	..	*1*	1	..	..	..	..	..	..	..	1	..	..	..	..	..	..	..	..	..	..	..	..	..	..	..	..	..	..	..	..	..	..	..	..
12. Nander	..	..	..	..	..	..	..	..	..	..	..	..	..	..	..	..	..	..	..	..	..	..	..	..	..	..	..	..	..	..	..	..	..	..	..	..	..
13. Parbhani ..	..	..	..	..	..	..	..	..	..	..	..	..	..	..	..	..	..	..	..	..	..	..	..	..	..	..	..	..	..	..	..	..	..	..	..	..	..
14. Gulbarga ..	*5*	3	2	..	..	..	..	..	..	..	..	..	..	..	..	..	..	..	..	..	*5*	3	2	1	..	..	..	..	1	..	..	1	1	1	..	..	..
15. Osmanabad ..	..	..	..	..	..	..	..	..	..	..	..	..	..	..	..	..	..	..	..	..	..	..	..	..	..	..	..	..	..	..	..	..	..	..	..	..	..
16. Raichur ..	*10*	4	6	*7*	4	3	1	2	..	..	..	1	2	..	..	..	1	..	..	..	*3*	..	3	..	..	..	..	..	..	..	1	..	..	..	1	..	1
17. Bidar	..	..	..	..	..	..	..	..	..	..	..	..	..	..	..	..	..	..	..	..	..	..	..	..	..	..	..	..	..	..	..	..	..	..	..	..	..

TABLE XIX.

Part B—Anglo-Indians by Age.

(B) ANGLO-INDIANS.

DISTRICT	All Ages			0—3		4—6		7—13		14—16		17—19		20—29		30—39		40—49		50—59		60—69		70 & Over	
	Persons	Males	Females	Males	Females	Males	Females	Males	Females	Males	Females	Males	Females	Males	Females	Males	Females	Males	Females	Males	Females	Males	Females	Males	Females
1	2	3	4	5	6	7	8	9	10	11	12	13	14	15	16	17	18	19	20	21	22	23	24	25	26
Hyderabad State ..	**3,370**	**2,188**	**1,182**	**115**	**97**	**116**	**75**	**140**	**99**	**119**	**74**	**224**	**123**	**545**	**222**	**306**	**134**	**397**	**192**	**120**	**81**	**78**	**60**	**28**	**25**
1 Hyderabad City ..	*2,832*	1,889	943	82	66	83	48	95	54	110	58	201	106	507	189	259	103	360	172	97	70	72	54	23	23
2. Atraf-i-Balda ..	*2*	1	1	..	..	..	..	..	..	..	..	..	..	..	..	..	..	..	..	..	1	1	..	..	..
3. Warangal ..	*155*	78	77	8	7	10	9	19	22	4	4	4	4	8	4	9	13	13	8	1	2	..	3	2	1
4. Karimnagar ..	*11*	3	8	..	1	1	..	..	1	1	..	..	..	..	3	1	..	..	1	..	1	..	1	..	..
5. Adilabad ..	*2*	1	1	..	..	..	..	..	..	..	..	..	..	1	..	..	1	..	..	..	..	..	..	..	..
6. Medak ..	..	..	..	..	..	..	..	..	..	..	..	..	..	..	..	..	..	..	..	..	..	..	..	..	..
7. Nizamabad ..	..	..	..	..	..	..	..	..	..	..	..	..	..	..	..	..	..	..	..	..	..	..	..	..	..
8. Mahbubnagar ..	*30*	21	9	..	..	..	..	8	3	..	1	7	1	..	1	2	1	1	..	1	1	1	..	1	1
9. Nalgonda ..	*13*	9	4	..	..	..	..	..	..	..	..	2	1	1	..	..	2	2	..	2	1	2	..	..	..
10. Aurangabad ..	*16*	13	3	1	..	..	1	2	1	..	..	1	..	..	..	3	1	4	..	2	..	..	..	..	..
11. Bir ..	*6*	2	4	..	1	..	1	..	1	..	..	..	1	..	..	1	..	..	..	1	..	..	..	..	..
12. Nander ..	*27*	19	8	3	1	4	1	1	..	..	2	1	1	4	1	3	1	1	1	1	..	1	..	..	..
13. Parbhani ..	*167*	87	80	15	15	10	10	8	9	2	6	4	5	13	14	20	9	10	5	5	5	..	2	..	..
14. Gulbarga ..	*64*	30	34	5	3	5	3	1	8	1	3	2	4	5	8	3	..	4	5	3	..	..	..	1	..
15. Osmanabad ..	*29*	22	7	1	2	2	1	5	..	..	..	1	..	2	1	4	3	1	..	5	..	1	..	..	..
16. Raichur ..	*16*	13	3	..	1	1	1	1	..	1	..	1	..	4	1	1	..	1	..	2	..	..	..	1	..
17. Bidar ..	..	..	..	..	..	..	..	..	..	..	..	..	..	..	..	..	..	..	..	..	..	..	..	..	..

TABLE XX.

AREA, POPULATION, VARIATION, DENSITY AND RELIGION.

Summary figures for Districts and State. It shows the area, population variation, density and religion.

TABLE

TABLE XX.
AREA, POPULATION, VARIATION, DENSITY AND RELIGION.

Area, Population, Variation,

S.N.	DISTRICT	Area in Sq. miles	POPULATION, 1931			Population, 1921	Percentage of Variation		Number of persons per Sq. mile in	
			Persons	Males	Females		1921 to 1931	1911 to 1921	1931	1921
1	2	3	4	5	6	7	8	9	10	11
	HYDERABAD STATE	**82,698**	**14,436,148**	**7,370,010**	**7,066,138**	**12,471.770**	**+ 15·8**	**— 6·8**	**175**	**151**
1	Hyderabad City ..	58	*466,894*	247,623	219,271	*404,187*	+ 15·5	— 19·4	8,809	7,626
2	Atraf-i-Balda	2,651	*499,661*	253,975	245,686	*497,498*	+ 0·4	— 7·4	188	188
3	Warangal	7,944	*1,117,693*	575,819	541,874	*925,041*	+ 20·8	+ 2·2	141	116
4	Karimnagar	5,722	*1,241,405*	634,416	606,989	*1,095,444*	+ 13·3	— 3·1	217	191
5	Adilabad	7,294	*762,030*	389.754	372,276	*655,536*	+ 16·2	+ 5·6	104	90
6	Medak	3,198	*738,665*	373,475	365,190	*642,796*	+ 14·9	— 5·8	231	201
7	Nizamabad	3,265	*623,225*	313,556	309,669	*499,765*	+ 24·7	— 11·7	191	153
8	Mahbubnagar	5.326	*971,616*	494.061	477,555	*792,632*	+ 22·6	+ 0·2	182	149
9	Nalgonda	6,049	*1,133,409*	580,897	552,512	*948,301*	+ 19·5	— 8·4	187	157
10	Aurangabad	6,212	*944,793*	480,498	464,295	*714,008*	+ 32·3	— 17·9	152	115
11	Bir	4,182	*633,690*	325,396	308,294	*467,616*	+ 35·5	— 24·8	153	118
12	Nander	3,771	*722,081*	367,170	354,911	*671,019*	+ 7·6	— 3·9	191	178
13	Parbhani	5,125	*853,760*	434,777	418,983	*765,787*	+ 11·5	— 1·7	167	149
14	Gulbarga	6,975	*1,225,008*	621,687	603,321	*1,095,753*	+ 11·8	— 7·9	176	157
15	Osmanabad	3,526	*691,068*	357,489	333,579	*615,216*	+ 12·3	— 4·0	196	174
16	Raichur	6,630	*937,535*	473,161	464,374	*880,420*	+ 6·5	— 7·4	141	133
17	Bidar	4,825	*873,615*	446,256	427,359	*800,751*	+ 9·1	— 5·7	181	166

N.B.—*Hindu includes Adi-Hindus, Aryas and Brahmos who are as follows :—*

	Males	Females
Adi-Hindus	1,252,651	1,220,579
Arya	1,896	1,804
Brahmo	98	84

Others are Jew and Buddhist and minor religions not returned.

XX.

Density and Religion.

TABLE XX.
AREA, POPULATION, VARIATION, DENSITY AND RELIGION.

DISTRIBUTION BY RELIGION															
Hindu		Jain		Sikh		Muslim		Christian		Zoroastrian		Tribal		Others	
Males	Females	Males	Females	Males	Females	Males	Females	Males	Females	Males	Females	Males	Females	Males	Females
12	13	14	15	16	17	18	19	20	21	22	23	24	25	26	27
6,203,053	5,973,674	11,456	10,087	3,064	2,114	791,435	743,231	79,444	71,938	937	847	280,584	264,205	37	42
132,150	120,427	194	118	690	312	103,095	89,248	9,217	6,906	548	544	1,698	1,682	31	34
219,754	212,534	46	40	26	26	25,417	24,995	1,573	1,581	21	17	7,188	6,493	..	..
458,164	427,872	13	50	137	89	36,176	31,644	14,955	13,997	69	28	71,305	68,194	..	..
593,448	567,875	2	17	127	103	28,256	27,546	7,188	6,434	10	3	5,384	5,010	1	1
309,893	296,818	149	155	62	59	24,030	21,791	2,092	2,152	15	12	53,513	51,294	..	..
324,869	317,436	285	237	41	44	35,396	36,122	10,488	9,174	..	3	2,396	2,174	..	..
272,631	270,402	23	15	67	62	24,761	24,008	7,128	6,728	21	21	8,925	8,438	..	..
424,099	411,896	92	89	128	120	43,281	41,323	1,410	1,295	2	..	25,049	22,832	..	..
506,244	483,363	92	99	72	62	31,842	30,391	12,324	11,365	2	4	30,321	27,228	..	..
395,587	386,000	2,906	2,407	356	136	63,065	59,376	5,398	5,183	125	122	11,066	11,071	..	..
291,654	277,064	1,728	1,455	30	23	27,691	25,730	15	13	5	2	4,273	4,007	..	..
315,618	305,844	556	529	869	719	41,667	39,488	218	180	11	13	8,231	8,138	..	..
378,530	364,892	1,924	1,761	83	51	45,332	43,093	216	220	44	34	8,648	8,932	..	..
496,890	484,057	1,013	985	176	153	99,636	95,950	2,861	2,784	50	35	21,061	19,407	..	..
308,294	288,065	1,424	1,320	169	123	41,525	38,783	42	21	3	..	6,032	5,267	..	..
413,436	407,810	476	396	6	8	48,756	46,943	2,130	1,745	10	9	8,343	7,457	4	6
366,792	351,324	533	464	25	24	69,509	66,800	2,194	2,160	1	..	7,201	6,586	1	1

State Table I.

AREA, HOUSES & POPULATION BY TALUKS.

1. THIS table gives the details for the State by taluks of the area, number of towns and villages, occupied houses, population, percentage of variation in population for twenty years and density.

2. During the decade there was no internal adjustment except that of the Samasthan Amarchinta which was transferred from Raichur to Mahbubnagar District.

3. The Military population of His Exalted Highness the Nizam's has not been included under Chaderghat as in 1921 but it is treated as an independent sub-division and included in the City.

4. The differences in the areas in certain wards in the City of Hyderabad are due to the proper readjustment of divisions by the Municipality and the increase of 2 miles in the City area as a whole to the same reason as certain suburban tracts having come under the City limits.

5. The apparent increase in the Secunderabad British Administered Areas is due to the proper measurements.

STATE TABLE I.

Area, Houses and Population by Taluks

TALUKS	Area in square miles	Number		Number of occupied houses	POPULATION 1931			1921 Persons	Percentage of Variation		Number of persons per square mile in 1931
		Towns	Villages		Persons	Males	Females		1921 to 1931	1911 to 1921	
1	2	3	4	5	6	7	8	9	10	11	12
HYDERABAD STATE	**82,698**	**133**	**21,697**	**3,312,222**	**14,436,148**	**7,370,010**	**7,066,138**	**12,471,770**	**+ 15·8**	**– 6·8**	**175**
Hyderabad City.	**53**	**1**	..	**116,807**	**466,894**	**247,673**	**219,221**	**404,187**	**+ 15·5**	**– 19·4**	**8,809**
1 **City Municipality**	**30·8**	..	..	**74,057**	**306,646**	**160,889**	**145,757**	**293,493**	**+ 4·5**	**– 20·8**	**9,956**
(a) City Anderoon	**2·0**	..	..	**18,760**	**69,272**	**35,907**	**33,365**	**90,531**	**– 23·5**	**– 31·0**	**34,636**
Ward I. ..	0·56	..	..	4,539	*21,638*	11,223	10,415	25,598	– 15·5	– 25·5	38,639
" II. ..	0·50	..	..	4,165	*14,038*	7,096	6,942	22,064	– 36·4	– 30·0	28,076
" III. ..	0·65	..	..	5.041	*14,705*	7,908	6,797	21,354	– 31·1	– 38·4	22,623
" IV. ..	0·29	..	..	5.015	*18,891*	9,680	9,211	21,515	– 12·2	– 21·5	65,141
(b) City Beroon	**11·18**	..	..	**16,785**	**68,543**	**35,463**	**33,080**	**53,614**	**+ 27.8**	**– 29·6**	**6,131**
Ward V. Beroon I.	3·12	..	..	6,549	*38,307*	20,049	18,258	27,648	+ 38·6	– 24·6	12,278
" VI .. II.	4·81	..	..	6,906	*18,237*	9,217	9,020	17,796	+ 2·5	– 29·2	3,791
" VII. " III.	3·25	..	..	3,330	*11,999*	6,197	5,802	8,170	+ 46·9	– 42·7	3,692
(c) Chadarghat	**17·62**	..	..	**38,512**	**152,512**	**80,840**	**71,672**	**149,348**	**+ 2·1**	**– 7·5**	**8,656**
Ward VIII Chad. A	4·81	..	..	10,234	*35,203*	18,391	16,812	22,528	+ 56·3	– 9·5	7,319
" IX " B	4·31	..	..	5,593	*26,631*	14,512	12,119	27,123	– 1·8	– 29·7	6,179
" X " C	0·44	..	..	5,159	*12,832*	7,090	5,742	25,529	– 49·7	– 18·1	29,164
" XI " D	0·58	..	..	4,529	*14,209*	7,715	6,494	21,468	— 33·8	– 12·9	24,498
" XII " E	4·63	..	..	5.943	*25,328*	12,995	12,333	16,437	+ 54·1	– 18·4	5,470
" XIII " F	2·85	..	..	7,054	*38,309*	20,137	18,172	16,978	+125·6	+1,559.6	13,477
(d) Plague Camps	..	..	..	..	**16,319**	**8,679**	**7,640**	..	..	..	..
2 H.E.H. the Nizam's Cantonments ..	3·20	..	..	7,169	*24,975*	13,880	11,095	19,285	+ 29·5	– 12·5	7,805
3 Residency Bazaars ..	0·576	..	..	4,524	*14,472*	8,116	6,356	15,543	– 6·9	– 13·5	25,125
4 Secunderabad including Bolarum and Trimulgherry ..	19·0	..	..	31,057	*120,801*	64,758	56,063	95,151	+ 27·0	– 16·1	6,358
Atraf-i-Balda District	**2,651**	**2**	**932**	**128,871**	**499,661**	**253,975**	**245,686**	**497,498**	**+ 0·4**	**– 7·4**	**189**
5 Sharqi ..	673	1	196	34,396	*153,874*	78,689	75,185	144,405	+ 6·6	— 6·4	229
6 Gharbi	318	..	115	13,419	*52,564*	26,764	25,800	69,538	– 24·4	+ 4·0	165
7 Shumali ..	526	..	196	17,249	*68,240*	34,731	33,509	86,527	– 21·1	– 3·5	130
8 Junubi	462	..	176	23,315	*92,860*	47,195	45,665	83,072	+ 11·8	+ 13·9	201
9 Dharoor ..	510	..	150	25,229	*71,880*	36,083	35,797	64,972	+ 10·6	– 6·0	141
10 Khadka ..	132	..	75	9,213	*34,286*	17,321	16,965	31,124	+ 10·2	– 35·9	260
11 Homnabad ..	30	1	24	6.050	*25,957*	13,192	12,765	17,860	+ 45·3	+ 47·7	865
Warangal District	**7,944**	**7**	**1,443**	**232,340**	**1,117,693**	**575,819**	**541,874**	**925,041**	**+ 20·8**	**+ 2·2**	**141**
12 Warangal ..	933	2	207	57,324	*300,571*	156,539	144,032	245,107	+ 22·6	– 1·2	322
13 Mahbubabad ..	974	1	218	44.225	*210,228*	107,753	102,475	163,894	+ 28·3	+ 0.1	216
14 Khammamet ..	700	1	171	36,752	*165,746*	84,991	80,755	136,282	+ 21·6	+ 0·2	237
15 Madhra	966	..	196	29,934	*142,510*	72,854	69,656	122,645	+ 16·2	– 3·3	148
16 Yellandu ..	792	1	66	18.814	*84,591*	44,363	40,228	75,147	+ 12·6	+ 25·7	107
17 Pakhal	720	..	210	15,760	*74,633*	38,441	36,192	65,200	+ 14·5	+ 11·1	104
18 Mulag	1,096	..	196	8,542	*39,329*	20,315	19,014	31,856	+ 23·5	+ 16·6	36
19 Paloncha ..	1,763	..	110	7,406	*35,112*	17,677	17,435	30,225	+ 16·2	–0·2	57
20 Paloncha (Samasthan)		2	69	13,493	*64,973*	32,886	32,087	54,685	+ 18·8		
Karimnagar District	**5,722**	**11**	**1,217**	**264,619**	**1,241,405**	**634,416**	**606,989**	**1,095,444**	**+ 13·3**	**– 3·0**	**217**
21 Jagtial	860	3	244	61,875	*292,553*	147,880	144,673	236,227	+ 23·8	+ 0·4	340
22 Sultanabad ..	1,058	..	180	36,105	*164,920*	84,299	80,621	191,710	– 13·9	+ 1·6	156
23 *Karimnagar* ..	947	4	193	43,612	*221,947*	114.205	107,742	183,050	+ 21·2	– 8·8	234
24 Sirsilla	686	2	168	42,024	*188,221*	96,076	92,145	158,526	+ 18·7	– 6·0	274
25 Huzurabad ..	556	1	135	35,403	*173,761*	89,076	84,685	137,708	+ 26·2	– 8·9	318
26 Parkal	509	..	112	22.961	*116,493*	60,017	56,476	109,465	+ 6·4	+ 1·6	229
27 Mahdeopur ..	1,106	1	185	22,639	*83,510*	42,863	40,647	78,758	+ 6·0	+ 1·9	76
Adilabad District	**7,294**	**9**	**2,068**	**157,438**	**762,030**	**389,754**	**372,276**	**655.536**	**+ 16·2**	**+ 5·6**	**104**
28 Adilabad ..	940	1	202	16,014	*86,674*	45,356	41,318	76,325	+ 13·6	+ 1.1	92
29 Asifabad ..	803	1	201	14,880	*70,263*	35,992	34,271	61,718	+ 13·8	+ 2.8	88
30 Rajura	823	1	275	14,064	*62,462*	32,347	30,115	54,402	+ 14·8	+ 38.1	76
31 Chinnur ..	882	1	174	18,280	*84,609*	43,104	41,505	70,376	+ 20·2	– 5.7	96
32 Lakshattipet ..	517	1	152	17,732	*87,379*	44,755	42,624	62,720	+ 39·3	+ 17.0	169
33 Sirpur	880	1	218	17,758	*87,032*	44,257	42,775	73,206	+ 18·9	– 2.0	99
34 Utnur	344	..	178	4,591	*20,639*	10,758	9,881	27,042	– 23.7	+ 23.8	60
35 Nirmal	455	1	191	22,425	*102,816*	50,841	51,975	89,321	+ 15·1	– 1.4	226
36 Boath	575	1	240	11,949	*64,756*	33,323	31,433	53,880	+ 20·3	+ 13.7	113
37 Kinwat	812	1	171	14,289	*71,919*	36,831	35,088	68,726	+ 4·6	+ 9.7	89
38 Yelgadap (Paigah) ..	263	..	66	5,456	*23,481*	12,190	11,291	17,870	+ 31·4	— 11.5	89

STATE TABLE I

Area, Houses and Population by Taluks

TALUKS	Area in square miles	Number of Towns	Number of Villages	Number of occupied houses	POPULATION 1931 Persons	POPULATION 1931 Males	POPULATION 1931 Females	1921 Persons	Percentage of Variation 1921 to 1931	Percentage of Variation 1911 to 1921	Number of persons per square mile in 1931
1	2	3	4	5	6	7	8	9	10	11	12
Medak District	3,198	8	938	168,531	738,665	373,475	365,190	642,796	+ 14·9	— 5·8	231
39 Medak	594	1	161	31,157	*127,602*	64,614	62,988	116,372	+ 9·7	— 12.9	215
40 Andol ..	450	3	171	25,764	*118,059*	59,359	58,700	104,531	+ 12·9	— 7.7	262
41 Baghat	415	1	116	21,391	*81,068*	41,502	39,566	89,650	— 9·6	+ 14.9	195
42 Kalabgur ..	381	2	148	29,020	*122,206*	60,194	62,012	96,258	+ 26·9	— 21.4	321
43 Siddipet ..	1,171	1	254	51,057	*247,385*	126,419	120,966	200,874	+ 23·2	— 3.8	211
44 Narsapur (Paigah) ..	102	..	35	3,533	*15,312*	7,649	7,663	11,880	+ 28·9	— 26.2	150
45 Viqarabad (Paigah)..	85	..	53	6,609	*27,033*	13,738	13,295	23,231	+ 16·4	+ 1.1	318
Nizamabad District	3,265	10	857	159,296	623,225	313,556	309,669	499,765	+ 24·7	— 11·7	191
46 Armur	989	3	198	48,324	*170,556*	84,041	86,515	138,442	+ 23·2	— 10·6	173
47 Kamareddi ..	551	..	142	29,292	*117,950*	59,744	58,206	109,634	+ 7·6	— 1·1	214
48 Nizamabad ..	789	2	178	32,536	*131,891*	66,930	64,961	99,662	+ 32·3	— 10·9	167
49 Bodhan	579	3	180	26,527	*108,200*	55,387	52,813	85,599	+ 26·4	— 23·5	187
50 Yellareddi ..	357	2	159	22,617	*94,628*	47,454	47,174	66,428	+ 42·5	— 12·9	265
Mahbubnagar District	5,326	3	1,373	225,039	971,616	494,061	477,555	792,632	+ 22·6	+ 0·2	182
51 Mahbubnagar ..	676	1	197	39,242	*168,488*	85,698	82,790	119,618	+ 40·9	— 22·8	249
52 Pargi	377	..	318	38,236	*168,326*	85,493	82,833	121,088	+ 39·0	+ 4·5	447
53 Makhtal ..	612	1	165	33,113	*131,707*	66,931	64,776	114,967	+ 14·6	— 4·7	215
54 Kalvakurti ..	883	..	156	27,711	*129,741*	66,150	63,591	107,850	+ 20·3	+ 1·0	147
55 Nagarkurnool ..	575	..	172	29,751	*127,930*	64,515	63,415	122,572	+ 4·4	+ 14·4	223
56 Amrabad ..	1,080	..	79	12,515	*55,737*	28,225	27,512	45,641	+ 22·1	+ 17·0	52
57 Wanparthi (Samasthan) ..	605	1	149	20,848	*90,318*	46,283	44,035	78,184	+ 15·5	+ 4·0	149
58 Jatpol (do) ..	357	..	90	12,018	*50,442*	25,532	24,910	40,810	+ 23·6	+ 5·9	141
59 Amarchinta (do)	161	..	47	11,610	*48,927*	25,234	23,693	41,902	+ 16·7	— 3·3	304
Nalgonda District	6,049	3	1,236	237,793	1,133,409	580,897	552,512	948,301	+ 19.6	— 8.4	187
60 Nalgonda ..	986	1	184	41,708	*189,807*	97,144	92,663	170 ,884	+ 11·4	— 6·6	193
61 Bhongir ..	1,266	1	257	49,840	*229,437*	117,055	112,382	204,181	+ 12·4	+ 1·2	181
62 Mirialguda ..	795	..	156	23,445	*115,112*	59,017	56,095	99,390	+ 15·8	+ 9·1	145
63 Suriapet.. ..	720	..	168	33,727	*167,314*	85,328	81,986	127,464	+ 31·3	— 12·1	232
64 Devarkonda .	971	..	199	26,616	*128,073*	66,063	62,010	107,266	+ 19·4	— 8·2	132
65 Huzurnagar ..	573	..	85	19,786	*91,743*	46,916	44,827	79,432	+ 15·5	— 1·6	160
66 Cherial (Jangaon) ..	738	1	187	42,721	*211,923*	109,374	102,549	159,734	+ 32·6	— 14·7	287
Aurangabad District	6,212	5	1,953	225,371	944,793	480,498	464,295	714,008	+ 32·3	— 17·9	152
67 Aurangabad ..	752	1	274	31,838	*140,783*	72,591	68,192	108,312	+ 29·9	— 9·0	187
68 Ambad	900	..	214	29,099	*121,329*	61,586	59,743	88,522	+ 37·2	— 27·5	135
69 Bhokardan ..	909	..	337	35,186	*146,248*	74,494	71,754	123,345	+ 18·5	..	161
70 Gangapur ..	546	..	223	20,848	*71,452*	36,390	35,062	40,225	+ 77·6	— 37·8	131
71 Jalna	744	2	213	28,992	*134,501*	68,638	65,863	108,890	+ 23·5	— 20·9	181
72 Kannad ..	687	..	227	21,347	*97,746*	49,714	48,032	84,984	+ 15·0	+ 3·9	142
73 Paithan ..	608	1	185	20,649	*78,969*	39,555	39,414	56,803	+ 39·0	— 26·9	130
74 Vaijapur ..	572	..1	149	20,159	*75,575*	38,000	37,575	44,344	+ 70·4	— 40·4	132
75 Khuldabad ..	129	..	41	4,258	*18,625*	9,256	9,369	12,177	+ 52·9	— 51·3	144
76 Sillod	249	..	55	8,687	*44,241*	22,443	21,798	35,387	+ 25·0	— 0·1	178
77 Ajanta (Jagir) ..	82	..	23	2,720	*9,826*	5,030	4,796	8,174	+ 20·2	+ 2·8	120
78 Ladsangvi (Paigah)	34	..	12	1,588	*5,498*	2,801	2,697	2,845	+ 93·3	— 10·0	162
Bir District	4,132	8	1,039	154,792	633,690	325,396	308,294	467,616	+ 35·5	— 24·8	153
79 Bir	640	1	202	33,255	*130,156*	66,690	63,466	99,389	+ 30·9	— 21·4	203
80 Mominabad ..	983	5	252	42,173	*182,840*	94,295	88,545	159,502	+ 14·6	— 3.1	186
81 Ashti	740	..	130	22,609	*69,046*	35,125	33,921	39,245	+ 75·9	— 42·7	93
82 Georai	564	1	156	18,665	*87,953*	44,943	43,010	47,593	+ 84·8	— 44·8	156
83 Manjlegaon ..	702	1	225	28,645	*121,091*	62,794	58,297	97,258	+ 24·5	— 28·1	173
84 Patoda	503	..	74	9,445	*42,604*	21,549	21,055	24,629	+ 72·9	— 39·7	85
Nander District	3,771	8	1,394	190,366	722,081	367,170	354,911	671,019	+ 7·6	— 3·9	192
85 Nander	564	2	245	35,872	*132,191*	67,325	64,866	127,898	+ 3·3	+ 23·8	234
86 Qandahar ..	639	2	235	48,101	*141,623*	73,233	68,390	130,551	+ 8·4	— 5·7	222
87 Mudhol	660	2	255	30,244	*120,865*	60,269	60,596	118,816	+ 1·7	— 14·9	183
88 Deglur	696	2	261	36,642	*133,205*	67,544	65,661	113,252	+ 17·6	— 13·1	191
89 Hadgaon ..	704	..	215	24,035	*103,953*	52,693	51,260	98,096	+ 5·9	+7·8	148
90 Biloli	508	..	188	20,502	*90,244*	46,106	44,138	82,406	+ 9·5	— 14·2	178
Parbhani District	5,125	12	1,566	186,341	853,760	434,777	418,983	765,787	+ 11·5	+ 1·7	167
91 Parbhani ..	534	2	255	26,544	*142,511*	72,814	69,697	129,905	+ 9·7	+ 0·2	267
92 Basmath ..	667	2	207	28,784	*123,374*	62,588	60,786	111,254	+ 10·9	+ 8·1	185
93 Hingoli	725	1	222	26,280	*116,616*	60,183	56,433	97,002	+ 20·2	— 8·3	161
94 Jintur	1,473	1	336	31,321	*147,172*	74,493	72,679	131,773	+ 11·7	— 0·8	100
95 Pathri	595	3	170	27,825	*120,413*	61,637	58,776	108,785	+ 10·7	— 18·0	202
96 Kalamnuri ..	588	2	215	20,528	*94,271*	47,630	46,641	85,068	+ 10·8	+ 7·9	160
97 Palam	543	1	161	25,064	*109,403*	55,432	53,971	102,005	+ 7·2	— 2·4	202

STATE TABLE I.

Area, Houses, and Population by Taluks.

TALUKS	Area in square miles	Number of Towns	Number of Villages	Number of occupied houses	Population 1931 Persons	Population 1931 Males	Population 1931 Females	1921 Persons	Percentage of Variation 1921 to 1931	Percentage of Variation 1911 to 1921	Number of persons per square mile in 1931
1	2	3	4	5	6	7	8	9	10	11	12
Gulbarga District	**6,975**	**12**	**1,698**	**298,571**	**1,225,008**	**621,687**	**603,321**	**1,095,753**	**+ 11·8**	**− 7·9**	**176**
98 Gulbarga ..	807	1	247	48,368	*220,957*	113,695	107,262	197,707	+ 11·8	− 7·2	274
99 Chincholi ..	823	..	172	22,598	*83,451*	41,798	41,653	73,054	+ 14·2	− 5·8	101
100 Kodangal ..	622	2	160	30,539	*133,304*	67,685	65,619	115,322	+ 15·6	− 3·8	214
101 Seram	440	1	109	22,233	*80,257*	39,944	40,313	85,198	− 6·2	+ 22·5	182
102 Yadgir	507	2	135	30,061	*130,951*	65,719	65,232	108,957	+ 20·2	− 2·6	258
103 Andola	709	..	159	20,342	*81,167*	41,305	39,862	62,937	+ 28·9	− 28·9	115
104 Shahpur.. ..	546	1	162	27,885	*104,038*	52,040	51,998	91,397	+ 13·8	− 16·3	191
105 Shorapur ..	527	..	186	26,778	*100,677*	50,700	49,977	81,133	+ 24·1	− 24·9	191
106 Kalvani (Jagir) ..	272	1	73	12,840	*43,547*	22,303	21,244	40,254	+ 8·2	− 8·0	160
107 Chitapur (do) ..	360	1	34	12,190	*60,900*	31,310	29,590	60,776	+ 0·2	+ 1·8	169
108 Shahabad (Paigah) ..	256	1	26	8,500	*32,555*	16,616	15,930	32,226	+ 1·0	+ 11·6	127
109 Aland (Paigah) ..	402	1	69	11,838	*50,723*	26,459	24,264	48,402	+ 4·8	− 19·8	126
110 Tandur (Jagir) ..	211	1	75	8,679	*36,167*	18,105	18,062	37,013	− 2·3	+ 19·8	171
111 Bashirabad (Paigah)	121	..	36	6,620	*27,791*	13,967	13,824	32,085	− 15·4	+ 0·1	230
112 Afzalpur (do)	372	..	55	9,100	*38,523*	20,041	18,482	29,292	+ 31·5	− 19·4	104
Osmanabad District	**3,526**	**7**	**813**	**156,623**	**691,068**	**357,489**	**333,579**	**615,216**	**+ 12·3**	**− 4·0**	**196**
113 Osmanabad ..	473	2	100	24,751	*98,700*	50,905	47,795	97,173	+ 1·6	+ 0·8	209
114 Kalam	605	1	142	24,966	*112,532*	58,174	54,358	104,225	+ 7·9	− 1·0	186
115 Tuljapur ..	600	2	135	29,725	*128,364*	66,352	62,012	115,316	+ 11·3	− 6·7	214
116 Latur ..	340	2	116	23,436	*118,447*	61,911	56,536	96,318	+ 22·9	+ 7·8	348
117 Parenda ..	734	..	142	21,417	*95,162*	48,138	47,024	79,543	+ 19·6	− 18·4	130
118 Lohara (Paigah) ..	450	..	103	17,618	*77,868*	40,603	37,265	70,788	+ 10·0	..	173
119 Ganjoti (Paigah) ..	324	..	75	14,710	*59,995*	31,406	28,589	51,851	+ 15·7	− 8·6	185
Raichur District	**6,630**	**16**	**1,748**	**202,860**	**937,535**	**473,161**	**464,374**	**880,420**	**+ 6·4**	**− 7.4**	**144**
120 Raichur ..	696	1	109	29,685	*140,033*	70,271	69,762	127,107	+ 10·2	− 9·1	201
121 Alampur ..	232	1	48	9,775	*30,148*	15,107	15,041	27,892	+ 8·1	− 9·6	130
122 Deodrug ..	547	2	187	16,329	*78,656*	39,277	39,379	82,537	− 4·7	− 7·2	144
123 Gangawati ..	458	1	158	15,234	*64,973*	33,160	31,813	58,990	+ 10·0	− 7·4	142
124 Kushtagi ..	715	2	228	17,707	*96,486*	49,053	47,433	83,021	+ 16·2	− 10·3	135
125 Lingsugur ..	773	2	195	15,991	*85,748*	42,793	42,955	79,071	+ 8·4	− 18·9	111
126 Manvi	676	2	168	18,525	*90,605*	45,341	45,264	93,382	− 2·9	− 1·9	134
127 Sindhnur ..	672	1	182	15,792	*75,061*	37,384	37,677	69,099	+ 8·5	− 11·4	112
128 Kopbal (Jagir) ..	551	1	162	21,306	*83,181*	42,204	40,977	77,768	+ 6·9	− 8·1	151
129 Yelbarga (do) ..	493	..	104	18,157	*73,498*	37,004	36,494	72,126	+ 1·9	− 0·3	149
130 Gadwal (Samasthan).	817	3	122	24,359	*119,146*	61,567	57,579	109,427	+ 8·8	− 3·8	146
Bidar District	**4,825**	**11**	**1,422**	**206,564**	**873,615**	**446,256**	**427,359**	**800,751**	**+ 9.1**	**− 5.7**	**181**
131 Bidar	627	2	197	28,891	*116,581*	58,422	58,159	110,248	+ 5·7	− 9·5	186
132 Udgir	684	1	178	27,710	*114,347*	59,428	54,919	100,376	+ 13·9	− 1·6	167
133 Ahmedpur ..	680	1	222	30,504	*125,807*	64,393	61,414	116,557	+ 7·9	+ 3·2	185
134 Janwada ..	440	1	132	16,287	*65,691*	33,906	31,785	62,732	+ 4·7	− 0·7	149
135 Nilanga ..	651	1	160	24,809	*100,254*	51,920	48,334	69,513	+ 44·2	− 17·9	154
136 Chitgopa (Paigah) ..	290	1	95	17,397	*73,798*	36,888	36,910	81,634	− 10·6	− 5·7	255
137 Narayankher (Paigah)	221	..	103	11,595	*54,677*	27,884	26,793	59,904	− 9·6	+ 16·9	247
138 Ghorwadi do ..	250	..	57	9,118	*39,128*	19,961	19,167	34,934	+ 12·0	− 16·5	157
139 Bhalki do ..	92	1	19	4,588	*18,564*	9,492	9,072	16,253	+ 14·2	− 30·6	202
140 Ekeli do ..	207	1	54	7,927	*34,035*	17,200	16,835	26,706	+ 27·2	− 2·8	164
141 Partabpur do ..	222	1	61	8,854	*52,015*	26,811	25,204	49,625	+ 4·9	+ 3·3	234
142 Hasanabad do ..	109	..	44	5,369	*23,058*	11,368	11,690	21,601	+ 6·7	+ 3·3	212
143 Chincholi do ..	192	..	54	6,212	*26,034*	13,107	12,927	25,064	+ 3·9	− 34·7	136
144 Murag (Deoni) do..	160	1	46	7,303	*29,626*	15,476	14,150	25,544	+ 15·9	− 7·2	185

State Table II.

POPULATION OF TALUKS BY RELIGION AND LITERACY.

Note:—1. This table shows the population of Taluks by Religion, and Literacy.

2. Under "Others" are included, Jews and Buddhists, whose figures are shown below:—

Religion	Population		Literates					
			0—15		15—20		20 and over	
	Males	Females	Males	Females	Males	Females	Males	Females
1	2	3	4	5	6	7	8	9
Jew ..	11	16	1	1	1	2	7	7
Buddhist ..	26	26	1	..	2	1	16	6

3. Under Hyderabad City, plague camps have been included, the population and the number of literates are shown hereunder:—

Religion	Population		Literates					
			0—15		15—20		20 and over	
	Males	Females	Males	Females	Males	Females	Males	Females
1	2	3	4	5	6	7	8	9
Hindu ..	3,520	2,461	458	303	589	94	504	479
Adi-Hindu ..	2,892	2,455	93	21	41	12	124	19
Muslim ..	1,545	1,694	341	191	528	93	491	224
Christian ..	540	733	83	24	112	19	181	93
Jain ..	168	279	12	2	8	1	28	5
Sikh ..	14	18	2	..	..	..	1	..
Others ..	..	..	..	..	..	..	..	..
Total ..	8,679	7,640	989	541	1,228	219	1,329	820

STATE TABLE II.

POPULATION OF TALUKS BY RELIGION AND LITERACY

STATE

Population of Taluks by

	District and Taluk	HINDU									
		Brahman				Other Hindu				Adi-	
		No. of Persons		No. of Literates		No. of Persons		No. of Literates		No. of Persons	
		Males	Females	Males	Females	Males	Females	Males	Females	Males	Females
	1	2	3	4	5	6	7	8	9	10	11
	HYDERABAD STATE	**196,654**	**179,814**	**117,663**	**12,294**	**4,753,748**	**4,573,281**	**237,983**	**23,794**	**1,252,651**	**1,220,579**
	Hyderabad City	**10,289**	**10,005**	**7,231**	**1,141**	**80,741**	**71,703**	**43,828**	**7,963**	**41,120**	**38,719**
1	City Municipality	5,504	5,529	4,176	742	47,289	42,571	25,869	5,889	26,147	24,162
2	H.E.H. the Nizam's Cantonment	240	176	218	32	1,307	1,029	774	101	1,700	1,381
3	Residency Bazaars	1,024	920	622	94	3,836	2,869	1,916	287	840	825
4	Secunderabad including Bolarum and Trimulgherry	3,521	3,380	2,215	273	28,309	25,234	15,269	1,786	12,433	12,351
	Atraf-i-Balda	**6,680**	**6,518**	**3,500**	**316**	**162,831**	**157,893**	**12,158**	**362**	**50,243**	**48,123**
5	Sharqi	1,332	1,540	812	82	55,055	52,967	2,462	38	14,667	13,679
6	Gharbi	551	528	178	14	14,624	13,880	843	15	5,804	5,766
7	Shumali	1,619	1,626	792	101	24,924	23,949	1,983	100	5,789	5,429
8	Junubi	1,164	1,148	824	32	28,172	27,757	1,428	73	11,437	10,756
9	Dharoor	646	630	320	21	20,412	20,177	3,831	24	8,668	8,703
10	Khadka	480	398	242	44	11,979	11,829	928	31	2,210	2,152
11	Homnabad	688	648	332	22	7,665	7,334	683	81	1,668	1,638
	Warangal	**10,104**	**8,281**	**7,387**	**1,175**	**352,138**	**334,826**	**24,129**	**685**	**90,922**	**84,765**
12	Warangal	1,865	1,316	1,339	396	105,143	98,104	4,187	181	29,219	26,847
13	Mahabubabad	975	957	723	61	68,394	66,023	2,110	54	15,333	14,013
14	Khammamett	1,246	1,031	939	124	53,064	50,929	1,841	38	13,079	12,431
15	Madhra	1,898	1,251	1,371	185	48,932	42,837	1,592	43	11,834	11,210
16	Yellandu	826	642	630	42	18,717	16,421	2,368	91	6,362	5,819
17	Pakhal	1,702	1,676	1,392	212	26,646	25,141	1,210	28	4,399	4,172
18	Mulag	560	535	360	115	12,147	11,452	4,621	112	2,730	2,553
19	Paloncha	776	723	512	28	10,836	10,987	2,772	29	3,301	3,109
20	Paloncha (Samasthan)	256	150	121	12	13,259	12,982	3,428	109	4,665	4,611
	Karimnagar	**9,038**	**9,188**	**6,737**	**1,074**	**468,119**	**447,704**	**10,521**	**772**	**116,291**	**110,983**
21	Jagtial	1,450	939	1,122	110	108,005	105,876	2,187	185	27,580	27,179
22	Sultanabad	1,822	1,332	1,254	128	62,133	59,952	1,561	88	15,754	15,084
23	Karimnagar	1,340	1,499	1,024	309	81,925	76,969	2,405	253	22,362	20,866
24	Sirsilla	1,236	1,459	982	124	70,552	67,696	1,627	68	19,510	18,512
25	Huzurabad	782	906	515	82	66,155	62,831	1,287	112	15,797	14,944
26	Parkal	1,196	1,546	924	192	46,130	43,043	893	38	10,056	9,471
27	Mahdeopur	1,212	1,507	916	129	33,219	31,337	561	28	5,232	4,927
	Adilabad	**7,469**	**7,088**	**5,165**	**597**	**244,581**	**232,014**	**7,285**	**468**	**57,843**	**57,711**
28	Adilabad	915	1,035	741	57	28,319	24,134	1,881	201	6,798	6,965
29	Asifabad	283	324	181	63	24,198	22,851	1,399	62	5,604	5,787
30	Rajura	326	351	168	28	20,996	19,158	328	14	3,187	2,977
31	Chinnur	496	568	261	63	34,120	32,907	814	28	4,078	3,905
32	Lakshatipet	216	228	111	63	31,172	29,464	563	15	7,284	7,243
33	Sirpur	533	575	214	83	25,136	24,148	328	31	10,469	10,432
34	Utnur	40	33	22	6	3,315	2,818	515	22	1,108	1,045
35	Nirmal	674	665	494	65	35,810	36,970	624	14	8,236	8,421
36	Boath	328	298	191	42	17,595	16,747	318	42	4,671	4,526
37	Kinwat	3,608	2,957	2,814	124	16,030	15,613	221	27	4,308	4,353
38	Yelgadap (Paigah)	50	54	18	3	7,890	7,204	294	12	2,105	2,057
	Medak	**6,241**	**5,925**	**4,099**	**303**	**250,685**	**245,855**	**11,526**	**366**	**67,943**	**65,656**
39	Medak	483	427	228	46	44,963	44,047	2,296	105	9,378	9,090
40	Andol	717	658	374	21	38,759	38,405	1,112	81	10,602	10,741
41	Baghat	455	447	192	22	28,571	27,113	1,427	32	8,482	7,926
42	Kalabgur	1,478	1,446	1,133	81	35,770	37,260	1,926	23	10,831	10,539
43	Siddipet	2,793	2,708	2,012	110	90,178	86,539	2,623	28	23,899	22,714
44	Narsapur (Paigah)	182	107	101	15	4,867	4,885	928	14	1,492	1,548
45	Vikarabad (Paigah)	133	132	59	8	7,577	7,606	1,214	83	3,259	3,098
	Nizamabad	**7,347**	**6,344**	**4,843**	**531**	**213,533**	**212,748**	**9,470**	**113**	**51,751**	**51,310**
46	Armur	1,720	1,337	1,212	102	61,218	63,507	1,278	14	12,158	12,720
47	Kamareddi	1,482	1,351	1,028	98	41,233	40,513	2,114	8	12,146	11,506
48	Nizamabad	766	674	512	62	44,940	44,085	2,736	58	10,258	9,826
49	Bodhan	2,103	1,888	1,583	181	35,094	33,384	1,928	15	9,710	9,785
50	Yellareddi	1,276	1,094	508	88	31,048	31,259	1,414	18	7,484	7,523

TABLE II.

Religion and Literacy.

STATE TABLE II.

POPULATION OF TALUKS BY RELIGION AND LITERACY.

HINDU		JAIN				SIKH				MUSLIM			
No. Literates		No. of persons		No. of Literates		No. of Persons		No. of Literates		No. of Persons		No. of Literates	
Males	Femal es	Males	Females	Males	Females	Males	Females	Males	Females	Males	Females	Males	Females
12	13	14	15	16	17	18	19	20	21	22	23	24	25
12,148	1,732	11,456	10,087	3,131	553	3,064	2,114	1,378	202	791,435	743,231	137,410	21,449
4,049	415	194	118	151	24	690	312	310	59	103,095	89,248	48,315	1,686
2,248	283	40	35	27	8	389	260	108	43	78,534	70,019	29,294	5,970
112	38	..	..	..	..	3	3	2	1	10,332	8,277	8,621	2,521
93	15	26	13	11	2	101	5	78	..	1,724	1,805	902	283
1,596	79	128	70	113	14	197	44	122	15	12,503	9,647	9,408	2,912
133	26	46	40	39	..	.. 26	26	18	4	25,417	24,995	3,817	421
..	..	..	..	..	..	2	1	1	..	4,367	4,191	1,143	149
..	..	..	..	..	..	14	20	10	4	4,542	4,420	320	1
114	6	..	1	..	..	8	5	6	..	1,414	1,596	1,417	206
2	..	1	..	..	..	..	..	..	..	4,714	4,539	182	..
..	1	15	9	18	..	..	..	..	..	5,232	5,187	466	30
..	15	10	7	8	..	..	..	..	..	2,286	2,222	187	..
17	4	20	23	18	..	2	..	1	..	2,862	2,840	143	35
531	163	13	50	8	2	137	89	83	9	36,176	31,644	7,021	1,013
882	105	..	..	..	..	84	51	60	4	12,817	10,796	8,425	759
26	2	12	9	7	2	6	..	5	..	4,773	4,160	1,005	84
38	..	..	..	..	..	..	1	..	..	6,418	5,976	948	57
25	11	1	41	1	..	5	4	3	..	5,123	4,683	858	23
36	28	..	..	..	..	6	4	5	..	2,818	2,834	429	80
4	11	..	..	..	..	12	5	5	..	1,388	1,195	281	16
5	..	..	..	..	..	1	..	..	..	889	717	803	18
..	..	..	..	..	..	6	6	3	..	798	739	155	14
15	11	..	..	..	..	17	18	2	5	1,150	1,093	117	12
464	78	2	17	2	2	127	103	72	6	28,256	27,546	5,428	431
171	68	..	..	..	..	78	72	46	3	6,535	6,646	960	150
46	..	2	2	2	2	5	..	4	..	3,834	3,588	366	11
195	5	..	..	..	..	12	10	10	1	6,726	6,700	2,614	181
8	..	..	..	..	..	9	5	4	1	3,734	3,591	459	87
29	..	..	15	..	..	5	4	3	..	3,544	3,576	391	68
15	5	..	..	..	..	14	10	2	..	2,339	2,157	247	16
..	..	..	..	..	..	4	2	3	1	1,544	1,288	391	28
233	23	149	155	42	19	62	59	9	..	24,030	21,791	3,613	256
44	2	42	53	3	2	..	..	..	..	5,090	5,667	396	1
22	5	4	2	..	..	..	..	..	..	2,156	1,602	192	21
..	..	13	13	4	8	..	..	..	..	931	761	302	75
1	3	..	..	..	..	..	..	..	..	1,600	1,402	427	43
10	5	..	..	..	..	..	..	..	..	1,541	1,302	232	4
4	1	2	4	..	..	..	..	..	..	1,874	1,700	300	4
..	..	..	..	..	..	..	..	..	..	369	288	35	24
5	4	6	7	2	..	8	4	2	..	4,415	4,114	1,263	49
57	..	88	40	29	8	..	..	..	..	2,156	1,773	170	19
78	..	44	34	4	6	25	31	3	..	3,131	2,499	167	7
12	3	..	..	..	..	34	24	4	..	767	683	129	9
49	46	285	237	19	3	41	44	18	1	35,396	36,122	4,085	512
22	24	8	11	4	..	19	17	7	..	5,098	5,450	897	29
2	1	33	26	10	3	5	2	2	1	6,039	6,000	322	19
4	2	119	120	..	..	..	1	..	..	3,611	3,694	1,003	240
4	3	119	74	4	..	16	22	8	..	10,686	11,862	570	128
13	14	..	..	..	..	1	2	1	..	7,273	7,187	1,276	74
2	1	..	..	..	..	..	..	..	..	642	695	110	..
2	1	6	6	1	..	..	..	..	..	2,047	1,734	407	22
91	28	23	15	7	..	67	62	16	2	24,761	24,008	3,031	309
34	22	..	..	..	..	2	1	2	..	4,628	4,835	452	30
7	..	..	..	..	..	..	5	..	..	2,974	3,132	156	39
50	6	23	15	7	..	48	44	11	2	6,420	6,041	1,020	190
..	..	..	..	..	..	2	..	1	..	6,803	6,285	1,050	42
..	..	..	..	..	..	15	12	2	..	3,936	3,765	353	8

STATE TABLE II.

POPULATION OF TALUKS BY RELIGION AND LITERACY.

District and Taluk	CHRISTIAN				ZOROASTRIAN				TRIBAL			
	No. of Persons		No. of Literates		No. of Persons		No. of Literates		No. of Persons		No. of Literates	
	Males	Females	Males	Females	Males	Females	Males	Females	Males	Females	Males	Females
1	26	27	28	20	30	81	32	33	34	85	36	37
HYDERABAD STATE ..	**79,444**	**71,938**	**14,874**	**6,820**	**937**	**847**	**808**	**677**	**280,584**	**264,205**	**2,171**	**105**
Hyderabad City ..	**9,217**	**6,906**	**6,604**	**3,971**	**548**	**544**	**508**	**476**	**1,698**	**1,682**	**212**	**84**
1 City Municipality ..	1,518	1,713	1,300	1,148	145	144	131	108	1,298	1,293	126	48
2 H.E.H. the Nizam's Cantonments ..	293	226	112	84	..	..	..	..	2	1	..	..
3 Residency Bazaars ..	473	337	268	178	65	61	58	54	25	21	2	1
4 Secunderabad including Bolarum and Trimulgherry	6,938	4,630	4,924	2,561	338	339	319	314	373	367	84	85
Atraf-i-Balda ..	**1,573**	**1,581**	**148**	**95**	**21**	**17**	**18**	**13**	**7,138**	**6,493**	**12**	..
5 Sharqi ..	560	571	40	37	1	..	..	..	2,505	2,236	..	..
6 Gharbi ..	179	176	5	..	19	14	18	12	1,031	996	2	..
7 Shumali ..	102	98	73	20	1	3	..	1	874	802	4	..
8 Junubi ..	53	52	19	20	..	..	..	..	1,654	1,418	..	..
9 Dharoor ..	431	445	9	18	..	..	..	..	679	646	6	..
10 Khadka ..	70	60	..	..	..	..	..	..	286	297	..	..
11 Homnabad ..	178	179	2	..	..	..	..	..	109	103	..	..
Warangal ..	**14,955**	**13,997**	**3,603**	**441**	**69**	**28**	**60**	**6**	**71,305**	**68,194**	**299**	**49**
12 Warangal ..	1,175	1,092	245	148	8	..	6	..	6,228	5,826	75	32
13 Mahbubabad ..	1,366	1,423	341	188	10	4	8	1	16,684	15,886	40	3
14 Khammamet ..	4,885	4,550	2,656	58	7	2	6	..	6,202	5,835	18	..
15 Madra ..	5,115	4,862	62	4	27	14	25	4	4,917	4,804	1	..
16 Yellandu ..	1,212	1,168	264	29	17	8	15	1	14,405	13,832	117	..
17 Pakhal ..	896	353	16	1	..	..	..	..	3,898	3,649	38	13
18 Mulag ..	168	167	6	8	..	..	..	..	3,820	3,590	10	..
19 Paloncha ..	139	110	3	1	..	..	..	..	1,821	1,761	..	1
20 Paloncha (Samasthan)	299	272	10	4	..	..	..	..	13,240	13,011	..	..
Karimnagar ..	**7,188**	**6,434**	**314**	**211**	**10**	**3**	**8**	**3**	**5,384**	**5,010**	**17**	**13**
21 Jagtial ..	2,990	2,854	87	113	1	..	..	..	1,241	1,107	13	10
22 Sultanabad ..	340	319	25	5	2	..	1	..	407	344	..	..
23 Karimnagar ..	1,198	1,098	189	67	1	1	1	1	640	598	4	3
24 Sirsilla ..	842	703	2	11	4	..	4	..	189	179	..	..
25 Huzurabad ..	1,681	1,347	4	15	1	2	1	2	1,111	1,060	..	..
26 Parkal ..	187	113	7	..	1	..	1	.	144	136	..	..
27 Mahdeopur ..	..	..	..	..	..	..	..	..	1,652	1,586	..	..
Adilabad ..	**2,092**	**2,152**	**105**	**67**	**15**	**12**	**14**	**6**	**53,513**	**51,294**	**155**	**87**
28 Adilabad ..	1	1	..	..	..	..	..	..	4,191	3,461	..	..
29 Asifabad ..	54	40	11	11	3	6	3	3	3,690	3,659	29	5
30 Rajura ..	..	..	..	..	7	..	6	..	6,887	6,855	..	..
31 Chinnur ..	18	28	6	10	..	..	..	..	2,792	2,695	2	..
32 Lakshatipet ..	1,664	1,661	47	17	..	..	..	..	2,878	2,726	4	..
33 Sirpur ..	2	2	..	2	..	..	..	..	6,241	5,914	72	82
34 Utnur ..	..	..	..	..	..	..	..	..	5,931	5,697	11	..
35 Nirmal ..	331	401	25	19	5	6	5	3	1,361	1,387	28	..
36 Boath ..	11	8	8	2	..	..	..	..	8,524	8,041	9	..
37 Kinwat ..	2	..	1	..	..	..	..	..	9,683	9,601	..	..
38 Yelgadap (Paigah) ..	9	11	7	6	..	..	..	..	1,335	1,258	..	..
Medak ..	**10,488**	**9,174**	**966**	**496**	..	**3**	..	..	**2,396**	**2,174**	**24**	**7**
39 Medak ..	4,491	3,787	606	145	..	..	..	..	174	159	1	..
40 Andol ..	2,449	2,203	44	44	..	..	..	..	755	665	17	6
41 Baghat ..	209	208	168	143	..	..	..	..	55	57	..	..
42 Kalabgur ..	1,229	1,242	17	38	..	..	..	..	65	67	2	..
43 Siddipet ..	1,762	1,339	7	8	..	..	..	..	513	477	..	1
44 Narsapur (Paigah) ..	184	184	2	..	..	..	..	..	282	244	..	..
45 Vikarabad (Paigah) ..	164	211	122	118	..	3	..	..	552	505	4	..
Nizamabad ..	**7,128**	**6,728**	**493**	**43**	**21**	**21**	**18**	**18**	**8,925**	**8,433**	**42**	**5**
46 Armur ..	2,329	2,338	73	..	5	6	4	4	1,981	1,771	..	..
47 Kamareddi ..	648	550	151	12	..	..	..	..	1,261	1,149	34	..
48 Nizamabad ..	2,026	1,838	226	10	2	1	2	1	2,452	2,442	..	..
49 Bodhan ..	116	110	35	14	6	2	5	2	1,553	1,459	8	5
50 Yellareddi ..	2,009	1,897	8	7	8	12	7	11	1,678	1,612	..	..

TABLE II.

Religion and Literacy.

STATE TABLE II.

POPULATION OF TALUKS BY RELIGION AND LITERACY.

OTHERS				No. OF LITERATES						Literate in English		Literate in Urdu	
No. of persons		No. of Literates		Aged 0-15		Aged 15-20		Aged 20 and over					
Males	Females	Males	Females	Males	Females	Males	Females	Males	Females	Males	Females	Males	Females
38	39	40	41	42	43	44	45	46	47	48	49	50	51
37	42	28	17	94,128	16,870	87,279	12,979	346,187	38,190	65,329	7,517	159,794	32,245
31	34	26	17	19,691	5,349	16,634	5,698	74,909	14,789	41,179	5,426	69,022	16,385
25	31	23	16	8,760	3,523	7,423	2,275	47,119	8,407	29,279	3,308	52,940	15,992
8	2	2	1	1,636	493	2,583	821	5,622	1,464	508	101	1,203	606
2	..	1	..	983	123	1,212	284	1,846	457	1,114	808	2,508	841
1	1	..	..	8,812	1,210	5,416	2,318	20,822	4,461	10,278	1,214	12,371	4,673
..	..	..	..	3,226	296	3,029	217	13,588	724	1,078	84	4,461	481
..	..	..	..	1,219	142	536	70	2,708	94	183	13	1,114	240
..	..	..	..	112	8	124	7	1,149	31	144	14	442	16
..	..	..	..	228	71	371	53	3,790	310	592	37	1,430	130
..	..	..	..	503	24	409	33	1,493	68	27	12	184	10
..	..	..	..	1,619	15	824	10	3,202	69	98	2	464	82
..	..	..	..	814	12	439	8	612	70	9	4	421	35
..	..	..	..	231	24	326	36	639	82	30	2	406	18
..	..	..	..	9,997	816	7,056	521	26,068	2,206	4,096	138	8,236	948
..	..	..	..	1,829	365	538	157	7,332	1,103	2,099	73	4,270	754
.	..	..	..	203	88	981	78	3,081	184	1,163	17	975	81
..	..	..	..	1,638	65	924	44	3,884	168	806	22	929	6
.	..	..	..	1,028	59	814	53	1,596	158	146	5	854	24
.	..	..	..	983	68	916	54	1,965	149	230	11	550	90
..	..	..	..	841	75	735	61	1,370	145	45	1	258	10
.	..	..	..	1,524	73	381	52	3,400	128	19	5	244	13
..	..	..	..	1,028	9	928	7	1,494	57	17	..	90	14
..	..	..	..	923	24	824	15	1,946	114	11	4	57	6
1	1	..	..	3,189	469	4,042	555	16,332	1,566	983	76	4,865	1,338
..	..	..	..	223	177	613	173	3,750	289	226	14	966	448
..	..	..	..	338	28	814	61	2,107	145	85	4	436	10
1	1	..	..	838	73	832	88	4,772	609	329	35	1,809	588
..	..	..	..	618	41	253	58	2,215	147	54	2	641	8
..	..	..	..	451	54	561	61	1,218	159	219	12	401	52
..	..	..	..	403	58	508	68	1,178	130	49	6	230	214
..	..	..	..	318	43	461	51	1,092	87	21	8	382	23
..	..	..	..	2,334	362	2,146	282	12,141	879	886	106	3,500	791
	..	..	..	271	102	232	98	2,562	63	204	47	445	288
	..	..	..	328	43	291	39	1,168	88	22	18	854	112
.	..	..	..	183	19	171	9	454	92	5	..	208	81
.	..	..	..	811	28	291	19	909	100	46	22	405	105
.	..	..	..	128	24	119	15	720	65	43	1	206	53
.	..	..	..	141	48	122	34	655	121	..	..	..	2
.	..	..	..	101	6	92	8	390	38	3	..	28	25
..	..	..	..	283	28	271	19	1,894	107	414	15	956	87
..	..	..	..	191	31	188	18	408	64	30	1	198	30
..	..	..	..	314	28	293	19	2,681	117	13	..	122	106
..	..	..	..	83	5	81	4	300	24	16	2	83	7
..	..	..	..	3,286	494	3,497	307	14,003	933	1,027	130	3,958	614
..	..	..	..	640	109	462	82	2,459	208	281	14	501	173
..	..	..	..	183	45	191	31	1,509	100	111	10	288	24
..	..	..	..	428	108	433	68	1,983	268	811	56	652	26
..	..	..	..	618	81	728	69	2,318	123	110	12	704	311
..	..	..	..	984	81	1,138	68	3,860	86	101	2	1,384	71
..	..	..	..	181	7	281	6	731	17	3	..	64	8
..	..	..	..	302	68	314	33	1,198	136	110	36	370	1
..	..	..	..	2,373	223	3,443	201	12,195	625	562	36	3,118	304
..	..	..	..	533	54	1,386	19	1,186	99	92	1	426	63
..	..	..	..	428	31	519	39	2,543	87	114	8	407	61
..	..	..	..	538	63	593	69	3,433	197	133	2	987	130
..	..	..	..	583	51	631	49	3,396	159	125	12	803	45
..	..	..	..	291	24	314	25	1,687	83	98	13	495	5

POPULATION OF TALUKS BY RELIGION AND LITERACY.

Population of Taluks by

Serial No.	District and Taluk	HINDU: Brahmans: No. of Persons: Males	Females	No. of Literates: Males	Females	Other Hindus: No. of Persons: Males	Females	No. of Literates: Males	Females	Adi-: No. of Persons: Males	Females
	1	2	3	4	5	6	7	8	9	10	11
	Mahbubnagar	**8,162**	**7,770**	**6,745**	**342**	**315,024**	**307,255**	**8,949**	**497**	**100,913**	**96,871**
51	Mahbubnagar	783	678	618	61	56,976	53,657	2,336	215	16,072	15,266
52	Pargi	1,115	995	924	71	51,013	49,779	1,214	85	19,891	19,145
53	Makhtal	745	759	611	22	44,518	43,425	983	94	12,294	11,712
54	Kalvakurti	1,305	1,327	1,128	47	40,970	39,612	876	24	15,310	14,816
55	Nagarkarnul	2,673	2,464	2,419	78	42,126	42,013	1,315	18	18,686	18,277
56	Amarabad	232	210	112	15	14,413	14,295	381	22	7,262	7,309
57	Wanaparthi (Samasthan) ..	766	784	622	26	32,512	31,268	682	19	7,757	7,351
58	Jatprol (Samasthan) ..	386	428	212	12	15,006	14,636	428	9	3,228	2,993
59	Amarchinta (Samasthan) ..	157	125	99	10	17,490	16,570	534	11	5,413	5,002
	Nalgonda	**9,823**	**7,387**	**6,584**	**202**	**389,524**	**373,893**	**14,544**	**704**	**106,897**	**102,083**
60	Nalgonda	3,357	1,732	2,064	38	66,437	64,576	3,448	233	18,018	17,118
61	Bhongir	1,233	1,053	921	29	85,527	82,377	3,216	115	20,284	19,015
62	Mirialguda	1,138	1,020	714	33	35,429	34,015	1,483	71	11,234	10,887
63	Suriapet	1,157	1,024	728	31	55,624	53,877	1,561	83	15,964	15,441
64	Devarkonda	477	478	318	11	40,317	38,142	1,762	94	11,800	11,727
65	Huzurnagar	1,233	1,039	916	38	29,587	28,584	1,111	23	7,972	7,696
66	Jangaon (Chirial) ..	1,228	1,021	923	22	76,603	72,122	1,963	85	21,630	20,199
	Aurangabad	**20,733**	**20,511**	**11,043**	**1,208**	**304,531**	**295,476**	**21,464**	**3,814**	**70,323**	**70,013**
67	Aurangabad	5,333	5,334	3,102	336	39,825	37,153	4,825	1,611	10,500	10,633
68	Ambad	1,570	1,443	763	94	41,636	40,869	2,531	614	9,718	9,575
69	Bhokardan	1,730	1,899	869	112	51,188	49,179	3,008	523	11,852	11,793
70	Gangapur	838	896	415	32	23,900	23,486	1,112	194	5,550	5,122
71	Jalna	1,705	1,642	824	99	42,016	40,429	2,314	202	11,367	11,128
72	Kannad	4,573	4,380	2,615	242	31,273	30,398	1,729	134	5,937	5,728
73	Paithan	1,330	1,565	614	88	26,522	26,652	1,615	143	4,807	4,910
74	Vaijapur	1,481	1,625	733	83	24,314	23,659	1,915	194	5,221	5,554
75	Khuldabad	638	567	315	31	5,349	5,356	214	21	1,100	1,162
76	Sillod	1,388	1,023	714	63	14,740	14,559	985	34	3,109	3,209
77	Ajanta (Jagir) ..	89	89	49	5	2,641	2,461	1,374	68	737	762
78	Ladsangvi (Paigah) ..	58	48	30	3	1,127	1,125	342	21	425	437
	Bir	**12,613**	**12,384**	**6,266**	**220**	**231,340**	**217,330**	**5,609**	**927**	**47,701**	**47,350**
79	Bir	2,064	2,240	1,135	57	47,789	45,017	1,674	307	9,740	9,593
80	Mominabad	3,592	3,212	1,786	33	66,128	61,670	717	181	14,035	13,835
81	Ashti	721	663	401	24	26,023	24,963	571	173	5,703	5,772
82	Georai	1,408	1,341	693	33	31,506	29,967	983	94	6,490	6,642
83	Manglegaon	2,973	3,228	1,324	31	43,669	39,702	803	124	9,621	9,472
84	Patoda	1,855	1,700	927	42	16,225	16,011	861	48	2,112	2,036
	Nander	**10,190**	**8,133**	**6,200**	**392**	**233,936**	**227,383**	**6,973**	**123**	**71,492**	**70,328**
85	Nander	1,036	1,086	709	138	40,361	38,147	2,367	64	12,871	13,582
86	Kandahar	1,316	1,188	714	12	49,450	45,956	1,502	11	14,851	13,518
87	Mudhol	2,698	2,050	1,823	64	38,633	39,738	927	5	10,215	10,506
88	Deglur	2,155	1,879	1,612	128	42,845	41,398	863	8	14,155	13,955
89	Hadgaon	1,440	1,198	714	11	32,110	32,338	716	14	11,831	10,415
90	Biloli	1,545	732	628	39	30,237	29,806	598	21	8,569	8,357
	Parbhani	**16,722**	**15,300**	**9,344**	**2,007**	**285,464**	**272,906**	**12,570**	**579**	**76,344**	**76,686**
91	Parbhani	1,977	1,624	1,320	780	48,727	46,678	3,916	119	11,616	11,811
92	Basmath	5,756	5,609	3,868	382	38,197	36,731	1,814	63	10,186	10,370
93	Hingoli	1,969	1,838	1,003	94	39,292	35,905	1,324	85	12,387	12,648
94	Jintur	1,358	1,280	684	87	43,911	42,508	1,929	91	16,364	15,708
95	Pathri	3,385	3,287	1,524	514	42,389	40,132	1,374	24	8,508	8,540
96	Kalamnuri	1,318	923	518	82	31,673	30,985	999	114	10,131	10,345
97	Palam	964	739	432	68	41,275	39,952	1,214	88	7,152	7,264

TABLE II.

Religion and Literacy.

STATE TABLE II.
POPULATION OF TALUKS BY RELIGION AND LITERACY.

HINDU		JAIN				SIKH				MUSLIM			
No. of Literates		No. of persons		No. of Literates		No. of Persons		No. of Literates		No. of Persons		No. of Literates	
Males	Females	Males	Females	Males	Females	Males	Females	Males	Females	Males	Females	Males	Females
12	13	14	15	16	17	18	19	20	21	22	23	24	25
130	**30**	**92**	**89**	**9**	**5**	**128**	**120**	**7**	..	**43,281**	**41,323**	**12,789**	**292**
17	10	..	..	..	..	6	5	3	..	6,794	6,687	3,767	74
31	4	..	..	..	..	4	..	1	..	8,983	8,823	3,164	65
25	2	31	31	4	3	2	2	..	..	7,691	7,384	2,127	12
10	1	12	9	1	..	..	..	..	..	4,717	4,368	1,027	10
5	..	..	..	..	..	..	..	..	..	4,084	3,974	801	28
..	..	49	49	4	2	112	109	3	..	1,822	1,537	173	26
3	..	..	..	..	..	2	4	..	..	2,949	2,675	276	6
..	..	..	..	..	..	..	..	..	..	4,308	4,823	649	32
39	13	..	..	..	..	2	..	..	..	1,783	1,602	205	44
459	**77**	**92**	**99**	**27**	..	**72**	**62**	**38**	**8**	**31,842**	**30,391**	**5,798**	**532**
147	12	19	24	17	..	40	34	27	4	6,071	6,132	1,977	144
18	2	17	17	7	..	18	18	10	1	6,640	6,566	840	147
15	7	..	..	..	..	7	4	1	..	3,812	3,065	375	41
201	28	24	32	3	..	..	..	..	..	3,849	3,700	616	55
7	8	..	..	..	..	..	..	..	..	2,522	2,329	268	69
..	..	..	..	..	..	1	3	..	3	3,185	2,858	489	7
71	20	32	26	..	..	6	3	..	..	6,254	5,746	1,233	69
1,919	**189**	**2,906**	**2,407**	**649**	**107**	**356**	**136**	**285**	**14**	**65,065**	**59,376**	**9,292**	**1,311**
1,105	90	323	420	262	34	310	98	255	9	14,898	13,404	6,358	848
27	7	429	400	82	6	11	10	7	1	5,619	4,980	496	51
395	12	143	128	38	1	..	..	..	..	9,131	8,294	864	102
42	..	360	289	51	24	8	4	6	2	3,965	3,468	110	12
89	24	407	343	42	4	11	6	8	1	9,206	8,425	425	86
8	6	302	281	40	11	..	..	..	..	6,197	5,663	59	16
5	7	261	158	31	4	..	..	..	..	5,338	4,905	407	68
18	..	402	342	82	..	16	18	9	1	3,519	3,269	232	24
8	3	43	26	15	..	..	..	..	..	1,741	1,875	222	29
70	34	34	25	6	3	..	..	..	..	3,100	2,921	28	10
8	5	..	..	..	..	..	..	..	..	1,470	1,420	55	48
4	1	..	..	..	..	..	..	..	..	861	752	36	32
68	**50**	**1,728**	**1,455**	**453**	**40**	**30**	**23**	**21**	..	**27,691**	**25,730**	**1,951**	**163**
12	28	315	298	124	7	10	11	9	..	6,246	5,781	626	47
40	25	261	230	108	30	12	7	10	..	9,297	8,709	286	28
4	2	494	481	106	2	..	..	..	..	2,010	1,887	179	14
6	..	409	233	88	..	..	..	..	..	3,814	3,569	293	18
..	..	148	118	..	..	3	1	1	..	5,169	4,661	374	85
6	..	101	95	27	1	5	4	1	..	1,155	1,123	193	21
85	**54**	**556**	**529**	**71**	**5**	**869**	**719**	**380**	**61**	**41,667**	**39,488**	**4,440**	**363**
15	31	138	137	24	1	685	562	356	60	10,382	9,387	2,415	280
22	14	119	129	23	3	100	100	18	1	6,590	6,325	286	29
24	3	48	29	2	..	43	32	2	..	7,864	7,580	829	44
1	..	37	41	1	..	39	25	2	..	6,849	6,934	276	80
5	1	93	89	21	1	2	..	2	..	4,524	4,181	138	10
18	5	121	104	..	..	..	..	..	..	5,458	4,961	476	20
1,032	**125**	**1,924**	**1,761**	**645**	**129**	**83**	**51**	**38**	**21**	**45,332**	**43,093**	**5,110**	**644**
340	37	259	147	47	17	19	3	10	..	9,292	8,336	1,531	153
295	38	271	281	185	96	10	6	8	7	7,317	6,970	949	81
108	27	469	488	168	8	30	17	9	11	5,963	5,465	624	189
19	5	195	193	88	..	..	..	..	..	6,112	6,088	487	66
12	1	339	297	119	6	4	4	3	2	6,624	6,149	498	14
158	12	287	220	72	..	12	11	2	..	4,255	4,157	587	180
100	5	154	185	21	2	8	10	6	1	5,769	5,728	434	52

STATE TABLE II.

POPULATION OF TALUKS BY RELIGION AND LITERACY.

STATE

Population of Taluks by

District and Taluk	CHRISTIAN				ZOROASTRIAN				TRIBAL			
	No. of Persons		No. of Literates		No. of Persons		No. of Literates		No. of Persons		No. of Literates	
	Males	Females	Males	Females	Males	Females	Males	Females	Males	Females	Males	Females
1	26	27	28	29	30	31	32	33	34	35	36	37
Mahbubnagar ..	**1,410**	**1,295**	**195**	**100**	**2**	..	**1**	..	**25,049**	**22,832**	**666**	**3**
51 Mahbubnagar ..	189	139	37	30	..	..	..	..	4,928	4,358	107	..
52 Pargi ..	30	27	4	3	1	..	1	..	4,456	4,064	105	2
53 Makhtal ..	366	360	21	5	1	..	..	..	1,288	1,158	..	..
54 Kalvakurti ..	378	316	17	6	..	..	..	..	3,458	3,143	99	..
55 Nagarkarnul ..	124	119	36	14	..	..	..	..	1,822	1,568	114	..
56 Amarabad ..	3	..	..	..	..	..	..	..	4,332	4,003	100	..
57 Wanaparthi (Samasthan) ..	358	323	71	38	..	..	..	..	1,939	1,680	..	..
58 Jatprol (Samasthan) ..	..	..	..	..	..	..	..	..	2,404	2,530	102	..
59 Amarachinta (Samasthan) ..	12	11	9	4	..	..	..	..	427	388	39	1
Nalgonda ..	**12,324**	**11,365**	**528**	**353**	**2**	**4**	**2**	**3**	**30,321**	**27,228**	**156**	**2**
60 Nalgonda ..	2,707	2,572	80	20	..	..	..	..	500	455	..	..
61 Bhongir ..	1,262	1,177	152	111	2	1	2	..	2,063	1,958	1	..
62 Mirialguda ..	1,541	1,420	11	18	..	..	..	..	6,356	5,684	20	1
63 Suriapet ..	2,601	2,414	91	80	..	..	..	..	6,109	5,498	9	..
64 Devarkonda ..	1 590	1,277	116	112	..	..	..	..	9,357	8,057	15	..
65 Huzurnagar ..	2,087	1,995	72	12	..	2	..	2	2,851	2,655	3	..
66 Jangaon (Chirial) ..	536	510	6	5	..	1	..	1	3,085	2,921	108	1
Aurangabad ..	**5,393**	**5,183**	**659**	**229**	**125**	**122**	**78**	**87**	**11,066**	**11,071**	**267**	**69**
67 Aurangabad ..	528	438	68	81	109	104	67	79	568	608	81	4
68 Ambad ..	435	405	24	2	1	3	..	2	2,167	2,058	61	21
69 Bhokardan ..	54	53	12	1	..	..	..	..	396	408	1	..
70 Gangapur ..	1,112	1,110	143	99	2	1	1	..	655	736	3	1
71 Jalna ..	1,412	1,398	235	69	9	6	7	8	2,505	2,491	5	1
72 Kannad ..	..	..	..	..	..	3	..	1	1,432	1,379	68	12
73 Paithan ..	568	525	73	11	..	4	..	2	709	700	7	2
74 Vaijapur ..	1,245	1,228	102	16	4	1	8	..	1,798	1,884	79	28
75 Khuldabad ..	36	33	2	..	..	..	..	..	349	350	9	2
76 Sillod ..	..	..	..	..	..	..	..	..	72	61	..	..
77 Ajanta (Jagir) ..	3	3	..	..	..	..	..	..	90	61	8	3
78 Ladsangvi (Paigah) ..	..	..	..	..	..	..	..	..	380	335	..	..
Bir ..	**15**	**13**	**8**	..	**5**	**2**	**5**	..	**4,273**	**4,007**	..	..
79 Bir ..	2	..	1	..	4	2	4	..	520	524	..	..
80 Mominabad ..	5	6	2	..	..	..	..	..	965	876	..	..
81 Ashti ..	..	..	..	..	..	..	..	..	174	155	..	..
82 Georai ..	6	3	4	..	..	..	..	..	1,310	1,255	..	..
83 Manjlegaon ..	..	..	..	..	1	..	1	..	1,210	1,115	..	..
84 Patoda ..	2	4	1	..	..	..	..	..	94	82	..	..
Nander ..	**218**	**180**	**67**	**10**	**11**	**13**	**10**	**5**	**8,231**	**8,138**	**10**	**48**
85 Nander ..	126	91	60	8	1	2	1	..	1,725	1,722	..	..
86 Kandahar ..	..	2	..	..	..	..	..	..	1,807	1,177	7	..
87 Mudhol ..	68	68	..	..	8	9	7	4	692	639	..	..
88 Deglur ..	10	14	1	..	2	2	2	1	1,452	1,898	..	..
89 Hadgaon ..	9	2	6	2	..	..	..	..	2,884	3,087	8	48
90 Biloli ..	5	8	..	..	..	..	..	..	171	170	..	..
Parbhani ..	**216**	**220**	**146**	**104**	**44**	**34**	**35**	**30**	**8,648**	**8,932**	**67**	**11**
91 Parbhani ..	32	41	18	13	18	7	6	6	879	850	28	11
92 Basmath ..	155	143	121	85	12	12	10	10	684	694	85	..
93 Hingoli ..	18	26	3	4	9	11	9	10	46	35	..	..
94 Jintur ..	..	..	..	..	..	..	..	..	6,558	6,907	..	..
95 Pathri ..	4	5	4	2	10	4	10	4	374	358	4	..
96 Kalamnuri ..	3	..	..	..	..	..	..	..	1	..	..	..
97 Palam ..	4	5	..	..	..	..	..	..	106	88	..	..

TABLE II.

Religion and Literacy.

STATE TABLE II.

POPULATION OF TALUKS BY RELIGION AND LITERACY.

OTHERS				No. OF LITERATES									
No. of persons		No. of Literates		Aged 0-15		Aged 15-20		Aged 20 and over		Literate in English		Literate in Urdu	
Males	Females	Males	Females	Males	Females	Males	Females	Males	Females	Males	Females	Males	Females
38	39	40	41	42	43	44	45	46	47	48	49	50	51
..	..	..	..	**4,507**	**259**	**4,726**	**232**	**20,258**	**778**	**800**	**35**	**5,762**	**693**
..	..	..	..	1,311	48	1,814	36	3,760	306	414	3	2,688	379
..	..	..	..	818	59	761	61	3,865	110	22	..	1,205	111
..	..	..	..	539	39	469	29	2,763	70	175	1	197	5
..	..	..	..	518	18	428	19	2,812	51	26	3	521	10
..	..	..	..	703	31	653	29	3,534	73	33	8	231	128
..	..	..	..	101	15	98	14	574	36	15	2	234	18
..	..	..	..	214	21	203	19	1,237	49	62	10	336	15
..	..	..	..	193	10	188	8	1,010	35	22	4	238	..
..	..	..	..	110	18	112	17	703	48	31	4	112	32
..	..	..	..	**3,853**	**584**	**4,587**	**303**	**19,696**	**994**	**694**	**138**	**5,237**	**452**
..	..	..	..	1,287	124	1,227	131	5,246	196	142	50	1,516	212
..	..	..	..	681	118	831	43	3,655	244	194	10	1,387	66
..	..	..	..	318	68	429	39	1,872	59	22	3	624	29
..	..	..	..	401	91	531	14	2,277	172	116	54	186	26
..	..	..	..	310	98	418	39	1,758	157	32	16	354	47
..	..	..	..	318	24	418	12	1,855	40	58	..	629	31
..	..	..	..	538	61	733	25	3,033	117	130	5	541	41
..	..	..	..	**8,848**	**1,763**	**7,317**	**997**	**29,491**	**4,268**	**4,366**	**296**	**11,481**	**3,415**
..	..	..	..	1,888	813	2,410	464	11,275	1.780	2,931	155	6,099	2,374
..	..	..	..	924	179	563	81	2,504	538	222	14	1,524	443
..	..	..	..	1,328	163	628	91	3,431	497	237	12	1,791	114
..	..	..	..	424	93	308	41	1,151	250	50	8	252	24
..	..	..	..	929	138	714	74	2,256	887	671	88	970	184
..	..	..	..	1,123	105	814	94	2,577	223	114	2	156	17
..	..	..	..	631	80	514	39	1,607	201	62	1	257	118
..	..	..	..	681	84	591	49	1,896	208	42	1	142	23
..	..	..	..	110	20	99	14	571	52	14	..	190	29
..	..	..	..	424	48	328	28	1,051	68	8	10	22	12
..	..	..	..	306	26	274	14	914	79	10	10	48	46
..	..	..	..	80	14	74	8	258	35	5	..	30	31
..	..	..	..	**2,911**	**356**	**2,756**	**242**	**8,714**	**802**	**649**	**21**	**3,130**	**676**
..	..	..	..	354	126	429	74	2,802	241	241	12	1,396	380
..	..	..	..	721	63	683	39	1,595	195	246	1	176	165
..	..	..	..	303	51	261	33	697	131	25	5	96	14
..	..	..	..	512	38	428	29	1,127	78	100	2	415	3
..	..	..	..	538	44	391	38	1,374	108	28	1	973	108
..	..	..	..	483	34	414	29	1,119	49	9	..	74	6
..	..	..	..	**3,130**	**243**	**2,794**	**195**	**12,312**	**623**	**1,261**	**36**	**3,597**	**253**
..	..	..	..	1,090	113	951	82	3,906	337	854	26	1,580	129
..	..	..	..	412	16	393	15	1,767	39	111	4	527	29
..	..	..	..	603	30	531	25	2,480	65	186	2	674	68
..	..	..	..	481	41	414	37	1,863	89	46	1	318	3
..	..	..	..	263	22	234	19	1,128	46	41	1	227	5
..	..	..	..	281	21	271	17	1,168	47	23	2	271	19
..	..	..	..	**4,844**	**1,282**	**3,627**	**811**	**20,516**	**1,557**	**1,093**	**46**	**5,806**	**1.287**
..	..	..	..	1,050	450	696	231	5,470	455	376	19	2,607	945
..	..	..	..	1,394	251	981	158	4,905	353	483	4	1,098	85
..	..	..	..	519	128	438	84	2,286	166	11	2	118	40
..	..	..	..	508	83	414	61	2,235	105	72	1	407	29
..	..	..	..	591	188	428	140	2,520	239	121	13	660	24
..	..	..	..	401	112	354	84	1,581	151	30	7	285	53
..	..	..	..	381	70	316	53	1,510	88	..	..	636	111

STATE TABLE II.

POPULATION OF TALUKS BY RELIGION AND LITERACY.

STATE

Population of Taluks by

District and Taluk	HINDU									
	Brahman				Other Hindu				Adi-	
	No. of Persons		No. of Literates		No. of Persons		No. of Literates		No. of Persons	
	Males	Females	Males	Females	Males	Females	Males	Females	Males	Females
1	2	3	4	5	6	7	8	9	10	11
Gulbarga	**17,351**	**15,481**	**10,445**	**911**	**381,289**	**372.016**	**14,111**	**3,661**	**98,250**	**96,560**
98 Gulbarga	4,063	3,250	3,065	237	65,418	62,180	3,265	1,856	17,278	16,679
99 Chincholi	3,185	3,171	1,933	101	21,290	21,552	1,518	188	6,376	6,624
100 Kodangal	1,224	1,044	528	42	45,217	43,990	1,291	168	11,326	11,179
101 Seram	1,448	1,058	863	69	24,227	25,209	1,008	185	6,747	6,949
102 Yadgir	1,463	1,410	796	81	39,911	39,561	2,189	112	12,317	12,124
103 Andola	427	395	215	30	27,680	26,622	1,211	192	5,455	5,877
104 Shahpur	512	530	190	18	32,043	31,851	924	185	9,875	10,068
105 Shorapur	1,909	1,896	1,281	92	35,389	35,061	421	139	5,278	5,285
106 Kalyani (Jagir)	970	770	464	32	12,746	12,268	214	188	3,808	3,570
107 Chittapur (Jagir)	632	631	312	28	19,317	18,178	1,000	185	4,337	4,188
108 Shahabad (Paigah)	168	98	63	4	10,440	10,139	261	21	2,494	2,334
109 Aland (Jagir)	400	395	194	68	15,266	13,816	185	14	4,574	4,268
110 Tandur (Jagir)	200	151	82	10	10,600	10,846	222	115	3,398	3,250
111 Bashirabad (Paigah)	416	328	261	71	8,095	8,270	193	1	2,411	2,295
112 Afzalpur (Paigah)	334	354	189	33	13,650	12,464	214	112	2,576	2,361
Osmanabad	**12,880**	**12,106**	**5,426**	**691**	**228,493**	**210,976**	**7,724**	**174**	**66,921**	**64,983**
113 Osmanabad	1,497	1,489	780	245	33,738	31,191	1,288	41	9,547	9,386
114 Kalam	4,823	4,800	2,010	102	29,595	27,629	1,212	28	12,584	12,228
115 Tuljapur	1,723	1,693	514	81	43,272	39,989	969	14	12,463	11,811
116 Latur	1,214	1,185	601	88	40,373	35,871	861	35	10,199	10,041
117 Parenda	1,350	1,158	594	64	34 351	33,750	1,314	15	8,090	8,185
118 Lohara (Paigah)	1,761	1,305	623	83	25,535	23,384	821	8	8,191	7,799
119 Ganjoti (Paigah)	512	526	304	28	21,429	19,162	1,114	33	5,847	5,588
Raichur	**19,146**	**17,848**	**10,183**	**734**	**338,564**	**332,696**	**18,849**	**2,330**	**55,726**	**57,266**
120 Raichur	5,148	4,712	2.462	179	42,386	43,134	5,514	989	12,204	12.011
121 Alampur	395	385	212	34	9,306	9,305	801	99	2,750	2,897
122 Deodrug	291	305	192	21	28,485	28,390	1,381	114	3,351	5,450
123 Gangawati	1,512	1,314	789	82	23,693	22,680	999	61	3,171	3,265
124 Kushtagi	873	668	364	61	40,271	38,938	1,591	89	3,054	3,178
125 Lingsugur	4,822	4,655	1,928	93	27,238	27,374	1,815	268	3,929	4,215
126 Manvi	665	686	314	22	38,809	38,308	969	34	3,881	5,572
127 Sindhnur	2,776	2,488	2,363	162	26,987	27,303	631	23	3,289	3,628
128 Kopbal (Jagir)	973	932	614	28	32,118	31,350	1,514	73	3,356	3,553
129 Yelbarga (Jagir)	900	916	561	34	29,274	28,936	1,391	102	2,945	3,253
130 Gadwal (Samasthan)	791	787	384	18	45,497	41,778	2,593	483	10,096	10,244
Bidar	**11,866**	**9,545**	**6,465**	**450**	**272,955**	**260,607**	**8,273**	**256**	**81,971**	**81,172**
131 Bidar	1,500	1,290	1,152	79	30,392	28,023	1,313	89	9,735	12,111
132 Udgir	2,263	1,896	1,213	35	35,629	33,248	617	21	12,012	11,386
133 Ahmadpur	967	778	374	11	44,920	43,872	394	9	9,821	8,974
134 Janwada	320	402	237	35	21,128	19,889	1,005	12	7,170	6,604
135 Nilanga	1.681	1,365	834	31	33,642	31,093	514	3	9,638	9,509
136 Chitgopa (Paigah)	412	330	193	22	21,119	21,253	933	8	6,748	6,807
137 Narayankher (Paigah)	662	438	261	12	16,654	16,240	824	19	5,336	5,153
138 Ghorwadi (Paigah)	934	700	394	19	12,710	12,464	791	5	3,622	3,448
139 Bhalki (Paigah)	207	195	83	3	6,622	6,267	668	33	1,854	1,209
140 Ekeli (Paigah)	305	150	162	12	9,346	9,246	591	15	3,185	3,253
141 Partabpur (Paigah)	958	806	683	81	18,031	16,920	222	25	4,423	4,304
142 Hasanabad (Paigah)	517	508	275	33	5,649	5,750	112	8	2,861	2,996
143 Chincholi (Paigah)	626	454	461	62	7,461	7,471	71	6	2,850	2,403
144 Murag (Deoni) (Jagir)	319	238	193	15	9,652	8,871	18	3	3,116	2,930

TABLE II.

Religion and Literacy.

STATE TABLE II.

POPULATION OF TALUKS BY RELIGION AND LITERACY.

Hindu		JAIN				SIKH				MUSLIM			
No. of Literates		No. of Persons		No. of Literates		No. of Persons		No. of Literates		No. of Persons		No. of Literates	
Males	Females	Males	Females	Males	Females	Males	Females	Males	Females	Males	Females	Males	Females
12	13	14	15	16	17	18	19	20	21	22	23	24	25
294	**97**	**1,013**	**935**	**379**	**77**	**176**	**153**	**16**	..	**99,636**	**95,950**	**8,296**	**1,107**
18	2	217	234	77	15	60	58	8	..	24,023	22,491	2,765	464
32	1	9	11	5	5	..	..	..	..	7,096	6,754	239	16
13	2	5	7	..	..	6	5	..	..	6,217	5,995	916	26
5	..	36	25	15	3	1	..	..	..	5,837	5,521	551	21
61	12	65	52	41	..	53	49	1	..	9,003	9,291	345	160
4	11	130	118	16	..	..	..	..	..	6,592	6,366	16	6
17	2	26	27	8	..	..	1	..	..	8,096	8,101	328	20
114	54	94	66	55	2	..	..	..	..	6,444	6,289	504	108
4	9	17	10	2	1	18	12	..	..	4,344	4,431	306	16
..	..	65	64	1	1	12	10	9	..	4,294	4,055	18	8
..	2	7	6	5	2	2	..	1	..	3,423	3,806	423	37
12	..	306	273	149	48	..	..	..	..	5,837	5,450	412	36
2	1	..	..	..	..	4	3	..	..	2,542	2,458	554	45
3	1	..	..	..	..	14	11	2	..	2,406	2,424	110	28
9	..	36	42	3	..	6	4	..	..	3,192	3,018	809	121
348	**113**	**1,424**	**1,320**	**304**	**54**	**169**	**123**	**47**	**17**	**41,525**	**38,783**	**1,221**	**592**
108	16	213	228	33	2	15	8	6	7	5,554	5,254	164	284
67	47	130	124	23	1	..	..	..	..	7,820	7,000	111	110
5	..	242	225	50	10	39	27	3	..	7,195	6,892	273	42
22	1	384	294	49	25	26	..	1	..	9,612	9,072	177	30
143	35	282	288	112	11	67	62	37	10	3,745	3,563	430	93
3	1	84	89	2	..	..	..	..	..	4,485	4,156	43	17
..	13	89	77	35	5	22	26	..	..	3,114	2,846	23	16
1,821	**81**	**476**	**396**	**233**	**51**	**6**	**8**	**1**	..	**48,756**	**46,943**	**8,641**	**1,139**
1,652	51	122	101	39	7	..	..	..	..	8,648	8,263	2,808	433
16	..	..	..	..	..	..	..	..	..	2,562	2,377	403	8
81	6	..	..	..	..	..	..	..	..	3,989	3,979	449	90
24	6	4	2	3	1	..	..	..	..	3,985	3,694	1,483	28
7	12	25	26	24	18	..	..	..	..	3,851	3,649	392	49
5	..	6	6	3	..	..	..	..	..	4,683	4,770	640	62
33	..	1	..	1	..	..	..	..	..	5,108	4,874	934	278
24	..	88	64	81	..	..	..	..	..	4,132	4,073	593	49
7	3	164	157	69	2	1	1	..	..	4,428	4,058	720	118
22	3	66	40	13	23	..	..	..	..	3,093	3,088	56	21
..	..	..	..	..	..	5	7	1	..	4,827	4,118	163	3
442	**137**	**533**	**464**	**93**	**35**	**25**	**24**	**19**	..	**69,509**	**66,800**	**4,562**	**678**
22	8	15	12	11	4	2	3	2	..	14,956	14,980	1,485	131
11	..	64	64	12	1	10	6	8	..	7,317	6,888	95	91
22	..	164	134	80	16	..	..	..	..	7,433	6,685	458	30
10	..	32	25	14	..	..	..	..	..	4,068	3,864	813	144
30	6	129	115	19	10	2	4	1	..	6,411	5,897	142	27
157	2	16	19	..	1	..	..	..	..	7,867	7,854	150	4
..	..	..	..	..	..	6	9	4	..	3,513	3,394	87	..
30	..	22	15	1	..	..	..	..	..	2,625	2,509	96	10
..	..	10	10	5	3	..	..	..	..	1,299	1,301	129	6
128	116	2	2	.. 1	..	..	..	..	..	4,036	3,844	235	4
12	4	51	46	..	..	..	..	..	..	3,261	3,048	50	5
5	1	6	5	..	..	..	..	..	..	2,168	2,256	193	4
..	..	22	16	..	..	..	..	..	..	2,452	2,423	59	28
15	..	..	1	..	..	5	2	4	..	2,103	1,857	625	194

STATE TABLE II.

POPULATION OF TALUKS BY RELIGION AND LITERACY.

District and Taluk	CHRISTIAN				ZOROASTRIAN				TRIBAL			
	No. of Persons		No. of Literates		No. of Persons		No. of Literates		No. of Persons		No. of Literates	
	Males	Females	Males	Females	Males	Females	Males	Females	Males	Females	Males	Females
1	26	27	28	29	30	31	32	33	34	35	36	37
Gulbarga ..	**2,861**	**2,784**	**229**	**58**	**50**	**35**	**39**	**24**	**21,061**	**19,407**	**64**	**43**
98 Gulbarga ..	96	131	20	26	30	19	26	17	2,510	2,211	8	1
99 Chincholi ..	766	767	11	..	2	..	2	..	3,074	2,774	..	..
100 Kodangal ..	810	769	11	7	1	..	1	..	2,879	2,630	2	..
101 Seram ..	9	9	2	..	..	..	..	..	1,689	1,342	..	..
102 Yadgir ..	569	546	105	4	..	..	..	..	2,338	2,199	43	30
103 Andola ..	9	4	..	..	1	..	..	..	1,011	980	2	..
104 Shahpur ..	102	80	26	2	1	..	..	..	1,383	1,340	..	..
105 Shorapur ..	3	2	..	..	2	11	1	7	1,581	1,367	1	..
106 Kalyani (Jagir) ..	3	2	..	..	4	1	2	..	193	180	2	..
107 Chittapur (Jagir) ..	56	56	23	..	..	..	..	..	2,597	2,408	..	..
108 Shahabad (Paigah) ..	36	27	20	17	8	4	7	..	38	25	..	..
109 Aland (Jagir) ..	..	..	..	..	..	..	..	..	76	62	..	..
110 Tandur (Jagir) ..	380	372	11	2	1	..	..	..	980	973	..	4
111 Bashirabad (Paigah) .	22	19	..	..	..	..	..	..	313	477	2	..
112 Afzalpur (Paigah) .	..	..	..	..	..	..	..	..	247	239	4	8
Osmanabad ..	**42**	**21**	**23**	**9**	**3**	..	**3**	..	**6,032**	**5,267**	**27**	**59**
113 Osmanabad .	15	6	13	4	1	..	1	..	325	283	..	6
114 Kalam ..	1	..	..	..	..	..	..	..	3,221	2,577	27	42
115 Tuljapur ..	6	..	2	..	..	..	..	..	1,412	1,375	..	..
116 Latur ..	19	14	8	5	2	..	2	..	82	59	..	..
117 Parenda ..	..	..	..	..	..	..	..	..	53	73	..	..
118 Lohara (Paigah) ..	1	1	..	..	..	..	..	..	546	581	..	7
119 Ganjoti (Paigah) ..	..	..	..	..	..	..	..	..	393	369	..	4
Raichur ..	**2,130**	**1,745**	**671**	**92**	**10**	**9**	**8**	**6**	**8,343**	**7,457**	**123**	**21**
120 Raichur ..	1,133	933	565	64	3	7	2	5	623	595	61	8
121 Alampur ..	45	41	6	..	..	..	..	..	49	36	3	3
122 Deodrug ..	273	224	14	11	1	2	..	1	887	829	..	..
123 Gangawati ..	..	..	..	..	..	..	..	..	845	858	12	2
124 Kushtagi ..	3	3	2	2	..	..	..	..	976	971	6	2
125 Lingsugur ..	69	39	47	..	..	..	..	..	2,046	1,896	24	..
126 Manvi ..	241	217	14	4	1	..	1	..	635	607	4	..
127 Sindhnur ..	1	..	..	..	4	..	4	..	107	121	..	..
128 Kopbal (Jagir) ..	10	7	5	2	..	..	..	..	954	919	4	..
129 Yelbarga (Jagir) ..	3	3	..	..	..	..	..	..	723	258	9	
130 Gadwal (Samasthan)	352	278	18	9	1	..	1	..	498	367	..	..
Bidar ..	**2,194**	**2,160**	**115**	**541**	**1**	..	**1**	..	**7,201**	**6,586**	**30**	..
131 Bidar ..	1,219	1,152	58	517	1	..	1	..	602	588	2	..
132 Udgir ..	37	47	16	12	..	..	..	..	1,495	1,383	3	..
133 Ahamadpur ..	110	89	19	..	..	..	..	..	978	887	8	..
134 Janwada ..	121	171	11	4	..	..	..	..	867	830	..	..
135 Nilanga ..	..	..	..	..	..	..	..	..	417	351	2	..
136 Chitagopa (Paigah).	186	147	1	3	..	..	..	..	540	500	2	..
137 Narayankher (Paigah)	122	156	..	..	..	..	..	..	1,591	1,403	..	..
138 Ghorwadi (Paigah) ..	..	..	..	..	..	..	..	..	48	36	..	..
139 Bhalki (Paigah) ..	..	..	..	..	..	..	..	..	..	..	..	..
140 Ekeli (Paigah) ..	264	265	9	4	..	..	..	..	62	75	18	..
141 Partabpur (Paigah) .	3	3	..	..	..	..	..	..	89	77	..	..
142 Hasanabad (Paigah).	130	130	1	1	..	..	..	..	37	45	..	..
143 Chincholi (Paigah) ..	2	..	..	..	..	..	..	..	194	160	..	..
144 Murag (Deoni)-(Jagir)	..	..	..	..	..	..	..	..	281	251	..	..

TABLE II. **STATE TABLE II.** **STATE TABLE II.**

Religion and Literacy. **POPULATION OF TALUKS BY RELIGION AND LITERACY.**

OTHERS				NO. OF LITERATES						Literate in English		Literate in Urdu	
No. of persons		No. of Literates		Aged 0-15		Aged 15-20		Aged 20 and over					
Males	Females	Males	Females	Males	Females	Males	Females	Males	Females	Males	Females	Males	Females
38	39	40	41	42	43	44	45	46	47	48	49	50	51
..	..	..	..	**6,249**	**1,593**	**5,263**	**789**	**22,361**	**3,596**	**1,579**	**358**	**8,568**	**1,358**
..	..	..	..	1,295	501	1,541	288	6,411	1,849	770	166	3,491	441
..	..	..	..	791	101	581	39	2,413	171	38	1	322	16
..	..	..	..	338	81	391	28	1,833	136	83	7	957	62
..	..	..	..	321	84	423	31	1,300	163	67	89	346	158
..	..	..	..	783	131	591	68	2,207	200	41	6	596	154
..	..	..	..	261	93	197	24	1,006	122	47	2	267	12
..	..	..	..	308	81	241	53	953	93	104	10	576	16
..	..	..	..	331	131	391	63	1,455	203	84	11	520	77
..	..	..	..	191	81	88	31	715	131	20	28	275	19
..	..	..	..	228	63	181	29	954	130	29	10	85	..
..	..	..	..	181	23	111	19	338	41	90	21	217	81
..	..	..	..	193	31	171	28	588	82	37	1	229	88
..	..	..	..	163	58	124	29	584	90	77	5	283	19
..	..	..	..	105	23	83	11	383	47	30	..	42	28
..	..	..	..	210	91	199	48	821	135	42	46	362	292
..	..	..	..	**2,690**	**488**	**2,683**	**358**	**9,750**	**863**	**923**	**46**	**2,313**	**468**
..	..	..	..	292	222	445	161	1,601	222	350	20	409	102
..	..	..	..	633	73	314	61	2,503	196	36	13	148	95
..	..	..	..	198	39	793	21	825	87	129	3	420	26
..	..	..	..	431	49	293	34	997	101	60	2	318	24
..	..	..	..	728	53	391	41	1,711	134	87	1	561	162
..	..	..	..	194	28	228	19	1,070	69	23	2	275	44
..	..	..	..	214	24	219	21	1,043	54	36	5	182	15
4	**6**	**2**	..	**9,849**	**1,660**	**8,186**	**806**	**22,497**	**1,988**	**2,873**	**220**	**11,309**	**2,185**
4	6	2	..	1,230	945	2,018	441	9,857	350	1,732	82	4,049	1,235
..	..	..	..	206	24	101	12	1,134	108	30	1	497	7
..	..	..	..	894	28	621	42	702	173	31	..	626	102
..	..	..	..	1,005	30	924	60	1,381	70	113	..	1,148	23
..	..	..	..	819	84	724	23	843	126	119	39	571	108
..	..	..	..	1,348	102	693	21	1,921	295	98	..	988	58
..	..	..	..	633	114	341	81	1,096	143	91	1	1,118	287
..	..	..	..	1,224	68	894	24	1,578	142	281	..	919	58
..	..	..	..	863	70	224	30	1,846	126	218	19	909	146
..	..	..	..	624	61	318	21	910	107	70	76	262	167
..	..	..	..	1,003	114	928	51	1,229	348	50	2	227	4
1	**1**	..	..	**3,151**	**633**	**5,493**	**465**	**11,356**	**999**	**1,034**	**221**	**5,431**	**597**
..	..	..	..	688	313	2,510	228	848	287	208	173	1,586	197
1	1	..	..	294	40	488	30	1,198	90	183	14	398	65
..	..	..	..	203	22	108	10	1,189	34	43	7	474	45
..	..	..	..	321	39	194	41	1,575	115	151	8	420	88
..	..	..	..	331	22	298	9	918	46	46	3	214	34
..	..	..	..	289	3	391	2	806	85	40	..	176	4
..	..	..	..	194	7	308	3	674	21	32	6	109	15
..	..	..	..	209	8	349	6	754	20	5	..	140	10
..	..	..	..	94	12	118	8	678	25	11	1	185	6
..	..	..	..	193	30	224	45	722	36	251	10	859	50
..	..	..	..	109	35	91	29	717	31	34	1	86	6
..	..	..	..	108	15	158	8	325	24	8	1	206	4
..	..	..	..	98	19	141	12	352	65	10	2	57	26
..	..	..	..	120	48	130	34	605	130	12	..	571	97

State Table III.

INFIRMITIES IN 3 PARTS.

Note.—1. Last time the table for Infirmities by castes was shown in the Imperial series but on the present occasion the table having removed from the All-India series, has been included as State or Local table, giving more statistical information e.g., occupations for the Infirms.

2. It comprises three parts ; part "A", number of Infirms by Religion ; part "B", by Castes, Tribes and Races and part "C", their distribution by occupation.

3. The selection and arrangement of castes in part "B" are governed by the same rule as followed in Imperial Table XVII.

4. Occupational figures are shown only for the main classes. There are 6,131 males and 3,892 females ("Principal Earners" 4,375 males and 2,306 females and "Working Dependents" 1,756 males and 1,586 females) whose occupation is begging.

STATE TABLE III—A.

Infirmities by Religion.

Serial No.	Religion	POPULATION DEALT WITH			INSANE			DEAF-MUTE			BLIND			LEPER		
		Persons	Males	Females	Persons	Males	Females	Persons	Males	Females	Persons	Males	Females	Persons	Males	Females
	1	2	3	4	5	6	7	8	9	10	11	12	13	14	15	16
	ALL RELIGIONS ..	14,436,148	7,370,010	7,066,138	2,200	1,337	863	3,742	2,209	1,533	12,516	6,480	6,036	3,738	2,630	1,108
1	Hindu	12,176,727	6,203,053	5,973,674	1,672	1,011	661	3,056	1,793	1,263	10,144	4,995	5,149	3,223	2,243	980
	(i) Hindu (Brahmanic) .	*9,699,615*	4,948,408	4,751,207	*1,307*	766	541	*2,199*	1,329	870	*7,782*	3,900	3,882	*2,256*	1,638	618
	(ii) Adi-Hindu ..	*2,473,230*	1,252,651	1,220,579	*361*	243	118	*850*	460	390	*2,344*	1,085	1,259	966	604	362
	(iii) Arya	*3,700*	1,896	1,804	*4*	2	2	6	3	3	*18*	10	8	*1*	1	..
	(iv) Brahmo ..	*182*	98	84	..	..	..	*1*	1	..	..	..	..	..	..	..
2	Jain	21,543	11,456	10,087	6	3	3	12	4	8	68	35	33	6	5	1
3	Sikh	5,178	3,064	2,114	1	1	..	..	..	..	8	4	4	..	..	..
4	Muslim	1,534,666	791,435	743,231	396	250	146	536	313	223	1,479	970	509	385	295	90
5	Christian	151,382	79,444	71,938	32	21	11	74	59	15	146	69	77	26	14	12
6	Zoroastrian ..	1,784	937	847	3	2	1	1	1	..	8	3	5	..	..	..
7	Buddhist	52	26	26	..	..	..	..	..	..	..	..	..	..	..	..
8	Jew	27	11	16	..	..	..	..	..	..	..	..	..	..	..	..
9	Tribal	544,789	280,584	264,205	90	49	41	103	59	44	663	404	259	98	73	25

STATE TABLE III—B.

Infirmities by selected Castes, Races and Tribes.

Caste, Race and Tribe	POPULATION DEALT WITH			INSANE			DEAF-MUTE			BLIND			LEPER		
	Persons	Males	Females	Persons	Males	Females	Persons	Males	Females	Persons	Males	Females	Persons	Males	Females
1	2	3	4	5	6	7	8	9	10	11	12	13	14	15	16
ALL RELIGIONS ..	14,436,148	7,370,010	7,066,138	2,200	1,337	863	3,742	2,209	1,533	12,516	6,480	6,036	3,738	2,630	1,108
Hindu (Brahmanic) ..	9,699,615	4,948,408	4,751,207	1,307	766	541	2,199	1,329	870	7,782	3,900	3,882	2,256	1,638	618
Balija	*39,300*	21,514	17,786	*12*	10	2	*30*	18	12	*72*	30	42	*7*	4	3
Bender	*237,774*	119,307	118,467	*16*	6	10	*22*	18	4	*76*	36	40	*24*	14	10
Bhoi ..	*285,273*	141,869	143,404	*36*	15	21	*22*	18	4	*145*	80	65	*38*	21	17
Bogam	*26,932*	12,535	14,397	*12*	3	9	*5*	2	3	*45*	25	20	*8*	2	6
Brahman	*376,468*	196,654	179,814	*76*	46	30	*141*	86	55	*342*	241	101	*54*	36	18
Burud	*34,777*	19,054	15,723	*28*	12	16	*15*	8	7	*22*	10	12	*2*	..	2
Darzi	*63,631*	32,220	31,411	*1*	1	..	*3*	2	1	*63*	40	28	*3*	3	..
Dasari	*3,220*	1,693	1,527	*8*	5	3	*12*	7	5	*26*	14	12	*8*	6	2
Dhobi	*269,492*	138,790	130,702	*50*	35	15	*152*	88	64	*360*	175	185	*92*	72	20
Erakala	*9,986*	5,049	4,937	*2*	2	..	*3*	2	1	*1*	1	..	..	..	..
Gosain	*29,227*	17,147	12,080	*3*	3	..	..	..	..	*2*	2	..	..	..	..
Gujarati	*8,063*	4,893	3,170	*1*	1	..	..	..	..	*3*	3	..	..	..	..
Gurav	*30,410*	15,676	14,734	..	..	..	*6*	5	1	*35*	13	22	*4*	4	..
Hajjam	*159,745*	83,855	75,890	*20*	12	8	*32*	22	10	*110*	56	54	*28*	26	2
Hatkar	*45,168*	24,337	20,831	..	..	..	*4*	3	1	*46*	21	25	*6*	5	1
Hindu (minor castes) ..	*17,610*	9,862	7,748	*23*	12	11	*169*	98	71	*265*	170	95	*176*	102	74
Julahi	*406,881*	211,803	195,078	*3*	2	1	*6*	4	2	*15*	3	12	*6*	2	4
Kalal	*426,836*	220,637	206,199	*7*	4	3	*37*	16	21	*127*	60	67	*18*	12	6
Kapu	*942,920*	490,183	452,737	*138*	70	68	*128*	78	35	*438*	220	218	*125*	95	30
Kasab	*81,165*	42,801	38,364	*14*	6	8	*12*	8	4	*23*	10	13	*11*	10	1
Kasar	*35,730*	19,036	16,694	*27*	12	15	..	..	..	*72*	40	32	*1*	1	..
Kayasth	*4,895*	2,813	2,082	*2*	1	1	..	..	..	*3*	3	..	..	..	..
Khatri	*4,739*	2,566	2,173	..	..	..	*2*	1	1	..	..	..	..	..	..
Kumbhar	*154,148*	80,919	73,229	*12*	8	4	*18*	8	10	*67*	33	34	*14*	6	8
Koli	*52,472*	29,264	23,208	*38*	29	9	*71*	41	30	*79*	42	37	*65*	39	26
Komati	*308,911*	163,432	145,479	*63*	33	30	*130*	70	60	*108*	50	58	*99*	80	19
Kshatriya	*88,434*	46,256	42,178	*6*	4	2	*2*	2	..	*32*	20	12	*4*	3	1
Kurma	*173,318*	89,646	83,672	*36*	12	24	*25*	15	10	*156*	73	83	*32*	19	13
Lingayat	*788,839*	397,604	391,235	*126*	66	60	*240*	137	103	*698*	311	387	*310*	280	30
Lodha	*6,908*	4,033	2,875	*5*	3	2	*2*	1	1	*12*	8	4	*1*	1	..
Lobar	*93,460*	51,365	42,095	*4*	2	2	*15*	8	7	*110*	55	55	*13*	8	5
Mali	*102,608*	51,611	50,997	*15*	10	5	*7*	4	3	*201*	90	111	*35*	25	10
Maratha	*1,491,558*	751,082	740,476	*155*	68	87	*313*	210	103	*1,620*	736	884	*585*	470	115
Marwari	*62,311*	34,572	27,739	*12*	9	3	*3*	2	1	*13*	7	6	*1*	1	..
Panchal	*69,874*	35,707	34,167	*26*	18	8	*5*	2	3	*42*	30	12	*2*	2	..
Pardhi	*5,466*	2,977	2,489	*3*	2	1	..	..	..	*14*	8	6	..	..	..
Patkari	*3,535*	1,949	1,586	*2*	1	1	..	..	..	*22*	14	8	..	..	..
Perka	*51,504*	25,723	25,781	*9*	6	3	*3*	1	2	*26*	15	11	*10*	8	2

STATE TABLE III—B.

Infirmities by selected Castes, Races and Tribes.

Caste, Race and Tribe	POPULATION DEALT WITH			INSANE			DEAF-MUTE			BLIND			LEPER		
	Persons	Males	Females	Persons	Males	Females	Persons	Males	Females	Persons	Males	Females	Persons	Males	Females
1	2	3	4	5	6	7	8	9	10	11	12	13	14	15	16
Pichakuntla	*8,957*	5,310	3,647	*7*	..	7	*8*	4	4	*32*	14	18	*4*	3	1
Rangrez	*26,751*	14,875	11,876	*2*	2	..	*4*	3	1	*38*	18	20	*7*	5	2
Sadhu	*3,493*	2,396	1,097	*19*	17	2	*10*	5	5	*22*	15	7	*2*	..	2
Satani	*54,396*	30,365	24,031	*8*	5	3	*7*	7	..	*35*	25	10	*4*	3	1
Sunar	*137,891*	72,550	65,341	*16*	13	3	*45*	33	12	*182*	80	102	*22*	18	4
Sutar	*110,350*	58,274	52,076	*14*	7	7	*12*	6	6	*140*	50	90	*39*	25	14
Telaga ..	*966,190*	448,805	517,385	*96*	53	48	*112*	73	39	*335*	142	193	*76*	56	20
Teli	*73,155*	38,773	34,382	*3*	2	1	*13*	10	3	*72*	60	12	*15*	9	6
Uppara	*79,492*	39,623	39,869	*4*	2	2	*31*	20	11	*14*	10	4	*8*	6	2
Velama	*51,988*	26,217	25,771	*5*	4	1	*12*	6	6	*130*	70	60	*18*	12	6
Vellala	*4,485*	2,339	2,146	*2*	..	2	*3*	1	2	*13*	7	6	*1*	1	..
Viramushti	*7,445*	4,118	3,327	*16*	10	6	*14*	7	7	*55*	40	15	*8*	6	2
Viswabrahman	*26,742*	14,293	12,449	*4*	2	2	*12*	8	4	*33*	19	14	*2*	2	..
Waddar	*138,082*	70,085	67,997	*32*	22	10	*44*	24	20	*185*	105	80	*17*	12	5
Wanjari	*70,936*	38,965	31,971	6	6	..	*32*	12	20	*280*	160	120	*39*	21	18
Yadava	*928,404*	471,464	456,940	*182*	92	90	*205*	130	75	*725*	340	385	*212*	152	60
Adi-Hindu	2,473,230	1,252,651	1,220,579	361	243	118	850	460	390	2,344	1,085	1,259	966	604	362
Adi Hindu (Minor caste) ..	*115,599*	60,822	54,777	*54*	31	23	*179*	103	76	*478*	210	268	*187*	122	65
Dher	*1,076,539*	552,632	523,907	*132*	102	30	*294*	152	142	*885*	445	440	*282*	175	107
Madiga	*1,281,092*	639,197	641,895	*175*	110	65	*377*	205	172	*981*	430	551	*497*	307	190
Tribal	544,789	280,584	264,205	90	49	41	103	59	44	663	404	259	98	73	25
Andh	*6,100*	2,800	3,300	*4*	3	1	6	4	2	*23*	13	10	*4*	3	1
Bhil	*15,052*	7,551	7,501	*3*	2	1	*12*	10	2	*36*	27	9	*2*	2	..
Chenchu	*2,264*	1,090	1,174	*3*	3	..	*2*	1	1	*24*	15	9	*1*	1	..
Erakala	*59,172*	32,002	27,170	*12*	8	4	*7*	4	3	*86*	47	39	*8*	5	3
Ghisadi	*2,171*	1,090	1,081	*4*	3	1	*2*	2	..	*13*	7	6	*1*	1	..
Gond	*113,280*	57,048	56,232	*26*	11	15	*26*	15	11	*245*	140	105	*38*	28	10
Koya	*33,638*	18,217	15,421	*4*	3	1	*7*	5	2	*13*	3	10	*2*	..	2
Lambadi	*300,466*	153,856	146,610	*23*	10	13	*24*	8	16	*176*	120	56	*25*	20	5
Pardhi	*7,172*	3,833	3,339	*4*	2	2	*3*	1	2	*12*	7	5	..	..	..
Pindari	*1,246*	671	575	*2*	1	1	..	..	..	*7*	6	1	..	..	..
Tribal-un-classified ..	*4,228*	2,426	1,802	*5*	3	2	*14*	9	5	*28*	19	9	*17*	13	4
Christian	151,382	79,444	71,938	32	21	11	74	59	15	146	69	77	26	14	12
Anglo-Indians	*3,370*	2,188	1,182	*4*	3	1	*2*	1	1	*12*	5	7	..	..	..
Europeans and other Races .	*2,613*	2,256	357	..	..	..	..	..	..	..	..	..	..	..	..
Indian Christians ..	*145,385*	74,988	70,397	*28*	18	10	*72*	58	14	*134*	64	70	26	14	12

STATE TABLE III.—C.

Number of Infirms and their distribution by Occupation.

	Males	Females
Total principal earners	5,419	2,902
Working dependents	2,265	2,385
Non-working dependents	4,972	4,234
Infirm population	*12,656*	*9,540*

Occupation	No. of Infirms following occupation as principal means of livelihood			No. of Infirms who are working dependants			No. of Infirms who follow the occupation as subsidiary means of livelihood		
	Persons	Males	Females	Persons	Males	Females	Persons	Males	Females
1	2	3	4	5	6	7	8	9	10
TOTAL WORKERS.	**8,321**	**5,419**	**2,902**	**4,650**	**2,265**	**2,385**	**205**	**153**	**52**
A. Production of Raw Materials	**1,210**	**818**	**392**	**931**	**421**	**510**	**102**	**72**	**30**
I. Exploitation of Animals and Vegetation ..	*1,207*	815	392	*931*	421	510	*102*	72	30
(a) Income from land rent	*12*	12	..	*6*	4	2	*3*	2	1
(b) Cultivators of all kinds	*360*	239	121	*300*	162	138	*58*	44	14
(c) Field Labourers, wood cutters etc. ..	*635*	425	210	*487*	201	286	*8*	6	2
(d) Raisers of Live stock, milkmen, herdsmen ..	*168*	111	57	*131*	47	84	*31*	18	13
(e) Fishing and hunting	*32*	28	4	*7*	7	..	*2*	2	..
II. Exploitation of minerals	*3*	3	..	..	..	..	..	..	..
B. Preparation and Supply of Material Substances	**98**	**80**	**18**	**38**	**22**	**16**	**13**	**9**	**4**
III. Industry	*41*	29	12	*20*	16	4	*7*	4	3
IV. Transport	*5*	4	1	..	..	..	..	..	..
V. Trade	*52*	47	5	*18*	6	12	6	5	1
C. Public Administration and Liberal Arts ..	**30**	**27**	**3**	**6**	**2**	**4**	..	..	..
VI. Public Force	*2*	2	..	..	..	..	..	..	..
VII. Public Administration	*4*	4	..	..	..	..	..	..	..
VIII. Professions and Liberal arts	*24*	21	3	*6*	2	4	..	..	..
D. Miscellaneous.	**6,983**	**4,494**	**2,489**	**3,675**	**1,820**	**1,855**	**90**	**72**	**18**
IX. Persons living on their own income ..	*4*	3	1	..	..	..	..	..	..
X. Domestic Service	*189*	57	132	*268*	27	241	16	12	4
XI. Insufficiently described occupation ..	*15*	15	..	*9*	3	6	..	..	..
XII. Unproductive	*6,775*	4,419	2,356	*3,398*	1,790	1,608	*74*	60	14

Hyderabad Census, 1931.

State Table IV.

COTTAGE INDUSTRIES.

STATE TABLE IV.

Cottage Industries.

Srl. No.	District	No. of Looms: Cotton	No. of Looms: Silk	No. of Looms: Wool	No. of spindles or charkas at work for spinning yarn out of cotton	No. of houses or establishments containing two or more persons not being weavers who are engaged on dying yarn or cloth	No. of houses or establishments engaged in printing cloth	No. of hand cotton ginning machines at work	No. of oil ghanies at work driven by hand or bullock or power	No. of sugarcane pressing mills at work driven by hand or bullock or power	No. of grinding machines at work driven by steam gas, hand or other power	No. of tailoring establishments composed of two or more tailors using sewing machines	Total No. of sewing machines used at tailoring establishments	No. of metal workshops	No. of potters establishments composed of two or more potters	No. of carpenters workshops composed of two or more carpenters including cabinet makers, wheels wrights, boat builders, etc.	No. of painters workshops where toys, painted boxes, plates, stationery playing cards, etc., are made	No. of smithy workshops composed of two or more blacksmiths	No. of dairy establishments where butter, ghee is manufactured	Modern cream separating machines at work
1	2	3	4	5	6	7	8	9	10	11	12	13	14	15	16	17	18	19	20	21
	Hyderabad State ..	**93,422**	**4.183**	**14,393**	**169,891**	**1,187**	**774**	**2,556**	**6.349**	**1,595**	**1,013**	**2,794**	**9,696**	**4,220**	**4,969**	**5,284**	**360**	**2,072**	**73**	**108**
1	Hyderabad City ..	1,687	298	591	1,039	383	510	101	694	8	204	992	5,991	1,042	894	1,998	194	1,294	6	51
2	Atraf-i-Balda ..	4,383	238	1,001	2,599	19	9	1,359	259	83	25	118	181	250	420	211	11	163	41	38
3	Warangal ..	4,690	88	432	13,829	24	10	273	239	1	42	82	96	268	603	452	65	156	23	19
4	Karimnagar ..	18,147	149	1,923	52,255	86	39	802	227	1	56	58	48	242	311	160	37	18	3	..
5	Adilabad ..	5.001	19	119	24,324	51	40	..	812	18	38	110	183	357	407	307	20	55	..	..
6	Medak ..	9,503	802	2,251	11,235	217	23	2	452	137	44	59	69	144	212	124	6	4	..	..
7	Nizamabad ..	5.025	264	653	15,928	45	33	..	379	199	28	62	31	159	174	117	3	..	..	..
8	Mahbubnagar ..	6,785	193	2,101	950	15	..	..	267	10	30	70	46	159	200	140	..	17	..	..
9	Nalgonda ..	10,532	148	1,035	32,686	..	26	..	..	..	21	112	134	304	397	340	7	43	..	..
10	Aurangabad ..	1,047	98	615	352	20	..	3	415	128	57	86	286	99	71	76	..	..	..	..
11	Bir ..	1,245	41	356	587	31	3	..	311	83	65	76	201	69	76	94	..	25	..	..
12	Nander ..	2,310	85	304	2,508	57	28	6	310	42	19	213	374	304	344	343	2	74	..	..
13	Parbhani ..	1,827	158	220	211	46	9	8	264	70	98	183	512	271	213	223	2	65	..	..
14	Gulbarga ..	10,716	1,203	1,044	5,518	131	27	2	659	102	77	219	493	262	378	371	3	82	..	..
15	Osmanabad	460	15	338	425	1	1	..	590	298	121	153	456	90	59	54	..	21	..	..
16	Raichur ..	7,444	359	302	655	15	..	..	101	35	37	66	201	56	78	72	8	17	..	..
17	Bidar	2.620	25	1,108	4,790	40	16	..	370	385	51	135	394	144	132	202	2	38	..	..

State Table V.

HYDERABAD CITY—NUMBER OF OCCUPIED HOUSES AND POPULATION BY MOHALLAS.

1. This table deals with the Capital of His Exalted Highness the Nizam's Dominions, showing the number of occupied houses and population by mohallas.

2. The arrangements of wards, mohallas and bazaars are kept in accordance with those followed by the Hyderabad Municipality and the Secunderabad Cantonment Authority though the number of occupied houses in a ward or bazaar may slightly be in variance with the figures of the Municipality or Cantonment in as much as "Occupied House" in the meaning of Census is "a dwelling place having a sep. rate entrance."

3. The City of Hyderabad (properly may be called as "Greater Hyderabad" like Greater Calcutta) includes not only British Administered Areas (figures for which have been separately given in this table) but also certain suburban areas lying partly within and partly without the Hyderabad Municipal limits. The areas so included have been printed in italics with the letters p. m. in brackets, showing they are partly municipal; while some areas which are wholly non-municipal are also printed in italics with the letters n. m. (non-Municipal) in brackets. Similarly a few tracts lying outside Cantonment boundary are treated and shown in italics with o. c. (outside Cantonment) in brackets.

4. Asterisks against a mohalla indicate that only a part of it has come under the ward in which it lies, while the other part or parts of the same mohalla may lie in any another ward or wards, which have been shown against it in brackets.

STATE TABLE V.

Hyderabad City—Occupied houses and population by Mohallas.

Serial No.	Name of Mohalla or Bazaar	Occupied houses	POPULATION		
			Persons	Males	Females
1	2	3	4	5	6
	HYDERABAD CITY	**116,807**	**466,894**	**247,623**	**219,271**
	I. Hyderabad Municipality (a)	**74,057**	**306,646**	**160,889**	**145,757**
	II. H.E.H. the Nizam's Cantonments ..	**7,169**	**24,975**	**13,880**	**11,095**
	III. Residency Bazaars	**4,524**	**14,472**	**8,116**	**6,356**
	IV. Secunderabad (including Trimulgherry and Bolarum) (b)	**31,057**	**120,801**	**64,738**	**56,063**
	CITY MUNICIPALITY.				
	(a) City Anderoon	**18,760**	**69,272**	**35,907**	**33,365**
	WARD I.	**4,539**	**21,638**	**11,223**	**10,415**
1	Dar-ush-shafa	238	1,255	648	607
2	Purani Haveli	183	1,389	783	606
3	Noor Khan Bazaar	699	4,471	2,141	2,330
4	*Daricha Rangeli Shah (VI)	51	125	63	62
5	Yaqutpura	251	682	356	326
6	Turab Jung Lane	84	252	134	118
7	*Dabirpura (V)	212	1,287	665	622
8	Atebar Chowk	148	659	333	326
9	Gachi Chabutra	83	257	138	119
10	Qadirulmulk Lane	97	194	108	91
11	Mandva-e-Chambeli	37	67	41	26
12	* Alijah Kotla (III)	64	140	75	65
13	Komatiwadi	157	730	378	352
14	Karwe Sahib Lane	62	321	166	155
15	Daricha Boodlay Shah	50	253	121	132
16	Kotla Ali-Yawar-ud-owla	67	262	128	134
17	Sultanpura	207	1,028	516	512
18	*Chaderghat (V.C.)	154	977	487	490
19	Daricha Rao-Rumbha	55	371	189	182
20	Jhatai-Karar Jung	73	288	140	148
21	Kotlai Akbarjah	54	511	284	227
22	Jilu -khana	57	155	92	63
23	Kaman Mahi	23	42	32	10
24	Charminar	110	161	133	28
25	Dewan Deori	104	429	259	170
26	Chatha Bäzaar	64	133	86	47
27	Yousuf Bazaar	91	189	133	56
28	Phatter-Gatti	90	389	232	157
29	Koochai- Naseem	66	518	265	253
30	Irani Galli	67	363	187	176
31	Kali-Kaman	196	946	487	459
32	Gulzar House	133	384	197	187
33	*Chowk Maidan Khan (II)	119	509	283	226
34	Mandy Meer-Alam	202	1,014	502	512
35	Kammalposh Lane	54	162	74	88
36	Kaman Elchi Baig	101	690	330	360
37	Fatehulla Baig Lane	36	85	42	43
	WARD II.	**4,165**	**14,038**	**7,096**	**6,942**
38	Gondki Bauli	62	383	191	192
39	Jalpalli	149	564	293	271
40	*Lal-Darwaza (VI)	115	440	193	247
41	*Aliabad (III, VII)	58	85	48	37
42	Chinta Bauli	43	161	75	86
43	Masjid Jali	32	67	28	39
44	Thatti Bucharmal	28	103	55	48
45	Nagul Chinta	71	297	160	137
46	Garaj Bazaar	42	76	42	34
47	Narayanrao Lane	15	45	26	19
48	Chinta Mahal	52	134	73	61
49	Feelkhana Chandulal	90	374	196	178
50	Murad Mahal	170	614	309	305
51	Ramkishan Lane	46	101	51	50
52	Bela Chandulal	116	206	126	80
53	Gowlipura	135	282	123	159
54	Daira	254	611	309	302
55	Jahandarjah Bazaar	65	146	70	76
56	Moghalpura	870	2,608	1,368	1,240
57	Hari Bauli	202	482	234	248
58	Makkhanlal Lane	50	83	42	41
59	*Chowk Maidan Khan (I)	105	368	220	148
60	Naimuddin Khan Lane	51	137	65	72
61	Sultanshahi	969	4,553	2,250	2,303
62	Andheri Bauli	44	118	59	59
63	Masjid Jafri Lane	66	251	124	127
64	Mir-jumla Tank	87	128	70	58
65	Beebi Bazaar	62	128	70	58

(*a*) *Includes the Suburban Population.*
(*b*) Includes also population outside Contonment limits indicated by (O. C.)